The Lawyer's Guide to

Retirement

Strategies for Attorneys and Their Clients

Third Edition

David A. Bridewell
Charles Nauts
Editors

Senior Lawyers Division ■ **American Bar Association**

The lawyer's guide to retirement / David A. Bridewell, Charles Nauts
   [editors]. -- 3rd ed.
        p. cm.
    ISBN 1-57073-612-X
    1. Lawyers--United States--Retirement.   2. Practice of law-
-Economic aspects--United States.   3. Estate planning--United
States.   4. Lawyers--Taxation--United States.   5. Lawyers--Medical
care--United States.   I. Bridewell, David A. (David Alexander),
1909–   . II. Nauts, Charles, 1930–   .
KF315.L39 1998
322.024' 344--dc21
                           98-30656
                            CIP

Discounts are available for books ordered in bulk. Special consideration is given to state bars, CLE programs, and other bar-related organizations. Inquire at Book Publishing, ABA Publishing, American Bar Association, 750 North Lake Shore Drive, Chicago, Illinois 60611.

www.abanet.org/abapubs

Contents

Contents

Contents

About the Editors

David A. Bridewell has practiced law in Chicago since 1940. He was managing partner of Russell and Bridewell from 1940 to 1983; a member of the firm Righeimer, Martin, Bridewell & Cinquino from 1983 to 1989; counsel to the firm of Spindell & Kemp from 1989 to 1991; and, beginning in 1991, counsel to the firms of Lewis, Overbeck & Furman and DeWolfe, Poynton & Stevens. He currently keeps his own office at 135 South LaSalle Street. He received his B.A. from the University of the South, Sewanee, Tennessee in 1930; his M.A. from Princeton University in 1932; and his LL.B. and J.D. from George Washington University Law School in 1938. He is admitted to the bars of the District of Columbia, Illinois, and Arkansas. He has been active in the Chicago, Illinois, and International Bar Associations, as well as the American Bar Association, where he was a member of the council of the Senior Lawyers Division and now serves as a vice chair of several committees, including the book committee. Bridewell is the author of several ABA books, including *The Lawyer's Guide to Retirement, Third Edition,* and *Reverse Mortgages.*

During 1993-34, Bridewell served first as a county attorney, then a district attorney for the Home Owners Loan Corporation, and in Washington from 1935 to 1940 as attorney and assistant to the general counsel of Home Owners Loan Corporation, Federal Home Loan Bank Board, and Federal Savings and Loan Insurance Corporation. Bridewell has also been outside attorney or counsel in trust matters to several Chicago banks, savings-and-loan associations, and insurance companies. He has been for many years a director of several Chicago-area banks and savings-and-loan associations.

Charles Nauts is of counsel to Harris & Harris, located in Lincoln, Illinois. Before 1995 he was associated with Chapman and Cutler, in Chicago, Illinois. He was chair of the ABA Housing for the Elderly Committee, Real Property, Probate and Trust Law Section, when that committee assisted Stephanie Edelstein of the ABA Commission on Legal Problems of the Elderly in producing its 1992 revision of *Attorney's Guide to Home Equity Conversion.* He is a former chair of the Chicago Bar Association Real Property Law Committee, and is a member of the American College of Real Estate Lawyers.

Preface

The third edition of this book on retirement revises and updates material on retirement planning supplied in the first and second editions by referring to or incorporating relevant interim legislation and by addressing additional subjects that we think a lawyer and spouse should know about before and after they retire. This edition not only deals with planning for retirement, it also discusses procedures necessary to do the planning. It is a practical guide that describes how to retire successfully, particularly by reducing income and estate taxes, as well as probate or succession costs.

Some chapters originally were written to be published in *Experience* or *Probate and Property,* or for presentation by participants in seminars at annual meetings of the American Bar Association—in Toronto in 1988, in Honolulu in 1989, in Chicago in 1990, and in San Francisco in 1997. All the chapters were written by recognized experts in their fields.

The seminars at which the presentations were made were cosponsored by six ABA sections— Senior Lawyers Division; Section of Real Property, Probate and Trust Law; Section of Law Practice Management; Section of Family Law; Section of Taxation; and Section of General Practice. This book should appeal to lawyers in every branch of practice, as well as to all retirees.

Our first two editions dealt mainly with the general areas of estate planning that help provide income and security in retirement, as well as minimize taxes and maximize inheritance. In the third edition, we are providing a more in-depth look at estate and tax planning and the available legal vehicles that enable one to attain those goals in retirement. As a result, more than half the chapters are new and deal with subjects relating to the the legal procedures that can help with retirement planning.

We have grouped the chapters into eight parts, dealing with the practical questions that arise *when* a lawyer and his or her spouse plan for retirement as well as those questions that arise *after* retirement.

Part I addresses the questions of if, to what degree, and when to retire and suggests consideration of alternate careers in retirement.

Part II outlines methods to get the most out of Social Security and pension income and addresses the various differences among retirement plans.

Part III discusses pre- and postretirement planning investment considerations.

Part IV looks at medical concerns retirees will face: Medicare, long-term care, advance healthcare planning, disability planning, and the insurance to take care of these concerns.

Part V provides tax and estate planning strategies: how to avoid excessive federal estate taxes when faced with a changing tax arena, such as we currently have; taxes and other techniques to achieve your planning goals; how to use Alaska and South Dakota law for perpetual trusts; estate planning for a remarried retiree; the problems that come with retirement distribution; the Uniform Custodial Trust Act; how to use discounts in estate administration; and saving on funeral costs.

Part VI describes numerous estate planning vehicles that retirees use to minimize the cost of estate administration (particularly small estates) and how to structure "of counsel" agreements and irrevocable life insurance trusts to minimize costs.

Part VII deals with the newly developing field of elder law, reverse mortgages and senior housing, and how to deal with questions of competency and undue influence that can arise in the handling of cases for elderly clients.

Part VIII addresses questions that may be faced by the survivors of a deceased lawyer; discusses what should be done with the lawyer's open and closed files; and tells how to handle the sale of the lawyer's law practice within the ethical regulations of the ABA and the rules of court.

All lawyers and their spouses planning for retirement should read this book and use it to attain their retirement goals.

Many people were of great importance in the production of this book. I would first like to thank all the contributors to the book; they took great pains to adapt their seminar presentation scripts or articles for inclusion as chapters. I would also like to acknowledge several current or former officers of the Senior Lawyers Division and thank them for their support: John Deacon, Lester Ponder, Harold Wren, John W. Storer, Victor Futter, John H. Pickering, Richard Allen, Leigh B. Middleditch, Jr., and Newton P. Allen all have been strong backers of the project. Finally, I would like to thank the staff members of ABA Publishing for their help in developing, editing, and producing this book: Joseph Weintraub, Richard Paszkiet, Denice Eichhorn, Holly Wehmeyer, Carol Siedell, and Richard Wright, president of Omega Publishing Services, Inc. But, above all, I wish to acknowledge the outstanding assistance of my extremely able secretary and paralegal who has labored long and hard with me in the production of this book from the beginning to the end.

My heartfelt thanks to all of them.

David A. Bridewell

Introduction

DAVID A. BRIDEWELL

When you should retire is a matter of personal choice or the decision of your spouse or law firm, but the sooner you begin to prepare for it financially, the better. Pensions and Social Security will take you only so far. The rest is up to you. You may decide to pursue a part-time law practice, a second career, or some other part-time efforts. Here are a few retirement planning suggestions, with indications of how you might attain them.

First, as you approach retirement age, begin to shift the managerial aspects of your law firm or practice to others. This will enable you to spend more time handling the private practice or public service you plan to enjoy during your golden years. It also will ensure that your firm and your clients' business will be carried on after you are gone. And, it will relieve the executor of your estate from attending to those aspects of your business affairs.

Next, simplify your estate so that the assets will be fewer and less complex by using a living or self-declaration trust with a pour-over will. You can transfer to the trust all stocks, bonds, real estate, and other assets, naming yourself as trustee with full powers as long as you live or are competent to administer it. You should also name your spouse or son or daughter and then a bank, in that order, as successor trustees. This way may help you avoid the probate of your will and estate and the resulting costs. If probate does become necessary, however, the will pours over all probated assets into the trust and thereby simplifies the details and costs of administration. See forms and discussions of self-declaration revocable trusts and pour-over wills in Part VI.

All your security investments can be handled by a securities firm, such as Merrill Lynch, in their street name in a cash management account or in your individual name as trustee under your self-declaration trust. The cash management account will collect all interest and dividends, segregate those that are taxable and nontaxable, and furnish you with monthly and annual statements that are a great help for reporting income, estate, and other types of taxes.

In the event you, as trustee, should die or become incompetent, your spouse or children, then the bank, would be empowered as successor trustees to continue the cash management account as provided in the self-declaration trust. You should also execute a durable power of attorney that gives your spouse or others the power to make family and property decisions if you become incompetent.

You should have in your safe-deposit box a letter of advice to your spouse with instructions about what should be done with the assets in your estate and the probate of your pour-over will if it becomes necessary. You should also list the names, addresses, and telephone numbers of the lawyer, accountant, insurance agents, and others who could help in the settlement of the estate and trust and to whom your successor trustees can turn for advice or assistance. A worksheet summarizing such information and organizing the record of your assets and liabilities is provided in Part VIII, chapter 75. This, along with other important documents, should be kept updated and held in your safe-deposit box.

For a full discussion of what a lawyer should include in this letter and a draft of a proposed letter, see "A Solo Practitioner's Letters of Instructions," by William D. Haught, at Part VIII, chapter 77. In addition to the letter, you should keep the following documents in your safe-deposit box. They will assist your spouse, or the executor or trustee of your estate, with the handling of your estate:

1. Your birth certificate and those of your children and grandchildren, or at least copies of the same;

2. Divorce or annulment decrees, if any;
3. Deeds for your home and other real estate;
4. Property tax receipts (last four years);
5. Income tax returns (last four years);
6. Titles to automobiles;
7. Social Security numbers;
8. Life insurance policies;
9. Medical, health, and nursing home insurance policies;
10. Homeowner's policies;
11. Schedules of employee benefits and copies of any pension plans;
12. Data with respect to all banks in which you have checking or savings accounts;
13. All prior wills and codicils; and
14. Partnership agreements relating to your law partnership.

Retirement planning, of course, includes estate planning, both before and after death, and estate planning requires a consideration of federal estate taxes. With the passage of the Taxpayer Relief Act of 1997, the previous $600,000 "Unified Credit" became $625,000 in 1998 and will increase at the rate of $25,000 per year for the next seven years until it reaches $1 million. There is no federal estate tax on estates with a value lower than the Unified Credit. On estates exceeding the Unified Credit, the tax is extremely heavy. It rises in proportion to the value of the net estate from 37 percent to 55 percent.

There is an additional 55 to 60 percent generation-skipping transfer tax on estates that are transferred to others after the death of the first recipient unless that tax is avoided by using a trust for the benefit of subsequent heirs. These taxes can reduce an estate to less than half of what it was when the original decedent died, unless various methods of tax planning are adopted.

The Revenue Reconciliation Act of 1993, under which we now operate, does provide a $1 million exemption for each estate owner and a $1 million exemption for his or her spouse with respect to grandchildren and nieces and nephews, which does permit tax planning through generation-skipping trusts in larger estates. To take advantage of this exemption, you must use these trusts. If you wish to provide for grandchildren and their heirs, it is possible to extend the benefits down for as long as a hundred years without incurring the 55 percent generation-skipping transfer tax

rate that might otherwise be collectible in addition to the regular federal estate tax. These federal estate taxes are, therefore, an important factor in retirement planning. (For a full discussion, see the chapters by Charles F. Newlin and Allan C. Bell in Part V.)

To plan for your estate, you must have a fairly accurate knowledge of your net worth. To determine that, you must know your assets and liabilities. So, one of the first things you, as a prospective retiree, should do is to prepare a balance sheet that shows assets, liabilities, and net worth for both you and your spouse. For a full discussion of this aspect of retirement planning, see chapter 75 by Walter T. Burke and chapter 77 by William D. Haught.

The unlimited marital deduction allows you to transfer to your spouse, on your death, any or all of your estate without a federal estate tax. You may also transfer any or all of your estate, up to the amount of the Unified Credit, to anyone else. Likewise, without reporting a gift tax, you may give your spouse any or all of your assets at any time;, and you may give up to $10,000 annually to any number of other individuals.

If you transfer everything to a spouse, however, the spouse's estate will be required to pay the federal estate tax on total assets when he or she dies. So you should consider how you can structure ownership to minimize the impact of federal estate tax on the total family assets. It may be desirable to equalize a spouse's assets by inter vivos gifts and trusts, thereby reducing the value of each estate and minimizing the federal estate tax (see Part VI).

While a decedent's estate usually includes the entire value of a joint tenancy or tenancy by the entireties property, there is an exception, known as the spouse's joint property rule, that applies to joint interests created and owned by spouses. Only half the property in such jointly owned property is included for tax purposes in the estate of the first spouse to die.

To minimize taxes on an estate larger than $1 million, it is possible for each spouse to declare in his or her trust or will that all assets exceeding the Unified Credit go to the surviving spouse and that all assets up to the amount of the Unified Credit be held in trust for children or other heirs, but that the surviving spouse is to receive a lifetime income from that amount.

From a tax standpoint, then, if the husband's estate is large enough, an amount equal to the Unified Credit should be in each spouse's name so that each can take advantage of the Unified Credit exemption to which he or she is entitled, regardless of who dies first. To achieve this equalization of value, it may be desirable for you, during your lifetime, to transfer assets in an amount equal to the Unified Credit and currently in your name. Tax decisions become more complicated with increased wealth and may require expert legal and financial counsel, but here are some suggestions:

First, look at the tax advantages of a principal home and, perhaps, a vacation home as well. Because real estate tends to increase in value, these homes probably will be one of the major capital assets during your retirement. They also are usually the best tax shelter. The interest on mortgages on both the primary home and a vacation home is income-tax deductible, regardless of whether the loan is for acquisition or improvement. State and local real estate taxes also are deductible from federal income tax.

In addition, effective in 1998, when you sell your primary home, up to $500,000 of your capital gain is not subject to federal income tax. If you leave the primary or vacation house, or both, to your heirs, the capital gain, if any, will not be taxed upon their sale, as the heirs take title to the property at the stepped-up market value on the date of your death.

Various types of trusts can also help you avoid federal estate tax. All of them are approved for use by the IRS and are discussed in detail in the following chapters. For instance, see the chapters on Family Limited Partnerships, Personal Residence Trusts, Tax Deferred Exchanges, Charitable Remainder Trusts, Irrevocable Life Insurance Trusts, and Roth IRAs in Part VI.

Second, with respect to investments: when you retire, the time for speculation and risk-taking has passed and 70 percent or more of your assets should be in gilt-edged assets—bank CDs, blue-chip stocks, corporate and municipal bonds, money market funds, mortgage-backed securities, real estate, and U.S. Treasuries. A discussion of retirement investing and portfolios can be found in Part III.

Third, a rule of thumb for financial planning for retirement is to save annually at least 10 percent of gross pretax income.

Fourth, it is usually less financially rewarding to work and earn income after you reach 65. Not only do you pay additional income, Social Security, and self-employment taxes, but you also lose part of your Social Security payments until you reach age 70. Therefore, it is desirable, if possible, to acquire your wealth before reaching age 65.

Fifth, you should have in writing all agreements made with your partners or law firm with respect to retirement or your status as a partner or as counsel, salary allotments, pensions, medical benefits, and other similar matters. You cannot expect everyone, even partners, to remember and carry out arrangements unless they are in writing.

Finally, retirees must work out and live by a budget of their anticipated monthly and annual income and expenses, because their income will normally be reduced and their expenses must be tailored so they do not exceed it. In preparing a budget, do forget that in addition to your savings and pension, if any, you also have your monthly Social Security and Medicare as assets. And remember that inflation generally eats away your assets at approximately 5 percent a year. Although this suggestion of a budget comes at the end of these so-called practical suggestions, it probably should be the first item considered by a person planning for retirement.

These are but a few suggestions that a retiree should consider, but they are enough to indicate the multitude of concerns that you must review and act on as you plan for your retirement. Many of these concerns are discussed in the following chapters.

Part I
Retirement?

1
Know Your Own Bone

Cathy L. Eberly

When the American Bar Association met in San Francisco in the summer of 1997, the Senior Lawyers Division's New Careers Committee presented its third program featuring lawyers who have started new careers or added dimensions to their current careers.

According to Milo Coerper, chair of the committee and a retired partner of the international law firm Coudert Brothers, presentations on new careers for lawyers have become popular at ABA meetings in recent years as the legal market has changed. "Changing employment trends and downsizing in the business world means that lawyers may no longer be able to stay with a firm for life," Coerper said. "In fact, it is best to realize that job security is a concept of the past. The new world marketplace necessitates having a flexible work force—including lawyers."

Fortunately, Coerper believes that lawyers, because of their intensive education and experience with client relationships, are in a good position to analyze the employment situations. George Cain, author of *Turning Points*, a best-selling book published by the ABA, challenges lawyers evaluating their careers to do some soul-searching by asking: "What drives me as a person?"

During the July meeting, six lawyers who asked themselves that question and made career choices that mirrored their interests, shared their stories with a large and enthusiastic audience. Five of the presenters are University of Virginia Law School alumni from different generations, and the sixth is professor emeritus at the law school. Their careers reflect a wide range of interests and motivations.

Cathy L. Eberly is director of communications for the Law School Foundation at the University of Virginia, where she edits the law school's alumni magazine, *UVa Lawyer.*

In the profiles that follow, six Virginia lawyers discuss—to borrow from Thoreau—their "bones," gnawing at them, burying them, unearthing them, and gnawing at them still.

John Corse, Fund-Raiser

When John Corse returned to the law school in 1992—nearly 40 years after his 1957 graduation—to help Virginia raise money during its $100 million capital campaign, he claims he had virtually no experience in fund-raising.

"About the only time I asked anyone for money was at the end of the year, when I was on my law firm's committee that attempted to collect overdue accounts from clients," he recalled. "Asking individuals for hundreds of thousands and even millions of dollars, as I do now, is quite different."

Yet Corse stepped into this new role with customary confidence because he shares something with each of the individuals with whom he meets: they are all graduates of the law school. "It's not hard to make a connection with people when you're talking about a place that was as important to each of you in your youth as the law school was to me," he said.

Because of his long and varied career, Corse can connect with people—whether or not they are graduates of Virginia—on a number of fronts. Following graduation from the U.S. Naval Academy in 1946, he served as a line officer in the U.S. Navy during the Korean War. He served eight years on active duty—including three years on surface ships and five years in submarines—and was qualified to command submarines. Following the war and law school, he joined Ulmer, Murchison, Ashby and Ball in Jacksonville, Florida, and became a partner in 1958. In 1972, Corse became managing trustee of Great American Mortgage

Investors, a real estate investment trust in Atlanta, and served as a director and officer of UniCapital Corporation, a related public company, from 1972 to 1975. In 1976, he joined Powell, Goldstein, Frazer & Murphy of Atlanta as a partner, where his practice continued to focus on commercial real estate transactions and bankruptcy matters representing lenders and developers.

Today Corse is senior director of development for the law school foundation. He spends a great deal of time on the road, meeting and connecting with alumni of all generations. Admitting that, as a senior member of the foundation staff, he is seen as somewhat of an "old gray beard" around the law school, the man who was a prep school classmate of George Bush and a Naval Academy classmate of Jimmy Carter brings a lifetime of experience to his position. "I was counting the other day, and I believe this career qualifies as my sixth," he commented.

As the law school's capital campaign nears its goal, Corse admits that he has been asked what his next career move will be. He isn't saying, but his collection of books and plans on houseboats and houseboating continues to grow, so at least a part-time return to saltwater cruising may be ahead. In addition, he's collected photographs of a charming old barn on an idyllic farm owned by his daughter and son-in-law. The word is that he is planning to renovate the barn, creating a cozy new home for himself and his wife, Muffet, that is only minutes away from his beloved law school.

Scottye Hedstrom, TV Executive

Scottye Hedstrom '79 wanted to get closer to the bright lights of television when she left her position with the Los Angeles firm O'Melveny & Myers in 1984 to conduct business affairs for the then-new daytime soap opera "Santa Barbara."

"I wanted to get closer to the action than I was when I worked in legal affairs at the firm," she explained. "Instead of drafting contracts based on deals with creative talent that others had negotiated, I wanted to work directly for a show and make the deals myself."

Hedstrom learned network television business affairs by meeting the demands of the soap opera's hectic daily schedule. When "Santa Barbara" was sold in 1985, she was ready for new television challenges, and quickly landed a spot with Walt Disney Studio's new network television division. Soon she was negotiating talent and production deals for many different types of programs, including "Dinosaurs," a comedy that linked puppets created by Jim Henson Productions with puppeteers, writers, "voices," and members of the Disney creative group.

According to Hedstrom, working in network business affairs requires adaptability and the ability to deal with strong egos. It also helps to have a sense of humor. "At Disney, I spent a lot of time negotiating with agents who were trying to get the best deal possible for their clients," she explained. "It seemed that, after every salary offer I made to a certain agency for one of their clients, they would tell me that they were 'highly insulted' by how low my offer was. Finally I began to anticipate their response by saying 'here's the offer; you're insulted; now let's move on.'"

Hedstrom admits that her job might seem a little confusing to those outside of the industry. "My mother was visiting me one time, and after watching me work for a day or so, she said: 'I don't understand your job at all. All you do is talk on the phone and say no!'"

But working in television business affairs requires more than well-developed negotiation skills. Hedstrom brought experience in entertainment law to Disney from her stint with O'Melveny & Myers. She also relied heavily on the education she gained at the law school. "It's important to know which issues are important to writers, producers, and other creative types . . . but, more importantly, you have to have the skills to know what makes a solid legal contract," she said.

Hedstrom's experience in the bright lights has served her well. In her eleven years with Disney, she rose to the position of vice president of network business affairs, where she was responsible for negotiating talent and production deals for most of the studio's network television shows, including the popular sitcoms "Home Improvement" and "Ellen."

Earlier this year, Hedstrom decided to take a break from network television to pursue another passion, scuba diving. In August she celebrated the first anniversary of her certification during a scuba diving vacation in Micronesia. Further plans for her sabbatical include a language immersion program in Mexico and more scuba diving in Belize and Indonesia.

But come next year, Hedstrom plans to be back in Burbank, working in the field that she loves. "In January, the networks begin to develop pilot TV shows," she explained. "I'd really like to work as a business affairs consultant for a new program." In helping the network folks get a new program off the ground, Hedstrom will be placing herself directly behind the television camera, which is exactly where she likes to be.

William Ide, Business Leader

Bill Ide has always been very curious about new challenges. He believes that curiosity and encouragement he received at critical points in his life from teachers and colleagues have motivated him to explore several different careers in the past thirty-two years.

Today Ide, a 1965 graduate of the law school, is closing in on his first year as senior vice president, general counsel, and secretary at Monsanto Company in St. Louis.

This is not a position he actively sought. Ide was a senior partner with Long Aldridge & Norman in Atlanta and president of the American Bar Association when a fellow lawyer with whom he worked in his ABA role approached him about the Monsanto job.

"I had no reason to want to leave Atlanta, because I had been there for thirty years," Ide said. "I had an instinct that this move would be a good one for me. As a global company, Monsanto would provide me important opportunities to learn and grow. My wife, Gayle, and I talked about it at great length before deciding to accept the challenge."

Ide brought significant experience as a lawyer and a manager to the Monsanto table. Following graduation from the law school, he clerked for the Honorable Griffin Bell of the U.S. Court of Appeals for the Fifth Circuit before joining Atlanta's King & Spalding. After receiving an MBA in finance from Georgia State University, he became a partner with Huie Brown & Ide in the mid–1970s and later served as vice chair of Kutak Rock. Ide took a leave from the law in the mid–1980s to work in the securities industry, then returned as a senior partner in the law firm Long Aldridge & Norman. He also served on the executive committee of Atlanta's committee to organize the Olympic Games. After the Olympics,

Ide became counselor to the U.S. Olympic Committee, and he has continued in that role since moving to St. Louis.

He already is impressed by Monsanto's willingness to invest in its employees to help them understand themselves and how they fit into the corporation. "Our CEO, Bob Shapiro, is very enlightened. He believes that if his employees understand themselves and their co-workers they are more likely to work together effectively and efficiently, and that increased productivity will improve our competitive position."

Ide believes that a key to career success is to know yourself, to understand what motivates you, and to follow your passion. He readily acknowledges that his willingness to follow his passion has increased since his surgery for prostate cancer about a year ago. "If you've ever had anything like that happen to you, then you'll understand it when I say that it causes you to look at your life differently," he said. "I realized that I was going somewhere in an awfully big hurry, and that I needed to take a little time to slow down and experience life a bit more."

While his decision to work for Monsanto had little to do with relaxation, Ide is certain that it was the right decision made at the right time. As always, he is looking ahead to new challenges. "I'd like to take on at least a couple more career challenges in my lifetime," he said. "One thing that I would like to do is to reach out a hand to someone who needs encouragement and help them. My sixth-grade teacher told me I was special, and I believed her. My headmaster at the Darlington School in Georgia made a call on my behalf to the folks at Washington & Lee and, because he believed in me, I was admitted. And at the law school, I was surrounded by faculty who, in addition to being magnificent intellectual forces, were also wonderful people. I want to be able to return the favor someday and help someone who needs me."

Toward that end, Ide has reached out to the law school, where he is an active volunteer. As a member of the Business Advisory Council, he and other business executives advise the dean on issues that link the worlds of law and business.

Ide's curiosity will always lead him to new challenges. "Every five or six years, I find that I have to walk to the other side of the mountain to see what's there," he admitted. "When I'm next on that journey, I will let my passion be my guide."

Charles Hobson, Visual Artist

When Charles Hobson was senior vice president of Comdisco Financial Services—the San Francisco-based finance firm he co-founded—during the early 1980s, he also was a fine arts student at the San Francisco Art Institute. And when the 1968 Law School graduate received his BFA in 1988 from the Art Institute and decided to become a full-time visual artist and teacher, he admitted that he gave "short shrift" to any contribution his legal training could possibly have made to his new career.

That was until his son, Parker, entered the law school last year. Then, a shift like the one that Hobson claimed marked his transition from lawyer also sparked in him a new acknowledgment for the role his legal education continues to play in his work as an artist. "Observing Parker's experience in Charlottesville has let me see the intellectual rigor that he's encountering and has made it obvious to me how integral that training is in my own work," Hobson said. "Even though my life seems to have taken me a vast distance away from the law school, the skills I learned there are solidly embedded in my working approach and sensibility."

Hobson describes these skills as a kind of "mental discipline" he learned at the law school that enables him to "turn facts over and over. again, pondering conflicting evidence, and becoming increasingly aware of the elusive nature of human language."

A longtime fan of artists' books, Hobson uses pastel, monotypes (an oil-painted image printed on paper), and other printmaking variations to construct images for books and works on paper. "I often follow an historical theme in my work and employ the monotype as a type of 'under painting' on which I apply pastel, acrylic, and printed texts," Hobson explained.

He cites as an example of this technique his new work, entitled "Shipwreck Stories." It was inspired by the true story of an 1865 shipwreck off the coast of California. The ship, overloaded with passengers, livestock, and other cargo, began to sink in a storm. Amid the ensuing chaos, one passenger—trained as a lawyer—sat down on deck and wrote a will and a final letter to the woman from whom he rented his house. Then he tucked the documents into his breast pocket and

donned two life jackets before drowning along with everyone else on board. In reading the story, Hobson became fascinated with the passenger's actions. How did he have the presence of mind to sit down and write a will? Why did he write to his landlady? "After mulling this over and over, I decided to take the facts of the shipwreck story and invent fictions based on that story which I presented through drawings," Hobson said.

In all of his work—which includes two books published as trade editions, fourteen limited editions, and nearly a dozen one-person exhibitions—Hobson's approach is equally thoughtful and exacting. He believes he has the law school to thank for some of his success. "It's clear to me that the intellectual tools I acquired at the Law School—which include acuity, judgment, and a sharp focus on the meaning of words—have served me far beyond what I expected or even imagined."

Richard Glanton, Foundation President

When Richard Glanton '72 boarded the train home from his corporate and finance practice at Philadelphia's Reed Smith Shaw & McClay twelve years ago, little did he know that, on that train, a colleague would ask him to join the board of nearby Lincoln University. He certainly did not know that soon he would be named Lincoln's general counsel and, as a result of that appointment, would be placed in charge of the Barnes Foundation, a major charitable trust controlled by Lincoln. In fact, Glanton's name might never have been recognized outside of Pennsylvania had not decisions he made regarding the trust engendered controversy throughout the art world.

The Merion, Pennsylvania-based Barnes Foundation had long been an unusual place. Founded in 1922 by Albert Barnes, a poor native of Philadelphia and a manufacturer of patent medicines who made a fortune by the age of 33 and devoted his lifetime to collecting some of the world's most famous paintings, the Barnes Foundation reflects Barnes's personal mission: to teach people to look at art in a less rarefied way than scholars do and to see the relationship of paintings to daily life. An eccentric, Barnes displayed his more than eleven hundred paintings—including works by Renoir, Cézanne, Matisse,

Picasso, Manet, van Gogh, and El Greco—throughout his home, hanging masterpieces next to works by unknown artists. He did not open the foundation to visitors, only to a small group of students who studied there, and reportedly would not allow art critics and other members of the world's intelligentsia to enter.

A year before his death in 1951, Barnes decided that Lincoln University, a primarily black school, should have the authority to supply trustees to the Barnes Foundation. Soon after Glanton became Lincoln's general counsel, the call came into the university that the foundation's president was retiring, and Glanton was tapped to fill the vacancy.

Glanton is the first to admit that he did not have the training one might expect from someone charged with overseeing one of the world's most impressive collections of art. "I took one art appreciation course as an undergraduate at West Georgia College, and that was about it," he said. Glanton did bring to the table a J.D. from the University of Virginia, a partnership in a center city Philadelphia law firm. and years of experience in trusts and estate work.

"When I got to the Barnes and looked around, I saw that we had $4 billion worth of art and no money to care for it," he said. Describing the foundation as an "arrested culture" where little has changed in years, Glanton was horrified to learn that the building that housed the paintings was deteriorating, and conditions were such that the art was not being adequately protected. While the foundation made available $1 million per year for repairs, that would not begin to cover the costs necessary to bring the Barnes up to code and to protect the precious artwork within.

"It was really clear to me that one way to help the foundation might be by loaning or de-accessioning some of the artwork, or by some other means," Glanton explained. "However, that action was expressly prohibited by the indenture. It was obvious to me that we would have to petition the court to change the indenture. But when I proposed this action to the foundation board and the word got out, I quickly became the 'bad boy' of the art world."

After a protracted legal battle, Glanton succeeded in amending the foundation's charter to permit the loan of some paintings as well as opening the Barnes to the public and making certain works available for exhibition domestically and overseas. Through it all, his goal was to raise money to protect the collection and to modernize the Barnes.

Since then, the Barnes Foundation has opened to the public on a part-time basis, and a collection of masterpieces has been exhibited at leading museums around the world, bringing in millions in fees and making the collection accessible to art lovers everywhere. A renovation of the Barnes has just been completed, and a major exhibition of the collection is being considered for 1999 in Europe.

Glanton is clear that he does not stand to benefit financially from his involvement with the Barnes. "I support my family with my law practice, and I will always do so." he said. Yet, when his five-year term as president of the foundation was up in 1995, he signed on for another term.

"We have accomplished a number of things already," Glanton said, noting that "we've put the Barnes collection on the map and created a worldwide interest in art appreciation. What we need to do next is to take on the foundations education policy." And there is little doubt in anyone's mind that Glanton is equal to the challenge.

Dan Meador, Novelist

In addition to his title of Professor Emeritus, longtime Law School faculty member Dan Meador also is called "novelist."

"It's true that I have written two novels, but I don't see novel writing as my second career," Meador said. "Since I am still very involved in academic pursuits, I view novel-writing as an added dimension to my current career, rather than as a completely new venture or a second career."

Meador's first novel, *His Father's House*, was published by Pelican in 1994. Part mystery, part romance, part lawyer's tale, it is about an American law professor who discovers in his deceased father's effects a photo of an attractive young German woman. His second novel, *Unforgotten*, has just been accepted for publication by Pelican and is scheduled for release in 1999.

Meador admits that he carried the idea for his first novel around in his head and his heart for years before he sat down to write. "The pressure to write just built up in me much like in a pressure cooker, until I had to let it out," he said. "I found that the only way to relieve the pressure was to sit down and get going."

Before starting the novel, Meador read widely on the art and craft of fiction writing, accepting some ideas he read and rejecting others. He found that, contrary to what several how-to-write books recommended, he was not able to outline the structure of the entire novel before writing it. "I found out that I could outline the first third of the novel but after that, I wasn't sure what the characters would do," he admitted.

He also discovered that conducting a lot of research into the subject of his novels was not his style. "I subscribe to the school of thought that claims one should write what one knows and sees, coupled with a lot of imagination," he said.

Meador did learn that writing a novel requires a great deal of perseverance. Fortunately, a dedication to writing was not foreign to this gifted teacher and scholar who has written extensively on the role of the American judiciary during his forty-five-year legal career. Meador has been a member of the Law School faculty since 1957 except for a four-year period during which he served as dean of the law school at the University of Alabama, where he received his J.D. in 1951. He also served in the U.S. Army, clerked for Justice Hugo L. Black of the U.S. Supreme Court, spent two years in private practice in Alabama, and served as assistant attorney general in the US Department of Justice's Office for Improvements in the Administration of Justice in addition to remaining active in the ABA and serving on a number of boards and commissions.

Meador wrote *His Father's House* at night and on weekends while still engaged full-time in teaching and research at the law school. "I found that it was necessary for me to write four to five days a week for 90 minutes to two hours at a time, to really see progress," he said. At this rate, he finished a first draft in 18 months, only to spend the next two years revising and rewriting it, and another two years getting the novel published.

His second novel, *Unforgotten*, progressed a bit more quickly. This time, the entire process—from writing the first word to securing a publisher—took only two years.

Meador believes that lawyers are uniquely suited to writing fiction. "Novels are about conflict and lawyers are trained to prevent conflict and to resolve it," he explained. He also noted that, in his travels since his first novel was published, lawyers who are also aspiring novelists have come "out of the woodwork" to talk with him about his avocation.

The advice he offers these individuals is simple. "Be certain that you want to write for the right reasons," he cautioned. "If you think that you're going to write a best-seller and make a lot of money, that's the wrong way to look at it. You should be writing to satisfy yourself, to create something of lasting value that uplifts the reader."

"I find novel-writing both an interesting and peculiar intellectual process and a diversionary exercise," Meador continued. "I think of it in the same way that someone said of William Faulkner: 'He looked into the heart of life and wrote what he saw.'"

2
Thoughts on a Second Career

GEORGE H. CAIN

Some years ago, Marilyn Monroe starred in a movie entitled *The Seven Year Itch*. The film suggests that all young marrieds become disenchanted after their seventh anniversary and seek a change of mate. It may be said that many lawyers get the same "itch" with respect to law practice. The desire for career change can come at any age; it is not a phenomenon limited to senior lawyers. Junior lawyers often move from private practice to join a corporate law department. Many senior lawyers have attained their seventieth or eightieth birthdays before making significant career changes. It is never too early, nor too late.

Before we proceed much further, we need to define what we mean by a *second career*. After all, is not a lawyer always a lawyer, no matter what he or she is doing? Well, that may be true, but for our purposes, we shall consider moving from, say, private practice into government, or from the bench into academia, or from the corporate world into institutional work as a career change—a *second career*.

Personal Considerations

Talents and Weaknesses

As you contemplate such a change, it is necessary to take inventory on a personal level. The assets you have available must be viewed in light of the requirements of the new course you are considering. The approach to a second career involves different considerations for the person about to

retire and for the person who is merely unhappy with his or her present position.

What about the person about to retire? Retirement is, for most active people, a traumatic experience. You should consider it well ahead of its happening and decide your best course. There are some who are "workaholics," who never want to retire from active work, and there are others who anxiously anticipate being able to spend every day sailing, golfing, or playing tennis—or maybe doing nothing.

Lawyers—young, middle-aged, or senior—need to do a thorough job of taking stock of talents and weaknesses. In the tough, highly competitive economy of today, every person must stand up against other people who are highly skilled. Should you be contemplating starting a second career in the foreign service, for example, you must evaluate your own competency and learning ability in foreign languages and whether your health is robust enough that service abroad is feasible.

This means that you need to take inventory. What is the state of your health and capacity for work? A new position may require more or less expenditure of physical energy than the job you are leaving. It may require considerable travel or long hours at the office or in a library.

Financial Factors

What are the financial stakes? Sometimes, career changes are made for the purpose of increasing income, particularly at a time in life when expenses are rising—as in the case of a person who is facing his or her children's higher educational expenses. At other times, the financial rewards are secondary, and a career change that may not have been feasible at one point in life becomes "doable" as the need for income declines. Nonetheless, lawyers are generally well-compensated, and they become accus-

George H. Cain, a retired partner of Day, Berry & Howard, is of counsel to the firm, Connecticut's largest. A lawyer for forty-five years, he was secretary and chief counsel to several national corporations before returning to private law practice in 1980.

tomed to incomes above those of society in general. In embarking upon a second career, a lawyer must decide whether it will produce sufficient income and, if not, whether the family has other assets that will make up the difference.

In order to inventory the family's financial resources, consider the size of your investment portfolio. How much income will it produce? Then determine how much you will draw in Social Security payments. Do you have any other pension income? How much will you have to pay in federal and state income taxes, keeping in mind that you must start withdrawing from your Keogh and IRA accounts in the year after you reach age 70½? While the IRS bases the required amount for withdrawal upon the life expectancies of the taxpayer and his or her spouse, in general, the amount to be withdrawn is approximately 5 percent annually of the total in all the taxpayer's Keogh and IRA accounts; this sum is added to the taxpayer's taxable income. Also, remember that the amounts withdrawn represent your capital, and if you spend it, that amount will no longer produce income.

Next, determine what you plan to do with your lifestyle. Must you maintain the same lifestyle or are you willing to sacrifice a bit? As a rule of thumb, it is said that you need about 60 percent of preretirement income during retirement to maintain an acceptable lifestyle. Will your second career require capital investment on your part? Will your second career provide income so that you can afford to use some of your capital as security to borrow whatever capital the second career requires?

Malpractice Insurance

Whether you decide to perform legal services pro bono or for compensation, a major consideration is the cost of malpractice insurance. Lawyers working with legal service organizations usually have protection under the organization's malpractice insurance policy, but you should check to make sure that the organizations you propose to serve will give you that coverage. Should you decide to hang out your shingle or become of counsel to a law office that may expect you to provide your own coverage, then you must consider the premium cost. Rates vary considerably from state to state and depend upon the nature of, and the degree of risk in, the lawyer's practice

and his or her experience. Suffice it to say that for a $100,000/$300,000 per claim, $1,000 deductible policy that can be purchased for as little as $350 the first year in a smaller state, premium rates range upward to almost $9,000 per year for $5,000,000 of coverage in a larger state. These premiums may increase substantially if your practice is in a "volatile area." The insurance providers list a number of "volatile areas," for example, corporate law, estates and trusts, and personal injury law on the plaintiff's side. Unfortunately, each lawyer or law firm is evaluated separately, and the premium is assessed separately, so it is difficult to know ahead of time what the premium cost will be.

Your Own Office

There is also the expense associated with starting your own office, if that is your choice for a second career. Most of these costs are self-evident: rent, utilities, secretarial salary and benefits, law library services, and office equipment rental or purchase (computer, printer, photocopier, facsimile machine, telephone system, file cabinets, reception room furniture, and so on). Then there are costs that are easier to overlook. The active lawyer is usually assessed more in the way of occupational tax, bar membership fees, and so on than the inactive lawyer. There are taxes related to the business of lawyering, such as license fees and unemployment taxes. There are bills for subscriptions to legal periodicals that are essential to active practice.

This should not discourage you from opening your office. Just be sure that your best estimate of the fees you can generate from your practice indicates that your income will be sufficient to cover the expenses and provide some profit. After all, that is why you decided to remain an active practitioner, is it not?

Even if you are committed to working pro bono every day as a practitioner, remember that you will have expenses for travel, automobile, parking, luncheons, and the like that you will not have if you elect to retire from practice altogether. You need to factor those expenses into the equation when you are about to make your decision as to what to do.

Psychological Issues

The psychological issues in reaching a second-career decision should not be ignored. Experts tell us that people should address these issues two to three years before their retirement date. The various alternatives open to the future retiree—remaining in the same area, moving to the Sun Belt, continuing to practice for compensation or pro bono, leaving the law altogether—need to be discussed with spouse, relatives, close friends, and business associates. Bear in mind that your decision affects these people as much, or even more than, it affects you; you owe it to them to have them share in your choice.

Often a retirement program involves not only a change of work, but also a change of residence. It is stressful to move to an area where nobody knows you and you have to cultivate new friends. To move to a new place where nobody knows you, where your income is limited, and where you are not important to anybody else is a big shock. Psychologists recommend that retirees join previous friends or acquaintances in whatever colonies may have established. These are generally recognized retirement communities either abroad or in this country.

Your mood as a retiree has an effect on those around you. Consequently, it is important to find out what they think about your plans. Is your spouse in accord with your proposal for life and, perhaps, work as a retiree? How will the new assignment affect your spouse? And how will others—family, friends, and peers—view you in your new post? The answers to these questions and the effect on you are factors to be taken into careful consideration.

Often, if the choice seems especially painful, the assistance of a professional counselor may be desirable and helpful. Conscientious people reach retirement age and at that point reassess their lives. What did I do? What have I accomplished? Where am I now? Where should I go from here? It is important that these questions be answered satisfactorily. When they are, the individual's new career will have meaning, and he or she will enjoy self-esteem.

Choosing the New Career

Remaining in Law Practice

In seeking a second career, lawyers may hesitate to move outside the profession. The law is a jealous mistress and has a way of captivating its members.

Moving to the Large Firm

Many lawyers have spent their entire lives as solo practitioners or as partners in small law firms. Their lives were stressful because it was necessary to keep abreast of developments in many areas of the law. For a lawyer in this group, a second career in a large firm may seem attractive. It would be a welcome relief to concentrate on a single legal discipline and to let one's colleagues in the firm provide the expertise on the others. Finding a large law firm willing to take on a senior lawyer may not be an easy task; it only becomes possible if the firm needs a lawyer in a particular field of practice and the senior has the experience being sought. Locating an office with a requirement for your talents involves contact with partners you know in the large firms, use of all your networking skills (particularly with fellow lawyers familiar with your abilities) and, possibly, discussions with search firms specializing in serving law firms. If you have a client base that you can bring along, the firm will find it easier to make an offer, provided that the clients are not dying off or retiring to the Sun Belt. You may also be expected by the firm to develop or expand your own stable of clients; doing that after age 65 is difficult.

Shifting to the Small Office

Other lawyers have worked a lifetime in a large firm. They may believe it would be a pleasant shift of gears to work with a small firm or to open their own office. However, you must be realistic. A smaller office may prove to have as great a pressure point as the larger office, depending upon the nature of its practice. Lawyers in the entertainment field may find that their clients call them at all hours and on any day of the week; on the other hand, lawyers with a substantial tax practice may be extremely busy only at particular portions of the year. Before making a shift to escape "large office burden," you should look carefully at the alternative. The shift to a small office or to your own office may be practical if you can retire early enough so that friends and business associates are still active and can become clients. The law office without clients is a very boring place! You must also consider whether the people who came to you as their lawyer when you were with a large firm would continue to retain you if you are lawyering with a small firm or working as a solo practitioner.

11

The older lawyer may find opening an office entirely feasible if attempted early enough—say, age 60—to allow time for the building of a client base. Of course, if you have independent means, so that income from law practice is not essential to your survival, then lack of money is not a barrier to opening an office.

For some, the problems associated with opening an office or establishing a new firm may be formidable. In these instances, it might be preferable to seek an of counsel relationship with a law firm with which you already have a good relationship.

Serving as Of Counsel

The of counsel position is also an attractive alternative for the partner in a firm who is faced with mandatory retirement. Your clients know you, are familiar with your firm, and are comfortable in their dealings. Should you move to another firm after you retire, these clients may not follow you. If you move and they do follow you, they will have to become familiar with the customs of the new firm and your new colleagues. To stay with your former partners avoids the stress that comes with change. In any case, should you decide to establish an of counsel arrangement, it should be reflected in a written agreement.

The Of Counsel Agreement

The purpose of the of counsel agreement, as with any other, is to avoid misunderstanding between the parties. Many law firms do not have a written agreement with their retired partners. The of counsel agreement supplies that deficiency. In the case of the retiree who joins an organization with which he or she had no prior affiliation, it is equally important—for somewhat different reasons—to have a written contract.

The first thing to be decided before setting the arrangement on paper is to determine what type of relationship you contemplate. Do you want to be an employee or an independent contractor? The answer to this question may have a number of consequences, such as, for example, the effect on your taxes, your health and disability insurance coverage, your malpractice insurance protection, and your independence in your activities. Because of these factors, you may want to be an employee for some purposes and an independent contractor for others.

Opinion 90-357

No matter which relationship you have, you probably will be called "of counsel" or "counsel" or some similar title. Because of Formal Opinion 90-357 of the ABA Standing Committee on Ethics and Professional Responsibility issued on May 10, 1990, there are both requirements and limits with respect to use of the title "of counsel."

What about use of the title? The caption to the Opinion states it succinctly:

> The use of the title "of counsel," or variants of that title, in identifying the relationship of a lawyer or law firm with another lawyer or firm is permissible as long as the relationship between the two is a close, regular, personal relationship and the use of the title is not otherwise false or misleading.

But apart from title, there are other reasons to be very clear in defining the relationship with your firm. Certainly, you want to avoid having the liability of a partner, so you must avoid the indicia of partnership. The doctrine of apparent authority applies here.

What should go into the of counsel agreement?

Employee or Independent Contractor

Do you want to be an employee of the firm or an independent contractor? If you are an employee, there are certain advantages: as an employee, you are entitled to fringe benefits, such as medical and disability insurance and malpractice coverage; as an employee, usually you will have no minimum hours. And there is a disadvantage: as an employee, you cannot report your unreimbursed expenses on Schedule C, and you will be subject to the 2 percent floor; that is, the only expenses you can deduct are those exceeding 2 percent of adjusted gross income.

If you are an independent contractor, you will not be controlled in your activities, as you would be if you were an employee. You can deduct your unreimbursed expenses without being subject to the 2 percent floor. As Harold Wren has pointed out, as an independent contractor, you may have to pay only one-half the 15.3 percent Social Security tax. This is so because the independent contractor is permitted an adjustment of one-half the tax on line 25 of Form 1040, so that filing in that capacity cuts in half the amount that must be paid. The independent contractor, therefore, receives the same tax treatment for the Social Security tax as an employee. On the flip side, as an independent contractor, you might be excluded from medical and disability benefits. Your safest bet is to choose the best of all worlds: establish yourself as an independent contractor for purposes of your relationship with your firm, but commit the firm to treating you as an employee for health insurance and other benefit plans.

In any event—whether employee or independent contractor—it is important that you think about malpractice insurance, and you should plan to include in the agreement the understanding between you and your firm as to whether as of counsel you will be covered.

Malpractice policies are "claims made" policies. Consequently, policies that may have covered you before retirement no longer cover you thereafter—unless you have a specific agreement with your former firm. And premiums are very high. Rightly or wrongly, some carriers take the position that the more experienced the lawyer, the more complicated and sophisticated the transactions he or she undertakes and the greater the risk of substantial exposure to the carrier. As we have mentioned above, the premium also varies depending on the type of practice in which the lawyer plans to engage.

Duties as Of Counsel

The of counsel agreement should spell out the nature and extent of your duties. Will you have responsibilities to clients and, if so, exactly how will they change, if at all, from your responsibilities as a partner? Will you be required to turn over responsibility for your clients to other partners in the firm? Will you be required or permitted to perform legal services either for your old clients, for new clients you have obtained, or for other clients of the firm? Will you have any administrative duties? Will you be permitted to attend firm meetings? Will you be required or permitted to serve on firm committees? Will you have any client development obligations? Will you have any obligation to assist in the hiring or training of new lawyers for the firm?

The importance of spelling out the duties that a lawyer who is of counsel is to perform cannot be overemphasized. If you, as of counsel, are allowed to participate in the various benefit programs that normally accrue only to persons active in the firm, then you must expect to have responsibilities that you must discharge. And certain medical programs permit enrollment of only those persons who work a minimum number of hours—usually about thirty—per week. Some duties, therefore, are in your best interest.

Requirements for Title

You should be aware that Opinion 90-357 does not permit the use of the title "of counsel" in the situation where the lawyer is affiliated only for a particular case, although it seems permissible to list a lawyer or firm as of counsel in the pleadings, where it is clear that the relationship pertains only to that particular case. The title may not apply for "casual collaborative efforts" or where the relationship is that of an outside consultant. The relationship must be close, regular, and personal; the assignment of duties should reflect that situation.

In New York, according to a Nassau County ethics opinion, a lawyer may affiliate as of counsel to two law firms; but in Ohio, the same lawyer may not practice law with more than one law firm at one time. In New York, again, according to a Nassau County opinion, a lawyer may not be designated as of counsel when his or her sole function is the referral of clients to the firm; use of the title must involve the performance of legal services by the lawyer; fee-splitting is not permitted. Just to show that you must look at the local rules in the state where you might plan to serve, note that in Arizona, a firm can split fees with its of counsel lawyer if the fee is split on the basis of the amount of work done by the firm and the lawyer. However, in Texas, fee-splitting is permitted with the of counsel who has a regular, continuing, and substantial relationship with the firm. In March 1993, the Los Angeles County Bar Association adopted Ethics Opinion 470. This opinion states that the payment of a year-end bonus to an of counsel attorney who is not a partner, associate, or shareholder of the law firm and whose relationship to the law firm consists primarily of the reciprocal referral of business is prohibited without client consent under the California rule against fee-splitting.

The Firm's Responsibilities

Not every of counsel is a lawyer retired from a law firm, and many are persons retired from a corporation, government, or academia. The working standards in each of these institutions vary greatly from each other and from those of most law firms. To avoid misunderstandings during the course of the new relationship, it is important that the duties of "second career" people be described clearly and adequately.

The firm should have certain duties toward you and these, also, should be spelled out. Must the firm provide you with an office? Of what size? What office services are to be available to you, and will you be obliged to pay for any of these services, or will they be provided at no charge to you? Will the firm pay, or reimburse you for, dues to, or expenses in attending meetings of, professional organizations and, if so, which entities? Will the expenses of your spouse in attending meetings of professional groups be reimbursed? And, as mentioned previously, the firm's obligations to cover you under medical and disability insurance programs and for malpractice insurance should be expressly stated. The agreement also should be explicit as to who must pay the premium for this coverage.

Compensation

Whatever the arrangement you have with the firm regarding compensation, it should be spelled out in writing in the of counsel agreement. And there are, perhaps, as many variations of compensation arrangements as there are lawyers.

Often a lawyer will become of counsel to the firm from which he or she retires as a partner. In that case, the partnership agreement may spell out what the retired lawyer is to receive. If the partnership agreement is silent, then the of counsel agreement must supply the omission.

Assuming that, as of counsel, you will have duties, then it is reasonable to presume that the firm expects to pay you for performance. Where the duties are those for which the firm will be compensated—such as working on a client's matters—then the agreement may provide that you will receive some percentage of the fee. If this is the case, the of counsel agreement should give you the right to approve the hourly rate being charged for your services. If you are producing the business but not working on the matters produced, the of counsel agreement should be certain to give you other duties giving rise to your right of compensation; otherwise, you may find yourself in the position of engaging in prohibited fee-splitting with your firm, especially if you are

an independent contractor. Where the duties are noncompensated—such as client development activities—then it may be appropriate to pay you an agreed upon annual stipend, payable monthly or at some other interval. In the most preferable arrangement, and the one likely to give rise to the least controversy, the firm will elect to pay you a negotiated amount on an annual basis to cover all of your work for the firm and will not make any charge for firm services provided to you.

Hours of Work Annually

When a lawyer joins a law firm as of counsel, particularly from corporate, government, or academic life, it is important to understand the work ethic expected by the firm. Since a lawyer who is of counsel is supposed to be retired and "taking it easy," he or she, theoretically at least, will not be working as hard. But both the lawyer and the firm should be clear on this. Therefore, the of counsel agreement should state specifically how many hours the firm expects you—as of counsel—to work per year. It should be clear that those hours may include time spent in performing services of benefit to the firm that do not necessarily result directly in compensation to the firm, such as attendance at professional meetings, legal writing, client development efforts, and the like. The number of hours required should bear some reasonable relationship to the rate of compensation, taking into account the value of the benefits being provided by the firm, in order to avoid dissatisfaction on both sides with the arrangement.

Conflicts of Interest

In deciding upon an of counsel arrangement, a lawyer must give careful consideration to any possible conflicts of interest that may arise. If the difficulties should appear insurmountable, perhaps it will be necessary to seek an arrangement elsewhere. Confront the conflicts issue early on, and make sure there is no problem so you can avoid frustration and disappointment further down the road.

Most conflict problems are caused by a lawyer's simultaneous or successive representation of clients with adverse interests. But conflicts situations arise in other contexts. Suppose a lawyer wishes to serve of counsel to two or more firms, as is permissible in New York. For purposes of applying the rules governing conflicts, it is as if both or all of these firms were a single firm. Even if lawyers associate together for office space but practice independently, if they have access to one another's files, they are treated as partners for conflicts purposes.

Most lawyers recognize that simultaneous representation of two clients with adverse interests is prohibited. Constant monitoring of any potential situation is essential to ensure that no conflict exists that requires attention.

In the matter of successive representation of clients with adverse interests, a different sort of problem is presented. Here it is a matter of preserving loyalty to the former client and confidentiality of matters disclosed during the representation. These factors must be evaluated carefully.

Presumptions

When lawyers are associated, there is an irrebuttable presumption in the case of present associates that confidences have been shared. Thus, the client of any one lawyer is the client of all for the purpose of determining conflicts. In the case of past associates, the current trend seems to be that the presumption of shared confidences is rebuttable. It then becomes a matter of fact as to what the lawyer, now seeking to be of counsel, knew as to matters handled by other lawyers in his or her former firm. Several cases are mentioned in Harold Wren's book dealing with this problem, and I will commend them to you if you are confronted with this question.

"Chinese Walls"

The rules applied to former government lawyers are, in a sense, less restrictive; the "Chinese wall," which does not receive many accolades when lawyers in the private sector are involved, appears to be more tolerable where government lawyers are concerned.

Lawyers moving from the corporate world or from government to the private sector often are called as witnesses with respect to matters formerly handled by them in their corporate and government jobs. Most states prohibit a lawyer— and the law firm with which he or she is associated—from handling a matter as counsel when the lawyer is to be a witness for the client. One should keep this in mind in considering where to establish an of counsel arrangement.

Potential Client Conflicts

There is an important recent opinion of the Committee on Professional and Judicial Ethics of the Association of the Bar of the City of New York, Formal Opinion 1991-1, dated April 30, 1991, and reported in the October 1991 issue of *The Record of the Association*. This opinion, stated as simply as possible, says that if a lawyer is representing a particular client, and he or she is seeking to represent another client whose interests are, or may be, adverse to the present client, this fact must be disclosed to both clients, and both must consent or the future employment must be declined. Since lawyers becoming of counsel in many instances are attempting to market their services to new clients, it is important, in light of this opinion, to make sure that the effort to obtain representation of the new clients will not have to be disclosed to present clients of the firm.

Term

As with any agreement, the of counsel agreement should have a definite term. However, the of counsel arrangement is a little different. All does not come to an end with a termination in this situation. Some aspects of the relationship undoubtedly will be retained. For example, the lawyer who is of counsel may continue to have an office and some office services available to him or her. Similarly, he or she may have some responsibility after termination of the formal arrangement. Whatever the understanding, it should be spelled out.

Should it not be feasible to determine now what the arrangement is to be after the term ends, the agreement should provide for orderly conclusion of the arrangement. The parties can always reach a new agreement, and it is unnecessary to state so in the current agreement.

The nature of the of counsel agreement is discussed in more detail in the volume entitled *The Of Counsel Agreement*, written by Harold G. Wren and Beverly G. Glascock and published by the Senior Lawyers Division of the ABA.

Moving from Private Practice into Other Fields

There are almost limitless reasons why lawyers choose to leave private practice for other fields of law—the judiciary, politics, academia, or the corporate law department, for example. Such changes would rarely be dictated by economics since, I believe, they are seldom more remunerative than private practice. Rather, personal goals and desires are the motivating factors. For many, politics holds an almost mystical attraction; for some, there is the opportunity for the prestige of a judgeship; for others, the desire to teach or the challenge of business. Age is a limiting factor in the ability to make a career change to these categories. While one may shift into politics at practically any age, a seat on the bench or an opportunity to teach usually requires some experience and a degree of maturity. On the other hand, senior lawyers are not likely to commence a political career, receive a judicial appointment, or join a corporate law department.

Sometimes, a person must have a spirit of adventure to accept particular career changes. The lawyer who chooses to enter the foreign service may find himself or herself living abroad in a strange country where American citizens travel to their offices by different routes each day to avoid being kidnapped and where families live behind well-gated walls for security. One adventurous lawyer chose to undertake a solo circumnavigation of the world. Then there are other possible choices to consider. Lawyers have opted to move from private practice to the trade association, to become expert witnesses, to serve as arbitrators or mediators, to become professional directors, and to become authors of fiction.

There is a degree of uncertainty in every career change. Perhaps the new position will not offer the rewards or the security you anticipate. It may even thrust you into the public spotlight of controversy. Witness the plight of the lawyer who left the security of a large Manhattan law firm to take over the deanship of the University of Bridgeport Law Center and found himself one day a virtual prisoner in his own office.

Moving from the Judiciary to Other Fields

Faced with state law regarding mandatory retirement, judges are often asked to step down from active work before they are ready. Fortunately, judges usually have many second careers from which to choose. There are opportunities to serve as a law school dean, to return to private law practice, or to serve as a judicial hearing officer. It is feasible to change careers after serving in the judiciary. Sometimes the opportunity presents

itself, but at other times, you must use your imagination to seek out a new course. As always, contact with friends and networking are the most valuable sources of possibilities.

Moving from Academia into New Pursuits

Few lawyers in academia make the transition into the corporate world or private practice. However, it is possible. As we know, many well-known professors at major institutions find advisory positions to the media and serve as trial counsel in highly visible litigation. For the lesser-known academician, the opportunities are more limited. Business is often skeptical of the practical approach of the law professor, and law firms may question whether a teacher of law will be a source of sufficient business, unless he or she has numerous contacts stemming from earlier phases of his or her life.

Opting for Public Service

Pro Bono Service

In many cities, there are hundreds, if not thousands, of public and private entities, charitable in nature, needing legal assistance on almost a daily basis. For example, in New York City, the need was perceived to be so great that the Association of the Bar of the City of New York created a Committee of Senior Lawyers, a principal function of which would be the coordination of pro bono assistance between the Association's hundreds of members interested in providing assistance and the organizations needing the help.

Many eleemosynary institutions lack the resources necessary to have a lawyer on staff or to pay for retained legal services. In any event, even if such funds are available, any not-for-profit institution will welcome the opportunity to save on legal expense. A retired lawyer—particularly one who is experienced as a general practitioner—will be able to contribute handsomely by volunteering his or her legal services.

Many retired lawyers could render a valuable service by serving as counsel to a worthy cause. Since concern about proper malpractice insurance is always present, many recognized groups provide an umbrella of coverage for those lawyers willing to give of their time and energy.

Arbitration

Arbitration, mediation, and alternative dispute resolution are burgeoning fields related to the law. The services of retired lawyers can be used in all of these areas. In some instances, those who volunteer their services receive no compensation in the initial stages of a case but are paid if the matter becomes extended over time. The American Arbitration Association has offices in many cities throughout the United States, conducts training programs for arbitrators, and offers the services of those on their panels who, by experience, have become qualified in the subject matter of a dispute. The advertising pages of the major national and regional legal newspapers contain the names and addresses of organizations devoted to other phases of dispute resolution. A letter and résumé sent to these organizations could start the ball rolling toward a new career as an arbitrator or mediator.

Lawyers have a wealth of experience in matters beyond the law: in organization, financial planning, and human resources. Aside from providing purely legal assistance, helping in these other areas will be both challenging and interesting. There are organizations of retired executives who provide uncompensated assistance to start-up companies and charitable institutions; lawyers who have knowledge and talent in bringing people together and in the area of finance would be valuable additions to these groups. Other lawyers have undertaken to become professional experts in fields of law in which they have superior knowledge. In some states, lawyers may function as real estate brokers or agents without any license other than the license as an attorney-at-law.

Politics

Still another interesting second career possibility is in the field of politics. Politics carries a financial cost. It takes a considerable amount of money to run for the town council, considerably more to run for the state legislature, and large sums indeed to run for the Congress. Consequently, a prospective candidate must have either substantial financial resources or the ability to raise large sums. The person approaching or in retirement is not always able to spend the campaign funds required.

If you elect to proceed on a political course, there is the considerable task of securing a nomination or a party endorsement. If you have not paid your political dues by working diligently in election after election during your lifetime, you may not be greeted by the political leaders with any degree of enthusiasm. Nonetheless, if you are a charismatic individual with the speaking voice of a Patrick Henry and you appear to be a sure vote-getter, then you may get the party endorsement you will need.

Lawyers are usually successful in politics. They have the talents and skills needed in the political arena: they are accustomed to mastering new subjects rapidly, and they are accustomed to compromising opposing viewpoints. Not so inviting is the sacrifice that politicians must make respecting life with family and friends. The considerable amount of time spent in traveling and attending vote-gathering and fund-raising events requires the politician to be away from home more than many other professionals.

Government

For many senior lawyers, a period of government service in the judicial or executive branch would be worthwhile. One might seek a judgeship, although the material required to be assembled in preparing a dossier for a federal judgeship—and for most state judicial appointments—is staggering. In a state where judges are elected, there is always the possibility of running for the post. This avoids the dossier problem but carries the burdens of running for political office, which were discussed above.

However, there are many opportunities to assist courts, short of a judgeship, if you are ready to assist on an unpaid basis. A meeting with the chief judge in your federal district or the chief administrative judge in the state court system where you reside will develop the areas in which you may be able to help. Given budgetary restraints and the overburdened system, many judges welcome the help of willing and capable hands. You may be of service in bringing parties to a better definition of the issues in litigation and to a satisfactory resolution of their problems without the necessity of a trial.

Some states offer reciprocal treatment to retired judges from other states and, as in the case

17

of Florida, permit them to sit as trial referees. But "mere lawyers" do not receive this treatment.

Foreign Service

Government service outside the judiciary also offers the possibility of service. The U.S. Department of State and the U.S. Department of Commerce are assembling groups of lawyers willing to travel abroad on an "expenses only" basis. These lawyers assist eastern bloc countries in developing laws and procedures consistent with democracy and capitalism. A clearinghouse for this effort is the Central and Eastern European Law Initiative, headquartered with the American Bar Association's Washington office. Also, the State Department considers lawyers for careers in the foreign service, but candidates must be willing to undergo exhaustive training in a foreign language and accept assignment in areas of the world that lack most of the amenities we in this country take for granted.

Conclusions

A second career for a lawyer is possible at any age, and particularly upon retirement. However, you must make a careful analysis of your personal attributes, financial condition, and psychological setting. There are many second careers from which to choose, depending on the results of your analysis. If you remain in law practice, especially if you decide to become of counsel to a law firm, be sure to have a written agreement with the law firm to avoid misunderstandings about its role and your responsibilities and privileges. Should you determine to leave the law, there are many opportunities to serve your fellow humans in the public arena

3
When a Solo
Takes Down the Shingle

ALAN E. DeWOSKIN

LAW PRACTICE AVAILABLE: Library, furniture, equipment, building, and the practice of a sole practitioner. Goodwill included. Purchaser may be appointed assistant Prosecuting Attorney for balance of term and take over active practice.

Most lawyers, after accomplishing their professional and financial goals, wish to take life a little easier and leave the rigors of practice. A law practice, like a medical or accounting practice, is primarily a service business in which the most valuable component from a financial standpoint is goodwill. Of course, law is a profession, not merely a business. But unlike doctors and other professionals who have long been capable of including goodwill in the valuation of their practices, until recently a solo practitioner's goodwill had no recoverable value for the lawyer who built the practice.

These days, in twenty-three jurisdictions, the solo practitioner who sells a practice is finally getting a square deal financially. He or she may benefit in a way that until recently was assured only to members of firms.

That financial fairness is embodied in the wide-ranging Rule 1.17 (Sale of a Law Practice),[1] which the ABA House of Delegates incorporated into the ABA Model Rules of Professional Conduct in 1990 (1983, as amended) ("Rules").

Most states either have adopted or are seriously considering Rule 1.17, which wipes away long-standing disparities in the treatment of both the clients and lawyers of solo practices. This chapter will review the provisions of Rule 1.17 and the versions adopted by several states. It will be concerned primarily with the ethical parameters of

the sale and briefly with the financial aspects, such as valuation, negotiating a sale, or obtaining financing.[2] The ethically planned sale of a law practice serves the dual purpose of protecting clients during a transitional period and providing equitable compensation to the lawyer or the lawyer's estate

Protecting the Client When a Solo Practitioner Retires

The Rule addresses much more than financial matters: It ensures that a sale is handled ethically and with client confidentiality in mind. Protecting

---

Alan E. DeWoskin is a solo practitioner of Alan E. DeWoskin, P.C. in St. Louis. He was a writer of ABA Model Rule 1.17 and Missouri's Rule 4.1.17.

1. Model Rule 1.17 states as follows:
   A lawyer or a law firm may sell or purchase a law practice, including goodwill, if the following conditions are satisfied:
   (a) The seller ceases to engage in the private practice of law [in the geographic area] [in the jurisdiction] (a jurisdiction may elect either version) in which the practice has been conducted;
   (b) The practice is sold as an entirety to another lawyer or law firm;
   (c) Actual written notice is given to each of the seller"s clients regarding:
      (1) the proposed sale;
      (2) the terms of any proposed change in the fee arrangement authorized by paragraph (d);
      (3) the client"s right to retain other counsel or to take possession of the file; and
      (4) the fact that the client"s consent to the sale will be presumed if the client does not take any action or does not otherwise object within ninety days of receipt of the notice.
   If a client cannot be given notice, the representation of that client may be transferred to the purchaser only upon entry of an order so authorizing by a court having jurisdiction. The seller may disclose to the court *in camera* information relating to the representation only to the extent necessary to obtain an order authorizing the transfer of a file.
   (d) The fees charged clients shall not be increased by reason of the sale. The purchaser may, however, refuse to undertake the representation unless the client consents to pay the purchaser fees at a rate not exceeding the fees charged by the purchaser for rendering substantially similar services prior to the initiation of the purchase negotiations.
2. For a discussion of these factors, see F. E. Lieber, "Primer on the Valuation of Law Practices," and Edward Poll, "Placing a Value on a Law Practice," in VALUING PROFESSIONAL PRACTICES AND LICENSES (Ronald L. Brown, ed., Prentice Hall, 1994).

clients is the most important issue addressed by Rule 1.17. Clients cannot be sold, but the opportunity to represent those clients, with their consent, can be sold to a lawyer competent to represent them under the new Rule.

When a lawyer practicing in a law firm leaves the practice, the firm continues to handle all pending client matters, and the transition for clients is usually smooth. However, if the lawyer was in solo practice in a state that has not adopted Model Rule 1.17 or a similar measure, the transition is not so smooth because there is no law firm ready to take over. To ensure that unfinished client business is taken care of and to avoid losing compensation for the goodwill of the law practice, some sole practitioners enter into haphazard, ill-conceived partnerships with younger partners before leaving the practice. The tacit understanding is that the elder partner will soon retire and receive compensation for the goodwill of the practice, leaving the remaining partner with the client base. However, partnership is not for everyone. There is no logical reason why a lawyer should be forced to establish a partnership simply to benefit from the appreciated value of the practice.

Other lawyers nearing retirement negotiate an inflated value for the physical assets of a law practice with the seller's agreement to refer clients to the purchaser. Such contrived arrangements may harm clients. See, for example, *Geffen v. Moss*, 125 Cal. Rptr. 687 (1975), in which the sales contract terms expressed the seller's intention to encourage clients to use the buyer's services in the future and called for payments to the seller in excess of the stated value of the physical assets.

The adoption of Rule 1.17 removes the incentive for such indirect methods. A direct sale without intervening partnerships or contracts is reasonable and fair and is far more likely to provide a smooth transition in which client affairs are handled competently.

Equitable Compensation for Solo Practitioners or Their Estates

When a solo practitioner who practices in a state without Rule 1.17 dies, the payment to the estate from the lawyer who completes the unfinished client matters is limited by the Rules and similar language in the predecessor Model Code of Professional Responsibility ("Code") to "that proportion of the total compensation which fairly represents the services rendered by the deceased lawyer." (Rule 5.4(a)(2) and DR 3-102(A) of the Code.) Thus, sale of "goodwill" is not permitted and is subject to discipline in those states without a rule specifically permitting it.

For example, in *Raphael v. Shapiro*, 587 N.Y.S.2d 68 (1992), an agreement for the sale of a lawyer's interest in a law firm, and for his goodwill, was found void and unenforceable as violative of the New York Code of Professional Responsibility. The purchasing lawyer succeeded in dismissing the selling lawyer's action for payment. However, because the purchasing lawyer had also knowingly violated the Code, he was not entitled to the return of the purchase price already paid.

Other Rules also limit the amount that may be paid to a sole practitioner who retires in jurisdictions without Rule 1.17. Rule 1.5(e) allows the division of a legal fee between lawyers not in the same firm only in proportion to the services performed or where "by written agreement with the client, each lawyer assumes joint responsibility for the representation." Disciplinary Rule 2-107(A) of the Code permits a division of fees only in proportion to the services performed and responsibility assumed by each lawyer.

In *O'Hara v. Ahlgren, Blumenfield & Kempster*, 537 N.E.2d 730 (Ill. 1989), the widow of a deceased lawyer contracted with a law firm to sell the right to all current and former files and records of her husband's practice in return for a percentage of the fees earned by the law firm, with the percentage gradually diminishing and ending after five years. The clients were notified of the sale after the fact. The Illinois Supreme Court held, inter alia, that the sale was against public policy because of the incentive it provided to the widow to recommend the services of the law firm without regard to the best interest of the clients.

Under agreements between a lawyer not in solo practice and the lawyer's firm, partner, or associate, the estate of the lawyer may receive payments over a reasonable period after the lawyer's death under Rule 5.4(a)(1) and the Code's DR 3-102(A). There is no requirement that the payments be related to any services the lawyer performed. Thus, in effect, the payments to the estate from the deceased lawyer's firm can include the value of the goodwill of the practice, while the compensation received by the estate of a sole practitioner cannot.

This is unfair. No distinction is justified between the solo practitioner and the member of a firm regarding what payments may be received upon retirement or death. A law firm's provisions for payments to a retiring partner and a law firm's requirement that a new partner contribute an equity investment to the firm are financial principles fundamentally identical to those involved in the sale and purchase of a practice.

Solo practitioners, therefore, are unfairly hampered and inconsistently treated in states without Rule 1.17 because they or their estates are prohibited from realizing the value of the goodwill of their practice when they retire or die.

Rule 1.17 Permits the Goodwill of a Law Practice to Be Sold

The sale of the physical assets of a law practice, such as office machines, library, furniture, and the payment of accounts receivable to a retiring or deceased lawyer for work already performed, were and still are allowed in all jurisdictions. For example, an agreement to purchase a law practice from the estate of a deceased lawyer, for which the purchaser would pay a percentage of all fees received pursuant to retainers on the books of the practice over four years, or any formula calculated to reasonably compensate the lawyer or the estate for past services, is permissible everywhere because the formula is merely a way of compensating for past services performed.[3]

What is new about Model Rule 1.17 is that it permits the sale or purchase of a law practice, including its goodwill, if the purchaser is qualified to assume the practice, avoids disqualifying conflicts, and protects information relating to the representation. "Goodwill" is the value assigned to the expectation of future business.[4] Most courts permit a value to be placed on a continuing law practice's goodwill in valuing marital property in a divorce action. See *McLean v. McLean*, 374 S.E.2d 376 (N.C. 1988). But prior to the adoption of Rule 1.17, the goodwill of a law

3. *See, e.g., Detroit Bank & Trust Company v. Coopes*, 287 N.W.2d 266 (Mich.App. 1979).
4. *Id.*

practice was something only members of firms could count on when retiring.

Who Can Sell and Who Can Buy a Law Practice?

Under Rule 1.17, a solo practitioner's practice is saleable to another solo practitioner or to a law partnership or a law professional corporation. The seller must be terminating the practice of law, at least in the same geographic area, and may enter into a covenant not to resume the practice of law in the same area.

The seller must offer the practice as an entirety to a single purchaser. The purchaser may not increase fees charged clients by reason of the sale. The purchaser must accept all of the seller's clients who are willing to retain the purchaser as their new lawyer; except those who refuse to accept the customary fees the purchaser charges and those whose matters would create a conflict of interest. If an entire firm ceases to practice, its clients are left without representation just as if they had been represented by a single lawyer. Therefore, Rule 1.17 also permits a law firm to sell a law practice. If approval of the substitution of the purchasing lawyer for the selling lawyer is required by the rules of any tribunal before which a matter is pending, such approval must be obtained before the matter can be included in the sale.

The law practice of a deceased, disabled, or disappeared lawyer may be sold by a nonlawyer representative not subject to professional responsibility constraints. Since, however, no lawyer may participate in the sale of a law practice that does not conform to the requirements of this rule, the representatives of the seller, as well as the purchasing lawyer, can be expected to see to it that the requirements are met.

The seller has an obligation to exercise competence in identifying a purchaser qualified to assume the practice; the purchaser has an obligation to undertake the representation competently (see Rule 1.1), to avoid disqualifying conflicts and to secure client consent after consultation for those conflicts that can be agreed to (see Rule 1.7). Both seller and purchaser have the obligation to protect information relating to the representation (see Rules 1.6 and 1.9).

The lawyer who purchases the practice of a deceased lawyer or who acquires the practice of a disabled or disappeared colleague may pay the lawyer's representative for the practice without engaging in illegal fee-splitting with a nonlawyer. Contemporaneously with the adoption of Rule 1.17 by the ABA House of Delegates in February 1990, Rule 5.4(a)(2) was amended to allow the purchaser of a law practice to pay a deceased lawyer's estate an amount that does not necessarily represent the same proportion to the total fees as that of the services rendered, thereby allowing for the concept of goodwill. The Comment to Rule 5.6 was also expanded to make it clear that certain right-to-practice restrictions are permissible when a practice is sold.

What Is and Is Not Saleable?

Rule 1.17 lays out the ground rules for satisfying all the ethical duties, including confidentiality, competence, notice, and informed consent, that are involved in transferring client files. It is essential for any lawyer contemplating the sale or the purchase of a law practice to be fully informed of the ethical rules and laws of the applicable jurisdiction and to read the Rule and its Comment in their entirety. Both the seller and the buyer are bound by certain ethical duties. The sales contract should be carefully drawn so it does not violate any ethical rules.

Neither clients nor their files can be sold. The selling lawyer does not own the clients or the clients' records. The clients' legal files may be transferred to another practitioner; but only for safekeeping. They should not be read by the buyer of the practice unless and until the client gives written permission. The client owns all confidential material in the file, and the lawyer cannot sell what the lawyer does not own.

Model Rule 7.2(c), which prohibits a lawyer from giving "anything of value to a person for recommending the lawyer's services (with specified exceptions)," was amended at the same time Rule 1.17 was adopted to allow payment to the seller of a law practice in return for client referrals to the practice purchaser.[5]

5. Model Rule 7.2(c) now reads as follows:
A lawyer shall not give anything of value to a person for recommending the lawyer"s services except that a lawyer may
(1) pay the reasonable costs of advertisements or communications permitted by this Rule;
(2) pay the usual charges of a not-for-profit lawyer referral service or legal service organization; and
(3) pay for a law practice in accordance with Rule 1.17.

Informed Consent

The seller's clients must be notified in writing—before the sale is consummated—of the intended sale; of the purchaser's identity; of any proposed change in the terms of future representation, including any effect on the fees; and of the clients' rights to choose a different lawyer and to reclaim their files. They must be told that the decision to consent or make other arrangements must be made within ninety days or their consent to the sale is presumed and the purchaser is authorized to act on the clients' behalf.

If the lawyer is dead and the practice is sold by the estate, then the purchasing lawyer must alert each client, receive written confirmation of the clients' willingness to be represented, and can presume client compliance if receiving no notice to the contrary within ninety days. Court action is required for clients who cannot be reached.

Of course, when a solo practitioner dies, a lawyer representing the estate of the deceased lawyer or appointed or otherwise responsible for review of files of the deceased lawyer has urgent duties that must take precedence over any negotiations for sale of the practice. That lawyer should (1) review files to the extent necessary to determine which need immediate attention; and (2) contact all clients to notify them of their lawyer's death and to request instructions in accordance with Rule 1.15(b), which requires the prompt notification and delivery to the client or third person of any funds or other property such person is entitled to receive. Fee records must be reviewed and unearned fees refunded pursuant to Rule 1.16(d).[6] The ABA urges the state, local and territorial jurisdictions to address the issue of death or disability of lawyers. By developing procedures for the protection of clients' interests and property and ethical closure or disposition of the practices, the profession will be best served. Among the features recommended for such pro-

6. The ABA Standing Committee on Ethics and Professional Responsibility, in Formal Opinion 92-369, concludes it is the ethical responsibility of every solo practitioner to have a plan in place that will ensure, insofar as is reasonably practicable, that client matters will not be neglected in the event of the lawyer"s death.
For a further discussion of the issues and duties that arise in these circumstances, see Connecticut Op. 92-10; Nassau County (New York) Ops. 89-43, 89-23; Maryland Op. 89-25; Mississippi Op. 114 (1986); Oregon State Bar Opinion 1991-129; Wisconsin Op. E-87-9 (digests of these opinions are available in the ABA/BNA LAWYERS' MANUAL ON PROFESSIONAL CONDUCT).

grams is the incorporation of the principles of Rule 1.17.[7]

Rule 1.17 Is Spreading and Changing

California Rule of Professional Conduct 2-300 has permitted the sale of a law practice, including goodwill, since 1989, predating Model Rule 1.17. Alaska, Colorado, Florida, Hawaii, Idaho, Indiana, Iowa, Massachusetts, Michigan, Minnesota, Missouri, New Jersey, New York, North Carolina, North Dakota, Oklahoma, Oregon, South Dakota, Washington, West Virginia, Wisconsin, and the Virgin Islands have all adopted a version of Rule 1.17 and made the corresponding changes to Rules 5.4, 5.6, 7.2, and/or their Comments. The Supreme Courts of Arkansas, Mississippi, Ohio, Pennsylvania, and South Carolina are considering the adoption of a version of Rule 1.17. The Rules Committee of the Supreme Court of Utah has the matter under study. The Supreme Court of Illinois has rejected the rule to date even though the State Bar Association endorsed Rule 1.17. Currently, the state bar associations of Georgia, Louisiana, Maine, Montana, Nebraska, New Hampshire, Ten-

nessee, and Vermont are considering the adoption of Rule 1.17. Texas and Puerto Rico have taken preliminary steps toward reviewing Rule 1.17. A detailed comparison of the different provisions of the rule by each state is presented in Tables 3–1a, 3–1b, 3–1c, and 3–1d.

There are interesting variations among the adopting states.

Florida's Rule 1.17, (1993), has substantially the same provisions as Model Rule 1.17 except that the purchaser must honor the fee agreements entered into between the seller and the seller's clients. Model Rule 1.17 permits the purchaser to "refuse to undertake the representation unless the client consents to pay the purchaser fees at a rate not exceeding the fees charged by the purchaser for rendering substantially similar services prior to the initiation of the purchase negotiations." Wisconsin also requires the purchaser to honor all existing fee arrangements with clients. And this provision is also part of the Hawaii Rule 1.17 and North Dakota Rule 1.17.

The rule in Florida, Wisconsin, North Dakota, and Hawaii works against the spirit and purpose of Rule 1.17. The purchasing lawyer is not a party to the retainer contract between the selling attorney and his/her clients. The client should be fully informed by the lawyers involved. By not permitting the purchasing lawyer to refuse the representation of clients who will not consent to pay the purchaser's usual fees, the proposed sale may be thwarted or the good-faith effort to protect the client may be circumvented. If there was no sale and the lawyer retired or died, the client would have to pay the existing usual fees in order to hire a lawyer to represent him or her. Therefore, retaining the provision to permit the purchasing lawyer to refuse the representation of clients who will not consent to pay the purchaser's usual fees does not harm the client who can refuse the representation in any event.

Alaska (1993) and the Virgin Islands (1990) have adopted the rule verbatim. Alaska declined to add the following comment to Rule 5.6 Restrictions on Right to Practice: "This Rule does not apply to prohibit restrictions that may be included in the terms of the sale of a law practice pursuant to Rule 1.17."

Colorado (1997) has adopted the Model Rule with the following additions/changes: The notice requirement adds the identity of the purchaser

---

7. The ABA House of Delegates on August 6, 1997 adopted the following Resolution:

RESOLVED, that the American Bar Association urges, state, local and territorial jurisdictions that do not now have programs in place, to address the issue of the death or disability of lawyers and to develop and implement through court rule or other appropriate means effective procedures for the protection of clients' interests and property and the ethical closure or disposition of the practice.

FURTHER RESOLVED, that, without attempting to be exhaustive, the following features are recommended for such programs:

(1) Plans should adhere to the recommendations and precepts of Rule 28 of the ABA Model Rules for Lawyer Disciplinary Enforcement, which outlines procedures for the inventory of files and the protection of confidentiality.

(2) If a practice is to be sold, plans should incorporate the principles of Rules 1.17 of the ABA Model Rules of Professional Conduct ("Sale of Law Practice"), which in the comment states that it applies to the sale of a law practice by a representative as well as other applicable provisions of the Model Rules.

(3) Plans should consider and be guided by the principles stated in Formal Opinion 92-369 of the ABA Committee on Ethics and Professional Responsibility with respect to the disposition of client files and property.

(4) Plans should be jurisdiction-wide but should recognize differences among types of practices and practice settings—rural and urban—and allow flexibility of arrangements appropriate to those differences such as providing, when necessary, that practicing attorneys periodically designate a survivor signatory/trustee; or appoint fiduciaries to close or dispose of practices under jurisdictional supervision.

(5) Plans should provide for expense reimbursement for trustees and fiduciaries closing practices, and consideration should be given to the provision of compensation for services.

Table 3–1a

Rule 1.17 Sale of a Law Practice—Analysis by State

State	Date Adopted	Effective	Ceases to Exist Juris	Geo	Silent	Disclosure Client Info Negotiation	Restrictive Covenants Yes	No	Client Notice of Sale	Before	> At Sale by Buyer	Honor Existing Ks	W/ Client Consent
ABA	2/7/90	– – –	X or X			X	X		X	X	X		X
CA	5/27/89	– – –			X		X		X	X			X
VI	– – –	2/7/90	X or X			X	X		X	X	X		X
MI	5/31/91	10/1/91			X	X	X		X	X	X		X
WI	10/25/91	– – –	X	X			X		X			X	X
NJ	10/16/92	– – –	X				X		X				X
FL	7/23/92	1/1/93			X	X	X		X			X	
AK	4/14/93	7/15/93	X			X	X		X	X	X		X
HI	– – –	1/1/94	X	X					X			X	X
MO	8/19/94	7/1/95			X	X	X		X	X	X		X
OR	3/9/95	– – –	X			X	X		X	X			X
IA	6/28/95	8/1/95		X					X			X	X
OK	12/14/95	– – –	X					X	X			X	X
MN	12/11/95	– – –			X	X	X		X			X	
WA	5/3/96	– – –			X	X	X		X	X	X		X
NY	5/22/96	– – –		X		X	X		X			X	X
WV	1/16/97	2/1/97	X				X		X	X	X		X
ND	3/1/97	– – –	X	X		X			X	X		X	X
MA	6/9/97	1/1/98			X			X	X	X	X	X	X
CO	7/1/97	– – –			X				X	X	X	X	X
NC	7/24/97	– – –	X			X	X		X	X	X		X
ID	8/28/97	9/1/97	X	X					X				X
IN	11/25/97	– – –	X						X		X		X
SD	3/10/98	7/1/98			X				X		X		X

and the client's right to retain other counsel or to take possession of the file, and the client's consent will be presumed if there is no response within sixty days instead of ninety days as in the Model Rule. Special provisions are added for handling conflicts of interests which cannot be waived. The notice may describe the purchaser's qualifications and the seller's opinion as to the purchaser's suitability and competence to assume representation of the client.

Florida (1993) specifies that the purchasing lawyer must be authorized to practice law in Florida. Written notification to clients must be by certified mail. The client is given thirty instead of ninety days to object. The court must authorize substitution or termination of counsel in pending litigation. If the client objects to the substitution of counsel, the seller must comply with the requirements of Rule 1.16(d). For clients who cannot be served, their matters are not included in the sale. The purchaser must honor the fee agreements between the seller and clients.

Hawaii's Rule 1.17 (1994), deletes the Model Rule 1.17 provision that permits the purchasing lawyer to refuse the representation of clients who will not consent to pay the purchaser's usual fees. Hawaii's Rule 1.17 also requires the purchaser to honor existing agreements between the client and the seller relating to fees and the scope of the work, unless the client consents in writing after consultation. [The rule is silent about what occurs if the client does not consent.] The seller must cease practicing law in the Federal District of Hawaii as well as the state courts.

Idaho (1997) adopted the Model Rule and added "in the substantive practice area" in paragraph (a) of the rule. None of the Model Rule comments were adopted.

Indiana (1997) specifically provides that if a client cannot be given notice or fails to respond to notice of the sale, the representation of that client may not be transferred to the purchaser.

Table 3–1b

Rule 1.17 Sale of a Law Practice—Analysis by State

State	Notice to Clients Date Time Period Begins When Sent	When Received	Time Period (Days) 30	60	90	Role of Nonlawyer Sellers Silent	Authorizes	Disclosure of Confidential Info During Sale Process W/Client Notice
ABA		X			X	X		X
CA	X				X	X		X
VI		X			X	X		X
MI		X		91 Days		X		X
WI		X			X	X		X
NJ	X			X		X		X
FL			X			X		X
AK		X			X	X		X
HI		X			X	X		X
MO	X				X	X		X
OR	X			45 Days		X		X
IA	X		X			X		X
OK						X		X
MN		X			X	X		X
WA						X		X
NY	X				X	X		X
WV					X	X		X
ND		X			X	X		X
MA		X			X	X		X
CO		X		X		X		X
NC		X	X			X		X
ID		X			X			X
IN								X
SD	X			X		X		X

Iowa (1995) has adopted the Model Rule, changing the ninety-day notice requirement to thirty days, adding that existing agreements between the seller and the client relating to fees and the scope of the work must be honored by the purchaser unless the client consents in writing after consultation. Provisions are added that the sale will not be effective for clients to whom notice was not given as required, pending litigation where the court refuses to give permission to withdraw, and where conflicts are present and cannot be resolved. Further, the sale agreement shall include a clear statement concerning the parties' respective responsibilities to maintain and preserve the records and files of the seller's practice, including client files.

Massachusetts (1997) has adopted the Model Rule verbatim with the exception of the provision of ceasing to engage in the private practice of law and selling the practice as an entirety.

Michigan (1991) allows the purchaser and the seller to negotiate a "reasonable period of time" within which the seller will not practice law in the geographic area covered by the practice. This covenant not to compete assures the purchaser the right of access to the seller's former clients and requires that written notice be given to clients at least ninety-one days before the sale. Notice should advise that if the purchaser had identified an unwaivable conflict of interest, the client should obtain substitute counsel. Sale of goodwill may be conditioned upon the seller's ceasing to engage in the private practice of law for a reasonable period of time within the geographical area in which practice has been conducted.

Minnesota (1995) requires that the purchaser be licensed to practice law in Minnesota. The rule specifies that clients with inactive files should also be notified. Purchaser may not increase the fee for at least one year. The rule specifies that

Table 3-1c

Rule 1.17 Sale of a Law Practice—Analysis by State

State	Defines Goodwill Yes	Defines Goodwill No	Judicial Review Files Yes	Judicial Review Files No	Same Fees Charged to Client of Buyers	One Buyer Rule	Piecemeal Sale Yes	Piecemeal Sale No
ABA		X	X		X	X		X
CA		X		X		X		X
VI		X	X		X	X		X
MI		X	X		X			X
WI		X	X			X		X
NJ		X		X		X		X
FL		X	X			X		X
AK		X	X		X	X		X
HI		X	X			X		X
MO		X		X	X	X		X
OR		X		X			X	
IA		X		X		X		X
OK		X		X		X		X
MN		X		X		X		X
WA		X		X	X			
NY		X		X				
WV		X	X		X			X
ND		X	X				X	
MA		X	X		X	X		
CO		X		X	X			
NC		X	X		X	X	X	
ID		X	X		Silent			
IN		X		X	X			X
SD		X		X	X	X		X

cases in which there is a conflict, the lawyer is not competent in that field, or the court has denied the seller's motion to withdraw are not to be considered part of the "entirety." The rules require a summary of the purchaser's professional background. The transaction may include a promise by the selling lawyer not to engage in the practice of law or solicit clients for a reasonable period of time and in a certain geographic area.

Missouri's Rule (1995) does not require an attorney to cease practicing. The parties may agree on restrictions of practice for the seller. The client must respond within sixty days. When the seller is a deceased lawyer's estate, the purchaser must give the clients notice. There is no requirement for a judge to review files prior to transfer.

New Jersey (1992) specifies that conflict cases are not considered part of the "entirety." The purchaser has authority to act on behalf of a client during the notification period if the client's rights would be prejudiced by the failure to act. The notification period is sixty days. The purchaser must publish a notice of the purchase in the *New Jersey Law Journal* and *New Jersey Lawyer* at least thirty days in advance of the transfer date. The fees charged shall not be increased. The selling lawyer is forbidden from "the private practice of law in this jurisdiction."

New York (1996) provides that during negotiations, the sellers may provide buyers with a list of clients, a description of their matters, and the payment status of each client's account. However, no client confidence can be revealed without client consent. Added written notice requirements are agreements between the seller and the seller's clients as to fees that will be honored by the buyer, proposed fee increases allowed by the rule, and the identity and background of the buyer or buyers including listed detail.[8]

8. See Gayle L. Coy, *Note—Permitting the Sale of a Law Practice: Furthering the Interests of Both Attorneys and Their Clients*, 22 HOFSTRA L.R. 969 (1994).

Table 3–1d

Rule 1.17 Sale of a Law Practice—Analysis by State

	Who Can Sell			Who Can Buy		Nonlawyers			Notice to Clients		
State	**Sole Practitioners**	**Law Firms**	**Estates**	**Sole Practitioners**	**Law Firms**	**Yes**	**No**	**Written**	**Regular Mail**	**Certified Mail**	**Newspaper**
ABA	X	X	X	X	X		X	X			
CA	X	X	X	X	X		X	X			
VI	X	X	X	X	X		X	X			
MI	X	X	X	X	X		X	X			
WI	X	X	X	X	X		X	X			
NJ	X	X	X	X	X		X	X			
FL	X	X	X	X	X		X	X	X		
AK	X	X	X	X	X		X	X			
HI	X	X	X	X	X		X	X			
MO	X	X	X	X	X		X	X			
OR	X	X	X	X	X		X	X	X		
IA	X	X	X	X	X		X	X			
OK	X	X	X	X	X		X	X			
MN	X		X	X	X		X	X			
WA	X		X	X	X						
NY	X	X	X	X	X		X	X			
WV	X	X	X	X	X		X	X			
ND	X	X	X	X	X		X	X		X	
MA	X	X	X	X	X		X	X			
CO	X	X	X	X	X		X	X		X	
NC	X	X	X	X	X		X	X			
ID	X	X	X	X	X			X			
IN	X	X	X	X	X		X	X			
SD	X	X	X	X	X		X	X	X		X

North Carolina (1997) limits purchasers to another lawyer or law firm licensed to practice law in North Carolina. The sale may be by area of law and not by the entire law practice. The time of response is thirty days and not ninety days as provided in the Model Rules. Specific attention is given to the handling of conflicts of interest. The court addressed the terms of the payment of the sales price allowing for financing the purchase by borrowing the money.[9]

North Dakota (1997) has adopted the Model Rule, changing the provision dealing with fees charged to clients to provide that existing agreements between the seller and the client relating to fees and the scope of the work must be honored by the purchaser unless the client consents in writing after consultation. An additional provision states that the sale of any particular area of

practice must include all of the selling lawyer's files in the area of specialty or practice.

Oklahoma (1995) has changed the Model Rule to provide that no files shall be transferred without the consent of the client. The notice provision adds that the lawyer is ceasing to engage in the practice of law in Oklahoma and the existence and status of any funds or property held for the client, including but not limited to retainers or other prepayments. A specific provision is added to prohibit the release of confidential information to a purchaser without the client's consent. Further, the transfer of inactive files shall only be transferred by specific consent of the client.

Oregon (1995) requires that client notification must be by certified mail. Notification is more specific: There must be a description of the purchaser's law practice, and seller must specify whether he/she will withdraw absent consent to the transfer. Notification period is forty-five days. Seller must assure that substitution of counsel is

9. See Barton T. Crawford, *Comment—The Sale of a Legal Practice in North Carolina: Goodwill and Discrimination Against the Sole Practitioner*, 32 WAKE FOREST L.R. 993 (1997).

made when necessary. Fees may not be increased except upon agreement of the client. The sale may be conditioned upon reasonable restrictions on the right to practice.

South Dakota (1998) gives special attention to estates of a deceased lawyer as sellers of a law practice. The notice requirement is sixty days as opposed to ninety days in the Model Rule. Consent is presumed until the client notifies the lawyer. The purchaser must publish an announcement or notice of the purchase and the transfer of the practice in a newspaper of general circulation within the county in which the practice is located at least thirty days in advance of the effective date of the transfer.

Washington (1996) allows for a sale of a law practice by formal opinion 192 dated May 3, 1996. The basic provisions of the Model Rule is maintained except there is no provision for notice to clients. The opinion deals with the legality of the sale of a law practice and the ethical limitations on the sale of a law practice.

West Virginia (1997) adopted the model rule verbatim but declined to add the following comment to Rule 5.6 Restrictions on Right to Practice: "This Rule does not apply to prohibit restrictions that may be included in the terms of the sale of a law practice pursuant to Rule 1.17."

Wisconsin (1991) mandates that the seller must cease the private practice of law in the geographic area or jurisdiction where the practice was conducted. The existing fee agreements and scope of work must be honored by the purchaser unless client consent in given in writing after consultation.

Rule 1.17 works. The Rule clearly spells out the ethical requirements of the sale of a law practice so that clients and their matters and documents are not neglected, dumped, sold, or transferred without informed consent. It puts solo practitioners in a financial position equal to members of firms regarding the value of the goodwill of a law practice at retirement or death. Besides assuring evenhanded treatment between the solo practitioners and members of firms, it also operates to ensure the competent and confidential treatment of client files. Selling a law practice benefits lawyers and their clients. Clients appreciate the smooth, orderly transfer and continuity of representation offered to them and are relieved not to have to search for a new lawyer.

And the solo practitioner who conscientiously strives to provide for the competent, continuing representation of clients receives peace of mind without foregoing the financial rewards of a lifetime of practice.

Sale of a Law Practice and the Practical Problems Facing the Parties

The obstacles to a sale of a law practice appear to halt many prospective sales. Appraisal, valuation, factors impacting on value, methods of valuation, advertising availability for sale, and payment terms must be considered in any sale of a law practice.[10] While space does not allow a full discussion of these issues, a brief discussion would help you get started.

The Appraisal

To appraise a law practice in a meaningful manner, the following documents are helpful:

1. Financial statements for the previous five years
2. Income tax returns, both state and federal, for the previous five years
3. Fee schedules, if any, for the previous five years
4. Leases still in effect for the premises and all equipment
5. Accounts payable listing and current accounts payable aging schedule
6. Notes payable, mortgages (deeds of trust), and conditional sales contracts
7. Documents relating to the acquisition and obligations on real and personal property investments
8. Cash receipts, cash disbursements, sales, purchase, payroll, and general journals
9. General ledger
10. Bank statements, cancelled checks, and bank reconciliations
11. Accounts receivable listing and current accounts receivable aging schedule
12. Work in progress schedule
13. Data on key personnel of selling attorney

10. See Edward Poll, THE TOOL KIT FOR BUYING OR SELLING A LAW PRACTICE (Edward Poll & Associates, Inc. General Practice, Solo and Small Firm Section, ABA (1995)). The author has granted permission to use his materials in this section of the chapter.

who will assist in the transition or remain employed by the buying attorney
14. Insurance policies in effect
15. Brochure(s), if any, of the firm
16. Annual appointment books
17. Additional relevant documents

A careful review of these documents should give you a pattern of the practice in question. Determining the income stream and any significant changes during the period under review will affect the value of the practice. The buyer should evaluate and consider the nature and distribution of the client base. A quick decision should be made as to whether or not the clients are likely to remain with the buyer. This early decision will save time and energy on the part of both parties to the proposed sale.

Important factors to consider are the variety of reasons a sale occurs or a purchase takes place. A sale may occur because the seller desires to retire, change careers or professional goals, or physically move from the jurisdiction. A purchaser may perceive that he/she should broaden the client base, enter a market not previously served, or expand the range of services. One cannot understate the importance of a properly drafted and prepared plan for the orderly transfer of a law practice. You will find a thorough discussion of guidelines for purchasing a law practice in *The Practical Accountant*.[11] Give careful attention to

client confidentiality, and the closing and post-closing relationships, at the beginning of the transaction—not at the end. See the end and you may be able to determine the easiest way to get to where you wish to be.

Valuation

The valuation of a law practice differs from valuing most closely held businesses. There are general standards and principles that must be understood and applied to obtain a fair and unbiased value. And it is prudent to give careful consideration to all the circumstances surrounding the lawyers in question.[12] A unique example is the contingency fee agreements part of many law practices.

Conclusion

The end of this chapter would not be possible without the beginning. The authors of Model Rule 1.17 knew that a new day was coming for the profession. They were correct. The solo practitioner is the heart and soul of the legal profession. While underserved and underrepresented in most legal professional associations and in the judiciary, the success of the profession depends on the success of the solo practitioner and the clients served by the lawyer toiling in this mode of practice.

11. See Denis A. Cohrs, *Guidelines for Purchasing An Accounting Practice*, THE PRACTICAL ACCOUNTANT 17–24 (Aug. 1989). While this article addresses an accounting practice, the information and process are applicable to the sale of a law practice.

12. See Edward Poll, THE TOOL KIT FOR BUYING OR SELLING A LAW PRACTICE (Edward Poll & Associates, Inc. General Practice, Solo and Small Firm Section, ABA (1995)). The author has granted permission to use his materials in this section of the chapter and Bruce H. Fairchild and Keith W. Fairchild, *How to Value Personal Services Practices* THE PRACTICAL ACCOUNTANT 27–40 (Aug. 1989).

The author acknowledges that this chapter was previously written by Joanne Petton Pitula, who was an assistant ethics counsel for the ABA Center for Professional Responsibility. The previous chapter forms the basis for this chapter, with the permission of Joanne Petton Pitula. The author also acknowledges the assistance of Henry M. DeWoskin, a lawyer with Alan E. DeWoskin, P.C., in the analysis and preparation of this chapter.

4

A Primer on Retirement: How to Cope with Junk Mail and a Slower Memory

SETH TAFT

Are you ready for "retirement"? I have been in it for nine years in Cleveland, Ohio, and I have some advice for you.

First off, I should admit something. I did not really retire. I just do not get paid.

So here is the advice.

Your body is not what it used to be. Your memory, that internal computer, has slowed down. Let's see. Did I brush my teeth? Easy. Check to see if the toothbrush is wet.

You must walk down Euclid Avenue, Cleveland's "Main Street," with your eyes up. If you see a friend fifteen feet away, there is a good chance your computer will produce his or her name by the time you are at hailing distance. If you look up and suddenly there the friend is, no chance! "Hi, good buddy!"

Keep a few blank 3" x 5" cards in your pocket. Write down anything you want to remember right away. It will not stick otherwise. How many times have you gone upstairs to do something, and then forgotten what it was when you got there?

Get yourself an electronic box, like my pocket organizer. I have a thousand telephone numbers stored in it, automatically alphabetized, including all the fax numbers that I should know and that are not in the telephone book. It has my kids' and grandkids' birthdays in it, e-mail addresses, the telephone number of my plumber (under "plumber," not the plumber's name—I have forgotten his name), my secret bank code, the combination to my club locker. It is a lifesaver. Do not

leave home without it. Beware of a crash! Learn how to transfer data to your computer.

You are clumsier! Use the banister, and do not have both hands full. You need one to catch yourself when you are about to fall. Your shoe will catch on a rug or crack that it never used to catch on. Watch where you are walking.

And you cannot lift that fifty-pound sack any more. Settle for the twenty-five pound bag, even if it costs more per pound.

You have aches and pains you never thought were possible. Grin and bear it! It beats the alternative.

Your spouse is more important than ever. First of all, he or she may love you dearly but quite possibly *not* for lunch. Remember that for a long time your career came first, and he or she was a great supporter. When I ran for mayor of Cleveland, my art-history-professor wife Franny was out campaigning every night, and even taught the morning after the election when we had been up until 4:00 A.M. Make your spouse Number One! You have the time.

Love your kids and grandkids, without being a burden on them. Take them to a ballgame. Take them on a trip, maybe one at a time. Make them special. On a young person's birthday, take him or her to a bookstore and say you will buy any book in the store for that person. Watch them puzzle and decide. It is fun. Offer to pay for summer camp or any other summer project.

We have issued a Granny Franny/Popsie Scholarship Certificate to each grandchild. It says that, until bankruptcy, we will pay for half of the cost of any education they wish to pursue, to the very end, provided they write us a letter asking for it

Seth Taft is a retired partner in the Cleveland law firm of Jones, Day, Reavis & Pogue, where he practiced general business law from 1948 to 1988.

and explaining why the education will help them. Our first three went to Yale—not the economy college.

Your home is your life. It reflects all the things you have done. Think hard before you leave it—to go south, to move to a more manageable house, to get that condo with no maintenance work and the ability to leave for long periods with no worry, to go to that life-support place.

My sister-in-law and her husband left their Rochester, New York, home (both are doctors) three times to retire—and got bored, in Northwest Connecticut, in Arizona, and then in North Carolina. Now they are back in Rochester for good. Clevelander Dick Tullis ran a big company, retired to Florida, and came back. For us, the excitement and interest and friends are in Cleveland. As soon as you move, there is no room for the family to visit you; your place is too small. You have to do all the visiting yourself.

We created a community called Pepper Ridge, we built a good part of our own house, and we added on to it four times to keep it as our dream house, with community pond, pool, tennis court, and ballfield right outside. Our kids come back twice a year, and we love it. The memorabilia are all around us, plus a special art collection—and every piece has a warmly remembered story of how we acquired it.

Your needs at home do change. You need more desk space. A copy machine is essential in dealing with Medicare, your IRA, Social Security, and everything else. A computer of some kind becomes a necessity. You need file space for things you used to keep at the office. You cannot put off getting an answering machine. And, a fax machine. If you are not going to have an office somewhere, get the fax. And e-mail is fun—all our family is on-line. We chat, and to respond you just type a little and click on "send."

You have probably learned the same lesson we have on those telephone calls asking for money. We have adopted a rule: "Send us anything you wish, and we will consider it. We do not make commitments over the telephone."

And how are you doing with junk mail? We have finally learned to throw it away, *before* opening, even if the envelope screams that we may have won a million dollars. My father used to say that he would send them a check, provided they took him *off* the mailing list.

Now, what about those volunteer organizations you used to give some time to, and what about that shop talk with your partners that was such a part of your business life, and those programs of the City Club, Council on World Affairs, bar association, and so on that you enjoyed?

My advice: Keep an office downtown! Make a deal with your law associates or partners that you can keep a cubbyhole. I have one, and it makes all the difference in the world—telephone, you are near meetings, fax, secretarial help, library, informal advice, delivery services, fewer distractions, computer (I take disks back and forth from home). It is a lot more efficient than trying to do volunteer or personal work from home.

You would be surprised how often someone is working on a legal problem and stops by to say, "Do you remember. . . ." And you do, and he or she is grateful you are around. I like that, and I think his or her letting me have a wee office and some services makes his or her life a little easier and pleasanter, enough to justify spending a little overhead on me.

Should you practice law?

I do not, except informally for me and some nonprofits I help. Be careful, because you really are not keeping up. But keep up your CLEs. It is not hard, and you will find plenty of programs to interest you. Estate planning and taxes are obvious ones.

Three times I have been judge for a day to marry people (including my daughter). Only lawyers in good standing can do this.

Are you the notary for your friends? Only lawyers in good standing can do this, too.

You might go to court to help with an adoption, a name change, or an estate, as a favor. Only lawyers in good standing are allowed to do so.

Creation and your community did well by you. Pay a little back. Volunteer at your favorite charity. You will discover they have a bottomless pit of needs and that, in fact, your career has made you an expert in getting things done.

I do mine in human services, substance abuse, international professional exchanges, trying to keep my political party on the right track, working for universal health care at a manageable cost, welfare reform, my college's and law school's quality survival, and more.

To hold it down, declare Friday (or Monday) to be part of the weekend. I'm trying, but haven't quite succeeded. And exercise at least twice a week!

Got a vacation home? Go there for a real break. Bring your kids and grandkids. But do not go for too long, or people will forget who you are back home. We have one, on the beach in Connecticut, but we limit our stays to a month at a time (June and August).

Like to travel? Take some interesting trips once a year. Get on the brochure mailing lists, from your college, from Lindblad, from museums, and so on.

Study up on where you are going. Take lots of pictures and make a scrapbook. Make your friends look at your pictures and book, and insist that they listen to stories about the Sphinx, that huge lizard, the soaring cathedral, the scenery. We take those trip regularly—China, the Lewis and Clark saga to the mouth of the Columbia River, the Nile, Mayaland, London, Greece, and Turkey. Our latest: the stone monuments of the British Isles and Brittany.

My final advice: Have fun making people smile.

Compliment people on how they dress—a handsome tie, a good-looking and capacious bag. And if their briefcase seems very full, ask if they brought their lunch. Wave to someone whom you might have competitively barged past in your previous life. Compliment the person confined to a powered wheelchair on how well he or she maneuvers. Sympathize with the stranger carrying a heavy load. Help the person in distress.

I got a "ten" one day on Chester Avenue in Cleveland when a woman caught her heel in a grate and tried to walk on as though she still had a heel attached to her shoe. When I tapped her on the shoulder and told her that a shoe repair shop was right around the corner, I got my smile of the day.

Say "thank you" more often—in person, by telephone, by sending a postcard. I keep a supply in my desk for that purpose, along with a batch of stamps. It just takes a minute. You would be amazed at the results. I have made "smiles" a very satisfying game.

So, you have no spare time. Your friends say you look great (I "fake it" on hair color and got three invitations to lunch from attractive persons of the opposite sex when I first tried it)! And I wonder how I ever had time to practice law. I love it!

5

So You Want
to Stay in Law

EDWARD E. BLAKESLEE

"Everything considered, work is less boring than amusing oneself."

Charles Baudelaire

I retired several years ago as a senior corporate legal officer but moved my base of operations. This article sets forth several practical ideas for like-minded lawyers who are considering retiring from what they are doing now, but who want to continue legal practice in some fashion.

But first, I need to say that my own decision to continue working is strictly that—my own decision. I fully respect the desires of others who wish to devote full time to golfing, fishing, playing tennis, traveling, managing their investments, or pursuing any of a multitude of other satisfying opportunities they did not have time for before retirement.

This article is based on a paper Samuel B. Witt III and I delivered to the Committee on Corporate Law Departments of the ABA Section of Business Law. It is tailored for corporate legal officers who are considering retirement, but I think lawyers in private practice will also find many helpful points to consider.

The Age 65 "Lid"

"How old would you be if you didn't know how old you were?"

Satchel Paige

Employers in interstate commerce, subject to the Federal Age Discrimination in Employment Act,

Edward E. Blakeslee is of counsel to Werner & Kennedy and serves on the board of directors of a Bermuda-based insurer of directors and officers for major U.S. life insurance companies. This article originally appeared in the Spring 1992 issue of *Experience*, which is published by the ABA.

are prohibited from using age as a basis of forced retirement. But there is an exception for individuals who have served for at least two years as executives or in other high policy-making positions and whose pensions are at least $44,000 annually, when calculated as a noncontributory straight-life annuity. Corporate general counsel usually fit neatly within this exception.

One rationale for this exception to mandatory retirement is that it gives younger people the chance for reasonably rapid advancement. I do not argue with this objective. But assuming good health, there is no reason why mandatory corporate retirement must mean the end of a career.

The age 65 convention is a rather recent historical development. In this country, the passage of the Social Security Act early in President Franklin Roosevelt's New Deal gave it official sanction as a way to cut unemployment. Yet, on the brink of the year 2000, there is little rationale for retaining this concept.

Check This List

Discard the arbitrary age 65 notion and move on to four real concerns as you ponder how to keep working after leaving your current practice. These four concerns are not necessarily listed in order of importance.

1. Your health, of course.
2. Your own emotional reaction to continuing practice. Are you looking for (and do you have a need for) a position with prestige and income comparable to the one you are leaving? Would you prefer to pursue new interests? Are you concerned that you may be risking failure after concluding a successful career?

3. Your family's financial needs. For example, do you have dependent parents or children in college or graduate school?

4. Your family's emotional needs. You have retired, not your spouse. If the two of you have developed separate interests, it will be important for both parties to have further opportunities to pursue them.

And you also need to consider the following matters, which are of less importance but still merit serious consideration:

5. Continuation of earned (not investment) income will cost you part or all of your Social Security retirement benefits. In 1997, retirees aged 65 to 69 lost $1 of Social Security benefits for every $3 earned in excess of $12,500. Retirees under 65 lost $1 for every $2 earned in excess of $8,280. Not until age 70 is one able to receive substantial amounts of earned income without forfeiting some Social Security income.

True, a delayed start in Social Security benefits results in somewhat larger payments eventually, but it takes a long time to offset the losses—until age 96 under one set of assumptions. And that loss tends to be understated, because not more than a portion of Social Security benefits are subject to income tax, whereas earned income generally is fully subject to income tax.

Furthermore, a portion of earned income of self-employed individuals is subject to a "tax" under the Self-Employment Contributions Act (SECA) of the Internal Revenue Code. Although the purpose of SECA is to fund Social Security retirement benefits and Medicare, the charge continues even while the benefit is forfeited under the earnings test.

From a purely financial point of view therefore, after age 65 and until age 70 you should limit annual earned income to $12,500 or aim at an amount substantial enough to provide a reasonable margin over tax costs and Social Security losses, or look into the rules on deferring income, or go in heavily for nontaxable "perks," or seek the nontaxable rewards of pro bono work.

Continuing with the points to ponder as you think of a new legal career:

6. Practicing by yourself, or for a small firm, may require more hours than your corporate position; you are not always able to tailor your schedule or work at your own pace and convenience.

7. There probably will be no one around to whom to delegate, so you will be working on some matters you consider routine or for which you may have no up-to-date expertise.

8. It may well be that for some considerable stretches of time you will find yourself working at your desk more intensely than you did as a corporate officer. You cannot always schedule vacations as readily as you could when you had someone to whom you could delegate problems.

9. It is easy to underestimate expenses. As a corporate legal officer, you may have questioned the hourly fees of outside counsel. But if you go into private practice, you will quickly see that 35 to 50 percent of those hourly fees are eaten up by office expenses.

10. Review charges for bar association and club memberships, and various seminars and conventions; recognize that, in the future, the money will come out of your own pocket.

Opening an Office

As you prepare to open your own office, pay attention to the following guidelines:

1. Prepare as if you mean it. Forget the sport jacket and suede shoes.

2. Make plans for secretarial assistance; part-time may be feasible. Hire someone who will not be penalized by the Social Security earnings test.

3. Order professional stationery before you retire.

4. Make arrangements to use top-of-the-line equipment, including photocopying, fax, word processing, and computer equipment.

5. Investigate congenial office space. A one-person office is lonely and lacks opportunity to exchange ideas. Frequently, arrangements can be made to sublease space from a law firm. If you sublease, you will enjoy the advantages of having a receptionist (which is essential if you have only a part-time secretary) and of using the firm's conference room, library, and equipment.

Also consider the growing trend toward shared-services arrangements being made available by commercial developers and managed by agents. A shared-services plan typically will include conference room, reception area, mail pickup and, for extra charges, additional features such as word processing and secretarial services.

6. Draft an announcement of your practice, and ask your secretary to start collecting a mailing list.
7. Keep yourself in circulation. Attend bar meetings, lectures, seminars, and the like.
8. Avoid stereotyping labels such as honorary, emeritus, and retired.

"The future is not what it used to be."

Paul Valery

Ways and Means

If you are headed for another legal career after a career as a corporate legal officer, you have several obvious options:

1. You can form an of counsel arrangement with your old firm. For many people, this requires the least amount of adjustment. However, the "chemistry"—the relationship with the current general counsel and other corporate officers—must be right.
2. Most financially rewarding, probably, is becoming affiliated with an outside firm. But you need to acknowledge to yourself that unless you have or develop a current specialized skill, you may be expected to contribute to the client base. In some instances, this arrangement proves to be merely a transition to full retirement. There are other instances of outstanding successes and second careers.

Define, in your own thinking, your prospective role in the firm: (a) as a specialist who will be sought out by other members of the firm or by clients; (b) as a continuing link between your former corporate employer and its principal outside counsel; or (c) as a "rainmaker" seeking to build clients for the firm more than for your own specialized talents.

3. Individual practice provides the most independence. But you might need to undergo some retraining and spend a lot of time and money providing office facilities and developing a practice. You must also be willing to take on a variety of functions. Individual practice, unless confined to a "boutique" spe-

ciality, is not going to attract high-level corporate clients with complex problems and needs for an in-depth array of legal experts. "Elder law" is a rapidly developing field for which you already have the major qualification of "being there."

4. One area that many about-to-retire lawyers tend to overlook is pro bono work. Specifically, you may consider assuming the pro bono responsibilities of a law firm.

Pro bono work requires technical expertise you may not presently possess. However, there are extensive training facilities available, usually through your local bar association. For example, in the New York City area, one should contact the Committee on Legal Assistance or the Senior Volunteer Lawyers Committee of the City Bar Association. For the first time in your life, you may enjoy the luxury of considering where your skills can be put to best use—without financial constraints.

5. Consider a position as chief executive, general counsel, or lobbyist for a trade association specializing in the business areas with which you are familiar. Many of the problems involve legislative and regulatory matters with which you have already dealt. You know the current issues, the people involved, and the law. (There are nearly thirteen thousand registered lobbyists in Washington.)
6. Use your experience as a manager to your advantage. Market this skill by seeking a position as managing director or administrative partner of a large- or medium-sized law firm or as its administrative vice president and corporate secretary, if it is incorporated. Such an opportunity, which might also develop after you have become of counsel to the firm, will enable you to maintain your identity as a lawyer and to make a real contribution while developing your specialized skill or your client base, or both.

It takes time to develop friendships and gain confidences, but eventually the firm will realize that your management experience and administrative efforts are making a real contribution to the firm's "bottom line." While you handle the often-neglected organizational details, the other lawyers will be free to devote their full time and efforts to their practices.

35

7. Senior Lawyers Division Council member Victor Futter, in a November 1990 article in *The Business Lawyer*, discussed the need for the corporate ombudsman. It is a role for which retired corporate counsel should be uniquely suited.

Rewards of Continuing

The rewards are clear for those lawyers who continue some form of legal practice after corporate work. Not necessarily in the order of importance, they are:

1. **Financial:** Unless one has accumulated considerable wealth, retirement reduces the amount of available money. On the other hand, income from continued practice, plus a reasonable pension, can produce quite the opposite result.
2. **Social:** Working involves more social and intellectual interchange with your colleagues during working hours than you may have realized.
3. **Professional satisfaction:** You continue the satisfaction you get from achieving in your chosen profession and making some contribution to society. There may be more opportunity for this rather than less when you are no longer subject to the restraints of a corporate organization; when half your time is no longer devoted to budgets, planning, personnel, and miscellaneous meetings.

Creative Transitions

Here are two ideas for transition to a second career:

1. **Early retirement plus retainer:** In some instances, it would profit both the corporation and an officer to provide a program for the officer to "step down" from a management role a few years prior to age 65 and resume full-time duties in his or her area of legal specialty within the corporate law department. The lawyer stepping down would take no cut in pay. Both parties benefit from this arrangement: The officer has an opportunity to hone professional skills, and the corporation has an earlier opportunity to advance a younger officer—at only modest cost to the corporation.

   Fertile imaginations will easily develop variations on the "step down" theme. For instance:

   (a) Two or three years prior to age 65, the officer might take early retirement and begin working for a firm, with the corporation retaining his or her professional services.

   (b) The early retirement arrangement might anticipate the officer's working half time for the corporation and at half pay—with an early-retirement pension sufficient to maintain income at preretirement levels.
2. **Sabbatical leaves:** Corporate employers might adopt colleges' longtime tradition of sabbatical leaves. One could then try a second career earlier than age 65, but without a final commitment.

   A survey several years ago of fifteen large corporations disclosed that while all fifteen granted leaves to employees for a variety of personal or educational needs, all of the programs fell short of what is commonly understood as a "sabbatical."

"To Live Is to Function"

Oliver Wendell Holmes, Jr., was appointed to the U.S. Supreme Court in 1902 at the age of 61. At that time, he had thirty years of service ahead of him. On his ninetieth birthday, in a radio talk, he expressed this philosophy: "The riders in a race do not stop short when they reach the goal. There is a little finishing canter . . . [but] the canter that brings you to a standstill need not be only coming to rest. It cannot be while you still live. For to live is to function. That is all there is in living."

Recognize the problems but do not be put off by them. Make your preparations well in advance of your retirement party.

"It ain't over 'til it's over."

Yogi Berra

6

Serving a New Clientele in a Second Career in Real Estate

STANLEY B. BALBACH

The largest financial transaction that an individual is likely to have in a lifetime is the purchase or sale of a home. This is particularly true of a senior citizen whose entire estate, with the exception of retirement benefits, may consist of home equity. This situation offers senior lawyers an opportunity for a second career in helping seniors while supplementing their own retirement income.

Who is to advise the would-be home seller in the drawing of the real estate brokerage contract? Who is to advise the would-be home buyer about the terms and conditions in the contract to purchase the home? What is negotiable about the listing contract? Certainly the sales price and, in most states, the terms of compensation for the broker, the terms of payment by the buyer, and the evidence of title, which is usually a deed supplemented by a title insurance policy except in most mineral transactions when a marketable abstract of title is required and in special situations where occupancy and ownership is based on contract.

Assuming that the time has come when the seniors (and we will presume that we are considering a husband and wife, both of mature years) are ready to make a change in housing, how can a lawyer help? Suppose this family of two seniors is considering the sale of a residence in which they have lived for a number of years. The first question in your mind as their counselor might be: "Why do the clients want to sell?" That may not be a legal question, but the answer may reveal legal and practical living questions.

Stanley B. Balbach is a partner in the Urbana, Illinois, law firm of Balbach and Fehr.

Let us assume one of the following reasons:

1. They want to live in a different climate. At this point, a lawyer might ask if the client has tried living in the different climate. Arizona, Florida, or Southern California may seem much different in the summer than in the winter. Colorado, Wyoming, the upper peninsula of Michigan, or the Maine coast may be delightful in summer, but has the client tried living there in the winter? The investment in spending a year in the contemplated climate is a modest one compared to the cost if a "permanent move" is made and the living conditions dictate another move.

2. They want to move closer to family. This decision should also be tested similarly to the test of a climate move. Try it out!

3. They want to move into a retirement home. It should be relatively easy to try this out on a rental basis, and if the retirement home is not willing to give your clients opportunity to test the living in that facility, they should possibly look elsewhere. Of course, if it is a local facility, visits with friends or as guests of the management should be considered.

4. They want to return to a family home or farm. While the individuals may have spent many happy times on the farm or in the family home as youths, things may have changed. Again, try it out.

5. They may have a shortage of funds. This is where thought should be given to a "reverse mortgage." The basic concept involves the transfer of title to the house to a lender who then pays the transferor a monthly amount for as long as the senior seller continues to

live in the house. This chapter is not a discussion of the mechanics of the reverse mortgage, as this question is treated in Chapter 70.

With the exception of reverse mortgages, leasing arrangements, and other alternatives to a reverse mortgage discussed in Chapter 70, all of the plans discussed in this chapter involve the sale of the residence. Why is it important in such a sale to have independent legal advice? The first thought of many prospective home sellers is to talk to the real estate broker. There is nothing wrong with this thought, but bear in mind that the broker is "across the table." The broker is interested in earning the largest commission possible in the shortest length of time. The seller wants the best price available, which may mean a different pricing structure and a different offering time than favored by the broker. The advertising by the broker, the methods of showing the house, the duration of the listing agreement, and the broker's personal commitment are all matters that need to be negotiated.

It is the duty of the lawyer for the seller to negotiate the contract with the broker that is in the best interests of the seller. In most parts of the country, all elements of the listing agreement are negotiable. It is important that the contract be clear about when a commission is earned and in what amount. Minimum advertising commitments should be stated, as well as the notice to be given on showing the property. The amount of the commission and when it is earned should be clearly defined. There is no rule against talking to several brokers, and lawyers are generally experienced in this negotiation. The lawyer is paid whether or not the house is sold so that the lawyer has no vested interest in a sale.

The lawyer recommended by the broker may not be the best one to use because that lawyer may have a relationship with the broker that would make it difficult for the lawyer to negotiate the brokerage contract in the best interests of the seller. Assuming that the brokerage contract is signed and the residence is in the process of being sold, then the plans for the next home of the would-be sellers should be moved along, if that decision has not been made. If the move is to Arizona, Florida, Southern California, Texas, a local retirement home, or a highly serviced community of any type, negotiations should be in process for an option so that this move will not be a problem when the residence is sold. It is part of the job of the lawyer to see that the client will be inconvenienced as little as possible while getting the best in legal, financial, and residential advice.

Practically every senior citizen is faced with the necessity or advisability of considering alternative living arrangements. The only real question is "How soon will the move be and where?" This chapter is intended to impress upon senior lawyers the necessity for independent legal advice when an individual, senior or not, is considering the living alternatives.

The lawyer is the only available advisor who does not have a conflict. The real estate broker wants the highest commission, payable as soon as possible, with the easiest contract terms so that the property will sell rapidly. The lender desires the highest interest rate with the least hassle in regard to the terms of the loan, resulting in a product that can be readily sold on the secondary market. The buyer's conflict about down payment, purchase price, possession, apportionment of insurance, designation of personal property, and realty is so obvious as to need little discussion. Bear in mind that if the original broker is not handling the deal but rather a buyer's broker has arranged the actual sale, the buyer's broker may be oriented toward the buyer, and the seller's broker does not want to lose a part of the commission. The protection of the seller obviously must be by the lawyer because the lawyer gets paid whether or not the deal goes through.

If your client is the buyer, then you should clarify his or her understanding of what is in the offer; you may find that your client's understanding is quite different from the terms in the document prepared and presented by the seller. In some parts of the country, there is a broker on both sides of the transaction. This would appear to offer some protection to the buyer, but frequently the buyer's broker is paid part of the commission negotiated by the seller, in which case the economic protection is limited. If you are retained by the would-be buyer to examine the contract, then you should do so carefully. This examination would not differ materially, whether the buyer is a senior or not, and consequently the reader is referred to state and local bar seminars and books for current procedures and law.

Home buyers and sellers need the benefit of independent legal counsel before they make the decision to sell the house, hire a broker, move to Florida, negotiate a reverse mortgage, or move into a retirement complex, and this need is particularly important to the senior citizen whose lifetime of savings may be involved.

In the case of a home seller, the listing contract with the real estate broker should be the subject of negotiation for questions of price, possession, terms of payment, the amount of commission and when it is earned, listing period, and legal descriptions, including easements and restrictions. Whether the seller is a first-time seller or more experienced, it is unlikely that the seller has the experience to negotiate with a broker, who has handled many transactions. In counseling the seller, the lawyer should inquire about the seller's reason for putting the home on the market. If the problem is a shortage of income, perhaps the reverse mortgage referred to earlier should be explored.

If the problem is too much house to care for, a suggestion to try a retirement facility or to rent a smaller house might be appropriate. Whatever advice is given by a lawyer would not be tainted with a conflict of interest on earning a commission, so, while it might be in error, it should not be because of self-interest. It is a sad situation when a residence is sold, an interest is purchased in a retirement facility, and the purchaser is miserable and without the finances to reverse the steps.

The lawyer who is retired, either from a law firm, the military, a corporation legal department, a judgeship, or other legal career, who desires a career in real estate but who lacks training in the handling of real estate transactions, will find educational opportunities provided by bar associations, law schools, title insurance companies (commercial and bar-related), and junior colleges and colleges. A second career in real estate is a natural outlet for a senior lawyer because his or her friends and acquaintances are likely to be of an age when a change of residence and living conditions is a likely and important step and one that can be disastrous after a lifetime of working and saving for a pleasant retirement or a change in careers. Remember that lawyers have no part in a real estate transaction in California or in Arizona by constitutional amendment, and real estate brokers can practice real estate law where they have been hired to sell the property. In some areas in the East, the buyer and seller each routinely has independent legal counsel.

The lawyer who is representing buyers or sellers of real property must be able to provide title insurance as a supplement to the legal opinion of the lawyer because of the requirement of the secondary loan market. The lawyer may be able to negotiate an agency contract with a commercial title insurance company, or the client can purchase title insurance from a nonlawyer agency; or, in approximately fifteen states including Colorado, Connecticut, Florida, Hawaii, Illinois, Indiana, Minnesota, North Dakota, Ohio, Pennsylvania, Utah, and Vermont, bar-related title insurance is available. Bar-related title insurance is provided to shareholder lawyers by a company owned and operated by lawyers who issue the policies when the lawyer finds the title to be merchantable. The need for "bar-related" title insurance is mostly due to the fact that commercial title insurance companies sometimes sell title insurance only through lay agencies, thus preventing the lawyer from providing a complete service. Many of those involved in real estate feel that a lawyer is not needed if there is a title insurance policy, not understanding the exceptions and, of course, that a nonlawyer may not have the fiduciary obligation to explain those exceptions.

The ABA Standing Committee on Lawyers Title Guaranty Funds and the Senior Lawyers Division have cosponsored presentations on how lawyers can organize bar-related title insurance companies. In the last year, programs have been offered in Alabama, Arkansas, Kentucky, Missouri, Montana, Nebraska, New Jersey, North Carolina, Oklahoma, South Dakota, Tennessee, Utah, Virginia, Washington, D.C., West Virginia, and Wyoming.

A bar-related title insurance company provides title insurance only to its lawyer shareholders and usually at a very competitive price (frequently $1 per $1,000 or less) due to the fact that the title information and opinion is the work product of the lawyer. A company that is organized, controlled, and operated by lawyers has the main purpose, not of selling title insurance, but of providing lawyers with the resource of fully serving the client.

An important service provided by the bar-related company is that of providing continuing education for its lawyer members. This function is closely coordinated with the work of the organized bar, and the leaders in the bar-related company are frequently the strongest supporters of the bar associations.

The fact is that a lawyer is needed by the seller and by the buyer. It is a field of law that is natural for the senior lawyer because it is the lawyer's friends who, because of their having home equity, are exposed to the greatest risk. A large part of the retirement "package" of a senior citizen is likely to be found in the residence. Also, it is a field of law where continuing education is available, either by the bar associations or by the title insurance companies (bar-related or commercial).

7
Of Counsel
and Retirement

HAROLD G. WREN

Most lawyers are not overly keen on retiring completely from the practice of law. Despite the lure of golf, hunting, fishing, or some other activity having no relation to the practice of law, few, if any, activities have the intellectual challenge—and joy—that law practice affords. Yet, for a lawyer to continue the high level of stress to which he or she may have become accustomed may not be in the best interest of his or her physical or mental well-being. There are, of course, workaholics who have no desire to change their patterns of living or to engage in some activity other than law practice. And, some lawyers, particularly those in very small law firms with weak, if any, retirement programs, may believe that they cannot afford to retire because they will have insufficient income to maintain the standard of living to which they are accustomed. But most lawyers want some form of activity related to the practice of law, with a substantial amount of free time to do those things that they have been unable to do during their active years. In the case of lawyers who have retired from the role of partner in a law firm, the of counsel arrangement not only offers a solution to the lawyer's problems in retirement, but also provides the law firm with an excellent opportunity to take advantage of the experience of a senior member of the bar.

If an attorney has practiced with a firm large enough to establish some form of pension planning, and there is a general notion—if not an express contract—within the firm that members of the firm will retire upon reaching a certain age, the of counsel agreement becomes the principal vehicle for establishing a relationship between the retired lawyer and the law firm of

which he or she was formerly a partner. In 1991, Beverly Glascock and I published the first edition of *The Of Counsel Agreement*. In 1998, when we published the Second Edition of the book we noted that there had been a number of cases in the interim involving the liability of law firms for of counsel's torts. The reader should refer to the new edition for a detailed discussion of these cases.[1]

In the Second Edition, we have included additional contracts which will be helpful to the drafter, whether representing the law firm or the practitioner. The of counsel agreement should be separate from the general partnership agreement. Both the individual lawyer and the law firm will realize advantages if they arrange their affairs under a carefully drafted of counsel agreement.

The of counsel arrangement between a retired partner and his or her former law firm is one of the four arrangements specifically permitted by Formal Opinion 90-357 of the ABA Standing Committee of Ethics and Professional Responsibility. In 90-357, the committee removed some of the restrictions that characterized its earlier Formal Opinion 330. It first eliminated the earlier requirement that of counsel be compensated only for the legal work that he or she performed, so that a retired partner would be free to draw a pension or other retirement benefit or share in the firm's profits. The committee disavowed any implication in the prior opinion that a lawyer would have to be in almost daily contact with the firm to retain his or her of counsel status. The thrust of 90-357 is that the requirement that a retired partner who is of counsel maintain a

Harold G. Wren is of counsel to the law firm of Voyles & Johnson, P.S.C., in Louisville, Kentucky.

1. See e.g., *Staron v. Weinstein*, 701 A.2d 1325, 1997 N.J.Super LEXIS 440 (1997), discussed in H. WREN & B. GLASCOCK, THE OF COUNSEL AGREEMENT: A GUIDE FOR LAW FIRM AND PRACTITIONER, 2nd ed. (Chicago, American Bar Association, 1998).

"continuing relationship" with the firm will be read more leniently than under 330.

The need for a well-drafted of counsel agreement becomes apparent in the case of the retired partner. The written agreement should make it clear that of counsel is neither a partner nor an associate of the firm. If of counsel is a retired partner, his or her name may be included in the firm name. The partnership, however, should give careful consideration to whether this is in the best interests of the firm as a whole. To avoid liability as an implied partner, of counsel status should be clearly communicated in the firm letterhead, professional announcement cards, shingles, directories, and law lists.

Most of counsel agreements should be built around the status of independent contractor, rather than the employer-employee relationship. The retired partner and law firm should anticipate as many problems as possible and draft a detailed agreement to meet their precise needs. In the Second Edition of *The Of Counsel Agreement,*[2] we included a number of written agreements to illustrate solutions to various problems presented by the of counsel relationship. Some of these agreements involve relationships of employer-employee; others are concerned with independent contractors. Typical of some of the problems reflected in these drafts are:

- *Compensation:* In 90-357, the ethics committee stated that it took no position on the manner in which of counsel should be compensated. This is a matter of contract between the parties. The parties may use a flat hourly rate, a percentage of gross receipts of business that originates with of counsel, a percentage of net income after deducting expenses related to such business, a drawing account, a draw plus a splitting of fees on matters that of counsel brings to the firm, or any one of many combinations or variations of these approaches.
- *Perquisites:* The of counsel agreement should spell out in detail those items of expense (e.g., car allowance, health insurance, malpractice insurance, bar association dues, travel and entertainment expenses, group term insurance, 401(k) plans, and so on) to be borne by the firm rather than by the individual lawyer.

2. See WREN & GLASCOCK, especially the appendixes.

- *Protection of Trade Secrets:* A law firm may wish to protect itself against the personal use or disclosure of trade secrets by of counsel. Alternatively, the of counsel agreement may incorporate this type of clause by reference to the general partnership agreement.
- *Malpractice Insurance:* Before a retired partner enters into an of counsel agreement, he or she should be certain that proper arrangements have been made for malpractice insurance. Since a lawyer's potential liability as of counsel is much less, the premium for coverage of of counsel's omissions and errors will be less than that for a partner. The of counsel agreement should provide that the law firm will make certain that of counsel has the necessary coverage.
- *Other Fringe Benefits:* In addition to coverage for malpractice insurance, of counsel agreements often provide for payment by the law firm of of counsel's professional dues and licensing, reimbursement of business expenses, health insurance coverage, and the like. Agreements often provide that, for these purposes, of counsel will be treated as an employee. The drafter must be careful, however, to avoid having the relationship between of counsel and the firm characterized as that of employer-employee, as distinct from independent contractor.
- *Duties:* The description of of counsel's duties and responsibilities for the firm, clients, and other parties will present some of the most difficult drafting problems surrounding the of counsel agreement. Obviously, contracts will vary greatly depending upon what the parties are seeking to accomplish. In the case of the retired partner, the parties may wish to state with some precision the extent and manner in which of counsel will cut back on the duties that he or she had as a partner. For example, they may agree that of counsel need no longer be required to take an active role in the litigation conducted by the firm. Or there may be a reduction in the number of hours that of counsel typically will be expected to be around the firm. Or there may be some indication of of counsel's retaining a more active role in serving some clients rather than others. However the duties of of counsel are outlined, there must be some consonant relationship between these duties and the compensation and perquisites that of counsel may be expected to enjoy.

In drafting the of counsel agreement, the parties should make every effort to have the relationship between of counsel and the law firm treated as one of independent contractor. In preparing this contract, the drafter must sail between the Scylla of the employer-employee relationship and the Charybdis of partnership. For some purposes, such as malpractice insurance, employee benefits, and health insurance, the parties may wish to treat of counsel as an employee. By careful drafting, they can make certain that this will not change of counsel's independent contractor status. At the same time, the parties must be very careful about assigning duties to of counsel that would place him or her in a managerial role or give him or her the semblance of the power to make decisions for the firm. An absence of care in this drafting might well cause the firm or of counsel to suffer some unnecessary vicarious liability.

The Of Counsel Agreement emphasizes that all phases of the relationship between a law firm and of counsel can be—and should be—governed by contract.[3] Lawyers are developing new clauses every day to meet new situations. Of counsel is not a new concept to the practice of law, but it has only been within the last twenty-five years that the bar has looked closely at this relationship. In 1972, the ABA's Standing Committee on Ethics and Professional Responsibility issued its first formal opinion on the subject. Formal Opinion 330 answered some, but not all, of the many questions that surround the of counsel relationship. In May 1990, the ethics committee promulgated Formal Opinion 90-357 in an effort to conform ethical requirements more closely to the realities of the practice in the late twentieth century.

Of counsel relationships may be premised either on an independent contractor or an employer-employee relationship at common law. In 90-357, the committee recognized that of counsel and the related law firm were free to make contractual arrangements that would satisfy their own particular needs. Some of counsel relationships are based on an independent contractor status; others use the employer-employee paradigm as the basis for the contract between the parties. The committee noted that two situations involved employers and employees, as distinct from independent contractors: (1) the

3. *Id.*

probationary partner-to-be and (2) the lawyer who became an employee of the law firm in a permanent status between partner and associate. It placed these two relationships under the overarching concept of "of counsel," along with the retired partner, the part-time practitioner, and the lawyer entering a second career. In the latter situations, the independent contractor status is probably the more common arrangement, but even here there may be situations in which the parties would prefer to use an employer-employee relationship for some particular reason.

In the case of the retired partner who becomes of counsel, some special problems not involved in some of the other relationships may arise. Retiring partners and their respective law firms must be especially careful about the manner in which the agreement is drafted. Within the concept of "retired partner," there are a number of different situations requiring separate treatment. For example, some retired partners will have no connection—and may not want any connection—with their former partnership, other than to receive periodically that portion of partnership profits or pension proceeds to which they are entitled by virtue of being retired. At the other extreme is the partner who is unwilling or unable to give up the control and prestige that he or she has enjoyed by virtue of being a partner in past years. Most retired partners fall somewhere between these two extremes. They no longer desire to maintain control over the partnership's operations, but they wish to remain active to some extent. It is in this precise situation that of counsel provides a necessary and desirable concept for both the lawyer and the law firm involved.

If you are contemplating retirement or have already retired but still wish to remain active, we urge that you and your firm enter into a detailed written agreement about your of counsel relationship. If you are concerned only with drawing your pension benefits or your share of partnership profits, you may need nothing more than your basic partnership agreement. But if you plan to do any work at all for the firm, we recommend that you approach the problem almost as though you were drafting a second agreement—totally separate from the partnership agreement—in which you spell out the details of your rights and duties as of counsel. In drafting this agreement, you must think through the pros and cons of the independent contractor status as compared with the employer-employee relationship. The principal advantage of the former is that the parties are not restricted in the terms they may wish to place in the contract. But there may well be times when you would prefer to be in an employer-employee relationship. For example, you may wish to be treated as an employee for purposes of health or malpractice insurance. A well-drafted, detailed agreement will give both the law firm and of counsel the security necessary for an effective and successful law practice.

The Of Counsel Agreement emphasizes the importance of such a detailed written agreement.[4] Although Formal Opinion 90-357 has spelled out the ethical parameters that govern the relationship, the ethics committee felt it inappropriate to comment on such matters as compensation and malpractice insurance. Yet every of counsel agreement must deal with these problems. The parties must work out the details of how the benefits and the burdens of the of counsel arrangement will be shared. In addition, they must be aware of how their relationship will affect third parties. Problems of conflicts of interest, malpractice, lawyer advertising, and the like are seen in a different perspective within the of counsel relationship.

Most of counsel agreements are negotiated upon the retirement of a senior lawyer who desires to take a lesser role in the practice. The parties to the agreement are usually the law firm and the retired or retiring partner. In this factual setting, most lawyers and law firms find that the independent contractor, rather than the employer-employee, relationship is more advantageous to both sides of the agreement. The former partner will want to retain the independence that the relationship connotes and to gain the substantial tax advantages that the independent contractor status affords.

As an independent contractor, the retiree may take his or her business deductions "above the line" (that is, prior to determining adjusted gross income) on Schedule C of Form 1040. Of counsel then will have the option of itemizing nonbusiness deductions or taking the standard deduction. He or she will not be limited by the 2 percent floor on miscellaneous business deductions applicable to employees, since these amounts will be shown as part of the cost of doing business on Schedule

4. *Id.*

C. For 1998, he or she will have to pay a 12.4 percent tax on the first $68,400 of earnings for purposes of the Social Security taxes (FICA and FUTA) and a 2.9 percent tax on *all* earnings for purposes of Medicare. A self-employed person who earned $100,000 during 1998 would have a Social Security tax of $8,481.60, and a Medicare tax of $2,900.00, or a total tax of $11,381.60. Of this amount, 50 percent would be deductible as a business expense on Schedule C of Form 1040, to give an independent contractor a net tax attributable to Social Security and Medicare of $5,690.80.

The law firm also gains substantial tax advantages from the independent contractor relationship. It retains the use of the money that it would otherwise be required to withhold for the income tax payable by the lawyer if he or she were classified as an employee. Instead, the firm files an information return, using Form 1099, and the independent contractor is responsible for the taxes. The lawyer files Form SE in conjunction with Form 1040.

The Internal Revenue Service has enforced the tax rules with respect to the employer-employee, as distinct from the independent contractor, relationship. It has required those of counsel who are practicing as independent contractors to answer elaborate questionnaires designed to elicit factual data about the extent to which one party has "control" over the other. If the common law element of control is present, the relationship is that of employer-employee; if not, then the parties are independent contractors. If some of the following questions are answered in the affirmative, the relationship of the firm with the lawyer will be that of employer-employee, rather than independent contractor:

1. Must the lawyer comply with the firm's instructions regarding the work?
2. Does the lawyer receive training from or at the direction of the firm?
3. Does the lawyer provide services that are integrated into the firm's business?
4. Does the lawyer provide services that must be rendered personally?
5. May the lawyer hire, supervise, and pay assistants for the firm?
6. Does the lawyer have a continuing relationship with the firm?
7. Must the lawyer follow set hours of work?

8. Does the lawyer work full-time for the firm?
9. Does the lawyer work on the firm's premises?
10. Must the lawyer work in a sequence set by the firm?
11. Must the lawyer submit regular reports to the firm?
12. Does the lawyer receive regular amounts at set intervals?
13. Does the lawyer receive payments for business or traveling expenses?
14. Does the lawyer rely on the firm to furnish tools and materials?
15. Does the lawyer lack a major investment in the facilities used to perform the services?
16. Is the arrangement such that the lawyer cannot make a profit or suffer a loss from his or her services?
17. Does the lawyer work for one firm at a time?
18. Is the arrangement such that the lawyer does not offer his or her services to the general public?
19. May the lawyer be fired by the firm?
20. May the lawyer quit work at any time without incurring liability?

No single affirmative answer—or even several affirmative answers—is necessarily determinative of whether the firm is in fact in "control" of the lawyer. But the questions provide a guide for one drafting an of counsel agreement to ensure that a particular contract between a lawyer and a law firm will be construed as establishing an independent contractor, rather than an employer-employee, relationship. The drafter of the agreement should make certain that more than half of the above questions will be answered in the negative. This should not be too difficult since there are only one or two questions (for example, the sixth question, dealing with the continuing relationship) that require an affirmative answer to maintain the of counsel arrangement.

Of counsel should make certain that the agreement that he or she executes with the law firm treats him or her as an employee for purposes of the firm's malpractice insurance coverage and health care. By careful drafting, of counsel can be certain that he or she will participate in these programs without jeopardizing independent contractor status.

As noted above, Formal Opinion 90-357 included two categories within the definition of of counsel that are based on the employer-employ-ee, rather than the independent contractor, relationship. These are the probationary partner-to-be and the permanent lawyer-employee who is neither an associate nor a partner and does not expect to become the latter. Some have urged that these two categories are not comparable to the retired partner, the part-time practitioner, or the former judge or governmental or corporate official who enters upon a second career. The latter categories lend themselves to contractual arrangements wherein the precise rights and duties of of counsel may be spelled out in detail. Of counsel under these agreements may be either independent contractors or employees, depending on the terms of the agreement. Some have argued that the two employee categories specifically mentioned in 90-357 should be excluded from the designation "of counsel." Others take the view that 90-357 properly reflects the practice within the profession of designating a number of different relationships as being "of counsel," without regard to the nature of the relationship as a matter of law.

The two employee categories specifically mentioned in 90-357 have quite different economic origins from the others that are specifically named. The common pattern of the past was for a young lawyer to associate himself or herself with a law partnership and, after a period, say, of five to seven years, to become a partner. Throughout most of the country, the profession was built around only these two categories of lawyers—partners and associates. The partners took the risks but also reaped the rewards. Associates were employees of the law partnership who took none of the risks and drew a salary from the firm. The partnership was free to terminate the employment of an associate, and the associate was free to leave the firm, at any time.

During the past two or three decades, the movement of lawyers from one firm to another has increased with the growth in the size of law firms. As law firms have opened new offices or merged with firms in other cities, additional employment patterns beyond the traditional two levels of partners and associates have developed. Some have established two or more levels of partners, associates, or both. Others have become professional service corporations or have formed partnerships of such corporations. Whatever the cause, law firms have undergone many changes.

A firm desiring to attract a particular lawyer to itself might find it necessary to offer him or her something more than an associate's position. But it might be reluctant to make him or her a partner until it had some experience working closely with him or her. The result might well be the designation of the newly employed attorney as a probationary partner-to-be. Such a person remains an employee while in probationary status that terminates with completion of the probation period. He or she is then elevated to partner status; or, if the firm and the probationary partner are unable to agree on this, the lawyer and the firm are free to go their respective ways without embarrassment to either of them.

Closely related to the probationary partner-to-be is the permanent employee who is neither a partner nor an associate. Traditionally, an associate who failed to become a partner within, say, five to seven years would leave the firm to join a smaller firm, go into practice on his or her own, or perhaps become a member of the legal staff of one of the firm's corporate clients. In recent years, some of the larger law firms have recognized that it may be more appropriate for such an attorney to remain with the firm in a status other than that of partner or associate. The lawyer involved may be a highly skilled specialist or may have dedicated himself or herself to serving one client's very special needs, or the partnership may have decided to limit the number of partners in the firm. Whatever the reason, such firms have created a category of permanent employee who may stay on with the law firm as "senior attorney," "tax counsel," "special counsel," or some similar title. The arrangement is desirable from the standpoint of the lawyer who is seeking security, since he or she steps into a position comparable to that of a tenured law professor. He or she is assured a steady income, without the strain, stress, and risk of loss that characterizes partnership status. The law firm can avoid losing a valued employee, retain his or her particular skills with less of a financial burden, and free the lawyer from management responsibilities so that he or she can more effectively carry out the assigned tasks of his specialty.

Under Formal Opinion 90-357, the probationary partner-to-be and the permanent employee are included within the phrase "of counsel" along with the retired partner, the part-time practitioner, and the former government or corporate official who has entered the practice of law as a second career. But the relationships created by all of these categories, as well as any not specifically mentioned in the opinion, are controlled by the precise terms of the agreement between the parties. Although the ethics committee has subsumed all of these situations under the concept of "of counsel," those who draft of counsel agreements must be careful to use traditional concepts such as independent contractor status or the employer-employee relationship to achieve the optimum arrangement for the parties involved. The legal profession must first gain some experience under 90-357 before any change is made in the existing concept of of counsel. In the meantime, all those interested in of counsel arrangements will continue to draft these agreements with sufficient care and detail to satisfy the needs of both of counsel and the related law firm in any particular situation. For the lawyer who has retired or is about to retire, the of counsel agreement offers an opportunity to both the individual attorney and to the law firm to reach an agreement that can be beneficial to both parties.

8
Going It Alone

PHILOMENE A. GATES

It can happen. No, it *will* happen. If you are part of a couple, one of you will die first. Though older couples often refuse to think about that, they had better sit down together, *now*.

As lawyers, you already know the specifics of counseling recently widowed or divorced clients. An article in *Experience* in Fall 1991 by Shirley Bass set out many basic caveats. What I am proposing here is a simple checklist to serve anyone over voting age who is someday going to be married or have a serious relationship that may come to an end. Most of the survivors will be women. When advising anyone who is living with a commitment to someone to think about his or her future, the following may be valuable to have on hand. There are several steps to take if someone is left alone, and it is good to know about those steps *before* that happens, so that the partners can discuss and plan.

A young husband or wife can die in an accident or, as has just occurred in my own family, can die of cancer. Whatever the cause of a spouse's death, however long the couple had to plan the survivor's future, no one is ever fully prepared for his or her loss of a life partner.

It is *very* important that a couple discuss what each partner needs to know about the couple's finances, their wishes about their children, how they would prefer to be buried—all of which are difficult to discuss when things are going well. Now is the time to have that kind of conversation.

I was barely 60 and in perfect health, as apparently was my husband when he died after suffering a ruptured aneurism while driving from Philadelphia to New York. He lived eleven days in the hospital, fighting for his life, and we believed

he was going to make it. Surely I was not about to discuss such things during those eleven days, even though I was frantic to ask him many vital questions. To have done so would have made him think that I did not believe he would live. Similarly, many wives are loath to have this sort of discussion during the latter part of their marriages because they believe their husbands will think, "She's going to leave me for someone else!" Furthermore, more and more women are handling their families' finances and related activities.

The time is *now!* Please advise your husband, wife, client, or friends to do it. Today's survivors of a marriage or a long-term relationship need help. There are many of the latter: Good people who love each other or want to share their lives without the complications of marriage. As a lawyer who has a subspecialty in matrimonial cases, I can emphasize that it is much easier to get married than to get divorced. Most lawyers know this full well, and many more each year are finding kindred souls who share interests, are friends, and simply do not want to live alone. They "get together" and, being lawyers, they usually have a carefully drafted list of rules in their relationships. If they do not have such a list, they should.

Mindful of modern-day tolerance of homosexuality, the above-described joint living arrangement frequently is one in which the committed individuals are of the same sex. This does necessarily connote that a homosexual relation exists. It sometimes simply means that two people decide to cohabit and to work it out in an orderly way so that each has his or her own duties toward the union. Whatever the arrangement, as in a successful long-term marriage, each must give the other "space."

Learning to live with another person, whether within the legal framework of a marriage or not, takes working at *every day*. Usually undertaken with love, affection, and respect, it will work out

---

Philomene A. Gates, a solo practitioner in New York City, is the author of *Suddenly Alone: A Woman's Guide to Widowhood*, published in paperback by Harper Perennial in 1990.

fine. The loss of a partner in any kind of long-term relationship is as real and painful as the loss of a legal mate. One does not even need to have shared a household to feel desolate upon the death of a dear and devoted companion.

Many of my male friends who are successfully living alone have criticized my previous publishing efforts directed to managing one's financial, emotional, and legal affairs after the loss of a mate. They say my writings are too focused on the woman being the surviving partner. I plead guilty. Many of my male friends living alone have very wisely decided not to marry again—enjoying, as they do (fortunately for those of us who are female and live alone), female companionship.

First, they have had to conquer the mechanics of their households. How the laundry equipment, stoves, and refrigerators work. They do their own laundry, defrost their own refrigerators, plant their own gardens (usually cut back to a size they can manage), and handle the maintenance of their homes and equipment therein. Normally, their wives took care of these matters.

Second, they decide, when they can face making the effort, that their friends have made all of the overtures thus far since their loss, and it is time for them to begin to reciprocate. One widower, now aged 88, has been doing this very successfully for ten years. He likes women and men, enjoys coed travel (he plans and executes it with his favorite female traveling companions), and likes very much spending evenings with a small group of men and women in his village. He reaches out, in other words. He has learned to prepare excellent soups, starting with a commercially canned variety and adding his own fish, meat, chicken, mushrooms, vegetables, herbs and spices, and wine or brandy. A hearty soup, a salad, and a buttered loaf of French bread, which he picks up at the local bakery early the day it has been baked, and he has a glorious and festive lunch. Most people over 60 do not want to gain weight. They are happy with a cookie, ice cream, or a candy—something that is not hard to fix. And it can be refused without hurting anyone's feelings! If my friend's group of four to six has played croquet or golf or been to a seminar at a local college in the morning, it is nice to end their morning at his home for a cocktail and his delicious lunch. He does the same for dinners. He has learned to prepare two or three delicious meals of poultry or fish that he can barbecue outdoors or, in winter, in his own fireplace. Everyone finds his main dish irresistible. He adds a vegetable, French bread, salad, and store-bought sweets, and he has it made. Naturally, he has all of the invitations he can comfortably accept and sees the people he really prefers.

Third, a man, particularly a retired lawyer, is in much demand in his adopted retirement community. Women are, as well, sought after for committees, boards, ad hoc task forces, and the like. Well-educated people have much to offer their fellow citizens once they do not have to punch a time clock every day. Their fellows find out very quickly who and where they are. One enormous caveat: Do not commit yourself to too many of these endeavors in an effort not to be lonely. One at a time will be rewarding and fun. Another large caveat: Do not undertake any work that will require a great deal of night driving. Most of us do not like to drive at night; in fact, it is downright dangerous. It is vital to make it clear, if volunteering for an effort you feel you want to be a part of, that night meetings outside your immediate neighborhood are out.

It is difficult to face the question of remarriage. There are many success stories of the "second time around." Unless there is enormous respect and a great basis for real friendship between you and a prospective mate, I would go very cautiously about it. When left alone, men are much more vulnerable to a second marriage than are women. In the first place, men are used to being taken care of. Some men I know could not even find all of the pieces of their clothing when their wife of many years was no longer there!

The many problems resulting in remarriage can, in themselves, ruin a second romance. Suppose both parties have houses they have lived in and love and possessions they cherish—but the other dislikes. Where do they summer? If one part of a couple has always gone to one vacation spot and the other to an entirely different one, how do they choose? One month or six weeks at each one is one solution many of my friends have adopted. They complain, however, that they just become a part of their old "group" and begin to feel that they belong when they have to pick up and move to the summer place.

Caution is wisdom before plunging into matrimony a second time. Just to have some companionship when one is lonely is not reason enough. A truly loving and respectful relationship can be built, and waiting a few months or years will not endanger it if it is meant to be. Analyze the pros and cons of remarriage as you would analyze a merger or an acquisition.

My suggested opening is, "Darling, you love me and I love you, but so many of our friends have been left alone with inadequate knowledge of what their husbands or wives would want them to do, that I will sleep a lot easier if you would tell me and if I tell you how much we have, how much we owe, and how we would manage if a truck would suddenly hit one of us as we crossed the street."

My husband and I were lawyers with a great family and a wonderful professional and social life. He was on his way toward being sworn in as the next president of the American College of Trial Lawyers. People expected that I should cope well, having practiced law (some of it matrimonial) continuously since 1942 (with an eleven-year sabbatical for child-raising). In the first year after his death, I most certainly did not cope well. Armed with a law degree and a CPA certificate, I found myself unable to absorb the simplest financial statement. All of a sudden, despite all of the communication we had about our affairs, I knew the agony of my clients who had been widowed or divorced.

What follow are the steps one must take in the long struggle after the sudden loss of a partner—just to put one foot in front of the other.

Step One

After the will has been read or the divorce is final, and family and friends have rallied around as long as their lives permit, sit down with a pad of paper. Telephone or meet with your lawyer, banker, investment adviser (if you have one), insurance agent, and perhaps a wise friend whose counsel you trust. If your spouse was a partner in a law partnership or other privately owned business, talk to one of his or her knowledgeable former partners or business colleagues.

Write down all of the questions you think about during the day and in the middle of the night. List what you think you own, free or encumbered, and what obligations you have. I still do this every six months, and I have been a widow for fourteen years.

Step Two

Have separate meetings with each of these professionals. Take with you any documents that you feel they might need to study so that they can guide your future plans. Do not hesitate to ask a lot of questions, preferably written down ahead of time.

Preface your inquiries with, "I know it might sound dumb, but I am not at my best right now, and I *must* understand every word of these papers now that it is up to me alone to make decisions." The exception is the insurance policies—the language is arcane, and no one understands it except your insurance agent. The widowed or divorced person at least must have tried to fathom the contents of what he or she is bringing to these meetings beforehand.

Step Three

Go through all canceled checks for the past year and preferably the past three years (and divide by three to get an average). A divorced person might not have access to all of the bank accounts in the other spouse's name, but a person can try to have them made available so that he or she can plan a budget.

This examination is the most important step in achieving peace of mind. At least when you finish the exercise you know what it has cost you, as a couple, to live. Many business and professional men admit to me today that they really have no idea how much it costs them to live. A man or woman alone *has* to know.

Step Four

Prepare a budget. Put your past canceled checks and credit-card statements in piles designating categories: rent, utilities, food, clothes, travel, charity, car and other transport, meals out, gifts, church, home maintenance, clothes maintenance (everything has to be cleaned and repaired someday), and any other major category unique to your case. There may be minor children, school tuitions, dependent parents or relatives, children away at school who not only require tuition but need athletic equipment, long-distance calling, health coverage, travel, and so on. This important expense budget may have to be modified a dozen times, but you have to start somewhere.

Step Five

What do you own? Prepare a list of assets and the possible income from each. You may have owned certain real or personal property jointly. You must find out if it is all now in your name. If not, how can you get access to it? Insurance, pension funds, credit unions, a stock and bond portfolio— all have to be figured into your total asset picture, as it is from that ownership that you will have to live, unless you have an outside income of your own or a lucrative personal career.

Step Six

Analyze your insurance. Confer with your insurance agent. If you are not happy with your current agent, ask your wise friends who seem to handle their own affairs well for a suggestion. Divorced persons have a specific problem, and their participation in the benefits from their ex-spouse's policies have probably already been a part of the divorce settlement.

Be sure not to leave this area of concern without insisting on a schedule of the insurance you carry. This schedule should list the policy number, the deductible, what it insures, and how much the premium is and when it is due. This document should be kept in a very handy place as you will want to refer to it often.

You Must Act

The steps I have laid out above are what you should know and do before being alone. Being lawyers, my husband and I talked about his retirement, how we would live, how much we might have to live on. We had, I believe, more communication than most happily married couples and told each other everything. Well, almost everything. After a lifetime of matrimonial practice, I am convinced that no couple tells each other everything!

One matter that is rarely discussed between couples (married, homosexual, or just platonic couples living together of the same or opposite sex) is, "If I die, which of your friends and relatives do you want to receive what?" Each of us has personal property, not just clothing and jewelry, but furniture, especially cherished paintings or other forms of art, silver, or porcelain—we are all collectors of one thing or another. Our libraries may have been disposed of by will or codicil, but there are usually some volumes that may have special meaning to one or more of our friends or relatives. I advise making lists of all friends and relatives to whom a special thing should be given. Most surviving spouses are too grief-stricken or too addled by all of the arrangements of the funeral to think about such a thing. So many friends have said, "Oh, I know Joe would have liked me to have his four-volume Carl Sandburg, as he said many times that he was willing it to me." But Joe never did put anything in writing, and the books went with all the rest to the thrift shop, his college, or the local library. Men and women should list the friends they wish to have something to remind them of their relationship and pleasure in one another's company. Beside each name they should specify what each should be given. The survivor's life would be much simplified if that is done well in advance of a terminal illness.

Couples should certainly review their holdings of securities, real estate, and so on; know the location thereof; have a list of anyone else who has control or access to same; and know exactly how to handle the securities and other matters in the other's absence. The sooner couples sit down together and do this, the better off they will be and the more calmly they will face tomorrow.

After I wrote a book on this subject, more than five hundred letters came my way, mostly from people I do not know, telling me how much my suggestions helped them. That is reward indeed, and the steps above are only a small part of what it takes to rebuild a life without the one person in the world whom you loved and depended on, and who loved you. You can be alone and not lonely. Your friends may move away to sunny retirement climates, so making new friends and developing new horizons is essential. Rise above the pain and anxiety. You must, and only you can do that. No one can do it for you. But if you plan ahead, grit your teeth, and just "do it," life ahead won't be fearful. Being alone and being older is not for sissies. There is a pillow embroidered, "Screw the Golden Years."

Not so! If you sow seeds of satisfaction and pleasure by giving to others and cultivate the garden of your mind and soul, there will be flowers in your heart and in your life. I guarantee it.

9
Sole Survivor

JILL SCHACHNER CHANEN

Ah, solo practice. No one to look over your shoulder. No one to tell you how many hours to bill. No one to breathe down your neck. No one to check up on whether you are working late nights and Saturdays—or not working.

So go ahead. Hang a shingle, rent an office, hire a secretary and tell the decorator to do the space up right.

Ah, if it only were that easy. For even the savviest consumers, the office, personnel, and technology options for today's sole proprietor can be dizzying. For lawyers—notorious for their lack of office management skills—knowing what to budget can make the difference between experiencing a successful solo practice or desperately seeking to rejoin the rat race.

In 1998, with the economy booming, inflation low, and business showing little sign of retrenching, the time may seem all the more inviting to strike out on your own.

But consider that for every $100,000 a solo practitioner grosses, only $30,000 likely will be taken home after office expenses and taxes, says Joel P. Bennett, a solo employment-law practitioner in Washington, D.C., who chairs the ABA's Law Practice Management Section. In large cities, Bennett says, solos could see overheads as high as $50,000 to $100,000 a year.

"Approximately 50 percent of your income goes to overhead if you have employees," says Bennett. "Once you know what your overhead is, what your fee structure is, and what your living expenses are, then you can figure out how much money you need to make."

After careful consideration of the costs of solo practice, the question may not be whether you

really want the responsibilities of a solo practice. The question may be, can you afford it? Here's where to start counting.

Office Space

Whether your vision of solo practice places you in a towering skyscraper offering breathtaking views, a corporate office park in suburbia, or a storefront in a heavily trafficked area, be prepared for rent to be a significant annual expense. Especially in this year's humming economy with businesses vying for space, rates can cause jaws to drop.

Office rents depend on varying factors, including the city, vacancy rate, length of lease, and type of space. The newest office buildings in an urban business district—commonly referred to as Class A—command the highest rents, while Class B rentals, in older or more remote buildings, are more affordable. Very old office buildings—Class C—offer significantly cheaper rents, but they may lack the mechanical or electrical systems to handle required technology.

In Chicago, for example, this year's gross rents—not including utilities and maintenance costs—for Class B office buildings in the city's downtown Loop business district range from $18 to $23 per square foot, says John Niemi, a senior vice president at Equis, a national real-estate brokerage company that works with law firms of all sizes. At those rates, the base rent for a 500-square-foot office—room for a lawyer and a secretary—can easily amount to $10,000 a year.

What about a downtown office in a midsized city? In Minneapolis, gross rents in Class B office buildings are $16 to $22 per square foot, according to Niemi. In Portland, Oregon, gross rents are $11 to $20 per square foot, according to CB Commercial Real Estate Group.

Rents for suburban office parks are comparable to downtown office spaces. Portland's CB

Jill Schachner Chanen is a lawyer and a freelance writer in Chicago. Her work is regularly published in *The ABA Journal, The New York Times, Crain's Chicago Business,* and the *Chicago Tribune.*

51

Commercial reports average gross rental rates of $14 per square foot. In Raleigh-Durham, North Carolina, where suburban office parks predominate, gross rents are $16 to $24 per square foot, says Scott Stankavage, a principal in Goodman Segar, a commercial brokerage in Durham.

If a storefront law office is your ideal, brace yourself. Storefronts are classified as retail and can command rents as high as downtown office buildings. In Chicago, on a busy neighborhood street in a mixed-use area, storefronts are renting for $10 to $15 per square foot.

And don't forget to budget for annual increases. Chicago rents have increased by nearly $1 per square foot over the past year, with the trend showing no sign of reversing itself.

Rents in Raleigh-Durham have increased 5 percent a year for the past five years because of a dearth of new office space. Stankavage expects the trend to diminish in the next few years because 2 million square feet of office space is planned for the area.

Because of the tight market and escalating rents, Niemi sees many solo practitioners opting for offices in suites, where tenants can get private offices and services such as use of conference rooms and secretarial assistance.

Companies such as San Francisco-based HQ Business Centers operate office suites with rents ranging from $300 per month to several thousand dollars, depending on the city, size of the office, and length of lease.

For example, a single office in San Francisco's financial district can be leased for as little as $900 per month; in Chicago's Loop, $500; and in downtown Seattle, $675, according to HQ spokeswoman Beverly Mann.

Support Staff

With advances in technology, a full-time secretary has become a luxury that many solos are finding they can do without.

Bennett is one of those lawyers. When he opened his practice in 1976, Bennett desperately wanted a secretary but could not afford one. Now that he can pay the salary, he no longer needs one.

"In my judgment, with technology today, you may not need any support staff at all," says Bennett, who co-authored the book *Flying Solo,* published by the ABA's Law Practice Management Section.

Bennett estimates that he has reduced his overhead 15 percent by eliminating the need for a full-time secretary. For solos who still cannot dream of a practice without a secretary, expect that salary to be the largest part of expenses.

According to the most recent National Association of Legal Secretaries' (NALS) salary survey, in 1996, annual salaries for entry-level legal secretaries range from $18,000 in the South-central states to $30,000 in the Pacific states. In the Northeast and Midwest, entry level is $25,000.

Experienced secretaries cost more. The NALS survey shows that those salaries range from a low of $22,000 in the South-central states to $37,000 in the Pacific states. In both the Northeast and Midwest, the average is $30,000 a year.

Like salaries, annual increases—or decreases—vary by region. Legal secretaries in the Northeast saw salaries decline by 10 percent from 1993 to 1995, while those in the Middle Atlantic region reported a 22 percent increase in wages over the same period. In the Rocky Mountain states, legal secretaries' salaries fell by 2 percent between 1994 and 1995, while salaries in the Midwest have held steady.

Bennett also points out that solo practitioners must consider employee benefits to attract support staff. According to the survey, almost every secretary received health insurance and more than half received retirement benefits like a 401(k) plan. These benefits can add thousands of dollars to the annual cost of a secretary.

As a way to reduce support staff costs, consider hiring students from local secretarial schools for tasks like filing and data entry, suggests Los Angeles attorney Theda C. Snyder, who wrote the Law Practice Management Section book *Running a Law Practice on a Shoestring.* These interns can be hired for hourly rates of $5 to $15.

Snyder also has hired secretaries and paralegals through temporary agencies for short and long terms. Hourly rates from temporary agencies may be higher, but the secretaries and paralegals receive all of their benefits from the agency, eliminating administration of health care and retirement plans for the solo practitioner.

According to John O'Neill, office director for the Chicago branch of Interim Legal Services, a nationwide agency for temporary employees, hourly rates for paralegals range from $20 to $30. The agency's affiliate, Interim Office Staffing, can provide secretarial service at hourly rates ranging from $20 to $27.

Furniture

Though furniture may be an expression of style, above all it should be functional. Interior designer Diana Horvat of the Washington, D.C.-based architecture firm CORE, suggests that solo practitioners invest in quality office furniture with a special emphasis on storage and seating.

According to Horvat, a lawyer's office should contain an executive-sized desk, a credenza, two bookcases and two guest chairs. If a lawyer does not plan to have a conference room for client meetings, Horvat suggests a separate computer table to remove clutter from the primary work surface. Expect to spend a total of about $7,000 for pieces made in solid wood from a high quality furniture manufacturer, she says. The same pieces in less-substantial materials can be purchased at national discount office supply stores for as little as $750.

Desk chairs will add $300 to $1,500, depending on the covering used. Horvat advises lawyers not to be swayed by the price or the fabric. Some lawyers may find the $300 desk chairs more comfortable than the higher-end ones. "Ergonomics is more important than leather when it comes to desk chairs," she says.

If cash is tight, consider used furniture. Los Angeles lawyer Snyder has purchased used furniture from other law firms and from secondhand stores. She recently purchased a wood desk and return for $90, and a four-drawer lateral file cabinet for $100 at a used furniture store.

Another possibility is renting, although long-term costs will be greater. At Cort Furniture, a national furniture rental company, an executive desk, credenza, and filing cabinet can be leased for an average of $165 per month.

A secretary also needs workspace. A desk and return may be purchased for as little as $150 from a discount office supply store. They can be rented for an average of $90 per month. And don't forget a desk chair for the secretary, which can add $50 to $250 to the total.

If the secretarial station doubles as a receptionist's desk, Horvat suggests investing in storage cabinets to hold fax machines, printers, and office supplies. Prices for these cabinets begin at $100.

Office Equipment

Equipping a law office may be one of the most difficult tasks a solo practitioner will confront. The problem lies not in what equipment to purchase—computers, laser printers, modems, fax machines, telephones, and copiers are necessities—but in how powerful the equipment should be and what bells and whistles to choose.

When it comes to computers, "Buy the biggest and fastest you can afford, because what you buy today will be outdated in six months," says Bruce Dorner, a Londonderry, New Hampshire, solo practitioner and computer consultant.

Dorner says solo practitioners should plan to budget $5,000 for a high-power computer, which should include 64 megabytes of memory, a Pentium II chip, a Microsoft Windows operating system, a 32x CD-ROM drive, a 56K capable modem, and a 17-inch color monitor.

For those on a tighter budget, James Eidelman of Eidelman Associates, computer consultants in Ann Arbor, Michigan, says $3,000 will buy a quality starter business computer. These computers should have 32 megabytes of memory, a Pentium I processing chip, a 15-inch monitor, and a 20x CD-ROM drive. Prices for lap-tops with the same features can run twice the price of the desktop version.

Both Dorner and Eidelman advise lawyers to buy the same computer for their secretaries as for themselves. It will double the budget but, says Eidelman: "It will ease the support nightmare if there is a problem with one. You can swap the components back and forth."

For printers, Dorner and Eidelman advise lawyers to purchase laser printers instead of ink jet printers. Although more expensive, laser printers not only produce better-looking documents, but they print more quickly. Laser printers can be purchased for $1,000 or less; ink jet printers for as little as $200.

Expect to spend $200 for a thermal-paper fax machine or $400 for a plain paper one. The plain paper machines are a better investment, suggests Christina Kallas, a solo practitioner in New York City, who uses hers as a copy machine as well. For large copying jobs, Kallas goes to a local office supply store where the inexpensive copies are more economical than purchasing or leasing a copy machine.

Copy machines can range from a reasonable $350 for one that copies at a rate of three pages per minute to $8,500 for a speedier machine that can collate, reduce, and enlarge. Copy machines also can be leased, thereby reducing upfront expenditures. A machine that retails for $5,000 and makes eighteen copies per minute can be leased for $89 a month for a three-year lease; one that retails for $8,500 and makes twenty-six copies per minute can be leased for $202 per month.

LPM chair Bennett advises fellow solos to shop around for deals on copiers through bar associations. He recently purchased one at an ABA Midyear Meeting for $850; it makes ten copies per minute and comes with an automatic document feeder.

No matter how powerful the computers and faxes are, the single most important piece of equipment for lawyers is still the telephone. Bennett says solo practitioners need at least four lines: two for telephone use, one to dedicate to the fax machine, and one for a modem.

Two-line telephones that have speakers, memory, and conference-calling capabilities cost approximately $150. Bennett recently invested $150 for a phone equipped with a headset, allowing him to have two free hands while talking.

While good quality business computers, printers, copiers, fax machines, and telephones are essentials, Dorner and Eidelman also suggest a variety of low-cost options that can help simplify new solos' professional lives.

On the top of their respective lists is hiring a computer consultant. Spending $2,000 will not only get the computer set up, it will provide new solos with valuable advice on how to use the computer and maximize its capabilities.

"Think about using a computer like the first time you drove a car," says Dorner. "You needed an instructor there. Trying to learn the complexities of computers while trying to practice law is dangerous."

Two of the most overlooked pieces of equipment that many solos say they cannot live without are a postage meter and scale. The time saved by not having to wait in line at a post office is worth the monthly leasing fee for the meter, New York solo Kallas says.

Because of government regulations, meters must be leased. Expect to pay from $25 to $75 per month, plus the price of postage. Scales, however, may be purchased for approximately $75.

Reference Materials

When it comes to reference materials, choices abound. The most common path is the one Kallas follows. She subscribes to an on-line research service for state law and purchases three or four substantive treatises and practice guides each year from her state's continuing legal education provider.

The on-line subscription, which she obtained through a bar association, costs $60 per month; she has spent $500 a year the past several years for treatises and practice guides. If she needs federal law materials or those of other states, Kallas uses the library at the federal courthouse, which is open to the public at no charge.

Like most solos, Kallas finds the idea of maintaining a full library impractical and cost-prohibitive. Books require storage space, and in a city like Manhattan—rents are among the highest in the nation—the square footage necessary for a library could add several thousand dollars a year to rent.

In addition, the cost of hard-bound books is high. The price of a new, hardbound federal law library from West Publishing—including the Federal Reporter, Federal Supplement, Supreme Court Reporter and U.S. Code Annotated—costs more than $60,000.

Secondary materials, including the Federal Criminal Code & Rules, the Federal Sentencing Guideline Manual, and Federal Jury Practice and Instruction, add another $3,700 to the tab.

State law libraries also are costly. Expect to pay more than $20,000 for a complete hardbound library of California law from West, while a new library of Massachusetts law costs more than $16,000.

Dealers of used law books provide another way to purchase hardbound materials. A complete used federal library can be purchased for $10,000, a complete used state library for less than $5,000, according to a spokesman for National Law Resources in Chicago, a used-book seller.

Some legal publishers report that they are discontinuing many of their hardbound materials because of the ease of delivering and updating information electronically through CD-ROMs or through on-line services

The costs of the electronic formats, however, are comparable to the hardbound books.

For example, Commerce Clearinghouse's Federal Securities Law Reporter, per year, is $1,524 in print and on CD-ROM, and $1,645 on-line. Annual costs for the Riverwood, Illinois, legal publisher's Federal Tax Guide are $701 in print, $815 on CD-ROM, and $800 on-line. Its Payroll Management Guide costs $529 in print, $499 on CD-ROM, and $549 on-line.

Similarly, West's federal law library on CD-ROM may be licensed for a monthly fee of $1,150. Its state law materials on CD-ROM may be licensed for a monthly fee of $345 for California and $217 for Massachusetts.

Both Westlaw and Lexis now offer low-cost subscriptions to their respective on-line research services that cater to the solo practitioner. Most of these programs are available through bar associations, and lawyers are advised to shop around for the best deal.

ABA members, for example, can subscribe to the Lexis Illinois state library and its federal library for $125 per month for unlimited access.

Additional state law libraries may be added for $75 per state. A subscription to a federal library on Westlaw is priced from $55 per month, and individual state library subscriptions are priced at an average of $150 per month.

Insurance

There is disagreement among solo practitioners over the need for professional liability insurance.

New York lawyer Kallas has taken the risk of not carrying it. She cites lack of assets and, more important, she says, her careful manner of practice is the best insurance she can have.

The good news for those who err on the side of caution is that professional liability insurance is readily available for solo practitioners of all experience levels.

This was not the case as few as ten years ago, says Paul Clauss, vice president and director of New England operations for Bertholon-Rowland, a Boston-based insurance broker.

"It is relatively easy in 1998 for a new [solo practitioner] to obtain professional liability insurance. There was more difficulty in the 1980s because of the economy. But now there is more capital in the market, and a lot of companies are offering lawyers' professional liability insurance," says Clauss, whose company administers such programs for bar associations in Boston and New York.

When shopping for professional liability insurance, Clauss recommends checking with bar associations first. Their programs are not necessarily less expensive, but they usually have been researched to ensure that the carrier is reputable, a prime concern in a crowded insurance market.

Costs for insurance also vary by city. Lawyers will find premiums higher in litigious states like California and Texas, says Paul Dorroh, a vice president of Kirk-Van Orsdale, which administers malpractice insurance programs for state bars in California, Washington, and Iowa.

Most bar-sponsored insurance programs also provide significant discounts to new admittees.

In California, for example, a new lawyer can obtain malpractice insurance for premiums of $500 per year. The insurance provides minimum coverage limits of $100,000 per claim with a $300,000 annual aggregate and a $1,000 deductible. A more seasoned attorney in California going into solo practice would find similar coverage for as low as $1,200 a year, Dorroh says.

In Boston, a newly admitted lawyer could pay as little as $300 per year for the same coverage, while the experienced lawyer might have to pay as little as $400 for the coverage, according to Clauss.

In Cincinnati, a newly admitted lawyer might be able to obtain this insurance for $600 a year, while the experienced lawyer would pay $1,400, says Hope Porter of Robert G. McGraw & Co. in Cincinnati, which administers the local bar's insurance program.

Unlike malpractice insurance, health insurance is seen as more of a necessity. Under certain situations, health care insurance from a previous employer may be carried into a new employment situation such as a solo practice.

However, the health care portability legislation that permits this sets no limits on premiums, and new solos may find their insurance quickly becoming unaffordable, says Janice MacFerrin, a principal of Attorney Benefit Specialists in Phoenix, who administers a health insurance program for the Maricopa County Bar Association.

55

For lawyers who find themselves in this situation or for those looking for new health insurance, check local and state bar associations. Many offer affordable programs for members, their families, and support staff.

The ABA's American Bar Endowment offers several insurance packages, including group term life insurance, disability, and office overhead expenses insurance. Premiums are, of course, based on the age and health of the insured individual. (For information, call 800/621-8981 or 312/988-6400.)

Phoenix lawyers, for example, can enroll in a managed care plan through the county bar association for as little as $100 per month. Family plans may be purchased for $480 a month. Lawyers in Cincinnati can find health care coverage through the Cincinnati Bar Association, provided that they are insuring at least one other employee.

Premiums for a health maintenance organization plan could be as low as $120 per month.

Make sure to budget for increases in premiums. MacFerrin says insurance costs nationwide are rising an average of 5 percent to 7 percent a year.

Marketing

Just because people are opening the office door, solo practitioners cannot forget about the need for marketing. Some practice management experts say marketing dollars are the most important a solo practitioner can spend, and there are plenty of ways to spend them. Those little items like business cards, brochures, and memberships in bar associations and clubs can add up.

According to a 1997 survey of law firms by Altman Weil, a legal services consulting firm, these small-ticket items cost the typical small-firm lawyer some $4,000 a year. If, by this time, the expense of taking a flier as a solo seems a bit daunting, just remember: It takes money to earn money.

10
Postretirement Volunteer Opportunities: An Update

JOHN H. PICKERING AND STEPHANIE EDELSTEIN

Introduction

The prospects of retirement are enticing: time to visit with family and friends, to work around the house, to travel, to write, to read, to paint, to improve the golf game, or to do volunteer work. But the attraction may be somewhat illusory. Work around the house can rapidly lose its charm. Family and friends may have competing interests. Travel may be difficult to manage on a fixed income. Lawyers who have had neither the time nor the interest to develop hobbies, and whose real hobby is their professional work, may find their days rather empty.

Accordingly, in planning for retirement, consider putting your professional experience to good use by some form of voluntary service. Paid employment may be an option in some cases, but by volunteering, you will reap personal rewards while providing a much-needed public service. Despite all that the profession and government have done in providing legal services to persons who are poor and disadvantaged, it is estimated that only 20 percent of legal needs are met. Senior lawyers can help fill the gap, while finding continuing, and very real, professional and personal satisfaction.

Compensated Professional Service

Some retired lawyers hope to supplement their retirement income with paid employment. Unfor-

tunately, opportunities for compensated professional service are slim without some prior relationship or special expertise. There are the fortunate few, of course, but they generally have connections or expertise in a particular area. For example, retiring senior partners could arrange part-time "of counsel" relationships with their firms. Eminent law professors may be employed as consultants in their fields of expertise. Some retired judges find employment in the "rent-a-judge" field, which is growing because of the increasing delay in the processing of our civil dockets. Retired government lawyers may be called back temporarily in emergencies to assist on major studies or projects of their former agencies. Some practitioners may find positions as arbitrators, or as adjunct professors or clinicians in local law schools.

Without some prior connection or special skill that is in demand, however, retired lawyers are not likely to be hired by law firms with which they have had no connection. Similarly, they are not likely to be employed as consultants, or to be selected as arbitrators. Consequently, job fairs for senior lawyers are frequently disappointing as senior lawyers learn they do not have the training, the expertise, and the reputation that are generally prerequisites for what few opportunities may exist for compensated service.

Planning ahead is essential. Firms that terminate their relationships with older associates and active partners and replace them with lower-paid recent graduates are unlikely to continue "of counsel" relationships with their seniors. And, despite the substantial gains wrought by the Age Discrimination in Employment Act, workplace

John H. Pickering, of Wilmer, Cutler & Pickering, Washington, D.C., is past chair of the Senior Lawyers Division and a former chair of the ABA Commission on Legal Problems of the Elderly, and Stephanie Edelstein is associate staff director of the commission.

57

discrimination against older practitioners still exists—it just may not be as blatant as in the past.

Uncompensated Service

In sharp contrast, the opportunities for volunteer service by senior lawyers, in both nonprofessional and professional capacities, are limitless. Senior lawyers' skills and experience make them ideally suited for service on the boards of nonprofit organizations, on the governing bodies of condominium and cooperative apartments, and in general community service activities. And the need is great. But these activities are frequently nonlegal, and may not suit those who prefer to continue practicing their profession. Fortunately, there are also numerous rewarding opportunities for providing volunteer legal services.

Volunteer Legal Practice

Few endeavors are better suited to the unique skills of senior lawyers than pro bono legal work for persons and organizations of limited economic means. Across the nation, senior lawyers are contributing their talents to the provision of legal services to low-income and older persons and to nonprofit organizations in their communities. They come from solo and large-firm practices, from corporate and government work, from the judiciary and from academe. Their reasons for volunteering may vary. Career government lawyers may be continuing the commitment to public service on which their careers were founded. Private practitioners may have decided to give something back to their particular communities. Corporate lawyers may volunteer in recognition of their professional obligations. What do they gain? Some find new venues for addressing issues with which they are familiar. Others are learning about legal issues that they did not encounter in their years of practice. Most are enjoying the company of their colleagues and younger lawyers. What they all have in common is a sense of personal and professional satisfaction.

Pro bono activity raises a host of questions for senior lawyers. Where does one find the volunteer opportunities? What kind of work is involved? Is the senior qualified in the field or is training needed and, if so, where can training be obtained? How can a lawyer accept pro bono cases once he or she has retired? What if the lawyer no longer maintains an office and has assumed inactive bar status? What about malpractice coverage?

In 1991, the American Bar Association's Commission on Legal Problems of the Elderly and Legal Counsel for the Elderly of the American Association of Retired Persons (AARP) embarked on a study of senior lawyer volunteer efforts. Most programs then in existence had begun informally, with individual lawyers seeking volunteer opportunities in local legal services offices or bar-sponsored programs, and had expanded as those volunteers encouraged their friends to join them. The ABA Commission and Legal Counsel for the Elderly initiated a demonstration project in cooperation with the Legal Aid Society of Middle Tennessee (Nashville), to identify problems and find solutions to barriers to senior lawyer volunteerism. The two organizations have also collaborated in the production of *Senior Attorney Volunteer Projects: A Resource Manual*, which discusses the elements of a successful senior lawyer volunteer program, provides guidance on establishing a program, offers suggestions for overcoming obstacles, and gives innovative ideas for pro bono activity. The organizations continue to conduct workshops at the ABA Pro Bono Conference and other venues, encouraging providers of legal services to utilize senior lawyer volunteers.

Where Are the Pro Bono Opportunities?

With active encouragement by the judiciary and the organized bar, retired lawyers are volunteering in increasing numbers—in Atlanta, Chicago, Denver, Los Angeles, Nashville, New York, St. Louis, Savannah, Washington D.C., and numerous other cities. They enjoy flexibility in the scheduling of their time and in the kinds of work they do; they receive training, substantive and administrative support, and malpractice coverage; and they have the opportunity to socialize with colleagues.

Traditional Legal Services Programs

The federal government funds two major legal services programs for the poor. The first provides civil legal services through agencies funded primarily by the Legal Services Corporation (LSC). These programs provide legal advice and representation to indigent persons of all ages. They are staffed by lawyers and paralegals, and are required to limit their services to persons who meet strict income guidelines. The available resources are extremely limited and must be allocated sparingly. As a result, programs must establish case priorities, which vary according to the needs of the community and the level of staffing. Priority areas vary among programs, but most provide counseling and representation in housing, government benefits, and consumer and domestic relations issues.

The second major federally funded legal assistance program is civil legal assistance to older persons under the Older Americans Act (known as Title III legal assistance). Federal funds flow from the U.S. Administration on Aging to each state's office on aging and, in turn, to smaller service areas, each coordinated by an area agency on aging. These area agencies are charged with planning and coordinating programs for older persons. They contract with local providers for legal assistance and other services. Legal services may be provided through contracts with the local federally funded legal services office, by freestanding elder law projects, by solo practitioners or independent lawyer panels or, in some states, especially in rural areas, by community service workers or client advocates.

Unlike LSC programs, Title III legal assistance programs have no specific financial eligibility guidelines, but the Older Americans Act requires that services be targeted to older persons who are in greatest social and economic need. Programs establish priority areas, which may include government benefits, pensions, housing and long-term care, planning for incapacity, guardianship and conservatorship, and consumer issues. Title III programs also provide outreach and community education programs, sending staff to senior centers to speak on specific topics or even to interview clients. As in the LSC programs, pro bono assistance is needed to stretch inadequate resources.

One innovative project, initiated by volunteers, benefits from its alliance with the local legal services program, while retaining some independence. The Utah Senior Lawyer Volunteer Project, which began with funding from two private foundations, is a joint effort of a variety of interested organizations and individuals, including a group of senior lawyers, a law professor at the University of Utah, the state bar association,

the legal services developer, Utah Legal Services (ULS) and the Utah Senior Citizens Law Center. The project, which provides wills and estate planning for low-income, elderly Salt Lake County residents, is staffed by volunteer lawyers, assisted by a paid paralegal-coordinator responsible for intake, screening, and management of the office. While essentially self-contained, the Utah project is affiliated with Utah Legal Services. It is located on the floor immediately below ULS, and is connected to the computer network and telephone system of that program. Utah Legal Services also provides professional liability coverage, the services of a part-time secretary, and access to its library.

Nontraditional Programs

Not all legal services to low- and moderate-income persons are provided by traditional LSC and Older Americans Act funded programs described above, and not all volunteers are affiliated with traditional legal services programs. Retired lawyers have found satisfaction working with court-annexed dispute resolution programs and health insurance counseling projects. In Maryland, a retired lawyer volunteers in the long-term care ombudsman program, visiting nursing home residents, investigating complaints, and helping to resolve disputes.

In 1995, faced with harsh funding cuts and significant restrictions on the kinds of activities in which they were permitted to engage, LSC programs joined with the legal community to examine alternative ways to deliver legal services to low- and moderate-income persons. Statewide planning groups are now considering (or in some cases, have already initiated) projects using computers and other technology to broaden access to the legal system. They are starting self-help programs, courthouse resource centers, discrete task legal services, and telephone hotlines for information and advice. All of these methods provide new opportunities for volunteers.

A number of states are developing hotlines to serve the general population, modeled on the statewide legal hotline for the elderly developed by AARP's Legal Counsel for the Elderly. Staffed by lawyers, including pro bono volunteers, hotlines offer a toll-free telephone number through which people can obtain free counsel and advice in simple matters, or referrals to legal services programs, reduced fee panels, or social service agencies. Hotlines serving older people are now operating in Arizona, northern California, Florida, Georgia, Hawaii, Maine, Michigan, New Mexico, Ohio, Pennsylvania, Puerto Rico, Texas, and Washington, D.C., and those serving the general population are cropping up in several other states.

Court-based alternative dispute resolution programs offer other interesting opportunities for pro bono work by senior lawyers. In Washington D.C., senior lawyers have volunteered as mediators in local and federal court-based mediation programs for several years. In the United States Court of Appeals for the District of Columbia Circuit, experienced senior litigators mediate selected civil cases pending on appeal. Volunteers receive specialized training in mediation techniques and find the work interesting and worthwhile. While it is professionally challenging to try to mediate at the appellate level a case that one side has won below, it can be done. About one-third of the cases referred to mediation are settled—resulting in valuable service to the court and great satisfaction to the volunteer.

Also in the District of Columbia, senior partners and other lawyers from the city's most prestigious law firms actively participate in the Superior Court's Multi-Door Dispute Resolution Program. This program was originally sponsored by the American Bar Association. It involves mediation, arbitration, and early neutral evaluation of civil cases in the trial court. Volunteers are trained in these techniques and find the work professionally satisfying and interesting. They also provide a valuable service to an overburdened trial court. Indeed, the efforts of these volunteers have helped cut the Superior Court's backlog to the extent that the court has been able to institute an individual calendar assignment system for civil cases.

How to Get Involved

It is relatively easy for senior lawyers to get involved in some form of pro bono legal service. It is not necessary to have a background in areas such as poverty or consumer law to make a significant contribution as a volunteer. Substantive skills are frequently transferable, and many legal services programs employ experienced staffs who stand ready to train volunteers on specific issues. Opportunities are not limited to litigators. There

is a need for corporate, tax, transactional, probate, real estate, and many other nonlitigation specialties.

When Legal Services of Eastern Missouri was considering whether to lease or purchase a building, a volunteer in that program was able to advise the director on commercial lease considerations. Senior lawyers at the Savannah office of Georgia Legal Services screen cases, do public speaking, serve on community boards, and mentor staff on legal writing, planning, management, and personnel matters. Retired lawyers with administrative law backgrounds apply their skills to Social Security, Medicare, and Medicaid cases.

At Legal Counsel for the Elderly in Washington, D.C., senior lawyers co-counsel probate and guardianship cases with staff attorneys, prepare powers of attorney, work on the telephone "Hotline," and handle portions of complex litigation. Retired administrative law experts (including administrative law judges) are a perfect match for the myriad cases involving administrative regulations and government benefit programs.

Lawyers who volunteer in the Nashville office of Legal Services of Middle Tennessee assume responsibility for many cases from start to finish. The Nashville volunteers have also made it possible for the program to expand beyond its traditional areas of service. The program now covers probate and real estate matters, including the real property issues that are particularly important in rural areas.

Since the concept of postretirement pro bono is relatively new, the range of roles for retired lawyers has not yet been fully explored. Much will depend on the volunteer's area of expertise, creativity, and willingness to tackle a new area, and on the needs of the program. Volunteers can conduct initial intake interviews, assist staff lawyers on cases, and share with staff their expertise on general practice of law issues. Volunteers with transactional experience can be a valuable resource in areas that usually are not handled by legal services organizations, but that have a significant impact on the lives of low- and moderate-income clients, such as administrative law, health care, real estate, tax, and probate matters. Experienced litigators or appellate advocates might choose to go into court, or they may prefer instead to offer guidance to staff lawyers in these practice skills. Senior lawyers can conduct self-help clinics on government benefit programs (Social Security and disability benefits, food stamps, and Medicaid), powers of attorney and other advance directives for health care and financial matters, bankruptcy, and uncontested divorces. They can assist older clients obtain reverse mortgages, or help community groups establish not-for-profit corporations. They can even do some legislative advocacy, serve as liaisons to community or professional boards or bar committees, or help with fund-raising or the recruitment of other volunteers.

What Are the Stumbling Blocks; How Are They Resolved?

In traditional pro bono representation, requests for assistance are screened by the local bar association or legal services pro bono program. If the prospective client meets the income eligibility guidelines and the case is within the program's established priorities, the matter is referred to a volunteer lawyer, who handles the case from beginning to end.

The traditional system is not well-suited to retired lawyers who no longer maintain an office or have secretarial support, or who are unfamiliar with the kinds of issues on which low- and moderate-income individuals most commonly seek advice. Today's programs address these issues. Senior volunteers usually work out of legal service program offices, where they are provided a desk, a telephone, a place to keep files, and secretarial support. This arrangement may involve sharing space, but this does not present a problem, especially if volunteers are in the office on different days. In fact, it can be a benefit. Many senior volunteers report that they enjoy the fellowship and collegiality of other volunteers and the opportunity to become acquainted with younger lawyers.

Even in retirement, time commitments must be accommodated. Senior lawyers may do other volunteer work, need to handle family and health issues, or want to travel, perhaps even wintering in another state. For these reasons, senior volunteers may prefer to handle only those matters that allow them to maintain a flexible schedule. This can be worked out in a variety of ways, depending on the wishes of the volunteers and the needs of the legal services program. Some volunteers choose to steer clear of responsibility for litigation. Others find it convenient to devote a specific block of time to the program. They come into the office one or two days a week, attend meetings, and handle cases or other matters in which they are involved. Some spend less time, some more. One enthusiastic retiree actually volunteers in a legal services program in Savannah in the winter and in a program in Denver in the summer!

Not all senior lawyer volunteers have maintained active bar status. Some have converted their bar membership to inactive status to avoid the expense of mandatory bar dues and continuing legal education programs. Others have retired to a state in which they are not licensed. To address these issues, Arizona, California, Delaware, Florida, Idaho, New York, Oregon, South Carolina, and Texas have developed emeritus rules, which allow recent retirees who are not members of the bars of those states to do pro bono work, usually with supervision by a lawyer licensed in the jurisdiction. The Arizona, Florida, Idaho, South Carolina, and Texas programs are open to lawyers who are licensed in other states, while California, Delaware, New York, and Oregon limit the application of the rule to those who are licensed in the respective state. Bar rules should not pose a significant barrier, however, since many of the roles described above allow retired lawyers to contribute to the pro bono effort without actually engaging in the practice of law.

Another issue to consider is professional liability. Under the traditional scheme, volunteer lawyers engaged in active practice either carry their own malpractice insurance or, in some cases, they obtain coverage for the particular representation from the referring pro bono program. Retired lawyers are unlikely to maintain such insurance. However, the programs in which they volunteer should be able to extend their policies to cover the volunteers at minimal cost. Indeed, volunteers should insist on malpractice coverage! The fact that services are rendered pro bono, without compensation, is no defense against liability.

What to Expect As a Volunteer

Like any other lawyers beginning a new undertaking, senior lawyer volunteers should expect orientation to the program, training, and ongoing supervision. Training in these projects can be a two-way street. Program staff can train volunteers on poverty, consumer, housing, and other relevant law issues. In turn, the senior volunteers can teach program staff about other substantive areas in which the volunteers are experienced. These areas could include real estate, probate, tax, and corporate law, including incorporation and tax treatment of nonprofit organizations. Volunteers can also help staff develop practice skills in the areas of trial or appellate advocacy, legal writing, or negotiations. One reason for volunteering given by senior lawyers is the opportunity to interact with their colleagues and younger lawyers. Regular, short meetings are often used for discussing cases and general information sharing. "Brown bag lunches," with informal training on a topical subject, can provide staff and volunteers with the chance to get to know one another.

As previously discussed, these projects can be fashioned to provide the flexibility that seniors may need to participate. Unlike traditional pro bono representation, where one lawyer or law firm is responsible for all parts of a case from start to finish, the legal services or other program remains ultimately responsible for the volunteer's work. It is essential that the supervising lawyer be kept informed of the volunteer's activities on a particular case or project—also important in case the supervising lawyer needs to take over in the event the volunteer is unavailable. The supervising lawyer should also take steps to ensure that the volunteers are recognized by the rest of the staff as an integral part of the program. This creates a collegial environment that serves the interests of the staff, the volunteers and, first and foremost, the clients.

Recruiting Senior Lawyer Volunteers

The ABA Senior Lawyers Division is a strong supporter of pro bono by its members, and has published accounts of individual experiences in *Experience* and *Senior Lawyer,* and in the 1997 book *Senior Lawyers Organizing and Volunteering.* The Division also has established the Senior Attorneys Volunteering for the Elderly (S.A.V.E.) Program. This program, in cooperation with Legal Counsel for the Elderly of AARP and the ABA's Commission on Legal Problems of the Elderly and Center for Pro Bono, matches prospective volunteers with programs in their communities. The S.A.V.E. program provides a convenient way for interested senior lawyers to find out about volunteer possibilities and has made a number of successful "matches."

In addition, legal services programs and other providers of legal assistance have come to recognize the valuable contribution that senior lawyers can make to the delivery of needed legal services. Their recruitment has taken several different forms. Some have placed notices in bar bulletins, and sent letters to the senior lawyer sections of their state and local bar associations. One of the most successful means of attracting volunteers is by peer recruitment (a great job for a committed volunteer).

In starting up its demonstration project, Legal Services of Middle Tennessee combined a mailing to senior lawyers with peer recruitment and other creative strategies. Three respected senior lawyers, including the former dean of the local law school, a past president of the bar association, who is a senior partner in a major law firm, and a retired bank counsel, reviewed membership lists from state and local bars and the American Bar Association, including senior lawyer sections. They worked with program staff to compile a list of about one hundred lawyers who they believed would be interested and available. Letters were mailed to each person on the list and followed by telephone calls. A recruitment lunch was arranged for a core group of twenty-five individuals. During the months leading to the startup of that project, the program director discussed the project at bar meetings and other social functions, even at the bar association Christmas party. Ultimately, twelve retired or semiretired lawyers volunteered; several of them are still actively involved in the program.

In Washington D.C., the Legal Counsel for the Elderly (LCE), which is affiliated with AARP, used AARP mailing lists in its initial recruitment drive, but once the program was up and running, its own reputation and the enthusiasm of its volunteers generated additional offers of assistance. LCE now includes about ten senior lawyers among its volunteers. The Legal Aid Society of the District of Columbia has made creative use of the media: one longtime senior lawyer volunteer was featured in newspapers and on television in a campaign entitled "Help Harry." And in St. Louis, Legal Services of Eastern Missouri and the bar jointly recruit volunteer lawyers.

The need is critical and the time is ripe. Even before the recent federal funding cuts and program restrictions, it was estimated that 80 percent of our nation's poor have no access to legal services; they do not have the benefit of the legal help that can open doors to other essential services and opportunities, such as government benefits, transportation, housing, health care, employment, and social services. Not only have those cuts and restrictions further limited the availability of legal services, but in recent years there has been an increasing need for assistance in advance planning for incapacity, for health-care decisions (including managed-care issues), and for other issues of personal autonomy.

The challenge is there. Bar associations and state access to justice coalitions are working to meet the growing need, and volunteers are an integral part of the plans. Don't wait to be called. Call yourself, or contact the S.A.V.E. program for referral to a program in your area. You will be glad you did. Nothing can be more satisfying to a lawyer than obtaining justice for those who cannot help themselves. Senior lawyer volunteers can help close the gap between the poor who have access to legal services and the poor who do not.

For further information about how to get involved, contact S.A.V.E., the Senior Lawyers Division, or the Commission on Legal Problems of the Elderly of the ABA.

11
Senior Lawyers Organizing

MARY PAT TOUPS

When the thought of retirement first surfaces in the mind of a lawyer, the second thought is often the concern that retirement will result in the loss of the legal lifestyle that has offered intellectual stimulation and friendships developed over the years of practicing law. Fear not, for there is an answer to deal with this concern. Across the United States, senior lawyers are organizing at both the state and local levels. In 1992–1993, the ABA's Senior Lawyers Division's State and Local Bar Groups Committee surveyed the nation to discover that fourteen states and sixteen localities had organized senior lawyers groups.

The original survey showed that the following thirteen states and the District of Columbia had organized senior lawyers groups: Connecticut, Florida, Georgia, Illinois, Kentucky, Maryland, Missouri, New Jersey, New Mexico, New York, North Carolina, Ohio, and Virginia.

That survey showed that the following sixteen localities had organized senior lawyers groups at the city or county level: Akron, Ohio; Camden County, New Jersey; Chicago, Illinois; Cleveland, Ohio; Denver, Colorado; Houston, Texas; Indianapolis, Indiana; Lancaster, Pennsylvania; Louisville, Kentucky; New York, New York; New York County, New York; Philadelphia, Pennsylvania; St. Joseph County, Indiana; St. Louis, Missouri; Sun City, Arizona; and Tulsa, Oklahoma.

The Division always has a committee devoted to helping senior lawyers organize a senior lawyers group at the state and local level. Frequently, Division members are active in organizing a state or local group, since their membership has made them aware of the value of interacting with other lawyers of a similar age.

Since more groups are organizing from year to year, the committee decided to produce an Annu-al Directory of State and Local Bar Associations with Senior Lawyer Groups. The 1997 directory listed thirty-five state and local senior lawyers groups, noting that others are in the formation stages. Write the ABA Senior Lawyers Division, 750 North Lake Shore Drive, Chicago, IL 60611, to request a copy of the most recent directory.

If you are lucky enough to live in a state or locality that already has an organized group, contact them now, and join in the fun.

If not the time has come to ask yourself, "Why not?" Do not wait until your retirement is in effect. Telephone a few friends who might be considering retirement themselves, and start the ball rolling. Do not be discouraged if your bar is negative toward the idea of senior lawyers organizing. Many senior lawyers have found a way to overcome the negatives. Also, many bars are delighted at the thought of senior lawyers organizing, since they realize they tend to lose their older lawyers from membership. An organized senior lawyers group is an extremely effective membership-retention device.

Three examples of ways to begin organizing a senior lawyers group follow. For additional ideas, feel free to contact already organized groups. Senior lawyers are always willing to help another senior lawyer.

In 1984, the ABA's Standing Committee on the Retirement of Lawyers, chaired by Stephen N. Maskalaris of Morristown, New Jersey, sent a brief notice to ABA members 60 years of age or older referring to a "plan" to create a Senior Lawyers Division. The notice asked interested members to mail in the first years dues of $15.00. More than thirty-five hundred checks were received. Later, the ABA House of Delegates, after considerable debate, approved the establishment of the Senior Lawyers Division. For several years the Division was the fastest growing group in the ABA. The ABA immediately realized the Division

Mary Pat Toups is an Orange County, California, elder law lawyer and freelance author.

is an excellent membership-retention device, because the Division meets the needs of the other lawyers that were not being met as the ABA had been previously structured.

In 1991, Robert D. Inman of Denver, Colorado, began cutting back on his practice and wondering if he might begin to feel isolated and separated from his comrades. He approached the Denver Bar Association with the request that a senior section be organized for social purposes and also to provide the seniors with a vehicle that would allow them to give something back to the community. The Denver Bar Association agreed, appointed a committee with funding for mailings, and designated every member lawyer older than 65 as an automatic member of the senior section, The group held a few well-attended social events, such as "roasting" dinners and golf tournaments, and then implemented their own pro bono project. They were off and running, in numbers and in spirit. They continue to expand their activities from year to year.

In January 1996, Mary Pat Toups, having been appointed by four Orange County Bar Association presidents to chair a nonexistent Senior Lawyers Committee, persuaded the incoming president, Jennifer Keller, to appoint a group of twenty-four senior lawyers to serve on this committee to meet the needs of senior lawyers. The committee developed so many activities, and recruited so many additional members, that the following year President Franz Miller suggested the committee develop into a section, which would allow the group expanded opportunities to serve senior lawyers. Creating the section in July of 1997, the group ended the year with eighty-five members enjoying speaker luncheons, several projects and, most importantly, wonderful camaraderie. These lawyers remember the days when every lawyer in Orange County knew every other lawyer. With about 10,000 lawyers practicing in Orange County today, it seems no one knows anyone.

For big-city senior lawyer activities, consider those of the Senior Lawyer Committee of the Association of the Bar of the City of New York. It has established a mentor program in which some eighty lawyers meet on a one-to-one basis once or twice a month with minority high-school students to discuss any matter or problem on the students' minds. It has held a program on retire-

ment planning. It has participated in the ABA's Central and East European Law Initiative. It has sought to promote the concept that corporations appoint ombudsman at the senior level who are responsible to the board of directors as an early-warning device to prevent serious corporate misconduct.

For a dynamic example of a state bar senior lawyers group, consider Virginia. The Virginia State Bar organized a Senior Lawyers Section as a separate unit in February 1987. The section has sponsored various articles on the subject of elder law and the needs of senior lawyers in the *Virginia Lawyer,* with some issues especially dedicated to senior lawyers. They have sponsored workshops and symposiums on various subjects, such as "Legal, Environmental, and Other Issues in the Perspective of Aging"; "Guardianship on the Crossroads of New Social Development"; "Senior Citizen Handbook"; "Senior Lawyers Advising Senior Clients"; "Counseling the Dying Client and His Family"; "Pro Publico Bono—Filling the Gap"; "Representing and Planning for the Elderly"; "All You Want to Know About Lawyers' Retirement but Are Reluctant to Ask"; "Comprehensive Services for the Senior Citizens"; "Death and Dying—Whose Business Is It?" and others. They, in conjunction with the Young Lawyers Section, repeatedly revise the *Senior Citizens Handbook,* which has been proven to be a most popular publication.

One committee of the Virginia Senior Lawyers Section developed a manual for lawyers on laws affecting senior citizens. Another committee addressed the issue of the rising cost of health care and the increasing demand for health care. The section's interest in organ donation led it to publicize the fact that drivers can record an anatomical gift at death on their licenses. They also worked with the Virginia Transplant Council to disseminate information about organ transplants.

The section has been involved in estate planning matters, including analyzing and publicizing living wills, the financial power of attorney, and the medical power of attorney. The section has worked with the state bar's pro bono committee to encourage Virginia senior lawyers to contribute their services to the elderly poor. The board of governors of the section is comprised of twenty-four lawyers who also adopt various resolutions from time to time outlining the senior lawyers' perspective on matters relating to senior lawyers throughout Virginia.

If you are considering relocating from your current home state to a sunny, warmer climate, you might want to consider the status you would hold in that state's legal community. If the state is not an integrated mandatory bar state, you would have no problem. But if the state is an integrated mandatory bar state, you might find that you would be precluded from practicing law, even as a pro bono lawyer. No dues paid, no pro bono practice of law. This from a profession under constant criticism for our failure to serve the poor!

However, some of the integrated state bars have adopted emeritus attorney rules to encourage retired lawyers to participate in pro bono programs. Mandatory dues are waived or reduced under these rules. Many states, including Arizona, Florida, Idaho, and Texas, welcome retired out-of-state lawyers into their emeritus attorney programs. However, California limits the program to California lawyers who have been active state bar member for several years. Recently the California Emeritus Attorney Rules were relaxed a bit, but they continue to be onerous. Some retired lawyers, wanting desperately to continue to do pro bono work after relocating to California, work as a paralegal or legal assistant to another lawyer who signs the papers and appears in court. Other relocated senior lawyers find this demeaning and simply walk away. This deprives the indigents of California, a major retirement state, of the services of a number of highly qualified, previously successful, now retired lawyers. You might want to consider these factors as you weigh the advisability of relocating and to help you determine which state you would most enjoy. You might want to avoid California.

If you are interested in information on the emeritus attorney programs already developed, please request the free "Info Pack for Senior Lawyers" available from the ABA Center for Pro Bono, 541 North Fairbanks Court, Chicago, IL 60611-3314.

State and local senior lawyer, although quite capable of developing their own original missions, goals, bylaws, and committee structure, are welcome to use our Senior Lawyer Division Informational Packet, which is filled with a wealth of information. To request a free packet, write the ABA Senior Lawyers Division, 750 North Lake Shore Drive, Chicago, IL 60611.

Also available is the book *Senior Lawyers Organizing and Volunteering: A National Profile*, which includes a chapter on all fifty states, the District of Columbia, the Senior Lawyers Division of the American Bar Association, and the SAVE (Senior Attorney Volunteers for the Elderly) program. The state chapters were written by senior lawyers recommended by the state bar executive director; the writing reflects the personality of each state, as well as the personality of each author.

The book presents valuable information about why and how senior lawyers' organizations and efforts are developed and about why and how senior lawyers volunteer. It includes information on topics such as: organizing at the state and local level, developing pro bono projects, emeritus attorney rules, reduction or waiver of bar fees and dues, and much more. It motivates the readers to develop strategies for tapping into the interests, resources, talents, skills, and commitment of this group.

To order this book send $15.00, shipping and handling included, to the ABA Pro Bono Center, 541 North Fairbanks Court, Chicago, IL 60611, attention Bridget Howard.

A successful retirement is a well-planned retirement. Keep in mind that the bar needs you as much as you need the bar, even though you are retirement age—whatever that is. Plan now to keep in touch with those people with whom you have most in common, lawyers. Join or organize a senior lawyers group today!

12
Professional Liability Insurance and Retirement

BONNIE L. YAKLEY

Upon retirement, a lawyer may find that canceling professional liability insurance is not a simple matter. This difficulty is based on most policies being "claims-made" rather than "occurrence" policies.

An occurrence policy provides coverage for an injury or damage that takes place during the policy period, regardless of when the claim is reported. This is how homeowner and auto policies are written. For example, if an accident occurs during the year 1988, but a claim is not brought forward until 1989, the policy in effect in 1988 will apply to the loss. Thus, an occurrence policy will respond to a loss that occurred during its policy term no matter when the claim is brought.

Claims-made coverage was introduced as a way to keep professional liability insurance available. Under a claims-made policy, coverage is provided only for claims made and reported to the insurance company while the policy remains in force. The claim itself will trigger the coverage under the policy that is in force when the claim is made, not when the loss actually occurred. In other words, if a lawyer missed a statute of limitations in 1988 and it was not discovered until 1989 and the claim is not brought until 1989, the policy in effect in 1989 will provide coverage. Herein lies the problem with the claims-made policy.

If the policy must be in force at the time the claim is made, what does the lawyer do to cover exposure for past claims after he or she retires?

Bonnie L. Yakley, CPCU, AAI, RPLU, is program manager for the lawyers professional liability department at Scottsdale Insurance Company in Scottsdale, Arizona.

The answer is a section in the claims-made policy called an "extended reporting period." The policy states that an extended reporting period may be purchased under certain conditions to provide coverage for possible future claims that result from events that occurred before the lawyer retired. Commonly referred to as "tail" coverage, this is a very important section of the policy and should be reviewed carefully by the lawyer in advance of his or her retirement.

There are many different forms of extended reporting period coverage. Some companies will offer the coverage only if the policy is canceling. An individual lawyer who is retiring from a firm that will be continuing its policy may not be offered the opportunity to purchase the extended reporting period at the time of his or her retirement. This is because some policies state that the extended reporting coverage will be available if the policy is terminating for any reason other than failure to pay the premium or the deductible, or if the policy is not being renewed by the insurance company. Therefore, if the policy is not terminating, the coverage cannot be offered. What does the lawyer do in this situation?

Many policies will provide coverage for a lawyer who is retiring and the policy is not terminating under the definition of *insured* in the policy. For example, the definition of *insured* may include any lawyer who has left the firm and is no longer in the active practice of law as long as his or her license to practice law has not been revoked or suspended, including the estate of a deceased lawyer. Therefore, a lawyer may not need to purchase an extended reporting period if the following conditions apply:

1. The policy remains in force after the lawyer has retired, as the other members of the firm wish to continue coverage.
2. There is prior-acts coverage being offered under the present policy.
3. The definition of *insured* includes a retired lawyer.

This situation should be reviewed very carefully by the lawyer with advice from his or her insurance representative to make sure that it is not necessary to purchase the extended reporting option.

In the case where the lawyer does not have to purchase the extended reporting option, or where it is not available because the policy is not being canceled, it may be necessary for the lawyer to keep track of the policy in case the option is offered at a later date. For example, suppose a lawyer retires and is not required to purchase the extended reporting option because the other lawyers in the firm continue the policy. What happens to the coverage for the retired lawyer when the firm dissolves five years later and the policy is canceled? The answer is that there may be no coverage after the policy is canceled unless the lawyer purchases the extended reporting option. For this reason, it is important that the retiring lawyer request that the firm notify him or her when and if the policy is being canceled. The lawyer should then review the situation with his or her insurance representative to determine if the extended reporting period should be purchased.

What about the situation where the lawyer is retiring, the policy is being canceled, and the extended reporting period coverage is made available by the company? At this time, the lawyer must determine what coverage options are available and what the cost will be.

Most companies offer at least a one-year reporting period. This means that for an additional premium, the lawyer may, in effect, extend present coverage for one year to cover claims brought for the past acts of the lawyer. The cost may be anywhere from 100 percent to 150 percent of the last annual premium. Each company's rates are different; the lawyer should investigate the cost well in advance of retirement.

With various statutes of limitations existing in each state, the one-year reporting period may seem very inadequate. A number of insurance companies realize this problem and have responded by offering additional coverage in the form of a one-, two-, or three-year reporting period. Some companies also offer the option to renew the one-, two-, or three-year reporting period at current rates. Other companies offer an unlimited reporting option that will provide coverage indefinitely into the future. The cost of these various options vary by company and the length of the option being purchased; it may be anywhere from 100 percent to 300 percent of the last annual premium. The unlimited reporting period is obviously the best option, if it is available and affordable by the lawyer.

A lawyer who is an individual practitioner most likely will need to purchase an extended reporting period for after-retirement coverage for wrongs occurring during the time he or she practiced law. A lawyer who is with a multi-lawyer firm may or may not need the extended reporting period at the time of retirement. In fact, the extended reporting period may not be offered or available at the time of retirement, if the firm is continuing its coverage.

Another option has become available in the last few years. More and more companies are now offering an individual tail for lawyers retiring from a multi-lawyer firm. If this coverage is available it should be stated in the policy. The extended reporting option is almost always only offered and available for up to thirty or sixty days from the cancellation of the policy. If the lawyer does not exercise the option available within those thirty or sixty days, he or she may lose that option forever and could be severely damaged financially should a claim come forward after his or her retirement.

But what about the lawyer who chooses to semiretire and become in effect of counsel to the firm? A lawyer who begins to wind down his or her practice, taking on a limited number of cases, may find that, with the decrease in his or her income, the cost of a full-time policy is difficult to afford. In this situation, the lawyer may wish to inquire into a part-time policy, which many companies provide at reduced annual rates. To qualify for such a policy, the lawyer may have to spend less than 50 percent of his or her time in the practice of law or may have to be receiving less than a certain dollar amount in income from the practice of law. Each company has its own criteria and should be investigated by the lawyer and his or her insurance representative. The coverage offered under the new policy should be reviewed to make sure it is as broad as that of the full-time policy, including the options and cost available under the extended reporting period coverage.

What about a lawyer who is with a multilawyer firm and is winding down his or her practice? In this situation, a lawyer may have coverage under the firm's policy without being named on the policy or paying a premium for the coverage. Many insurance policies will include under the definition of *insured* any attorney who is retained as lawyer of counsel. Coverage will apply only to services rendered on behalf of the "named insured" or a predecessor firm. The key to coverage is in the company's definition of *of counsel*. Many companies define *of counsels* to mean those lawyers who are not members of the firm but are utilized on a case-by-case basis for their expertise in a particular area of law. The definition also extends to include retired members of the firm who will provide services for their former firm because of their experience in an area of law or with a former client. If the lawyer fits this definition, many companies will agree to provide coverage at no charge, under the definition of *of counsel*. The lawyer's name is normally not listed on the insurance policy in this case. Because each case is different and all circumstances must be reviewed, a lawyer in this situation should consult with an informed representative of his or her insurance company before withdrawing from the firm's policy and assuming that the of counsel coverage will apply.

A lawyer with a multilawyer firm who retires and finds that he or she is automatically covered under the firm's present policy may need to make a determination about extended reporting period coverage when the firm dissolves at a later date. If the firm is in actuality merging with another firm, coverage for lawyers who have retired from the original firm may still apply under the new policy of the merged firms; the extended reporting period coverage need not be purchased. The key is in the insurance company's definition of *predecessor firm*.

One insurance company defines *predecessor firm* as a partnership or professional corporation that has undergone dissolution and in which at least 50 percent of the lawyers are still affiliated with the named insured. Another company defines *predecessor firm* as any law firm or professional legal corporation engaged in the practice of law to whose financial assets and liabilities the firm listed as named insured in the declarations is the majority successor in interest.

Thus, depending on the definition of *predecessor firm*, a lawyer who retires from one firm may still have coverage under a new firm merger. This occurs if the new policy considers the old firm a predecessor firm and provides coverage for retired lawyers of the predecessor firm. This situation can be very technical, and the lawyer should consult with an insurance representative of the company before assuming that the new firm still provides coverage for him or her and, therefore, he or she does not need to purchase the offered extended reporting period coverage.

A new feature provided by some insurance companies today is "individual retirement extended reporting coverage." This feature allows the retiring lawyer to purchase an individual extended reporting endorsement. This endorsement provides coverage for only that lawyer. The individual purchasing the coverage may then be excluded from coverage under the firm's policy, to avoid stacking of limits. The insurance company may have stipulations for purchasing the "individual retirement extended reporting coverage," such as requiring that the lawyer be insured with the company for at least five consecutive years previous to the purchase of the endorsement and that the lawyer be at least 50 or 55 years of age. However, more and more companies are allowing the purchase of an individual tail with few restrictions. Once again, this is an option that should be reviewed by the lawyer with his or her insurance representative. It does allow the lawyer the option of purchasing his or her own tail and not having to worry about monitoring his or her old firm for future purchase of the extended reporting period option when the firm dissolves or cancels its policy.

Because there are many circumstances that come into play and can affect coverage or lack of coverage, each lawyer needs to seek the advice and direction of his or her insurance company representative before retiring. No one can afford to go into the situation blindly.

13
No Retreat
in Retirement

KIRSTEN L. CHRISTOPHE

Every year, thousands of lawyers retire from their law firms.

Many retire in the traditional sense. For others, however, "retirement" simply means leaving a current practice setting for other work.

Whatever the nature of their retirements, lawyers changing their status should consider the professional liability ramifications of the change. In particular, lawyers should take steps to assure they will continue to be covered for claims that may arise from the practice they are leaving.

A crucial step in accomplishing this is for the departing lawyer to review the partnership agreement, professional liability insurance policy, and recent claims at the firm.

Partnership agreements and insurance provisions can vary greatly from firm to firm. Often, for instance, the partnership agreement is silent about the firm's ongoing indemnity or insurance obligations to former members.

While reviewing a law firm's professional liability insurance policy, a departing lawyer should note that professional liability insurance typically is written on a "claims made" basis.

A claims-made policy covers any claims filed during the policy period, even if the events giving rise to claims occurred before a policy went into effect. This coverage encourages firms to keep liability insurance in force in the future to pay for claims related to today's work.

At the same time, however, gaps may develop even in claims-made coverage, which could pro-

foundly affect the departing lawyer. An insurer, in some instances, may restrict or exclude coverage of a law firm's activities in a given practice area.

By operation of the claims-made coverage trigger of the policy, any exclusion added in a later year would be applied to all the work ever performed in the area, therefore eliminating coverage against claims filed in the future.

Departing lawyers also should note the coverage limits under the firm's insurance policy. Because those limits cover all claims made and reported within that policy period, there may be few or no insurance funds remaining to cover claims against retiring lawyers if the firm already has submitted many claims—or even one serious one—during that period.

Careful attention also should be paid to how the insurance policy defines "insured."

In an of counsel relationship, for instance, the lawyer may be an employee or an independent contractor. Under some policies, coverage of employees or contractors is limited or unavailable.

Retiring lawyers should carefully review policy conditions that outline key responsibilities of the firm regarding policy renewal and claims. To assure that coverage is available for a claim against a retiring lawyer, the lawyer should clarify his or her individual responsibilities to report claims.

Risky Assumptions About Firm Survival

It has become risky for a departing lawyer to assume that the firm will continue to exist and buy appropriate insurance on an ongoing basis.

In smaller firms and among solo practitioners, dissolution is a common byproduct of the retirement of a key partner. In recent years, however,

Kirsten L. Christophe is vice president and director of risk management services for the Attorneys' Advantage program at Aon in New York City. She has served on the council of the ABA Section of Tort and Insurance Practice and on the standing committees on Lawyer Competence and Lawyers' Professional Liability.

dissolutions have become common among large firms, as well.

In any dissolution, it is vital that the firm and former partners maintain insurance coverage. All too frequently, however, money to pay insurance premiums or costs of an "extended reporting period" is scarce during the dissolution, and it often is unclear who in the firm has authority to make spending decisions.

While a retiring lawyer may wish to protect his or her own interest by purchasing an individual extended reporting period, this option is largely unavailable under law firm policies.

Since the time period for acting on various insurance coverage options often is limited, it is important that lawyers leaving firms meet promptly with their insurance representatives to evaluate coverage status and options.

In ideal circumstances, a "retiring" lawyer and the firm will consider indemnification and insurance issues well in advance of the status change. Doing so in consultation with appropriate insurance professionals to address unresolved issues and specific insurance needs before they arise will help the transition unfold as smoothly—and risk-free—as possible.

14
Retirement of Partners in the Modern Age: Taxation Problems in Second Careers

GEORGE H. CAIN

When most senior lawyers entered law practice, it was genuinely a profession. Law firms were run not by a committee or committees, but by the partners—sometimes by one or two partners who were martinets. But, more often than not there was a sense of family in the firm. Once aboard, a lawyer stayed unless guilty of some breach of ethics or discipline, or a display of incompetency.

Nor was it proper to sever one's partner from the partnership just because the fellow might have aged a bit and lost some of the spring in his step or, perhaps, seen some of his clients go astray.

Greater economic pressures on families have driven younger lawyers to seek higher compensation by calling for elimination of highly compensated partners.

Clients have themselves to blame, too, for this loss of professionalism. Law firms are treated somewhat the same as "discount houses." Clients shop for attorneys much as they look for a new television set; price is the main determinant, with service coming in second. The law firm's reputation, character, and personnel selection have diminished importance in the eyes of clients who want only to get a desired result at the cheapest price.

As a result there have been dramatic changes in the legal profession. In essence, two groups of firms have tended to survive: the largest, which serve corporate clients able to afford significant legal bills, and the smallest, which provide a boutique service in a carefully carved niche of the law. Medium-sized firms discovered they were unable to deliver an acceptable level of service to large clients and were too expensive for smaller ones. Many found it necessary to merge with other medium-sized firms to achieve the size and breadth of coverage desired by large corporate clients.

At the same time, many of the largest firms, subjected to constant pressure to cut costs to win the bidding wars for business, were downsizing. This is a euphemism for firing lawyers, along with support staff. To date, partners have not been immune in the restructuring process and there is no reason for them to expect immunity in the future.

Apart from downsizing in relatively few firms, there is no pattern of law firm behavior with respect to retirement. Some partners simply never retire as partners; we all hear tales of lawyers who continue in the management and operation of their firms well into their eighties. Other firms require partners to retire according to a rigid set of rules. Still others have no policy and each partner decides for himself or herself when it is time to depart as a partner.

Should a Lawyer Be Forced to Retire?

There are many arguments in favor of forced retirement of lawyers, and a mandatory retirement age has many negatives.

Some humans deteriorate physically and mentally with age. While many people retain their

George H. Cain is a former member of the Council of the Senior Lawyers Division and present chair of its Book Committee. He has written two books published by the American Bar Association since retiring from Day, Berry & Howard in 1990: *Turning Points: New Paths and Second Careers for Lawyers* and *Law Partnership: Its Rights and Responsibilities*.

mental acumen into advanced years, others lose their sharpness or their ability for cognitive work; mental disability is common in older society. The loss of a lawyer's mental ability is disastrous for a client. It is vital for the profession that clients receive advice only from competent advisors. In a firm where collegiality is important, few are willing to tell a colleague that he or she is no longer competent. If everyone must retire at a particular age, the unpleasant decision need never be reached.

Older lawyers continue to be successful "rainmakers." On the other hand, circumstances may result in the loss of an older lawyer's client base and the firm may no longer afford to carry the senior lawyer; either he must retire voluntarily or be forced out of the firm. If there is a mandatory retirement age, this difficult decision can be avoided.

Adoption of a mandatory retirement age has its negatives.

First, there is the loss of wisdom. Once an experienced lawyer retires, the firm loses the expertise of that individual. If several lawyers in a particular practice area happen to reach a mandatory retirement age simultaneously, it can turn out to be a crippling blow.

Another negative is loss of continuity with long-term and valued clients. Adopt a mandatory retirement policy and the senior lawyer is gone—and so is the legal business for the firm attributable to him.

Have You Retired?

It is often important to know whether or not you have retired from your firm, because significant consequences flow from your status as a partner.

For example, if you are no longer a partner, you may find it difficult to enforce payment of your retirement benefits. In *Bane v. Ferguson,*[1] Mr. Bane had been a partner with Isham, Lincoln & Beale of Chicago, which had awarded him a pension. The Isham firm then had a disastrous merger and Bane's pension was terminated. He sued his former partners. The court said that because Bane had been a partner, he could not claim under ERISA nor was he protected under the Illinois Uniform Partnership Act because he was no longer a partner; and because he was no longer a

partner, his former partners owed no fiduciary duty to him and had no tort liability for the dissolution of the firm that ended his benefits. Mr. Bane was "up the creek without a paddle."

In general, courts will not permit partners to assert claims for age discrimination under ADEA nor under most state workmen's compensation statutes because the statutory language limits the beneficiaries to persons with employee status.

Protecting Your Tax Position in Your Second Career

When contemplating a "second career," one should keep in mind the fact that the Internal Revenue Service does not look kindly upon your efforts to have a "trial run" to see whether you are likely to be successful, especially if that means writing off expenses in the trial effort against income from your "regular job."

There is Nicholas A. Sloan. Mr. Sloan, a veteran of the Korean conflict, held a doctorate in electrical engineering. He taught at George Washington University, entered its law school, and received a law degree in 1977. He then went to work with the Department of Justice, not as a lawyer, but as a computer systems analyst. He planned to take early retirement from the government in 1981 and set up his own law practice. This would be his "second career."

In the late 1970s, while working in the DOJ, he accepted a variety of cases to gain some experience. He assisted clients in matrimonial matters, prepared wills, and handled Medicaid and workmen's compensation claims. He charged his clients very little or nothing at all.

In a more committed effort to establish himself, he purchased a house in Chestertown on the Eastern Shore of Maryland. His wife looked after his mail and answered the telephone. Mr. Sloan, who maintained his primary residence in a Washington suburb, visited Chestertown on the weekends.

The IRS determined a deficiency in the 1981 tax return of Mr. and Mrs. Sloan of more than $11,000 plus a penalty. They filed a petition for relief and the matter reached the United States Tax Court.[2]

The court observed that Mr. Sloan based his fees on estimates of the time that he worked on a

---

1. 890 F.2d 11 (7th Cir, 1989).

2. *Sloan v. Commissioner,* T.C. Memo 1988-294, 1968 Tax Ct. Memo LEXIS 324 (1988).

case. He carried no malpractice insurance in 1981. He spent $480 in 1981 on bar dues and publications but did not subscribe to publications that related particularly to the kinds of cases he was handling, and he attended no bar association functions related to those cases. The Sloans had purchased a houseboat in 1980 and, in 1981, Mr. Sloan used it for his office; he met a half dozen people on the houseboat in connection with his practice. He also used the boat for recreational purposes.

In their tax return for 1981, the Sloans deducted expenses in connection with the houseboat and for the cost of publication subscriptions and legal education courses. The Sloans reported gross receipts of $640 from Mr. Sloan's practice. However, they reported losses in 1979 through 1983.

The commissioner determined a deficiency for 1981 on the ground that the losses claimed by the Sloans were not incurred in furtherance of any trade or business. The tax court agreed.

First, it said that Mr. Sloan

> . . . did not conduct his law practice in a business-like manner. Despite working long hours on cases, he rarely charged his clients for his services. Mr. Sloan failed to keep detailed records of the time that he spent performing legal services. On those few occasions that he did bill clients, he based his fees upon estimate [sic] of the time he worked on each case. Moreover, he charged extremely low fees for his efforts. He testified that on two instances, he charged clients a fixed amount, which worked out to a fee of less than $2 per hour.[3]

The first lesson in protecting your tax position: keep accurate records and don't give away your services. Says the IRS: "Sock it to those clients!"

Mr. Sloan had conceded that his job at the Department of Justice provided his primary source of income. He had indicated that he wanted to gain legal experience from his activities in 1981 that would be useful when he practiced in earnest after retirement. Said the tax court:

> Such an intention shows that he was not so much interested in current gain from his practice as he was in attempting to build a foundation for a practice which he hoped to establish in the future (citation omitted). In our judgment, it also indicates that Mr. Sloan did not engage in the practice of law with the primary purpose of earning a profit (citation omitted).[4]

The second lesson is that you don't get a deduction for amounts spent in anticipation of a "second career." Unless you are already in it, your deductions are at risk.

With respect to Mr. Sloan's attempt to establish a law practice in Chestertown, the court noted that Mr. Sloan was only there on weekends when the courts were not in session and that he and his wife did not socialize with members of the community,

> . . . the very individuals who might have hired Mr. Sloan to represent them. In our view, such actions show that he failed to make a serious effort to establish a practice in Chestertown during 1981. In addition, such conduct also indicates that Mr. Sloan was not involved in his law practice with "continuity and regularity." (citation omitted)[5]

Another lesson from the Internal Revenue Service: If you want to demonstrate a good-faith effort to earn a profit (and earn those deductions), work at it "full-time" and show some endeavor in the marketing area. Don't ignore your most obvious potential clients.

Summing up, the tax court opined:

> Because we hold that Mr. Sloan did not conduct his legal activities with the primary purpose of earning a profit and was not involved in such activities with continuity and regularity, we conclude that Mr. Sloan's activities in connection with his law practice did not rise to the level of a trade or business. For such reason, the petitioners are not entitled to the deductions claimed by them with respect to such practice.[6]

The Internal Revenue Service also seems to keep an eye out for lawyers looking for a second career outside the law.

Lew Warden, a lawyer, had been a solo practitioner in California for more than twenty years. After extensive litigation involving a sale of real property owned by Mr. and Mrs. Warden was concluded, they received more than $350,000. They treated half of the property as business use and half as residential use on their 1989 return. They then rolled over $85,000 of the business portion of the sale proceeds into a yacht, which they had previously purchased in 1986.

The yacht, christened *Rocking Chair*, turned out to be a "disaster" for the Wardens. When they bought it, Mr. Warden was age 66 and looking

3. *Id.* at 12.
4. *Id.* at 14.

5. *Id.* at 14.
6. *Id.* at 14.

forward to retiring to a warmer climate. He was dissatisfied with his law practice and had decided that he and his wife could earn a living from chartering the boat.

Mr. Warden was an experienced sailor, had worked as a seaman in his youth, and had been an Air Force navigator and pilot. While practicing law, he and his wife had enjoyed cruising and yacht-racing as a diversion in the San Francisco Bay area and offshore.

Rocking Chair was chartered on only a few occasions despite advertisements in several publications. In the years 1987 through 1992, the Wardens claimed yearly losses in a range of $45,000 to more than $81,000 from their chartering activities. In most of these same years, Mr. Warden reported net earnings from law practice, although in 1992 the Wardens showed a zero net income. The Internal Revenue Service disallowed the 1989 loss from the yacht claimed by the Wardens for 1989. The case reached the tax court.

In its opinion,[7] the court said:

> We must first decide whether petitioners' ownership and operation of Rocking Chair were activities that were "not engaged in for profit" within the meaning of section 183(c). Section 183(a) provides generally that if an activity is not engaged in for profit, no deduction attributable to such activity shall be allowed, . . .

The court then reviewed each of the various factors leading to that determination.

First was the manner in which a taxpayer carried on the activity. The court noted that the Wardens had opened a separate bank account for *Rocking Chair,* although expenses were not always paid from that account. They had obtained a business tax declaration, obtained a seller's permit, filed sales and use tax returns, obtained an employer ID number, obtained additional insurance, maintained a telephone on the yacht, advertised the yacht's availability, and attempted to sell it. However, they had no written business plan, nor did they attempt to verify chartering income forecasts, or the income's sufficiency to cover expenses. The Wardens made no showing that they had used data from their records to try to improve the profitability of the operation.

Second was the expertise of the taxpayer or his advisers. There was no evidence to show the spe-

cific nature of the information Mr. Warden obtained from talking with other boatmen or from studying yachting magazines.

Third was the effort spent by the taxpayer in carrying on the activity. The court said that the time spent by the Wardens in cleaning and maintaining *Rocking Chair* was consistent with use of the yacht for recreation.

Fourth was the taxpayer's expectation that the assets used in the activity would appreciate. In this case, the Wardens offered no evidence as to what they anticipated.

Fifth was the taxpayer's success with other similar activities. The Wardens had no "track record" in this respect.

Sixth was the historical record of income and losses and any occasional profits. The court observed:

> A record of substantial losses over many years and the unlikelihood of achieving a profitable operation are important factors bearing on the taxpayer's intention (citation omitted). The presence of such losses in the formative years of a business is not inconsistent with an intent to achieve a later profitable level of operation; however, the goal must be to realize a profit on the entire operation, which presupposes sufficient future net earnings from the activity to recoup the losses (citation omitted). In the present case, petitioners reported losses over 6 years of operation totaling $370,377.[8]

Next, was the financial status of the taxpayer. In 1986, when the Wardens purchased *Rocking Chair,* they had a net worth of $1,027,000. Mr. Warden's law practice and some securities supplied income while the Wardens wrestled with the *Rocking Chair* problems. The court noted that the Wardens "did obtain a tax benefit from the losses generated by the chartering activities."[9]

Finally was the presence of elements of personal pleasure or recreation. The items that the tax court noted as this factor was being considered were stated in the opinion:

> Mr. Warden was no longer happy in his practice of law, and he was at an age where he was ready to retire. Petitioners wanted to live in a more pleasant, recreational setting. They clearly enjoyed sailing and had engaged in sailing activities for recreation for at least 20 years prior to purchasing Rocking Chair. The yacht was custom built and was equipped with all the amenities. Beginning in 1988, Mr. Warden lived on the yacht and used it as his residence. Peti-

7. *Warden v. Commissioner,* T.C. Memo 1995-176, 1995 Tax Ct. Memo LEXIS 170 (1995).

8. *Id.* at 22.
9. *Id.* at 23.

tioners admittedly used Rocking Chair for activities unrelated to chartering, but did not document these trips in their operating log.[10]

The tax court said that, to prevail, the Wardens must show that their activities with *Rocking Chair* were primarily to make a profit. It said that it was not enough that the Wardens had profit as one objective of their activity.

The court said that where the taxpayer has both a personal and profit objective in an activity, the court must decide which activity is "primary." Based on the entire record, the court was not "convinced that the petitioners' primary objective was to make a profit."[11] Consequently, the deduction of the loss associated with the yacht would have to be limited (in accordance with section 183 of the Internal Revenue Code) to an amount equal to the gross income of the activity.

Perhaps you are a lawyer anticipating retirement and anxious to conduct, after retirement, some professional or business activity which has long been your dream. If your objective is to engage in a profitable enterprise, but foresee a period of buildup before it turns the corner, stop and review your income tax picture. Should you be counting on losses from your new activity to cushion the income tax burden on your other earnings, you might first consult the tax experts in your law firm on the question: What should you do, in the light of cases like *Sloan* and *Warden,* to protect your position?

A License for Postretirement Activities?

Have you retired when your postretirement activities are such that one does not need to be a licensed lawyer to perform them? Maybe so, but maybe not—if they are activities which lawyers sometimes undertake. This was the situation confronting Robert E. Mahoney, an Iowa lawyer.[12]

Mr. Mahoney was a law firm partner. He had practiced for thirty-three years and was 58 years old. When he failed to turn over some estate assets to a successor, he was disciplined by the state bar and his license was suspended. Before his license was to be reinstated, he withdrew from his law firm. In his probation report, he advised the disciplinary committee, formally, that

10. *Id.* at 23-24.
11. *Id.* at 26.
12. *Committee on Professional Ethics & Conduct of the Iowa State Bar Ass'n v. Mahoney,* 402 N.W. 2d 434 (Ia. 1987).

he had retired from the general practice of law and that the firm name had been changed.

Mr. Mahoney's partners agreed to give him a pension, under the terms of which he was not to compete with the firm in the practice of law but could perform tax work and labor negotiation work.

Mr. Mahoney formed a corporation, called ConsulCorp. From its office, he drafted tax returns and acted as a labor negotiator. He also obtained a real estate license. In addition, he rendered business and investment advice, and prepared real estate documents, some contracts, and one will. He appeared in court on a pro bono basis. He obtained the necessary continuing legal education and maintained the client security fund necessary to keep his law license current.

The Committee on Professional Ethics and Conduct brought a proceeding against Mr. Mahoney, on the ground that his formal announcement of retirement from the practice of law was misleading. In upholding the committee's recommendation for further disciplinary action against Mr. Mahoney, the court rejected Mr. Mahoney's contention that he was no longer in the general practice of law:

> . . . [Mr. Mahoney] did not terminate his status as a practicing lawyer when he changed offices. Doing tax preparation and labor negotiation is not necessarily the practice of law and properly may be done by nonlawyers. When these tasks are done by a licensed lawyer, however, they constitute the practice of law.[13]

The court held that Mr. Mahoney's statement to the committee was misleading and suspended him for six months.

> It is important to know whether or not you are "retired." As we observed in the *Bane* case, your partners have no fiduciary duty to you once you retire. If they fail to pay you a pension as agreed, it may be a breach of contract, but it is not a breach of fiduciary duty. Furthermore, as Mr. Bane found out, the partners had no obligation to forego a dissolution of the firm to pay him his pension.

For the partner who wants to retire and receive a benefit from his former law firm, it is important to know that he or she has actually retired. To impose a legitimate restriction on the retired partner's ability to continue law practice, it is vital to assure that the partner is, in fact, retired; a payment characterized as a payment for a law

13. *Id.* at 436.

practice in all but a few states will be illegal. And forfeiture-for-competition clauses are legal in most states only when coupled with payment of a retirement benefit.

15

Retirement Provisions in the Partnership Agreement: Forfeiture-for-Competition

GEORGE H. CAIN

Forfeiture-for-Competition Clauses in Retirement Arrangements

One of the more controversial elements in arrangements between partners and law firms is the freedom, or lack thereof, accorded lawyers who leave their firms. Whether the lawyer withdraws or retires, many firms seek to eliminate or sharply curtail his or her ability to continue to practice. The reason may be fear of competition from the lawyer, the cost of maintaining his or her malpractice insurance, or simply ignorance of the implications of ABA Model Rule of Professional Conduct 5.6.[1]

In recent years, considerable litigation has ensued. It has had the effect of establishing some limits as to when practice restrictions are permissible and when they will be prohibited. The bottom line is that the clause must strike a fair balance between protection of the right of the individual to practice law for livelihood and the right of the firm to protect itself against predatory action by a former partner.

The California Cases

The courts in California have given careful attention to the issue. For example, in the *Haight* case, the partnership agreement was drafted to provide:

Each Partner agrees that, if he withdraws or voluntarily retires from the Partnership, he will not engage in any area of the practice of law regularly practiced by the law firm and in so doing represent or become associated with any firm that represents any client represented by this law firm within a twelve (12) month period prior to said person leaving the firm, within the Counties of Los Angeles, Ventura, Orange, Riverside or San Bernardino nor within any City in such Counties for a period of three (3) years from the date of withdrawal or retirement, so long as continuing members of this firm engage in practice in the same areas of law.

The agreement further provided that:

A Partner . . . may violate this [section]. However, by so doing, he forfeits any and all rights and interests, financial and otherwise, to which he would otherwise be thereafter entitled as a parting Partner under the terms of this agreement.[2]

Certain of the Haight, Brown partners left the firm and set up practice in violation of the noncompetition clause. The California Business and Professions Code contained a section authorizing any partner to agree not to carry on a similar business within a specified county or city where the partnership business was transacted so long as any other member of the partnership carried on a like business in the area, At the same time, under Rule 1-500 of the California State Bar, a

George H. Cain is a former member of the Council of the Senior Lawyers Division and present chair of its Book Committee. He has written two books published by the American Bar Association since retiring from Day, Berry & Howard in 1990: *Turning Points: New Paths and Second Careers for Lawyers* and *Law Partnership: Its Rights and Responsibilities.*

1. Rule 5.6 provides that "a lawyer shall not participate in offering or making . . . (a) a partnership or employment agreement that restricts the right of a lawyer to practice after termination of the relationship, except an agreement concerning benefits upon retirement; or (b) an agreement in which a restriction on the lawyer's right to practice is part of the settlement of a controversy between private parties."

2. Haight, Brown & Bonesteel v. Superior Court of Los Angeles Cty., 234 Cal. App. 3d 963 at 966, 1991 Cal. App. LEXIS 1123 at 2, 285 Cal. Rptr. 845 at 846 (Cal. Ct. App. 1991).

lawyer licensed in California may not be a party to an agreement if the agreement restricts the right of the lawyer to practice law; however, the restriction is not prohibited if it is a part of a partnership agreement and the restriction does not survive termination of the partnership. The court was faced with resolving the inconsistency between the code and the rule of the state bar.

The withdrawing partners argued that the forfeiture had the effect of dissuading departing partners from handling cases for clients in competition with the firm or from practicing law in competition with the firm. Thus, they said, it was an impermissible restriction on the practice of law in violation of the public policy behind Rule 1-500.

The *Haight* court said:

> We do not construe rule 1-500 in such a narrow fashion. In our opinion, the rule simply provides that an attorney may not enter into an agreement to refrain altogether from the practice of law. The rule does not, however, prohibit a withdrawing partner from agreeing to compensate his former partners in the event he chooses to represent clients previously represented by the firm from which he has withdrawn.[3]

The court also observed:

> We recognize the personal and confidential relationship which exists between lawyers and their clients. We do not, however, believe that such a relationship places lawyers in a class apart from other business and professional partnerships. We find no reason to treat attorneys any differently from professionals such as physicians or certified public accountants, for example, by holding that lawyers may not enter into noncompetition agreements in accordance with [the Business and Professions Code].[4]

The court enforced the provisions of the partnership agreement.

The California Supreme Court had occasion to consider the issue and to revisit the decision in *Haight* two years later in *Howard v. Babcock.*[5] There, the partnership agreement had language resembling that in *Haight*. The partners of Parker, Stansbury, McGee, Babcock & Combs in 1982 had entered into a partnership agreement containing a clause providing:

> Should more than one partner, associate or individual withdraw from the firm prior to age sixty-five

(65) and thereafter within a period of one year practice law . . . together or in combination with others, including former partners or associates of this firm, in a practice engaged in the handling of liability insurance defense work as aforesaid within the Los Angeles or Orange County Court system, said partner or partners shall be subject, at the sole discretion of the remaining non-withdrawing partners to forfeiture of all their rights to withdrawal benefits other than capital as provided for in Article V herein.

Subsequent to the execution of that partnership agreement, several new partners were elected, although they did not sign the partnership agreement. Three other partners then terminated their relationship with the firm and announced that they would begin practice in competition with the firm. The other partners of Parker, Stansbury replied that they would withhold a portion of the withdrawing partners withdrawal benefits because of the latter's violation of the noncompetition clause. There then ensued a battle over the withdrawing partners' share of the accounts receivable, work in progress, and unfinished business of the firm.

In litigation between the parties, the trial court decided that although the partnership was dissolved by operation of law when the withdrawing partners terminated their relationship with the firm, the partnership agreement, including the noncompetition clause, remained binding in all its terms. On appeal to the court of appeal, the latter declared the noncompetition clause void on the ground that Rule 1-500 of the Rules of Professional Conduct banned the noncompetition agreement. A further appeal to the California Supreme Court followed.

The supreme court noted that there was a conflict among the courts of appeal in California and that the *Haight* court had found that clause enforceable. As for the Business and Professions Code, it found "no demonstrated legislative intent to create a silent exception for lawyers" and said that it would apply the statute according to its terms. It concluded that the statute applies to partners in law firms.[6] The court then had to deal with the issue of whether the Code of Professional Responsibility, Rule 1-500, prohibited the clause. Said the court:

> We are not persuaded that this rule was intended to or should prohibit the type of agreement that is at issue here. An agreement that assesses a reasonable

3. *Id.* at 969, 1991 Cal. App. LEXIS 1123 at 9, 285 Cal. Rptr. at 848.

4. *Id.* at 971, 1991 Cal. App. LEXIS 1123 at 15, 285 Cal. Rptr. at 849.

5. 6 Cal.4th 409, 863 P.2d 150, 1993 Cal. LEXIS 6006, 25 Cal. Rptr. 2d 80 (Cal. 1993).

6. *Id.* at 417, 863 P.2d at 154, 1993 Cal. LEXIS 6006 at 16.

cost against a partner who chooses to compete with his or her former partners does not restrict the practice of law. Rather, it attaches an economic consequence to a departed partner's unrestricted choice to pursue a particular kind of practice.[7]

Significantly, the court said "we agree with the court of appeal in Haight [citation omitted] declaring an agreement between law partners that a reasonable cost will be assessed for competition is consistent with rule 1-500."[8]

The opinion states

> We are confident that the interest of the public in being served by diligent, loyal and competent counsel can be assured at the same time as the legitimate business interest of law firms is protected by an agreement placing a reasonable price on competition. *We hold that an agreement among partners imposing a reasonable cost on departing partners who compete with the law firm in a limited geographical area is not inconsistent with rule 1-500 and is not void on its face as against public policy* (emphasis in original).[9]

The supreme court sent the case back to the trial court to determine whether the clause at issue was reasonable. The trial court found that the clause was reasonable and the plaintiffs again appealed.

Finding that the trial court had failed to consider further evidence about the extent of the penalty exacted by the questionable clause, the appellate court again remanded the case to the trial court. It referred to the earlier decision by the California Supreme Court, saying

> Citing rule 1-500 of the Rules of Professional Conduct, the court concluded an agreement may only assess "a reasonable cost against a partner who chooses to compete with his or her former partners . . ." (Howard v. Babcock, supra, 6 Cal. 4th at p. 419.) The penalty is reasonable when it "operate(s) in the nature of a tax on taking the former firm's clients [in consideration of] the financial burden the partners'-competitive departure may impose on the former firm . . ." (Id. at 424) "To the extent the agreement merely assesses a toll on competition within a specified geographical area, comparable to a liquidated damage clause, it may be reasonable. . . . (Id. at p. 425.) Such a liquidated clause is valid if it represents compensation for the firm's losses "that may be caused by the withdrawing partner's competition with the firm . . . ." (Id.)[10]

California's liberal approach appears to be more the exception than the rule, and in many jurisdictions such clauses are prohibited and will not be enforced.

The New York Cases

In New York, the Court of Appeals in a 1989 decision struck down such a clause as being in violation of the Code of Professional Responsibility, DR 2-108(A), the same section as is incorporated into California's Rule 1-500.[11] In the *Cohen* case, Mr. Cohen had been a partner in Lord, Day & Lord for some 20 years. In 1985, he withdrew from the firm to join another New York City firm. The partnership agreement provided for payment to a withdrawing partner of a share of the firm's profits, including those stemming from services performed but not yet billed at time of departure. A withdrawing partner was paid, based on a formula, over a three-year period, thus avoiding the necessity of a detailed accounting. In addition, the partnership agreement contained this clause:

> Notwithstanding anything in this Article . . . to the contrary, if a Partner withdraws from the Partnership and without the prior written consent of the Executive Committee *continues to practice law in any state or other jurisdiction in which the Partnership maintains an office or any contiguous jurisdiction,* either as a lawyer in private practice or as a counsel employed by a business firm, he shall have no further interest in and *there shall be paid to him no proportion of the net profits of the Partnership collected thereafter, whether for services rendered before or after his withdrawal.* There shall be paid to him only his withdrawable credit balance on the books of the Partnership at the date of his withdrawal, together with the amount of his capital account, and the Partnership shall have no further obligation to him. (Emphasis in Original)[12]

When Lord, Day failed to pay Mr. Cohen his departure payments, Mr. Cohen sued.

Lord, Day & Lord relied upon the forfeiture-for-competition clause and complained that Mr. Cohen had taken some of the firm's clients with him.

In the trial court, it was ruled that the "no competition" clause was unenforceable as violative of Disciplinary Rule 2-108(A).[13] The appellate divi-

---

7. *Id.* at 419, 863 P.2d at 156, 1993 Cal. LEXIS 6006 at 19.
8. *Id.*
9. *Id.* at 424, 863 P.2d at 160, 1993 Cal. LEXIS 6006 at 33.
10. Howard v. Babcock, 40 Cal. App. 4th 569, 575, 1995 Cal.App. LEXIS 1136 (1995).

11. Cohen v. Lord, Day & Lord, 75 N.Y.2d 95, 550 N.E.2d 410, 551 N.Y.S.2d 157 (N.Y. 1989).
12. *Id.* at 97, 551 N.Y.S.2d at 157.
13. DR 2-108(A) of the New York Code of Professional Responsibility provided "A lawyer shall not be a party to or participate in a partnership or employment agreement with another lawyer that restricts the right of a lawyer to practice law after the termination of a relationship created by the agreement, except as a condition to payment of retirement benefits."

sion reversed, holding that the clause was valid as a financial disincentive to competition and did not prevent Mr. Cohen from practicing law in New York or any other jurisdiction. Mr. Cohen appealed and the court of appeals reversed.

The court of appeals said that the retirement exception in the disciplinary rule was just that—an exception limited to payments in respect of retirement—and did not extend to payments for any other reason. On the firm's argument that the forfeiture clause was justified because of the economic hardship suffered by the withdrawing partner's taking clients with him, the court observed:

> While a law firm has a legitimate interest in its own survival and economic well-being and in maintaining its clients, it cannot protect those interests by contracting for the forfeiture of *earned revenues* during the withdrawing partner's active tenure and participation and by, in effect, restricting the choices of the clients to retain and continue the withdrawing member as counsel.[14]

Further, the court noted that, unless there is an agreement to the contrary, withdrawal of a partner constitutes dissolution of the law partnership, but when there is an agreement to avoid automatic dissolution, the withdrawing partner may forego the ordinary and full accounting which would take place in the event of dissolution. The court then said that the agreement forged by the Lord, Day & Lord partnership had to be struck down because such an agreement "must not conflict with public policy" as reflected in DR 2-108(A).[15]

Of significance, also, is the discussion of the provision depriving a competing withdrawn partner of fees previously earned. The court made two points. First, it said that "while a law firm has a legitimate interest in its own survival and economic well-being and in maintaining its clients, it cannot protect those interests by contracting for the forfeiture of *earned revenues* during the withdrawing partner's active tenure and participation and by, in effect, restricting the choices of the clients to retain and continue the withdrawing member as counsel." (citation omitted)[16]

The *Cohen* case was revisited several years later

14. Cohen, *supra*, 75 N.Y.2d at 100, 551 N.Y.S.2d at 160 (emphasis in original)(citation omitted).
15. *Id.*
16. Cohen, *supra*, 75 N.Y.2d at 101, 551 N.Y.S.2d at 160.

when the New York Court of Appeals decided *Denburg v Parker, Chapin, Flattau & Klimpl.*[17]

Howard S. Denburg withdrew from Parker, Chapin in May 1984 and joined a firm in New Jersey. According to the partnership agreement, the capital account of a withdrawn partner was to be paid to him without interest at the end of the fifth fiscal year after his withdrawal. When Mr. Denburg had received none of his capital account funds by the end of the fifth year after his withdrawal, he sued the firm. The firm set up as its defense a paragraph of the partnership agreement which read, in pertinent part, as follows:

> (a) . . . Any active Partner may withdraw from the firm at any time on not less than sixty (60) calendar days notice to the firm. If an Active Partner withdraws from the firm and shall engage in the private practice of law individually, through another law firm, or otherwise . . . . , the Withdrawn Partner shall, on demand, pay to the firm a sum equal to the greater of (i) 12½% of the share of the firm's profits allocable to him . . . during the two complete fiscal years of the firm immediately preceding the date on which he . . . withdrew from the firm (except that no amounts shall be payable by the Withdrawn Partner whose share of the firm's profits allocable to him . . . during the fiscal year of the firm immediately preceding the date on which he . . . withdrew from the firm was less than $85,000 provided that such Withdrawn Partner directly or through another law firm renders no services to clients of the firm during the 24 months following the date on which he . . . withdrew from the firm), or (ii) 12½% of the total billings to former clients of the firm made by such Partner or other law firm in which he . . . is a partner . . . , with respect to services rendered during the 24 month period following his . . . withdrawal from the firm. The firm shall apply the whole or a portion of the capital account of the Withdrawn Partner to the payment of the obligation referred to in the preceding sentence. Withdrawn Partners shall not be entitled to any accounting or other payment for work in process, uncollected accounts, good will or any other matter or cause."[18]

One of Mr. Denburg's former partners testified that Parker, Chapin had moved into new quarters and had borrowed $4.5 million to finance the move. There was also evidence that the partners had agreed to stay together for five years to share the burden of the increased costs and had agreed that any who left would compensate the firm appropriately.

17. 82 N.Y.2d 375, 624 N.E.2d 995, 1993 N.Y. LEXIS 3931, 604 N.Y.S.2d 900 (1993).
18. As quoted in 184 A.D.2d 343, 586 N.Y.S.2d 107, 1992 N.Y.App. Div. LEXIS 8133 (N.Y. App. Div. 1992).

The trial court denied Mr. Denburg's motion for summary judgment and he appealed.

The court of appeals agreed with the conclusion of the appellate division that the clause was a forfeiture-for-competition provision and violative of public policy.

Thus, it appears that the New York Court of Appeals holds to the traditional ban against non-competition clauses. It is a signal to you to be aware of the policy in your state, should you determine to include such a clause in your partnership agreement.

Nonetheless, in a recent decision by the appellate division in New York,[19] the court appeared to say that the scope of the ruling of the court of appeals in the *Cohen* case should be limited to the facts of that case. In *Feldman*, the limited partners in a realty partnership sued the general partner and its president, one James Haber, for breach of fiduciary duty and other claims. The defendants, including Haber, were represented by the law firm of Beigel, Schy Lasky Rifkind Goldberg Fertik & Gelber (the "Beigel firm"). The plaintiffs sought to disqualify the Beigel firm, claiming that it was in violation of the provisions of a settlement agreement entered into between the plaintiffs, Mr. Haber, and themselves in a case in Illinois. In the Illinois case, the agreement provided:

> As an inducement to the settling defendants [including Haber] to enter into this Settlement Agreement, and as a material condition thereof, [the Beigel firm] warrants and represents to the settling defendants that neither such firm nor any of its employees, agents, or representatives will assist or cooperate with any other parties or attorneys in any such action against the settling defendants arising out of, or related in any way to the investments at issue in the actions or any other offerings hereinbefore or hereafter made by the settling defendants . . . nor shall they encourage any other parties or attorneys to commence such action or proceeding.[20]

Shortly after the Settlement Agreement was executed, the Beigel firm wrote some of the settling plaintiffs, saying that some of the limited partners who had settled had asked the firm to "conduct an investigation . . . to determine whether limited partners may have claims for damages." A year later it commenced the suit that became the subject of the *Feldman* case.

The trial court had found that the language of the Settlement Agreement was "clear and unambiguous"; it held that an interpretation that would prohibit the Beigel firm from assisting plaintiffs but allow it to represent them would be absurd. The trial court did not disqualify the Beigel law firm because it violated the terms of the Settlement Agreement but because the agreement violated Code of Professional Responsibility DR 2-108, which prohibits lawyers from entering into an agreement restricting their right to practice law.

On appeal, the plaintiffs relied on the *Cohen* case. However, said the appellate division, it did not support their position. It noted that *Cohen* dealt with a law firm partnership agreement that conditioned payment of "earned but uncollected partnership revenues upon a withdrawing partner's obligation to refrain from the practice of law in competition with the former law firm, and was found to be a violation of DR 2-108 (A) and thus unenforceable as against public policy."[21]

The appellate division then distinguished *Feldman* on the facts. It noted that it had solicited the plaintiffs to take part in the lawsuit and then said:

> Even assuming, arguendo, that a settlement agreement that forbids an attorney to represent other clients against the settling defendants in similar litigation is against public policy, as expressed in the Code of Professional Responsibility, an agreement not to solicit clients is not likewise against public policy.[22]

Though it was not necessary to do so, the court indicated it would not support the view that DR 2-108 (B) would represent the public policy of New York and, in dicta, it impliedly accepted the outcome and reasoning of the California court in *Howard v. Babcock*, supra. However, the ultimate decision in *Feldman* was for the plaintiffs on the ground that the Biegel firm had "solicited" plaintiffs in violation of its agreement.[23]

The New Jersey Cases

The effect of a forfeiture-for-competition clause has also been judicially reviewed in New Jersey,[24] which has followed the *Cohen* and *Denburg* deci-

---

19. Joel Feldman et al., v. Harvey Minars et al., 230 A.D.2d 356, 658 N.Y.S.2d 614, 1997 N.Y.App. Div. LEXIS 6516 (1997).
20. *Id.* at 357.

21. *Id.* at 358–9.
22. *Id.* at 359.
23. *Id.* at 361.
24. Jacob v. Norris, McLaughlin & Marcus, 128 N.J.10, 607 A.2d 142, 1992 N.J. LEXIS 376 (1992). *Jacob* arose in the context of an agreement involving a professional corporation, rather than a partnership, but this factor was not discussed by any court that heard the case.

sions in New York. Norris, McLaughlin & Marcus is a professional corporation with a law practice in New Jersey. It was sued by two partners who, together with an associate, terminated their membership in the firm to recover sums they claimed were due them under a "service termination agreement." After leaving Norris, McLaughlin, they commenced practice under the firm name of Collier, Jacob and Sweet.

The terms of their departure were governed by two agreements entered into by the parties in 1986—a buy-sell agreement which required the firm to buy back the shares of any shareholder whose employment with the firm was terminated for any reason. This agreement was carried out and was not in dispute. The second agreement was the aforementioned service termination agreement providing for compensation above the member's equity interest in the firm, calculated pursuant to a formula set out in the agreement.

The service termination agreement provided for different benefits depending upon whether the departure was competitive or noncompetitive. A departure was "competitive" if the lawyer within one year of the date of termination either (a) engages in the practice of law involving service to clients of the former firm who were clients of the former firm at the date of termination, or (b) solicits other professional and/or paraprofessional employees of the former firm to engage in the practice of law with the departed attorney.[25]

The departing lawyers, Messrs. Jacob and Collier, together requested $81,125 as compensation under the service termination agreement. The firm declined the payment, asserting that the lawyers had retained clients in violation of the antisolicitation provision and had solicited employees in violation of the antiraiding provision.

The departing lawyers filed suit, arguing that the competitive departure provisions were void as against public policy because they contravened Rule 5.6 of the Rules of Professional Conduct. This rule, similar to DR 2-108(A) considered in *Cohen* (see fn. 11, *supra*), provided that:

> A lawyer shall not participate in offering or making: (a) a partnership or employment agreement that restricts the rights of a lawyer to practice after termination of the relationship, except an agreement concerning benefits upon retirement.[26]

Norris, McLaughlin defended on the ground that the plaintiffs had engaged in a "competitive voluntary departure" and under the terms of the service termination agreement, they were entitled to no termination compensation and received only the right to purchase from the law firm certain life insurance. Had the departure been a "noncompetitive departure," the firm would be obligated to pay the departing member, among other benefits, an amount equal to 25 percent times 110 percent of the member's annual draw, applicable immediately prior to departure.

The case reached the New Jersey Supreme Court. Norris, McLaughlin argued that the court should distinguish between agreements that require departing lawyers to forfeit their equity interest in a firm and those that merely deprive them of additional compensation unrelated to their vested interest. The court said it did not have to resolve the question of whether it was "earned" or "additional" compensation. The court held that, if the agreement creates a disincentive to accept representation of a client, it violates the Rules of Professional Conduct. It declined to accept the distinction in *Cohen* as to the departing lawyer's right to receive "earned income" as distinguished from "future profits," since either disincentive would discourage client choice.

The court discussed the argument that the old firm had a need to protect its commercial concerns. The court declared that:

> Moreover, although law firms are understandably concerned about their financial well-being in view of the increasing fluidity of law-firm membership, that fluidity also justifies a heightened vigilance against any form of restrictive covenant.[27]

Nonetheless, the court tossed out a modicum of comfort to Norris, McLaughlin, indicating that the value of a departing partner's capital account could be adjusted to reflect the lesser value of the firm resulting from its change in circumstances:

> In computing a withdrawing partner's equity interest in the former firm, accounting for the effect of the partner's departure on the firm's value is not unreasonable. Although the departing attorneys always have a right to receive the value of their capital accounts, in computing the value of any additional interest they have in the firm, the value they contributed can be offset by the decrease in the firm's value their departure causes.[28]

25. *Id.* at 15, 607 A.2d at 142, 1992 N.J. LEXIS 376 at 4.
26. *Id.* at 17, 607 A.2d at 142, 1992 N.J. LEXIS 376 at 8.

27. *Id.* at 27, 607 A.2d at 142, 1992 N.J. LEXIS 176 at 27.
28. *Id.* at 28, 607 A.2d at 142, 1992 N.J. LEXIS 376 at 28.

The court referred to its decision in an earlier case, *Dugan*,[29] which had established that goodwill is nothing more "than the probability that old customers will resort to the old place" and the further probability that future patronage can be translated into prospective earnings.

> Accordingly, we recognize that if a partner's departure will result in a decrease in the probability of a client's return and a consequent decrease in prospective earnings, that departure may decrease the value of the firm's goodwill. It would not be inappropriate therefore for law partners to take that specific effect into account in determining the shares due a departing partner.[30]

The court then held that the loss of a firm's client revenue following the departure of a member was another of the many factors to be taken into consideration in determining the value of the departing member's share in the corporation.

The court then considered what effect should follow from striking down the offending clause in the service termination agreement and noted that the departing lawyers would receive a windfall by receiving compensation despite their violation of the rule in signing the agreement. If they were barred from receiving the additional compensation, the firm would receive a windfall from a covenant that violated public policy. The court indicated that the solution lay in determining whether the public interest would best be served by giving one party or the other the benefit of the decision. It decided that lawyers Jacob and Collier should receive the additional compensation.

> We note that equitable principles might bar a plaintiff's recovery if the plaintiff had been a senior partner instrumental in drafting a restrictive agreement, imposing it on his or her fellow partners or employees, and then sought to have the provision declared unenforceable when he or she decided to leave. Nothing in the record indicates that Jacob or Collier played such a role in developing the Agreement. Therefore, Jacob and Collier are entitled to the compensation provided by the Service Termination Agreement.[31]

Consequences of the Caselaw

There are numerous lessons to be drawn from *Cohen, Denburg,* and *Jacob.* First, it is extremely difficult to conceive of a forfeiture-for-competi-tion clause that will stand in the courts. Secondly, should you be the departing partner seeking to escape judicial censure for becoming a party to an agreement containing such a clause, make sure that you had no hand in its drafting. Thirdly, as a partner in a firm seeking to protect itself against the losses following the departure of a departing "rainmaker," note that *Jacob* teaches that a downward adjustment in "goodwill" can be made in valuing the value of the departing lawyer's interest. But beware. As appears from a number of other decisions, whether "goodwill" can be valued at all is a question.

The *Denburg* decision also illustrates that the rule in New York is more restrictive, and securing to the withdrawing competing partner his or her capital account is insufficient. A forfeiture-for-competition clause will not survive judicial scrutiny in New York. The court's language is expansive on the point. Speaking of the language in the partnership agreement, it said:

> Whatever other incidental objectives the provision may have had, it is evident that its principal function was to prevent withdrawing partners from competing with their former firm. The provision, after all, exacts a penalty only from those withdrawn partners who continue to practice law privately, and, therefore, potentially in competition with the firm, and exempts from the penalty only those who, inter alia, do not in their new situations continue to serve their former firm's clients. Indeed, the exemption is inexplicable if a principal purpose of the provision was not to prevent competition. Moreover, even if the firm's motive in assessing the penalty was benign, it is clear that the effect of the penalty provision would be to discourage departing counsel from continuing to represent clients of the firm and concomitantly to interfere with the clients' choice of counsel. Accordingly, we are of the view that [the provision] is void on its face as a forfeiture-for-competition provision. . . .[32]

J. Edward McDonough, upon leaving Bower & Gardner in New York, found to his satisfaction that the prohibition against forfeiture is meaningful.[33] He was one of eleven equity partners in the firm and the partnership agreement provided that each of them was entitled to a special distribution amount; in Mr. McDonough's case, it amounted to $800,000. The amount was adjusted

---

29. Dugan v. Dugan, 92 N.J. 423, 457 A.2d 1 (1983).
30. Jacob, *supra,* 128 N.J. at 30, 607 A.2d 142, 1992 N.J. LEXIS 376 at 30.
31. *Id.* at 36, 607 A.2d 142, 1992 N.J. LEXIS 376 at 42.

32. Denburg, *supra,* 184 A.D.2d at 345, 586 N.Y.S.2d at 109, 1992 N.Y.App. Div. LEXIS 8133 at 6.
33. J. Edward McDonough v. Bower & Gardner, 226 A.D.2d 600, 641 N.Y.S.2d 391, 1996 N.Y.App. LEXIS 4307 (N.Y.App. Div., 2nd Dept., 1996).

by reducing the total in an amount paid annually in any year in which the firm earned "excess profits." The agreement further provided that "in the event a Special Distributee, inter alia, died or permanently retired from the practice of law, the remaining Special Distribution Amount would be paid in the form of a Special Departure Distribution. However, if the departing Special Distributee voluntarily left the firm or was discharged for cause, he or she would not receive any of the Special Distribution Amount."[34] By the time Mr. McDonough had departed from the firm, his special distribution amount had been reduced to $600,000. Bower & Gardner declined to pay Mr. McDonough on the ground that he had not "permanently ceased the practice of law after he left the firm."[35] The firm claimed that it was a contingent retirement benefit. The trial court granted summary judgment for Mr. McDonough and the firm appealed.

The appellate division affirmed the action of the trial court:

> Succinctly stated, the effect of the Partnership Agreement is that if the plaintiff wishes to continue practicing law after withdrawing from the firm, he must forfeit $600,000 in earned but uncollected partnership monies. Under the rule established in Cohen v. Lord, Day & Lord . . . , such a provision is an unenforceable restraint on the practice of law.[36]

Illinois Supports the Prohibition

Illinois has joined its voice in support of the ban against forfeiture-for-competition clauses.

William M. Stevens was a partner in Rooks Pitts & Poust in that state from 1981 until he voluntarily withdrew on May 31, 1992. In 1984, he had signed an agreement that stated:

> In the event of the death of a General Partner, or the withdrawal of a General Partner by reason of (i) permanent disability, (ii) retirement, or (iii) voluntary or involuntary withdrawal of a General Partner pursuant to subparagraph (c) of ARTICLE FIRST hereof, the interest of the estate of any such deceased General Partner and the interest of any such withdrawing General Partner (hereinafter in this Article called the "Ex-Partner"), shall be limited as follows:
>
> * * *
>
> (B) The interest of the Ex-Partner in the tangible and intangible assets of the Partnership shall be limited to an amount equal to the net balance of the Ex-

Partner's capital account, supplemental capital account, current account and any other account, on the dates of death or withdrawal, together with the Ex-Partner's share of collections, if any, received within three (3) years after death or withdrawal for work performed prior to January 1, 1984 in accordance with the income sharing percentages applicable to the year the work was performed ("Old Runoff") plus the Ex-Partner's share of collections, if any, received within three (3) years after death or withdrawal for work performed after December 31, 1983 and before July 1, 1987 in accordance with the income sharing percentages in effect on June 30, 1987, ("New Runoff") and plus the Ex-Partner's income sharing percentage at the time of death or withdrawal collected within three (3) years after such death or withdrawal ("Inventory"), which shall be paid as set forth below, subject to the adjustments, offsets and holdbacks set forth below. . . .

> (iii) If the Ex-Partner has voluntarily or involuntarily withdrawn from the Partnership, the Ex-Partner shall be paid within a reasonable time after June 30 and December 31 in each year thereafter an amount equal to four-fifths (4/5th) of his share of the collections of Old Runoff, New Runoff, and Inventory. *If the Ex-Partner is not directly or indirectly engaged in the practice of law, in competition to the legal practice of the Partnership existing immediately prior to his withdrawal either individually or in association with another law firm in the Chicago metropolitan area including the City of Chicago and the seven (7) surrounding counties in Illinois and Indiana . . . for a period of one (1) year subsequent to becoming an Ex-Partner, the Ex-Partner shall as soon as practicable thereafter receive an additional payment equal to one-fourth (1/4th) of the amount previously paid to the Ex-Partner hereunder* (emphasis supplied) and shall thereafter be paid all of his share of Old Runoff, New Runoff, and Inventory within a reasonable time after June 30 and December 31 of each year and each year thereafter.[37]

Less than a year after he left Rooks Pitts, Mr. Stevens became associated with another Chicago law firm engaged in general practice. Rooks Pitts paid him 80 percent of the compensation due him under Article Ninth, and refused to pay the balance, subtracting $60,640 from the total he claimed of $303,202. Mr. Stevens sued, seeking a declaratory judgment.

The trial court denied the motion.

The Illinois Appellate Court considered the opinions of the New Jersey Supreme Court in *Jacob,* and of the New York Court of Appeals in *Cohen* and *Denburg* upholding the restrictions in

---

34. *Id.*
35. *Id.* at 601.
36. *Id.* at 601.

37. William v. Stevens v. Rooks Pitts and Poust, 682 N.E.2d 1125 (Ill. App.Ct. 1997), *appeal denied,* 689 N.E.2d 1147 (1998).

Rule 5.6, as well as the ruling of the California Supreme Court in *Howard v. Babcock* allowing a reasonable cost against an ex-partner who chooses to compete with his former firm in a limited area.

The court observed that, while, in Illinois, courts have employed a reasonableness test as to noncompetition clauses for other professions, Illinois law provides "little basis for allowing lawyer noncompetition clauses."[38] The court said:

> While we acknowledge the rationale behind the "rule of reason" cases, our research has revealed no Illinois case law which would support a finding that subsection (b)(iii) of Article Ninth is not violative of Rule 5.6. By requiring the departing lawyer to give up certain compensation due to him if he competes with the firm in a certain geographic area within one year after his departure, this financial disincentive provision hinders both the departing lawyer's ability to take on clients and the clients' choice of counsel. We conclude that subsection (b)(iii) of Article Ninth is in contravention to the public policy underlying Rule 5.6 and is unenforceable.

The court also considered that fact that the parties were in pari delicto and whether, under such circumstances, it should aid either party. It said that to do that would "eviscerate" Rule 5.6 and its underlying public policy. It remanded the case to the trial court to enter summary judgment in favor of Mr. Stevens and to "compute the remaining departure compensation, prejudgment interest, and costs due to him."[39]

Only a few months after the decision in *Stevens*, the Illinois Supreme Court struck down a noncompetition clause that banned, for a period of two years following the termination of an employment contract with a professional law corporation, any effort to "solicit or endeavor to entice away any clients of the Corporation without the prior written consent of the Corporation." The court's opinion was that "the foundation for Rule 5.6 rests on considerations of public policy, and it would be inimical to public policy to give effect to the offending provisions.[40]

If you wish to have a forfeiture-for-competition clause in your firm's partnership agreement it is wise to check carefully the decisions in your state to determine just how far the courts will allow you to go in building a protective wall against the competing withdrawn partner.[41] It is likely to be only an inch, rather than a mile.

We have discussed the ethics and enforceability of forfeiture-for-competition clauses in the context of drafting a partnership agreement, and in the context of withdrawal of a partner from a law firm. May a law firm enforce a forfeiture of retirement benefits against a partner who does not merely withdraw, but actually retires, and then resumes the practice of law?

Judicial Enforcement of the Prohibition

A reading of the cases in New York would indicate that a properly drawn clause can be judicially enforced against a retired partner, provided that the payments to him or her are, in fact, retirement benefits. When Robert Silagi retired from the firm of Guazzo, Perelson, Rushfield & Guazzo, P.C. in 1981, he received certain benefits. Then, after a six-month leave-of-absence, he decided to return and a new agreement was executed. Under this agreement, Mr. Silagi would act as counsel to the firm, with use of an office and services, and would receive half salary; in addition, he would receive 25 percent of the fees in two matters. He agreed that he would not solicit any past, present, or future clients of the firm for a four-year period nor accept any clients whose interests were in conflict with interests of the firm's existing clients for one year. The agreement provided for binding arbitration of disputes.[42]

Mr. Silagi sought arbitration of his claim for a share of a fee. When the trial court ordered arbitration, the law firm filed an answer seeking damages against Mr. Silagi for competing in violation of his agreement. Mr. Silagi then moved for a stay of arbitration, contending that the issue of the applicability of DR 2-108 was not subject to arbitration. The firm filed a cross-motion requesting a hearing on whether DR 2-108 applied. The trial court denied the hearing, and it ordered arbitration of Mr. Silagi's claim and a trial of the firm's counterclaims.

38. *Id.*
39. *Id.*
40. Dowd &. Dowd, Ltd. v. Gleason, 3693 N.E.2d 358 (1998).
41. Note that California goes further than most states in upholding forfeiture-for-competition clauses. *See* Note, *Why Anti-Competition Clauses Should be Unenforceable in Law Partnership Agreements: an Argument for Rejecting California's Approval in* Howard v. Babcock, 8 GEO. JNL. LEG. ETHICS 669 (1995). The New York position, which severely restricts such clauses, is supported by a report of the Committee on Professional Responsibility, Association of the Bar of the City of New York. See 20 FORDHAM URB. L. JNL. 897 (1993).
42. *In re* Silagi, 146 A.D.2d 555, 537 N.Y.S.2d 171, 1989 N.Y.App. Div. LEXIS 745 (N.Y.App. Div. 1989).

In reversing the trial court, the appellate division distinguished *Matter of Silverberg*,[43] saying:

> That case involved an agreement to terminate a partnership and not the retirement of a partner from an ongoing firm, as is alleged by respondent herein. Should this threshold issue be resolved in respondent's favor, there would be no public policy barring arbitration of the claims and counterclaims. Respondent's motion for a hearing should therefore have been granted and the arbitration stayed.[44]

Resuming Practice and Foregoing Benefits

On the other hand, the New York courts have followed the *Cohen* case[45] and permitted enforcement of a forfeiture-for-competition clause where the retiree abandoned practice in exchange for benefits and then was permitted to resume practice by agreeing to relinquish the retirement benefits. In *Graubard Mollen Horowitz Pomeranz & Shapiro v. Moskovitz*,[46] the court said:

> A more important consideration is the purpose behind DR 2-108. Restrictive covenants are limited in the case of attorneys in order to serve the greater social purpose of providing clients with full and free choice of counsel. The retirement benefits exception therefore ought to be narrowly read. A firm may, for instance, require an attorney not to represent its client or not to practice law at all while receiving retirement benefits, but if the attorney decides to forego those benefits, then he may practice and clients may freely avail themselves of his services.

Expulsion and the Prohibition

The Supreme Court of Kansas has addressed the issue somewhat indirectly.[47] Malcolm Miller was a partner who did not retire in a literal sense, but was forced out of his firm. A dispute arose after his expulsion when the firm did not pay certain fees to him, which he claimed he was due. Mr. Miller sued.

The partnership agreement among the partners of the firm provided that any partner who was expelled and who, under certain provisions of the agreement is entitled to retirement rights, would not be regarded as an expelled partner, but considered for all purposes as being a retired partner. The agreement further provided that to be entitled to retirement rights, a partner had to meet one of three criteria: attained age 60, have served with the firm for thirty years, or be unable to continue because of physical or mental disability. These rights were subject to forfeiture and required the retired partner to return any benefits paid to him if the retired partner, "without the express consent of all continuing partners, reenters the practice of law or becomes otherwise gainfully engaged or employed at an occupation associated with or related to the practice of law."[48] Mr. Miller qualified for retirement benefits because he had attained age 60 and had been with the firm for more than thirty years.

The Kansas Supreme Court held that DR 2-108 allows restriction of the practice of law if it is a condition to payment of retirement benefits. It held that the application of the provision to Mr. Miller was within the exception.[49]

In attempting to settle the issues between the firm and Mr. Miller, one of the continuing firm's partners wrote to him, offering to continue payment of retirement benefits to Mr. Miller if he would restrict himself to certain permitted activities, that is:

> You may rent office space and employ a secretary, with the understanding that you will identify and utilize it as a "private office" and not a law office. You agree that you will not list or advertise yourself by stationery, letterhead, building address, telephone listing, or otherwise as a lawyer or attorney. Within that setting you may consult with persons and counsel them, but you may not represent them in judicial or administrative proceedings. If you refer such persons to other lawyers, you will either make no charge for any service rendered by you either before or after the referral or you agree that it shall not be your practice to make such referrals to any particular lawyer or law firm.[50]

If Mr. Miller observed these restrictions, the firm would pay him $2,000 per month for ninety-six months.

The Kansas Supreme Court held that the facts were distinguishable from the facts in the *Cohen* case,[51] since Mr. Cohen was not "retiring" but "withdrawing" from Lord, Day & Lord. Here, Mr. Miller was qualified for retirement benefits and was being treated as if he were retiring from Foulston, Siefkin. Said the court:

43. 81 A.D.2d 640 (N.Y.App. Div. 1981).

44. *In re* Silagi, 146 A.D.2d at 556, 537 N.Y.S.2d at 172, 1989 N.Y.App. Div. LEXIS 745 at 3.

45. *Supra* note 11.

46. 149 Misc.2d 481 at 485 (N.Y.Sup. Ct. 1990).

47. Miller v. Foulston, Siefkin, Powers & Eberhardt, 246 Kan. 450, 790 P.2d 404, 1990 Kan. LEXIS 78 (1990).

48. *Id.* at 455, 790 P.2d at 408, 1990 Kan. LEXIS 78 at 12.

49. *Id.* at 459, 790 P.2d at 411, 1990 Kan. Lexis 78 at 19.

50. *Id.* at 460, 790 P.2d at 411, 1990 Kan. LEXIS 78 at 21.

51. *Supra* note 11.

Nor was the offer of retirement benefits here coercive. Plaintiff did not voluntarily withdraw from Foulston-Siefkin. He was forced to leave under threat of being expelled. Because of his longevity with the firm, he qualified to receive retirement benefits. To receive these benefits, however, plaintiff had to meet certain conditions. Plaintiff had to choose between retiring, including stopping the practice of law and receiving over $190,000 in retirement benefits, or continuing the practice of law, in which case he lost retirement benefits. The provisions of the 1965 agreement making the payment of retirement benefits conditional upon plaintiff's retirement by not continuing to practice law was not unethical or unenforceable and did not violate DR 2-108(A).[52]

Clarity in the Agreement

A partner about to retire and the continuing partners should have a clear understanding as to what limitations, if any, are to be placed upon the retiring partner's right to continue to practice law after retirement. All need to be cognizant of the ethical restrictions imposed by DR 2-108 and be aware that no restrictions are permissible unless, and only so long as, retirement benefits are paid to the retiring partner.

Retirement Provisions in Partnership Agreements

Scale-Down of Compensation

One of the more accepted provisions applicable to retiring partners in modern-day partnership agreements is a scale-down clause. To ease the transition of partners from active to retired status, the partnership agreement or the firm's stated retirement policy will provide for a gradual reduction of partner compensation beginning in the year after the partner reaches age 65 and continuing through age 70, when the partner is required to retire. An example of a scale-down of a major firm is set out in the *Vinson & Elkins* case,[53] which was described thus:

Further, the partnership agreement provided that after reaching fixed-basis status and continuing into retired status for the remainder of the partner's life, former percentage partners would be paid as a guaranteed payment a percentage of their base compensation. This guaranteed payment was to be 75 percent of their base compensation in the first year and 50 percent the second year, and ultimately

---

would reach 25 percent in the fifth year and thereafter. (*Id.* at 45).

Not all firms can be, or are, as generous as Vinson & Elkins. Variations of the Vinson & Elkins formula might include a scale-down of 20 percent in each of the years after the partner reaches age 65 through age 70, with some specified minimum, say, a percentage of the lowest partner draw in the firm. More importantly, payments usually cease after age 70.

Supplemental Retirement Benefits

If a firm has no mandatory retirement age, it is unlikely that it will provide any retirement benefits to retired partners. Each partner will have to rely on a combination of resources—Keogh Plan and IRA, Social Security, and personal investments—usually without firm assistance. When retirement is mandatory, the firm's financial resources determine whether retired partners receive anything after reaching the firm's retirement age.

In any event, whether the firm provides the benefit or the partner is left to his or her own resources is a distinction without a difference. Remember, to a partner "it is your money."

Long-Service Partners Versus Others

In today's law firms, there is a difference between the lawyer who joined the firm forty-five years ago upon graduation from law school and the "lateral partner," who became part of the organization within, say, the last ten or fifteen years. The person who has given his entire life to the firm may receive more generous treatment in the form of a supplemental retirement benefit that is not offered to those retiring with less service.

Such supplemental payments do not put a great strain on the budgets of larger firms. Forty-five years ago, the number of partners in most firms was quite small, compared with the number of partners in those firms today. Thus, the supplemental payments to a small number of "old-timers" is spread over a large number of active partners. They can afford it!

Attending to Client Relations

As the retirement age approaches, all partners must devote proper attention to clients' matters. The retirement of a partner inevitably will be

---

52. *Id.* at 462, 790 P.2d at 412, 1990 Kan. LEXIS 78 at 26.
53. 1992 U.S. Tax Ct. LEXIS 54 (1992), aff'd 7 F.3d 1235, 1993 U.S. App. LEXIS 31000 (5th Cir. 1993).

viewed differently by the firm and by clients. If a partner has served his clients well, the partner, from the client's view, is "my lawyer"; from the firm's view, the client is "our client."

Thus, the buzzword in the profession today is "institutionalize." Law firms want to institutionalize the clients—to try to make the clients loyal to the firm rather than to any individual lawyer. Clients resist such attempts; even large corporate clients, speaking through their general counsel, will say that they do not retain law firms; they select lawyers.

Under these circumstances, continuing partners should plan, well in advance of their partner's retirement, to gather clients into the inner circle. They should be exposed to other partners and senior associates, both professionally and socially, to establish good rapport. The retiring partner should be part of this effort. If the firm waits until the retirement date has arrived before commencing the "institutionalization" process, a time lapse occurs before good relations can be cemented. This lapse can prove disastrous for retention of business.

Even though a partner has retired, the firm should provide incentives to him or her to remain active in the client retention process. An occasional invitation to join a business conference with the client, or a social gathering involving the client, will assist in moving the client toward the view that there has been no real change in the "tender loving care" provided by the firm.

Defining the Particulars

Partners about to retire need to consider, and to discuss with the continuing partners, the services that will be provided to them after retirement. Most law firms will offer retired partners an office (often smaller than when the partner was active), secretarial assistance, and office services. The firm can offer other items depending upon its philosophy, generosity, and financial resources. It might elect to pay membership dues in professional associations or social clubs, on the theory that the retired partner's participation in these organizations is a good marketing tool. The firm may permit the retired partner to participate in employee benefit plans, particularly life and health insurance programs. The retired partner may also be permitted to attend partnership meetings and to continue to have access to the firm's financial and operating information.

Whatever the nature of these arrangements, they should be agreed upon in advance of retirement and included in a separate agreement to cover the postretirement status of the individual lawyer. If the retiree is to serve as of counsel to the firm, the agreement[54] should define the duties and responsibilities of that position and, in particular, the understanding as to malpractice insurance coverage should the lawyer be providing legal advice other than to the firm's lawyers.

54. See HAROLD WREN & BEVERLY GLASCOCK, THE OF COUNSEL AGREEMENT 2ND EDITION (American Bar Association (1998)).

Part II
Retirement Income: Getting the Most Out of Social Security and Pensions

16
A Survey of Retirement Plans of Law Firms

DAVID A. BRIDEWELL

In an effort to determine the extent to which law firms have retirement plans in place, a survey was recently completed of some six thousand individual lawyers. The Retirement Planning Committee of Real Property, Probate and Trust Law Section, in cooperation with the Committee on Retirement Plans of Law Firms of the Senior Lawyers Division, mailed questionnaires to more than six thousand members of the probate and trust division of that section regarding retirement planning in their law firms. It was hoped that the results of the survey would assist lawyers and their law firms in evaluating their own plans or lack thereof.

The questionnaires asked the size of their firm; at what age partners were required to retire; the compensation paid upon retirement; how compensation was determined; whether retiring partners were encouraged to remain with the firm; whether the retiree was paid a percentage of the fees brought in; whether the retirement plan was funded by insurance or investments; whether the plan was qualified under federal law so that it was a deductible expense prior to tax reporting of annual firm income; and, if not qualified under federal law, how and when that status was determined.

The responses to the questionnaire were divided into four groups: (1) solo practitioners; (2) small firms of two to ten lawyers; (3) medium-size firms of eleven to fifty lawyers; and (4) large firms of more than fifty-one lawyers. These groups were then further separated into the following categories: (1) those that have retirement

David A. Bridewell serves as counsel to the Chicago law firm of DeWolfe, Poynton & Stevens.

plans; (2) those that do not; (3) those that have funded and qualified plans; and (4) those that do not. The results of the survey reflected only those firms that had retirement plans.

The interesting overall results of this study show that (1) the larger firms have the largest number of retirement plans and the largest number of funded and qualified plans, and (2) individual practitioners and the smaller firms are the ones having no plan or plans that are neither funded nor qualified. The smaller the firm, the smaller the number having a retirement plan; and of those that have plans, many are not funded and qualified.

From the percentages shown, this study demonstrates that individual practitioners and smaller and medium-size firms need to revise their plans for retirement and to fund and qualify those plans so that they are fully funded and qualified as an ongoing tax-deductible expense and not as an after-tax deduction from net income and profits.

The results show that an unfunded, nonqualified plan is dangerous because the cost of paying out benefits to retiring partners could eat up the net income and profits of the year's operation. This is particularly the case in older firms where a majority of the partners are nearing retirement age or in a small firm in which many of the lawyers are approximately the same age.

The study also shows that many retirement agreements of old law partnerships provided for payout without any type of limitation to retiring partners based on their accustomed percentage draw from the net profits or accounts receivable.

Such payouts could possibly exhaust or extensively deplete the income of the firm, particularly

93

if the retirees had been or still were the principal income producers of the firm. Some limitation on retirement payout to retirees is essential, particularly in cases where the plan is not funded with securities or insurance and where the plan is not qualified under federal law as a tax-deductible expense for the firm.

Now that income taxes are so high, it is essential that retirement plans be qualified under federal tax laws so that payouts to retirees are paid from net income *before* tax, as an expense of doing business, rather than from net income *after* taxes are paid. It is also essential that retirement plans be funded or at least partially to ensure that all retirees receive their retirement income when due.

Table 16–1, which summarizes the answers received from the ABA members who answered the questionnaire, supports the conclusions stated above.

Table 16–1

	Large Firms	Medium Firms	Small Firms	Solo Practitioner
1. Number of lawyers	51+	11–50	2–10	1
2. Have an established retirement plan	92%	82%	41%	28%
Do not have an established retirement plan	8%	18%	59%	72%
3. Have set retirement age for partners	73%	41%	28%	11%
*Do not have set retirement age for partners	25%	58%	72%	83%
4. Provide established compensation upon retirement	75%	48%	25%	11%
Do not provide established compensation upon retirement	25%	51%	71%	72%
5. Compensation is a percentage of previous salary	47%	36%	17%	11%
Compensation is not a percentage of previous salary	34%	33%	39%	17%
6. Firm pays 100% of compensation	62%	55%	43%	17%
Firm makes joint contributions with partners	13%	14%		
Partners make 100% of contribution	11%	6%	2%	17%
7. Encourage or permit retirees to continue with firm	87%	67%	49%	†
Do not allow retirees to remain	7%	10%	9%	
8. Pay compensation for legal work brought in after retirement	33%	30%	25%	†
Do not pay compensation for legal work brought in after retirement	59%	33%	26%	
9. Retirement plans funded entirely or partially through investments or insurance	63%	77%	79%	94%
Retirement plans unfunded	34%	23%	14%	6%
10. Provides for actuaries to compute amounts set aside for each retiring partner	18%	9%	11%	17%
Do not provide for actuaries	72%	85%	78%	61%
11. Have retirement plans that are qualified under federal law	72%	84%	80%	100%
‡Have nonqualified retirement plans	38%	29%	13%	
Of those with nonqualified plans:				
Plans that provide part compensation after specified age or disability payment	69%	56%	36%	
Plans that pay part of salary to surviving spouse or other beneficiary in case of death before or after retirement	55%	40%	45%	
12. Just one qualified plan	33%	58%	62%	83%
More than one qualified plan	42%	24%	14%	17%
13. Types of plans:				
Profit Shoring	x	x	x	x
Keogh	x	x	x	x
Defined Benefit	x	x	x	x
Defined Contribution	x	x	x	
Target Benefit	x	x	x	
HR-10	x	x	x	
401 (k)	x	x	x	x
Money Purchase	x	x	x	x
Pension	x	x	x	
SEP		x	x	x
ESOP		x		
Defined Compensation			x	
IRA			x	x

*The answers for questions 3 through 13 represent only those firms that have retirement plans.

†This question is not relevant to the solo practitioner.

‡These numbers exceed 100 percent because some firms offer both qualified and nonqualified plans.

17
Retirement Plans for Law Firms

JOSEPH H. GORDON

Every law firm should have at least four retirement plans. Most already have three, but many still lack that important and indispensable fourth, despite being urged to do so by the first two editions of this book.

First, there is Social Security, to which partners have contributed, probably for many years, as self-employed persons. Retirees can start drawing these benefits as early as age 62, but if they continue to have earned income, the benefits are curtailed. By waiting to age 70, they can increase the monthly payments by 15 percent or more. Nearly every lawyer has maximum coverage under Social Security because they have paid the tax on the maximum amount of earnings to which the tax has applied over the years. There's more detailed information in the chapter "Social Security," by Harold G. Wren. But there's one salient fact to understand: Social Security was not conceived or intended as a pension plan but only as a safety net—a basic level of sustaining income.

Second, there are provisions in almost every law partnership agreement relative to the retirement or death of a partner, or to the dissolution of the partnership. These provisions should provide for the distribution of assets, such as earned but undistributed shares of fees, and the division of capital accounts of the firm. Many firms seem now to take care of their retirement plans by a policy statement adopted by the board of directors and approved by the plan. The partnership agreement, or bylaws (if the firm is incorporated), should and usually does provide for the payment of the capital account to a terminating

Joseph H. Gordon is of counsel with the firm Gordon, Thomas, Honeywell, Malanca, Peterson & Daheim in Tacoma and Seattle, Washington.

member or partner. Equity holders are referred to in this chapter as "partners," whether or not the firm is incorporated.

Third, most law firms have Keogh or 401(k) plans in which retirees will have accrued a nestegg for retirement, depending and based on when the plan was put into effect. In some instances, partners may have an IRA. In effect, these are forced savings plans, since the money contributed to them is deducted from the partners' income. Income taxation of the contributions to the plans, as well as accumulated investment income in the plans, is postponed until money is withdrawn. The amounts saved in these plans are likely to be significant by the time of retirement.

Three Plans Are Not Adequate

Are these three plans adequate for retirement in the style most partners would like to become accustomed? The answer is an emphatic "No." While the income from the three might be sufficient to provide basic economic benefits, they do not serve as guidelines for when retirement will occur, or compensate the seniors for the years of loyal service to their law firms, or the goodwill or client base they have helped to create.

Nor are the three basic plans adequate for the firm, because they do not provide any control by the firm over the future of aging partners, nor do they provide for retiring partners' future services or loyalty to the firm. They do not provide the compensation for past services that would have been rewarded had, for instance, the partners become federal judges, bank or corporate executives, or government employees, all of which positions would have provided generous retirement benefits.

Why shouldn't lawyers who have worked hard all their lives be entitled to as good a retirement as a federal judge or an executive of a corporation? Why shouldn't a well-run law firm have the same ability to dictate the time and terms of the retirement of partners in the same manner that it controls the hiring of new associates?

Benefits to All

The fourth and most important plan is a comprehensive and well-designed law firm retirement plan. The benefits are many for both lawyers and the firm.

To the firm, a retirement plan gives (1) the ability to save clients when partners retire; (2) the ability to fix the time and manner for partners' retirement; (3) the ease of business transfer from partners to younger lawyers; the salving of the firm's conscience about doing the "fair" thing in the treatment of retiring partners; (5) the increased loyalty and tenure of the partners; and (6) the increased image of stability of the firm.

To the retiring partners, a retirement plan affords economic and psychological advantages. A definitive plan helps partners in the transition from active practice to retirement and in planning for the activities of the future. Law firm retirement plans can provide for the continued participation and interest of retired partners in the firm and retain them as members of the team. Partners' feelings of usefulness is a valuable asset in retirement and will be beneficial to their health and welfare. The retirement "option" must be made sufficiently attractive to lessen the trauma of the change in status and compensation.

The three basic plans are to a great extent the personal plans of retiring lawyers, to which they have contributed their own money. The plans go a long way, but not all the way, to providing what is needed for retirement and retirement planning. It is obvious that the fourth plan is necessary.

Fourth Leg of the Stool

Now comes the hard part. Since the first edition of this book some ten years ago, not only time but more research has convinced me that there is more to be said about retirement plans of law firms, particularly the larger firms. And there are more of them now than then. But how to do it?

The law firm retirement plan should take into consideration the needs of both the firm and the retirees. There are so many questions to be answered and so many different varieties of retirement plans that it is little wonder that many law firms throw up their hands in despair and never face up to adopting a workable plan.

The content and type of plan depends on many factors, including (1) the culture of the firm; (2) the demographics of the firm; (3) the age of the firm; (4) the compensation system of the firm; (5) the selfishness or the goodwill of the majority; (6) the stability of the firm; (7) the loyalty of the partners; (8) the geographical location of the firm; and (9) the existence of one or more partners who will tackle the problem and see it through.

Some of the questions to be answered are (1) should the plan be funded or unfunded; (2) should the plan be mandatory or optional; (3) if mandatory, at what age; (4) should retirement be gradual, with a period of "of counsel" or "special counsel" status; (5) how much should retiring partners be paid and over what period of time.

It is almost impossible to cover the many situations that are encountered in the retirement or termination of any partner relationship. In addition to those listed above, one might add (1) the culture of the area and of the firm itself, (2) the family and financial circumstances of the retiring partner, (3) the size and prosperity of the firm; (4) the health of the retiring partner, as well as many other things so diverse that in no way can they be accommodated under one instrument. It is highly desirable, however, to have either the retirement plan or the policy of the firm fix a definite date at which the questions involved will be discussed and determined. That date may be at age 62, 65, 70, 75, or any other age the firm desires to fix. Embarrassment and ill feelings will be avoided if the date is agreed on at the time of the entrance into the partnership. Any agreement must be flexible to cover all situations. Unfortunately, it seems that this has to be done on an ad hoc basis.

The provisions for the appraisal of the value of the capital account should include a consideration of the value of the work in progress and of the accounts receivable. Other types of businesses usually include a value for "goodwill." But in computations for law firms, there usually is no value placed on goodwill. Either the firm or the retiring partner should have the option of paying out the capital account on a monthly basis over a period of time with suitable interest calculations to protect not only the financial condition of the firm, but also the financial integrity of the retiring partner.

Sample Plans

The sample plans included in the second edition of this book are still valid and useful.

Plan A is the simplest and, for that reason, perhaps the easiest to sell. Note that it is called a policy of the firm and not a contractual plan. Plan B also is a policy program and provides for an optional five-year step-down retirement in lieu of a payout as set forth in the partnership agreement. Plan C is a more comprehensive plan based on a flat amount per month instead of an average of previous compensation.

The reader should note that all three of the plans have noncompete clauses, the validity of which may be in doubt because of recent court decisions. These plans should be used only as a checklist of provisions. Each firm should tailor the agreement to its needs.

A Look at One Firm

Some personal research of my own firm may be instructive as to the reasons for termination or retirement of partners. The firm is 104 years old, having been started in 1894 by a graduate of the University of Michigan Law School who took the advice of Horace Greeley to heart and went west, as did a number of the firm's original partners. In the firm's 104-year history, there have been 104 partners, and it has been my privilege to know all of them and their individual circumstances. Half of them are still active partners and working successfully at the practice of law.

But what has happened to the other half? Why are they no longer partners? Let's take a look at the reasons.

- Death before retirement (6). There is little that could be done about the demands of the grim reaper. We lost six good lawyers, mostly from cancer, while they were in the prime of their careers.
- Illness (2). Two became too ill to continue to practice.
- Assumed judicial positions (4). Four partners,

while in the prime of their practice, were elevated to judicial positions, two being elected to the state trial court bench and two being appointed to the federal bench.
- Went to competing firms (13). As the firm grew bigger, more and more of the partners seemed to chafe under the regimentation and the diminishing restrictions of a large firm and terminated to go to a smaller firm or into individual practice.
- Entered business (2). The banking business looked better for two of our good lawyers, and so they went to work for their clients.
- Early retirement (12). Our partnership agreement provided that a partner could take early retirement at age 62, and twelve of our partners have chosen to do so, with most of them becoming "of counsel" and entering into a special contract with the firm for their practice after age 62. It is obvious that more and more of the good lawyers in the profession are retiring early, either because they have financial security from the sources mentioned in this article or from other sources and do not want to work as hard as they have in the past. For those who became "of counsel," most of their contracts provided that they would be furnished with an office, a secretary, and their continuing legal education expenses and bar association dues, and that they would be entitled to 50 percent of any fees that they brought in.
- Normal retirement (12). Only twelve of the partners retired in what could be considered a normal manner. In the early days of the firm's history, there was no such thing as "retirement." Lawyers practiced to the end and died with their boots on. Fortunately, only a few of these were past their prime and should have retired earlier.
- Special case (1). One lawyer is reluctant to abandon the ship and is in his sixty-fourth year of practice at age 89. He sold his equity position to the firm for the payout of his capital account when he was 75, using the formula in the partnership agreement, and entered into a contract under which he agreed not to practice any further and to turn over any of his old clients and future business to other members of the firm. He is active in the administration of the firm's affairs, including marketing and hiring. (Guess the identity of this special case.)

Incidentally, all the "of counsel" contracts are written on a year-to-year basis and may be terminated on thirty days' notice by either party.

The difficulty of trying to draft a retirement agreement that would cover all of the situations our firm has experienced is obvious. It probably would be preferable to have a contract covering the necessary items, but with a provision that the executive committee or special committee or whatever governing body the firm chooses has the power to enter into one-year contracts with retiring partners according to their particular situations.

The retirement scene in the legal profession is constantly changing, and my opinions have changed from those expressed in the first two editions of this book, and they will probably change from day to day as the profession itself changes. What effect, for instance, will the advent of more women in the profession have on retirement plans? What new tax programs will become available? What programs will insurance companies offer for retirement?

A specific example of an insurance program is the new variable universal life insurance program developed by the American Bar Insurance Plans Consultants Inc (ABIPC). It provides not only death benefits, but also various other options without additional expense as a substitute for current group insurance policies. Unfortunately, it is available only to law firms with more than fifty partners. Many of the firms of that size or larger are finding it attractive. A brief description of the program by Tim Pfeiffer, executive director of ABIPC, follows as Exhibit 17–1, with instructions as to how to get further information.

The tax and insurance considerations in any discussion of a retirement plan are an absolute necessity. Unfortunately, the nature and the lack of priority in the large firm agenda of the retirement question place a roadblock to solving a vital problem in firm administration.

Exhibit 17–1
Retirement Plans for Law Firms:
Variable Universal Life
By Tim Pfeiffer

If you already offer a 401(k) or other qualified program, your partners probably are searching for additional ways to accumulate retirement dollars on a tax-favored basis. Now, there is an increasingly popular way for firms to provide partners with additional retirement flexibility, often without the necessity of spending additional dollars. That way is group variable universal life insurance. It provides a death benefit, plus flexible side fund options that allow an insured to select from a menu of investment-grade funds for tax-favored cash-value growth.

To use variable universal life, the firm may simply replace the group term life insurance plan that is currently in place for partners, often at a comparable cost to premium rates already being paid. Sometimes this means removing the partners from the group term life plan. By doing this the firm incurs little to no additional cost, and it provides partners with a valuable funding tool to enhance other firm benefits—or to supplement personal retirement funding objectives.

Of course, if there is no current life insurance plan in place for partners, the firm may establish a new variable universal life plan for that purpose. Depending on the percentage of partners who participate, underwriting concessions may be available that will guarantee each partner has a certain amount of life insurance coverage. The higher the percentage, the more generous the guarantees.

Variable universal life insurance is uniquely suited for retirement planning because it allows the insured to take maximum advantage of Internal Revenue Code Section 72, which allows earnings under a life insurance contract to be not taxable on withdrawal until they exceed the death benefit premiums paid in. Under variable universal life contracts, insureds are able to make additional premium deposits beyond what is needed to pay for the death benefit and, thereby, "over fund" the policy up to limits prescribed by the internal Revenue Service.

This means that by using after-tax premium dollars, an insured can realize investment earnings equal to all the death benefit premiums paid in before owing any income tax on withdrawals. Importantly, variable universal life insurance products typically allow the insured to direct the cash values among several fund selections. Transfers of cash values among the policy's funds and growth of fund values due to reinvested dividends do not trigger taxable events, which further enhances the value of the variable universal life insurance strategy.

This is an excellent way to accumulate money on a tax-favored basis.

Variable universal life insurance is both permanent and portable. It typically can be continued to age 99 and withdrawals can begin at any age. Therefore, if retirement is deferred beyond age 65, an insured can continue to make premium payments for as long as desired until initiating the withdrawal phase of the contract. Also, partners taking early retirement incur no penalty charges for distributions prior to age 59½, as is the case with annuities and qualified plans. Partners leaving a firm must be able to take their policies with them, and companies offering these plans typically switch a terminating partner from the firm's list bill to a direct bill basis at that time.

The ABA's insurance affiliate, American Bar Insurance Plans Consultants Inc., offers a group variable universal life insurance product, called ABA Preferred, for law firms of fifty lawyers and more, and an individual variable universal life policy for ABA members called ABA Premiere. Both feature both low costs and low loads, including for investment flexibility a spectrum of fourteen fund choices within five brand name fund portfolios, including such managers as Putnam, T. Rowe Price, and Scudder.

ABI will be happy to explore ways that this strategy can complement the retirement options that you currently offer. ABI can be reached at 1-800-445-3540, or via e-mail at info@abiins.com.

PLAN A
Retirement Policies and
Supplemental Pension Plan

1. Retirement at age 70 is mandatory. A person's birthday shall be considered to have occurred on the first of January of the calendar year in which it actually occurred.

2. Full retirement benefits shall be payable to a retiring partner (not an associate) who has attained age 65 and who has either twenty-five years of service with the firm as a partner or thirty years total service as a partner and associate.

3. A partner may voluntarily retire with full retirement benefits prior to the mandatory retirement age at the end of any calendar month after completing the mentioned years of service with the firm and attaining age 65.

4. Early retirement is permitted for any partner who has completed the mentioned years of service with the firm at the end of any calendar month after the partner's 55th birthday, but in such case retirement benefits are reduced by .33 percent per month (4 percent per year) for each month that the early retirement anticipates the time at which the partner would qualify for full retirement benefits.

5. A retiring partner shall not receive any payment for accounts receivable at the time of such partner's retirement or any payment in consideration of the value of work in process at the time of retirement. Nor shall a retiring partner be entitled to share in any particular business for which the firm is likely to be paid in the future, regardless of such partner's involvement with that business. Such partner shall not be entitled to a share of any particular fee that will be received in the future for work done in the past. A retiring partner shall not be entitled to share in fees paid after such partner's retirement by any particular client or clients for which such partner has been responsible during such partner's career.

6. A retiring partner shall not be permitted to retain fees to which such partner might be entitled as an executor/executrix, trustee, receiver, or other fiduciary, if those fees would have been income of the firm under the partnership agreement were such partner an active partner.

7. A retiring partner shall be obligated prior to such partner's retirement, as well as subsequent thereto, to the fullest extent such partner is able to do so, to see to the gradual turnover of clients to the younger lawyers, and wherever possible, such partner also shall try to turn over directorships and fiduciary positions to the younger lawyers.

8. The only payment other than retirement benefits that the retiring partner shall be entitled to receive is a return of such partner's capital contributions to the firm, payable in such manner as shall be mutually agreed upon.

9. A retired partner may not engage in competitive activities of any kind.

10. A retired partner shall be entitled to an annual pension for life equal to 20 percent of the average of such partner's annual earnings (excluding earnings under the "windfall" clause of the Partnership Memorandum) during such partner's best five consecutive years as an active partner, payable in equal monthly amounts.

11. Should such supplemental pension payments extend beyond thirty-six months, there shall be an upward or downward cost-of-living adjustment between the thirty-sixth and thirty-seventh monthly payments in such amount as to cause the thirty-seventh monthly payment to have the same purchasing power as the first monthly payment had (followed by similar cost-of-living adjustments each subsequent thirty-six months that payments are being made). Such cost-of-living adjustments shall be based on the Consumer Price Index for All Urban Consumers (CPI-U) issued by the Department of Labor office in Philadelphia.

12. A retired partner may become of counsel, but not automatically. Such partner may enjoy status only by mutual agreement with the continuing firm, which means by invitation on an annual basis, and such status shall terminate at such time as the continuing firm thereafter determines.

13. A retired partner who is of counsel and whose yearly pension payments exceed $36,000 shall not be entitled to receive from the continuing firm any additional compensation for such partner's of-counsel services except such as may be awarded such partner under the "windfall" provision stated in paragraph 16 below.

14. A retired partner who is of counsel and whose yearly pension payments are less than $36,000 shall be entitled to receive compensation for such partner's of-counsel services at the yearly rate of 50

percent of the sum of such partner's service credits since retirement on any bill submitted by the firm and paid since retirement during that year. In no event, however, shall such yearly of-counsel compensation exceed such amount as causes that compensation when added to such partner's yearly pension payments to exceed the aggregate sum of $36,000.

15. There shall be an upward or downward cost-of-living adjustment to the aforementioned $36,000 limit each year hereafter, to the nearest $1,000 based upon the Consumer Price Index for All Urban Consumers (CPI-U) issued by the Department of Labor office in Philadelphia, so as to cause such limit in subsequent years to have relatively the same financial impact it had on January 1, 1990.

16. Should the continuing firm receive a fee in excess of $200,000 (sometimes referred to as a "windfall") attributable in whole or large measure to the service, effort, or other influence of a retired partner, the continuing firm, in its sole discretion, may grant such partner an equitable portion of such fee, and any such windfall allowance shall not be subject to the of-counsel compensation limit prescribed in paragraph 14 above.

17. In the event of the death of a retired partner, whether of counsel or not, prior to such partner's receipt of sixty monthly payments of the mentioned supplemental pension, such partner shall be considered to have a vested property right in at least sixty months of retirement payments, and to the extent that such partner did not receive that number of payments, the balance of said vested payments, as they fall due monthly, shall be paid to such partner's estate or designee.

18. The firm shall never in any one year be obligated to make aggregate disability, pension, and death payments (current or in arrears) that exceed 10 percent of the firm's net income that year as reported for federal income tax purposes.

    If the aggregate payments for all such categories of obligations would exceed that limit, then the priority shall be to pay current disability payments first, current pension obligations second, current death payments third, and prior arrearages last, in the same order of priority.

    If any disability, pension, or death payment otherwise due is not paid by reason of the 10 percent limitation, it shall be paid in future years, but only out of the excess that may exist in any fiscal year in the difference of the amount of the current obligations for such year for those purposes and the maximum limitation of 10 percent of the net income for the year.

    Unpaid disability, pension, and death obligations for past years shall not bear interest, but they shall have no cutoff date beyond which the same are no longer obligations, the only limitation being the ability of the continuing firm to pay both accruing obligations and past due obligations out of 10 percent of the net income, except that the continuing firm's obligations to pay pension arrearages to any retired partner shall terminate upon such partner's death.

19. In the event of the liquidation of the firm, its obligation to pay retirement benefits shall be subject to the prior return to the continuing partners of their capital contributions and shall be limited to the remaining assets (including accounts receivable and the value of work in process) and the income of the continuing firm and its net assets. There shall be no personal liability of any individual partner in connection therewith.

20. There can be no modification of retirement benefits affecting the interest attributable to any partner after such partner's retirement without such partner's written consent or the written consent of such partner's successor in interest; there can be no modification of the retirement plan as it affects benefits for any active partner after he or she has attained age 55 without his or her consent.

21. Subject to the preceding paragraph, any change or modification in the retirement plan, once adopted, may be made only by the affirmative vote of two-thirds of the partners in interest, and on such questions, those partners who have attained age 55 shall also vote.

PLAN B
Retirement, Death, and Disability Policy

The following is the policy of _____ as to the retirement, death, and disability of partners.

1. Purpose—Right to Change

The firm desires to be fair and equitable in compensating senior partners who have retired while at the same time maintaining the highest quality of service for its clients. Although no two individual situations are alike, in order to maintain uniformity and to allow future planning, both on the part of the partner and of the firm, it is necessary that certain rules and policies be established. The firm reserves the right to change the policy in the future if it should appear to the firm that the policy is no longer fair and equitable, either to the partners affected thereby or to the firm.

2. Executive Committee Power

Nothing herein contained is intended to restrict the executive committee of the firm or the firm itself from making continuing contracts with retired partners relative to their participation in firm affairs, either legal or administrative, provided such contracts shall be on a year-to-year basis only and shall be for the calendar year. It shall be the general policy that a retired partner shall be entitled to an office, secretarial service, and other fringe benefits, including participation in health and welfare benefits and club dues where appropriate.

3. Birth Date

For the purposes of this policy, the birthday of all partners shall be considered to occur on the last day of the year in which their birthday actually occurs.

4. Partnership Agreement

The partnership agreement shall remain in full force and effect, including the provisions for retirement, death, and disability, except as specifically altered or amended by the provisions contained in this policy.

5. Retirement Age

Any partner after age 62 may elect to take full retirement or planned retirement as set forth herein, but such election must be made no later than on attaining of age 67. If full retirement is elected, it shall be governed by the provisions in the partnership agreement.

6. Planned Retirement

If planned retirement is elected, the compensation to the partner shall be as follows:

6.1   The capital account of the partner shall be computed in the normal manner as of the date of the election and shall include the partner's percentage of the accounts receivable. The amount so computed shall be divided into sixty payments and paid monthly commencing January 1.

6.2   The partner's percentage used for the allocation of partnership profits in the year prior to retirement shall become the fixed percentage of the partner, but this percentage figure shall be adjusted up or down each year by the same amount that 100 divided by the number of partners changes from the retirement year.

6.3   The partner shall be paid 90 percent of the amount that would be computed using the fixed percentage figure the first year of planned retirement, 80 percent the second year, 70 percent the third year, 60 percent the fourth year, and 50 percent the fifth year.

6.4   It is contemplated that the partner will reduce his or her legal activity and the time spent on firm business by a similar percentage, but it is understood that the reduction in time and effort will not be uniform and the partner may want to take a sabbatical leave or extended vacation in any particular year or years during the planned retirement and that the objective is to have the work load reduced to 50 percent by the end of the fifth year.

6.5   At the end of the fifth year, the partner's interest shall be terminated and he or she shall cease to be a partner, but shall be entitled to one-half of the extended draw amounts that were paid during the fifth year for life, payable monthly. He or she may become of counsel or assume such other status and receive such other compensation as the executive committee may determine.

7. Duties of Retired Partner

It is understood that the retired partner will continue to promote the interest of the firm and will not in any way enter into any competition with the firm during the time when he or she is receiving the benefits. If a retired partner practices law outside of the firm without the consent of the firm, the partner may forfeit the right to receive all or part of further benefits pursuant to this plan.

8. *Group Life Insurance*

The firm will maintain its group life insurance policy on the partner retiring at the maximum amount to age 75 and will pay any benefits from said policy to the heirs of the partner. Such payment shall be in full discharge of any and all interest that the partner may have in the firm or to future payments. The firm shall have no obligation to make any other payment to the estate of a deceased partner other than from insurance proceeds, except for amounts due on the capital account, which shall be paid on schedule.

9. *Disability*

In the event of the total or partial disability of the partner during the planned retirement program, the payments set forth hereunder shall continue for a period of one year, after which time the executive committee shall be authorized to reduce the payments and the benefits under the program in accordance with the situation then existing, but in no event shall said payments or benefits be reduced by more than one-half.

10. *Payment Limits*

In no event shall the payments to the retired partners under the planned retirement program exceed 10 percent of the net income of the partnership for the previous year. If it appears that said payments might exceed the limited amount, the executive committee shall have the power to proportionately reduce the payments to each beneficiary in order that the amount may stay within the limit.

11. *Effective Date*

This policy shall become effective on January 1, 1993, and shall not apply to any partner who has reached age 67 by that date.

PLAN C
Retirement, Death, and Disability Policy

The following is the policy of _____ as to:

1. The retirement of partners;
2. Payments to be made to partners who hereafter retire, partially retire, become disabled, or withdraw from the firm;
3. Payments to be made upon the death of a partner.

The right of a partner to withdraw his or her capital as reflected on the books of the partnership upon retirement, death, or disability is not covered by this plan since provisions therefor are or will be set forth in the partnership agreement of the firm. The provisions herein contained for payments to a partner upon retirement, death, disability, or withdrawal are intended to provide complete compensation to the partner for services rendered to the firm prior to retirement, death, disability, or withdrawal and are in lieu of any other form of compensation therefor.

In the past the firm has endeavored to be fair and equitable in compensating partners who have retired or become disabled and the beneficiaries of deceased partners, and the firm intends to continue to do so. The policy herein stated represents the present view of the firm as to what will be fair and equitable in the future. The firm reserves the right to change the policy in the future if it should appear to the firm that the policy is no longer fair and equitable either to partners affected thereby or to the firm.

Sec. 1 *Definitions.* When used herein the following terms (and adaptations thereof) shall have the following meanings:

   1.1 *Retirement* means complete or substantial cessation of the practice of law as a member of the firm. Retired partners include both those who after retirement continue affiliation with the firm and those who withdraw from the firm. "Retired partners" do not include partially retired lawyers. Retirement may be of three types:

      1.1.1 *Normal retirement* is retirement after reaching normal retirement age.

      1.1.2 *Retirement on account of disability* is retirement by a partner who has not reached normal retirement age or who has not elected early retirement, as the result of a determination that the partner suffers from disability.

      1.1.3 *Early retirement* is retirement prior to normal retirement age with the consent of the firm by a partner who has reached sixty years of age and who has completed twenty or more years of service with the firm as a partner.

   1.2 *Partial retirement* means reduction of activity in the practice of law and continuation of affiliation with the firm.

   1.3 *Withdrawal* means severance of affiliation with the firm. Withdrawal may be for a purpose that the firm does or does not regard as competitive.

   1.4 *Disability* means that in the judgment of the firm a partner has become physically or mentally incapacitated to the extent that he or she is unable to perform work to the firm's standards.

   1.5 *Normal retirement age* of a partner is the first day of the fiscal year of the firm nearest to the birthday on which the partner becomes sixty-seven years of age.

   1.6 *Net income* means the gross income of the firm excluding the proceeds of life insurance policies paid to the firm, less all expenses incurred in producing such income. Such expenses shall include, but not be limited to:

      (a) normal retirement benefits paid (2.3);

      (b) early retirement benefits paid (2.4);

      (c) disability benefits paid not covered by insurance (5.3.2);

      (d) death benefits paid under 6.2.3. and 6.3 to the extent not covered by insurance payable to the firm;

      (e) death benefits paid to the beneficiary of a disabled partner pursuant to 6.4 to the extent that the same are based upon or in lieu of those for which provision is made in 6.2.3 and are not covered by insurance payable to the firm;

      (f) premiums paid for life insurance and disability insurance for partners;

      (g) depreciation of the fixed assets of the firm as reported for federal income tax purposes; and

(h) interest on amounts borrowed by the firm.

Such expenses shall not include:

(a) payments to a withdrawing partner (section 3);

(b) distributions to a partially retired partner (section 4);

(c) payment to a partner of the proceeds of a disability insurance policy maintained by the firm for a partner (5.2);

(d) payments to a disabled partner based upon a percentage of the firm's income (5.3.1); and

(e) payments to the beneficiary of a deceased partner based upon a percentage of the firm's income (6.2.1, 6.2.2, and 6.4).

1.7 *Adjusted net income* shall mean net income plus the expenses referred to in subparagraphs (a), (b), (c), (d), (e), and (f) of the second paragraph of 1.6.

Sec. 2 *Retirement.*

2.1 *Voluntary retirement.* Each partner shall have an absolute right to retire and to receive the benefits herein provided upon reaching normal retirement age.

2.2 *Compulsory retirement.* The firm will have the right to require any partner to retire in any case in which the firm finds that the partner has become disabled. A partner will automatically be retired upon the first day of the fiscal year of the firm nearest to the birthday on which the partner becomes 72 years of age, unless he or she and the firm agree that he or she shall thereafter continue in the practice of law. A partner who has been required to retire will receive normal retirement benefits if he or she retires after reaching retirement age. Otherwise he or she will receive disability retirement benefits.

2.3 *Payments to a partner who retires after reaching normal retirement age.* A partner who has retired after reaching normal retirement age shall receive for the remainder of his or her life the normal retirement benefit. The normal retirement benefit shall be the sum of $3,000 per month adjusted at the beginning of each fiscal year of the partnership in proportion to the percentage, if any, by which the cost-of-living index for _____ published by the Bureau of Labor Statistics of the Department of Labor of the United States has increased or decreased between September 1, 1967, and the beginning of the applicable year. In the event that the Bureau of Labor Statistics shall cease to publish a cost-of-living index for _____ , the firm shall elect in lieu thereof such other index as it deems most nearly approximate the index now published for _____ . Adjustments in the normal retirement benefit will apply both to partners who are retiring in the year in which the adjustment is made and to partners who have retired in any previous year.

2.4 *Payments to partners upon early retirement.* A partner who has elected early retirement with the consent of the firm shall be entitled to receive for the remainder of his or her life the normal retirement benefit reduced on an actuarial basis to reflect the longer period for which the partner may expect to receive benefits.

2.5 *Office space and secretarial service.* A retired partner who continues to be affiliated with the firm will be entitled to reasonable office space and reasonable secretarial assistance.

2.6 *Restriction on activities of a retired partner.* A partner who has retired will not engage in the practice of law except with the consent of the firm. If a retired partner practices law outside of the firm without the consent of the firm, the firm may cancel his or her right to receive all or part of further benefits pursuant to this plan.

Sec. 3 *Withdrawal.*

3.1 *Payment to be made to all partners who withdraw from the firm.* Any partner who withdraws from the firm shall be entitled to receive for his or her services during the portion of the fiscal year of the firm prior to the date of withdrawal a sum equal to such partner's percentage of the net income of the firm for the year in which the withdrawal occurs multiplied by a fraction in which the numerator is the number of full calendar months that have elapsed during the fiscal year prior to the date of withdrawal and the denominator is twelve. There shall be deducted the amounts of such net income that such partner has already received prior to the time of his or her withdrawal.

3.2 *Additional payment to withdrawing partner who does not propose to compete with the firm.* The firm shall pay to a partner who withdraws from the firm for the purpose of engaging in an activity that the firm does not regard as competitive an additional sum equal to one-third the partner's percentage of the net income of the firm for the year in which the withdrawal occurs. The partnership may as a condition of making such payment require the withdrawing partner to execute a covenant with the firm that he or she will not engage for such period as the firm regards as reasonable in activity that the firm regards as competitive.

3.3 *Time for payments.* Payments to be made pursuant to this section shall be paid to the partner entitled thereto as of August 31 of the fiscal year of the partnership in which withdrawal occurs as soon after such date as the amount thereof is determined by the firm's accountants. The firm may if it so elects make advances against the payments due.

Sec. 4 *Partial retirement.* Upon reaching normal retirement age a partner will be deemed to be partially retired. Commencing with the year in which a partner is deemed partially retired his or her participation in the profits of the firm will normally be reduced in accordance with guidelines set forth below. Participation may be varied, however, at the discretion of the partnership either upward or downward from the guideline basis in cases in which there is a sound reason for such variation. It is contemplated that the effective input of a partially retired partner will gradually decline because of a combination of naturally existing factors. These would include reduction in vigor because of age and perhaps ill health, gradual withdrawal from assumption of primary responsibility for servicing particular clients, a reduction in intensity of work, a shift of emphasis from original work and major direct responsibility to a more often advisory function, and a reduction in the hours per day and days per year spent in the office. It is the expectation of the firm that partially retired partner's contribution to the firm, considering all of these factors, will remain generally commensurate with his or her percentage of participation under the guidelines. Because the partner's contribution depends upon many relevant factors in addition to time spent in the office, it is not contemplated that a partially retired partner's work year would be automatically reduced in proportion to his or her guideline level of compensation.

The normal adjustment will be made in accordance with the following guideline:

(a) There shall first be determined the average percentage paid to all partners during the five years preceding the first year of partial retirement. This is obtained by dividing into 100 the number of persons who were partners during each of such years and averaging the results. For the purpose of determining the number of partners in each year, each partially retired partner shall be given the same weight as the portion of the basic percentage to which he or she was entitled during the year in question. _____ shall be given the weight of 50 percent in each year in which his or her percentage is to be taken into account.

For example, if in a given year there were twenty-five active partners and one partially retired partner receiving 83.33 percent of his or her basic percentage as hereinafter set forth, the total of 25.833 would be divided into 100 and the average percentage for that year would be 3.88.

(b) The partially retired partner's actual percentage during each of the five years preceding the first year of partial retirement shall then be averaged.

(c) The difference between (b) and (a) will be divided by (a) to obtain the partner's "basic deviation from average."

For example, if a partner's average percentage during the five-year period preceding the year of partial retirement were 6 percent and the average partnership percentage were 4 percent, the partner's basic deviation from average would be plus 50 percent.

(d) During each year of partial retirement the partner's "basic percentage" will be calculated by adding or subtracting his or her basic deviation from average to or from the average partnership percentage for that particular year. This is determined by dividing 100 by the number of persons who will be partners during such year, including all partially retired partners, on a weighted basis as described in (a) above.

For example, if the average partnership percentage for the particular year were 3.8 and the partially retired partner's basic deviation from average were plus 50 percent, his or her basic percentage would be 5.7 percent.

(e) The partner shall receive a portion of his or her basic percentage in each year of partial retirement as follows:

First year	83.33 percent
Second year	66.33 percent
Third year	50 percent
Fourth year	33.33 percent
Fifth year	25 percent
Sixth year	Fully retired

However, in no year would a partially retired partner receive less than the then-current full retirement benefit.

For example, assuming that a partner's basic deviation from average is plus 50 percent and the average percentage of the partners remains at 4 percent during each of the partner's partial retirement years, his or her basic percentage would be 6 percent and the actual percentage during the first year of retirement would be 5 percent; during the second year 4 percent; during the third year 3 percent; during the fourth year 2 percent; and during the fifth year 1.5 percent. In the sixth year he or she would be considered fully retired.

For the purpose of these calculations amounts paid to partners other than in accordance with percentage will be disregarded.

Sec. 5 *Disability.*

5.1 *Determination of disability.* The firm will have the absolute right to determine whether or not and when a partner has become disabled and when such disability has ceased. Such determination may be made retroactively at any time after the disability occurs, including a time after the death of a partner.

5.2 *Insurance payments upon disability.* In the event that the firm shall maintain a policy of disability insurance for the benefit of the partner, the partner will be entitled to receive the entire proceeds of such insurance policy in the event of his or her disability.

5.3 *Payments by firm upon disability.*

5.3.1 *Payments for first year following disability.* A disabled partner will be paid his or her percentage of the net income of the firm for a period of one year from the date upon which the firm finds that the disability occurred, subject to proration as provided in 6.2.1 in the event of death. The firm shall have the right to adjust the partner's percentage at the beginning of the fiscal year of the partnership during the period of disability in accordance with the firm's normal practices as if no disability had occurred. The amount paid during the second fiscal year shall be calculated by multiplying the partner's income for the year based upon such

new percentage by a fraction in which the numerator is the number of days during such year for which such partner was entitled to disability benefits and the denominator is 365. Payments shall be made at such time as may be fixed by the firm, provided that final payment shall be made at the time that the audit of the books of the firm is complete for the fiscal year with respect to which the last payment is to be made.

5.3.2 *Payments following first year of disability.* Upon the expiration of one year from the date upon which the firm determines that a disability has occurred, the disabled partner will cease being compensated by the partnership on a percentage basis. Effective upon the expiration of such one-year period the firm will pay to such partner for the remainder of his or her life or until the firm finds that the disability has ceased the normal retirement benefit for a partner who has retired upon reaching normal retirement age actuarially reduced to take account of the longer period for which the benefit may be paid, related back to the date of disability. The firm shall be entitled to deduct from monthly payments to be made pursuant to this section the amount of any payment due the partner on account of disability insurance provided for the partner by the firm. The firm will not be entitled to reimbursement for any amount by which the insurance payment exceeds the disability payment due.

Sec. 6 *Death.*

6.1 *To whom payments made.* Payments to be made pursuant to this section shall be made to any person designated by the partner to receive such payments pursuant to written instrument executed by the partner and filed with the firm by the partner prior to his or her death. In the absence of such designation such payments shall be made to the estate of the deceased partner. The one who is to receive such payments is herein called "the partner's beneficiary" or the "beneficiary of a partner."

6.2 *Payments upon death of a partner who has not retired.* The beneficiary of a partner who dies prior to retirement, other than retirement on account of disability, shall be paid the following sums:

6.2.1 The beneficiary shall be paid a portion of the net income of the firm for the year in which death occurs equal to that deceased partner's percentage of such income for such year multiplied by a fraction in which the numerator is the number of calendar months that have elapsed in such fiscal year to the date of death, including the month in which death occurs, and in which the denominator is twelve. There shall be deducted therefrom the amount of such net income already withdrawn by the deceased partner prior to the date of death. Payments to be made pursuant to this section shall be paid to the beneficiary entitled thereto as of August 31 of the fiscal year of the partnership in which death occurs as soon after such date as the amount thereof is determined by the firm's accountants. The firm may if it so elects make advances against the payments due.

6.2.2 The beneficiary shall be paid an additional sum equal to one-half of the partner's percentage of the net income of the firm for the year in which death occurs. Such sum shall be paid in monthly installments equal to the then-applicable normal retirement benefit commencing on the first day of the second month following the month in which death occurs and continuing until the entire amount due is paid, provided that by agreement between the parties the firm may make advances of the amount due pursuant to this section.

6.2.3 The beneficiary will be entitled to receive a normal retirement benefit for a period of sixty months. The first payment will be made on the first day of the month succeeding the month in which the last payment to be made in the full amount of the normal retirement benefit is paid pursuant to subparagraph 6.2.2 above.

6.2.4 If a partially retired partner shall die in a year in which his or her percentage of the net income of the firm is less than the then-current full retirement benefit payable with respect to such year, the benefits payable pursuant to 6.2.1 and 6.2.2 will be based upon the then-current full retirement benefit with respect to such year rather than upon the deceased partner's percentage of the net income of the firm for such year.

6.3 *Payments upon death of a retired partner.* The beneficiary of a partner who has retired for reasons other than disability shall receive a normal retirement benefit or benefit payable upon early retirement, whichever the partner was receiving prior to the date of death, for a period of sixty months following the date of death less the number of months in which he or she has already received normal retirement benefits or early retirement benefits.

6.4 *Payments upon death of a partner who has retired on account of disability.* The beneficiary of a partner who dies following the date as of which the firm finds that the partner was disabled will be entitled to receive the benefits specified in 6.2, except that there shall be deducted therefrom amounts that such partner was entitled to receive pursuant to 5.3.1 and except that if the partner was receiving payments pursuant to section 5.3.2 at the time of death such payment shall be continued for a period of sixty months from the date of death in lieu of the payment to be made pursuant to 6.2.3.

6.5 *Limitation on benefits to be paid pursuant to this section.* No payments need to be made pursuant to 6.2.3 or 6.3 or of the benefits provided in 6.4 that are based on or in lieu of the provisions of 6.2.3 if at the time payment is due neither a spouse nor minor child of the deceased partner shall survive him or her.

Sec. 7 *Limitation on amount to be paid.* If in any year the sum of all payments to which reference is made in subparagraphs (a), (b), (c), (d), (e), and (f) of the second paragraph of 1.6 shall exceed 20 percent of the adjusted net income of the firm for such year, each of those who have received the payments referred to in such subparagraphs (a), (b), (c), (d), and (e) shall rebate to the firm on a pro rata basis a sufficient amount of such payments so that the total of such payments shall not exceed 20 percent of the adjusted net income of the firm for such year. Any repayment to be made pursuant to the preceding sentence may be made over a period of twelve months. If in any year the firm anticipates that the limitation set forth in this section will be applicable it may reduce payments with respect to which the limitation is applicable in accordance with its estimate of the adjusted net income for such year. At the end of any such year an appropriate adjustment will be made so that the amounts paid for such year shall be in accordance with the provisions of this plan including the provisions of this section.

Sec. 8 *Determinations.* The determination as to the amount of net income and adjusted net income of the firm in any year shall be made by the certified public accountant regularly employed by the firm, whose determination shall be binding. All other determinations to be made pursuant to this plan shall be made by the firm. In the event that there is ambiguity in this plan or if any provision of the plan needs interpretation the firm shall have the right to resolve the ambiguity or to make the interpretation and its decision shall be final.

18
The Social Security Cash Machine

JONATHAN BARRY FORMAN

As a theoretical model of social planning and reward for hard work, the Social Security System's Old-Age and Survivors Insurance (OASI) program is a thing of beauty. In this largest U.S. social welfare program, which collected $317 billion in payroll taxes in 1996 and distributed $299 billion in benefits that same year, workers pay taxes with the assurance that, when they retire or die, they or their families will receive their just rewards.

If only reality fit the model. The truth is that the OASI's outflow of benefits is based on calculations that unfairly favor some workers and their families over others. Simply stated: Low earners do better than high earners. Married couples do better than single individuals. Single-earner couples do better than dual-earner couples. And elderly retirees do better than elderly workers.

Cash In, Benefits Out

OASI benefits are overwhelmingly financed through payroll taxes imposed on individuals working in employment or self-employment that is covered by the Social Security system. For 1998, employees and employers each pay a tax of 5.35 percent on up to $68,400 of wages earned in covered employment, for a combined OASI rate of 10.7 percent (the lion's share of the total rate of 15.3 percent that is collected for OASI, disability insurance, and Medicare, the three components of Social Security). Self-employed workers pay an equivalent OASI tax of 10.7 percent on up to $68,400 of net earnings.

Jonathan Barry Forman is a professor of law at the University of Oklahoma in Norman. He holds degrees in law, economics, and psychology. He is the author of numerous articles on Social Security, tax, and pension law.

In addition, as much as 85 percent of a taxpayer's Social Security benefits is subject to income taxation. The actual amount to be included is determined by applying a complicated two-tier formula. Basically, single taxpayers with incomes greater than $25,000 and married couples with incomes greater than $32,000 must include as much as half of their Social Security benefits in income, and single taxpayers with incomes greater than $34,000 and married couples with incomes greater than $44,000 must include as much as 85 percent of their Social Security benefits in income.

Workers older than age 62 generally are entitled to OASI benefits if they have worked in covered employment for at least ten years. Benefits are based on a measure of the worker's earnings history in covered employment known as the average indexed monthly earnings (AIME). Basically, the AIME measures the worker's career-average monthly earnings in covered employment.

The AIME is linked by a formula to the monthly retirement benefit payable to the worker at normal retirement age, a benefit known as the primary insurance amount (PIA). For a worker turning 62 in 1998, the PIA is equal to 90 percent of the first $477 of the worker's AIME, plus 32 percent of the AIME over $477 and through $2,875 (if any), and plus 15 percent of the AIME over $2,875 (if any). It is worth noting that, on its face, the benefit formula is progressive, meaning it is designed to favor workers with relatively low career-average earnings.

A worker's benefits may be increased or decreased for several reasons. Most important, benefits are indexed each year for inflation as measured by the increase in the Consumer Price Index. Also, benefits payable to workers who choose to retire after their normal retirement age are actuarially increased through the delayed retirement credit. On the other hand, workers who retire before age 65 have their benefits actuarially reduced. The so-called retirement earnings test can reduce the benefits of individuals who continue to work after retirement. For example, in 1998, workers age 65 through 69 lose $1 of benefits for every $2 of annual earnings greater than $14,500.

The retired worker, of course, is not the only beneficiary of OASI. Dependents and survivors of the worker may also receive additional monthly benefits. These so-called auxiliary benefit amounts are also based on the worker's PIA. For convenience, worker and auxiliary benefits are generally combined into a single monthly check.

For example, a 65-year-old wife or husband of the retired worker is entitled to a monthly spousal benefit equal to 50 percent of the worker's PIA. Consequently, a retired worker and spouse generally can claim a monthly benefit equal to 150 percent of what the retired worker alone could claim. Alternatively, a 65-year-old widow or widower of the worker is entitled to a monthly surviving spouse benefit equal to 100 percent of the worker's PIA. Auxiliary beneficiaries can begin receiving actuarially reduced benefits before age 65.

These auxiliary benefit amounts are subject to a variety of limitations. For example, the retirement earnings test also limits the benefits paid to auxiliary beneficiaries who continue to work. Also, the maximum monthly benefit that can be paid with respect to any worker is limited to between 150 and 188 percent of the worker's PIA. Under the so-called dual entitlement rule, when an individual is entitled both to a worker's benefit and also to a benefit as an auxiliary of another worker, only the larger of the two benefits is paid.

Your Money's Worth?

So how well do workers who have paid into the Social Security system fare when the time comes for them to be on the receiving end? The best way to understand OASI's distribution features is to evaluate the program's impact over the course of a worker's lifetime. This lifetime perspective leads to a comparison between the OASI taxes paid by a worker and the expected benefits.

For example, one might compare the expected value at age 65 of the OASI taxes that a worker paid over a career, together with interest at a market rate on those tax payments, with the expected value at age 65 of the stream of OASI benefits that the worker can expect to receive for life. The worker will receive his or her "money's worth" if the expected value of benefits to be received equals the expected value of all taxes paid. If the expected value of taxes paid exceeds the expected value of benefits, then the worker would, in effect, be paying other program participants. But if the expected value of benefits exceeds the expected value of the taxes paid, then the worker would be receiving extra benefits from other participants.

Numerous studies have made just such comparisons. Their results clearly show that the linkage between the OASI taxes paid by a worker and the expected benefits is quite loose and can vary dramatically depending on such factors as family status, income, and age. If we compare the current OASI program to a model in which each worker earned an actuarially fair rate of return on taxes paid, we can see that the current program results in significant transfers that favor some workers over others.

In short, not everyone gets his or her "money's worth." In particular, the current OASI program favors early generations of retirees over later generations, low earners over high earners, married couples over single individuals, larger families over smaller families, single-earner couples over dual-earner couples, and elderly retirees over elderly workers. We'll discuss these in turn.

1. *Early generations versus later generations:* Early generations of OASI beneficiaries have received disproportionately greater benefits than their meager tax contributions might otherwise justify. Their rich rewards were the inevitable consequences of two facts: (a) early participants paid relatively low taxes over relatively short coverage periods, yet (b) they received relatively generous benefits over relatively long benefit periods. Subsequent retirees have also benefitted from low tax rates and frequent increases in benefit levels. Thus, the OASI program favors early generations of beneficiaries over later generations.

Fortunately, the OASI program is close to maturity, with most workers having been in covered employment or self-employment throughout their careers. And both the OASI tax rate and tax base have been increased for actuarial soundness. Accordingly, studies project that by the time the baby boomers retire (starting around 2010), the value of the OASI benefits they will receive should roughly equal the value of the OASI taxes they paid. Generations retiring prior to 2010 will receive more favorable treatment, but the size of these intergenerational transfers will diminish over time. Consequently, in coming years a worker's generation will be a factor of decreasing significance.

2. *Low earners versus high earners:* Because of the progressive formula used to compute OASI benefits, workers with low earnings over their careers tend to receive disproportionately greater benefits than workers with high earnings. We need to note, however, that this redistribution occurs only within the limited range of covered earnings (up to $68,400 in 1998), and that above this cap, earnings are not redistributed. Also, this progressive redistribution (from high-income to low-income workers) may be somewhat offset by the longer life expectancies of high-income workers and their spouses and by the greater likelihood that spousal and surviving spouse benefits will be paid to spouses of high earners.

3. *Married couples versus single individuals; larger families vs. smaller families:* Because of spousal and surviving spouse benefits, married couples tend to receive relatively more benefits than single individuals. Similarly, because of other auxiliary benefits, larger families fare better than smaller families. In essence, the benefits received by larger families are subsidized by the taxes paid by individuals and smaller families, regardless of their ability to pay.

Indeed, perhaps one of the most significant features of the OASI program is that married couples are so heavily favored over single individuals. Specifically, a single worker with no dependents will receive a benefit at normal retirement age of just 100 percent of the worker's PIA, while a worker with a spouse will receive 150 percent of the worker's PIA, and a surviving spouse can receive 100 percent of the worker's benefit long after the worker's death.

Furthermore, providing auxiliary benefits for other dependents favors larger families over smaller families and single individuals. In that regard, a worker with a spouse and additional dependents could receive a monthly benefit of as high as 188 percent of the worker's PIA, yet a worker with a spouse and no other dependents would receive a monthly benefit of just 150 percent of the PIA. A single worker would receive a monthly benefit of just 100 percent of the PIA.

4. *Single-earner versus dual-earner couples:* Two additional problems result from providing spousal and surviving spouse benefits based on the earnings of the retired worker. First, two-earner couples generally receive lower total benefits than one-earner couples with the same earnings. Second, because married women with earnings usually have earned less and worked a shorter time than their husbands, they often receive little or no additional OASI benefits from their OASI tax payments. Let's examine these two types of inequities.

(a) *The penalty on dual-earner couples:* The individual income tax is based on individual income, but married couples may file jointly and enjoy preferential tax rates. On the other hand, the OASI tax is based on individual filing units (workers), but OASI benefits are paid based on certain family unit relationships (workers and their auxiliaries). Consequently, the OASI tax and benefit structure can result in significant penalties on dual-earner couples as opposed to single-earner couples.

Table 18–1 compares the OASI benefit entitlement of four couples with various average annual lifetime earnings. All of the couples reached age 65 in 1992.

Even though the Cleavers, Bunkers, and Keatons all had the same average annual lifetime earnings and so paid the same total OASI taxes, their respective OASI worker and spousal benefits vary dramatically, depending upon the relative earnings of the two spouses.

The Cleavers, a single-earner couple, end up with the highest combined worker and spousal benefit ($1,435 per month). That's $250 a month more than either the Bunkers or the Keatons, the dual-earner couples with identical family earnings ($24,000 per year). Moreover, the Seavers receive absolutely no family benefit over the Cleavers, despite the fact that the Seavers consistently paid OASI taxes on $8,000 a year more family earnings.

Similar inequities can be observed when surviving spouse benefits are considered. The table

Table 18-1

Average Annual Lifetime Earnings and 1992 Monthly Social Security Retirement Benefits[a]

	Cleavers	Bunkers	Keatons	Seavers
Earnings				
Husband	$24,000	$16,000	$12,000	$24,000
Wife	0	8,000	12,000	8,000
Family Total	$24,000	$24,000	$24,000	$32,000
Benefits				
Husband	$957	$712	$591	$957
	WB[b]	WB	WB	WB
Wife	$478	$468	$591	$478
	SB[b]	WB	WB	SB
Family Total	$1,435	$1,180	$1,182	$1,435
Survivor Benefits				
Amounts	$957	$712	$591[c]	$957
As Percent of Couples Benefit	67%	60%	50%	67%

[a]For workers retiring at age 65 in 1992.
[b]WB = Workers Benefit; SB = Spousal Benefit.
[c]Spouse continues to collect on her own benefit. Survivor benefit does not apply.

shows the amount of surviving spouse benefits that each wife could claim if she survived her husband. There again, even though the Cleavers, Bunkers, and Keatons all had the same average annual lifetime earnings, the Cleaver widow, in the single-earner couple, ends up with the highest surviving spouse benefit ($957). Moreover, the Seaver widow gains absolutely no additional surviving spouse benefit over the Cleaver widow, even though the Seavers consistently paid OASI taxes on $8,000 a year more in family earnings.

(b) *The penalty on secondary workers:* In fact, the tax penalty really falls on the secondary workers, those married individuals who earn less than their spouses. When a secondary worker is entitled to OASI benefits both as a retired worker and as a spouse (or surviving spouse) of a primary worker, the dual entitlement rule prevents the secondary worker from receiving both the full worker's benefit and the full spousal (or surviving spouse) benefit. Instead, only the larger of the two benefits is paid. The effect is that the secondary worker gets no return on OASI taxes paid unless the secondary worker's worker benefit exceeds the spousal (or surviving spouse) benefit based on the primary worker's earnings record.

Indeed, for many secondary workers in dual-earner couples, additional OASI taxes they paid will produce absolutely no more OASI benefits than if they had not worked at all and paid no OASI taxes. For spousal benefits, this inequity will occur any time the worker benefit earned by a husband is more than twice the worker benefit earned by his wife. She would then receive a greater OASI benefit as a spouse than as a retired worker.

For example, compare the Cleavers to the Seavers in the table. The Seavers' combined worker and spousal benefit is no larger than the total received by the Cleavers. In effect, the Seaver wife received absolutely no OASI benefit from the OASI taxes she paid on her $8,000 a year of earnings.

The situation is even worse regarding surviving spouse benefits. A surviving spouse will receive absolutely no OASI benefit from the OASI taxes that she paid unless her earnings were greater than her husband's.

In short, there are substantial penalties on dual-earner couples, in general, and on secondary workers, in particular.

As more and more women enter the workforce, these two inequities will become increasingly important. In 1930, women constituted just 22 percent of the workforce, yet by 1994 they had more than doubled their presence—to 46 percent of the workforce. Of the 20.8 million women 62 or older who received Social Security benefits in 1994, 7.5 million were entitled to benefits based only on their own earnings record, 8 million were entitled solely as wives or widows, and 5.3 million were dually entitled.

5. *Elderly retirees versus elderly workers:* Monthly OASI benefits are paid as a matter of right to any covered individual who retires at age 62 or older. But if such a person continues to work, his or her OASI benefits may be reduced by the OASI earnings test. Further, an individual who continues to work must continue to pay Social Security and income taxes on those subsequent earnings and may also have to pay income tax on a portion of the OASI benefits. Together, the earnings test and these tax provisions combine to subject some elderly individuals to astronomical marginal tax rates that unfairly discourage them from working. For example, a worker who faces the 28 percent income tax rate, the inclusion of 85 percent of his or her OASI benefits in income, and the 7.65 percent Social Security tax rate will face an effective marginal tax rate of almost 60 percent. Worse still, elderly workers who are also subject to the Social Security retirement earnings test can face even higher effective marginal tax rates.

Recent Proposals to Reform the Social Security System

The Social Security system is also in financial trouble. The trustees of the Social Security funds estimate that benefits will exceed income starting around 2010, and the program will be unable to pay full benefits after about 2029. In fact, the trustees estimate that the deficit over the traditional 75-year projection period is about 2 percent of payroll. In short, the federal government will need to either raise Social Security taxes or cut Social Security benefits. Not surprisingly, Social Security reform has become a hot topic in the past year or so.

1. *The 1994–1996 Social Security Advisory Council:* In January of 1997, the 1994–1996 Social Security Advisory Council issued a long-awaited report on how to reform the Social Security system. The council members were not able to achieve a consensus. Instead, three different reform proposals were offered for consideration. Under the so-called Maintain Benefits (MB)

approach supported by six of the thirteen council members, the current Social Security system would remain pretty much as it is, except for a few changes around the margins.

On the other hand, a majority of the Advisory Council (seven of the thirteen members) did favor making some fairly major changes to Social Security. In particular, these seven council members agreed that at least a portion of Social Security payroll tax contributions should be redirected into individual retirement savings accounts (IRSAs) that would invest in the stock market. Under the so-called Individual Accounts (IA) approach, these individual accounts would be held by the government, invested in secure equity funds, and annuitized on retirement. Alternatively, under the so-called Personal Security Accounts (PSA) approach endorsed by five council members, these individual accounts would be held by financial institutions and their investment would be directed by individual workers.

For example, under the Personal Security Accounts (PSA) plan, the current Social Security system would be replaced with a two-tiered system. The first tier would provide a flat retirement benefit for all workers, and the second tier would provide workers with privately owned individual retirement savings accounts, referred to as Personal Security Accounts (PSAs). The PSA plan called for the new system to be implemented on January 1, 1998. The PSA plan would be fully effective for workers under the age of 25; workers between 25 and 54 would receive a mix of benefits; and current retirees and workers age 55 and older would continue to be covered by the current Social Security system, with a few minor changes.

Under the first tier, workers younger than 25 in 1998 who work at least thirty-five years in covered employment would receive a flat dollar benefit equivalent to $410 monthly in 1996 dollars. These benefits would be financed by employer Social Security contributions. Workers age 25 to 54 would receive a composite tier-one benefit that would include their accrued benefit under the current Social Security system and a prorated share of the new tier-one flat benefit.

Under the second tier, the plan would create Personal Security Accounts (PSAs) that would be dedicated to retirement savings. These PSAs would be financed by reallocating 5 percentage points of the employee's share of OASI taxes. Every worker under the age of 55 in 1998 would participate in the 5 percent payroll reallocation and receive PSA benefits based on their accumulations plus interest. Individuals could begin withdrawing funds from their PSAs at age 62, and any funds remaining in their accounts at death could be passed on to their estates.

2. *The Committee for Economic Development:* Also this past year, the Committee for Economic Development issued a report on Social Security reform in which it advocated leaving the basic Social Security system pretty much intact but creating a second tier of privately owned, Personal Retirement Accounts (PRAs). Both employers and employees would be required to contribute 1.5 percent of payroll to these PRAs, and the self-employed would be required to contribute the entire 3 percent.

3. *Chilean-Style Privatization:* A number of analysts suggest that we should privatize Social Security, specifically by completely replacing the current Social Security system with a system of Individual Retirement Savings Accounts (IRSAs). Proponents of privatization typically point to the country of Chile, which began to privatize its Social Security system in 1981. Under Chile's new Social Security system, workers are required to contribute at least 10 percent of their salary to IRSAs held by private pension funds of their choosing. About twenty different companies manage these new IRSAs, subject to extensive regulation by the government.

The Chilean example is already being followed by a number of other countries, including Argentina, Colombia, Mexico, Peru, and Uruguay. For that matter, the World Bank has begun to encourage most countries to include IRSAs in their Social Security systems. Replacing a portion of Social Security with IRSAs has also found a good deal of support in Congress, in academic circles, and in the press.

Conclusion

This chapter raises some serious questions about the fairness of Social Security's OASI program. The current OASI program seems particularly unfair to single workers, dual-earner couples, and elderly workers. The OASI program also has financial problems. In short, it is time to reform the OASI program.

19
Social Security

HAROLD G. WREN

What Is Social Security

Every person thinking about retirement must think about Social Security. There is often a tendency to discount the significance of Social Security in the overall estate plan. But for most people, this is an unsound approach. For example, if your annual income will be $320,000, then your Social Security income of $16,000 a year (or 5 percent) may seem relatively unimportant. If your retirement income is going to be around $64,000, then the $16,000 a year that you receive from Social Security amounts to 25 percent of your retirement income; it is now much more significant.

Most of us will find that we are in the latter category. Hence, it makes sense to give some serious thought to our financial planning, using Social Security as the base for our retirement program.

What, then, is Social Security? These are the benefits that are paid monthly to the beneficiaries under the Old-Age, Survivors, and Disability Act (OASDI). While Social Security is sometimes used as a generic term to include several different solutions to social problems, such as unemployment or disability insurance, we use it here to refer to the benefits that are paid by the United States to those persons who have paid the OASDI tax throughout their working lives, with a view to receiving back an annuity for the rest of their life after they have retired. Most lawyers today will receive the maximum Social Security benefit when they retire. This monthly payment of their annuity then becomes the base of all of their retirement income.

Who Is Eligible?

Once you have decided to retire, the first step to take is to go to the Social Security office in your area and make application for receipt of benefits. The Social Security Administration suggests that you visit their office approximately six months before you plan to retire. Very few people in our society today are not covered by Social Security. The three most common groups that are ineligible for Social Security are (1) federal government employees hired prior to 1984, (2) about 30 percent of state and local government employees, and (3) railroad workers. Anyone else, age 62 or over, is eligible to apply for Social Security benefits.

When Social Security was first started, 65 was considered the normal retirement age. Under the Age Discrimination in Employment Act (ADEA), this normal retirement age was first increased to 70 and then eliminated altogether. As a result, most lawyers can continue to work indefinitely, if they should choose to do so. Most lawyers are covered by Social Security.

What Benefits Are Available?

Retirement Benefits

One of the first responsibilities of the retiring lawyer is to determine exactly what his or her entitlement will be upon retirement. Once you are 55 or older, the Social Security Administration (SSA) will figure your benefits before your retirement. You simply fill out a Request for Earnings and Benefit Estimate Statement form [Form SSA–7004–SM (SPEC) (4-95)]. (See the copy of the form on page 118.) Within six weeks or less, you will receive a statement telling you how much your monthly benefit check will be when you retire and how much Social Security will pay you and/or members of your family should you become disabled or die. With this knowledge, you will be much better able to determine your investment strategy to prepare for those years when you will be living on a fixed income.

Harold G. Wren is of counsel to the law firm of Voyles & Johnson, P.S.C., in Louisville, Kentucky.

Request for Earnings and Benefit Estimate Statement

Form Approved
OMB No. 0960-0466

☐ SP

☐ Please check this box if you want to get your statement in Spanish instead of English.

Please print or type your answers. When you have completed the form, fold it and mail it to us. (If you prefer to send your request using the Internet, contact us at http://www.ssa.gov)

1. Name shown on your Social Security card:

First Name _____ Middle Initial _____

Last Name Only _____

2. Your Social Security number as shown on your card:

☐☐☐ – ☐☐ – ☐☐☐☐

3. Your date of birth (Mo.-Day-Yr.)

☐☐ – ☐☐ – ☐☐☐☐

4. Other Social Security numbers you have used:

☐☐☐ – ☐☐ – ☐☐☐☐
☐☐☐ – ☐☐ – ☐☐☐☐

5. Your sex: ☐ Male ☐ Female

For items 6 and 8 show only earnings covered by Social Security. Do NOT include wages from State, local or Federal Government employment that are NOT covered for Social Security or that are covered ONLY by Medicare.

6. Show your actual earnings (wages and/or net self-employment income) for last year and your estimated earnings for this year.

A. Last year's actual earnings: *(Dollars Only)*

$ ☐☐☐ , ☐☐☐ . 0 0

B. This year's estimated earnings: *(Dollars Only)*

$ ☐☐☐ , ☐☐☐ . 0 0

7. Show the age at which you plan to stop working.

☐☐ *(Show only one age)*

8. Below, show the average yearly amount (not your total future lifetime earnings) that you think you will earn between now and when you plan to stop working. Include performance or scheduled pay increases or bonuses, but not cost-of-living increases.

If you expect to earn significantly more or less in the future due to promotions, job changes, part-time work, or an absence from the work force, enter the amount that most closely reflects your future average yearly earnings.

If you don't expect any significant changes, show the same amount you are earning now (the amount in 6B).

Future average yearly earnings: *(Dollars Only)*

$ ☐☐☐ , ☐☐☐ . 0 0

9. Do you want us to send the statement:
  • To you? Enter your name and mailing address.
  • To someone else (your accountant, pension plan, etc.)? Enter your name with "c/o" and the name and address of that person or organization.

Name _____

Street Address (Include Apt. No., P.O. Box, or Rural Route) _____

City _____ State _____ Zip Code _____

Notice:
I am asking for information about my own Social Security record or the record of a person I am authorized to represent. I understand that if I deliberately request information under false pretenses, I may be guilty of a Federal crime and could be fined and/or imprisoned. I authorize you to use a contractor to send the statement of earnings and benefit estimates to the person named in item 9.

▲

Please sign your name (Do Not Print)

_____

Date _____ (Area Code) Daytime Telephone No. _____

Form SSA-7004-SM Internet (6-98) Destroy prior editions

You will become entitled to the full benefit at age 65, the present normal retirement age. But the law allows you to take an early retirement, beginning at age 62, with a decreased benefit, or to delay your retirement until age 70, with an increased benefit.[1]

Beginning in 2004, the normal retirement age will increase by two-month increments for the next five years (2004 through 2008), reaching 66 in 2009. It will remain at that level through 2020, at which time it will begin another increase by two-month increments until it reaches 67 in 2026. The normal retirement age for surviving spouse's benefits will have a similar progression two years after the changes in the normal retirement age for worker benefits. Thus, the first two-month increment will be in 2006; the normal retirement age will reach 66 in 2011, and 67 in 2028.

All monthly benefits are based on the primary insurance amount (PIA). The formula for calculating your PIA is complicated, but personnel at the SSA will help you figure it out. If you are thinking of retiring, plan to visit the Social Security office nearest your home no later than three months before you reach the birthday after which you plan to retire.

To figure your PIA, you need to know your average indexed monthly earnings (AIME), based on your lifetime earnings history. If you were born in 1936 or later,[2] for each year, beginning with 1951, calculate either the maximum taxable amount or your taxable earnings for that year,[3] and multiply this amount by an index factor to account for inflation. This factor ranges from 9.25774 (that is, more than nine times) in 1951, to 1.00000 for 1996 and later years.

Next determine the number of years to be used in figuring your AIME. For most lawyers, this will be ten years. Assume that you plan to retire at 65. These would be your calculations: First, count the number of years after the year you turned 21 through the year that you became 61.[4]

1. See discussion of the delayed retirement credit, *infra* p. 121.
2. Persons born during the years 1928 through 1935, normally retiring during 1993 through 2000, use a special factor for each one of these years.
3. Most lawyers will use the maximum taxable amount for each year, but there may be years, especially in the early stages of a lawyer's career, when taxable earnings are controlling. Since only thirty-five years (out of forty) are considered in calculating your AIME, these early years will probably have little effect on your ultimate calculations.
4. For persons born in 1929 or earlier, count the years from 1950 through age 61.

This figure (40) represents the number of quarters of coverage (or ten years) you need to be fully insured. Divide your total earnings for the thirty-five highest years by 420 (i.e., 35 x 12) to get your average indexed monthly earnings (AIME). For most lawyers, this figure will be the maximum AIME permitted, or $4,144.

By referring to the appropriate tables, you can calculate your PIA and derive your monthly benefit. For most lawyers, in 1998, the maximum monthly benefit for an age-65 retiree is $1,342, or $16,104 annually. If you are married, your total monthly benefit will be 150 percent of this amount, or $2,013 ($24,156 annually).

If you elect to retire at 62, you will receive 80 percent of the PIA, which gives you a monthly benefit of $1,109,[5] or $13,308 annually. If you are married, your benefit will be $1,109 plus 37½ percent of your age-65 PIA ($520), or a total monthly benefit of $1,629 ($19,548 annually).

Spouse's Benefits

While retirement benefits are the most important part of Social Security, you should be familiar with some other benefits. If both spouses have worked all their lives, their monthly and annual benefits would be doubled to $2,684 monthly and $32,208 annually for an age-65 retirement and $2,218 and $26,616 for age 62. In the event of your death, your surviving spouse will continue to receive the Social Security to which you are entitled. If your spouse continues to care for a child under 16 (or any age, if the child was disabled prior to age 22), he or she will be entitled to an additional 50 percent of your entitlement.

Your divorced spouse may be entitled to benefits as early as age 62 if he or she was married to you for at least ten years. Divorced spouses are normally entitled to the same benefits as spouses. Ironically, however, the divorced spouse may receive more financial protection than the spouse, since the benefits for divorced spouses are not subject to the maximum family benefit. This benefit will terminate if the divorced spouse should remarry. And your divorced spouse can receive benefits if you are at least 62, whether retired or not, or if you are receiving Social Security disability benefits. If you are 62 but not

5. This figure represents the maximum benefit for a person electing benefits in 1998 who is 62 in that year. Because of actuarial factors, it is not precisely the same as 80 percent of the maximum monthly benefit for a person retiring at 65.

retired, then you must have been divorced at least two years earlier before the divorced spouse can receive benefits.

Child's Benefits

The Social Security law is very liberal in its definition of *child*. The term includes both legitimate and illegitimate natural children, adopted children, stepchildren, and dependent grandchildren (if their parents are deceased or disabled). To be eligible, a child must be under 18, under 19 if in high school, or any age if disabled before age 22. Each child is entitled to 50 percent of your PIA. Thus, if a child qualifies for Social Security on the facts above, he or she would be entitled to $671 per month.

Other Benefits

Survivors' benefits under Social Security are largely the same as those that the retiree, his or her spouse, and/or child might receive during retirement. A disabled surviving spouse age 50 to 59 who cannot work because of a severe mental or physical impairment will receive 71.5 percent of your PIA. There are also some special payments for persons who became 72 before 1968. These are designed for older persons (they would have to be at least 102 years old in 1998) who had little chance of becoming fully insured during their working years. There is also a lump-sum death benefit of $255, payable to the surviving spouse who was living with a deceased retiree at the time of his or her death. If no such person survives the decedent, payment may be made to certain other persons who qualify.

Disability Benefits

Up to this point, we have been dealing with those Social Security benefits that accompany retirement or death. But a person may be disabled even before he or she becomes eligible for retirement. Disability means that you are so severely impaired, either mentally or physically, that you are incapable of performing any substantial gainful work. To qualify for disability benefits, you must have earned a minimum number of quarters of coverage, and some of these must have been earned in recent years. The number of quarters required ranges from thirty-nine for those born in 1928 to six for those born after 1969. Disability benefits begin after a waiting period of five

months. To qualify, you must have been disabled throughout this period. Benefits can be paid retroactively for up to twelve months, not including the five-month waiting period. If a disabled person dies before filing a claim, the family can apply for the disability benefits within three months of his or her death. The amount of the disability benefit is the same as the normal retirement benefit at age 65, unless the person is already receiving a benefit reduced by having taken early retirement.

Calculating the Amount of Your Social Security Benefits

Importance of the Earnings Record

The most important single bit of information that you will need to calculate your entitlement will be your earnings record. As stated above, you can obtain this information from the SSA by filing a Request for Earnings and Benefit Estimate Statement. You can then calculate your AIME and PIA.

Effect of Other Pensions

In industrial America, corporations often integrate their pension plans with Social Security. Normally, this would not be true in the case of lawyers. Your primary problem will be the coordination of your Social Security with your other forms of retirement income and your investment program. For example, you may be drawing a pension from the military. This, along with your Social Security and sometimes a portion of your pension income, cannot be changed. You will continue to draw these amounts as long as you live, and your survivor will continue to draw a reduced benefit.

Some lawyers or their spouses may have worked for federal, state, or local government and were not covered by Social Security when that employment ended. In that event, two-thirds of the pension benefits from the government employment will be offset against any Social Security benefit for which you are eligible as a spouse, widow, or widower. This rule does not apply to certain persons who were beneficiaries during certain past time periods, for example: (1) those entitled to Social Security benefits before December 1977; (2) women (or men dependent on their wives) who received government pensions from December 1977 through November 1982; and (3) persons who received government pensions from December 1982 through January 1983, who were dependent on their spouses.

Once you have learned how much you and your spouse will need to live on in retirement, you are then free to budget any excess for investment purposes. Typically, you will have ninety days from the time you retire to roll over tax-free any portion of your pension.

Effect of Early Retirement

As indicated earlier, you can take early retirement at any time between age 62 and 65. For each month that you retire early, your PIA will be reduced by five-ninths of 1 percent. In other words, if you retired at exactly age 62, you would receive 80 percent of your normal PIA.

Delayed Retirement Credits

As noted earlier, you can increase your benefits by delaying your retirement to age 70. For those who reach 65 in 1998 or 1999, the amount of the delayed retirement credit (DRC) is an additional 5.5 percent. It then increases at the rate of one-half of 1 percent for every two-year period (6 percent for 2000–2001; 6.5 percent for 2002–2003; 7 percent for 2004–2005; 7.5 percent for 2006–2007) until it reaches 8 percent for 2008 and subsequent years.

A lawyer born in 1943, will reach 65 in 2008. If he then delays his retirement for five years until he reaches 70 in 2013, he will increase his monthly benefit by 40 percent to $1,879 per month, or $22,546 annually. If both spouses continue to work and then retire at age 70, their total annual income from Social Security for the family unit will be $45,092. As more and more people live beyond traditional life expectancies, more persons will opt for retirement at 70. This is consistent with the increase of the normal retirement age to 66 in 2009, and to 67 in 2026.

Earnings Limitations

By waiting until age 70 to retire, a lawyer may avoid the earnings limitations for years between 65 and 70. In 1998, the earnings limitation for persons under 65 is $9,120; for those who are 65 through 69, the limitation is $14,500. During the years 1999 through 2002, the limitation increases each year. For example, if a lawyer retires in 1998 at age 65, the limitation is $14,500. It then increases to $15,500 in 1999, $17,000 in 2000, $25,000 in 2001, and $30,000 in 2002.

For those younger than 65, the limitation reduces the lawyer's Social Security benefit by $1 for every $2 over the earnings limitation. For those 65 or older, the benefit is reduced by $1 for every $3 over the earnings limitation. If, for example, a lawyer retires on January 1, 1998, at age 65, and continues to earn $50,000 per year for the next five years, his Social Security benefit would be reduced each year by the following amounts:

Year	Age	Limitation	Excess	Reduction
1998	65	$14,500	$35,500	$11,833
1999	66	15,500	34,500	11,500
2000	67	17,000	33,000	11,000
2001	68	25,000	25,000	8,333
2002	69	30,000	20,000	6,667

When he reaches age 70 in 2003, his Social Security benefit would no longer be subject to the earnings limitation.[6]

If you are self-employed, you are also subject to the earnings limitation until age 70. The annual limitation is the same as that for employees. Under the special alternative test for the calendar year in which benefits begin, your work is examined to determine the months in which you performed *substantial* services in self-employment. The rule of thumb is that less than fifteen hours per month is not substantial; more than forty-five hours a month is substantial. Between these two figures, your actual services are examined.

If you have more than one business, the profits and losses of all of your businesses must be consolidated for purposes of the earnings limitation. If your total profit was over the earnings limitation, your Social Security benefits will be reduced even though one of your businesses may have lost money. Similarly, if self-employed and also employed by others, you must combine your salary and wages with any net profit or loss from self-employment for purposes of determining your earnings limitation.

Many items that would be taxable income for purposes of the federal income tax do not qualify as earnings for purposes of the earnings limitation. The following are typical examples:

1. Pensions and retirement pay
2. Payments from certain tax-exempt trust funds

---

6. If he reaches his 70th birthday in 2003 after January, he would be subject to the limitation for months in the calendar year before the month in which he reaches 70.

3. Dividends and interest from investments, and capital gains
4. Rental income (unless you are in real estate)
5. Noncash payments for domestic services
6. Tips not in cash or less than $20 per month
7. Sick pay
8. Workers' compensation and unemployment insurance benefits
9. Veterans' training pay
10. Reimbursement for travel or moving expenses
11. Damages, fees, interest, or penalties received in a court judgment (but not back pay)
12. Contest or lottery winnings

Applying for Benefits

When to File

Once you have decided that you are going to retire, how do you apply for benefits? Suppose you expect to reach age 70 on May 19, 1994, and retire sometime after that birthday. You should contact the SSA no later than three months before your seventieth birthday, that is, February 19, 1994. Actually, we urge you to file in January in the year in which you intend to retire.

Where to File

Normally, you will file your application for Social Security benefits with the office of the SSA that handles your particular zip code. The telephone service of the SSA is now fully automated, and you can dial 800-234-5772 for help. The SSA will often have one of its employees listening in on your conversation to guarantee that you receive prompt and courteous service. The district office of the SSA will give you precise instructions about what to bring when you file your application. Normally, you will want to have the earliest possible application date.

Evidence Required in Support of Application

An applicant for Social Security benefits must submit evidence to prove his or her identity and fulfillment of all requirements for the benefit being sought. In the case of someone who is retiring and who is not disabled, this usually means proving his or her age and any family relationships (for example, spouse or child) for whom benefit is sought. You should have little if any dif-

ficulty proving these facts. While the SSA prefers original records, it will accept certified copies. Birth certificates, religious birth records, marriage licenses and/or certificates, divorce decrees, and death certificates are the kinds of documents that you typically will be asked to present. It would be wise to call the district office prior to your visit to get precise knowledge of exactly what documents will be required.

If you are filing for disability benefits, you will have to present somewhat more complicated proof. All medical impairments are listed on Form SSA–3368–F8. Use the earliest possible date of initial disability. Give the full details about any medical treatment, including the names of providers. If it appears that it will take a while before all the details can be provided, give the SSA clerk a written statement of an intent to file so that the application will be dated as of the earlier date, rather than the one on which the completed form is actually received.

Time Limits

In the case of applications for benefits for Social Security during your retirement, it is wise to file well in advance of the time that you will become entitled. But applications may be filed after you have become entitled or even ceased to be entitled. The difficulty is that the latter applications may cause the person who is filing or members of the family to lose some benefits. For example, applications for old age and survivors' benefits that are filed after the first month of entitlement result in benefits only for a period preceding the filing of no more than six months. Applications for disability benefits are accepted up to twelve months after the disability is ended. If the delay is due to the applicant's physical or mental condition, such applications may be accepted up to thirty-six months after the disability has ended, if the disabled person is still alive.

Your Right to Appeal

The law provides a series of steps by which you may appeal a determination of the SSA on your entitlement to benefits. After the initial determination, you may request a reconsideration by filing Form SSA–561 within sixty days after the initial determination (within ten days to request continuation of benefits, and thirty days in the case of overpayment). You may appoint a representative, who need not be a lawyer, to help you review the case file and/or present additional evidence. The SSA reviews your case file and any such evidence and eventually issues a decision about its reconsideration.

Within sixty days thereafter, you may file a request for a hearing before an administrative law judge (ALJ) on Form HA–501. At the hearing, you and/or your representative may review the case file, provide new evidence, and present, subpoena, and cross-examine witnesses. Within sixty days after receiving the ALJ's decision, you may request (on Form HA–520) that the SSA Appeals Council review your case. This is the central review body within the SSA, which will normally reverse an ALJ only if it finds an abuse of discretion, error of law, a finding unsupported by evidence, or a broad policy issue affecting the public interest. Neither you nor your representative is present at this appellate review within the agency, but you may obtain copies of documents in the record and a copy of the transcript of oral evidence at the hearing. You may also file a brief and/or provide new evidence. All of the proceedings on this review go into your case file.

Within sixty days after receipt of the Appeals Council decision, a claimant may seek judicial review in the federal district court. The court reviews the entire case file and reaches a decision as in other cases of judicial review of actions of administrative agencies. In one situation, a claimant may obtain an expedited appeal to the federal district court following a reconsideration determination, an ALJ decision, or the filing of a request for appeals council review but with no final decision. This is where the claimant and the SSA agree that the only factor preventing a favorable determination for the claimant is a provision of the law that the claimant believes is unconstitutional. The claimant may then file an action in the federal district court within sixty days after he or she receives notice that such an agreement has been signed.

A lawyer who represents a client before the SSA in administrative proceedings may charge a fee with the approval of the SSA. If there should be litigation in the federal court, under the Equal Access to Justice Act (EAJA), the prevailing party may recover lawyers' fees, expenses, and costs of litigation.

Amount of Social Security Tax

Tax Rate

The tax rate for Social Security taxes has increased from 1 percent on the first $3,000 of earnings during the period from 1937 through 1949, to 7.65 percent on the first $68,400 of earnings in 1998. The employee maximum annual tax this year is $5,232.60. The tax rate is established by Congress. The maximum taxable amount increases each year, based on increases in the average wages and salaries of all employees in the country.

OASDI and HI

In legal theory, there are two Social Security taxes: (1) Old-Age, Survivors, and Disability Insurance (OASDI) and (2) Hospital Insurance (HI). OASDI pays for the typical Social Security benefits, and HI pays for Part A of Medicare—that is, hospital benefits for those who are covered. These two separate payroll taxes are added together and withheld from employees' wages. Since 1990, the tax rate for OASDI has been 6.20 percent on a maximum taxable amount, which reached $68,400 in 1998. For HI, the tax rate has been 1.45 percent on earnings, but with no limit on the taxable amount.

Beginning in 1994, *all* earnings are subject to taxation for purposes of hospital insurance, even though the concept of a maximum taxable amount will be retained for purposes of OASDI. Self-employed persons pay at a tax rate double that of employed persons—12.4 percent for OASDI and 2.9 percent for HI, or a total of 15.3 percent. But the self-employed person is permitted to reduce his or her adjusted gross income by one-half of this tax on his or her income tax return. The result is to equalize the tax effect on the self-employed person with that on the employee.

What Is Taxed?

What constitutes earnings for purposes of the Social Security taxes is roughly the same as what constitutes earned income for purposes of the federal income tax. Thus, meals and lodging provided by the employer are included, unless provided for the convenience of the employer. Similarly, tips, if they are $20 or more a month, are treated as regular wages. If you have two or more employers during a calendar year, each employer must withhold the Social Security taxes up to the maximum taxable amount (that is, $68,400). If your total earnings from all employers exceed this amount, you typically will overpay your taxes, and any amount over the maximum annual tax may be applied against the payment of your income taxes on Form 1040, or you may file a claim for refund.

Taxes After Retirement

A portion of your Social Security benefits (SSB) may be included in your gross income after you retire. Benefits include any social security payments plus any amounts withheld for Part B of Medicare. To place the burden of this tax on those best able to pay it, Congress adopted concepts of a "base amount" (BA) and "modified adjusted gross income" (MAGI) to provide a rule for taxing a portion of SSB. MAGI is defined as adjusted gross income plus tax-exempt interest plus certain foreign-source income. The law requires the recipient of SSB to include in gross income the *lesser* of (1) one-half of the SSB, or (2) one-half of the MAGI, plus the SSB, minus BA. For most taxpayers, the amount included in gross income will be simply one-half of the excess of Social Security benefits over the base amount.

The base amount for single persons (or married persons living apart for the entire year) is $25,000, and for married persons filing a joint return, $32,000. Taxpayers include 50 percent of the excess over these thresholds in adjusted gross income. Since 1994, single persons also include in gross income an *additional* 35 percent of SSB above $34,000; married persons filing a joint return, an additional 35 percent above $44,000. In other words, 85 percent of Social Security benefits above these thresholds will be included in the adjusted gross income of a recipient beneficiary.

20
The Simplified Retirement Plan Alternative

DAVID L. HIGGS

"Our life is frittered away by detail. . . . Simplify, simplify."[1] Few of us seem able—or willing—to follow Henry David Thoreau's advice to adopt a simple lifestyle. Perhaps the best we can hope for is to simplify some of the more complex tasks before us. Given increased technical requirements and government red tape, Thoreau's advice can be profitably applied to retirement plans in the 1990s.

The simplified employee pension (SEP) is indeed a simplified retirement plan alternative. A SEP operates in much the same manner as a traditional profit-sharing plan but with substantially reduced administrative time and expense. A SEP may be easily adopted (normally by use of a preprinted government form), requires neither submission to nor advance approval by the Internal Revenue Service, requires no annual tax return, and eliminates fiduciary responsibility.

A SEP permits deductible contributions by an employer in the same manner and amount as a traditional profit-sharing plan, and benefits accumulate on a tax-deferred basis for participants. A SEP allows an employer to substantially eliminate administrative expenses and at the same time maintain a retirement plan for its employees.

As is discussed below, some requirements associated with SEPs, such as expanded coverage and vesting requirements, may make SEPs less desirable for some employers than for others. A SEP is, however, a retirement plan alternative worth considering, especially for small employers.

Accumulation of Wealth

A SEP permits the tax-deferred accumulation of benefits for each participant in the same manner

as a traditional retirement plan. Contributions to the SEP by the employer are not included in the income of participants at the time such contributions are made. Employer contributions are made to the individual retirement account (IRA) of each SEP participant. The participant does not include the contribution amount in income until such time as a withdrawal is made from the IRA, which need not occur until the participant attains age 70½.[2]

As with any IRA, the earnings on investments are not subject to current income taxation. Earnings, like the SEP contributions, are not taxable to the participant until the participant receives an actual distribution from the IRA. More simply stated, the SEP/IRA permits tax-deferred growth of investments.

The tax-deferred growth within the SEP/IRA permits the accumulation of substantial wealth for a participant. The chart below illustrates the potential for accumulation of wealth within a SEP/IRA, assuming a regular annual contribution and a consistent rate of return of 10 percent annually.

Annual Contribution	Ten Years	Twenty Years	Thirty Years
$ 5,000	$ 79,687	$ 286,375	$ 822,470
$10,000	$159,374	$ 572,750	$1,644,940
$20,000	$319,468	$1,145,500	$3,289,880
$30,000	$479,202	$1,718,250	$4,934,820

Even if contributions are made for only ten years and then left to accumulate on a tax-deferred basis, the IRA amount will be substantial. For example, if the $159,374 (amount accumulated

David L. Higgs is a partner in the Peoria, Illinois, office of Husch & Eppenberger, LLC.

1. HENRY DAVID THOREAU, WALDEN 66 (Signet Classic edition, 1854).
2. 26 USC §§ 408(a)(6) and 401(a)(9). Distributions from an IRA must commence by April 15 of the year following the calendar year in which the participant attains age 70 and a half. (Hereafter, the Internal Revenue Code of 1986 (chapter 26 of the USC) will simply be referred to as "Code.")

after ten years of an annual $10,000 contribution) continues to grow for twenty more years (without further contributions) at 10 percent per year, the IRA value increases to over $1 million.

A SEP permits the accumulation of substantial wealth that may be available at retirement. While the benefits of compounding interest and tax-deferred growth are not peculiar to a SEP, this is one of the principal reasons for establishing and maintaining any retirement plan, including a SEP. By adopting a retirement plan and making consistent annual contributions, an employer can provide some retirement security for its employees and thereby make available a significant employee benefit.[3]

SEP Advantages

The tax-deferred growth within the SEP/IRA is not unlike the growth permitted in a participant's account in a traditional retirement plan, such as a profit-sharing plan. There are, however, certain distinct advantages of a SEP as compared to other tax-qualified retirement plans.

Simplified Adoption

For most employers, a SEP may be adopted by execution of a preprinted Internal Revenue Service form.[4] The form is only twelve lines (*not pages*) long. The form has been approved by the Internal Revenue Service to qualify as a SEP.

A SEP may be adopted by the employer at any time on or before the due date of the employer's income tax return for the year involved.[5] For example, if the employer is a sole proprietor who files income tax returns on a calendar-year basis, the employer could adopt a SEP for any given year until April 15 of the following year. A traditional retirement plan, by comparison, must be in writing and executed on or before the end of the

plan year to which it relates. (Funding of the traditional retirement plan need not necessarily be made before the end of the plan year, however.)

Because adopting the SEP document is so simple, the employer may save money that might otherwise be spent for professional services in adopting a traditional retirement plan. The Internal Revenue Service form is free, so there may be no need to pay a lawyer or benefit consultant to draft a specific plan or to pay any other person for a plan document. The SEP form is preapproved, so there need be no professional expense in securing a favorable ruling from the Internal Revenue Service in connection with its qualified status, and no user fees[6] will be paid to the Internal Revenue Service. Compared to a traditional retirement plan, adopting a SEP is usually easier and less expensive.

Simplified Administration

Once the SEP is adopted, the administration of the SEP is also simpler than for a traditional retirement plan. A SEP is funded through each participant's IRA; that is, the employer contribution is allocated and contributed to each IRA. There is no single trust that holds all the assets for the benefit of all plan participants. In a SEP, each participant has responsibility for investing his or her IRA account; the employer is not responsible for SEP/IRA investing. In fact, once the employer determines the annual contribution amount and contributes it to each participant's IRA for the year, it has no further administrative responsibility for the SEP.

Simplified Reporting and Disclosure

For a traditional retirement plan, a summary plan description must be prepared that summarizes the plan's content. The summary plan description must be furnished to each participant.[7] No such description is required for a SEP. A SEP participant need only be furnished a copy of the preprinted Internal Revenue Service form and the corresponding questions and answers on the back of the form.[8]

For a traditional retirement plan, employers must prepare and file an annual information

---

3. An employer must consider the direct cost of providing the retirement benefit for all employees and weigh that cost against the tax benefits for owners and the value of the employee benefit in attracting and retaining employees. An additional benefit to owners is that contributions to a retirement plan will generally not be subject to employment taxes.

4. Form 5305-SEP. This form may not be used if the sponsoring employer maintains any other tax-qualified plan or has ever maintained a defined benefit pension plan. This form may likewise not be used if the employer utilizes the services of leased employees as that term is defined in Code § 414(n). An employer who is not permitted to use the preprinted government form may be able to adopt a prototype SEP document from a brokerage firm or financial institution or may adopt an individually designed SEP.

5. Prop Regulation § 1.408-7(b).

6. On ruling requests submitted to the Internal Revenue Service, a user fee is required. For plans with fewer than 100 participants, the fee may be as much as $700. See Form 8717.

7. ERISA Regulation § 2520.104b-2(a).

8. Form 5305-SEP, Q&A-13. If the employer adopts a non-model SEP, the employer should furnish employees with a copy of Notice 81-1, 1981-1 C.B. 610.

return with the Internal Revenue Service on Form 5500 series. No such annual return is required for a SEP.[9]

A traditional retirement plan is obliged to furnish a statement to each participant each year of the participant's account balance, earnings and losses, and contributions. An employer that maintains a SEP is required only to furnish an annual statement to each active participant of the amount of the SEP contribution, if any, paid to the participant's IRA.[10]

Simplified Fiduciary Duties

A traditional retirement plan is administered by a plan administrator (often the employer), and plan assets are invested by a trustee (generally either a commercial trustee or an individual, such as the principal owner or the employer). Because of the discretion vested in these persons, they are considered fiduciaries with respect to the plan. As fiduciaries, they owe specific legal duties to plan participants, including the prudent investment of the plan assets.[11]

Since a SEP is funded through participant IRAs, the employer is in no way responsible for investing a participant's assets. Participants have complete responsibility for their own investing. The employer simply has no fiduciary duty with respect to investing assets.[12]

Simplified Summary

A SEP is indeed a simplified alternative to a traditional retirement plan. It may easily be adopted and administered with very little time or expense. And perhaps most importantly to some employers, a SEP can be operated without periodic reporting to or involvement by the Internal Revenue Service or the Department of Labor.

Technical Requirements for a SEP

A SEP is statutorily authorized by Internal Revenue Code section 408(k). Compared to a traditional retirement plan, a SEP calls for few technical requirements. Those few requirements are discussed below.

Written Plan

To establish a SEP, an employer must adopt and execute a written SEP document on or before the due date of the employer's income tax return for the year involved.[13] The written document should specify the manner in which the contributions are to be made, the eligibility requirements for participation, and the manner in which contributions are to be allocated to participants.

Participation

The eligibility requirements for a SEP are simpler and more liberal than those for a traditional retirement plan. Each employee who has attained age 21, has performed service for the employer during at least three of the preceding five years, and receives at least $300 (as indexed) in compensation from the employer during the year must participate in the SEP.[14] Part-time employees may not be excluded from participation, unless their compensation is below the threshold amount. The expansive coverage requirements for a SEP are a price of simplicity.

Leased employees are treated as employees for purposes of the participation requirement and may not be excluded from the SEP coverage.[15] Further, the term *employer* includes all corporations in a controlled group of corporations,[16] all commonly controlled trades or businesses,[17] and all members of an affiliated service group.[18] Each employee of the *employer*, as that term is defined in the aggregate, must be permitted to participate in the SEP.

The foregoing discussion notwithstanding, certain employees may be specifically excluded from participation in the SEP.[19] Employees who are covered by a collective bargaining agreement in which retirement benefits were the subject of good-faith bargaining and certain nonresident aliens are not required to participate in the SEP. Employees who have not met the minimum age, service, and compensation requirements may

---

9. Form 5305-SEP; ERISA Regulation § 2520.104-48.
10. Form 5305-SEP, Q&A-13.
11. ERISA § 404(a).
12. An employer that maintains an individual account plan, such as a profit-sharing plan, may reduce its fiduciary responsibility for plan investments if it allows for participant-directed accounts in accordance with ERISA § 404(c).
13. Code § 408(k)(5); Prop Regulation § 1.408-7(b).
14. Code § 408(k)(2).
15. Code § 414(n)(3). A leased employee is defined in Code § 414(n) and may be generally described as a person, other than an employee, who provides services to the recipient employer pursuant to an agreement with a third party and does so on a substantially full-time basis and at the primary direction of the recipient.
16. Code § 414(b).
17. Code § 414(c).
18. Code § 414(m).
19. Code § 408(k)(2).

also be excluded from participation until such time as those requirements are satisfied.

Contributions and Allocation Method

As with a traditional profit-sharing plan, employer contributions to a SEP are made at the discretion of the employer. The contribution amount may be varied from year to year, and in some years the employer may elect to make no contribution at all. Contributions that are made to the SEP may not impermissibly discriminate in favor of any highly compensated employee.[20] The method by which employer contributions are to be allocated to participants must be specified in the SEP document.[21]

In general, the allocation of contributions by an employer to a SEP must bear a uniform relation to compensation, and for this purpose compensation in excess of $150,000 (as indexed) may not be considered. Under this basic mandate, each participant would receive the same percentage of compensation as a contribution to the participant's SEP/IRA. This basic allocation method is illustrated as follows:

Name	Compensation	Contribution Allocated
Craig	$150,000	$22,500
Carolyn	$ 40,000	$ 6,000
Scott	$ 20,000	$ 3,000

In this example, since each of the three participants receives the same percentage of his or her compensation, 15 percent, this allocation method meets the SEP requirements.

As an alternative to the basic proportionate allocation method described above, a SEP may permissibly allocate contributions in a manner that integrates with Social Security in accordance with the permitted disparity rules.[22] Under an integrated SEP, the more highly compensated employees will receive a greater percentage of the employer's contribution. Generally, integration is accomplished by allowing one contribution percentage for compensation in excess of the Social Security wage base and a different percentage for all other compensation.[23] An example of a permissible integration allocation is described as follows:

Name	Compensation	Contribution Allocated
Craig	$150,000	$22,500
Carolyn	$ 40,000	$ 4,673
Scott	$ 20,000	$ 2,336

As the example[24] illustrates, the more highly compensated employee, Craig, receives a disproportionate percentage of the contribution (15 percent) as compared to the lowest-paid employee, Scott (11.68 percent).[25] The integrated allocation method will allow an employer to provide a greater benefit to highly compensated employees than to rank-and-file employees.

Funding Through an IRA

A SEP must be funded through the IRA of each participant.[26] Each participant must establish a separate IRA into which the employer contributions are made each year.

Since contributions are made to a participant's IRA, the participant is in effect fully and immediately vested in the contribution; that is, the participant is entitled to the entire amount in the IRA whenever the participant desires. The distribution and taxation rules of an IRA apply, and the employer may not prevent a participant from withdrawing contributions from the IRA at any time.[27]

This full vesting requirement of a SEP is another liberalization of the rules that might otherwise be applied in the traditional profit-sharing plan. A traditional retirement plan may permissibly impose a graduated vesting schedule that states if an employee prematurely terminates service with the employer, the employee may forfeit all or a portion of the employee's plan benefit.

Federal Income Tax Consequences of a SEP

Employer

An employer is allowed a deduction for federal income tax purposes for contributions made to a SEP. An employer may deduct SEP contributions in an amount up to 15 percent of the aggregate

20. Code § 408(k)(3). "Highly compensated employee" is defined at Code § 414(q).
21. Code § 408(k)(5).
22. Code § 408(k)(3)(D).
23. Code § 401(1).

24. The example is based on an integration level at the 1996 taxable wage base and an integration rate of 5.7 percent.
25. A preprinted government form may not be used if the SEP utilizes an integrated allocation formula. In addition, if an integration formula is used and the SEP is top-heavy, certain minimum contributions may be required. Code § 408(k)(1)(B).
26. Code § 408(k)(1).
27. Code § 408(k)(4).

compensation paid to SEP participants during the year involved.[28] This is the same deduction limitation imposed on contributions to a traditional profit-sharing plan.

Employee

As is the case with a traditional retirement plan, an employee is not required to include in income the employer contributions to the participant's SEP/IRA. An employee may exclude from income contributions to the SEP/IRA in an amount equal to the lesser of 15 percent of compensation or $30,000 in any year.[29]

The normal rules of taxation of distributions from an IRA apply to the SEP/IRA. This means that the participant must include in income any distribution from the SEP/IRA in the year in which it is received. Distributions prior to age 59½ will normally be subject to an additional 10 percent early distribution penalty.[30]

The SIMPLE IRA Alternative

Prior to 1997, employees could include a salary reduction feature as part of a SEP. The salary reduction SEP allowed participating employees to elect to have a portion of their compensation contributed to the SEP on their behalf. After 1996, the salary reduction SEP may not be adopted. However, another simplified salary reduction arrangement is available—the SIMPLE IRA.[31] The SIMPLE IRA allows each eligible employee, along with the employer, to make contributions to the employee's IRA and accumulate funds for retirement on a tax-advantaged basis.

A SIMPLE IRA is an option for an employer with one hundred or fewer employees who receive $5,000 in compensation. In a SIMPLE IRA, all employees who receive at least $5,000 of compensation from the employer during any two preceding calendar years and who are expected to receive at least $5,000 of compensation in the current year must be eligible to participate. (Employees covered by a collective bargaining agreement and certain nonresident aliens may be excluded from coverage in the SIMPLE IRA.)

An employee participating in the SIMPLE IRA may make salary reduction contributions of up to $6,000 per year. (Unlike a 401(k) plan, there are no special nondiscrimination tests to be satisfied.) In addition, the employer must satisfy one of the following contribution formulas: (1) match employee contributions on a dollar-for-dollar basis up to 3 percent of compensation or (2) 2 percent of compensation contribution for each eligible employee whether or not the employee makes elective deferrals. (An employer may reduce the 3 percent matching contribution to 1 percent for limited periods of time.[32]) Other discretionary contributions by the employer are not permitted. Contributions to the SIMPLE IRA are excluded from employees' income for federal income tax purposes and are deductible by the employer. All contributions are fully vested.

Distributions from a SIMPLE IRA are generally taxed in the same manner as distributions from IRAs. A SIMPLE IRA account may be rolled over to an IRA after the employee has participated for at least two years. Also, during the first two years of participation, a distribution which is subject to the additional early distribution tax is taxed at a 25 percent rate rather than 10 percent.[33]

The SIMPLE IRA may be adopted by using a model form issued by the Internal Revenue Service.[34] As with the model SEP, the model SIMPLE IRA is not to be filed with the Internal Revenue Service. An employer may require that all contributions under the SIMPLE IRA be made to a particular financial institution, though there must be procedures in place to allow each participant to transfer the participant's contributions to another SIMPLE IRA or regular IRA selected by the participant.

The SIMPLE IRA also has simplified reporting requirements for both the trustee and sponsoring employer. The normal ERISA rules, such as filing the annual report with the Internal Revenue Service, do not apply. Also, fiduciary responsibility for investment performance will not apply to an employer to the extent the participant exercises control over the assets in the account.[35]

The SIMPLE IRA presents an attractive option for an employer who desires to allow employees to make salary-reduction contributions and for

28. Code § 404(h).
29. Code § 402(h).
30. Code § 72(t). There are exceptions to the early distribution penalty, including distributions that are part of a series of substantially equal periodic payments. See Code § 72(t)(2)(A)(iv).
31. The SIMPLE 401(k) is also similar to the SIMPLE IRA but is not discussed herein.

32. Code § 408(p)(2)(C)(ii).
33. Code § 72(t)(6).
34. Form 5305-SIMPLE or Form 5304-SIMPLE.
35. ERISA § 101(g).

which the employer will have limited contribution obligations and simplified administrative responsibilities.

Conclusion

An employer considering any retirement plan must give the matter thorough investigation and careful thought. For an employer looking to simplify its retirement plan, particularly a small employer, the SEP or SIMPLE IRA presents a simplified alternative. A SEP or SIMPLE IRA offers the benefits of a traditional retirement plan but with a simplified administrative process. Keep Thoreau's directive in mind: Simplify.

21
Rethinking Retirement

THOMAS A. HAUNTY

The only thing even more challenging than entering the practice of law today may be retiring from it. Economic, tax, and investment conditions are changing so dramatically that traditional methods and assumptions about retirement planning may no longer produce the nest egg that you need to support your retirement. Four important new financial realities must be addressed to assure a "successful" retirement.

Reality One

You will probably live longer. Through medical advances and improvements in diet and fitness, people can now expect to spend a longer portion of their lives in retirement. Unfortunately, this means your savings could expire before you do. Whatever your age, start saving for retirement now; through the magic of compounding, saving even a small percentage of your income can accumulate into a tidy nest egg over a number of years.

Reality Two

Pension plans are providing less.

In the past, retirement planning suggested that enough capital would be available for you to retire on as long as you contributed the maximum allowable percentage of income to your qualified pension plan each year. Today, this is no longer true because ceilings are being imposed on contribution levels, especially for firm owners, a category that generally includes most partners. Benefit payment levels also are limited and further reduced by taxes on mandatory distributions.

Thomas A. Haunty, a certified financial planner and registered health underwriter, is a senior associate at North Star Resource Group in Madison, Wisconsin, specializing in advising lawyers and law firms. Dionne C. Blaha assisted in the preparation of this article, which originally appeared in the July 1993 *ABA Journal*. Reprinted by permission.

Qualified plans should remain a part of your financial program because they offer the twin advantages of tax-deductible contributions and tax-deferred growth. However, they should no longer serve as the sole vehicle for developing retirement savings.

One supplemental retirement program gaining popularity is the Private Pension Plan (PPP), which provides the same tax-free buildup found in traditional qualified plans, but PPPs provide tax-free income at retirement. Because they are nonqualified, PPPs also do not have contribution ceilings.

Reality Three

Retirement is costing more. A common misconception is that personal and household expenses decline in retirement. The reality is that, while the nature of the expenses may be different, they are regularly increasing.

For example, many retirees face the same tax rate they did while working, due to deductions that have been curtailed or eliminated and additional taxes on Social Security benefits and mandatory distributions from individual retirement accounts and qualified pension plans.

Even taking into account the historical average 5 percent rise in the cost of living each year, general retirement expenses will double every fourteen years. Certain expenses incurred more frequently by retirees, such as health care, are actually increasing at almost double the general inflation rate.

Prudent planning suggests that retirees should employ the same strategies of tax elimination, reduction, and deferral that they sought to apply during their working years.

Reality Four

Personal saving is now a necessity. We tend to regard the federal government, through such sources as Social Security, and our employers as our primary sources of retirement income. In reality, many law firms are actually reducing contributions to pension plans to offset the rising costs of employee benefits, and Social Security is providing a lower percentage of preretirement income.

More than ever before, it is imperative that you redefine "living within your means" in order to contribute more to your savings. You must balance your financial priorities between today's lifestyle (while you have a paycheck) and tomorrow's anticipated retirement lifestyle, which will depend solely on the savings you have accumulated over your working life.

Try to live by the 80/20 rule, using 80 percent of your earnings for living expenses while saving the remaining 20 percent. Systematic savings programs, such as payroll deductions into pension plans and electronic transfers into mutual funds,

are invaluable at "forcing" you into the habit of saving.

Concentrate more of your investment holdings in common stocks, which have historically provided superior long-term returns.

How much will you need to have saved to provide a stream of income protected against inflation for thirty years? A reasonable estimate is twenty times your annual income goal. For example, a 65-year-old lawyer who plans to retire this year on a $50,000 annual income needs to have already saved $1 million in pensions and investments. However, for a younger lawyer planning to retire in twenty-five years or more, retirement income needs will likely be higher due to inflation, meaning that savings will have to be greater, as well.

If you do not save today, you will not be able to afford to retire later. Start now to make a comfortable retirement a reality.

22
ABA Members Retirement Program

SUSAN W. WHITE

The ABA Members Retirement Program is the most popular retirement program of its kind in America. It is a flexible, cost-effective, full-service program designed specifically to meet the retirement planning needs of the legal community. Working in partnership with the American Bar Retirement Association (ABRA), the sponsor of the program, State Street Bank and Trust Company serves as the program's investment manager, trustee, and administrator. This partnership combines ABRA's thirty years of experience in sponsoring the program with State Street's strength as a premier servicer of retirement plans.

From solo practitioners to large law firms, the ABA Members Retirement Program lets you design a retirement plan that meets your firm's unique requirements. By providing a broad menu of investment, administrative, and client services, the program answers the complex and diverse needs of law firms: responding to the financial requirements of partners, associates and staff; providing a variety of investment options; and assisting with both compliance testing and tax-reporting requirements, as well as providing ongoing employee communications programs. It provides you and your employees an effective way to build assets for your future while saving time and money. Whether your firm is establishing a plan for the first time or seeking to improve the design and service quality of an existing plan, we invite you to consider the advantages of a program that seeks to deliver exactly what today's law firms need: performance flexibility, and comprehensive, quality service.

Susan W. White is a vice president with State Street Global Advisors in Boston.

Our Commitment to You

The ABA Members Retirement Program's goal is to help law firms—both large and small—design retirement plans that incorporate the features that are most important to them. The program offers a wide range of plan designs, investment options, and participant services that make it very easy and cost-effective to provide your firm with a comprehensive retirement plan. Our aim is to provide you with the highest quality products and services possible.

A Single-Source Approach that Saves You Time and Money

The ABRA program's full-service approach eliminates the need for multiple-service providers. We manage all the components of an effective retirement program for you. The program combines the services of professional consulting, investment management, participant services, trust/custody, brokerage, recordkeeping, and administration. In addition to eliminating the time and resources needed to coordinate the activities of these key providers, the administration and the quality of your plan are enhanced by this streamlined approached. When you select the ABRA program, we work with you to develop a retirement plan tailored to your firm's needs. Then we make the rest easy for you.

Quality Investment Options Managed by Leading Advisors

To help reach those goals that will enable you to enjoy your retirement to its fullest, you need a wide range of high-quality investment options and confidence in the investment manager you choose. The ABRA program lets your participants take control of their financial future by enabling them to choose an investment mix best suited to their financial goals. Each investment option has distinct risk/reward characteristics—whether equities, balanced funds, fixed income options, or self-managed accounts. By effectively combining these options, participants can diversify their investment options, reduce their exposure to risk, and increase their opportunities for reward. The program's flexibility allows participants to change their investment strategy as their financial needs change. The program investment lineup includes:

- Core Fund Options. A wide selection of funds, ranging from equity and balanced funds to fixed-income options, to match a participant's investment objectives and outlook.
- Structured Portfolio Service. An asset allocation service that enables participants to choose a specific investment portfolio strategy—conservative, moderate, or aggressive—and have their retirement assets allocated automatically among the program's investment fund options to reflect the strategy selected.
- Self-Managed Account. A self-directed brokerage account providing access to publicly traded stocks, bonds, and thousands of mutual funds, many of which have no loads and no transaction fees.

A Full Range of Plan Designs

The ABRA program offers you a choice of retirement plans, each designed to fit specific needs and respond to the financial requirements of partners, associates, and staff.

"Profit sharing plans" offer firms the greatest flexibility in making contributions for participants. There need not be profits to make tax-deductible contributions to the plan. Each year you decide if and how much you will contribute to the plan—up to a maximum of all participants' compensation. Participants decide which investment options are right for their retirement goals.

"Money purchase pension plans," also called defined contribution plans, require the sponsoring firm to make regular contributions on behalf of participants. Contributions are determined by a formula based on each participant's compensation. The age of the participant does not affect contributions made on the participant's behalf. Employers are subject to tax penalties if the required contri-

bution is not made. Employers may contribute and deduct from their taxes up to a maximum of 25 percent of each participant's compensation or $30,000 per participant, whichever is less, subject to applicable deduction limits.

The 401(k) Options: Save for Your Retirement and Lower Current Taxes

Traditional 401(k) Plan

If you choose a defined contribution profit-sharing plan with a 401(k) option, your firm's eligible participants will have the opportunity to reduce their federal, and often state, income taxes through voluntary pretax savings contributions. If you choose to match employee contributions in whole or part, your firm will realize even greater tax savings. Contributions can be deducted automatically from participants' paychecks and may be invested in any of the program's investment options. Because it is the only employer-sponsored qualified retirement plan that allows participants to contribute current income on which taxes are deferred, the 401(k) plan is the fastest growing area of retirement planning.

SIMPLE 401(k) Plan

If you choose the SIMPLE 401(k), many of the administrative requirements that accompany the traditional 401(k) are eliminated. Like the traditional 401(k) plan, your firm's eligible participants will have the opportunity to contribute pretax dollars and reduce taxes. Unlike the traditional 401(k), the higher-paid employees deferrals are not contingent upon the lower-paid deferrals. This is due to the fact that SIMPLE 401(k) plans require the employer to fund the plan by matching participants contributions 100 percent up to 3 percent of annual compensation, or by making a flat contribution of 2 percent of all compensation to all eligible participants.

Choose from any of these plan designs and features. A plan consultant will work with you to identify your needs and help you choose the best solution.

Complete Accounting and Administrative Services

With the adoption of an ABRA plan, you receive plan accounting, participant accounting, and administrative services that use the most advanced technology to provide for the daily processing and valuation of investment funds. We assist you with both compliance testing and tax-reporting requirements and issue quarterly participant account statements. In addition, participants receive confirmation statements for all of their plan activity and are assured of accurate, immediate access to their accounts and plan information. From the beginning, the program team will work with you to ensure a smooth transition, and to keep your plan running smoothly.

Professional Plan Consulting Services

The ABRA program provides you with professional consulting services to assist you in establishing and maintaining your retirement plans(s). We will assist you in custom-tailoring annual contribution calculations to maximize the tax advantages of your plan. We will perform required 401(k) discrimination testing for your firm's profit sharing/401(k) plan. As regulatory resource consultants, we will help you keep abreast of IRS, Department of Labor, and Securities and Exchange Regulations that may affect your plan.

Our Commitment to Retirement Planning: Education and Access to Account Information

Travel. A retirement home. New hobbies. These are just a few of the dreams you and your colleagues may have for retirement. Since the ABRA program is an effective vehicle for tax-favored retirement savings and capital accumulation, it can help you realize these dreams. The success of your firm's retirement plan depends on how effectively it meets your participants' needs. The ABA Members Retirement Program offers a complete communications program designed to encourage participation and heighten enthusiasm. We provide easy-to-understand educational materials about the value of saving for retirement, the benefits of your firm's plan, the differences among the investment options, and the day-to-day mechanics of the plan—all the information your participants need to make informed investment choices. We offer a multimedia approach to communications that includes

enrollment packages, slides, quarterly newsletters, and phone lines. When you join the ABA Members Retirement Program, planning for your financial future is not a one-time event. Our ongoing communications approach keeps participants abreast of investment performance, changing market conditions, and tax laws. We will remind them that as their lives change, they can easily alter their investment selections.

An Unparalleled Commitment to the Legal Community and Retirement Planning

Founded in 1772, State Street has established a strong tradition of reliable and innovative services. Today, we focus on meeting demanding service requirements for managing and processing virtually all types of financial transactions. We provide custody services for nearly 40 percent of U.S. mutual funds, and we are the leading trustee for U.S. pension plans. With more than $300 billion in assets under management and more than $1.7 trillion under custody, State Street enjoys the confidence of thousands of institutional and individual investors.

Our expertise extends to all facets of defined contribution plans—investment management, participant and retiree services, trust/custody, brokerage, recordkeeping, and administration. More than 2.6 million defined contribution plan participants look to State Street for quality service every day.

Our approach is consultative, sharing ideas gained through years of experience working with our customers to help you build a plan that works—for today and tomorrow.

ABRA: Serving the Needs of the Legal Community

ABRA has been responding to the retirement needs of the legal community for more than thirty years. Our experience working in the retirement plan business enables us to draw on the knowledge and insight we have gained by working with the legal community. The ABA Members Retirement Program seeks to deliver exactly what today's law firms need: performance, flexibility, and comprehensive service. More than thirty-five thousand participants in 4,400 plans are taking

135

advantage of the ABA Members Retirement Program's wide range of retirement plans, investment options, and participant services to plan effectively for their futures.

An Unbeatable Combination

Today, the ABA Members Retirement Program proudly boasts more that four thousand member firms and retirement funds that total more than $3 billion. This unqualified level of success, with significant economies of scale, offers many benefits, not the least of which is the cost-effective approach we take to providing services to your firm. We are uniquely positioned to provide a broad investment portfolio, comprehensive administrative services, and professional custom service, while providing savings in enrollment, investment management, and administrative fees. So whether you are looking for a full-service program or wish to select stand-alone products, the ABRA program is a winning choice. Let us help you plan for your financial future.

To learn more about the ABA Members Retirement Program, please call (800) 826-8901.

23
Survey of Retirement, Death, Withdrawal, and Disability Partnership Agreement Clauses of Twenty Major U.S. Law Firms

STEPHEN N. MASKALERIS

The workforce in the United States is growing older. People are living longer and hence have the ability and desire to remain active on the job longer. The legal profession is not immune from such developments. Generally, it has become evident that firms are growing larger and their partners older, and, thus, the need to plan for the future security of firm members is a growing concern among young and old alike. In structuring a program, a firm must deal with the sensitive issues of determining the age of retirement; whether retirement should occur through a gradual phasing-out period or as a strict cutoff; the amount of retirement benefits; and what, if any, perquisites should be made available to the retiring partner. This article attempts to shed some light on the subjects of retirement, death, withdrawal, and disability programs through a review of the approaches taken by many of the largest law firms in the country as more particularly summarized in the attached bibliography.

Retirement

A review of retirement programs throughout the country indicates a uniform approach to retirement age. All of the firms surveyed allow for vol-

untary retirement, generally starting at age 60, with a requirement that the partner has been with the firm for a set number of years (usually fifteen to twenty years). Upon reaching the age at which they can voluntarily retire, partners must give their firms notice in advance, varying from as much as six months to as little as ninety days.

Mandatory retirement, on the other hand, is usually imposed on partners by their seventieth birthday, unless they are given permission to continue as active partners by a vote from the remaining partners. One firm in particular sets mandatory retirement at age 75, but only if a majority of the partners vote to impose this age limit. Such a policy leaves the matter of retirement to the individual whims of the partners. A formal, structured program would appear to be more desirable, however, as it eases the lawyer's transition into retirement and makes provisions for it.

The most equitable method is the structuring of a retirement program around a gradual reduction of active interest rather than an abrupt termination. An example of this would be a four-step phasing-out period starting at age 65 and continuing over a three-year time span. During each of the three years, the lawyer's partnership interest would be reduced by 16.67 percent, so that at the end of the third year, his or her partnership interest would be 50 percent of what it had been originally. This reduction in partnership

Stephen N. Maskaleris is the principal of Maskaleris & Associates, a Morristown, New Jersey, law firm. He founded the ABA's Senior Lawyers Division in 1984–85.

interest would correspond to a parallel reduction in the partner's workload and other responsibilities to the firm.

Upon mandatory retirement at age 70, the partner's retirement level of compensation would be determined by taking one-third of the highest interest the retiring partner received for any year following age 60. During this transition period, many firms require that the partners relinquish any administrative position, committee memberships, or offices presently held. This may appear to be somewhat harsh and unpleasant, but it is important to prepare the partner for the eventuality of retirement, and it also gives the firms time to find adequate replacements for the vacated posts.

Method and Allocation of Benefits

The firms vary greatly in determining the quantity and dispersal of retirement benefits. As a general rule, a standardized method of allocation should be employed. Perhaps the best way to explain the various programs of retirement allocation would be to present several examples. (See the Appendix.)

One firm led the way by setting a minimum monthly benefit of $3,000, calculated by taking one-half of 28 percent of the partner's final average annual compensation during the three highest years of the previous six years preceding retirement. From this amount, a "Keogh offset" was deducted in an amount equal to the monthly annuity payment that would be payable under a single-life annuity purchased at the time of retirement.

Some firms took a more simplified approach to allocating retirement benefits, and such a course of action is recommended, as is keeping the formula as simple and easy to understand as possible. For example, one firm simply pays 22 percent of an individual's average monthly compensation based on the partner's last two active years with the firm.

Another firm makes semiannual payments for the first ten years of retirement up to 25 percent of the partner's "normal average share," which is a figure used to determine the standard upon which percentage payments to the retiring partner will be based. In the particular agreement reviewed, the normal average share was determined by taking the average of one-third of the

sum of the partner's net income for the two years preceding his or her termination year. After the tenth year of retirement, the semiannual payments are reduced to 15 percent of the partner's normal average share.

An unusual approach taken by another firm used a lump sum method. This firm determined retirement income to be the greater amount of either:

1. $25,000 adjusted for the change in the Consumer Price Index; or
2. 25 percent of the retiring partner's average share of the firm's net income for the five consecutive years preceding the last ten years before the partner's sixty-fifth birthday during which his or her share of firm income had been the greatest.

Funding the Retirement Plan

Whether a firm pays retirement over the life of an individual or in a lump sum, the firm should set up funding for its program. Not to do so is foolhardy and financially unsound.

The great majority of firms reviewed funded their retirement programs through mandatory annual contributions by each partner to the firm's Keogh plan that range from 6 percent to 10 percent of each individual partner's total annual compensation. These firms estimated that such individual partner's mandatory contributions to the Keogh plan would fully fund the retirement benefits of those partners who are presently in their early to mid-40s. Older partners would receive supplementary payments from the current income of the firm, which would be added to the Keogh account to produce a straight-life annuity equal to 25 percent of the final average compensation for each retired partner.

Many firms finance Keogh plans on their own, without contributions from their members, while others contribute to the fund along with the partners. One firm in particular contributes the initial $7,500 to the retirement fund after which partners must pay 10 percent of their net earnings or $7,500, whichever is less, into the plan per annum.

Setting up some type of retirement reserve fund, therefore, as insurance against lean years of practice is obviously a sound idea. There is also a consensus among firms that a partner should receive his or her percentage interest of contribution paid into the firm's capital account as part of his or her overall retirement benefit package.

To insure against a firm's capital being drained by retirement benefit programs, most firms limit their aggregate benefit payments to a set percentage of the firm's net earnings for the fiscal year in question. The percentage limits range from 7.5 percent to 15 percent of the net earnings of the firm per fiscal year, with the majority opting for the latter limit. These fail-safe limits are an important part of any retirement program and should be included in any planned program.

Perks

Once a partner retires, his or her association with the firm should be encouraged to continue, unless the partner or the firm chooses otherwise. Most retired partners are either given the option of "of counsel" status or are voted such an honor. For the most part, firms also reserve office space and provide reasonable secretarial services to the retired partner. The only major limitation put on retired partners is that they may not continue to practice law outside of the firm in localities in which the firm maintains offices. Retired partners are very valuable firm assets and should be utilized where possible.

Death Benefits

Each firm has a different contingency plan for dealing with the death of a partner or former partner. One firm requires all partners up to the age of 65 to carry the group life insurance coverage the firm makes available. Thereafter, it is optional.

In addition to death benefits, most firms provide a deceased partner's estate with a portion of the partner's remaining pension benefits. Many firms make a distinction, however, between a partner who is already retired at the time of death and one who is still active. There is frequently a minimum number of years that a partner must have been with the firm prior to death before his or her estate can receive death benefits. Gradations in the size of death benefits are also common based on the number of years a partner has been with the firm.

Once eligibility for death benefits has been established, there are two common methods of payment:

1. Lump sum: A typical method of calculating a lump-sum payment is to average the partner's income over the previous three to five years. A percentage of this average yearly income becomes the lump sum. This percentage varies widely, ranging from 133 percent to 300 percent of the partner's average income. Other firms simply pay out whatever remaining funds are in a partner's retirement account.

2. Survivor's death benefits: Here the deceased names a beneficiary, or payments may be made to the deceased partner's estate if there is no named beneficiary. These benefit payments can range from 100 percent of what the partner would have received to a fractional percentage.

   The cutoff of these payments may be calculated in one of three ways: (1) when the partner's spouse dies; (2) when the partner's share of the retirement plan has been paid out (it should be noted that this is basically an extended form of the lump-sum payment, since the total payment is predetermined); or (3) when the partner would have achieved a certain age if he or she were alive; a frequent cutoff point is age 78.

Death benefits usually mirror retirement plans. The procedures by which a living retiree is paid determine the size and nature of death benefits. Death payments must be part of a holistic approach to retirement benefits.

Withdrawal

When a living partner withdraws from a firm before retirement age, payments are usually made in a similar fashion to death benefits. There is a minimum amount of time that a member must have been with the firm (typically two years) before being eligible to receive withdrawal payments. Withdrawal payments are universally lump-sum payments, although the firm may have a grace period of several months before it is required to pay a withdrawing member.

Some firms penalize a withdrawing partner by paying him or her only what was in his or her drawing account and earned income up to the date of withdrawal if the partner intends to practice law in the same jurisdiction. If the partner withdraws for another reason, he or she will receive retirement pay. Withdrawal should be in writing at least thirty days in advance. Usually, when a partner withdraws to compete with the firm, however, his or her withdrawal benefits are at peril.

It should also be noted that in the event of the death or withdrawal of a partner, his or her capital account balance is paid to the partner or estate, less any debts owed the firm.

In firms practicing as professional corporations, a dying, retiring, or withdrawing member's shares are bought back at face value upon the member's departure from the firm.

Disability

Many firms maintain health insurance coverage for their members as well. A distinction, however, is usually made between short- and long-term disability.

A typical provision is that a partner will receive full compensation during the first six months of disability; 66.66 percent during the next six months; and will be deemed to have withdrawn from the firm after one year of disability. A minority of firms immediately retire a partner deemed to be permanently disabled, relying on disability insurance provisions of their firm's agreements.

Conclusion

The common themes found running throughout the various retirement plans surveyed were security, predictability to ease the mind of the partners, and fairness so that each partner is dealt with equitably.

If a firm seeks to build, develop, and perpetuate an enduring professional organization, a structured program to deal with the eventualities of retirement, death, withdrawal, or disability is a necessity. The peace of mind such a program brings to a lawyer is of great benefit to the firm. Freed from the anxiety of an uncertain future, lawyers can devote their full energies to the practice of law without worrying about whether they are being treated fairly, whether they will be secure in their old age, or whether they will have to endure financial strain in the event of disability. A firm that is willing to offer an attractive ben-

efit package will be assured its partners will remain and will continue to work toward the expanded growth of the firm's practice.

In sum, much thought should be given to the topics of retirement, death, withdrawal, and disability, and simple, clear, and understandable agreements should be developed to effectuate the intentions of the partners of the firm. Any agreement is generally better than no agreement. The important thing is to make provision for these concerns in a firm's partnership agreement.

Research Note

This research has been compiled through a review of excerpts of partnership agreements dealing with the subjects of retirement, death, withdrawal, and disability from twenty of the largest law firms in the United States. Their cooperation has made this work possible, and I thank them for their aid. The author is also grateful for the services of Stephan Mashel, a second-year law student at Rutgers Camden Law School, and Robert Lavitt, an entering freshman law student at Boston University Law School.

The following is a breakdown of the sizes of the participating firms:

Total Number of Lawyers	Number of Firms
0–49	—
50–99	—
100–149	10
150–199	4
200–249	3
over 250	3

Total Number of Partners	Number of Firms
0–49	7
50–99	11
100–149	2
150–199	—
200–249	—
over 250	—

Total Number of Associates	Number of Firms
0–49	—
50–99	11
100–149	4
150–199	5
200–249	—
over 250	—

APPENDIX A

Retirement

Retirement is mandatory at age 70. After the age of 65, no partner is eligible to serve in an administrative or managerial capacity. In the event that a partner, other than a guaranteed partner, continues with the firm after the age of 65, his or her percentage interest in net distributable profits shall be reduced each year thereafter until the date of his or her mandatory retirement by one-fifth of the difference between his or her percentage interest at the end of the year in which he or she attains age 65 and the normal retirement factor applicable to him or her.

Retirement Benefits

A partner retiring on or after his or her normal retirement date (age 65) who, at the time of retirement, has been with the firm for at least twenty-five years, shall be entitled to a pension to be measured by such retiring partner's normal retirement factor.

A. Computation of Normal Retirement Factor

The normal retirement factor of a partner shall be a percentage computed as follows:

1. There shall be computed such partner's average annual remuneration (whether by way of participation in profits, capital payments, special fees, director's fees, interest on capital, or guaranties received by him or her) in the three of the ten years ending on such normal retirement date in which he or she received the highest remuneration; provided that if such partner's percentage interest in the net distributable profits of the firm shall have been reduced during such ten-year period, there may be included in such computation (if beneficial to such partner), in lieu of the lowest of the three years otherwise includable, the highest remuneration received by such partner in any year prior to such ten-year period.

2. There shall be determined the percentage that, if applied to the average net distributable profits of the firm for the three fiscal years ending on such partner's normal retirement date, would result in a dollar amount equal to 25 percent of such partner's average annual remuneration determined pursuant to clause (i) of this subparagraph A, and such percentage shall be his or her normal retirement factor.

Adjustment of Normal Retirement Factor for Less than Twenty-five Years with the Firm

If on retiring on or after the normal retirement date a partner shall have been with the firm less than twenty-five years, but at least twenty years, then the retirement factor shall be the normal retirement factor applicable to him or her multiplied by a fraction, the numerator of which shall be the number of years of his or her service with the firm and the denominator of which shall be twenty-five.

Computation of Joint and Survivor Pensions on Normal Retirement

If a partner elects, before retiring, to receive his or her pension as a joint and survivor pension, such partner's normal retirement factor (A) shall be adjusted by the firm's auditors on an actuarial basis to reflect a reduced retirement factor applicable to such partner and his or her survivor and such partner's election of a 100 percent, a 75 percent, or a 50 percent joint and survivor pension.

Normal Retirement After Less than Twenty Years with the Firm

If on retiring on or after normal retirement date, a partner shall have been with the firm less than twenty years, he or she shall not be entitled to any pension, but if he or she shall have been a partner in the firm for at least ten years, he or she shall be entitled to the payment of his or her inventory interest in equal monthly installments over a period of not more than five years. If with the firm less than ten years, he or she shall not be entitled to any payment of inventory interest.

B. Computation of Early Retirement Factor

The early retirement factor of a partner retiring as of an early retirement date shall be a percentage computed as follows:

1. There shall be computed such partner's average annual remuneration (whether by way of participation in profits, capital payments, special fees, director's fees, interest on capital, or guaranties received by him or her) in the three of the ten years ending on such early retirement date in which he or she received the highest remuneration; provided that if such partner's percentage interest in the net distributable profits of the firm shall have been reduced during such ten-year period, there may be included in such computation (if

beneficial to such partner), in lieu of the lowest of the three years otherwise includable, the highest remuneration received by such partner in any year prior to such ten-year period.

2. There shall be determined the percentage that, if applied to the average net distributable profits of the firm for the three fiscal years ending on such early retirement date, would result in a dollar amount equal to 25 percent of such partner's average annual remuneration determined pursuant to clause (i) of this subparagraph A.

3. The percentage determined in accordance with clause (ii) of this subparagraph A shall then be reduced by 5 percent thereof for each year by which such partner's early retirement date preceded his or her normal retirement date, and such percentage so reduced shall be his or her early retirement factor.

Adjustment of Early Retirement Factor for Less than Twenty-five Years with the Firm

If, on retiring early (age 60 to 65), a partner shall have been with the firm less than twenty-five years, but at least twenty years, then the retirement factor that shall be used in computing his or her pension shall be the early retirement factor applicable to him or her multiplied by a fraction, the numerator of which shall be the number of years of his or her service with the firm and the denominator twenty-five; less than twenty years with the firm, no pension. But if he or she has been with the firm at least ten years, he or she shall be entitled to the payment of his or her inventory interest over a period of not more than five years; less than ten years, no inventory interest.

Permanent Disability

Each partner in the firm agrees that the permanent disability of any partner shall be determined by a committee to be selected by the firm and to consist of five percentage partners; a majority vote of said partners shall determine if any partner is permanently disabled. If such a determination is made, he or she shall be entitled to such benefits.

Limitations Affecting Retirement Allowances

If the aggregate pensions payable to all retired partners shall exceed an amount equivalent to 10 percent of the net profits of the firm, such pensions shall be proportionately reduced so that the aggregate shall equal 10 percent of the net profits so increased.

If in any fiscal year of the firm (i) the total of all capital payments, director's fees, and payments to guaranteed partners in such year shall exceed 30 percent of (ii) an amount equal to the income of the firm less all expenses of operation for such year, then solely for the purpose of computing pensions based upon a percentage of net profits, the total of the items referred to in clause (i) of this sentence shall be deemed to be 30 percent of the amount determined pursuant to clause (ii) of this sentence.

Representing Clients

A retired partner who engages in the practice of law and in such practice, without the consent of the firm, represents clients who have been clients of the firm at any time within five years before the date for such partner's retirement shall be deemed to have waived all right to receive any further payments under any provision.

Death

A. If he or she was a guaranteed partner, a payment in an account equal to the annual guaranty to which he or she was entitled at the time of death;

B. If he or she was a percentage partner and at the time of his or her death shall have been with the firm as a partner for at least ten years, payment of his or her inventory interest in equal monthly installments over a period of not more than five years; and

C. If he or she was a percentage partner but at the time of death had been with the firm for less than ten years, a payment equivalent to his or her inventory interest multiplied by a fraction, the numerator of which shall be the number of full years that he or she was a partner and the denominator of which shall be ten.

Part III
Investment Strategies for the Potential Retiree

24
Your First Investment Advisor? You

ESTHER M. BERGER

The story is told of two rival Wall Street analysts who followed several major industries for their brokerage firms. Having disagreed about nearly everything for twenty years, these two amazed themselves by finally agreeing on something.

> "I'm not too sure what looks good to me right about now, Ed," Sam said.
> "Beats the heck out of me, too," Ed said.
> "Looks like we're not in Kansas anymore, Ed," Sam said.
> "Oz," said Ed, "we're definitely in Oz."

Rock-and-Roll Aftershocks

Ed and Sam are pretty much mirroring the confusion of many investors these days. Five-hundred-point drops in the Dow followed by consecutive one-hundred-point up days. Blue chips in favor, then small cap stocks leading the way. Investment truisms fall by the wayside as new "realities" emerge.

Whether or not you directly take part in this frenzy, your money is probably affected in some way. Indeed, you are among the lucky few if your bank savings rate, stock and bond investments, mutual funds, and—most important—pension plan assets have not been rocked by the aftershocks of the rock-and-roll markets.

Two Cs, Two Ds

Now more than ever is the time to understand—and return to—the basics of solid investing. Now more than ever is the time to reevaluate what you own and what you should own. By a simple investment strategy that I call the two Cs and two

Esther M. Berger is a certified financial planner and senior partner at the investment firm of Berger, Jaffe & Associates LLC in Beverly Hills. She is the author of *MoneySmart: Secrets Women Need to Know about Money* and *MoneySmart Divorce*.

Ds, you can maximize your investment dollars and help preserve the safety of your portfolio.

The first C is *common sense*—a simple tool that is surprisingly seldom used. Invest in what you understand, what makes sense to you. For example, the American population is clearly aging, so you might consider investing in companies that will benefit from an older population. The travel and leisure industries are obvious starting points, as are health-care providers and pharmaceutical companies. You should not invest in biotechnology if you do not really understand biotech. Stick with common sense.

The same logic applies to bond investments. Interest rates on short-term securities are at almost their lowest level in sixteen years. As billions of dollars worth of certificates of deposit and Treasuries mature, investors are experiencing the financial world's version of sticker shock—low, low interest rates. Many ultraconservative investors who are dissatisfied with current yields are considering their first foray into other types of financial instruments. Is this a good idea? Perhaps, but caveat emptor.

All sorts of investments are being touted these days as low-risk, high-yield alternatives. Some are; some are not. Government bond funds, for example, may be fine if they hold only government bonds. But if yields are boosted by adding corporate bonds, foreign bonds, or option strategies to the mix, be prepared for additional risk. While Treasuries and Treasury agencies (Ginnie Mae, Fannie Mae, Freddie Mac, and their relatives) are highly creditworthy, corporate bonds are only as creditworthy as the corporations that issue them and should be examined on a case-by-case basis, especially given the recent spate of downgradings.

Foreign bonds—even those of highly stable countries—have the potential drawback of currency risk. A weak U.S. dollar may result in capital gains, but a strengthening dollar may cut your total return substantially.

The Friendly Curve

The safest way to increase yield is by sticking with low-risk investments, such as Treasury securities, and by lengthening maturities. Look for value along the yield curve, but bear in mind that owning a thirty-year Treasury bond is considerably riskier than owning a three-month T-bill. Do not compare apples with oranges, even if they are both Treasury securities.

While long-term bonds *can* result in capital gains in a declining interest-rate environment, they carry substantial interest-rate risk if rates increase. They also carry substantial purchasing-power risk because they offer no inflation protection.

If you want to guarantee a specific and certain return for a future need, look into zero coupon bonds, which are issued at a discount and receive no interest payments (thus the "zero coupon") until maturity. The safest type of a zero is a zero coupon Treasury, which represents a future interest or principal payment on a U.S. Treasury bond or Treasury note. Zeros offer several benefits, including capital accumulation, attractive yields, liquidity, and a wide range of maturities.

However, zeros are volatile, and interest on those purchased outside a retirement plan may be taxed as current income even though you do not actually receive the income until the bonds mature. You can solve this problem by purchasing tax-free zero coupon municipal bonds.

Municipal bonds, zeros, corporate bonds, foreign bonds, and even U.S. government bonds must all be evaluated carefully. Perception does not always equal reality in the world of bonds, so never assume safety. Again, put your common sense to work.

Find a Comfort Zone

The second *C* in my investment strategy is *comfort level*. In simple English, don't do it if it doesn't feel right. Historically, stocks have proven to be excellent investments over time. From 1926 to 1996, blue-chip stocks, as represented by the Standard & Poor's 500, returned 10.7 percent versus 5.1 percent for U.S. government bonds. (More about this later.) But if stocks make you edgy, if you find yourself worrying too much about the day-to-day fluctuations of the stock market, you probably should not own stocks. Stay within your comfort level.

Some investments go in and out of favor, sometimes dramatically so. For a while, high-yield mutual funds (read "junk bonds") were popular. So, too, were second-trust deeds, gold, investing in penny stocks, investing in Japanese stocks, investing in Mexican stocks, and so on.

Always remember to trust your instincts in these situations. The "best" investment for this year, next year, or any year is the one that makes sense to you, helps you achieve your financial goals, and stays within your comfort level. If you are like many investors, you may be more comfortable owning mutual funds than attempting to construct your own do-it-yourself portfolio of stocks and bonds.

When the Feeling Is Mutual

Investing in a mutual fund is a way to invest in a professionally managed portfolio in which many investors' dollars are pooled. The investment dollars can be pooled in an income fund consisting of bonds, in a growth fund consisting of stocks, in a balanced fund that is a mix of stocks and bonds, or you can even go abroad with an international or global fund.

A mutual fund is a particularly good investment for people who want to start small, because the pooling of dollars allows for wide diversification. For instance, if you have $20,000 to invest, you will not be able to buy a well-diversified portfolio of stocks. But with the same $20,000, you can buy shares in a mutual fund and get a great deal of diversification. However, you do not get to make investment decisions on a day-to-day basis. A professional fund manager does all of the buying and selling and is the hands-on decision-maker.

So, the good news about owning a mutual fund is that you can diversify for very little money. The bad news is that the fund manager calls the shots, and if anything obscures the manager's vision, you could lose money and see red. Below are brief descriptions of six types of mutual funds:

Money-Market Mutual Funds

These are funds that buy and sell short-term financial instruments. Normally they keep a stable dollar price of one dollar per share. The interest rate changes every day because the investments are so short-term. Most banks, brokerages, and mutual fund companies offer money-market funds.

Stock Mutual Funds

Buying shares in a stock mutual fund means investing in a portfolio of stocks. Stock mutual funds come in all shapes and sizes, from blue-chip funds to small company funds to sector funds that invest only in one industry (such as health care or utilities). Stock funds can range from low-risk to high-risk depending on the type of stocks they hold.

Bond Mutual Funds

Bond mutual funds can be corporate bond funds, municipal bond funds, government bond funds holding only Treasuries or agencies, and so on. You should not just compare yields when you choose a bond fund. Compare quality and maturity, too. Short-term, higher-rated bond funds pay less but offer more safety.

Balanced Funds

Balanced funds contain both stocks and bonds. They are designed to yield both growth and income. Balanced funds provide a way of almost splitting the difference between a stock fund and a bond fund and can be a good middle ground for conservative investors.

Global and International Funds

International funds can invest anywhere outside the United States; global funds are free to invest in both U.S. and foreign securities. These funds offer good opportunities to own foreign stocks and bonds and to let a fund manager who is an expert in the overseas markets manage these investments for you.

Socially Responsible Funds

Investors who want to put their money where their hearts are can look to stock and bond mutual funds that own only specially screened investments. These can range from investments in environmentally friendly companies to municipal bonds issued to further education and health care. Many of these funds have performed excellently, proving that you can do good and do well at the same time.

Choosing a Fund

While looking for the right mutual fund, here are some things you should consider:

- How long has the fund been around? You do not want to invest in a brand-new fund, because you will not have any way to track its performance. If it did very well last year, so what? You need to know what it did five and even ten years ago when the markets were not so wonderful.
- Find out who the fund manager is and how long he or she has been around. This is very important because the manager is the person who will be calling the shots. A very well-known mutual fund was headed by a top manager for years. He left, and a second manager took over. Two years later, the second manager was replaced by yet a third manager. When the five-year track record of this fund is examined, it is important to remember that the new manager has nothing to do with the fund's history.
- Find out how frequently the fund you are interested in turns over its portfolio. Does it follow a buy-and-hold approach or a more active trading approach?
- If you are looking at a stock mutual fund, you will want to know what type of stocks the fund invests in. If it is a blue-chip mutual fund, you know it invests primarily in large, household-name companies. If it is a sector fund, be prepared for a fair amount of volatility.
- Whether it is a blue-chip fund, a sector fund, or any other type of fund, make sure you ask what its top ten holdings are. Six months from now they will change because of the trading within the portfolio, but at least you will get a good idea of the type of stocks the fund manager looks at. You will also get a sense of the manager's vantage point and the approach he or she takes to stock selection.

If you are shopping for a bond mutual fund, you will want to ask these questions:

- What is the credit quality or the average rating of the bonds in the portfolio?
- What is the average maturity of the portfolio? Let us assume that the average maturity of Bond Mutual Fund A is thirty years. This means that it will be a lot more volatile than a portfolio holding three-year bonds. Yields are usually higher with longer maturities, but so is risk.

- Find out the yield on the fund, but also check the total return. Total return means that even though you are getting a wonderfully high yield, you may be losing part of your principal at the same time. If you paid $10 a share for a bond mutual fund and it is now $9 a share, you have lost 10 percent of your principal. If you are getting a 10 percent yield, you are just breaking even.

- Finally, find out what the fund's yield and total return have been over the last year and over the last five and ten years. This will reflect what the fund has been yielding, as well as what happened to principal. If you are told that the yield on a bond fund was 9 percent last year and the total return was 7 percent, then 2 percent of the principal was lost. Total return is a much better indicator of the overall performance of a fund than the yield figure alone. Total return tells you not only what investors' principal earned, but also whether actual dollars increased or decreased.

Making the Decision

Why go through all of this before investing in a mutual fund when there is a fund manager making all the decisions? Because the mutual fund you invest in, whether it is a stock, bond, or balanced fund, should be in sync with your investment objectives and risk tolerance.

Egg-wise

The first *D* in my strategy is *diversification*, which is Wall Street jargon for "don't put all your eggs in one basket." The reasoning is clear. Even at only 2 to 3 percent inflation, putting every dollar that you own in the world into "safe" investments with no inflation protection is a surefire way to grow very poor very safely.

Historically, dollar for dollar, stocks have outperformed all other investments. From 1946 through 1996, large-company stocks returned an average of 12.6 percent. Small-company stocks did even better, returning 14.4 percent. Bonds, on the other hand, fared a lot less well. Intermediate-term U.S. government bonds posted an average annual return of 5.9 percent; long-term corporate bonds returned 5.8 percent.

According to a study done by Ibbotson Associates, Inc., a Chicago-based research firm, from 1926 through 1989, a hypothetical investment of $1 performed as follows:

$1 invested in the stock market grew to $534.00
$1 invested in government bonds grew to $17.30
$1 invested in T-bills grew to ....less than $10.00

Given the reality of inflation combined with this strong case for stock ownership, does this mean that you should fill your portfolio with nothing but stocks? Absolutely not. But it certainly does not make sense to leave them out altogether.

If owning stocks is within your comfort level, do consider investing in a "basket" of high-quality equities. You should not own just one or two stocks; chances are they may both go down. A well-constructed equity portfolio should include at least ten stocks diversified across industry lines. You can achieve similar diversification by investing with a professional money manager who will custom-tailor a portfolio to your specifications (minimum investment for such services is usually $250,000–$500,000).

If you decide to use mutual funds as your primary investment vehicle, do not invest all of your money in just one fund. Always diversify. Remember, each mutual fund's performance is only as good as the performance of the fund's manager, and the manager's luck could change rapidly. Some people sink as much as $500,000 into one mutual fund, which is a serious mistake in my opinion. These investors have put an awful lot of eggs in one basket.

Personally, I would not put more than $50,000 in any one mutual fund, especially if that represented all the money I had to invest. Again, it comes back to diversifying with what you have and applying common sense.

Of course, the flip side of this is that someone with $20,000 to invest should not own five different mutual funds. Two maybe, but not five. You should not diversify yourself to the point of absurdity.

Battling Inflation

Real estate, whether in the form of outright ownership or a managed investment such as a real estate investment trust (REIT), can provide your portfolio with much-needed inflation protection as well. If you are well-versed in the market for collectibles (art, antiques, and so on), you might consider including them in your portfolio.

Precious metals, especially gold, used to be owned extensively as an inflation hedge. Aside from the unsettling volatility in the precious metals markets in general, I am unconvinced that gold is the inflation hedge that it once was.

Mr. Bush, Mr. Disney

As a new world order emerges (to quote former President Bush), opportunities for international investing abound. And as we move toward twenty-four-hour global trading and an increasingly integrated world economy, it pays to remember that "it's a small world after all" (to quote Walt Disney).

Given the political, economic, and currency risk inherent in foreign stock and bond ownership, should you *still* consider investing outside the United States? Do the potential rewards of global investing outweigh these risks? For investors who can see far ahead, the answer is likely to be "yes."

The wisdom of investing globally—particularly in equities—is shown by the performance of international stocks as represented by EAFE (Europe, Australia, Far East Index) versus domestic stocks as represented by the Standard & Poor's 500. While the Standard & Poor's 500 posted a 14.6 percent average annual return from 1976 to 1996, EAFE stocks returned 15.3 percent. Even though there is no guarantee that foreign stocks will continue to perform as well as they have in the past, they have produced a remarkable long-term record.

Bond Options

For bond investors, diversifying globally can be profitable in both the higher yields available outside the United States and in the potential for capital gains should the dollar weaken against foreign currencies. Most money flows to countries with relatively high interest rates and with currencies that either closely follow the dollar or can be hedged without the substantial costs that eliminate yield differences. Canadian currency and, to a lesser extent, Australian and New Zealand currencies tend to follow the dollar.

Currency risk can be avoided entirely by investing in foreign money markets denominated in U.S. dollars. While the return on this type of investment is less than glamorous, the risk element is correspondingly low.

Investors willing to risk more to reach for a higher return may want to consider international bond funds. Most short-term funds are less volatile but pay less income than their longer-term counterparts. Short-term funds also typically try to hedge currency risk by using options, futures, and sophisticated cross-currency hedges. Long-term funds, however, have substantial currency risk exposure.

How much of your portfolio should be diversified globally? Conservative investors may want to shift 10 percent into short-term global bond funds and 5–10 percent into global stock funds. Growth investors may find a more appropriate allocation in a mix that is 5–10 percent global bond fund and 10–15 percent global stock fund.

Age "Equation"

A final word about diversification—or "asset allocation" in modern-day parlance. A good rule of thumb is to match your age to the percentage of fixed-income investments in your portfolio. For example, at age 65, consider allocating 65 percent to fixed-income investments (cash, money markets, bonds), with the remaining 35 percent of your portfolio in inflation hedges (stocks, real estate, collectibles).

The logic here is clear: At age 65, you will understandably be more interested in safety than risk. An investor in his or her 30s will also have to contend with the reality of inflation eroding his or her capital base and, as such, will require substantially more inflation protection than an older investor.

Patience, Patience

The second *D*, and arguably the most important part of my investment strategy, is *discipline*.

Discipline means taking a loss while it is still manageable and not always waiting to break even. Remember that an investment that is down 50 percent in value must increase 100 percent just to get back to square one.

Discipline means making a financial plan and *sticking to it*. It means not investing in the latest "going to the moon" stock tip unless you are prepared for a potential crash landing. Discipline means being an investor, not a trader. It means taking the long view and not letting your common-sense investment plan get derailed by the day-to-day vagaries of the financial markets.

Remember that one bad year does not a bad investment make. While "buy and hold" does not necessarily mean till death do you part, it also does not mean you should bail out right after the honeymoon. Or before it even gets started!

Investing, particularly in the case of retirement planning, should be carefully thought out. This is your serious money, and it deserves to be treated seriously. You should not gamble with retirement money or select investments only because they look safe. As in life, appearances can be deceiving, and what used to be safe is not necessarily safe anymore.

Take our Social Security system for example. Most of us grew up "secure" in the knowledge that our financial futures would be well-provided for by the U.S. government and our hard-earned tax dollars. Pretty clear case of perception versus reality, no?

The bad news is that Social Security accounted for only 38 percent of the average retiree's income in 1990. That year, the average benefit for all retirees was a paltry $602 per month, which is hardly enough to live on.

In fact, it is likely that you will need at least 75–80 percent of your annual preretirement income to maintain your standard of living once you do retire. It is equally likely that Social Security will provide just a tiny fraction of that amount.

Is it safe to assume that your pension plan will make up the shortfall? Maybe so, maybe not, especially if it is not indexed for inflation. And with interest rates at almost a sixteen-year low and stocks moving up, down, and sideways, it is becoming increasingly difficult to invest wisely today to achieve financial security in the future.

Strong Framework

Where should you turn for help? To your first—and, in my opinion, your best—investment advisor. You.

You do not need a Ph.D. in economics. Investing is not rocket science, and it is not magic. While my two Cs and two Ds are not a guarantee of investment success, they are an excellent framework for being moneysmart in the twenty-first century.

Common sense, comfort level, diversification, and discipline—smart tools for smart investors.

25
Retirement Portfolios: What Should They Look Like?

CONSTANZA ERDOES AND JOHN HENRY LOW

A common question from many investors is, "Now that I have retired. what changes should be made to my investment portfolio?" The typical answer looks somewhat like this:

- Cut back on equities
- Invest the majority of your portfolio in bonds or fixed-income securities
- Sell growth and international stocks and/or funds: they are too risky
- Focus on income rather than capital appreciation
- Invest in money market funds and bank certificates of deposit

Our answer to the same question may surprise you. What changes need to be made? Probably none. Assuming that your portfolio is already well diversified, that its long-term rate of return is satisfactory, and that its level of risk is well within your individual tolerance, then certainly, the answer is none. Why?

Today's life expectancies are dramatically different than they were even fifty years ago. We are living longer than ever thanks to advances in the medical fields. With current life-expectancies at the traditional retirement age of 65, a typical couple should expect that at least one partner will live another twenty-five years. At age 75, they should expect at least one partner to live an additional fifteen years. To put this in perspective, fifteen years is equivalent to saving for a college education. If you were doing so for your children or grandchildren, would you limit their investments to fixed income and money market securi-

ties? Of course not. Should not the same reasoning be applied to your retirement portfolio?

The most common concerns in retirement planning are outliving your assets, and/or ensuring that the surviving partner is well taken care of. While relying on an investment portfolio that is composed solely of fixed income and cash might seem a safe course, in reality, it is almost guaranteeing yourself and/or your spouse a declining standard of living. Why? Because of the one word that is most often ignored when discussing investing, and yet has the greatest potential impact on your portfolio's returns. Inflation. *Never forget to factor in inflation*. The fact is that investments such as money market accounts, bank certificates of deposit, commercial paper, and short-term Treasury bills barely stay ahead of inflation.

Let us take a closer look at how different investments have fared over the past twenty-five years. In Table 25–1, we see that the average annual rate of return over the past twenty-five years for 90-day Treasury bills been 7.1 percent. The average inflation rate for the same period has been 5.7 percent. Subtracting the rate of inflation from the investment return, we receive a net benefit of 1.4 percent, *before taxes*. Surely you expect your portfolio to give you a greater benefit. So let us next examine bonds. The diversified bond index, Lehman Aggregate Bond Index, had an annual rate of return of 9.1 percent for the same period. Now, 9.1 percent sounds like a very healthy average return for bonds. But factor in inflation, and you are left with a much weaker net benefit of 3.4 percent. Only in the case of equities, with the S&P 500 Index earning an average of 12.9 percent per year, do we see a net benefit that is significant.

Of course we realize that these are *average* figures, and that at today's level of 3 percent, infla-

Constanza Erdoes and John Henry Low are partners at Knickerbocker Advisors Inc., an investment management firm based in New York. The information contained in this chapter is intended for general information only and should not be acted upon without professional advice.

Table 25-1

Asset Class Performance over the Past 25 Years (1972–1997)

	Average Annual Rate of Return	Less Average Annual Rate of Inflation	Average Annual Net Benefit
90-day Treasury bills	7.1%	– 5.7%	1.4%
Lehman Aggregate Bond Index	9.1%	– 5.7%	3.4%
S&P 500 Index	12.9%	– 5.7%	7.2%

tion seems negligible. But even at a low rate of 3 percent per year, the buying power of $100,000 is eroded to $73,742 in ten years and to approximately half of its value, or $54,379, in twenty years. We also fully realize the psychological comfort in investments such as Treasury bills and money market accounts which generally cannot lose principal, while bonds and stocks can. But, the fact remains that over long periods of time, it is equities that boost portfolio returns.

Now, we are in no way advocating that a portfolio be invested 100 percent in equities. Every portfolio should be a mix of different asset classes, such as cash, fixed income, and equities. And that mix depends on three individual factors. These three factors are the guiding principals in properly structuring every portfolio, whether investing for retirement, a dependent's education, or general life savings. Let us take a closer look at these factors.

1. Calculate Your Portfolio's Return Requirement

First, calculate the individual rate of return that you need your portfolio to earn. If you have saved enough to comfortably retire on, then you may have the luxury of requiring a lower rate of return from your investments than someone who did not save enough. This, of course, is the best position to be in, giving you the greatest flexibility during retirement. In this situation, your only concern is that your portfolio stay ahead of inflation plus taxes, which can be done with a fairly conservative investment asset allocation that should leave you with fewer worries during the investment markets' zigs and zags.

If you are not in this position, then you need to calculate the rate of return your portfolio needs

to grow by on an annual basis, net of any withdrawals that you need to make. And don't forget inflation. Let us briefly consider the case of Investor A.

Conservative Investor A has a portfolio of $750,000, needs to withdraw $75,000 annually, expects to use his portfolio for fifteen years, and does not want to reduce the principal of the portfolio, intending to leave that to his children. At a quick glance you might think that Investor A's required rate of return should be 7.5 percent (or the equivalent of his annual withdrawals). And, 7.5 percent seems a reasonable return to achieve over the long term with a low- to moderate-risk portfolio. But you have not factored in inflation. Even at today's low rate of inflation of 3 percent per year, Investor A's required rate of return would need to be an average of 10.5 percent per annum, not 7.5 percent. And even more if you want to factor in taxes. Suddenly, a low-risk portfolio may not be aggressive enough to give Investor A the return he needs. So remember, to properly calculate your required rate of return, factor in your annual expenditures, how much principal (if any) you do not want to deplete, *and* inflation and taxes.

2. Invest According to Your Risk Tolerance

This is probably *the* most important rule of investing. A portfolio's structure or asset allocation should match the investor's tolerance for investment risk. A mismatched investment strategy is the biggest danger in investing. Portfolios that are too aggressive are often abandoned midcourse, or worse yet, sold as a panic response at the worst possible moment. Portfolios that are too conservative run the risk of not providing the investor with an adequate return that he or she may need during retirement.

How does one assess his or her risk tolerance? One way is to look at your reaction to recent market corrections. When the Dow Jones Industrial Average fell 7 percent in October, 1997, did you panic? Did you quickly calculate how much money you had lost? Did you start putting in sell orders for portions of your portfolio to capture gains before the market fell any further? Did you have trouble falling asleep wondering how you were going to make up for the loss in your portfolio? If so, then you are likely to have low investment-risk tolerance and your portfolio might be too aggressive for you.

If you watched the markets with some concern, but kept reminding yourself that market corrections are normal, and that over time, your portfolio should recover, and took no further action, then you probably have a middle-range investment-risk tolerance.

If you watched the market tumble and began to get excited as this presented a great buying opportunity and immediately committed additional dollars for more equity investments, then you are probably a highly risk-tolerant investor and can live with a very aggressive portfolio.

A great way to assess your particular risk tolerance, is to think of what percentage of your portfolio you could stand to lose in any one year. Assume that you have a portfolio of $500,000. If you lost 10 percent in one year, and at the end of the year your portfolio was worth $450,000, would you panic? What if it lost 15 percent and it was worth $425,000? 20 percent? 25 percent? Now, no one expects investors to be happy or unconcerned when the markets correct. But there is a difference between concern and a high level of anxiety bordering on panic. Everyone has a particular "pain threshold" which is important to know. Once identified, you can structure a portfolio that should not stray beyond that threshold, by looking at the historical ranges of returns of different asset classes over time. Look at the worst losses in each asset class over the past thirty years or so and how many years had losses versus gains. Do not be lulled by the bull market of the 1990s. The worst market loss in recent history was over the 1973–1974 period, during which the S&P 500 lost 14.7 percent and

26.5 percent respectively. It could certainly happen again.

So for example, a very conservative investor may not want to invest heavily in a very risky asset class such as gold after looking at the recent history of the S&P Gold Index, which over the past twenty-nine years has had twelve years with losses as high as 52 percent in one year. Contrast gold with a "risky" equity asset class, micro cap stocks, as measured by the CRSP/DFA 9/10 Portfolio Index, which had seven loss years out of the past twenty-nine, as high as 31 percent in one year. By contrast, the somewhat "less risky" S&P 500 Index of large-company stocks experienced six loss years, with the worst single-year loss being 26 percent in 1973. Bonds, which are characterized as "safer" and lower yielding and, as measured by the Lehman Aggregate Bond Index, had one loss-year of 3 percent in 1994.

A lower risk investor, then, might allocate a higher percentage to Treasury bills, fixed income, income-oriented stocks, and large capitalization stocks. A moderate risk investor would allocate less to Treasury bills, fixed income and more to equities, perhaps by adding some small cap stocks and international and emerging markets exposure. An aggressive investor would have a higher allocation of "riskier" and higher returning asset classes such as small cap stocks, international, and emerging markets.

Of course, risk tolerance has to be weighed against investment-return requirements. A low-risk investor may consciously choose a more aggressive portfolio to achieve a certain rate of return needed to fund his retirement

Remember that every portfolio should be well diversified among *many* different asset classes, but by adjusting the asset class weightings in accordance with your investment-risk tolerance, you are setting up a winning portfolio strategy.

3. Calculate Your Investment Time Horizon

Now for the good news. Despite all the misgivings you may have after calculating your risk tolerance, a long investment time horizon is the best way to reduce the risk of a portfolio. Let us repeat, the longer you have to invest, the more aggressive you can be. Why?

Because every market zigs and zags, has corrections, years with gains and years with losses. But over a period of ten years or more, these zigs and zags even out. Put another way, over time, investment returns revert to their mean. So even a conservative investor who gritted his or her teeth and held on through the 1973–1974 bear market earned an average of 6.65 percent per year on the S&P 500 Index in the 1970s. The timing risk is investing right before a downturn or bear market. But long-term investment time horizons smooth out the dips. Remember that over the past seventy years, there has never been a ten-year period in which any major asset class lost money.

If you have an investment time horizon of ten years or more, you can afford to allocate a more aggressive portfolio than if you only had five years. Keep your focus on the long-term, and not on short-term swings and corrections in the markets. Long-term investors tend to be satisfied investors.

So calculate the rate of return that you need to earn, and structure an investment portfolio that will provide you with that return at a level of risk that is comfortable for you. If you are not quite sure how to pinpoint these factors or allocate your portfolio, seek out an investment professional to help you determine an appropriate portfolio structure. Having the right investment strategy is the key to a successful long-term portfolio.

26
Life Insurance and Annuities for Retirement

BENJAMIN G. BALDWIN

The objective of this chapter is to familiarize you with the characteristics of life insurance and annuity contracts—the terms, the restrictions, the penalties, and the options—so that you can work with your chosen life insurance professional and make your life insurance assets enhance your retirement.

Basic Life Insurance Products

A life insurance product menu has been developed to give you a quick overview of the life insurance products on the market and what they can do for you (see Figure 5–1). Across the top of the matrix are the essential characteristics of life insurance products. Down the left-hand column are the six generic forms of life insurance contracts. The upper third of the matrix provides information regarding life insurance products into which you will pay only an amount sufficient to pay the mortality and expense charges for a very limited period of time, usually one year. The lower two-thirds shows the four generic forms of life insurance contracts into which you may pay funds in addition to the amounts required for the annual mortality and expense charges. These are referred to as the "plus" dollars for investment purposes. The matrix points out the fact that you can get a commitment from a life insurance company to pay life insurance benefits by merely paying these two expenses and therefore any additional dollars placed in the contract must be evaluated from the standpoint of

Benjamin G. Baldwin is president and owner of Baldwin Financial Systems, Inc., a registered representative of EQ Financial Consultants, Inc., and an agent of Equitable Life, in Northbrook, Illinois.

an investment on an "alternative use of funds" basis.

Nonguaranteed Term Insurance

Looking at the top of the product menu, we see that there are basically two types of insurance into which you only pay mortality and expense charges each year. Nonguaranteed term insurance means that the insurance company does not have to guarantee you anything. They do not have to guarantee to renew your policy and, indeed, in some cases, they may guarantee to cancel your policy after, for example, three years. When a policy does not guarantee the right to renew and does not guarantee you the right to convert and maybe even guarantees to terminate itself after a limited period of time, the insurance company does not have to charge you too much for the contract. The fewer the guarantees, the lower the price.

Renewable and Convertible Term Insurance

Should you wish to have the insurance company promise you that they will renew the policy at a stipulated rate and/or that they will allow you to convert that policy to some other type of contract offered by that insurance company, they will charge you for these privileges and your policy becomes renewable and convertible term. These privileges put the policyowner in a position of control with the insurance company responding to that control. The insurance company is, therefore, accepting more risk and will charge more for this type of contract. If you request six different term insurance quotes from six different com-

155

Figure 26–1

The Menu of Life Insurance Products

Term Only = Mortality and Expenses Only

	General Description	Investment Vehicle	Investment Flexibility	Premium Flexibility	Face Amount Flexibility	Appropriate For
Nonguaranteed-Term	Lowest cost No control	NONE	N/A	NONE Increases	NONE	Very limited situations.
Yearly Renewable and Convertible Term	Policyowner Control	NONE	N/A	NONE Increases	NONE	Limited cash flow, temporary needs protection now.

Term PLUS = Mortality, Expenses, and Investment

	General Description	Investment Vehicle	Investment Flexibility	Premium Flexibility	Face Amount Flexibility	Appropriate For
Whole Life	Fixed Life Basic Coverage. Dividends provide investment return.	Primarily insurance co. selected long-term bonds and mortgages.	NONE To change investment, borrowing and reinvesting is required.	NONE Dividends can reduce or eliminate fixed, billed premium.	NONE Want more? Buy new, if you can pass a physical.	The conservative older insureds, substandard insureds.
Variable Life	You direct the investment.	Common stock, bond funds, guaranteed interest rates, zero coupons, money markets, etc.	MAXIMUM Your decision: split it, move it, etc.	NONE Fixed premium remains level. Loans available.	NONE Want more? Buy new, if you can pass a physical.	The investor. An alternative to buying term; invest difference.
Universal Life	Current interest rate, flexibility, transparency.	Short-term interest investments.	NONE Borrow or withdraw.	MAXIMUM Enough for mortality and expenses, or as much as Law allows.	MAXIMUM Increase or decrease . . . stay healthy for major increases.	Younger insureds. Variable needs like short-term interest rate investments.
Universal Variable Life	Disclosure, flexibility, control.	Common stock, bond funds, guaranteed interest rates, zero coupons, money markets, etc.	MAXIMUM You name it. You split it. You move it. You withdraw it.	MAXIMUM Enough for mortality and expenses, or as much as law allows.	MAXIMUM Increase or decrease . . . Stay healthy for major increases.	The investor. An alternative to buying term; invest difference. I want it my way!

panies, you can expect to get six different costs. Although it may be tempting and seem very logical to accept the one offering the lowest cost, you must be careful and consider what rights you may be giving up in accepting the lowest possible price. In reviewing the higher-priced contracts, review what rights you are purchasing by paying those extra costs, and consider the value of those rights to you.

Whole Life Insurance

Whole life insurance takes in all the various life insurance policies sold in this country up to 1976. Up to that time, when you wanted to give more to the insurance company than just the mortality and expense charges, the companies took the extra funds and invested them in their general portfolio, which consisted primarily of long-term bonds and mortgages. The extra amount that you paid in was determined by the type of whole life insurance policy you chose. You could choose a whole life or ordinary life insurance policy into which you would promise to pay a stipulated sum annually for the rest of your life. This minimized the extra amount to be paid. Alternatively, you could choose a policy into which you wanted to pay ten annual payments or wanted to stop payments at age 65 and then have the policy continue for the rest of your life. The insurance company would stipulate how much you would have to pay for this ten-pay life or life paid-up at age 65 policy. These plus dollars for investment would go to work in the insurance company's long-term bond and mortgage portfolio. If your policy was with a nonparticipating company, your equity in the policy, the cash value, would grow by a contractually guaranteed amount for the rest of the policy's existence. If your policy was a participating policy, your equity would grow by the contractually guaranteed amount, which would be added to by the payment of dividends. The dividends would become payable if the insurance company found that their expenses were lower than they anticipated, their mortality experience was better than they expected (fewer people died than they had anticipated), and/or their investment results in their general portfolio of long-term bonds and mortgages did better than anticipated. If the combination of these three factors resulted in a divisible surplus, then the insurance company would divide that surplus among its policyowners and pay dividends. These dividends are considered to be a return of premium and thus are not taxable until the amount you have received in dividends exceeds the amount you have paid into the policy, your cost basis.

The investment within the whole life insurance policy—that is, within the insurance company's long-term bond and mortgage portfolio—acts much like a long-term bond account without the downside risk. That is, the insurance company guarantees what the guaranteed cash value of the contract will be and that it will not decrease below that amount. Thus, in spite of the fact that the value of the insurance company's portfolio of long-term bonds and mortgages does decrease in periods of increasing interest rates, this reduction is not passed on to the policyowner. However, this does not prevent policyowners from being disappointed in the rate of return they are receiving on the cash they have in their whole life insurance policies during times of increasing interest rates. They will evaluate that investment in terms of what the money could be earning if they could reinvest it at the higher interest rates available to them. Since it takes time to reinvest the insurance company bond portfolio at the higher rates, these rates will not be passed through to the policyowners for a number of years. During such

periods, whole life will not look good on a competitive basis. It will compete much more favorably if the economy moves into a decreasing interest rate cycle. At that point, the insurance company's portfolio, now made up of higher-interest-earning bonds and mortgages, begins to be able to pay out those higher earnings via dividends. This explains why many whole life insurance policyowners were very unhappy with the investment results of their policies in 1979 and 1980 (the prime rate in December 1980 was 21.5 percent). These same policyowners were pleasantly surprised in the late 1980s with the much more competitive return being offered by many of their whole life insurance policies.

The next three questions addressed by the product menu as you move from left to right concern flexibility: investment flexibility, premium flexibility, and face amount flexibility. In whole life insurance, the contract is rigidly structured and does not provide flexibility of investment vehicle, premium, or face amount. All three are stipulated by contract.

Variable Life

The original variable life insurance policy became available in the United States in 1976, well before universal life. The change from a whole life policy to a variable life policy was rather simple. The insurance company replaced the bonds and mortgages as the investment vehicle within the policy with stock and money-market accounts and gave the policyowner the right to choose. Since that time, the variety of accounts available within these contracts has expanded each year so that now they can be described as tax-sheltered families of mutual funds that provide and charge for life insurance. You will note that the flexibility available in the variable life contract is only available in the investment area; it is inflexible with regard to premium and face amount. Premium and face amount are stated in the contract, and you would have to apply for a brand-new contract if you should ever want additional insurance.

Universal Life Insurance

Universal life was born in the late 1970s because policyowners wanted to enjoy the relatively high interest rates available in the money-market accounts of that day. The insurance companies responded to the market demand for currently

157

competitive interest rates within their life insurance policies. They replaced the long-term bond and mortgage account with investments with which they could guarantee an annual interest rate that was competitive in the current market. On that first day when EF Hutton Life told the policyowner that the cash within his or her insurance policy would earn, for example, a 10 percent return for that particular year, a whole host of changes occurred within the insurance industry that assured that it would never be the same. The insurance company was guaranteeing a specific interest rate on a specific amount of money and therefore was accountable for those promises. The company had to detail the expenses that were deducted from any monies going into an insurance policy, such as state premium taxes and the expenses of issuing the policy. It had to account for the amount of the interest earnings within the account and how those earnings were being used by the insurance company to pay expenses and mortality costs. Life insurance policies had become transparent. The fact that expenses continue throughout the life of an insurance policy and the fact that mortality charges continue and increase with age became, for the first time, eminently clear in universal life insurance.

Universal life insurance provides you with premium flexibility. You may choose what you want to pay into the policy. As additional checks come in, the insurance company applies the proper state premium taxes and the associated expenses and credits the balance of the check to the investment account paying interest on the new balance. If you want more or less at risk, all you change is the amount being charged for mortality expenses.

The first generation of universal life insurance could therefore handle premium flexibility and face amount flexibility without difficulty. It could not, however, offer any investment flexibility. Monies that went into a universal life policy for investment purposes would get the interest rate promised by the insurance company. No other investment alternatives were available.

Universal Variable Life

Universal variable life is a hybrid built of everything that came before it. It took from universal life a duplicate of its annual interest rate guarantee and the flexibility of premium payment and face amount. To this it added alternatives for plus

dollars that you may decide to put into the policy for investment purposes. It is common today to have various funds available within universal variable life policy: common stock, aggressive stock, balanced, global, bond, high-yield bond, guaranteed interest, zero coupon, money-market accounts, and so on. Real estate funds are the most recent addition to some of the contracts. The positive side of this development is that when you choose to be insured—that is, when you choose to pay mortality and expense charges—you also may choose (within limits) how much extra you wish to pay in for investment purposes and where those investment dollars should be allocated. The negative aspect of this flexibility is responsibility. You may choose to pay the wrong amount into the policy and/or you may choose the wrong investments. October 19, 1987, the day the stock market dropped approximately five hundred points, has taught many variable life policyowners that the common stock accounts within these policies can go down as well as up.

Last-to-Die / Second-to-Die / Survivorship Life Insurance

A specialized type of life insurance insuring two lives and paying off at the death of the second to die is often known as survivorship life and second-to-die life insurance and is a product of ERTA 1981. It was legislated into existence by the fact that a couple can often choose to pay no estate taxes until the last of the two dies. Keep in mind that a change in tax law could seriously affect its usefulness. The idea of the policy is that it will deliver the cash when the estate tax bill needs to be paid. It is very popular since estate taxes are so confiscatory, and the cost of the coverage is relatively low. The chance of the insurance company having to pay is reduced since there are two lives that must terminate before it is called upon to pay.

These policies can be structured as either whole life, universal life, or universal variable policies and thus have the risks and rewards described above for policies funded in that way.

There is a tendency for insurance salespeople to appeal to people on the basis that, "I can sell it to you for less," meaning a lower premium. This usually means that the hoped-for future support of the policy is to come either from high assumed interest rates in the future and low mortality rates or high dividends that must support term insurance riders in the future. Both methods miss the idea that heavy initial funding of these policies starts them earning a tax-sheltered return for the policyowner that will likely make the policy perform better and be less likely to require additional substantial investment in the unknown future if interest rates and/or mortality costs turn sour. Since these policies are to provide an eventual death benefit, the funding method for the retiree would be to have the contract contain sufficient investment capital to generate enough return to pay all policy costs to life expectancy. If the policy is to provide the death benefit and, in addition, is to provide a place to invest assets within a nontaxable environment for future generations, then a universal variable type of policy may be more appropriate.

Keep in mind that there are a lot of assumptions in these policies that must remain true for a very long time in order for them to be as valuable as many assume they will be. First, the marriage must survive. Then the tax law must remain favorable, the financial assumptions in the policy must work out, and the insurance company must survive as long as the couple.

Life Insurance Inventory

Once you understand what kinds of life insurance are available, the next step is to inventory what you already own. By using a life insurance inventory page (see Figure 26–2), you can record all essential information needed to analyze the policies in regard to adequacy of amount and to evaluate the investment merits of the policies being used for that purpose.

How Much Is Enough?

The question of "how much is enough?" is a very personal one. In the event of your death, will someone else take an economic loss? If so, do you care to reduce that economic loss by purchasing life insurance so that insurance dollars will be available to mitigate that loss? The need or desire for life insurance can come from a business or a

Figure 26–2

LIFE INSURANCE INVENTORY

Insured/ Company	Type of Policy	Po;icy Number	Register Date	Death Ben.	Asset Value	Policy Loan	Ann. Cash Val. Inc.	Annual Premium	Annual Dividend
Name/									
1.									
2.									
3.									
4.									
5.									
TOTALS				____	____	____	____	____	____

Total Asset Value (husband and wife)	____
Total Policy Loans (husband and wife)	____
Total Annual Cash Value Increase	____
Total Family Premium	____
Total Annual Dividends	____

BENEFICIARIES OF POLICIES

Primary Beneficiary	Secondary Beneficiary	Policy Features	Loan Rate
1.			
2.			
3.			
4.			
5.			

personal relationship. In the personal financial planning area, we are primarily concerned with the insurance needs of a family. The life insurance needs analyzer (see Figure 26–3) is a checklist to help you determine your life insurance needs. The first section of the form deals with the immediate expenses that come up at an individual's death; it also includes some of the reserve funds that a family may want to establish for future needs, such as an education fund or emergency funds—when the single breadwinner is lost.

Figure 26–3

LIFE INSURANCE NEEDS ANALYZER
Funds Required for Cash Expenses and Sinking Funds

1. Probate and Administrative Expenses:
   a. 5% of Probate Property _____
   b. 2% of Nonprobate _____
   c. ?% for Complexity _____
2. Funeral Expenses _____
3. Special Obligations _____
   Pledges _____
   Contracts _____
   Divorce _____
   Business _____
4. Debts/Insurance Loans/Current Bills _____
5. Income Tax Liabilities:
   a. Year of Death Return _____
   b. Retirement Plan Payout _____
   c. IRA/KEOUGH/TSA _____
   d. Deferred Annuity _____
   e. Tax Shelter Liability Exceeds:
      1) Basis _____
      2) Fair-market Value _____
6. Federal Estate Taxes _____
7. State Inheritance Taxes _____
8. Education Fund (calculated or today's cost estimate) _____
9. Mortgage _____
10. Extra Fund for Error/Family Emergency Fund _____
FUNDS REQUIRED FOR CASH EXPENSES AND SINKING FUNDS: _____

Survivor Income Funds

	Number of Children	Years of Income	Monthly Income
Income Periods:			
#1. Children under 18	_____	_____	_____
#2. Children over 18	_____	_____	_____
Spouse under 60/65	_____	_____	_____
#3. Spouse Age 60/65			
for Life (recommend age 85)	_____	_____	_____
Period #1 Income Objective	_____		
Less: 1. Est. Social Security	_____		
2. Spouse's Earned Income	_____ *		
3. Other Assured Income	_____		
Net Unfunded Income Objective	_____ per month		
Discounted Present Value for _____	_____		
years assuming _____ % interest			Child Raising Fund

* (Rule of Thumb = Social Security Benefits, $300 per eligible beneficiary, maximum three)

Figure 26–3 (Continued)

LIFE INSURANCE NEEDS ANALYZER
Funds Required for Cash Expenses and Sinking Funds

Period #2 Income Objective _____
   Less: 1. Est. Social Security _____
        2. Spouse's Earned Income _____ *
        3. Other Assured Income _____
   Net Unfunded Income Objective _____ per month
        Discounted Present Value for _____ _____
        years assuming _____ % interest   Post-Children Fund
* (Rule of Thumb = Social Security Benefits STOP)

Period #3 Income Objective _____
   Less: 1. Est. Social Security _____
        2. Spouse's Earned Income _____
        3. Other Assured Income _____
        4. IRA and Other Retirement Plans _____
   Net Unfunded Income Objective _____ per month
        Discounted Present Value for _____ _____
        years assuming _____ % interest   Retirement Fund

      ANNUITY METHOD FOR INCOME IN EVENT OF DEATH _____
        (Principal ZERO ($0) at Spouse's Life Expectancy)
      ALTERNATIVE METHOD: CAPITAL RETENTION METHOD _____
        Assuming _____ % interest _____
        (Principal INTACT at Spouse's Life Expectancy)

TOTAL FAMILY CAPITAL REQUIRED FOR EXPENSES AND INCOME, LESS: ANNUITY or CAPITAL
    1. Present Family Investment Capital _____
    2. Existing Net Benefits of Life Insurance _____
    3. Retirement Plan—Generated Cash _____

ADDITIONAL FAMILY CAPITAL REQUIRED _____ _____
    or (Surplus) Family Capital Available   ANNUITY or CAPITAL

The second section of the form deals with survivor income and splits the income requirements of a family into three different periods. The first period covers children under age 18 in the home. The second period covers the time after the youngest attains age 18 and prior to the spouse's attaining age 60, which is the earliest time that the spouse can draw upon Social Security. The third and final period is the spouse's post-60 to -65 period and continues on for the rest of that surviving spouse's life, which is the only period most people approaching retirement will have to deal with. Fill in the blanks with how much income you wish to have for your surviving spouse. You calculate the amount of capital needed for each of the three periods as a discounted present value column calculation, using the income required, the amount of time that the income is required,

and some assumed interest rate or discount rate so that the discounted present value of that stream of payments can be determined. This particular form can be calculated by reproducing it on a Lotus spreadsheet or by using your financial calculator.

Provision has been made on the form for deducting the other sources of assured income that a surviving spouse may have, such as Social Security, spouse's earned income, income from employee benefit plans, veterans plans, state public schoolteachers plans, federal employee plans, and other survivor income plans.

The funds needed for income are then added to the funds needed for cash expenses and sinking funds to arrive at an amount of money that will accomplish all family objectives. The next task is to compare what the family has to this figure, which represents what the family needs. To do this, we add up the value of the amount of life insurance that would be available, the amount of accumulated investable capital available, the amount of all retirement-plan-generated cash, and any other assets that would be available to provide security for the couple. We subtract what is available from what is needed in order to come up with an amount of additional capital needed if such be the case. As you approach retirement, your objective is to have enough of these resources so that they are entirely adequate to support you and your spouse for the rest of your lives and at the same time pass those assets that you wish to pass to others with as much efficiency and economy as possible.

Life Insurance Action Letter

The life insurance action letter (see Figure 26–4) is a sample letter to your life insurance professional requesting information upon which you can base decisions regarding life coverage. The action letter asks how much it would cost for you

Figure 26–4

Life Insurance Action Letter

Dear _____:

I am evaluating my life insurance and I would appreciate your assistance.

I would be interested in your recommendations regarding the type of life insurance I now own, keeping in mind that my principal objective is to own enough to provide adequate security for my survivors at minimum after-tax cost for the protection.

I have not decided whether I need. or want, any additional life insurance. Please send me a ledger statement showing the cost of $ _____ of yearly renewable and convertible term insurance for a male non-smoker/smoker, age _____ and $ _____ for a female non-smoker/smoker, age _____ .

If you have an alternative policy that you would recommend, please send me the information, including a ledger statement for any contract you are recommending. If you will be offering Universal Life or Universal Variable, I will need a statement of monthly charges, mortality costs, credits, account values, and surrender values for the first eleven years and a statement disclosing the assumptions being used in the statement,

Sincerely,

Name and address

---

to pay only mortality and expense charges into a policy that is renewable and convertible at your option. This assumes that you are willing to pay a little bit more for term insurance than you might otherwise have to pay with a nonguaranteed type of insurance. The payment of this required premium, representing merely expense and mortality charges, will put the life insurance in force as quickly as possible with as little cash outlay as possible. Whether to invest with the insurance company is an investment alternative question on which you may cogitate leisurely after the insurance company is on the risk and your family is off the risk.

Request for Policy Information

If there is any question regarding the status of any individually owned life insurance policies, fill out the request for policy information form (see Figure 26–5) with the insured's name and policy number and address it to the appropriate insurance company. This form must be signed by the policyowner. Insurance companies vary in their response time to these forms. Keep a photocopy of the form and resubmit it periodically with a large note in red ink, SECOND REQUEST, if you don't get a response the first time.

What to Do with What You Own

Once you have determined what you have, the next step is to determine what task you wish to have each policy serve in retirement. Is it for eventual death benefits for personal beneficiaries? If so, the objective will probably be to have such policies continue with the smallest amount of cash flowing into them as is possible to sustain them. Personally paid-for conventional term life insurance policies probably will be terminated by this time because of the rapid increase in premium. Whole life policies will be redesigned to minimize cash flow by eliminating policy loans and applying dividends to reduce or eliminate premium. Other investment-oriented policies also will be redesigned with regard to policy investment, amount of life insurance, and allocation of investment to accomplish the policies' stipulated purpose.

Is the policy intended to supplement your retirement income or the retirement income required by both you and your spouse? If so, should the income be taxable or are there reasons that it

Figure 26–5

Request for Policy Information

To: _____   Date: _____
         (Company Name)

_____   Re: _____
         (Address)

_____   Policy No.: _____

Please forward the following information on the above policy for the items checked below. (You may use this form for your reply or a separate communication if more convenient.) Thank you.

  (1) Kind of policy _____

       Is additional indemnity included? _____   Disability premium waiver? _____

  (2) Register date _____ Age at issue _____

  (3) Face amount _____

  (4) Computed value of any family income type provision or decreasing term as of current date _____

       Expiry date _____

  (5) Owner of policy _____

  (6) Successive or contingent owner _____

  (7) Beneficiary: Primary _____ Secondary _____

  (8) How settled? (If other than single sum, please indicate withdrawal rights, power of appointment, and terms of simultaneous death provision.) _____

       _____

  (9) Assignments _____

 (10) Summarize any physical or occupational ratings _____

 (11) Amount of premium _____ Payable _____

 (12) Premium paid to _____

 (13) Current dividend election _____

 (14) Amount of current year's dividend _____

 (15) Supplemental one-year term insurance now in force through use of dividends _____

 (16) Cumulative amount of dividends now credited to policy:

       Paid-up additional insurance _____

       Cash value of additional insurance _____

       Accumulations at interest _____

 (17) Please send form for new dividend election

 (18) Outstanding loans _____

 (19) Cash values as of (previous year, current year, age 65) _____

       _____

 (20) Request policy loan forms _____

 (21) Request change of beneficiary forms _____

 (22) Provide policy cost basis and gain or loss position at this time.

Please send the required information
and/or necessary forms to:

_____   _____
                                                    Policyowner Signature

_____

should not be currently taxable? If the latter is the case, it may be essential that the policy remain "life insurance" and thus continue to make charges for mortality, that is, life insurance costs. If, however, income taxes are tolerable, then the policy can be turned into an annuity contract without the transaction being a currently taxable event by means of an IRC section 1035 tax-free exchange into an annuity.

Loans on Life Insurance Policies

In prior years, many corporations and individuals maintained their life insurance policies by borrowing the inside buildup of the policies to pay not only the ongoing premiums, but also to pay loan interest costs. Life insurance policies provided unexciting investment returns, policy loan interest charges were low, and policy loan interest payments were deductible when four of the first seven premiums were paid without direct or indirect borrowing. Consequently, there are many corporate and individual life insurance policies with very substantial loans against them.

The Tax Reform Act of 1986 and its new Internal Revenue Code Section 264(a)(4) addressed the manner in which corporations should treat policy loan interest. It provides that where interest is produced by borrowing on an insurance policy purchased after June 20, 1986, the interest is deductible as a business expense only on the first $50,000 of loan per individual. Policies acquired by June 20, 1986, have been grandfathered. Corporations will still be eligible for the full loan interest deductions on these grandfathered policies. This means that pre–June 21, 1986, life insurance policies have a special value to corporations: special good in that they can still deduct the loan interest; special bad in that as these policies age, the required loan costs are increasing as the loans increase. The old, underperforming life insurance policies that may be in force under corporate arrangements would not retain the grandfathered loan interest deductibility if they were to be exchanged for a new policy.

Individuals are treated more harshly. Generally, policy loan interest for both old and new policies (old policies were not grandfathered) is considered consumer interest and thus is no longer deductible. This may be another place where a corporate employer can help a shareholder employee. The ownership of highly leveraged, pre–June 20, 1986, personal policies could be conveyed to the corporate employer for their net asset value. The employer could then use this key employee life insurance to provide the employee and his or her family with salary continuation benefits in order to replace the security previously provided by the personally owned life insurance. This would shift the burden of servicing these policies to the corporate employer, who could continue to deduct the policy loan interest (pre–June 20, 1986, policies) whereas the employee would not be able to do so.

Policy Loan Rescue Plans

The existence of this problem with minimum deposit plans has given birth to a new marketing thrust in the insurance industry: minimum deposit rescue plans. The lead sentence of the article in the June 29, 1987, issue of *Forbes* magazine, page 112, "The Insurance Loan Dilemma," said it well: "If you own a minimum deposit life insurance policy, condolences are in order. Tax reform probably leaves you with nothing but unpalatable options." The options are:

1. Continue the policy as is. The ostrich option. Loans get bigger, dividends are held down, interest gets higher, deductibility gets lower, buildup of tax-deferred gain grows larger, and the day of reckoning becomes more onerous.
2. Pay off the loan with other assets and continue the policy without borrowing. The success of this strategy depends upon the quality of the life insurance policy, its expenses, mortality charges, and investment return offered by the contract.
3. Pay off the policy loan via a loan against other assets that provide for the legitimate deductibility of loan interest, such as a personal residential mortgage.
4. Put the policy on the reduced paid-up insurance option without paying off the loan. In most cases, this will significantly decrease your life insurance and therefore can be expected to create an ordinary income tax liability up to the amount of gain in the policy or the amount of loan relief, whichever is the smaller of the two. There are a number of variations of this reduced paid-up scenario, but remember that reductions in death bene-

fits are likely to trigger ordinary income tax liabilities.

5. Surrender the policy. This is a taxable event. If there is a gain over basis in the policy, it is taxable at ordinary income tax rates. If there is a loss relative to basis, it is not deductible. If most of the equity has been borrowed, there will be decreased net proceeds from the surrendered policy to pay the taxes due on the gain.

6. Exchange the life insurance policy for either another life insurance policy or for an annuity contract via a 1035 tax-free exchange either with or without loans on the policy continuing. Loan relief will result in an ordinary income tax liability to the extent of gain in the policy.

If you must continue the loan, ask the insurance company what is available under strategy 6, a 1035 tax-free exchange to another policy. The objective will be to move to a policy with lower expenses, lower mortality costs, and higher investment return. To avoid a taxable event in the process of the exchange, the loan should be moved intact to the new policy. In this way, the taxation of net debt relief may be avoided and higher yields within the new policy can be used to reduce or eliminate the loans.

To qualify for a 1035 tax-free exchange, you may have to pass a physical. In most cases, you will find a 1035 exchange is worthy of consideration. For example, if you are approaching retirement, you may be able to take old premium paying policies, 1035 exchange them into single premium whole life insurance policies, increase your death benefit, and eliminate premium payments. Many people can enhance return, provide flexibility to cash flow, and increase death benefits.

You could also donate the unneeded policy to a charity. You would take a charitable deduction for the amount of the net cash value and also continue to take charitable deductions for any payments to that charity. The charity could then use the future contributions to eliminate the policy loan and pay premiums and loan interest as required.

Charitable Opportunities with Life Insurance Assets

There is a way to give something away for estate tax purposes but to keep for yourself the income from what you have given away. A piece of property may be considered two pieces instead of one.

Part one is the income interest in the property and part two is the remainder interest, or what is left when you die. Part two may be given to charity while you retain part one for yourself. Although you may think it would be difficult to determine the value of these two parts of one piece of property, it is not, because the IRS mandates interest rates and issues valuation tables based on life expectancy that must be used.

If you want to give to your favorite charity, but also want income for your life, or for your own and your spouse's life, the best item to give would be an asset that you obtained at very low cost (low cost basis). This should be an asset that has and will continue to appreciate rapidly, thus increasing further estate taxes, but generates little or no current income for you. Your objective in giving this asset to charity would be to increase income, decrease future estate taxes, enjoy a current deduction for a charitable contribution, and enjoy the appreciation of the charitable organization now rather than after you have died.

The key to the way this works is that you give this highly appreciated asset to charity. The charity sells it and invests the total proceeds without paying any capital gains tax. They then can reinvest the proceeds to generate the income that they will pay to you. If you sold the appreciated asset personally, you would have to pay capital gains taxes of about 28 percent, which would net you 28 percent less capital available to generate income than is available to the charity.

For example, if you sold something for $100,000 that was entirely profit, you could assume that between the state and federal government you would be taxed 30 percent on the $100,000 profit and you would end up with $70,000 to put to work to generate income. Assuming an interest rate of 6 percent, your income would be $4,200 per year. However, if you gave that $100,000 asset to charity, the charity could sell the asset, pay nothing to the state and federal government, put the full $100,000 to work for you, earn 6 percent, and pay you $6,000 per year. This would increase the income you would receive from that asset by more than 42 percent.

Some people are reluctant to do this because the gift deprives their personal beneficiaries of the value of the asset at their eventual death. However, there is an easy solution for this also. It is entirely possible that the additional income provided by the charity would be enough so that you could gift part of it to your beneficiaries (present interest gifts so they would qualify for the $10,000 per person, per year annual exemption) so that they could buy life insurance on your life or, in a husband-and-wife situation, buy a second-to-die life insurance policy. These policies could be used to provide cash to replace the value of the asset you gave to charity in what is called a wealth replacement trust. Since ownership of the trust would be held by other than you and your spouse, it would not be included in your estate at your own or your spouse's death. In addition, you would have a current charitable deduction for the present value of the remainder interest you are giving to the charity plus their gratitude currently.

You will need the help of your favorite charity, attorney, accountant, and life insurance professional to get this done correctly, but it can be well worth the effort. This can be an everybody wins situation. You reduce your estate taxes and income taxes while receiving more income during your life. The charity receives a future gift, and Uncle Sam, while sacrificing tax revenues, has helped a charity remain economically healthy, doing what society might otherwise have to do.

Marital Deduction

If the "don't own" solution is not practical in your case, yet you are concerned with substantial estate taxes and the fact that the assets within your estate could not be easily liquidated for cash within nine months, you can eliminate estate taxes by making sure that you are married on the day you die. You give all your assets to your surviving spouse. The so-called marital deduction allows you to pass to your spouse an unlimited amount of assets at death, free from any estate taxes. Two things might make this strategy difficult. The first may be that not all of your assets should pass to your spouse, that some should pass to other beneficiaries. The second is that it loads up your spouse's estate so estate taxes are not avoided but simply deferred until the second death.

The strategy of giving all assets to the surviving spouse at the death of the first spouse will work once. It will not work at the death of that surviving spouse, assuming the spouse has not remarried and decided to pass all to the new spouse. At that time, the spouse, now a single individual,

will no longer qualify for any marital deduction. Any estate over the $600,000 exemption will be subject to federal estate taxes. Life insurance on the life of an estate owner is often a solution for making sure that the cash is available to pay estate taxes.

Second-to-Die Life Insurance

A strategy that is being used with greater frequency today is for the estate owner and spouse to do all they possibly can to minimize estate taxes at the first death. This involves using the marital deduction and the $600,000 exemption. This can eliminate estate taxes entirely on up to $1,200,000 in assets. Estates larger than this, or unplanned estates, probably face inevitable estate taxes. To ensure that the cash is available at the second death, you might purchase a second-to-die policy (it may be called a survivorship life policy). Such a policy will not pay off at the death of the first of the two to die but rather at the second death. As a result, this type of life insurance requires lower premiums than a regular life insurance policy. It also allows a couple to obtain life insurance even if one of the two is not in the best of health, whereas the not-too-healthy spouse may not have been able to qualify medically for regular first-to-die life insurance.

The objective of second-to-die policies is to maximize death benefits at the second death. They are very specific-purpose policies, and that purpose is to provide funds to pay estate taxes *for* an estate, rather than *from* an estate.

If the estate owner or the spouse of the estate owner is to own this policy, the full face amount of the death benefit will be includable in the estate and therefore could trigger estate taxes as high as 55 percent against the total death benefit. This is hardly an appropriate arrangement. The survivors of the estate owner and spouse receive the primary benefit of this policy. If it is sufficient in amount to pay all taxes, it will allow the survivors to take the full value of the assets willed to them at death rather than splitting those assets with Uncle Sam. Thus the beneficiaries of the estate owner and spouse are the obvious and appropriate purchasers and owners of such a policy. If these beneficiaries purchase and pay for the policy, most appropriately within some kind of living trust arrangement, the cash to pay the estate taxes will come into their hands at the exact time the taxes are due, at the death of the surviving spouse. The beneficiaries may use the cash from the life insurance proceeds to buy the estate assets, thus providing the estate with cash to pay federal estate taxes. This is a most efficient and economical method of making sure cash is available to pay these taxes. The second-to-die policy offerings are improving. Currently there are whole life, universal life, and universal variable varieties. The last variety can make the policies inside of a family trust very efficient providers for many family purposes—for example, gifting programs or college educations for grandchildren.

Creditor Projection and Life Insurance Products

The frightening example of how easily our lifetime accumulations can be decimated by unforeseen creditors is enough to make anyone stop and think, "What would happen to me!" Adequate and appropriate liability insurance is one answer; however, there always exists the possibility that under a particular set of circumstances the insurance may prove to be inadequate in amount or simply not comprehensive enough to cover the type of loss experienced. In this case, life insurance company contracts may be worth more than their weight in gold.

Under the laws of many states, the cash value and death benefit of a life insurance policy that is payable to the spouse, child, parent, or dependent of an insured cannot be levied by a creditor. It is not clear whether these beneficiaries must be direct beneficiaries or can be the indirect beneficiaries via a living trust. Another caveat is that monies paid into these policies cannot be paid under circumstances that would allow your creditors to prove they were paid in order to safeguard those assets from the claims of the creditor, that is, in fraud of the creditors' rights. You need to build up the asset values of these contracts while you are solvent and without known potential creditors for these assets to enjoy this special protection.

A 1987 bankruptcy case in Illinois against Roland M. Vogel affirmed that his life insurance policies payable to his wife and children were exempt from his creditors' claims.

Life insurance assets are not protected from all creditors, however. The most notorious of all creditors, the Internal Revenue Service, can always penetrate your policies. You also expose these assets to the claims of creditors if you make withdrawals from them.

You can protect your life insurance from creditors by giving it away. If you don't own it, no one can take it from you. Although such protection is as complete as you can get, it may mean that the life insurance contracts you have given away will not accomplish their intended purpose if the new owner chooses to exercise his or her ownership rights. To reduce the possibility of this happening, you might use an irrevocable trust to divest yourself of ownership, at the same time having some assurance that the policies will accomplish their intended purpose. Generally, these trusts do not rely on state law and, therefore, they continue to protect assets even when the insured policyowner moves to another state. When you set up such a trust and carefully choose an "independent" trustee, usually that trustee is sympathetic to the objectives of the grantor and will carefully adhere to the terms and the spirit of the trust document. Obviously, such a trust can protect not only insurance contracts but other assets as well.

Annuities

Basically, an annuity is an amount payable yearly or at other regular intervals for a certain or uncertain period. But an annuity contract should do more than that.

You should beware when insurance companies issue unchangeable and inflexible contracts that limit you and will not adapt to the changes in your life. Inflexibility is more risk than you should take. When you annuitize an annuity, you take the capital that has accumulated within an annuity contract and turn that capital into a fixed-period payout, a fixed-amount payout, or a lifetime payout. Since fixed is not desirable, you should avoid annuitization for as long as possible.

Immediate Annuities

Immediate annuities with structured payouts are defined as having amounts payable at regular intervals for a certain or uncertain period (see Figure 26–6). The immediate annuity is a contract that guarantees a monthly income to the annuitant as a result of a certain amount of capital being in the annuity contract. Pensions often

Figure 26–6

Annuities for Structured Payouts

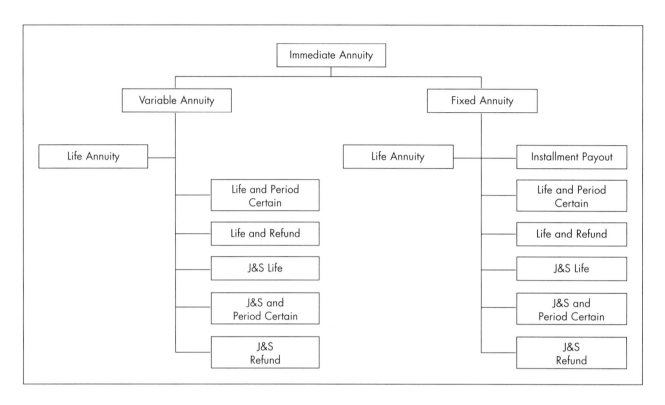

offer this type of annuity; in some cases, the pension plans themselves purchase such contracts from an insurance company as annuities for their retirees by means of a lump-sum payment.

The vast majority of these annuities are fixed (rather than variable) annuities. By looking at our diagram (see Figure 26–7), we see that the male, age 65, based on his life only, would receive a life annuity of $10,866 per year. Looking over the rest of the diagram, we see that this is the highest payment possible. What are the risks that this individual is taking?

The *first* risk is that this annuitant might receive one payment and then die. In that event, the balance left over at his death would be forfeited to the insurance company. That is an unacceptable risk. Suppose instead that he lives a long life and beats the annuity tables. What is the *second* risk he is taking? Suppose a few years down the road he needs access to the principal that he invested in the annuity. Can he get it? No! Once he has annuitized, he can no longer get at his capital. Finally, what is the *third* risk he is taking?

The amount of the monthly or annual payments will not change. Inflation severely erodes the value of fixed annuity payments. The three risks of immediate annuities are forfeiture of capital, loss of liquidity, and inflation.

The annuitant could request an installment payout, saying to the insurance company that he wanted them to pay him in equal annual installments, or monthly installments over the next five years. Alternatively, the annuitant could say that he wanted $1,000 per month from the investment for as long as it lasts. Under both of those decisions, no money would be forfeited to the insurance company under any circumstances. However, it is entirely possible that payments would cease before the annuitant died. Most people and pension plans want to be able to assure people that their retirement income will continue for the rest of their lives.

As a result, both pension plans and individuals often insist on life incomes. Since the life annuity entails the risk of forfeiture of capital at death, provisions are put into the contract to protect

Figure 26–7

Male Age 86 — Spouse Age 62

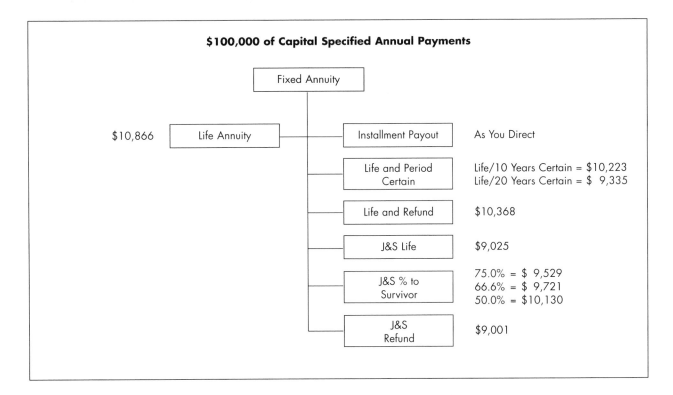

against that risk. The other options for the annuitant are life and ten years certain, life and twenty years certain, or life and refund certain. Under any of these scenarios, payments will be made to a single annuitant for life, but at least payments will be made to the annuitant's beneficiary for the time period guaranteed if the annuitant dies prior to the end of the guarantee period.

In our example, we have a spouse, so there are two lives for which we want to guarantee income. The spouse in this case is female and younger than the male annuitant, which drives down the amount of income that can be expected from the annuity contract, since women typically live longer than men.

For a straight joint and survivor annuity, the payout will be $9,025 per year. That means that the full amount of the $9,025 will continue during each individual's life for as long as the longer-living of the two shall live. If that income is insufficient, they could raise the amount of the payout by choosing to have the survivor of the two receive a reduced amount of income. The

more the income is reduced after the first death, the higher the income will be that they receive while both are living.

Now, what is wrong with all of these annuity contracts? Inflexibility! As soon as the decision is made to annuitize and the first check is accepted, it is fixed. The capital that has been invested in the annuity contract is no longer accessible. You cannot tell the insurance company that your personal circumstances have changed and you would like to change what is happening in the contract. Once you have accepted that first monthly check, the insurance company will not allow you to change the payout decision.

What else is wrong with this annuity contract? Let's say the couple in this scenario select the joint and survivorship annuity and they receive the $9,025 for a long, long period of time. Do you think that the income of $9,025 per year will look as good in the year 2000, 2010, or 2020 as it did in 1990? Prices will have increased manyfold during that period of time and that check for $9,025 per year will begin to purchase less and less goods and services. Inflation has the potential to severely erode this couple's standard of living.

Let's compare this $9,025 joint and survivorship annual income that our couple has accepted to the alternatives available.

Deferred Annuities

Deferred annuities (see Figure 26–8) are flexible annuities. A deferred annuity is an accumulation vehicle. Its function is to accumulate money for you for your retirement and, if your deferred annuity is flexible enough, to allow you to make periodic withdrawals from the contract without annuitization. Deferred annuities can be fixed or variable.

Fixed Annuity

Fixed deferred annuities are single-dimension annuities because they have only one investment opportunity. These are the ones that you hear the most about: They are widely advertised, promising a wonderful current interest rate. It is not a

Figure 26–8

Annuities for Accumulation and Periodic Withdrawals

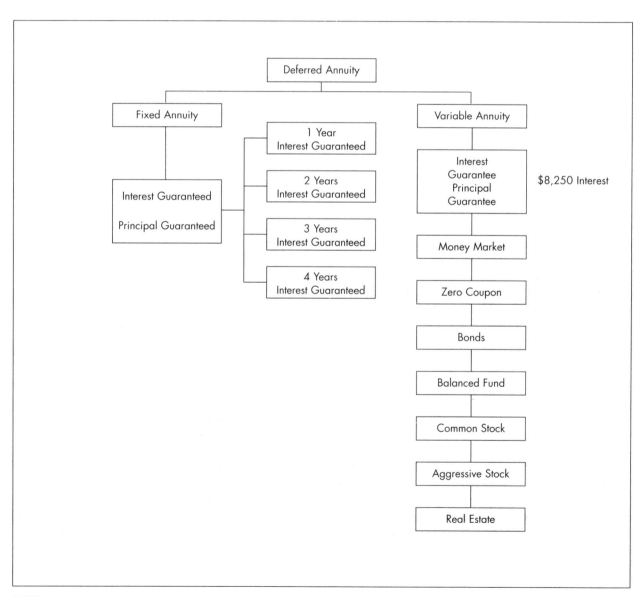

security, since there is only one investment vehicle within the contract. The insurance company chooses the investments from which they guarantee you a particular rate of interest and provide you with a guarantee of your principal. These annuities will typically guarantee an interest rate for periods from as short as three months to as long as four or five years.

A fixed annuity is a single-dimensional investment from which you receive only guaranteed interest. If this is what you want and need, it competes favorably for the money you may have in certificates of deposit and various mutual funds that invest in government securities, bonds, or mortgages. It also competes with the money you might invest in a municipal bond fund. The annuity typically has a degree of conservatism not found in your municipal bond funds or mutual funds in that as interest rates go up, its market value, in most cases, will not go down. But beware—there are some annuities coming into the marketplace that are called market-to-market contracts. If you buy one of these annuities and interest rates go up after the purchase, you will receive only the current market value of the contract if you try to cash it in. You are taking principal risk with this contract.

In most annuities, there is either a front-end sales charge, diminishing the funds you have going into the contract, or a contingent deferred sales charge, a back-end load that would diminish your principal if you chose to leave the annuity at an early date. This usually means that if you keep the annuity at least five, ten, or fifteen years, the charge disappears.

You will want to be very concerned about the financial strength and stability of the insurance company issuing your annuity contract. These contracts are long-term contractual arrangements. You want an insurance company that is going to last at least as long as you are. Additionally, these fixed annuity contracts are counted among the general assets of the insurance company and can be affected by the other things the insurance company does.

It is appropriate for the insurance company to invest the capital that you put inside of your annuity contract in intermediate term bonds and mortgages since that type of investment will match the rate at which they will have to pay you, the annuitant. In some cases and to varying degrees, most insurance companies will invest some portion of this capital in less-than-investment-grade securities. They lend this money to borrowers whose credit rating is less than the investment-grade level. Insurance companies will do this in the private market as well when they make direct arrangements with individual companies by direct placement of loans. The insurance company's ability to find borrowers that they feel certain will pay them back and yet will pay them a higher rate of interest has been one of the reasons for the success of annuities. The insurance company, after all, is a conduit into which you put your relatively small amount of dollars. They pool your money with a lot of money from other people and make very significant loans to companies that can use your capital. The companies using the capital pay you substantial interest for the use of it.

In such large, diversified portfolios, there inevitably will be borrowers who default on their loans. However, in most cases that will be a very small portion of the portfolio and will have very little impact on the insurance company's total portfolio. Such losses normally will be offset by the higher rate of interest they have been able to earn on the good loans they made. The insurance company will get in trouble only if they have a substantial portion of their portfolio in one type of security. If the marketplace suddenly loses faith in that type of security, and the policyowners descend upon the insurance company, demanding the return of their capital all at once, then we have problems. Such a run on the bank, so to speak, may force the insurance company to sell fixed income securities when their usual practice is to retain them until maturity, collecting the interest up until that time. If an insurance company is forced to sell those less-than-investment-grade bonds into a market in which their value is greatly depressed, they may be unable to raise sufficient capital to pay off the onslaught of policyowners. This is only a risk to those insurance companies that have a relatively undiversified investment portfolio comprised primarily of one type of security.

When shopping for fixed annuities, it is wise to put a high priority on a reasonable interest rate rather than seeking out the highest interest rate available. Remember that the weakest borrower must pay you the most to get you to invest in his or her contracts. Just look in the newspaper and you will find savings and loans and banks listed in order, with the weakest of them offering the highest interest rates. Institutions do not pay high interest rates because they love you, but because they have to.

Variable Annuity

You would think that a variable annuity automatically entails more risk than a fixed annuity and, yet, let me suggest that such variable contracts can offer *less risk* if they provide more flexibility and a safe haven account.

The safe haven accounts are the guaranteed interest/guaranteed principal accounts and the money-market accounts. If you bought a variable annuity contract and used only these portions of the contract, you would be emulating a fixed, deferred-annuity contract.

You will want to look for any charges against these accounts, however. In most quality contracts, the guaranteed interest/principal account provides you with a net rate of return without reducing your capital by the amount of a front-end load or investment account charges. If the insurance company is guaranteeing you 8 percent, they probably make 9 percent on reinvesting the capital that you have lent to them. Therefore, they can pay the expenses of your annuity contract out of the spread. In many cases, you will find a contingent deferred sales charge in these contracts that states that, should you terminate the contract early (for example, before the ten or fifteen years have elapsed), some portion of your annuity contract will be surrendered. The insurance company is telling you that the contract has not been in force long enough for them to recoup all of the expenses incurred in putting that annuity contract on the books. These expenses include the agent's commission.

Before you invest in any annuity contract, you will want to be fairly certain that you are not going to have to surrender the contract so early as to incur the contingent deferred sales charge or that you will not need to withdraw money in excess of what the contract allows without the imposition of a sales charge. You will want to evaluate the exact amount of the contingent deferred sales charge, determine the circumstances under which it is imposed, and see if that gives you the flexibility you need.

I would look for flexibility in the area of a free corridor, an amount of capital that you can get out of your annuity without having to pay a penalty. I also would hope that your interest earnings on your capital investment would be exempted from the contingent deferred sales charge. If your objective with your deferred annuity contract is to obtain long-term compounding with a deferral of taxation, it would be unlikely for you to want to withdraw more than 10 percent of the annuity account value. This would defeat your long-term investment strategy by using up your annuity proceeds too quickly. This type of variable annuity can give you what you seek in a fixed-dollar annuity and still offer you the opportunity of using the other funds should they at some point become attractive to you.

Remember when you were looking at the immediate annuities and we determined that the joint and survivorship income that our couple, age 65 and 62, could receive each year was $9,025? At that particular point in time under a variable annuity within the guaranteed interest/guaranteed principal account, this same couple could have earned 8.25 percent on their $100,000 of capital. This would mean that $8,250 in income alone could be generated by the contract. If they could live on that income alone and not delve into their principal for even one year, they would be better off. For the period of that one year, they would still have access to their full $100,000 capital, albeit exposed to potential insurance company penalties and ordinary income tax to the extent that it represents a return of funds that have never been taxed previously. As a result of delaying annuitization for one year, each one of the individuals would be one year older and, therefore, the annuity income available would be higher since it increases as their ages increase.

The best-case scenario would be if they really did not need of the income being generated by their annuity contract. In this case, the excess income generated by the contract could be dollar cost averaged into some of the alternative investment accounts in the contract in an effort to reduce the couple's exposure to inflation risk by increasing their investment in equities.

Over the years, as the equity accounts build as a result of their transfers, it is likely at some time the equity markets will be high relative to the couple's average investment in the plan. When this happens, and the amount of money in their equity account disturbs their peace of mind, they may easily sell out the equity account and transfer the assets back into the guaranteed interest/principal account. This would increase the amount that is generating interest, which will, in turn, increase the amount that they have either for spendable income as required or for reinvestment on a dollar cost averaging basis into the equity accounts.

These annuity accounts can be used for after-tax, personal accumulation of retirement capital, or as the receptacle for individual retirement accounts, tax-sheltered annuity accounts, 401(k) plans, and pension and profit-sharing plan monies. Many such annuity contracts have been used for the rollover IRA receptacle of distributions from employers to employees of retirement fund accumulations.

When you are dealing with capital that has taken a lifetime to accumulate, you are dealing with important core capital. The preservation of this capital can have a great deal to do with your mental attitude as you live on the fruits of that capital for many years.

After looking at the various options offered, you may find the rollover IRA strategy very satisfying and stress-free. If you can roll the funds into an IRA annuity contract and live on just the interest earnings (or less than the interest earnings and invest the excess income on a dollar cost averaging basis into one of the equity accounts), your capital will never diminish. It will always be equal to or greater than what you had when you retired. Distributions can be timed in a tax-wise fashion.

We have retirees coming into our office, asking for distributions in the early part of the year and withdrawing sums that they expect to take them through to the fall. They will deposit that money into a money-market account and use it for living purposes. When that is exhausted, they ask for another distribution of just enough to get them to the end of the tax year so that they do not have to pay income tax on more than they need within the current calendar year.

One of our favorite retirees is a gentleman who retired more than five years ago. He has watched his account balance increase at the rate of 3 percent per year while he has taken distributions to provide for his living expenses, paid cash for a new car, and gone to Las Vegas once or twice a year, while making sure that his distributions were taxed at the minimum bracket possible. If he had to take all of the interest income today, he would

be receiving more than he would have received five years ago had he accepted his employer's fixed life income monthly annuity payment. He now is beyond the back-end load period and therefore his funds are entirely available to him to the extent that he is willing to pay ordinary income tax on what he takes as distributions. In the event of his death, his spouse will have an amount of capital substantially larger than what was available when her husband retired. If we do everything right, she will enjoy that income by taking periodic withdrawals from the contract for the rest of her life and, at the death of the second of the two of them, the capital will then be paid out to their stipulated beneficiaries with none of the funds being forfeited to the insurance company. This is the kind of annuity that I like!

Annuities Available

Here is what is available in the annuity marketplace today. The left side of the diagram (see Figure 26–9), the immediate annuity selections, are for those people who are forced to annuitize either by their employer, by their economic situation, or by their contract provisions. An important criteria in purchasing an annuity would be that the contract not force annuitization or even encourage annuitization by paying higher interest rates if the annuitant annuitized rather than taking periodic distributions and avoiding annuitization.

Be very careful. There are many poor annuity contracts in the marketplace today. They can be hazardous to your wealth!

Forced annuitization can be very costly in terms of investment results and flexibility. You will want to avoid such contracts if you are seeking flexibility and control.

The annuity as an accumulation vehicle (that is, the deferred annuity that allows you to take periodic distributions) is a highly desirable contract. It gives you the ability to compound within the contract without current taxation. That ability allows you to build a bigger capital base faster that will someday generate income during your retirement years. Do not let people dissuade you by criticizing annuities and doing mathematical models that show that when you withdraw your capital from the annuity, if taxes go up there is a possibility that your net after-tax return would be smaller than if you invested outside of an annuity. Your objective in an annuity is to build a large

Figure 26–9

Annuities

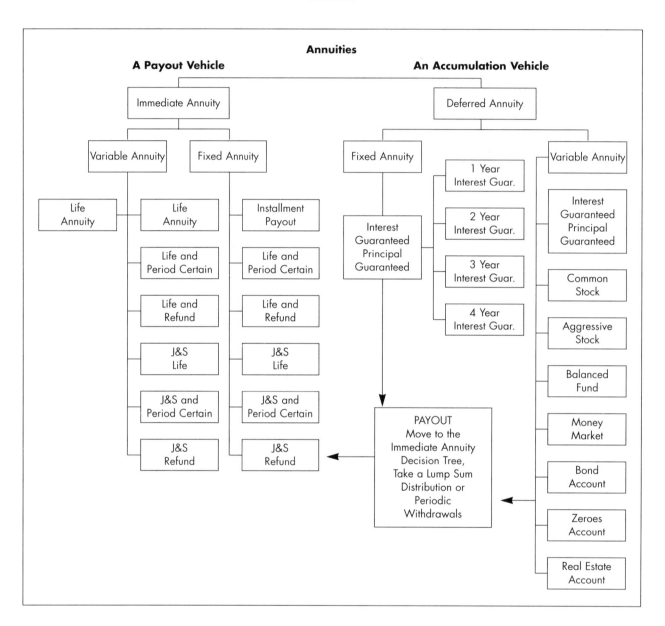

capital base inside of the contract to generate income, not to build a large capital base and then to erode that capital base by pulling out both principal and income. The bigger the capital base you build, the more likely you are to be able to live on interest only.

Figure 5–10 summarizes what we have been trying to accomplish. There are only two income generators in this world—the individual at work

and money at work. During a major part of our lives, the income is generated by the individual at work. However, it is essential that each one of us fill our capital wheel to the right on the diagram so that when we are no longer able to work or do not wish to work, there is sufficient capital in the wheel to generate income to provide for our standard of living and our independence. Any plan that assumes that principal can be taken from

Figure 26–10

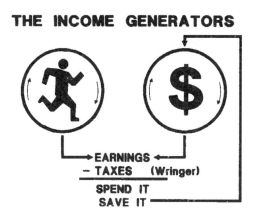

THE INCOME GENERATORS

that capital wheel over time because of the assumption that we will die by a certain age will create a very unhappy and insecure retiree. We will live in fear that the capital wheel will disappear before we do.

Alternatively, a retiree with a full capital wheel, generating sufficient income so that the invasion of principal is not required will, in all likelihood be a happy, healthier, secure, friendly, and longer-living retiree. It is worth working for.

Trading Life Insurance and Annuity Contracts

Flexibility is preferable to inflexibility in the life insurance and annuity contracts that you use to enhance your own and your family's financial security. If the contract you have purchased is adaptable to your economic circumstances as they change and develop, it is more likely to perform satisfactorily for you.

You may find yourself owning a life insurance or annuity policy that is no longer suitable. You should not just surrender the contract; the income taxes and penalties that may be required may cause you unnecessary expense. There is a provision of the income tax code referred to as section 1035 that allows you to make tax-free exchanges of a life insurance policy for another life insurance policy, a life insurance policy for an annuity contract, or an annuity contract for another annuity contract. You simply trade contracts. However, you cannot do a tax-free trade of an annuity contract into a life insurance contract.

To effect a 1035 tax-free exchange, you must direct company A to send the net proceeds of your contract to company B and direct company B, in writing, to put those proceeds into the company B life insurance contract or annuity that you prefer. If this is done properly, you should not have to pay income taxes on the transaction. You may, however, have to pay surrender charges to company A and acquisition charges to company B. If these are acceptable and the alternative contract is better suited to fulfilling your needs, then proceed.

The advantage of the tax-free exchange is that you will not have to pay any taxes on the gains earned in the original contract. What if there are no gains in the original contract, indeed, what if there is a loss? Surrendering the contract does not allow you to take a deduction for that loss on your income tax return. Losses as a result of surrendering life insurance or annuity contracts are not deductible. The reason you have a loss in that old contract is because your cost basis, your investment, exceeds the capital accumulated in the contract. The advantage of doing a 1035 tax-free exchange in this case is that you would be rolling that high basis into the new contract. The higher the basis in your new contract, the more you will be able to take out of that contract in living benefits without taxation. Those old policies that have not performed adequately can still be valuable to you in this way. In short, gain or loss in your old contracts, the 1035 tax-free exchange is likely to be to your economic advantage.

The 1035 tax-free exchange becomes advantageous also if you own a life insurance policy and at some point in the future determine that the life insurance is no longer needed or appropriate. You shouldn't be paying for it any longer. You can get the money that you have put into your contract (your basis) out of your life insurance policy by doing a 1035 exchange of that policy into an annuity contract. From that point forward, the investment return within the contract will not be subject to the mortality charges inherent in a life insurance policy, your tax-deferral will continue, and your cost basis in the contract will include all of your previously paid life insurance costs and expenses. Do remember, however, that the proceeds of the annuity contract will not be received income tax-free by your beneficiary as would be the case if you had retained the life insurance.

Many old annuity contracts were less flexible and provided less investment returns to the contract holders than do the ones that are being issued today. If you find yourself with such a contract, you may wish to do a 1035 exchange into an annuity contract that would better suit your present-day needs and provide you with greater investment returns and more flexibility.

You will note we have not suggested tax-free exchanges from an annuity contract into a life insurance contract, since section 1035 does not permit that type of tax-free exchange.

APPENDIX A
Annuity Purchase Checklist

1. The company issuing the contract: Financial strength and track record. An annuity contract is only successful when the relationship is long term, that is, lifetime.
2. Current interest rate: A fixed dollar annuity. Investment accounts, investment management, and competitive current interest, and guaranteed principal accounts if you are choosing a variable annuity.
3. Guarantee period for the guaranteed interest rate.
4. Minimum guaranteed rate of interest after the initial guarantee period is completed.
5. Bail-out provisions: Provisions that allow you to surrender the annuity contract without penalty if the interest rate falls below a contractually stated amount.
6. Cost of bail-out provision: Do you have the option of accepting higher interest and no bail-out provision or lower initial interest with a bail-out provision?
7. Interest rate track record for fixed annuities: Investment account track records and interest rate track records for variable annuities.
8. Free withdrawal privilege: How much cash can you withdraw from a contract each year without being subject to insurance-company-imposed withdrawal charges? Withdrawal from any annuity before age 59½ would be subject to the normal government penalty, currently 10 percent.
9. Front-end charges: Reducing your investment.
10. Surrender charges (back-end loads): At what point would such surrender charges no longer exist?
11. Under what circumstances are the surrender charges waived, such as death, disability, or an annuity payout?
12. Market value adjustment: If the annuity contract is surrendered, is the surrender value adjusted as a result of changes in prevailing interest rates? This would be typical of a variable annuity bond account. You would be wise to avoid this adjustment feature in a fixed annuity.
13. On surrender, can you choose to take your payments back instead of the cash surrender value?
14. At death, what is the situation for your named beneficiary? With a fixed annuity, it would be unusual for the beneficiary to be in a situation where the amount to be paid out was less than the amount invested. However, with variable annuities, a significant drop in the stock market could expose an individual to significant principal risk. You will find that with most variable annuities, the beneficiary will receive the annuity at market value or the owner's gross investments in the contract, whichever is greater. Within the prospectus you can expect to find approximately a .5 percent charge for this guarantee for the variable annuity. Look for it; it does offer a nice measure of security.
15. Are there any annual fees?
16. What is the commission, and what is its impact on your account?

27

Before You Buy That Mutual Fund: Factors to Consider

CONSTANZA ERDOES AND JOHN HENRY LOW

Mutual funds are unequivocally a great investment vehicle. They provide individual investors with a degree of diversification that is unbeatable. They also allow you to invest in markets that ordinarily might be very difficult to invest in, such as very small or international stocks.

Mutual funds have come a long way since they originated in the 1920s. They are the favorite investment vehicle of the baby boomer generation, which has poured trillions of investment dollars into mutual funds. Their popularity is evidenced by their number—there are far more U.S. registered mutual funds (approximately 11,000) than individual U.S. stocks (approximately 7,000). The sheer volume alone can make selecting mutual funds difficult, but there are other important factors to consider. Common questions that we are frequently asked include: Should I choose load or no-load funds? Shouldn't I just invest in last year's winners? Should I care who the fund manager is? What are these "A" and "B" shares anyway?

In this chapter, we offer ten tips on selecting great mutual funds for your portfolio.

1. Determine your asset allocation.

Determine your asset allocation, *then* look for mutual funds that invest in those asset classes or investment markets. Decide how much of your portfolio should be invested in equities and how

Constanza Erdoes and John Henry Low are partners at Knickerbocker Advisors Inc., an investment management firm based in New York. The information contained in this chapter is intended for general information only and should not be acted upon without professional advice.

much in fixed income, and then narrow the asset classes to include large *and* small cap stocks, international and domestic stocks and bonds, and value and growth stocks. Each asset class or investment market has different risk and return characteristics.

Your particular asset allocation should be based on your individual return requirements, investment risk tolerance and time horizon. If you have trouble determining the proper allocation, consult a professional. The proper asset allocation can be the single most important determinant of a successful investment plan. Studies have shown that asset allocation (rather than security selection or market timing) accounts for more than 90 percent of investment performance, so don't skimp on this crucial investment determinant.

2. Find mutual funds that invest in a single asset class.

Now that you have determined that a 10 percent allocation to small capitalization (cap), "value-style" stocks is appropriate for your portfolio, how do you find a mutual fund for this asset class? One way is to call an investment company and ask them about their mutual funds that invest in that asset class. A much better and more objective way is to use independent research material available from Morningstar, Value Line, or Micropal, or consult a professional.

Look for funds that tend to stay invested in their asset class, rather than "style shifters." Style shifters are funds that rotate among different asset classes at the manager's discretion in an attempt to chase performance by moving into the next "hot" investment style. Sometimes this practice has positive results (like Fidelity's Magellan Fund under Peter Lynch), but more often the results are disappointing. There are remarkably few managers who can sustain a constant level of outperformance through style shifting.

The main problem with a fund that style shifts is that you never really know where your assets are invested. The portion of your investments allocated to the small cap value asset class may, in two months, end up being invested in mid cap stocks or highly aggressive "growth" stocks. Style shifting is akin to market timing. The theory is fine, but in practice it usually washes out.

It takes a long time to develop the skills to invest with consistent excellence. Generally, fund managers who specialize in a single style become more proficient using that style than managers who always change styles (the jacks of all trades and masters of none). Your investment dollars are important. Finding a fund that invests in a single asset class gives you control over your portfolio's returns *and* risks.

3. Ask if the fund is "actively" or "passively" managed.

Each asset class has an appropriate benchmark or index. The S&P 500 is probably the best known index, representing the 500 largest stocks in the United States, which are a blend of both "value" and "growth" styles. Actively managed funds use research, techniques, models, or instinct to try to either *beat the returns* or *reduce the risk of* an index, in contrast with a passively managed or index fund, which seeks only to *replicate* the returns of an index.

For example, a fund that exactly matches the holdings and proportions of the small/mid cap Russell 2000 Index is an index or passively managed fund. This type of fund does not try to beat the returns of an index. So, if a Russell 2000 index fund exactly matches the holdings and proportions of the Russell 2000, the fund's returns will equal those of the Russell 2000, less the fund's fees and expenses. (This is why low fees on an index fund are crucial.)

By contrast, a fund that invests in S&P 500 stocks but buys different proportions or selects different securities to try to beat the returns of the S&P 500 is an actively managed fund. Actively managed funds represent an additional element of risk over index funds because investors rely on the manager's skills to outperform. (Remember, an active manager has to outperform the index plus his or her fund's fees.) This is not an easy task. In some years, barely 20 percent of actively managed funds beat their index.

4. Judge a fund's performance against the appropriate index or benchmark.

Unfortunately the risk and return performance of most funds are most often compared against that of the S&P 500 Index because it is the most recognized index among investors.

This practice is especially misleading for small cap and international funds. As they are inherently riskier than large cap funds, they are *expected* to have higher returns than the S&P 500 over the long run. So when a small cap fund compares its long-term performance against that of the S&P 500, it may look more favorable than if it compares its performance against its more appropriate small cap index.

Mutual funds that invest in the large cap blend asset class are the *only* funds that should be compared against the S&P 500. Be sure to ask which index the fund is benchmarking itself against. If the answer is the S&P 500 for any asset class other than large caps, you may want to look elsewhere. Also ask what the fund's correlation percentage to the index is. The correlation statistic tells us how much of a fund's behavior can be explained by the behavior of the index. Thus an S&P 500 index fund should have a nearly perfect (100 percent) correlation to the S&P 500. If it doesn't, then the fund is not investing exactly in the same proportion or with the same timing as the S&P 500. If a fund's correlation is materially less than 80 percent, then its movements are not materially linked to those of an index, and the fund is either benchmarking itself against the wrong index, style shifting, or investing in a different style.

5. Judge a fund's performance over the long term.

An almost foolproof way to pick the wrong mutual fund is to buy last year's winner. Look at a fund's performance over at least a three- or five-year period. Even better, focus on eleven or twelve years (rather than ten). Today, eleven years will still include the 1987 market crash, while the ten-year statistic will factor it out. Examine the fund's performance over different market and economic environments. Does the fund perform well only in bull markets? Is the fund so defensive that it only performs well in bear markets? How did it do in inflationary years? Years with slow economic growth, and so on?

6. Don't pay for loads if you don't have to.

And you don't have to anymore. Loads are simply sales commissions. When mutual funds began to appear on the markets, they were almost exclusively load funds. As the industry has grown, no-load funds have proliferated.

Does a load affect your investment that much? Absolutely. Assume you are choosing between two funds that invest in the same asset class, and have similar risk/return performance. If you invest $10,000 in the no-load fund, your entire $10,000 is invested immediately. If you invest that same $10,000 in a fund that carries a 5 percent load, only $9,500 is invested immediately, with the remaining 5 percent or $500, going to the salesperson as a commission. This is a high price to pay when you factor in the magic of compounding. Look at the chart below to see what happens to $10,000 invested in each fund over 10 years assuming a 10 percent annual rate of return:

	Load Fund Value	No-Load Fund Value
$ Invested	$ 9,500	$10,000
Year 1	$10,450	$11,000
Year 2	$11,495	$12,100
Year 5	$15,300	$16,105
Year 10	$24,641	$25,937

As you can see, over ten years, the load fund earned $1,296 or 13 percent *less*, just by charging a 5 percent commission during the first year. To lessen the appearance of upfront load costs, the industry has created different classes of shares, some of which ironically may cost the consumer even more. For example, "A" shares are usually front-end loads payable at the time of investment; "B" shares may be back-end loads, payable when you sell the fund rather than when you purchase it; "C" shares may be level loads, meaning some percent is charged each year. Either way, they erode your return. With the number of mutual funds available today, you should be able to find a great performing no-load fund in every asset class.

Also be wary of funds whose loads dissipate over time. These are funds that charge loads only if you sell them in five years or less (often, "B" shares). In reality, "B" shares often charge higher ongoing management fees to make up for potentially lost commissions. Besides, five years is a very long time to hold on to a potentially mediocre fund just to avoid a load charge.

7. Look for experienced managers.

We firmly believe that consistent performance is attributable to mutual fund managers who are highly experienced in their investment style or market sector. A successful European stock investment manager, for example, may not have the skill or the knack for investing in small, high-growth U.S. stocks. This holds true in most professions. A top-notch criminal litigator might be out of his element tackling complex corporate transactions. Investment professionals are no different.

Ask about the manager's background. How long has he or she invested in this asset class? Some mutual fund families, by policy, rotate their managers every few years—great training for investment managers but potentially disappointing results for investors.

With the rapid proliferation of mutual funds over the past ten years, the average age of mutual fund managers is in the early 30s. Think about the implications: A fund manager in his or her late 20s or early 30s probably has not experienced a major bear market (the last crash was in 1987 and the last major, prolonged bear market was in 1973-1974). This is not to say that there are not some fine young managers out there, but you may not want to have your *entire* portfolio run by someone with no experience in a market downturn.

8. Beware of funds with high manager turnover.

We invest our client's dollars with managers, not mutual funds. After all, it is the manager's vision and skill that determine a fund's performance, and not the mutual fund's name or legal entity status. When a new manager takes the reins of a mutual fund, you can't really be sure that he or she will manage the fund in the same style as the previous manager. Technically, a fund's risk and return performance can only properly be measured under the same manager. So when evaluating a fund, you should discard any performance prior to the last manager change.

Now, there are some terrific funds that are an exception and only hire managers who can succeed in carrying on the fund's investment style. Unfortunately, they tend to be the exception rather than the norm. Also watch out for funds managed by "teams," which often masks high manager turnover from the scrutiny of a fund analyst.

9. Don't rely on fund names.

What a fund can legally invest in is delineated in the fund's prospectus, often a difficult but worthwhile read. Most funds have great leeway to invest in a variety of instruments at the manager's discretion. It is important to find out how consistent a fund has been with its investment objective. For example, a few years ago, we came across a utility fund (supposedly low risk) that was trying to boost its performance by investing more than 50 percent of its assets in very risky high-tech stocks. The fund was perfectly within its legal rights to do so, but we suspect this might have come as a shock to many of the fund's investors.

Unfortunately, mutual funds are only required to disclose their holdings twice a year (some do disclose more often). Look at independent fund research and ask for old annual reports to find the fund's *actual* investments over the past few years, including the ratio of cash to invested assets. Consistently high cash ratios may indicate that the fund is growing so quickly that it can't put cash to good use or that the fund is defensive and is hedging against a downturn in the markets.

10. Watch those expenses.

Every fund has annual expenses that are used to pay for the manager's and staff's salaries, overhead, research costs, and such, but some funds carry unreasonably high expenses. Look at a fund's expense ratio, found in both the prospectus and annual report. The expense ratio expresses a fund's annual expenses as a percentage of each dollar invested. So an expense ratio of 1 percent means that 1 percent of every dollar invested ($.01) goes toward paying the fund's expenses. (Note that mutual funds disclose their investment returns *net* of expenses.)

As a rule of thumb, large cap blend funds should have expenses of 0.9 percent or lower. Index and bond funds, should be substantially lower (under 0.2 percent for index funds, under 0.5 percent for bond funds). Research-intensive, specialized, new and international funds will have higher expenses and thus higher expense ratios (1.5 percent). Many good funds will lower their expenses every year—a trend we heartily endorse.

Selecting the right mutual funds for your investment portfolio is part science, part art. Armed with the right questions and adequate research, you will be well on your way to selecting consistently great mutual funds for your portfolio.

Part IV
Health-Care Issues

28
Medicare: An Overview

HAROLD G. WREN

Medicare is a program of health insurance for people age 65 or older and disabled people. It consists of two parts. Medicare Hospital Insurance (Part A) pays for inpatient hospital care, some inpatient care in a skilled nursing facility, home health care, and hospice care. Medicare Medical Insurance (Part B) helps pay for doctors' services, outpatient hospital services, home health care, diagnostic tests, medical appliances, prescription drugs, and a number of other services and supplies not covered by Part A.

Part A: Hospital Insurance Eligibility and Benefits

How Do I Become Eligible for Medicare Part A?

If you are age 65 or older and are entitled to Social Security benefits or railroad retirement benefits, you generally qualify for Part A of Medicare. It is not necessary that you actually retire at age 65 or be receiving Social Security or railroad retirement benefits to be eligible for Medicare Part A. You can continue to work past age 65 and still be eligible for Medicare benefits, provided you file a Medicare enrollment application.

If you are under age 65, you may be eligible for Part A benefits if:

1. you have been receiving or are entitled to receive Social Security or railroad retirement disability benefits for more than twenty-four months; or
2. you suffer from end-stage renal disease.

If you are age 65 or older but are not entitled to Part A because you do not have enough work credits but are eligible for Part B benefits, you can purchase Part A insurance during a general enrollment period by paying a monthly premium. Persons over 65 who are ineligible for Part A may purchase Hospital Insurance (HI) at a premium cost of $309[1] per month in 1998, so long as they are eligible and enroll in Part B, and pay the monthly premium of $43.80. Disabled persons under 65 who lose their cash benefits because they return to work may continue under Medicare for a period up to thirty-six months, after which they may purchase Medicare coverage in the same way as do those over 65 who are uninsured.

HI is financed by payroll deduction in the same way as Social Security. The tax rate for Social Security benefits (SSB) is 6.2 percent of annual earnings, for hospital insurance (HI), 1.45 percent, or a total of 7.65 percent. Self-employed persons pay twice this amount, or 15.3 percent of annual earnings, but are entitled to deduct one-half of this amount. The net result is to treat such persons the same as employees.

Prior to 1991, the maximum amount taxable for Social Security benefits and HI was the same—$51,300. Beginning in 1991, the maximum taxable amount for SSB was increased to $53,400, and for HI, to $125,000. In 1992, these figures were raised to $55,500 and $130,200; and in 1993, to $57,600 and $135,000. Since 1994, *all* of an employee's earnings have been subject to the tax for HI, but the limitation ($68, 400 in 1998) has been retained for Social Security.

Harold G. Wren is of counsel to the law firm of Voyles & Johnson, P.S.C., in Louisville, Kentucky.

1. This amount is reduced to $170 for uninsured persons (and their spouses) who have at least thirty credits toward qualifying for Social Security.

What Does Medicare Part A Pay For?

Medicare Part A will pay for four kinds of medically necessary care:

1. inpatient hospital services;
2. skilled nursing facility services following a hospital stay;
3. home health services; and
4. hospice care.

Inpatient Hospital Services

Medicare will help pay the costs of inpatient hospital stays, but first, certain conditions must be met. A doctor must prescribe treatment for your illness or injury that can only be provided through an inpatient hospital stay. Second, the hospital you stay in must participate in the Medicare program. Finally, a utilization review committee at the hospital or a peer review organization (PRO) must not disapprove your stay.

ROLE OF THE PEER REVIEW ORGANIZATION

A peer review organization (PRO) is a group of practicing physicians and other health-care professionals who review the care given to Medicare patients to determine whether it meets the standards of quality accepted by the medical profession. PROs also investigate written complaints by beneficiaries or their representatives about the quality of care provided by hospitals, skilled nursing facilities, home health agencies, and other health-provider organizations.

PROs have the authority to decide whether the proposed care is reasonable and necessary and can deny payment for care given that was not medically necessary. The Department of Health and Human Services has designated a PRO in each state to be responsible for reviewing each case brought to them to determine whether the physician and/or hospital made correct judgments in the case.

For example, if the hospital denies you admission, you may appeal to the PRO to find out:

1. the reasons for the denial;
2. when and how to request reconsideration; and
3. where to file your request.

Suppose the hospital's utilization review committee determines that Medicare will no longer cover hospital inpatient care in your case. If your physician agrees with the hospital, you may demand a written explanation of the decision. The notice must explain your right of appeal, and it must give you the name, address, and phone number of the PRO in your area. If you wish, you may take an appeal to the PRO. The PRO will decide on the propriety of the committee's decision depending upon:

1. the necessity of the services requested;
2. the reasonableness of the services; and
3. the appropriateness of the setting.

If you are not satisfied with the decision of the PRO, you can appeal to an administrative law judge of the Social Security Administration.

The role of the PRO is not limited to decisions regarding your request for admission and length of stay in the hospital. The PRO in your area will also review your case following your hospital stay to determine whether you were discharged prematurely. Other issues commonly resolved by the PRO are:

1. whether surgical procedures are being performed only when medically necessary; and
2. whether admissions for elective surgery are being made only when outpatient care is either medically inadvisable or unavailable.

If all other conditions are met, and the PRO approves your inpatient hospital stay, Medicare will help pay the costs of covered hospital services.

SERVICES COVERED

Medicare will help cover the costs of covered hospital services for up to ninety days of hospitalization for each spell of illness. Medicare Part A fully covers the first sixty days of hospitalization after an annual deductible of $764[2] is paid by you. After the annual deductible is paid, Medicare Part A pays in full the cost of a semiprivate room (two to four beds) or a ward (five or more beds). It will pay for a private room only if the patient's condition requires isolation or if no semiprivate beds are available. If you wish to stay in a private room, but none of the above conditions are met, Medicare will pay only the rate charged for a semi-private room, and you will be required to pay the difference. For days sixty-one through ninety, you must pay a daily coinsurance amount of $191. Thereafter, you have the option of paying the hospital charges or up to $382 per day for as many as sixty

2. The dollar amounts for deductibles, coinsurance payments, and the like are based on 1998 figures, which may increase in coming years.

"lifetime reserve days." Your "benefit period" will expire sixty days after your discharge from the hospital. If you are later admitted for another hospital stay, you must again pay the deductible and coinsurance amounts for a new benefit period.

Other inpatient hospital services covered under Part A include:

1. regular nursing services;
2. special care units, such as intensive care and coronary care units;
3. drugs, vaccines, blood (whole and packed red blood cells), blood components, and the costs of blood processing and administration;
4. appliances, such as splints and wheelchairs, furnished by the facility;
5. lab tests, X rays, and radiation therapy;
6. operating and recovery room costs;
7. services provided by ancillary departments of the hospital, such as physical therapy, rehabilitation therapy, and occupational therapy.

SERVICES NOT COVERED

Medicare Part A will not pay for:

1. private duty nursing services;
2. the medical and surgical services of a physician;
3. the first three pints of blood (whole blood or units of packed red blood cells);
4. personal convenience items (such as telephone, television, and the like);
5. drugs, appliances, and supplies for use outside the hospital, unless a limited supply is necessary to facilitate your discharge from the hospital;
6. a private room, unless a private room is medically necessary or no semiprivate bed is available.

USING YOUR LIFETIME RESERVE DAYS

If you have to stay in the hospital for more than ninety days, Medicare will help cover the costs up to an extra sixty days of hospitalization. These sixty extra days, called lifetime reserve days, can be used only once. That means that once you use them, they cannot be reused during the same or a later hospital stay. Ordinarily, if you must stay in the hospital for more than ninety days, your excess lifetime reserve days will be used unless you elect not to use them. Your hospital is required to notify you if you have used or if it appears that you will use any of your lifetime reserve days. Coinsurance charges for reserve days are $338 per day. After

reserve days are used up, you will be responsible for the entire hospital bill.

Skilled Nursing Facility Care

Medicare Part A also covers the costs of inpatient care furnished by a Medicare-participating skilled nursing facility if certain conditions are met:

1. you must have been a hospital inpatient for at least three consecutive days before you were transferred to a skilled nursing facility;
2. you must be admitted to a skilled nursing facility within thirty days after leaving the hospital;
3. you must be transferred to the skilled nursing facility because you require extended treatment for a condition for which you received treatment in the hospital; and
4. a doctor must certify that you need, on a daily basis, skilled nursing or rehabilitative care or care that can only be given in a skilled nursing facility on an inpatient basis.

If all of these conditions are met, Medicare will help pay the costs of your stay in a skilled nursing facility up to one hundred days. Of those hundred days, Medicare Part A will cover the full cost for all covered services up to the twentieth day. From the twenty-first through the hundredth day, you will be responsible for a daily coinsurance amount of $84.50. After that, you will be required to pay the entire amount.

SERVICES COVERED

Medicare Part A coverage for skilled nursing facility services includes the costs of:

1. a semiprivate room, unless a private room is medically necessary;
2. regular nursing services, if it is furnished by, or under the supervision of, a registered professional nurse;
3. physical, speech, and occupational therapy when it is furnished by the skilled nursing facility;
4. medical social services;
5. drugs, vaccines, blood (whole and packed red blood cells), blood components, and the costs of blood processing and administration;
6. medical supplies, such as splints, oxygen, surgical dressing, casts, and the like; and
7. other diagnostic and therapeutic items provided by a hospital with which the facility has an agreement for the transfer of patients.

SERVICES NOT COVERED

Medicare Part A does not cover the costs of:

1. private duty nursing care;
2. a private room, unless medically necessary;
3. personal grooming and convenience items;
4. any item or service that would not have been covered as an inpatient hospital service.

Home Health Services

A home health agency is a private organization or a public agency that provides skilled health care and other services in your home. The services provided by home health agencies can be covered under both Medicare Part A and Part B, but Part A pays if you are eligible under both programs. Under both Part A and Part B, there is no deductible or coinsurance charge for home health services (except for a 20 percent coinsurance charge for durable medical equipment), and there is no limit on the number of visits and no requirement of prior hospitalization.

To qualify for Medicare coverage of home health care services, the following conditions must be met:

1. you must be confined to your home;
2. you must be in need of intermittent skilled nursing care or in need of physical or speech therapy;
3. you must be under the care of a physician who periodically reviews the care you receive;
4. the home health agency must be a Medicare-participating provider.

SERVICES COVERED

Home health services covered under both Medicare Part A and Part B include the following:

1. the intermittent or part-time services of a registered nurse, licensed practical nurse, or a licensed vocational nurse under the supervision of a registered nurse;
2. the skilled services of a physical, speech, or occupational therapist;
3. medical social services provided under the direction of a physician and furnished by a qualified medical social worker;
4. the part-time or intermittent services of a home health aide;
5. medical supplies and durable medical equipment;
6. the services of interns and residents-in-training; and

7. outpatient services (other than the costs of transporting an individual to the facility) provided under arrangements with an approved provider facility that require equipment that cannot readily be transported to the individual's residence for treatment purposes.

Medicare payment depends upon the patient demonstrating a need for intermittent or part-time care. That means the individual must have a recurring need for the services of a professional nurse or home health aide at least once every sixty days. Usually, individuals need home health care a few hours a day several times a week. At the most, Medicare covers home health services up to thirty-five hours per week on a less than daily basis (that is, less than four days a week). In a few instances, Medicare will cover full-time skilled nursing care and home health care services needed seven days a week, but only up to twenty-one consecutive days.

SERVICES NOT COVERED

Medicare excludes from coverage of home health care:

1. services that would not be included as a covered hospital inpatient service, such as private duty nursing services and items of personal convenience and comfort;
2. drugs and biologicals;
3. food services, such as Meals-on-Wheels and similar services;
4. housekeeping services; and
5. transportation services to a facility for outpatient treatment.

Hospice Services

Hospice care is a program of services provided by public or private organizations to terminally ill people. Services are aimed at supportive therapy, such as pain relief, rather than invasive cure-oriented approaches. Hospice emphasizes home care assistance, rather than institutionalization.

SERVICES COVERED

Medicare covers the following hospice services:

1. nursing care provided by, or under the supervision of, a registered professional nurse;
2. medical social services provided by a social worker under the direction of a physician;
3. physician's services;
4. counseling services to the terminally ill individual and the individual's family;
5. medical appliances and supplies, including

drugs and biologicals used primarily for pain relief;

6. short-term inpatient care at a hospital or skilled nursing facility that meets special hospice standards;

7. the services of home health aids and homemakers, including personal care and household services;

8. physical, speech, and occupational therapy services to control symptoms or enable the individual to maintain activities of daily living and basic functional skills.

Medicare covers a total of 210 days of hospice care during an individual's lifetime. Of these days, a terminally ill patient is limited to two ninety-day periods and one subsequent period of thirty days. If a patient elects to receive hospice care, he or she must choose from which program he or she will receive care. He or she waives the right to use Medicare coverage for other services related to his or her condition, as well as the right to receive hospice care from a program other than the one he or she has chosen. This election is revocable.

Part B: Medical Insurance Eligibility and Benefits

How Do I Become Eligible for Medicare Part B?

If you are eligible for Medicare benefits under Part A, you are automatically eligible for benefits under Part B. If you are not eligible for Part A benefits, you can still apply for Part B benefits if you are age 65 or older and a resident and citizen of the United States or a permanent resident alien who has resided in the United States for the five years immediately before the month of application for enrollment. This means that persons not entitled to Social Security benefits, such as federal and state employees, are nonetheless eligible for Part B benefits.

How Do I Enroll for Part B Benefits?

Enrollment for benefits under Part B occurs either automatically or voluntarily.

Automatic enrollment occurs once you qualify for benefits under Part A (by reason of entitlement to Social Security or disability payments or benefits under the end-stage renal disease program).

You must opt out of Part B if you do not want its coverage. If you are not entitled to Part A benefits, you can voluntarily apply for Part B benefits, but only during a general enrollment period.

Once you enroll for Part B benefits, your period of coverage under Part B depends upon whether you enrolled during an initial or general enrollment period.

Enrollment Periods and Periods of Coverage

There are two kinds of enrollment periods: (1) an initial enrollment period, for those who automatically qualify for benefits under Part A, and (2) a general enrollment period, for those who want to re-enroll after termination or who failed to enroll during the initial enrollment period. There is also a special enrollment period for those who were covered by an employer-sponsored group health plan when they first became eligible for Medicare.

INITIAL ENROLLMENT PERIOD
Enrollment should take place during the first three months of the initial enrollment period in order to obtain the earliest possible coverage for Part B benefits. The initial enrollment period begins on the first day of the third month before the month in which you first become eligible for Part A benefits and ends seven months later. For instance, if you first become eligible for Social Security retirement benefits or otherwise become entitled to Part A benefits in June 1998, your enrollment period begins on March 1, 1998, and runs to the last day of September 1998. To determine when Part B coverage begins, you must determine when your enrollment occurred within the seven-month period. You are deemed to have enrolled in the third month of your initial enrollment period if you are already receiving or apply to receive Social Security cash benefits (or benefits under the renal disease program) or Part A benefits during one of the first three months of the initial enrollment period. Coverage under Part B begins on the first day of the fourth month (the month you first become eligible).

There is a slight gap in coverage if you enroll during the last four months of the initial enrollment period.

GENERAL ENROLLMENT PERIOD
On the other hand, if you fail to enroll during the initial enrollment period and wish now to enroll,

there is a greater delay before coverage begins. You can apply for benefits only during the general enrollment period, which runs each year from January 1 to March 31. Coverage will not begin until July 1 of that year. There is no limit on the number of times you can re-enroll for Part B benefits, but there is a premium penalty for delayed enrollment. If you enroll more than one year after you became eligible for Part A benefits, your monthly premium will be at least 10 percent higher than the basic premium amount.

EXAMPLES

Howard Sprague will turn 65 and become eligible for Social Security retirement benefits on April 13, 1998. His initial enrollment period began on January 1, 1998, and will run to the end of June 1998. If he applies for Social Security benefits before the end of the third month of his enrollment period (i.e., before the end of March 1998), his period of coverage under Part B begins on April 1, 1998.

Oliver Douglas elected to retire and take his Social Security benefits when he reached age 62. He will reach age 65 in July 1998 and will become entitled to benefits under Part A of Medicare. His initial enrollment period under Part B begins on April 1, 1998, and extends to the last day of October 1998. Since he is already receiving Social Security benefits, he is automatically deemed to have applied for Part B in June 1998 (the third month of his initial enrollment period) and coverage will begin on July 1, 1998.

SPECIAL ENROLLMENT PERIOD
FOR ELDERLY EMPLOYEES

If you are age 65 or older and covered under an employer-sponsored group health plan at the time you first became eligible for Medicare, you may delay enrollment without incurring a penalty and without waiting for the general enrollment period to apply. Instead, you may enroll for Part B benefits during a special enrollment period. The special enrollment period begins on the first day of the month you are no longer covered under the group health plan and runs for seven months thereafter. If you fail to enroll during the special enrollment period, you must wait for the general enrollment period to file an application.

Premiums

Medicare Part B is financed from premiums paid by enrollees with some support from the Medicare Trust Fund and general tax revenues. Enrollees pay a regular premium for each month of coverage. If you participate in Part B this year, you will pay a monthly premium of $43.80, which is usually deducted from your monthly Social Security check. If you are not receiving Social Security cash benefits, you will be billed directly on a quarterly basis.

In addition to the monthly premium, you must also pay a yearly deductible of $100. After the deductible is paid, Medicare Part B will cover 80 percent of the Medicare-approved cost for each covered item. You must pay the remaining 20 percent. If your doctor or supplier does not agree to take payment from Medicare "on assignment," you may owe more than the remaining 20 percent plus the difference between the Medicare payment and the physician's actual charge.

The Assignment Method of Payment

Many doctors and suppliers have entered participation agreements with Medicare. This means that they have agreed in advance to "take assignment" for all services provided to all Medicare patients.

The assignment method of payment simply means that you assign to your doctor or supplier your rights to Medicare payment for covered services. In turn, your doctor or supplier agrees to accept the reasonable charge determined by the Medicare carrier as his or her full charge for covered services. Your doctor or supplier fills out the claim forms and sends them to Medicare. Medicare then pays your doctor or supplier 80 percent of the cost of the reasonable charges. You are responsible only for the coinsurance amount (the remaining 20 percent of reasonable charges) and the yearly deductible, if it has not already been paid. Your doctor or supplier cannot charge you (or your private supplemental insurance or Medigap carrier) more than the reasonable charge amount. He or she can, of course, charge you for services not covered by Medicare.

Each year, the names, addresses, telephone numbers, and areas of specialties of all local Medicare-participating physicians and suppliers are published in a directory. These directories are distributed to local Social Security offices, senior citizen organization centers, and hospitals.

If your doctor or supplier has not entered into a participation agreement, he or she might still accept assignment on a case-by-case basis. If he or she refuses to accept Medicare assignment in your case, you will be responsible for amounts that exceed 80 percent of the reasonable charges. In addition, you may have to fill out and send in the claim form yourself. Many nonparticipating doctors and suppliers will fill out the claim forms for their patients. As of September 1, 1990, all physicians and suppliers, whether or not they accepted Medicare assignment, had to fill out and send in claim forms for their Medicare patients.

Are the Fees of Nonparticipating
Physicians Limited?

In the past, nonparticipating physicians and suppliers were not limited in the amount they could charge for services provided to Medicare patients. Medicare would pay for 80 percent of the reasonable charges, and the patient would be required to pay the difference between the Medicare payment and the physician's or supplier's actual charges. Today, the fees of the physician or supplier who does not accept Medicare assignment are limited to a maximum allowable actual charge. Although the formula is complicated, the result is that the fees of the nonparticipating physician or supplier fall somewhere between the carrier's reasonable charge for Medicare patients and the actual charge used by nonparticipating physicians for non-Medicare patients. Sanctions are imposed upon a physician or supplier who knowingly and willfully bills above his or her maximum allowable actual charge amount. As of 1991, new rules replaced the maximum allowable actual charge with a limiting amount.

If your physician or supplier does not accept Medicare assignment for elective surgery, he or she is required to give you a written estimate of your out-of-pocket expenses if the total charge is $500 or more. If he or she fails to do this, you are entitled to a refund of any amount you paid over the Medicare-approved amount. Such a physician or supplier is also subject to certain sanctions and penalties.

If your physician or supplier does not accept Medicare assignment for otherwise covered services, and a PRO or carrier determines that the services were not reasonable or necessary, you are entitled to a refund from the physician of any payments collected by him or her for those services.

COVERED SERVICES

Medicare Part B covers the following services:

1. physicians' services, including diagnosis, therapy, surgery, and consultation. These services are covered only if they are provided in the home, office, institution, or at the scene of an accident. They are covered only if they are furnished by a duly licensed doctor of medicine or osteopathy, a dentist (excluding dental care), a podiatrist, an optometrist, or a chiropractor who is licensed by the state;

2. services and supplies, including drugs and biologicals, incident to physicians' services, which represent an expense to the physician;

3. rural health clinic services, including the services of a physician, a nurse-practitioner, or a physician's assistant, and the supplies incident to the services;

4. outpatient hospital services, including services incident to physicians' services, diagnostic services, such as X rays and lab services, surgery services, physical, speech, and occupational therapy services;[3]

5. X-ray, radium, and radioactive isotope therapy, including the services of technicians;

6. the rental or purchase cost of durable medical equipment if it is furnished for use in the home, is used to serve a medical purpose, and is generally not useful to a person in the absence of illness or injury;

7. ambulance services when use of other transportation would endanger the patient's health and the vehicle and its crew meets certain standards of quality;

8. prosthetic devices that replace all or part of an internal organ, including cardiac pacemakers, prosthetic lenses, breast prostheses, colostomy bags, and supplies;

9. artificial limbs and eyes, and braces for limbs, back, or neck;

10. antigens, pneumococcal vaccines, and immunizations required because of an injury or immediate risk of infection, hepatitis-B vaccine for certain persons at risk, blood clotting factors, and immunosuppressive drugs;

11. services and related care provided by a certified registered nurse anesthetist;

12. nurse-midwife services and supplies used incident to those services;

3. Services of *independent* physical therapists and occupational therapists are covered up to $750 per year for each type.

13. qualified psychologist services provided at a community mental health center;
14. HMO services of physician assistants, nurse practitioners, and clinical psychologists;
15. dialysis services and supplies furnished in approved end-stage renal disease centers, and home dialysis equipment and supplies and support services;
16. some Pap smears on or after July 1, 1990;
17. periodic mammography screening;
18. blood for transfusions, after the first three pints per year (including any considered under Part A);
19. drugs that cannot be self-administered, blood-clotting factors for hemophilia, injectable osteoporosis drugs, and immuno-suppressive drugs during the first year after an organ transplant; and
20. home health services (the same as those provided by Part A, but with payment from either Part A or Part B).

Medicare is designed to cover all sorts of medical services, but there are borderline situations where the services may be covered partially or not at all. Dental services are normally not covered, but if such services involve surgery to the jaw or other facial bones, they will be covered.

SMI does not include routine eye care, but services performed by qualified optometrists are included if they would be covered when performed by a physician. Similarly, the manual manipulation of the spine by a Medicare-certified chiropractor to correct out-of-place vertebrae, as shown by an X ray, would be covered, but other diagnostic or therapeutic services of chiropractors would not.

Medicare will pay for the services of a podiatrist who treats a patient with a condition affecting the lower limbs, such as diabetes, but not for routine services, such as hygienic foot care, the treatment of flat feet, or the removal of corns, calluses, and most warts.

A special rule governs the payment for outpatient treatment of mental illness. If the illness is such that it would normally have required admission to a hospital for treatment, Medicare will pay 80 percent of the allowable charges; if not, it will pay only 50 percent.

In some situations, Medicare will pay the full cost of certain health services which are not subject to the annual deductible nor the 20 percent coinsurance payments. These include flu shots, certain outpatient clinical diagnostic laboratory tests, and home health services prescribed by a physician. Other services are exempt from the deductible, but subject to the 20 percent coinsurance. These include mammography screening, Pap smears, colorectal screening tests, and diabetes self-management training.

SERVICES NOT COVERED

Even though numerous services and supplies are covered by Medicare Part B, many others that are frequently needed by the elderly are not. Some of these include:

1. routine physical, eye, and ear examinations;
2. routine foot care;
3. examinations for prescribing or fitting eyeglasses or hearing aids;
4. cosmetic surgery;
5. routine dental care, including care for the treatment, filling, removal, or replacement of teeth, root canal therapy, surgery for impacted teeth;
6. diagnostic and laboratory tests performed in a laboratory independent of a hospital and the attending physician's office, unless it meets certain specified conditions;
7. drugs and biologicals that can be self-administered;
8. personal comfort items;
9. eyeglasses, contact lenses, or hearing aids;
10. orthopedic shoes, except where the shoe is an integral part of a leg brace;
11. most immunizations;
12. the first three pints of blood for transfusions, per year;
13. acupuncture;
14. meals delivered to the patient's home;
15. private duty nurses;
16. extra charges for a private room; and
17. homemaker services.

Medicare Supplementary Insurance

A lawyer who retires at age 65 when he or she becomes eligible for Medicare will probably find that Medicare alone does not provide sufficient health insurance for the lawyer and his or her family. The situation becomes acute if the lawyer is so unfortunate as to suffer a catastrophic illness. For this reason, most lawyers should try to find some kind of affordable Medicare supplementary (or "Medigap") insurance.

A large law firm, corporation, or other entity will often provide such coverage at a relatively low cost, as part of its overall retirement program. But the solo practitioner or the member of a small law firm must purchase this insurance on his or her own. Typically, the cost ranges from $52.75 to $169.75 per month, depending on the extent of the coverage. Since 1992, providers have made available ten standard plans, with the following coverages:

- Basic benefits:
  Parts A and B coinsurance (the 20 percent coverage not paid by Medicare);
  Coverage for 365 additional hospital days after Medicare benefits end; and
  First three pints of blood each year (all ten plans)
- Skilled nursing coinsurance (eight plans)
- Part A deductible (nine plans)
- Part B deductible (three plans)
- Excess of actual over allowable charges under Part B (three plans, 100 percent; one plan, 80 percent)
- Medicare coverage when outside the United States, that is, during foreign travel (eight plans)
- At-home recovery (four plans)
- Prescription drugs (three plans: two with $1,250 limit; one with $3,000 limit)
- Preventive care (two plans).

Health-Care Reform

In 1997, Congress amended the basic Medicare law to provide new options with respect to health care. Consumers will no longer be limited to traditional fee-for-service Medicare and Medigap insurance to cover health care. They may elect plans wherein a Health Maintenance Organization (HMO) provides basic services, including preventive care, often at less cost. But they must use the HMO's physicians and hospitals, and will be unable to select their own. Alternatively, they could join a Preferred Provider Organization (PPO) and receive medical services from providers outside the HMO, but at a higher cost. Still another alternative would be to join a Provider Sponsored Organization (PSO), operat-

ed by a group of (typically, local) physicians and hospitals, wherein insureds may select their own providers.

For insureds aged 65 and older, the traditional fee-for-service arrangement remains the principal vehicle for health care. Until Congress enacts a comprehensive health care program for all citizens, including the forty million persons who are uninsured, most consumers will probably prefer fee-for-service plans over HMOs, PPOs, and PSOs. Meanwhile, the most important concern for the retired or retiring lawyer is to make sure that he (and his spouse) are fully covered by the combination of Medicare and Medigap.

Long-Term Care Insurance

Neither Medicare nor Medigap will provide financial relief for the lawyer who suffers a condition that demands that he or she be placed in a nursing home. With the lengthening of our life expectancy, the chance that a senior family member will be placed in an institution with facilities less than a skilled nursing facility or hospital, has greatly increased.

In the absence of insurance protection, family fortunes can be dissipated because of the high cost of such long-term care.

In recent years, many insurance companies have developed programs to protect the older person from such misfortune. The average cost of nursing home care ranges from $62.00 to $200 per day.[4] At $100 a day, an individual in a nursing home for five years would have to spend $182,500. Long-term care insurance provides the funds to pay for this care.

Long-term care insurance policies contain a variety of provisions. Select the program that is right for you. These are the most important considerations:

- Should the policy be for a term of years or for life? Although the average length of stay in a nursing home is only two-and-a-half years, it could be much longer in an individual case. But a policy that would pay benefits for life might cost 30 to 40 percent more.
- Should you buy a policy that provides for automatic increases in benefits for inflation, or one that allows you periodically to upgrade your coverage? Depending upon the age of the

4. THE WALL STREET JOURNAL, March 21, 1997.

insured, the policy providing for automatic protection against inflation can be nearly twice as expensive.

- Should you buy nursing home care only, or nursing home plus home care? Most people would rather remain in their own homes, if possible. If the daily benefit of the long-term care insurance is the same for both a nursing home and home care, the additional premium can be 30 to 40 percent higher than coverage for nursing home care only. Alternatively, the policy may have the same premium for the two situations, but with a reduction in benefits where the care is at home. Normally, the cost of care at home should be less than that in a nursing home.

In addition to the above, long-term care insurance policies may contain other provisions which may or may not add to the cost of the policy. Here are some of the more common provisions:

- *Third party notification:* This provision requires the insurer to notify a third party (a lawyer, accountant, or relative) if a policy is about to lapse for nonpayment of premium. This makes it possible to protect the older person who may inadvertently fail to keep up payment of premiums.
- *Waiver of premium:* Some policies provide for waiver of premium once benefits begin. Others may have a waiting period for sixty or ninety days after the beginning of benefits. This feature may apply only to nursing home situations, as distinct from home care.

- *Restoration of benefits:* This provision is for situations where an individual may be in and out of long-term care. Suppose, for example, an insured has a policy with a maximum benefit of $100,000. He uses up $10,000 of his benefits in a nursing home. He then fully recovers, and returns to his home, receiving no more benefits. If he later returns to the nursing home, his maximum benefit is restored to $100,000, and is not $90,000.
- *Nonforfeiture benefits:* If the insured drops his long-term care insurance policy, the insurer may provide the insured with a reduced paid-up policy or, alternatively, return all or a portion of the premiums after a certain number of years.
- *Death benefit:* These benefits provide for a refund of premium upon the death of the insured.

As in life insurance, these provisions may cost the insured somewhat more than the usual long-term care insurance policy. The insured should include one or more of them, depending upon the individual situation. The reader is referred to chapter 29 for a more detailed discussion of long-term care insurance.

29
Providing for Long-Term Care

TIMOTHY C. PFEIFFER

Americans are living longer now than ever before. Advances in medicine, healthier lifestyles, and the gradual elimination or control of most contagious diseases have contributed to longer and more productive lives. According to the American Association of Retired Persons (AARP), 6,000 Americans now reach age 65 each day. Statistically, a 65-year-old now has a 56 percent chance of living to age 80. According to the Brookings Institution, the number of people age 65 and over will double by the year 2030. The number over age 85 will triple.

With longer life has come an increased probability that at some point many of us will require some form of long-term care. Many diseases that once were fatal now entail lengthy treatment programs and protracted care. Other conditions such as senility and motive disorders are derivatives of a longer lifespan. According to the U.S. Census Bureau, the fastest growing segment of the population is age 85 and over, and one out of four people in that segment are nursing-home confined. Further, the American Health Care Association projects that the number of elderly Americans living in nursing homes will increase 58 percent by the year 2020. According to the National Center of Health Statistics, the average nursing home stay is 2.2 years for elder Americans over age 65, with women having a longer stay (2.4 years) versus men (1.9 years). For a person age 65 the chances are two in five that some form of long-term care will be required during the remainder of life—and a 40 percent chance that it will be a nursing home.

Long-term care essentially takes three forms: skilled, intermediate, and custodial care. Skilled care is generally confinement in a nursing care facility offering 24-hour skilled nursing care under the care of a physician and with a treatment plan. Intermediate care is generally medically necessary care but is administered on a less-frequent basis— often two or three times per week. Custodial care is assistance with "activities of daily living" for those who need it. Activities of daily living are activities such as bathing, toileting, dressing, transferring, eating, and continence.

While a bargain compared to hospital confinement charges, long-term care is not cheap. According to the American Health Care Association, it now costs an average of $41,000 per year to live in a nursing home ($112 per day). The cost varies widely by state and region and by metropolitan and rural areas. Home health care costs average approximately one-half confinement costs.

Who pays for long-term care? According to a 1997 study conducted by John Hancock Mutual Life Insurance Company and the American Council on Aging, 73 percent of Americans mistakenly believe that long-term care costs are funded primarily by Medicare. In fact, while $77.9 billion dollars was spent on long-term care in 1995, only 9.4 percent was paid by Medicare. Medicaid paid 46.5 percent of the costs, individuals paid 35.8 percent, churches and other groups paid 4.1 percent, and insurance paid 3.2 percent.

Why doesn't Medicare pay? Medicare pays for daily skilled care in a Medicare-approved skilled nursing facility. There must have been a hospital confinement of at least three days, admission to the facility must be within thirty days of discharge from the hospital, and a physician must certify that daily skilled care is necessary. Most nursing care is not skilled care, falling instead into the intermediate or custodial categories. In fact, according to a Harvard University survey for the government, 95 percent of all confinements are for custodial care, 4.5 percent are for intermediate

Timothy C. Pfeiffer is the executive director of American Bar Insurance Plans Consultants, Inc., a wholly owned subsidiary of American Bar Endowment.

care, and .5 percent are for skilled care. This, plus the additional Medicare "gatekeeper" requirements noted above, makes it highly unlikely that Medicare will be the payor for a long-term care confinement for most Americans.

Medicare does much better on the home health care side. Of the $28.6 billion spent on home health care in 1995, 40.6 percent was paid by Medicare, 21 percent by individuals, 14.3 percent by Medicaid, 11.6 percent by insurance, and 12.2 percent by other sources such as church and community groups. It should be noted, however, that a significant portion of Medicare home health care expenditures are for hospice care.

Medicaid, as noted, currently shoulders the major portion of the confinement-care burden and a significant portion of the home health care burden. Medicaid is, however, a program for the indigent, and to qualify under Medicaid one must demonstrate that all other resources are substantially exhausted. A primary reason that Medicaid bears so much of the long-term care tab is not because so many elderly people are poor but because they have spent their available assets on long-term care expenses and must now turn to the government for assistance. This process is often called "spend down," and entails spending down all "countable assets" to Medicaid thresholds. Countable assets include all cash over $2,000, all stocks and bonds, IRAs and Keoghs, savings bonds, T-bills, investment properties and vacation homes, CDs, single premium deferred annuities, cash value life insurance, and second vehicles. Not counted are cash under $2,000, a primary residence (if used by the nonconfined spouse) and household effects, a car, personal jewelry, burial accounts and prepaid funeral arrangements, and term life insurance. Some states also have income caps that specify, regardless of the asset level after spend down, one cannot qualify for Medicaid if income exceeds a certain monthly threshold. Medicaid also allows the nonconfined spouse to retain his or her income and Social Security benefits (subject to spousal impoverishment limits). Income can also be transferred to trusts.

Until recently, a common strategy in long-term care planning has been to transfer assets to a trust to qualify for the Medicaid limits, thereby preserving the original intended purpose for the assets—for example, as gifts to children. States have taken an increasingly dim view of such asset transfers in anticipation of Medicaid qualification and have

enacted "look back periods" that establish a period of ineligibility for Medicaid long-term care payments based on the time between the asset transfer and the long-term care confinement. States have tightened their "look back" periods, most recently from thirty to sixty months. Finally, in certain circumstances it can be unlawful for a lawyer or a financial planner to counsel clients for a fee on such divestitures—further reflecting governmental concern that Medicaid is being overused as the primary funder of long-term care. The government is not poised to increase funding for long-term care and it has begun to provide incentives to increase the private sector's role in this process.

To that end the federal government included long-term care under "HIPAA" or the Health Insurance Portability and Accountability Act (HR-3103), which was passed on August 21, 1996. The act became effective on January 1, 1997, and establishes guidelines for tax qualification of long-term care insurance plans. Importantly, all insurance policies in force on January 1, 1997, were automatically grandfathered as tax qualified—thus assuring all current long-term care insureds the benefit of the new tax advantages. The law provides that a portion of premiums for tax-qualified plans are treated as medical expenses and are eligible for deduction, along with other medical expenses that exceed 7.5 percent of adjusted gross income. The amount of premium eligible for deduction increases by age—from $200 under age 40 to $2,500 over age 70. More importantly, the benefits received under a tax-qualified long-term care policy that reimburse long-term care expenses are not taxable as income.

As is often the case with new legislation, HIPAA raised several additional tax issues as well as addressing some: In defining tax-qualified plans, some benefits are not as favorable as benefits under nonqualified plans. Tax-qualified plans, for instance, *require* certification by your doctor that your nursing home stay will likely exceed ninety days. Nonqualified plans typically do not have such a requirement. Also, a qualified plan cannot offer cash value benefits such as spouse paid-up features, while nonqualified plans commonly have such features. While it is clear that benefits under tax-qualified plans are not taxable, the taxability of benefits under nonqualified plans remains an open question. HIPAA did not specify that benefits received under nonqualified plans are taxable, only the extent to which benefits received under qualified plans are not. Perhaps the greatest benefit under HIPAA goes to employer-provided tax-qualified plans—premiums paid by the employer are deductible as a business expense and benefits received are not included in employee income. If you want to buy long-term care protection, which is for you: qualified or nonqualified? While the conservative long-term care shopper will opt only for a tax-qualified plan, many carriers offer a choice between tax qualified or nonqualified plans. You may want to consider both.

We have now considered several possible funding sources for long-term care. Medicare probably won't help us much, and Medicaid, for most of us, is not an acceptable alternative. Therefore we have only two strategies left: self-insurance (if asset levels support that option), or long-term care insurance. Before you decide to self-insure your long-term care risk, consider the $41,000 average annual cost of care. Not counting inflation, if you or a loved one require two-and-a-half years of care, the expense could be $102,500. If the stay is five years, the total could be $205,000. If you assume 5 percent annual inflation, that $41,000 annual expense increases to $52,316 in five years and to $66,789 after ten years. Are these the levels of risk that you would choose to insure by yourself? Carefully weigh your risk factors in making your decision: your family health history; your current state of health; your care network (family and friends who might help provide care for you); your financial condition; and the impact that self-insuring can have on your overall financial plan and/or your estate plan. Most of us will decide that we would benefit from at least a minimal amount of long-term care insurance, and many of us will want long-term care insurance to cover the greater portion of the costs of care if we should ever need it.

Look for this in a long-term care insurance policy:

- *A secure insurance company.* Long-term care insurance, like life insurance, anticipates a long time between purchase and the need for benefits. We want our insurance company to be there when we need to use the benefits. Select a company with top financial credentials. Look for A.M. Best Company ratings of A++; Duff & Phelps ratings of AAA; Moody's Ratings Service Ratings of Aaa; and Standard & Poor's ratings of AAA.
- *Coverage for all levels of care.* Be sure the policy covers skilled, intermediate, and custodial care, and be sure that it covers confinements in nursing homes and assisted living facilities.
- *Coverage for home- and community-based care.* Be sure that the policy covers all levels of care and services including visiting nurses; home health aides; physical, speech, occupational, and respiratory therapists; adult day care; respite care; hospice care; and therapeutic devices.
- *Inflation protection.* Simple and compound options are often offered, typically offering a 5 percent benefit. Look for plans that offer a compound option that increases each year for the life of the policy.
- *A range of options.* Tailor the policy to your needs and your pocketbook. Look for a maximum daily benefit range (typically up to $250 or $300 per day); waiting period choices (typically from 20 to 180 days)—the longer the waiting period, the lower the cost; and coverage duration from two years to lifetime—the shorter the duration, the lower the cost.
- *A pool of money approach to benefit utilization.* If your expenses do not reach the benefit level you selected when you bought your policy, your benefit period should be adjusted to allow you to use the total dollar value of your maximum benefit.
- *Attainable benefits.* Be sure that there are no waiting periods for preexisting conditions and no prior hospitalization requirements that would stand in the way of your ability to collect benefits.
- *Guaranteed renewability.* Coverage should be renewable indefinitely. Many policies also guarantee rates for an initial period of two to five years. Following that period, rates can be adjusted if they are adjusted for the entire class of policies or insured group.
- *Waiver of premium.* No further premiums should be due once you are eligible to receive benefits, for as long as benefits continue.

Consider your long-term care risk as part of your overall financial plan and the financial impact that a condition requiring long-term care could have on you and your family's life. As with other medical risks, carefully consider the ways that this risk can be funded. In balance, private long-term care insurance is becoming the mechanism of choice in planning for long-term care needs. Be sure that you include a detailed long-term care funding evaluation in your overall retirement plan.

30

Interaction of Long-Term Care Insurance and the Estate Tax

JAY A. SOLED

The Health Insurance Portability and Accountability Act of 1996 (HIA)[1] provides taxpayers with various tax incentives to purchase long-term care (LTC) insurance. Subject to certain limitations, the premiums on this insurance are now deductible;[2] employer-provided LTC insurance premiums are not includable in the employee's gross income;[3] and amounts received from such policies are statutorily exempt from tax.[4] Before taxpayers rush to buy LTC insurance, however, they should carefully evaluate the impact of the federal estate tax on their plans.

Background

Prior to enactment of the HIA, premium payments for LTC insurance were outside the scope of "medical care" and consequently were not deductible.[5] And it was not entirely clear whether the proceeds from these policies were subject to income tax.[6]

Despite these possible tax shortcomings, over the past decade the purchase of LTC insurance has enjoyed appreciable growth.[7] No doubt the demographics of an aging nation is one of the chief reasons for this phenomenon,[8] coupled with an average lifespan in this country that now approaches 77 years.[9] Also, the cost of LTC has risen at a rate disproportionate to the rate of inflation. Older taxpayers are therefore ideal candidates to purchase LTC insurance to reduce the

risk that they will have to bear the entire cost of nursing home care.

From an economic perspective, taxpayers' concerns regarding the expenses of LTC are probably well-founded. The cost of nursing home care can wreak financial hardship. The Health Insurance Association of America (HIA) indicates that the average cost of nursing home care in 1990 was about $72 per day and, by 1995, this cost had risen to more than $100.[10] The magnitude of these figures captures the attention of even many well-to-do taxpayers.

In the past, taxpayers sought guidance from practitioners to protect their hard-earned assets from erosion by nursing home expenses and to ensure passage of their estates to family members. To make clients eligible for Medicaid, advi-

Jay A. Soled is a lawyer and an assistant professor at Rutgers University in Newark, New Jersey. The author would like to thank Herbert L. Zuckerman for his helpful comments and insight in the preparation of this chapter.

1. P.L. No.104–191 (8/21/96), §§ 321–323, 325–326, amending Code § 213(d) and enacting Code §§ 4980C, 6050Q. and 7702B.

2. § 213(d)(1)(D).

3. § 106(a).

4. § 104(a).

5. § 213(d).

6. See, generally, § 104(a), which exempts from tax "amounts received through accident or health insurance (*or through an arrangement having the effect of accident or health insurance*) for personal injuries or sickness. . . . (Emphasis added)

7. Health Insurance Association of America, "Policy and Research Findings: Long-Term Care Insurance 1994" (March 1996) ("By the end of 1994, more than 3.8 million people have purchased long-term care insurance policies compared with 815,000 by December 1987. From 1987 to 1994 long-term care insurance sales grew at annual average rate of 25 percent.").

8. See U.S. Senate Comm. on Aging, "Aging in America: Trends and Projections," S. Rep't No. 59, 101st Cong., 1st Sess. 1, 3 (1989) (estimates that by the year 2000, the number of Americans age 65 or older is projected to exceed 34.8 million).

9. U.S. Bureau of Census, *Current Population Reports* (1995).

10. Health Insurance Association of America, "Who Buys Long-Term Care Insurance: 1994–95 Profiles and Innovations in a Dynamic Market" (1995).

sors often used numerous trust devices that simultaneously gave clients entry to nursing homes and protected the bulk of clients' estates from being consumed by nursing home charges.[11] Establishment of these specialized trusts represented a form of insurance for those interested in protecting their assets.

Section 217 of the HIA made it a criminal offense for taxpayers to "knowingly and willfully dispose of assets . . . in order . . . to become eligible for [Medicaid]" or for lawyers to abet taxpayers in this activity.[12] The Balanced Budget Act of 1997 removes liability from clients and places it on anyone who "for a fee knowingly and willfully counsels or assists an individual to dispose of assets (including by any transfer in trust) in order for the individual to become eligible for medical assistance under a state plan under Title XIX, if disposing of the assets results in the imposition of a period of ineligibility for such assistance. . . ."

While Medicaid restrictions have been tightened, Congress generally has made the purchase of LTC insurance more affordable by providing a deduction for LTC premiums and an exclusion for LTC proceeds. The deduction for eligible LTC premiums is subject to the floor of 7.5 percent of adjusted gross income (effectively reducing the availability of this deduction for many high income taxpayers),[13] and the premium deduction is limited to amounts, based on the age of the taxpayer, that are to be adjusted annually for inflation after 1997.[14] (Table 30–1 shows the limits on deductible LTC premiums.) Nevertheless, the scope of the medical care deduction has been broadened to allow deductions for qualified LTC insurance contracts.[15] Qualified LTC insurance contracts are generally those arrangements that provide "necessary diagnostic, preventive, therapeutic, curing, treating, mitigating, and rehabilitative services, and maintenance or personal care services, which are required by a chronically ill individual, and are provided pursuant to a plan of care prescribed by a licensed health care practitioner."[16]

Table 30–1

Limits on Deductible LTC Premiums

Age Before the Close of Tax Year:	The Limitation Is:
40 or less	$ 200
More than 40 but not more than 50	375
More than 50 but not more than 60	750
More than 60 but not more than 70	2,000
More than 70	2,500

LTC insurance proceeds are also excludable from income, subject to a cap of $175 per day, or $63,875 annually (also adjusted annually for inflation after 1997).[17] The cost of employer-provided LTC insurance—except if provided through a flexible spending account or cafeteria plan—is similarly excludable from income.[18]

When taxpayers scrutinize the advantages and disadvantages of LTC insurance, there is little doubt that the deduction and exclusion relating to this insurance make its purchase more appealing. A key factor taxpayers may overlook in their LTC analysis, however, is the impact of the federal estate tax and the bearing it may have on whether they should purchase LTC insurance.

Analysis

The federal estate tax potentially applies to the estate of every decedent.[19] A decedent's estate includes not only the value of assets held directly (that is, probate assets that pass via the will),[20] but also the value of nonprobate assets (for example, jointly held property and the proceeds from life insurance policies).[21] The federal estate tax graduated rate schedule ranges from 18 percent to 55 percent based on the size of the taxable estate.

In many instances, two significant factors cause the estate tax burden to be deferred, reduced, or eliminated. The first is the estate tax marital deduction, which allows a married taxpayer the option of passing assets tax deferred to the surviving spouse.[22] The second factor is the

11. Schlesinger, Scheiner, and Schneider, "Medicaid Planning Ideas: What Works and What Doesn't," 20 EP 331 (Nov/Dec 1993); Barreira, "Using Special Powers in Medicaid Trusts," 4 PROB. & PROP. 42 (Jan/Feb 1990).
12. 42 U.S.C. § 1320a-7b(a)(6).
13. § 213(a).
14. §§ 213(d)(10) and 7702B(d).
15. § 213(d)(1)(D).
16. § 7702B(c).

17. § 7702B(d).
18. § 106(c).
19. § 2001.
20. § 2033.
21. See, e.g., §§ 2037 and 2042.
22. § 2056(a).

unified credit of $192,800 (in 1997) that permits a taxpayer, who has made no prior taxable gifts, to pass at death up to $600,000 of assets tax free.[23] (For 1998, the applicable credit amount, formerly known as the unified credit, will be $202,050; and the applicable exclusion amount, formerly referred to as the exemption equivalent, will be $625,000.[24])

Even with the help of the marital deduction and the unified credit, many taxpayers engage in sophisticated estate planning to reduce their taxable estates and minimize the impact of the estate tax. Common techniques include the use of irrevocable life insurance trusts,[25] personal residence trusts,[26] grantor retained annuity trusts,[27] and family limited partnerships.[28] A common goal of these strategies is to provide taxpayers the opportunity to reduce their estates by allowing them to transfer assets free of transfer tax or subject to a reduced gift tax.

Yet the very same taxpayers, who engage in sophisticated estate tax planning to decrease their estates, purchase LTC insurance in a somewhat contradictory endeavor to maintain the value of their estates.[29] In other words, LTC insurance proceeds that offset nursing home costs leave an equivalent amount of dollars in the taxpayer's gross estate. These dollars are often exposed to estate tax. Therefore, taxpayers whose estates will be subject to estate tax receive less than what they bargained for when they initially purchased the LTC insurance.

Example

A, age 60, is a widow with a net worth of $5 million. She purchases an LTC insurance policy for an annual premium of $3,000. The purchased policy provides LTC coverage up to $50,000

annually. Assume that after twenty years, A enters a nursing home costing $50,000 a year and that she resides there for two years before dying. Have A's premium payments protected her estate from $100,000 worth of depletion (A's intended goal), thereby permitting A to pass these savings on to her intended beneficiaries?

No. Assume that the estate tax rate to be applied to A's estate of $5 million is a flat 55 percent.[30] In such a case, the payment of LTC insurance premiums ensures that only $45,000 will pass to A's beneficiaries [$100,000 minus ($100,000 times .55) = $45,000]. Certainly, had A considered this result, she may not have originally purchased the LTC insurance. Instead, she may have engaged in other estate planning techniques.

Another way to make this identical point more vividly is to consider the consequences had A not secured an LTC policy. The nursing home expenses would have depleted A's estate by $100,000, but the real cost of this expenditure to the beneficiaries of her estate would be only $45,000. In effect, for every dollar A spends on nursing home care, $.55 is effectively borne by the federal government.

The impact of the estate tax is only slightly less dramatic in the case of smaller estates. In the prior example, suppose the value of A's estate is only $700,000, and her marginal estate tax rate is 37 percent. In this situation, out of every dollar of LTC insurance proceeds paid on A's behalf, the beneficiaries of her estate would only effectively receive $.63.

LTC insurance, however, is obviously purchased for a number of diverse reasons. The imposition of estate tax certainly does not negate all the advantages LTC insurance offers. But the purchase of this insurance should be selective, and the estate tax should be made part of the analysis.

The purchase of LTC insurance by a single taxpayer whose net worth exceeds the exemption equivalent ($600,000 in 1997; $625,000 in 1998), for example, requires circumspection: On the one hand, in the absence of LTC insurance, entry into a nursing home could cause a serious erosion of capital, particularly if the taxpayer's illness requires an extended stay (for example, ten

23. § 2010(a).

24. Taxpayer Relief Act of 1997, P.L. No. 105–34 (8/5/97).

25. See, e.g., Blattmachr and Slade, "Life Insurance Trusts: How to Avoid Estate and GST Taxes," 22 EP 259 (Sep/Oct 1995).

26. See, e.g., Harrison, "Calculating the Potential for Transfer Tax Savings in Personal Residence GRITs," 80 J. Tax'n 232 (Apr 1994).

27. See, e.g., Woodson and Johnson, "GRATs Let Grantor Retain Control and Reduce Transfer Tax," 56 Tax'n for Accts. 68 (Feb 1996)

28. See, e.g., Jones, "Family Limited Partnerships Achieve Tax and Nontax Goals," 23 Tax'n for Law. 196 (Jan/Feb 1995).

29. See, e.g., Feldesman and Canning, "Long-Term Care Insurance Helps Preserve an Estate," 20 EP 76 (Mar/Apr 1993); Saks, "Update on Long-Term Care Insurance and Checklist for this Wealth Protection Tool," 23 EP 276 (Jul 1996).

30. Of course, because of the graduated rate schedule of the transfer tax system, the effective rate of tax would be slightly less, but the assumption regarding the flat 55 percent tax rate simplifies this illustration.

years).[31] On the other hand, it should be made clear that the dollars that these taxpayers are intent on passing to their beneficiaries by protecting the assets from nursing home debts may instead be subject to estate tax.

The application of this analysis in the case of married taxpayers is more complex, but no less pertinent. In general, married taxpayers whose net worth exceeds $1.2 million (in 1997) and who have properly planned estates that make maximum use of the unified credit should consider the consequences of the estate tax on their LTC planning. The analysis regarding married taxpayers differs from that applicable to single taxpayers, and is made more complicated by the fact that each spouse wishes to safeguard the economic well-being of the spouse who may need no nursing home care. (Entry into a nursing home by one spouse may possibly impoverish the other spouse because in that situation, the taxpayers

31. Based on telephone conversations with various insurance companies offering LTC insurance, this author was told that the average length of a nursing home stay is currently three years.

must, in effect, maintain two households.) Aside from the issue of their combined net worth, other factors to consider in determining whether to buy LTC insurance include the couple's respective ages and health.

It would be nice to conclude this analysis with a chart that indicates when taxpayers, in light of the estate tax, should or should not purchase LTC insurance. Unfortunately, the circumstances of taxpayers are too varied to make such a chart meaningful. Instead, each client's situation must be weighed on a case-by-case basis to determine whether the merits of purchasing LTC insurance outweigh the costs of the estate tax.

Conclusion

Certain income tax incentives now make the purchase of LTC insurance more attractive. High net worth taxpayers, though, should not overlook the fact that, in many instances, a large percentage of the proceeds provided by these policies may ultimately pass to the government in the form of estate tax, rather than to the taxpayers' beneficiaries.

31

Medical Insurance Needs in Retirement

BENJAMIN G. BALDWIN

The basic objective of medical insurance is to make sure that you and your family are never exposed to medical bankruptcy.

With this objective in mind, the first specification for a policy is that it have an "unlimited" maximum. That is not always possible. It used to be more readily available than it is now. Many insurance companies have reduced their lifetime maximums to one million dollars. Although the one-million-dollar maximum sounds like a significant amount it is not necessarily enough. Your strategy should be to go for the best, request the unlimited, and compromise only if you find that the best is unavailable or impractical.

Optimally, the policy should cover all physician-prescribed treatments to diagnose and correct a medical condition. In an indemnity plan (insurance company reimburses you for your expenses after you have been treated by your chosen provider), the insurance company should pay your bills after you have paid an acceptable deductible. In addition, you will participate in the payment of the bills up to some percentage, called "coinsurance." The coinsurance percentage you pay could range between 10 percent and 50 percent. The insurance company then would pay the balance of those bills. It is entirely possible that you could go medically bankrupt paying the coinsurance percentage of unlimited bills. As a result, hopefully you will find a policy that has a "stop-loss provision" which obligates the insurance company to pay 100 percent of the bills for the balance of the calendar year, after some stipulated limit on your coinsurance payments. It is

important that you know how much would have to be paid out of your own pocket in the way of deductibles and coinsurance if you and others in your family suffered a number of severe illnesses in one year. Once you have determined the maximum "out-of-pocket" amount, you can make sure that you have an emergency fund sufficient to provide for this worst-case scenario.

We would like your medical coverage to provide you with an unlimited maximum, comprehensive coverage, reasonable deductibles and an acceptable stop-loss. Complete your Medical Insurance Inventory (see Figure 31–1) to see how you are doing on meeting the specifications.

Preexisting Conditions

Preexisting conditions may be an obstacle you will have to face. Often when applying for insurance coverage you have to answer questions regarding your medical history. This will reveal anything that has happened in your past that would affect the insurance company's ability to provide health insurance for you profitably. You may not have to complete medical questions on employer-provided group medical insurance, but the policy is likely to state that it will not pay benefits for conditions that manifested themselves before the policy was put in force.

Preexisting conditions may be excluded entirely or they may be excluded only for a certain period of time. In some cases, insurance companies will pay some benefits for preexisting conditions but limit the amount of the total payments. Any condition that has been diagnosed by a physician should be revealed on the application. It does not pay to turn in fraudulent applications to insurance companies. When you file a claim for an unrevealed preexisting condition, the insurance com-

Benjamin G. Baldwin is president and owner of Baldwin Financial Systems, Inc., a registered representative of EQ Financial Consultants, Inc., and an agent of Equitable Life, in Northbrook, Illinois.

Figure 31-1

Medical and Dental Insurance Inventory

Insured	Company	Policy Number	Policy Maximum	Deductible	Coinsurance	Stop-Loss	Annual Premium
1 _____	_____	_____	_____	_____	_____	_____	_____
2 _____	_____	_____	_____	_____	_____	_____	_____
3 _____	_____	_____	_____	_____	_____	_____	_____
4 _____	_____	_____	_____	_____	_____	_____	_____
5 _____	_____	_____	_____	_____	_____	_____	_____
					Total Annual Family Premium:		_____

pany will, and must, refuse to pay. You are much better off being candid and thorough with the insurance company, so that if and when they do issue a policy, you have reasonable assurance that the promised benefits will be paid and the policy will not be rescinded because of any erroneous or misleading statements on the application.

The fact that insurance companies exclude preexisting conditions has caused many people to become disenchanted with the insurance industry, which has resulted in pressure for reforms and health insurance legislation. This resulted in the Health Insurance Portability and Accountability Act of 1996 (HIPAA).

One of the objectives of HIPAA is to improve portability and continuity of health insurance coverage in the group and individual markets. Full enforcement of the act began January 1, 1998.

The portability provisions limit preexisting conditions and give employees credit for coverage in a prior group, that is, an employee, having had what is referred to as "creditable coverage" with a prior health insurance plan would get credit for that term of coverage toward the preexisting condition limitation of the new employer.

The law specifies that a preexisting condition is a condition either mental or physical, regardless of cause, for which medical advice, diagnosis, care, or treatment was recommended or received within the six month period ending on the enrollment date and if such a condition does exist, then that condition may be excluded from coverage for up to twelve months.

The result of this is that any employee having completed all preexisting conditions require-

ments under one employer's plan could join a new employer and not have to requalify for the new employer's plan.

There is a requirement that the employee's "creditable coverage" be continuous and not have a break in coverage of more then sixty-three days.

The states may create comparable programs to accommodate individuals, but should the state fail to adopt "acceptable alternative mechanisms," those individuals leaving the group market must be guaranteed issue provided they have first exhausted their COBRA rights.

Inside Limits

Many policies today contain "inside limits" that restrict the benefits that are payable for a number of conditions. Limits on benefits paid for mental or nervous disorders, and also drug and alcohol problems, are common. Insurance companies have found that bills for these types of problems can be unending. Conditions that are difficult to diagnose and difficult to treat with measurable results are often excluded within a policy and/or subject to limits on what the insurer will pay. Know the limits in your policy.

Guaranteed Renewable

Individual health insurance policies may be guaranteed renewable, meaning that the insurance company cannot cancel or change the policy benefits once the policy is issued. However, the insurance company does reserve the right to change the cost of the policy on what they refer to as a *class basis*. This means that all people with similar policies would be exposed to the same cost increases at the same time. In effect, the insurance company would not select you *individually* for a rate increase. The company must file the change in cost with your state insurance commissioner and get approval before it can impose a change.

Employer-Provided Medical Insurance

The best source for medical insurance today is your employer-provided policy. If you have access to an employer-provided medical insurance policy, it is highly likely that the employer is subsidizing it. The advantage to this arrangement is that you need not report what the employer pays for that policy as taxable income as long as the employer is treating all employees equally. The employer also is allowed to deduct the cost as an employee benefit. Deductible by your employer and not taxable to you is about as good as it gets. From an income tax standpoint, your employer is the efficient purchaser of medical insurance.

Generally speaking there are four types of medical insurance plans; indemnity plans, service provider plans, preferred provider plans, or health maintenance organizations.

Indemnity Plans

After you have experienced a loss, indemnity plans reimburse you for that particular loss in accordance with the policy provisions. Indemnity plans offer you the advantage of selecting your own physician and/or hospital. You may choose the best provider, even though "the best" may also be the most expensive—this is both the advantage and the problem with indemnity plans. The giver of care and the receiver of care have no personal incentive to keep costs reasonable. More recent medical insurance plan designs involve both you and the caregiver in providing cost-efficient medical care to bring down the costs. These generally are referred to as "managed care" plans and the more "managed" they are, the less they usually cost.

Service Provider Plans

Blue Cross/Blue Shield service organizations offered some of the first "fee for service" types of plans in which the insurance organization also is the provider of care. Blue Cross/Blue Shield provides their participants with the facilities of the member hospitals and physicians for a monthly subscriber's fee. If the insurance company and the provider are one and the same, the insurance company has a better opportunity to control costs. Theoretically, this makes them better able to estimate the charge to subscribers. Many Blue Cross organizations contract with the hospital to provide the benefits required by its plan. Since it is supplying that provider with a substantial amount of business, it will negotiate discounted rates with that provider which thus reduces costs below that of an indemnity plan.

Preferred Provider Plans

Preferred provider organizations (PPO) are arrangements established by commercial insurance companies following the Blue Cross/Blue Shield example. Coalitions of insurance companies negotiate with providers to obtain discounted rates for their insureds based upon the fact that they will be able to send a substantial number of patients to those providers. You will be encouraged to use these preferred providers because there will be lower deductibles than with the indemnity plan, lower coinsurance and, often, less paperwork and lower costs. The preferred providers agree to charge less so they can get the "business." You agree to use the preferred provider because it costs you less and it is less hassle than the indemnity plan.

Health Maintenance Organizations

A health maintenance organization (HMO) is an assemblage of insurers, physicians, and hospitals joined together in one business arrangement to provide medical care to its members on a prepaid basis. In effect, they state to their members that they will "maintain their health" for a stipulated amount of money per month.

Health maintenance arrangements can work well if the organizations are economically sound and have good facilities and personnel. However, if any of these factors deteriorate, the whole system may deteriorate. In 1989, a major health maintenance organization failed financially, leaving hundreds of thousands of people in doubt about their coverage. Imagine how a member of a failing HMO would feel if his or her health was failing at the same time.

Gatekeepers—The Keeper of the Keys to Managed Care

In PPOs and HMOs, management of your care is primarily through what is called a primary care or "gatekeeper" physician. All your medical services will be funneled through this physician. If you need a specialist, this gatekeeper will assign that specialist and if that specialist wants to take an X ray, he will ask permission of your gatekeeper to do so. If the organization providing your care works properly and all participants are confident in each other's fairness, permission will be granted for your X ray. However, don't be surprised if the gatekeeper doctor demands that the request for the X ray be in writing and insists on responding to that request in writing, a process which could delay your X ray ten days or more. Managed care is a constant process of balancing costs with medical benefits. If the cost side of the equation is emphasized too much, you find hassle and delay, which can result in unsatisfactory medical care and thus higher costs than would otherwise be the case.

> Associated Press August 25, 1995
>
> PORTLAND, Ore. — Jane Harrison was surprised that she had to fight with her doctor to see a specialist about her multiple sclerosis.
>
> Although diagnosed 15 years ago, Harrison never had seen a neurologist who specializes in the debilitating nerve and muscle disease.
>
> She finally found one on a list provided by her insurer, a health maintenance organization, but they ran into a problem: Her primary care doctor wanted her to see his clinic's neurologist —one who did not specialize in MS.
>
> She had to change primary care doctors before she got to see the specialist.

HMO Limitations

When you enroll in an HMO, you have accepted that organization as your exclusive provider of care for some period of time, usually one year. If the organization has a talented staff and is healthy financially, you are likely to be a satisfied member. However, if they are not healthy financially, they will begin to lose talented physicians and you may find that your gatekeeper seems to be more concerned with costs than with your health. When you think about the boom going on in new HMO offerings, keep in mind that when they start up and enroll new members, there is a lot of money coming into the organization and little going out. The new enrollees are healthy, so demands on services are relatively low. It is easy to be profitable under these conditions and this entices start-up companies into this business. However, over time, the population of the HMO grows older and sicker and, although incoming revenue may not be increasing, services going out will be. If you're in an HMO facing these problems and become seriously ill, you may be unhappy with your HMO. Fear of this type of scenario has caused many people to avoid the HMO type of plan.

All HMOs are going to have to work together and police themselves if they are going to keep concerns such as this from appearing in the paper and scaring their healthy membership away. These problems have encouraged the development of hybrids of HMOs. The PPO and indemnity plan combination (often referred to as point of service or POS) gives you more choice and control so that you can use the HMO and/or PPO options with less fear of losing control.

Point of Service Plan

An alternative offered by many commercial insurance companies and adopted by many employers is the combination indemnity plan/PPO option. Under this arrangement, you do not commit to the indemnity or the PPO plan in advance. You decide which to use at the time care is needed. The employer will attempt to "steer" you toward the PPO by means of lower deductibles, lower coinsurance, lower cost, and lower hassle than is available under the indemnity plan, but ultimately it is your choice. If the care is needed for something you feel can and will be handled well by the PPO, the PPO will be the choice. You can expect the services to be cheaper and easier since the benefits are delivered often without annoying paperwork (no claim forms) and with low, or no, deductibles and coinsurance.

Freedom of choice encourages you to *choose* to use preferred providers and go through gatekeepers rather than being mandated to do so as is the case with an HMO. As the doctors have seen that more of their patients are willing to use PPOs under this type of plan, they themselves have joined the organizations, which thus increases the available talent. Indeed, many doctors have found that they generally are better off negotiating rates up front with a PPO and collecting what is due them, rather than maintaining an individual practice and their own collection department to try to collect their billings. Some have found that their individual collection percentage is less than what they can negotiate with a PPO. You may be staying with the indemnity plan so that you can choose your own doctor, but one day you'll probably find that your own doctor is in your optional PPO and you can use his or her services at a discounted rate.

The indemnity plan with the PPO option is referred to as the dual option plan or point of service plan. You may, however, be given the option to choose between the indemnity, preferred provider, or health maintenance organization, a triple option. Cost-wise and benefit-wise, you will be encouraged to move from indemnity to PPO to HMO. If you elect the HMO, you'll probably have to live with that election for at least a year but then you probably would be able to elect another type of option.

Medical Savings Account (MSA) Medical Insurance Plans

Medical insurance plans that qualify the participant to establish a medical savings account (MSA) were created by the Health Insurance Portability and Accountability Act of 1996. MSAs are government incentive experiments to drive down the cost of health care by making people more careful in the manner in which they shop for health-care services.

The stand-alone government-designed health insurance plan is based upon a relatively high deductible plan ($2,250 per individual per year or $4,500 per family per year). Such a plan design would not be an acceptable option to most people. However, the opportunity to participate in an MSA, which provides a financing mechanism for the high deductible, may be sufficient to make such a high-deductible plan acceptable. If it is, insureds under these plans will be spending "their own money" out of their MSAs to pay medical bills up to the deductible amount and, as a result, are expected to be much more careful how they spend MSA dollars.

According to the IRS, 9,720 MSAs had been opened as of April 30, 1997. People ask, "Why so few?" Here are some of the reasons for the initial lack of interest in MSA qualifying medical insurance plans:

- MSA and eligible medical plan rules have been a moving target. In April 1997, the Treasury Department ruled that the family deductible for MSAs could no longer be a multiple of a single deductible of between $1,500 and $2,250, but now would have to be a flat amount . . . between $3,000 and $4,500—a disadvantage to families.
- Companies have been reluctant to enter the market because of the government limit on the number of allowable plans—to 750,000 by 1999 with interim caps for September 1, 1997 and September 1, 1998.
- Company uncertainty over compliance and product design.
- MSAs are available only to the self-employed, employees of firms without health insurance, and employer groups of fifty employees or less (during either of two years prior to MSA start-up) and up to two hundred employees after the MSA has been put in force.
- The sale of an MSA is more difficult and less rewarding for agents.
- MSA statute dictates a PPO plan design, but with insufficient penalties for out-of-network charges to make the PPO plan work. The maximum out-of-pocket for singles is $3,000 and $5,500 for families in or out of network.

Figure 31–2 outlines the specifications for an early MSA qualifying medical insurance policy, and Figure 31–3 provides specimen rates for such a policy.

Such a medical insurance plan design would qualify participants to establish their own individual MSAs, which they could fund themselves or have funded by their employer, but not both. In order to facilitate payments from their MSAs, the account, held by any financial institution that can establish IRA accounts, could incorporate the following features:

- A medical savings card—present the card for payment of services to any dentist, physician, pharmacist, or other health-care provider who accepts MasterCard®
- Checks
- Balances exceeding $3,500—such balances may be transferred to a brokerage account and then invested in a wide variety of mutual funds and equity investments.

Figure 31–2

Specifications for an Early MSA Qualifying Medical Insurance Policy

Deductible:	$2,250/individual; $4,500/family
Out-of-pocket expense limit:	$3,000/individual; $5,500 family (includes deductible)
Plan maximum:	$5,000,000
Optional maternity available 365 days after effective date.	
PPO plan:	80% Coinsurance; 60% Out-of-Network
Outpatient services for mental illness, substance abuse are included in out-of-pocket expense limit (usually subject to lower maximums).	
Outpatient emergency care:	No deductible
Issue ages:	19 to 64. Children birth to age 19 (Age 25 if unmarried, dependent, full-time students)
Maximum annual contribution:	65% x $2,250 = $1,462 75% x $4,500 = $3,375 (May be made for current year up until April 1st of the following year).

Employee free to choose any MSA Trustee.

Figure 31–3

MSA Qualifying Medical Insurance Policy
Specimen Rates for the Chicago Area

Attained Age		Nonsmoker			Smoker	
	Male	Female w/ OB	Female w/o OB	Male	Female w/OB	Female w/o OB
Under 25	56.50	162.23	76.26	70.30	201.87	94.89
25-29	60.75	166.58	79.43	75.59	207.29	98.84
30-34	68.80	169.60	90.41	85.62	211.05	112.51
35-39	80.38	175.20	100.46	100.03	218.02	125.01
40-44	100.46	186.90	116.53	125.01	232.57	145.01
45-49	128.49	198.50	136.62	159.90	247.11	170.01
50-54	160.56	214.52	158.42	199.80	266.95	197.14
55-59	207.81	241.72	178.50	258.60	300.79	222.12
60-64	259.11	276.10	203.88	322.43	343.58	253.71

Plus 1 child: 46.70
Plus 2 or more children: 110.96

Accumulations in MSA Plans

These are not "use it or lose it" plans like the Section 125 flexible spending account plans that allow people to fund their coming year unreimbursed medical expenses with a pretax deduction from their compensation. The money in a 125 plan must be used up by the participant or it is forfeited.

MSA plans, on the other hand, allow unused contributions to be carried over from year to year to be used sometime in the future. While waiting to be called upon to pay medical expenses, they may be invested within financial instruments as the participant directs and they compound on a tax-deferred basis.

Spending MSA Money

The government incentive (contributions deductible from gross income) to create MSAs is with the understanding that the money is supposed to be used to pay deductibles and other uninsured medical expenses. If distributions are taken from an MSA for other than medical expenses for the insured and eligible dependents covered under the high-deductible plan, they must be included in gross income and are subject to a 15 percent penalty tax, under Code Section 220 (e)(4), if the recipient is younger than 65. After age 65, the nonmedical withdrawals will be subject to income tax but no penalty. Distributions as a result of death, or total and permanent disability, also are exempt from the 15 percent penalty tax. The qualifying medical expenses for which tax-free distributions from MSAs can be used generally are the same as those that qualify for deduction as an itemized medical expense and include:

- Deductibles under qualifying MSA plans
- Coinsurance payments under qualifying MSA plans
- Uninsured medical expenses such as dental care and vision care

Under the conference committee report, distributions may not be used to pay insurance premiums other than premiums for long-term care insurance, COBRA, or premiums for coverage while the individual is receiving unemployment compensation. In the event of death, the spouse of the deceased MSA participant may use the MSA account as his or her own during his or her lifetime. If a nonspouse is the beneficiary of the account, the death distribution will, like IRAs, be subject to both income and applicable estate taxes.

One attraction of MSAs is the very significant amounts of money that could be accumulated during your young and healthy years to be used tax-free for medical expenses when your health deteriorates.

Medicare Plus Choice Medical Savings Accounts

This is not effective until tax years after December 31, 1998. It is a pilot program and will be open only until December 31, 2002. The plan will be available only to eligible seniors who apply.

The medical insurance plan which entitles someone to use an MSA may not have a 1999 deductible exceeding $6,000. A $6,000 deductible would entitle a participant to contribute 75 percent of that amount, or $4,500, to his or her MSA.

Seniors opting for the plan, who as a result of this decision reduce the government's cost of their health insurance, may find a portion of this premium savings contributed by the government to their MSA.

COBRA

On April 7, 1986, the Consolidated Omnibus Budget Reconciliation Act (COBRA) was enacted. It is a federal law applicable to employers providing health benefits to groups of twenty or more employees. It allows you to continue your group insurance even after your employment has terminated. You pay the full cost of what the employer was paying for the plan and possibly up to 2 percent more for administrative expenses. The continuation of your coverage may extend up to eighteen months. Your spouse and children may have up to thirty-six months of continued health insurance. As a rule of thumb, if you qualify, sign up. *Don't ever go even one day without health insurance!*

The second rule of thumb is to get other health insurance in effect as soon as possible. COBRA coverage has what I refer to as a "brick wall" at the end of your allowable coverage. The brick wall is an unknown as a result of the 1996 Health Insurance Portability and Accountability Act

(HIPAA), which requires the availability of health insurance coverage for individuals who have exhausted available group health coverage. However, passing a law does not guarantee that the insurance provider you would prefer will be the one providing the coverage. You would choose at the price you will be willing to pay. If you are on COBRA and healthy enough to get your own coverage, get off COBRA and on your own coverage with a carrier and coverage of your choice at an acceptable cost. Your own or your family's health may deteriorate while you are on COBRA and you will find yourself stuck with what your state chooses to provide.

The COBRA provisions are a boon to terminating employees and dependents since they make health insurance available regardless of physical condition. Premium payments to continue the coverage must be made promptly. It has been estimated that an employee or dependent covered under COBRA receives $2 in benefits for each dollar of premium paid. As a result, employers have been advised to terminate employees' COBRA coverage if they don't pay their premiums on time, so don't be late.

Employer and Employee COBRA Responsibilities

Of the lawsuits related to COBRA, approximately one-third are related to inadequate completion of the "Initial Notice" requirements that outline the rights of COBRA qualified beneficiaries and their responsibilities. It is up to the employee to notify the employer in case of divorce or a dependent no longer being eligible for regular group coverage.

It is up to the employer to provide "Initial Notice." COBRA guidelines dictate that the notice is to be mailed via first class mail to employee and spouse. It is the "and spouse" part that has created problems. Envelopes not properly addressed to include the spouse, new spouses the employer did not know about, and other administrative foul-ups have created havoc for employers. It is important for employers to administer COBRA carefully. A $100 million class action suit has been filed against a company by 2,000 former spouses and dependents alleging lack of compliance with the notice requirements of COBRA. The COBRA statutory penalty against employers for COBRA violations is $100 per day per beneficiary.

Figure 31–4

COBRA

COBRA Qualifying Event	Qualifying Individual	Maximum Time Period
Death of a covered employee	Covered dependent spouse and covered children	36 months
Termination of the covered employee's employment (other than for gross misconduct) or reduction in a covered employee's hours of employment	Covered employee and covered dependents	18 months
		29 months*
Divorce or legal separation of covered employee from spouse	Covered dependent spouse and children losing coverage	36 months
The covered employee's group health coverage terminates due to coverage by Medicare	Covered dependent spouse and/or covered children	36 months
The dependent child ceases to be an eligible dependent under the terms of the employer's group health plan	Covered dependent child ceasing to be eligible	36 months
	* If disabled at the time of termination or reduction of hours	36 months

Conversion

Your final chance to continue your health insurance without having to requalify medically would come at the end of your COBRA benefits, or the state-mandated continuation under the HIPAA laws as implemented by your state. This is the right to convert to an individual policy. Typically, these conversion policies are relatively expensive and the benefits are very restrictive. The conversion privileges are of value only to those who cannot obtain health insurance in any other way.

State Programs

Many states have passed legislation for employer groups of less than twenty employees that is patterned after COBRA so that employees have a right to continuing health care after termination; Illinois, for example, provides for a nine-month extension of health coverage. Your employer's insurer will provide you with the information and paperwork you need.

Should none of these alternatives for health insurance be available to you, the next step would be to contact your state insurance commissioner's office and ask for the enrollment materials, price list, and benefits description of the state-sponsored health insurance pool. Most states have created state pools for those who cannot get health insurance elsewhere. We would suggest you get the papers and sign up for the state pool, but while you are awaiting acceptance, keep trying for alternative coverage for each member of your family.

Individual Medical Insurance

If employer-provided health insurance is not a viable alternative, you will apply directly to an insurance company for an individually issued policy. The advantage of this procedure is that you can more or less dictate the type of benefits you want. The disadvantage is that you have no employer to help you pay for the insurance. Unfortunately, individual insurance is most readily available if you are healthy. In applying for an individual health insurance policy, the insurance company will ask you a dizzying array of medical questions. They will want to know your personal health history and that of everyone in your family. It is in your best interest to divulge everything

because, even if you have a particular health condition that the insurance company might not wish to cover, they may be able to issue the policy with an exclusion rider. The policy would cover everything but that particular condition, certainly a better alternative than no health insurance at all. Another advantage of an individual policy is the availability of a guaranteed renewable contract, which allows the insurance company to adjust the costs for the insurance as long as it does so on a class basis and has the approval of your state insurance commissioner to make the change. The following action letter is designed to help you define your medical insurance needs to a provider or insurance agent.

Figure 31–5

Individual Medical Insurance
Action Letter

Dear Sir:

I am in need of private medical insurance. I am male / female born _____ I am a smoker/nonsmoker in excellent / good / fair health.

My spouse is a male / female born _____ and is a smoker / nonsmoker in excellent / good / fair health.

We have / do not have children. Their names, dates of birth, sex, and basic health condition are listed on the back of this letter.

I would like a comprehensive major medical policy that is Lifetime Guaranteed Renewable and has an Unlimited Lifetime Maximum.

Other plan features are:
1. Individual deductible $100 / $200 / $500 / $1,000 / $2,000/ $ _____.
2. Coinsurance Provision 80/20 (Insurance company pays 80%, I pay 20%)
3. Stop-Loss Provision—What is my maximum out-of-pocket requirement?
   For the family _____
   For how long _____
4. A PPO and/or HMO option.

Please send me quotes from a number of companies including any descriptive material you have on the plans along with enrollment forms and instructions.

I would appreciate your evaluation of the coverages regarding which one you feel is fairly priced and sufficiently comprehensive to provide for my family.

Sincerely,

The action letter to request quotes regarding private health insurance first lists the specifics regarding those who need health insurance (dates of birth, smoker or nonsmoker, health conditions) for all members of the family. It then requests a comprehensive major medical policy that is guaranteed renewable throughout your lifetime that has an unlimited lifetime maximum. You then select an appropriate deductible. You can ask the insurance professional to provide you with quotes at various deductibles so that you may choose the one that is most cost-effective for you. It states your requested coinsurance provision—that is, what percentage of the medical bills you would pay and how much the insurance company would pay, stipulating the most typical split of 80 percent being paid by the insurance company and 20 percent by you. Keep in mind a 50 percent/50 percent split normally will cost you less and may not increase your out-of-pocket maximum. You would pay a greater percentage of the smaller bills but then it would shift the responsibility to the insurance company. The letter next asks for the maximum out-of-pocket exposure so that you would know what your medical costs could be under a worst-case scenario.

Association Medical Insurance

You also may be able to obtain medical insurance from an association of which you are a member. Some organizations sell insurance to provide an extra benefit for their membership and/or to make a profit for their organization. You obviously would prefer the former. Some are designed to pay you a stipulated amount of money each day you are in the hospital. Keep in mind that the average stay in the hospital is less than ten days. A $50 per day indemnity policy paying you $500 for the ten days is not going to be much help and may not be worth what it costs. Policies that will pay benefits only if your medical condition is caused by an accident or some specific illness have enjoyed a resurgence of popularity as managed care has continued to limit payments under the conventional forms of health insurance. The consumer is beginning to see a need for coverage that is not under the jurisdiction of managed care but will pay if what is stipulated in the policy happens to the insured. These policies cost less, but you should be very careful to make sure that

they do give you the peace of mind that you seek. As competition heats up in this area, we have seen quality improve and prices go down, especially when provided through employer-sponsored voluntary purchase programs.

Federal Government Provided Medical Insurance

Both federal and state governments provide medical insurance benefits. The Medicare program of the federal government provides mandatory basic hospitalization benefits for most U.S. citizens over the age of 65 and some other special classes of individuals. The hospital coverage, referred to as Part A, is supplemented by Part B of Medicare at a cost to you of $43.80 per month for 1997. Part B is a voluntary program that provides for the payment of doctor bills. All eligible individuals should sign up for both of these plans three months prior to their 65th birthday since Medicare normally is insufficient by itself. We recommend that a supplemental plan be purchased.

Caution to Medicare Participants

Medicare has been primarily an indemnity insurance plan. Your chosen doctor and hospital are reimbursed for the services they provide to you within the benefits approved by Medicare. The yeas and nays of managed care are coming. HMOs all over the country are soliciting your business and telling you in wonderful ads what good care they will offer you, but please be careful. Ask them if signing up with them mandates that they must be your exclusive provider and, if so, when and how could you terminate the relationship. What freedoms are you giving up? What happens when you get sick away from home? You also will want to know how financially solvent they are and whether they are a new start-up company or one with a mature book of business and a good reputation for quality care. No, it is not easy for Medicare patients to select a provider today. Too many new providers are trying to leverage our fear of costly illness into business for themselves. Shop with a healthy degree of skepticism.

Which Medigap Plan?

There are ten standard medicare supplemental benefit plans. Figure 31–6 highlights the benefits

Figure 31–6
Ten Standard Medicare Supplement Benefit Plans

	Plan A	Plan B	Plan C	Plan D	Plan E	Plan F	Plan G	Plan H	Plan I	Plan J
CORE BENEFITS										
Pan A Hospital (Days 61–90)	X	X	X	X	X	X	X	X	X	X
Lifetime Reserve Days (Days 91–150)	X	X	X	X	X	X	X	X	X	X
365 Life Hospital Days (100%)	X	X	X	X	X	X	X	X	X	X
Parts A and B Blood	X	X	X	X	X	X	X	X	X	X
Part B Coinsurance (20%)	X	X	X	X	X	X	X	X	X	X
ADDITIONAL BENEFITS										
Skilled Nursing Facility Coinsurance (Days 21–100)			X	X	X	X	X	X	X	X
Part A Deductible		X	X	X	X	X	X	X	X	X
Part B Deductible				X		X				
Part B Excess Charges						100%	80%		100%	100%
Foreign Travel Emergency			X	X	X	X	X	X	X	X
At-Home Recovery				X			X		X	X
Prescription Drugs								$250 Ded 50% to $1,250	$250 Ded 50% to $1,250	$250 Ded 50% to $3,000
Preventive Medical Care					X					X

provided by each. Our recommendation as the most cost-effective choice is plan F. The reason for that recommendation is that it covers all the basics plus 100 percent of the Part B expenses, the doctor's bills. We have seen doctor bills that far exceed what Medicare mandates as "reasonable and customary" and consider it a significant area of exposure for you. Another reason for our recommendation is that it does not include the at-home recovery, prescription drugs, and preventive medical care, benefits that we consider too limited to be worth what they typically cost. You may have a very good reason for choosing the more costly and comprehensive plan J. If you know that you will use up the full prescription drug limitation of $3,000 per year each year, or really want the extra benefits of the more comprehensive plans then, by all means, select one of them.

One reason for a Medigap policy is the need for coverage for that portion of the doctor bill that Medicare deems "excessive." A doctor who accepts just what Medicare allows is a "participating" physician, others are "nonparticipating." About one out of every three physicians are participating. It is probable that this number will fall as Medicare continues its cutbacks. When Medicare refuses to pay too often, it becomes impossible for these physicians to maintain their practices. You can obtain a good Medigap policy for approximately $80 to $100 per month. You should be able to locate a good one by consulting your doctor or, better yet, his billing department to find out which ones they and their patients like best. But only one plan please—multiple Medigap policies are a waste of money.

The good news about Medigap policies is that if you apply in time (start three months prior to

Figure 31–7

Medigap Action Letter

Dear Sir:

I am in need of private Medigap insurance. I am male / female born _____ I am a smoker/nonsmoker in excellent / good / fair health.

My spouse is a male / female born _____ and is a smoker / nonsmoker in excellent / good / fair health.

I would like a comprehensive Medigap policy that is Lifetime Guaranteed Renewable and has an Unlimited Lifetime Maximum.

Other plan features desired are:
1. Cost-effective benefits that fill in the gaps by paying what Medicare Parts A and B commonly exclude.
2. Usual and customary expense coverage so that the Medigap policy will pay the excess charges between the usual and customary costs and the more limited Medicare eligible expenses.

Please send me quotes from _____ companies including any descriptive material you have on the plans along with enrollment forms and instructions.

I would appreciate your evaluation of the coverages regarding which one you feel is fairly priced and sufficiently comprehensive to provide for my family.

Sincerely,

---

your 65th birthday) or without a break in your existing coverage, you can get a policy without any medical questions asked. Make sure you and your clients apply promptly. Even after you have a plan, you can move to another without medical questions or preexisting condition limitations as long as there is no break in coverage.

One more caution. Doctors in some areas are signing their patients up for "wellness" benefit plans, annual physicals, and so on, for a monthly or annual retainer and a promise to waive the Medicare deductible. First, the deductibles for Medicare may be picked up by your Medicare Supplement insurance. Second, if the doctor is selling "insurance" it is probably not legal. And third, it is probably not worth the money. If you know of one that you consider a fair, legal arrangement, we would love to hear from you. If you are aware of those that are not, take it up with your state insurance commissioner.

Summary

Although you may not be seeing health-care reform on the evening news anymore, you can be sure that it is still going on. Insurers, legislators, health-care providers, employers, and combinations of all these players are working daily to devise systems of delivering health care more effectively. "Managed care" is the buzz word of the day. This is your new medical care world and you are going to have to cope with:

- Networks rather than individual physicians
- Financial incentives to accept more controlled care (by them not you) j Change, as the providers work at trying to balance quality of care with cost of care
- Gatekeepers—the general or primary physician who will need to approve your use of specialists
- Utilization review to determine the "necessity" of the medical care you are receiving
- Preadmission certification
- Dental PPOs

The bottom line on medical insurance is that you shouldn't go a day without it. A lack of medical insurance can be hazardous to your economic health.

A Word About the National Health-Care Crisis

"Crisis?" Yes, crisis. The only people you will encounter who do not think it is a crisis are those who have not been affected personally by having someone they care about fall through the cracks of the current U.S. health-care system. However, crisis does not mean it can't get worse. It is getting worse as we continue to ignore it.

You see, health insurance, as it is structured today, is not *insurance*. Insurance, by definition, is a pooling of your payments with those of others to have your losses, if any, paid by the insurer because you have paid a premium. But, today most consumers obtain their health insurance through their employers. In the past, employer-provided health insurance would terminate when we were too sick to work and had exhausted our rights under COBRA and conversion policies. It ceased to reimburse us for our losses even though we paid the premiums while we were healthy and employed. This is the problem that the HIPAA law of 1996 has tried to address. In spite of the law that mandates that you have continuity of coverage and access to individual insurance after COBRA, the law does not have the ability to force insurance companies to provide the coverage or to mandate the cost of that coverage.

HIPAA has not solved the problem that you have health insurance while you are a healthy, employed, fortunate worker and, since the cost is deductible, it costs you no more than $.70 per dollar after the tax benefit (assuming you're in the 30 percent tax bracket). Then, when you are an individual purchaser, the system increases your cost. It gives you an opportunity to pay for COBRA, conversion insurance, or state pool health insurance with your *after-tax* earnings. You not only have to pay 100 to 102 percent of the cost of your coverage but also full income tax on the money with which you pay the premium. In the 30 percent tax bracket, you have to earn $1.42 in order to spend $1.00 to buy health insurance.

How is that for public policy. Health insurance costs you $.70 if you are a healthy, employed worker but twice that much if you're too young, too old, or too ill to get your health insurance through an employer.

It remains to be seen at this point whether HIPAA will provide solutions to some of today's health-care problems or exacerbate the situation by driving more and more insurance companies out of the health insurance market, thus increasing costs and reducing supply.

You do not want government being the *provider* of health insurance or health care for two reasons. One, dollars that go through government are eaten up by inefficient bureaucratic expenses and two, you can't complain to city hall about city hall. Government's function should be to do what it does best, serve and protect you if the private health-care system lets you down.

What kind of private system would work? One that could not get rid of you no matter what happened. One that could not use "closed blocks" of policies. These "closed blocks" enable insurance companies to increase premiums on certain blocks of policies, those with the older insureds experiencing higher claims, until all of those who had been insured give up because of the cost and lose their coverage. We must have a system that *must* provide your care forever. Economically, in such a system, it would be best for the system to keep you healthy and, if you are sick, to get you well as soon as possible—just the opposite of the current system.

What's wrong with this new system? There is no room for "little" systems. They have to be big so that they can serve you throughout the country, spread the risk, and be efficient. You won't get to choose your own doctor. Professionals whose primary concern is making you well will choose for you. And, worse yet, you will all have to agree to pay for your coverage forever, even if you pay for it out of welfare, health-care stamps, or charity. There's the rub—there can be no "free lunch" in the new health-care system. Spreading the risk and spreading the cost is essential.

There must be constant pay, constant coverage, and professionals directing your treatment. Uncle Sam should be there to measure, evaluate, and report quality of coverage and results, and to assist you when the system fails to provide quality care. The competition between the systems will be to keep their populations healthier at lower cost than the other systems. Efficiency and quality will pay. But you will have no choice regarding participation, provider, or paying. Impossible! Americans won't accept it! What do you mean, it sounds like Social (Medical) Security to me?

Of course, you can keep your present system. You can hope you and yours don't fall through the cracks of the system dragging all of you down emotionally and economically. The current system does allow you to choose your own doctor, choose not to pay, and choose not to be covered—and that obviously is important to you.

32
Advance Health-Care Planning

KRISTEN LEWIS GRICE

Advance health-care planning has become a major concern for people of all ages and backgrounds who fear that a future incapacity or disability will keep them from exercising their rights to direct the course of their medical treatment and health care. Estate planning practitioners report an ever-increasing number of inquiries about effective ways to address this concern.

Inadequacy of Living Wills

Many have enthusiastically embraced the concept of a living will, which typically applies only when an individual is in a terminal condition and death is imminent. However, the living will addresses only a single health-care decision: the withdrawal or withholding of life-sustaining treatment. Many (if not most) duly executed living wills are ultimately not utilized in clinical practice, often because the terms of the documents are too vague for any practical application.

The living will was not intended to address most of the health-care decisions that are made during an individual's lifetime and is often ineffective in the very situation it was designed to address. The living will gained much of its acceptance as a perceived response to a significant medical concern expressed by many individuals: the fear of having life prolonged, or death delayed, solely by virtue of artificially supplied nutrition and hydration. It is ironic that many existing living will statutes specifically exclude from the definition of life-sustaining treatment any type of nourishment,

Kristen Lewis Grice is counsel in the tax section of Smith, Gambrell & Russell, LLP, in Atlanta, Georgia. This chapter first appeared as an article in *Probate and Property,* the magazine of the Section of Real Property, Probate and Trust Law of the ABA.

including intravenous or nasogastric feeding. A significant majority of the courts that have considered the issue have found that such artificial feeding constitutes medical treatment that may be rejected like any other such treatment.

Ineffectiveness of "Family Consent" Laws

Most people would agree that medical decision making is a private matter that typically belongs outside of the court system. In recognition of this concept, many states have adopted so-called family consent statutes that provide a prioritized list of individuals, generally close relatives, who are authorized to make medical decisions on behalf of an incompetent or incapacitated individual without the intervention of a guardian or court. Like intestacy laws, family consent statutes represent the legislature's considered opinion about who an individual would likely want to make medical decisions on his or her behalf in the event the individual is unable to do so.

Although family members may generally be the best persons to make such medical decisions, this is not always the case. For example, an AIDS patient may prefer that a sympathetic friend rather than an estranged family member act on his or her behalf. And many elderly people have outlived those who typically are designated in family consent statutes for surrogate medical decision-making.

Additional difficulties often arise under family consent statutes when individuals who are equally entitled to make medical decisions for an incompetent person disagree as to the proper course of action. In such situations, and in those states without family consent statutes, health-care providers have no clear indication of who has the right to make medical decisions on behalf of incompetent patients. Court intervention, including the possibility of a court-appointed guardian, is virtually assured in such cases.

Filling the Void: The DPAHC

The durable power of attorney for health care (DPAHC) is filling the void left by living will and family consent statutes that are often restrictive and ineffective. With patience and careful drafting, a DPAHC may be tailored to reflect the precise preferences and values of each individual regarding personal and health-care matters. Unlike most living wills, a DPAHC may be drafted for use in connection with a broad range of lifetime, and even some post-death, health-care, and personal decisions. The DPAHC also may be used to ensure that an individual (the principal) can delegate decision-making authority in such matters to a person or persons of his or her choice (the agent) and not the choice of the state legislature or the courts.

The concept of a durable power of attorney—one that survives the principal's subsequent incompetence or incapacity—is particularly appropriate in health-care decision-making. An agent acting under a DPAHC does not usurp the principal's right to make health-care decisions, but rather exercises that right on the principal's behalf only if the principal is unable to do so.

Statutory Basis for DPAHC

According to the national organization now known as Choice in Dying, Inc. (formerly known as The Society for the Right to Die and Concern for Dying), as of June 1, 1997, forty-six states and the District of Columbia had legislation authorizing both living wills and the appointment of health-care agents. Of the four states that did not specifically authorize both of these planning opportunities, Alaska authorized only living wills, while Massachusetts, Michigan, and New York authorized only the appointment of health-care agents. The specifics of the enabling legislation in each state vary greatly and are in many situations modified by case law from state to state. (For statutory and case law citations for a particular jurisdiction, contact Choice in Dying, Inc., 1035 30th Street, N.W., Washington, D.C. 20007, or call (800) 989-9455. This organization maintains current information on living wills and DPAHCs for all jurisdictions that authorize them.)

Even if a particular state does not expressly recognize the concept of a DPAHC under case law or specific enabling legislation, the execution of a DPAHC may still serve a valuable purpose. A DPAHC could, in appropriate circumstances, constitute clear and convincing evidence of an individual's desires with respect to the matters covered by the DPAHC. The Missouri Supreme Court, in *Cruzan v. Harmon,* 760 S.W.2d 408 (Mo. 1988) *cert. granted as Cruzan v. Director, Missouri Department of Health,* 109 S.Ct. 3240, denied the application of Nancy Cruzan's guardians to discontinue the artificial nutrition and hydration responsible for keeping her alive in a persistent vegetative state because, among other reasons, there was no "clear and convincing" evidence of Nancy's desires in this regard.

Nonstatutory Authority for DPAHC

Case law is virtually unanimous in holding that a person who has become unable to make medical decisions for himself or herself does not by virtue of such incapacity lose the common law right of self-determination and the concomitant right to direct the course of his or her medical care and treatment. A number of state courts, by extending the reach of an individual's right to privacy, have even asserted a constitutional basis for an individual's right to direct the course of medical treatment. The American Bar Association, at its 1990 midyear meeting, endorsed the following general principles:

1. individuals who are capable of making health-care decisions generally have the right to consent to or refuse suggested health-care interventions, even if the result would be to shorten life's span; and
2. an appropriate surrogate may exercise this right on behalf of an individual who is incapable of making such decisions.

However, an individual's right to consent to or refuse medical treatment is not absolute and must be weighed against certain other important interests, including

- the preservation of life;
- the protection of innocent third parties, such as minor children who are dependent on the individual;

- the prevention of suicide; and
- medical ethics.

All of the above are generally described as "compelling state interests." (For an excellent discussion of the legal bases of an individual's right to direct the course of his or her medical treatment and the necessary balancing of this right against countervailing state interests, see Collin, Lombard, Moses, and Spitler, *The Durable Power of Attorney: A Systems Approach, 2d ed.,* (Shepard's/McGraw-Hill, Inc., Colorado Springs, Colorado, 1987.)

Involvement of Estate Planners

In the course of estate planning, it is most appropriate to consider executing a living will and a durable power of attorney to cover financial and property matters. Both of these standard documents tie in directly with the relatively novel concept of a DPAHC.

Although estate planning lawyers are accustomed to discussing death and disability with their clients, such discussions typically occur in the abstract. In order to formulate a DPAHC that will meaningfully reflect their clients' desires in this sensitive area, lawyers must learn to discuss in detail particular types of medical and health-care situations and decisions of concern. However, drafting a DPAHC is a multidimensional exercise that involves more than purely medical considerations. The lawyer should be ready to discuss the clients' relevant values, life history, and religious convictions, all of which may, and should, affect the scope and content of a DPAHC.

Lawyers have thus far been afforded relatively little guidance in the area of drafting an effective and meaningful DPAHC. Many have attempted to address the sensitive and complex issue of surrogate medical decision-making in the context of the standard general durable power of attorney covering property and other financial matters by including a cursory right "to make health-care decisions for the principal." Such an approach, however, is not likely to affect the individual's desires and is unlikely to be accepted as sufficient authority by many medical practitioners.

Drafting an Effective DPAHC

A DPAHC should ideally be contained in a separate document (that is, not included as part of a power of attorney that covers property and financial matters). Just as it may be undesirable for a power of attorney covering financial matters to be made a part of the principal's medical records, it may be equally inappropriate for the agent's authority regarding health-care matters to become part of the public record—for example, if the document is filed in the local real estate records in connection with a transfer of the principal's real property.

The DPAHC statutes in some states provide detailed forms for use. Although some states mandate strict adherence to the statutory forms, many of these forms are nonexclusive and provide a good starting point for discussion. (Copies of all statutory DPAHC forms are available from Choice in Dying, mentioned above.) The American Bar Association Commission on Legal Problems of the Elderly has also prepared a sample form for a "Power of Attorney for Health Care," set forth in the Appendix (pages 509–514). Notwithstanding the existence of such useful standardized forms, it is important to remember that one of the greatest virtues of a DPAHC is that it can, and should, be tailored to reflect the specific desires of an individual, to the extent permissible under applicable local law.

Appointment of Agent and Successors

Perhaps the most important element of a DPAHC is the appointment of the individual who will serve as the principal's agent for making medical and personal-care decisions in the event the principal cannot do so personally. Some states specifically preclude the appointment of any health-care provider as an agent under a DPAHC, while others may limit the restriction to a health-care provider who is involved, directly or indirectly, in rendering medical or other care to the principal under the DPAHC.

A family member is often the best surrogate decision-maker in health-care matters. Such individuals are most likely to be familiar with the principal's preferences and values and able to apply them in specific contexts. Typically, however, such individuals would also be likely to benefit from the principal's death, either under the principal's will or the laws of intestacy. Such conflicts of interest may influence an agent acting under a DPAHC to make a medical decision that could hasten the principal's death contrary to the principal's desires. On the other hand, it is also possible that a family member could err on the side of preserving the principal's life contrary to the wishes of the principal, due to feelings of guilt or remorse.

It is important at the outset to raise and discuss these and other potential conflicts of interest with the nominated agent, before the agent is called on to act under the DPAHC. Health-care providers should also be sensitive to the possibility that conflicts of interest may occasionally translate into a serious abuse or misuse of a DPAHC. Court intervention and the possible appointment of a guardian should be invited when appropriate to safeguard the interests of the principal. Although it is preferable in most cases to conduct medical decision-making in private, the courts can and sometimes should play a role in ensuring that such decisions are made in good faith and in the best interests of the principal.

The nominated agent under a DPAHC, however carefully chosen, may balk when called on to exercise this authority. Since a nominated agent cannot be forced to act under a DPAHC, it is advisable for the principal to designate one or more successor agents in the event the nominated individual fails to act by reason of resignation, death, disability, or unavailability. The principal may also wish to appoint co-agents under a DPAHC. For example, a person with several adult children all living nearby might require the advice and consent of all the children as co-agents under a DPAHC. However, as in the case of family consent statutes, irresolute conflict among co-agents may effectively defeat one of the primary benefits to be gained by executing a DPAHC.

Breadth of the Agent's Authority

The grant of authority under a DPAHC may be as broad or as limited as the principal desires. The DPAHC is basically a neutral document that can be molded and precisely tailored to reflect the concerns and preferences of the individual. Typical DPAHC-enabling legislation permits the delegation of all powers or rights an individual may have—to be informed about, to consent or refuse to consent to, or to withdraw any type of health care, which may be defined to include any care,

treatment, service, or procedure to maintain, diagnose, treat, or provide for the principal's physical or mental health or personal care.

A DPAHC may be used to advise the agent and health-care providers of any particular medical care, procedures, treatment, or medications to which the principal is opposed, on religious or other grounds, or which he or she definitely favors. The DPAHC may even address certain post-death health-care matters, such as authorizing an anatomical gift or autopsy or disposing of the principal's remains.

Some states, as a matter of public policy, specifically provide that certain medical procedures, such as psychosurgery, abortion, or sterilization, may not be covered by a DPAHC. A DPAHC may not be used to authorize euthanasia or any other action or course of action that would violate state or federal criminal or civil laws.

Standards for Exercise of Agent's Authority

An agent acting under a DPAHC should exercise his or her powers in a manner that is consistent with the intent and desires of the principal, as manifested in the DPAHC or otherwise. If there is no clear and convincing evidence of how the principal would want the agent to act in a particular situation, the agent should be guided in the decision-making process by the principal's values and beliefs. However, this so-called substituted judgment standard for surrogate decision-making is not accepted by all jurisdictions. If a particular jurisdiction does not recognize the substituted judgment approach, or if that approach fails to yield a clear decision, the agent should act in the principal's best interests.

It is essential that any DPAHC provide as much evidence as possible of the principal's wishes regarding health-care decisions so that the agent may take comfort in and rely on such guidance when exercising authority. An agent who is confident that he or she is implementing the principal's desires is more likely to undertake the required medical decision-making when called on to do so. Furthermore, health-care providers may be more willing to rely on the agent's decisions under a DPAHC if there is adequate evidence of the principal's desires regarding a particular health-care decision.

Continued communication between the principal and the nominated agent after a DPAHC has been executed may help assure the agent's ongoing willingness to exercise the decision-making authority at the appropriate time.

When powers granted under a DPAHC are exercised, the agent is required to use due care to act for the benefit of the principal in accordance with the terms of the DPAHC. The DPAHC-enabling legislation in many states provides that if the agent under a DPAHC acts in good faith with due care for the benefit of the principal, and in accordance with the terms of the DPAHC, the agent will not be subject to any type of civil or criminal liability.

Life-Sustaining Treatment

Many individuals desire to execute a DPAHC for the primary purpose of addressing decisions regarding the provision or withdrawal of life-sustaining treatment, including artificial nutrition and hydration. In contrast to a living will, a DPAHC may be used to require that maximum care, including life-sustaining treatment, be afforded in certain situations. In light of the sensitivity of the subject of life-sustaining or death-delaying treatment, it is advisable to deal with this topic specifically when drafting any DPAHC, in a manner that makes it clear that the principal has carefully considered the issue.

One approach is to set forth in the DPAHC a general statement of the principal's views about life-sustaining or death-delaying treatment. For example, the principal may state that life-sustaining treatment is to be provided only if the agent believes that the burdens of the treatment will outweigh the expected benefits thereof or, at the other end of the spectrum, that such treatment shall be afforded to the greatest extent possible without regard to chances of recovery or quality of life considerations, or some appropriate middle ground. The DPAHC should also afford the principal an opportunity to designate whether any particular form of life-sustaining treatment is to be excluded from coverage under the DPAHC.

If the principal has previously executed a living will, the DPAHC should specifically address the effect of the living will on a DPAHC that authorizes the agent to deal with the precise circumstances covered by the living will. This is especially important if there is a conflict between the terms of the living will and the DPAHC regarding the withdrawal of life-sustaining treatment, which may be defined under the state's living will law to exclude artificially supplied nutrition and hydration. However, even in states that have living will laws that specifically preclude the withdrawal or withholding of artificially supplied nutrition and hydration, courts have held that such legislation does not limit an individual's broader common- law, and possibly constitutional, right to decline such life-sustaining treatment by other lawful means. Most living will laws provide that they are cumulative in effect and do not purport to set forth the sole means by which an individual may exercise medical decision-making powers.

Nomination of Guardian

To the extent permitted under local law, the principal may wish to use a DPAHC to nominate the agent or someone else as his or her guardian in the event a court determines that a guardian should be appointed. Although one of the primary purposes of executing a DPAHC is to preclude the need for a court-appointed guardian, such an appointment may be desirable despite the availability of an agent under a DPAHC. The principal should recognize, however, that such a nomination is typically not binding on a court, which will respect the nomination only if it is determined to be in the best interests of the principal.

The laws in some states provide that the appointment of a guardian automatically terminates the authority of a previously appointed agent under a durable power of attorney. Individuals have attempted to use such laws to deliberately and maliciously terminate the authority of an agent under a DPAHC. Using the DPAHC to nominate the agent as the principal's guardian may discourage this type of tactic and may ultimately serve to uphold the wishes of the principal.

The powers of a guardian of the person typically extend to making health-care decisions for the ward. Therefore, to the extent that someone other than the agent under the DPAHC may serve as the guardian of the person of the principal, the DPAHC should specifically address their interaction and respective duties.

Medical Facilities and Personnel

The principal may use a DPAHC to authorize the agent to admit or discharge the principal from hospitals, institutions, nursing facilities, treatment centers, and other health-care institutions. On the other hand, a principal may use the DPAHC to make it clear that he or she does not want to be committed to a nursing home or other long-term care facility under any circumstances. The DPAHC should also grant the agent specific authority to hire and fire the health-care personnel who will be responsible for the principal's care at such institutions or at home. Although the agent is not permitted to delegate his or her authority, the agent should be permitted to act through others employed by the agent as reasonably necessary to implement the exercise of the agent's powers.

The agent under a DPAHC should be specifically permitted to contract for any required health-care services in the name of the principal and to bind the principal to pay for all such services. However, in light of the significant costs of health-care services, the DPAHC should address the relative duties and responsibilities of an agent acting under a DPAHC and any guardian of the property who may be appointed for the principal.

Access to Medical Records

A DPAHC may be used to grant the agent access to the principal's medical records as well as the right to disclose the contents of such records to others in the course of acting under the DPAHC. This power is especially important if it is ever necessary for the agent to arrange for the transfer of the principal—for example, from a health-care provider who refuses to respect the agent's authority or to follow the agent's directions under the DPAHC.

Third-Party Compliance

Health-care providers often cannot be forced to follow the directions of an agent acting under a DPAHC. Refusals to act may be based on the provider's medical judgment, ethical position, the fear of malpractice, or other liability. Furthermore, the DPAHC-enabling legislation in some states provides that health-care providers have the right to administer treatment for the patient's comfort or alleviation of pain, notwithstanding the directions of an agent acting under a DPAHC.

The principal may consider granting the agent the power to seek court intervention for the purpose of securing compliance with the directions under a DPAHC. However, to the extent the agent actually finds it necessary to request court assistance, one of the primary purposes of the DPAHC has been defeated. A less drastic method of encouraging third-party reliance on and compliance with the directions of an agent acting under a DPAHC may be to include in the text of the DPAHC a statement to the effect that any person who relies in good faith on directions of the agent shall be protected to the same extent as though such person had dealt directly with the principal as a fully competent person.

Relevant DPAHC-enabling legislation often provides that health-care providers and others shall not be civilly or criminally liable to the principal or the principal's estate for complying with the decisions or directions of an agent acting under a DPAHC, even if death or injury to the principal ensues. Such legislation also typically provides that if the principal's death results from withholding or withdrawing life-sustaining or death-delaying treatment in accordance with the terms of the DPAHC, the death will not constitute a suicide or homicide for any purpose.

In some states, liability for failure to comply with the directions or decisions of an agent acting under a DPAHC may be avoided completely if the provider promptly informs the agent of such noncompliance and permits the agent to arrange for the transfer of the principal to another provider. To the extent a health-care provider's noncompliance with the agent's directions necessitates a transfer of the principal to another facility, health-care providers in some states are obligated to continue to give reasonably necessary consultation and care pending completion of the transfer.

Immediate Effectiveness of DPAHC

There is no real risk in providing that a DPAHC becomes effective immediately upon execution. If the principal is capable of consenting, or refusing to consent, to a particular course of medical treatment, a DPAHC is, by its terms, inoperative. A determination of the principal's decisional capacity should ideally be made by the principal's attending physician in consultation with the agent under a DPAHC.

Termination of Agent's Authority

Specific consideration should also be given to the termination of the authority granted to an agent under a DPAHC. The principal may provide that the agent's authority shall terminate upon the principal's death, or that the agent's powers shall extend beyond death for the purpose of authorizing the autopsy of the principal's body, an anatomical gift, or the disposition of remains, as permitted by local law. Some DPAHC-enabling legislation imposes strict time limits on the validity of a DPAHC, such as seven years from the date of execution, often corresponding to similar limits for living wills.

Although a DPAHC by definition may survive the incapacity of the principal, the principal may wish the agent's authority to terminate upon the appointment of a guardian for the principal.

It is important to remember that if durability is desired—that is, the agent's authority under the DPAHC is to survive the principal's incompetency or incapacity—some states require a specific statement to that effect. The laws in other states provide that a power of attorney is durable unless expressly provided otherwise.

Revocation and Amendment

The DPAHC should also specifically address the revocation of the agent's authority. Clearly, the principal may revoke the DPAHC at any time simply by physically destroying the document. However, the principal may wish to require that any revocation be effected by a written instrument delivered to the agent or health-care provider. On the other hand, the principal may wish the revocation threshold to be quite low and to permit revocation orally or by any other expression of an intent to revoke. Local law may impose specific requirements for the effective revocation of the DPAHC.

The principal should also consider whether a divorce or separation subsequent to the execu-

tion of a DPAHC that appoints the principal's spouse as the agent should operate to revoke the former spouse's authority automatically. Automatic revocation might also be appropriate where the principal marries subsequent to the execution of a DPAHC that appoints as the agent a person who is not the principal's spouse. Some DPAHC-enabling legislation provides for automatic revocation in such cases. If the principal does not wish such revocation to occur, the issue should be specifically addressed in the DPAHC.

The principal may also wish to amend, but not revoke, a DPAHC from time to time. The DPAHC may speak directly to the issue, but local law requirements should also be considered.

Formalities of Execution

The formalities of executing a DPAHC should be sufficiently stringent to assure that the principal knowingly and voluntarily signs the document. However, overly restrictive execution formalities may be invalid to the extent that such requirements infringe on the individual's right to delegate health-care decision-making powers. DPAHC-enabling legislation varies considerably from state to state regarding witness and notary requirements. Some states provide that if the principal is a patient in a health-care facility at the time the DPAHC is executed, the principal's attending physician or another health-care provider must also witness and attest to the execution of the DPAHC. Unfortunately, the experience of many practitioners has been that medical personnel are typically unwilling to participate in the execution of medical consent documents.

Conclusion

The DPAHC, and its growing acceptance by health-care professionals, represents a desirable trend that can give new meaning to the right of an individual to direct the course of personal health-care and medical treatment. Yet, the current paucity of law in the developing area of surrogate health-care decision-making assures that this will remain a challenging aspect of estate planning for the near future.

Part V
Tax and Estate Planning Issues for Consideration

33

The Ten Most Common Estate Planning Mistakes (And How to Avoid Them)

STEPHAN R. LEIMBERG

This entire commentary is devoted to the types of problems that can cost you and your family tens of thousands of dollars and unbelievable heartache. Since only a fool learns from his own mistakes, this commentary is dedicated to the wise person who can profit from the lessons so many have expensively learned the hard way.

Here are ten areas of common (and serious) mistakes that can be easily solved with the assistance of a financial services professional. Have you made one or more of these mistakes? If you haven't checked, how do you know?

Mistake 1: Improper Use of Jointly Held Property

If used excessively or used by the wrong parties (especially by unmarried individuals) the otherwise "poor man's will" becomes a poor will for an otherwise good man or woman. In short, jointly held property can become a nightmare of unexpected tax and nontax problems including:

A. When property is titled jointly there is the potential for both federal and state gift tax.

B. There is the possibility of double federal estate taxation; if the joint ownership is between individuals other than spouses, the entire property will be taxed in the estate of the first spouse to die—except to the extent

the survivor can prove contribution to the property. Then, whatever the survivor receives and does not consume or give away will be included (and taxed a second time) in the survivor's gross estate.

C. Once jointly owned property with right of survivorship has passed to the survivor, the provisions of the decedent's will are ineffective. This means the property is left outright to the survivor who is then without the benefit of management protection or investment advice.

D. The surviving spouse can give away or at death leave the formerly jointly owned property to anyone she wants regardless of the desires of the deceased spouse. In other words, holding property jointly equates to a total loss of control since the surviving spouse can ignore the decedent's wishes as to the ultimate disposition of the property. This loss of control can be especially horrendous when the joint owners are not related.

E. Since the jointly held property passes directly to the survivor (who then could possibly squander, gamble, give away, or lose the property to creditors), the decedent's executor could be faced with a lack of adequate cash to pay estate taxes and other settlement expenses.

F. A well-drawn estate plan is designed to avoid double taxation—often by passing at least a portion of the estate into a CEBT (Credit Equivalent Bypass Trust). In this manner up to $600,000 can be sheltered from federal estate tax at both the first decedent's death and then again (since the surviving spouse has only an income interest) escape estate tax

Stephan R. Leimberg is CEO of Leimberg and LeClair, Inc., an estate and financial planning software company, and president of Leimberg Associates, Inc., a publishing and software company, in Bryn Mawr, Pennsylvania. He is a best-selling author and a nationally known speaker on estate and financial planning.

at the death of the surviving spouse. But holding property in joint tenancy thwarts that objective. Instead of going to a bypass trust to avoid a second tax, the property goes directly to the survivor and will be taxed at the survivor's death. So the credit of the first spouse to die is wasted.

Mistake 2: Improperly Arranged Life Insurance

A. The proceeds of life insurance are often payable to a beneficiary at the wrong time (before that person is emotionally or physically or legally capable of handling it) or in the wrong manner (outright instead of being paid over a period of years or paid into trust).

B. There is inadequate insurance on the life of the key person in a family (the "breadwinner") or the key person in a corporation (the "rainmaker").

C. Often no contingent (backup) beneficiary has been named. The "Rule of Two" should be applied here: In any dispositive document there should be—for every name in the document—at least two backups.

D. The proceeds of the policy are includible in the gross estate of the insured because the policy was purchased by the insured and then transferred within three years of the insured's death. The solution is to have the ultimate beneficiary acting without direction from the insured and using her (or its) own money, purchase and own the insurance from its inception. That party should also be the beneficiary.

E. When the policyowner of a policy on the life of another names a third party as beneficiary, at the death of the insured the proceeds are treated as a gift to the beneficiary from the policyowner. For example, if a wife purchases a policy on her husband's life but names her children as beneficiaries, at the husband's death she is making a gift in the amount of the proceeds to the children.

F. If a corporation names someone other than itself (or its creditor) as the beneficiary of insurance on the life of a key employee, when the proceeds are paid the IRS will argue that the proceeds are not income tax free and should be treated as either dividends if paid to or on behalf of a shareholder, or compensation if paid to an employee who is not a shareholder (assuming the premiums were never reported as income or there was no split-dollar agreement or no "P.S. 58" income reported). Worse yet, if the insured owned more than 50 percent of the corporation's stock, he or she is deemed to have incidents of ownership (that means federal estate tax inclusion of the proceeds) in the policy on his life. So, for example, the same $1 million proceeds could be taxed as a dividend for income tax purposes ($280,000 income tax) and *also* be taxed as an asset in the estate for estate tax purposes ($550,000 maximum tax).

G. Whenever life insurance is paid to the insured's estate, it is needlessly subjected to the claims of the insured's creditors and in many states unnecessarily subjected to state inheritance tax costs. Probate costs are increased without reason and the proceeds are then subjected to the potential for an attack on the will or an election against the will.

H. If a life insurance policy—or any interest in a life insurance policy—is transferred for any kind of valuable consideration in money or money's worth, the proceeds may lose their income-tax-free status. For example, if a wife buys the $1 million term insurance policy owned on her husband's life from his corporation or business partner, when she receives the proceeds, the entire $1 million will be subject to ordinary income tax ($280,000).

I. Where a husband is required by divorce decree or separation agreement to purchase or maintain insurance on his life, he will receive no income tax deduction for premium payments if he owns the policy—even if his ex-wife is named as irrevocable beneficiary. No alimony deduction is allowed on the cash values in a policy the husband is required to transfer to his ex-wife under a divorce decree. The safest way to assure a deduction is for the husband to increase his tax deductible alimony and for the ex-wife to purchase new insurance on his life, which she owns and of which she is the beneficiary. It is extremely important for each spouse recently divorced to immediately review his or her own life, health, and disability insurance situation.

Mistake 3: Lack of Liquidity

A. Most people don't have the slightest idea of how much it will cost to settle their estates or how quickly the taxes and other expenses must be paid. Worse yet, they don't realize that a forced (fire) sale of their most precious assets, highest income—producing property, or loss of control of their family business will result from an insufficiency of cash. (If you haven't checked, how do you know your executor will have enough cash to avoid a forced sale?)

B. Liquidity demands have increased significantly in the last few years and should be revisited by those who have not done a "what if. . ." hypothetical probate. Among the expenses that demand cash from the estate's executor are:

1. Federal estate taxes
2. State death Taxes
3. Federal income taxes (including taxes on pension distributions)
4. State income taxes (including taxes on pension distributions)
5. Probate and administration costs
6. Payment of maturing debts
7. Maintenance and welfare of family
8. Payment of specific cash requests
9. Funds to continue operation of family business, meet payroll and inventory costs, recruit replacement personnel, and pay for mistakes while new management is learning the business
10. Generation skipping transfer tax (55 percent)
11. Excise tax on excess pension accumulations (15 percent)

Most larger estates will be subjected to almost all of these taxes and costs.

Mistake 4: Choice of the Wrong Executor

A. Naming the wrong people to administer the estate can be disastrous. The person who administers the estate must—with dispatch—often without compensation, with great personal financial risk, and without conflict of interest:

1. Collect all assets
2. Pay all obligations
3. Distribute the remaining assets to beneficiaries

Although this three-step process seems simple, in reality these tasks are highly complex, time-consuming, and, in some cases, technically demanding. Is the named executor capable?

B. Selection of a beneficiary as an executor can result in a conflict of interest. That person may be forced to choose between his interest and that of the other beneficiaries. This problem can be solved by adding an independent third party such as a bank trust department to serve alone or together with a family member.

C. Selection of a business associate may result in a conflict of interest. If the executor's job is to decide whether or not to sell the business interest or the task is to obtain the highest possible sales price, the executor will be responsible for the course of action that will best serve the beneficiaries' interests. Yet that may be diametrically opposed to his own. He may be selling himself out of a job or demanding a higher price for the business than he is willing to pay.

D. Sometimes the selected executor has neither the time nor the inclination to devote to the sometimes long and drawn out process of estate administration. Does the executor even live in the state of the testator?

E. The appointment of executors who do not know or get along well with the family members they are to serve sometimes results in chaos.

Mistake 5: Will Errors

A. One of the greatest mistakes is dying without a valid will. This results in "intestacy," which is another way of saying that the state will force its own will upon the heirs if it chooses.

B. Too many wills have not been updated. A will should be reviewed at least:

1. At the birth, adoption, or death of a child
2. Upon the marriage, divorce, or separation of anyone named in the will
3. Upon every major tax law change
4. Upon a move of the testator to a new state
5. On a significant change in income or wealth of either the testator or a beneficiary
6. On any major change in the needs, circumstances, or objectives of the testator or the beneficiaries

Mistake 6: Leaving Everything to Your Spouse

A. Many people feel that there will be no federal estate tax because of the unlimited estate tax marital deduction and so they leave their entire estates to their spouses. But upon the death of the surviving spouse, everything that he or she received (assuming it has not been consumed or given away) is then piled on top of the assets that spouse owns. It is then that the "second death wallop" occurs with federal estate tax starting at a minimum of 37 percent on taxable amounts in excess of $600,000 and reaching up to a confiscatory maximum of 60 percent. The solution can be simple: The establishment of a CEBT (credit equivalent bypass trust). Up to $600,000 of assets can be left to a trust that provides income to the surviving spouse as well as other financial security but will not be taxed in his or her estate no matter when he or she dies or no matter how large trust funds grow. The balance of the estate can go in trust or outright to the surviving spouse. If that amount together with the surviving spouse's own assets doesn't exceed $600.000, this portion will also pass estate tax free when the surviving spouse dies.

B. Some individuals leave huge amounts outright to a surviving spouse that they themselves have never managed (few people have ever managed huge amounts at one time let alone managed spouses at any time). Often the survivor doesn't have the slightest training or experience in handling and investing a large stock portfolio, real estate holdings, or running a family business.

Mistake 7: Improper Disposition of Assets

A. An improper disposition of assets occurs whenever the wrong asset goes to the wrong person in the wrong manner or at the wrong time. Leaving an entire estate to a surviving spouse or leaving a large or complex estate outright to a spouse unprepared or unwilling to handle it is a good example. Leaving a sizable estate outright to a teenager is another.

B. "Equal but inequitable" distributions are common. If an estate is divided equally among four children who have drastically different income or capital needs, an equal distribution can be very unfair. Consider for example four children, the oldest of whom is a brilliant and financially successful medical doctor and the youngest of whom has serious learning disabilities and is still in junior high school. Think of a family with a physically handicapped child and one with three healthy children with no physical problems. Obviously. their needs and circumstances are not the same. Should each child receive an equal share? The proper solution may be a "sprinkle" provision in a trust that empowers the trustee to provide extra income or principal to a child who needs more in a given year.

C. Obvious examples of improper dispositions include the gift of a high-powered sports car to a child or senior citizen who no longer drives. "That can't happen in my estate," many people would be tempted to say, but upon the death of a primary beneficiary at the same time or soon after the testator, quite often there is no secondary beneficiary or the second beneficiary who is named shouldn't receive the asset in the same manner as the primary beneficiary. The solution is to consider a trust or custodial arrangements and to provide in the will or other dispositive instruments for young children and legally incompetent people. Consider also the importance of a well-considered "common disaster" or "simultaneous death" provision so that the asset avoids needless second probates and double inheritance taxes and goes to the right person in the right manner.

Mistake 8: Failure to Stabilize and Maximize Value

A. Many business owners have not stabilized the value of their businesses in the event of the disability or death of a key person. What economic "shock absorbers" have been put in place to cushion the blow caused if a key employee was lured away by competition at the wrong time? Who will pay for the fixed expenses of the practice or business if the key employee is not there to generate income? Key employee life and disability insurance, coupled with good business overhead coverage, will certainly help.

B. Buy-sell agreements are essential to a business that is to survive the death of one of its owners. Yet many businesses have no such agreement. Or the agreement isn't in writing. Or the price (or price-setting mechanism) doesn't reflect the current value of the business. Or the agreement isn't properly funded. So there is no guarantee that the heirs will receive the price they are entitled to—or no assurance that the surviving owners will have the cash they need to buyout the heirs (especially the dissident ones who want to tell them how to run their company).

C. Wills, trusts, life insurance contracts, HR-10 (Keogh) plans, IRAs, tax-deferred annuities, without "backup" beneficiaries mean that money that could otherwise pass outside of the probate estate may instead be subjected unnecessarily to such costs and risks. The value of all those instruments and wealth transfer tools can be enhanced at no cost by merely naming secondary beneficiaries.

Mistake 9: Lack of Adequate Records

A. It can drive your executor crazy—and cost thousands of dollars of expenses—if estate financial documents are hard to find. Take out a safe deposit box. Tell your executor where it is and make sure your executor has or can get the key and has access to it. Put all your important documents in that box. Each year, put an updated list of the names and phone numbers of advisors your family can count on in the box. Check with your lawyer on the rules that apply at death: some safe deposit boxes are "frozen" (the state requires that the bank seal the box from entry until the inheritance tax examiner can inventory the contents) and there can be lengthy delays in getting to the papers in the box.

B. It is possible for an executor to obtain new copies of old income tax returns from the IRS—but why put the executor to the trouble and expense? Be sure to keep tax returns and records at least six years.

C. Many survivors have never been told what the decedent's goals were, what assets they can rely on for income or capital needs, or how best to utilize the available resources. Most widows or surviving children never had

a meaningful discussion with the decedent about their financial security if. . . .

Mistake 10. Lack of a "Master Strategy" Game Plan

A. Do-it-yourself estate and financial planning is the closest thing to do-it-yourself brain surgery. Few people can do it successfully. Yet, even do-it-yourself planning—from taking courses or reading books or listening to radio shows on the subject—is preferable to no planning. Actually, an intelligent layman can learn and do quite a bit if the time is taken at least once a year to quantify in dollar terms financial needs and objectives ("here's what we must have and here's what we'd like to have"), current financial status ("here's where we are"), and a game plan for getting to the goal in the most efficient and effective way. Using the right team of CPA, lawyer, life insurance agent, trust officer, and other financial services professionals to conduct an annual "financial fire drill" to help formulate and execute that plan can make all the difference.

References

To learn more about these and other common (and costly) estate planning mistakes, and the solutions to them, contact a financial services professional.

The Bottom Line

The key principal in my book, *Keeping Your Money*, is that *you can't eliminate the big mistakes in your estate until you've identified them.* Every family (and single person)—every year—should stage a "financial fire drill," Become informed. Educate yourself now. Educate your survivors—before they *are* your survivors! Teach them how to handle money and make decisions. Show them, by example, how to read the bottom line on where their financial security stands.

A "financial fire drill" means that, with the assistance of a competent financial services professionals—you annually measure your needs. Establish an order of priorities and then develop and put into effect plans to make certain that you are on target to meet your financial security needs.

34
Basic Estate Planning in a Changing Tax Environment

DAVID A. BRIDEWELL

As a result of the Taxpayer Relief Act of 1997, a new day has dawned for lawyers engaged in estate planning for themselves and others. The act has corrected many deficiencies and eliminated many ambiguities in the old law, and now is the time to bring existing wills and other estate-planning documents into line with the new legislation.

Previously, federal estate taxes started at 37 percent on estates in excess of $600,000, escalating to 47 percent on amounts over $1,000,000 and to 55 percent for estates over $3,000,000. With no change in the rates, the estate tax burden has risen steadily over the years as a result of inflation. On the other side of the equation, the burden has also risen because the unchanged $600,000 exemption has been eroded by inflation. A recent IRS report showed that only 5.5 percent of estate taxes on returns filed in 1995 came from estates with assets of less than $1,000,000, a clear indication that a reduction in rates and/or an increase in the exemption were long overdue. Congress opted for the latter as part of its revision of the entire tax structure in 1997.

The New Tax Law

Although the Taxpayer Relief Act has reduced taxes, experts agree that the complexity of the code has been significantly increased. There are more than 300 new separate tax provisions with layers of different effective dates, phase-ins, and transaction rules. Buried in the fine print are

changes that will affect all lawyers, their businesses, and their estate plans. The only way to resolve their impact on the individual is to research each question as it arises.

First, let us see how some of the more important provisions of the act have changed our approach to the drafting of wills and other estate-planning documents, both from an income tax and estate tax point of view.

On the income tax side, one of the most significant provisions is the reduction in capital gains rates on the sale of certain assets (stocks, real estate, etc.) after May 6, 1997, the rate having been reduced from 28 percent to 20 percent (10 percent for those in the lowest bracket). Effective in 2001, the 20 percent rate will drop to 18 percent for assets acquired after 2000 and held for more than five years. This provision will be of concern to almost everyone, yet it is one of the most complicated in the new tax structure.

Next in importance is the $500,000 exclusion of profits on the sale or exchange of a principal home after May 7, 1997, made jointly by husband and wife ($250,000 for singles). To qualify, the taxpayer must have owned and used the property as a principal residence for at least two of the five years before the sale or exchange. This exclusion should greatly simplify record keeping for many senior taxpayers, as it will eliminate much of the burden of keeping track of improvement costs over the years.

Another new income tax benefit, although of more interest to younger taxpayers than seniors, is the child tax credit of $400 to 500 per qualifying child; new education credits for college costs; and more flexible, tax-free, nondeductible rules governing contributions to IRAs.

David A. Bridewell serves as counsel to the Chicago law firm of DeWolfe, Poynton & Stevens.

From a federal estate tax viewpoint the most important change is a gradual increase in the individual exemption available to all taxpayers for their lifetime gifts and transfers on death from the present $600,000 to $1,000,000 in 2006. The figure for 1998 is $625,000 and $650,000 for 1999; thereafter the increases vary, although mostly in $25,000 increments until the $1,000,000 figure is reached in nine years. Therefore, on a combined basis, husband and wife will eventually be able to transfer up to $2,000,000 of assets free of estate and gift taxes.

In addition, the act provides, with respect to deaths occurring after 1997, an exclusion for certain "qualified family-owned business interests" to the extent that such interests plus the available exemption do not exceed $1,300,000. The statute contains complicated rules for determining whether a family-owned business qualifies, a subject beyond the scope of this limited review. Suffice it to say that the total combined exclusion for husband and wife could run as high as $2,600,000 if there is in the picture such a qualified business interest.

These changes and many others too numerous to mention here will simplify income and estate tax planning and should eventually decrease significantly the number of people who must be concerned at all with gift and estate taxes. However, these matters require the attention of trained specialists and are not to be addressed by those unfamiliar with the intricacies of the new law.

Consequences of Inaction

Having thus established that the recent amendments to the federal income and estate tax laws necessitate a review of existing wills and other testamentary documents, we now turn to a consideration of the unhappy results that may stem from inaction. Before looking at the one-page home-grown will of the late Justice Warren E. Burger, the former Chief Justice of the United States Supreme Court, let us examine, in a hypothetical example, one of the commonest deficiencies in estate planning—the failure to take advantage of the full $600,000 exemption in both the husband's and the wife's estates in order to shelter from tax the full $1,200,000 in their combined estates.

Suppose the bulk of Mr. X's family assets, amounting to about $1.8 million, had been in the joint names of himself and wife who predeceased him. On her death the entire estate would have passed to Mr. X by operation of law without tax consequences, and on his subsequent death the entire $1.8 million would have been subject to tax, less, of course, his own $600,000 exemption. This would have produced an estate tax of about $564,000 at the 47 percent rate.

However, with rudimentary estate tax planning, Mr. and Mrs. X could have transferred to the wife during her lifetime $600,000 out of the jointly owned property and into her sole name. She could then have put this money into a testamentary or living trust for her husband's benefit during his life with remainder to the children. On her death this $600,000 would have been sheltered by her individual estate tax exemption, and still no taxes would have been occasioned by her death. But by failing to do so, in effect she waived her $600,000 exemption. Even more importantly, Mr. X's gross estate could have been reduced from $1.8 million to $1.2 and, after application of his own $600,000 exemption, the tax thereon at the 37 percent rate would have been only about $225,000. Thus, the children stood to lose $339,000 in estate taxes that any competent estate planner could have saved. Moreover, in some states—Virginia, for example—because of the application of the federal credit for state death taxes, the maximum amount that can be sheltered from the federal tax is almost $1.3 million in the combined estates of husband and wife.

This is substantially the scenario that was widely reported to have been the product of Justice Burger's amateurish attempts at testamentary draftsmanship. It was based principally on an article by George W. Dodge that appeared in the Arlington, Virginia, *County Bar Journal* pronouncing the will "woefully inadequate" and suggesting incompetent estate planning in the wasting of $600,000 of Mrs. Burger's exemption, reminiscent of the costly inaction described in the hypothetical example given above. But, as Professor Paul L. Caron of the University of Cincinnati College of Law has pointed out in *69 Tax Notes 1020*, November 20, 1995, this is not at all what happened.

Mrs. Burger *did in fact leave a will* bequeathing $650,000 to her children and effectively consuming her federal exemption. The estate tax on the remaining $1.8 million was thus deferred until the Chief Justice's death one year later. There were also two inter vivos trusts and lifetime gifts made by the Burgers as part of their estate plan. Professor Caron has appropriately entitled his article "Chief Justice Burger: A Better Tax Lawyer Than His Critics."

This is not to suggest, however, that the Burger will should be held up as a model of testamentary draftsmanship. Among the most obvious defects are the following:

1. The will was lacking in the affidavit required by Virginia law to make it "self-proving," thus necessitating the appearance of the attesting witnesses in court to prove the will by their oral testimony.

2. The will contained no waiver of surety bond, thus requiring payment of premiums to a bonding company to indemnify the executor against the claims of creditors and others.

3. The will did not grant adequate powers to the executor, including, among others, the power to sell real estate, thus necessitating a petition and court order to approve such sales. These and many other standard clauses would have been included in any will written by an experienced member of the probate bar.

4. The residue was left to the two children, but there was no condition of survivorship or gift over in the event of a prior death. Had this occurred, the estate might have passed otherwise than in a way the testator would have wanted.

In further defense of the chief justice, however, it should be noted that his will was prepared only nine days after the death of his wife, at a time when he may have still been in a state of shock. Perhaps, therefore, the will was intended as a stop-gap, but, if so, it conveys another lesson: sometimes a stop-gap will can become one's last will and testament.

Some Basic Principles of Estate Planning

We close this discussion with a brief overview of some of the guiding principles by which most estate planners abide:

As a general rule intestacies are to be avoided.

In almost every case a properly drawn will is essential to any estate plan, regardless of the size of the estate. Without a will the devolution of an estate is controlled by the state laws of descent and distribution. Although these laws vary from state to state, they could leave a spouse with insufficient assets to cover living costs, or they could place substantial assets in the hands of young adults who lack the financial acumen to handle them properly. A person who elects an intestacy abdicates his citizen's right to control the disposition of his own property when he dies.

Except for small estates, joint ownership of assets by husband and wife is no substitute for a will.

Joint ownership has sometimes been referred to as a "poor man's will," and it does have its place where tax considerations are not a significant factor and all probate costs can be avoided by the automatic devolution of property to a co-owner. However, in any estate of substance the joint ownership form is unwise, except for a few assets such as joint checking accounts, where they may provide convenience during lifetime. Rarely, however, should invested assets (stocks, bonds, etc.) be held in joint names, since as shown in the hypothetical case stated above, it can sometimes result in the waiver of an individual's $600,000 exemption and the payment of hundreds of thousands of dollars in needless estate tax. In the case of a common disaster affecting husband and wife, a circumstance normally covered in any well-drawn will, a joint ownership may cause the property to pass to the next generation in shares quite different from those that would have been selected by a testator in consultation with his estate planner.

Estate planning begins with a review and calculation of individual and combined marital assets.

In relatively small estates ($600,000 under today's tax laws) only minimal estate planning is necessary.

In moderate estates (between $600,000 and $1.2 million under today's tax laws) a division of assets between spouses should be considered along with the use of trusts structured to take advantage of the $600,000 exemption for each spouse, provide lifetime income for the survivor, and the reduce or eliminate estate taxes on their respective deaths.

In larger estates more sophisticated estate planning is required, and one or more of the following trusts can be utilized to effectuate the individual's wishes and minimize the tax bite:

- Self-declaration, revocable trusts
- By-pass trusts
- Marital trusts
- Q-tip trusts
- Charitable remainder trusts
- Grantor retained income trusts
- Qualified personal residence trusts
- Generation-skipping trusts
- Life insurance trusts

If a family business is involved, there are special provisions that can be incorporated into an estate plan to produce significant tax savings, such as:

- Buy-sell agreements

- Key employee insurance
- Survivor income benefit plans
- Private annuities
- Limited liability family partnerships
- Limited liability companies
- Subchapter S corporations

Conclusion

We have seen other instances where lawyers are diligent in taking care of their clients but sadly remiss in taking care of themselves. But in no area of the law is it more important for them to put their house in order than in the estate planning field. This is a subject that merits their close attention not only on behalf of their clients but also on behalf of themselves and their families.

35
Spotlighting the Taxpayer Relief Act of 1997

GRACE ALLISON AND DAVID HIRSCHEY

"Tax relief" is here in the form of the Taxpayer Relief Act of 1997 (TRA '97), which President Clinton signed on August 12, 1997. Despite the professed interest on Capitol Hill in tax simplification, TRA '97 contains more than 300 separate provisions and dozens of different effective dates, phase-ins, and transition rules. Buried in the fine print are changes that will affect many estate plans.

This chapter provides an overview of some of the important provisions of TRA '97, a few of which were modified by additional tax legislation enacted in mid-1998 as part of the IRS Restructuring and Reform Act (IRRA '98). Many of these changes affect estate planning, including changes to income taxes, estate and gift taxes, individual retirement accounts, and charitable giving. Real estate lawyers also will be interested in many of the changes. The intent is to provide enough detail to give a flavor of the complexity of the new law and to offer a framework for more in-depth and individualized analysis.

Individual Income Tax Changes

Capital Gains Tax Cut

Prior law taxed gains from the sale of capital assets at a maximum 28 percent rate. TRA '97 contains new capital gains rates and holding period rules for sales occurring after July 28, 1997. Under TRA '97, the maximum rate on gains from the sale of capital assets held more than eighteen

months is 20 percent. The 28 percent maximum rate continues to apply to gains from the sale of assets held for more than one year but not more than eighteen months. TRA '97 contains a special transitional rule imposing a maximum 20 percent rate on gains from capital assets held for more than one year and sold after May 6, 1997 and before July 29, 1997. In addition, TRA '97 makes a 10 percent capital gains tax rate available for taxpayers in the 15 percent income tax bracket for gains on assets held more than eighteen months. The 15 percent income tax rate currently applies to taxable income of $41,200 and below for couples filing jointly and to taxable income of $1,650 and below for an estate or trust. Two important exceptions are (1) gains from the sale of collectibles, such as art and coins, which remain subject to the 28 percent maximum rate; and (2) depreciation recapture, which becomes subject to tax at a 25 percent maximum rate.

TRA '97 further decreases the maximum tax rate on capital gains to 18 percent for assets purchased after 2000 and held more than five years. A lower 8 percent rate is available to individuals, trusts, and estates in the lowest income tax bracket for such sales. Again, these lower rates do not apply to gains from the sales of collectibles or depreciation recapture. A special rule allows investors to treat assets as sold on January 1, 2001, recognize gain, and then qualify for the 18 percent rate on additional gain if held until 2006. *Note:* IRRA '98 reduces the holding period necessary to qualify for the maximum 20 percent capital gains rate from "more than eighteen months" to "more than twelve months," generally effective for tax years ending after December 31, 1997.

Grace Allison is tax counsel and David Hirschey is a senior lawyer with the Northern Trust Company, headquartered in Chicago, Illinois.

The capital gains tax changes have important implications for investors. Clients with concentrations of highly appreciated securities in their portfolios should reconsider reducing those concentrations and diversifying investments. If a client already is in the process of diversifying his or her portfolio, the client should consider accelerating the diversification program. Clients may also want to reevaluate relative after-tax advantages of tax-deferred or tax-exempt investments versus taxable investments. The reduced capital gains tax rates should favor financial assets, such as stocks, over "hard" assets, such as collectibles. Finally, the cut in the capital gains tax rates means that growth-oriented investments generally will enjoy higher after-tax returns than income-oriented investments.

Sales of Personal Residences

Before TRA '97, homeowners could defer gain on the sale of a principal residence by "rolling over" the sales proceeds into a new residence of equal or greater value. Code § 1034. Those aged 55 or older could exclude up to $125,000 of gains on the sale of a principal residence. Code § 121. TRA '97 significantly changes these rules. It provides that a married couple filing jointly is entitled to exclude $500,000 of gain on the sale of a principal residence from income, while a single taxpayer receives a $250,000 exclusion. The new rules do not require the taxpayer to purchase a replacement residence, and can be used once every two years. These new rules (generally effective for sales on or after May 7, 1997) replace current law rollover and "one time only" $125,000 exclusion provisions.

These changes will allow many families and single persons to relocate without paying any capital gains tax on the sale of a home. Examples of those likely to benefit include mature homeowners with a large, highly appreciated home but no more than $500,000 of built-in gain who are moving to smaller quarters; wage earners relocating to less expensive regions or neighborhoods; and divorced couples, widows, and widowers moving to smaller homes, retirement communities, or extended-care facilities. The new rules also eliminate the need to reconstruct records of capital improvements when the sales price of a residence is $500,000 or less. The "price" of the changes, however, is that taxpayers can no longer

roll over and thus defer gains on the sales of residences in excess of $500,000 or $250,000, as the case may be, by purchasing replacement homes.

Estate and Gift Tax Law Changes

The act tinkers with more than two dozen transfer-tax provisions. The new rules range from the purely administrative to changes that immediately affect estate plans. This section describes the major changes.

Increased Unified Credit

Under current law, an individual may transfer $600,000 during life or at death or a combination of both without paying gift or estate tax. Code § 2010. After the person has exceeded the $600,000 exemption equivalent, gifts and bequests are generally subject to gift or estate tax, with a maximum rate of 55 percent. TRA '97 does not change the gift and estate tax rates but gradually increases the unified credit exemption equivalent as follows:

Decedents Dying and Gifts Made in	Unified Credit Exemption Equivalent
1998	$ 625,000
1999	650,000
2000 and 2001	675,000
2002 and 2003	700,000
2004	850,000
2005	950,000
2006 and thereafter	$1,000,000

The increase in the unified credit has several implications for clients' estate plans. For clients who already have made lifetime transfers totaling $600,000, TRA '97 provides an opportunity to make additional lifetime tax-free gifts. Lawyers who have clients with smaller estates should consider whether formula provisions in their clients' wills and living trusts would result in funding the credit shelter trust with $1 million, leaving a correspondingly smaller amount in the marital trust, which could adversely affect the surviving spouse.

Exclusion for "Qualified Family-Owned Businesses"

TRA '97 introduces Code § 2033A, which provides an exclusion from a decedent's gross estate for the decedent's interest in a "qualified family-owned business" (which includes some farms). The maximum exclusion is $1.3 million, although the amount of exclusion must be reduced by the unified credit exemption equivalent in effect at the date of death. For example, assume a decedent dies owning a "qualified family-owned business" worth $2 million in 1998, when the applicable unified credit exemption equivalent is $625,000. Code § 2033A allows the estate to avoid tax on $1.3 million. $675,000 will be excluded under the qualified family-owned business provisions, and $625,000 will be sheltered from tax under the unified credit. The Code § 2033A exclusion, which is elective, is generally effective for estates of decedents dying after 1997.

Unfortunately, it is not easy for an estate to qualify for the exclusion. Among the eligibility requirements are:

- The "adjusted value" of "qualified family-owned business" includable in the decedent's estate (plus certain lifetime gifts of interests in the business) must exceed 50 percent of the decedent's "adjusted gross estate."
- The business must pass complex "material participation" tests that require the involvement of the decedent or members of decedent's family in the family business during the eight-year period before the decedent's death.
- A "qualified heir," including certain unrelated long-time employees, must acquire the business.
- The qualified heirs must agree to pay an additional estate tax if, within the ten-year period after the decedent's death, certain disqualifying events occur—for example, the heirs do not "materially participate" in the business, the business is sold to outsiders, the business is no longer located in the United States, or the heirs cease to be U.S. citizens.

Code § 2033A provides an important tax saving opportunity for those who intend to pass management of a family business or farm on to family members or long-time employees. Lawyers and their clients, however, must carefully plan to meet the complex statutory requirements. Lawyers should also consider whether a client's current will or trust provisions governing disposition of a family-owned business will satisfy these requirements. Of course, as the unified credit increases over the next decade, the value of the Code § 2033A exclusion will decrease. For instance, in 2006, the maximum exclusion under Code § 2033A will be only $300,000 ($1.3 million less $1 million generally applicable unified credit

exemption equivalent). Note: IRRA '98 changes the qualified family owned business exclusion into a deduction—and moves the provision from Code § 2033A to Code § 2057.

Reduced Interest Rates on Estate Tax Installment Payments Attributable to Closely Held Businesses

Before TRA '97, an estate with a closely held business could under certain circumstances pay estate tax attributable to the business over fourteen years, with interest only for the first four years and a special 4 percent interest rate on the first $1 million of value. Code § 6166. TRA '97 retains Code § 6166 but reduces applicable interest rates for estates of decedents dying on or after January 1, 1998. The new provisions reduce both the interest rate on estate tax attributable to the first $1 million of taxable value from 4 percent to 2 percent and also the interest rate on the balance of estate tax attributable to the business. The trade-off for the reduced interest rates is that interest on installment payments of estate tax no longer qualifies as an estate or income tax deduction.

Inflation Adjustments for Certain Gift and Estate Tax Exclusions and Exemptions

Unlike the income tax, the code has not generally adjusted exemptions and exclusions for estate, gift, and generation-skipping taxes for inflation. In a major change, TRA '97 introduces inflation adjustments for some (but not all) transfer-tax exclusions and exemptions. The following major exclusions and exemptions will now be adjusted for inflation:

- $10,000 gift tax annual exclusion. Adjustments will be based on changes in the Consumer Price Index, with 1997 as the base year, effective for gifts made on or after January 1, 1999. The annual exclusion will be adjusted in $1,000 increments only, rounded to the next lowest multiple of $1,000.
- $1 million generation-skipping transfer tax (GSTT) exemption. Again, adjustments will be based on changes in the Consumer Price Index, with 1997 as the base year, effective for transfers made on or after January 1, 1999. The GSTT exemption will be adjusted in $10,000 increments only, rounded to next lowest multiple of $10,000.

In a period of single-digit inflation, adjustments may occur only once every two or three years. In light of these changes, lawyers may want to advise their clients to revise their wills and living trust agreements to the extent that they incorporate the fixed dollar exemption amounts of prior law, such as a gift of $1 million intended to use the client's GSTT exemption.

Repeal of 15 Percent Excise Tax on Excess Retirement Distributions and Accumulations

Prior law provided that if an individual received more than $112,500 (adjusted annually for inflation) in one year from IRAs and qualified plans, this "excess distribution" was subject to a 15 percent excise tax. Code § 4980A. At death, Code § 4980A(d) imposed a 15 percent additional estate tax on the decedent's actuarially determined excess accumulation in IRAs and qualified plans. In 1996, Congress suspended the application of the tax to lifetime distributions during 1997–1999, although the 15 percent additional estate tax continued to apply.

TRA '97 completely repeals the 15 percent additional tax for lifetime distributions from qualified plans and IRAs after 1996 and for decedents dying after 1996. The repeal should encourage contributions to IRAs and qualified plans and maximum deferral of amounts invested in IRAs and qualified plans. In some situations, however, early withdrawals from IRAs remain beneficial, including when the client uses withdrawn funds to make lifetime gifts to reduce taxes on his or her estate at death.

IRA Changes

The Roth IRA

Before TRA '97, an employee and his or her spouse each could contribute $2,000 to an IRA and deduct those amounts from gross income unless the employee participated in a qualified employee benefit plan and the employee's adjusted gross income exceeded $50,000 for married couples filing jointly or $35,000 for single filers. Earnings on nondeductible contributions were subject to income tax when the employee withdrew them from the IRA.

Under TRA '97, an employee and his or her spouse each may contribute $2,000 to a new Roth IRA. Phase-out begins for couples filing jointly with adjusted gross income in excess of $150,000 and for single filers with adjusted gross income in excess of $95,000. Contributions are nonde-

ductible, and the $2,000 amount must be reduced by any IRA contributions made by the employee. The employee's withdrawals, however, are not subject to income tax or the 10 percent penalty tax if (1) five years have passed since the employee made his or her first contribution, and (2) the employee makes his or her withdrawal:

- after age 59½;
- to buy a first home for the employee or a family member (for example, a child or a grandchild); or
- after the employee's death or disability.

If the withdrawal does not satisfy these requirements, the earnings portion of the withdrawal will be subject to income tax and, if the employee is under age 59½, the 10 percent penalty tax on early withdrawals will also apply. Amounts contributed are treated as withdrawn first on a tax-free basis as a return of basis.

A client with adjusted gross income of less than $100,000 may convert a regular IRA to a Roth IRA. The conversion will be taxed in the same manner as a withdrawal from a regular IRA, with the important exception that the 10 percent penalty tax on early withdrawals will not apply. If a taxpayer completes a conversion before 1999, the taxable income resulting from the withdrawal can be spread over four years. Finally, in a major change, the minimum distribution rules of Code § 401(a)(9) do not apply to a Roth IRA while an individual is alive, although they do apply after death. The nonapplication of the minimum distribution rules provides a significant opportunity to defer income taxes while investing in a tax-free environment.

The Roth IRA is likely to have significant estate and financial implications for clients. A client can use the Roth IRA as a tax-free investment account in which interest, dividends, and capital gains will never be subject to income tax. For instance, assume a client contributes $2,000 to a Roth IRA, the Roth IRA has earnings, and the client withdraws earnings tax-free after age 59½ and after waiting the five year period. Even if the client is under age 59½ and his or her withdrawal from the Roth IRA is not qualified, the client can at least withdraw his or her contributions to the Roth IRA first on a tax-free basis. Given the income tax advantages, many clients and their spouses might establish Roth IRA accounts. Because conversion triggers immediate income tax, however, it is unclear whether many will convert existing IRAs into Roth IRA accounts.

Education IRA

Before TRA '97, a child with no earnings from employment could not contribute to an IRA, and a parent could not establish an IRA for a child. TRA '97 changes these rules by creating a new "Education IRA" that allows a person to establish and fund an IRA for any beneficiary under age 18. An individual can contribute only $500 cash per year to the Education IRA and cannot make a contribution to an Education IRA if his or her "modified adjusted gross income" exceeds $160,000 for married couples filing jointly or $110,000 for single filers. Education IRAs are tax exempt, allowing earnings to accumulate tax-free.

In addition, distributions from Education IRAs are tax exempt if the beneficiary uses the distributed funds to pay post-secondary education expenses, including tuition and room and board. If distributions exceed education expenses during any year, the earnings portion of the distribution is subject to income tax and a 10 percent penalty tax. Contributions to Education IRAs are not tax deductible but qualify for the gift tax annual exclusion. An Education IRA must have a bank as custodian or trustee. The beneficiary of an Education IRA may be changed to another family member with no income tax consequences.

The obvious benefit of the Education IRA is that it allows parents and others to make tax-free investments to help finance a child's college education. Anyone who qualifies under income limits—including a parent, grandparent, aunt, or uncle—can establish an Education IRA; multiple Education IRAs are possible for the same beneficiary. An individual's contributions to a Education IRA are separate from (and in addition to) contributions to the individual's own IRA. Multiple contributions of $500 apiece, however, are not allowed, and the aggregate contributions to a beneficiary's Education IRA(s) may not exceed $500 per year.

Deductible Contributions to IRAs

Under prior law, an employee and his or her spouse each could contribute $2,000 to an IRA and deduct the contributions for income tax purposes. The employee and his or her spouse, however, could not deduct the contributions if (1) the employee or the spouse participated in a qualified employee benefit plan, and (2) adjusted gross income exceeded $50,000 for married couples filing jointly or $35,000 for single filers.

TRA '97 now allows a spouse who does not participate in a qualified plan to make a deductible $2,000 contribution to an IRA, even if the other spouse participates in a qualified plan, so long as the couple's adjusted gross income does not exceed $160,000. TRA '97 also increases the general income limitation on deductible contributions to an IRA in 1998 to $60,000 for married couples filing jointly or $40,000 for single filers. TRA '97 provides for additional increases to the income limitations of $1,000 per year from 1999 to 2002, with larger increases beginning in 2003. By 2007, the income ceilings will be increased to $100,000 for couples filing jointly and $60,000 for singles. These changes provide obvious retirement savings opportunities for single-income families.

No 10 Percent Penalty on Early Withdrawals from Individual Retirement Accounts for Higher Education Expenses or First-Time Homebuyer Expenses

Under current law, early withdrawals from an IRA or qualified employee benefit plan before age 59½ are generally subject to a 10 percent penalty tax as well as regular income tax. The code provides limited exceptions to the 10 percent penalty tax, for example, for payments after death or disability, substantially equal periodic payments, or deductible medical expenses. TRA '97 adds another exception that allows early withdrawals from IRAs without the imposition of the 10 percent penalty tax if the IRA owner uses the withdrawn funds for higher education expenses or first-time homebuyer expenses. The waiver of the 10 percent penalty tax applies to any amount of higher education expenses but has a lifetime limitation of $10,000 for homebuyer expenses.

Although this change will help a parent finance a child's post-high school education and first-time homebuying expenses, a tax-free loan from a qualified plan may be preferable to a taxable withdrawal from an IRA. Alternatively, a person could take a distribution from a qualified plan, roll the distribution over to an IRA, and then make a withdrawal from the IRA for educational or homebuying purposes without a 10 percent penalty.

Charitable Contributions

Gifts of Appreciated Publicly Traded Stock to Private Foundations

After May 31, 1997, individuals who contributed appreciated publicly traded stock to private foundations could no longer claim an income tax charitable deduction based on the fair-market value of the stock. Rather, the income tax charitable deduction was based on the adjusted basis of the stock, which for many clients was far below current fair-market value. TRA '97 retroactively changed this rule to allow taxpayers to claim a fair-market value charitable income tax deduction for contributions of certain appreciated, publicly traded stock to private foundations from May 31, 1997 through June 30, 1998. This is the third time Congress has opened this "window of opportunity" for those holding low-basis publicly traded stock to offset ordinary income with a large charitable income tax deduction by contributing the stock to a new or existing private foundation.

New Rules for Charitable Remainder Trusts

TRA '97 now requires that the present value of a charity's remainder interest in any transfer to a charitable remainder trust equal at least 10 percent of the initial fair-market value of the amount transferred. This rule applies to additions to charitable remainder unitrusts as well as to initial fundings of both charitable remainder unitrusts and charitable remainder annuity trusts.

Congress also imposed maximum payout rules for charitable remainder trusts in TRA '97. Under TRA '97, payments made in any year by a charitable remainder annuity trust to individual beneficiaries may not exceed 50 percent of the initial fair-market value of the trust's assets. Similarly, payments made in any year by a charitable remainder unitrust to individual beneficiaries may not exceed 50 percent of the fair-market value of the trust assets on the most recent valuation date.

Congress directed these new rules at planners who advised clients to use charitable remainder trusts primarily as vehicles to defer payment of capital gains tax on highly appreciated assets, rather than as deferred charitable giving vehicles. The 10 percent rule will also limit a client's ability to establish or make additional tax deductible contributions to charitable remainder trusts with successive interests in parents and children or grandchildren. Clients may need to amend wills or trusts that will create charitable remainder trusts at death to comply with these rules.

Conclusion

This chapter highlights the provisions of TRA '97 about which clients are most likely to contact their lawyers. TRA '97 also contains other changes that will not generate phone calls from clients but will still affect estate plans and probate (for example, new rules for waiving the estate tax recovery rights in Code §§ 2207A and 2207B; application of the 65-day rule to probate estates as well as to trusts). Although TRA '97 does not simplify the tax law, it does provide new opportunities for clients and the need for clients to consult with their lawyers.

36
TRA '97 Has Broad Impact on Estate and Gift Tax Provisions

EDWARD KESSEL AND KATHLEEN A. STEPHENSON

The Taxpayer Relief Act of 1997[1] (TRA '97 or the act) was passed by Congress and signed by the president with the usual fanfare that accompanies such events. As is typical with tax legislation, TRA '97 is both a boon and a bane. Any hope of tax simplification has been reduced to a mere echo. While TRA '97 could more accurately be called the "Tax Practitioner Relief Act" as estate plans are reviewed and in some instances revised, its hasty drafting and glaring omissions may cause practitioners to seek relief from the act rather than under it.

Analysis of the New Rules

Unified Credit
(Act Section 501; Code Section 2010)

The most publicized change in the new law is the replacement of the "unified credit" with two new phrases: the "applicable credit amount" and the "applicable exclusion amount." The "applicable credit amount" is the tax that would result if the tax were computed on the "applicable exclusion amount." While the words may have changed, the melody remains the same. The effect of the change is simply to increase the exemption equivalent from $600,000 in 1997 to $1 million in the year 2006. The phase-in of the increased applicable exclusion amount starts very slowly, rising to only $700,000 in the first five years, and saving the largest increases for the years 2004, 2005, and 2006.

Year of Death	Exemption Equivalent
1997	$ 600,000
1998	625,000
1999	650,000
2000	675,000
2001	675,000
2002	700,000
2003	700,000
2004	850,000
2005	950,000
2006	$1,000,000

Although both the House bill and the Senate bill provided for indexing after the $1 million figure was reached, indexing did not make it into the final bill.[2]

The new law does not contain a transitional rule such as that enacted when the unlimited marital deduction was introduced in 1981. In view of this, it is expected that most existing wills and revocable trusts containing formula "minimum" marital deduction clauses or "maximum" bypass trust provisions will be considered to increase the amount passing under the bypass trust automatically unless state courts rule otherwise. A safer and more prudent approach, however, may be to review existing wills and revocable trusts and to amend those that do not anticipate subsequent changes to the unified credit. Where the dispositive provisions of the bypass trust and marital deduction trust are not similar, the increase to the bypass trust as a result of the change in the applicable exclusion amount may have an unintended impact on the interest passing to or for the benefit of the surviving

Edward Kessel is of counsel to the Philadelphia law firm of Pepper Hamilton, LLP. Kathleen A. Stephenson is a lawyer with Pepper Hamilton, LLP, in Philadelphia.

1. P.L. No. 105-34 (8/5/97).
2. TRA '97 § 501; Code § 2010.

spouse. Reviewing clients' overall gift giving strategy may be appropriate as well.

Family-Owned Business Exclusion
(Act Section 502; Code Section 2033A)

One open question regarding the family-owned business exclusion of Section 2033A has been the subject of much debate.[3] Section 2033A frames this new benefit as an "exclusion" rather than a "deduction" from the value of the gross estate. This distinction is important for capital gains purposes.

The basis of property acquired from a decedent is stepped up to its fair market value (FMV) at the decedent's date of death (or the alternate valuation date), but only if the property is included in the gross estate for estate tax purposes.[4] The family-owned business exclusion applies to family business interests acquired by a qualified heir from the decedent.[5] Characterizing the benefit as an "exclusion" from the gross estate casts a shadow over whether the family-owned business interest is included under Section 1014(b)(9). If the interest is, in fact, excluded from the estate for estate tax purposes, the qualified heir would not be entitled to a stepped-up basis.

A counter argument is that the business interest is included in the gross estate and only its "value" is excluded. A liberal reading of Section 2033A would seem to support this conclusion. Comments by representatives of the Treasury Department's Office of Legislative Counsel indicate that allowance of a stepped-up basis was, in fact, intended by the drafters. It is not clear, though, whether a family-owned business interest passing to a qualified heir will receive a full step-up or will be afforded the same treatment as property that has been given a special-use valuation under Section 2032A and, as a consequence, takes the Section 2032A valuation as its basis for capital gains purposes. This issue should be clarified by a Technical Corrections Act.

Qualified Conservation Easement
(Act Section 508; Code Section 2031(c))

For federal estate tax purposes, the FMV of real estate subject to a conservation easement is reduced by the value of the easement. Section 2031(c) now adds the option of permitting the personal representative to elect to exclude from the gross estate up to 40 percent of the value of land subject to a qualified conservation easement after reduction for the value of the easement and after subtracting the value of any retained development rights. If the value of the easement is less than 30 percent of the value of the land without the easement (reduced by the value of any retained development rights), then the 40 percent figure noted above is reduced by 2 percent for each percentage point by which the value of the easement is less than 30 percent of the value of the land.

The amount of the exclusion from the gross estate cannot exceed the "exclusion limitation," which is phased in as follows:

Year of Death	Exclusion Limitation
1997	$ 600,000
1998	625,000
1999	650,000
2000	675,000
2001	675,000
2002	700,000
2003	700,000
2004	850,000
2005	950,000
2006	$1,000,000

The conservation easement may be placed on the land by (1) the decedent, (2) a member of his family, (3) the personal representative of his estate, or (4) the trustee of a trust that holds the real property. "Member of the decedent's family" is defined in Section 2032A(e)(2), and includes the individual's ancestors, spouse, lineal descendants, and the spouses of lineal descendants.

For purposes of Section 2031(c), the conservation easement must qualify under Section 170(h)(1). In addition, the property subject to the easement must have been owned by the decedent or a member of his family at all times during the three-year period before his death. The property must be within twenty-five miles of a metropolitan area, national park, or wilderness area, or within ten miles of an urban national forest. The secretary of the treasury may refuse to recognize the proximity of land near a national park or wilderness area that is part of the National Wilderness Preservation System if such land is not under significant development pressure.

---

3. For a comprehensive analysis of the family-owned business exclusion, see Katzenstein and McArthur, "Planning for the Family-Owned Business Exclusion Under TRA '97," 24 EP 465 (Dec. 1997).
    4. § 1014(b)(9).
    5. § 2033A(b)(2).

Debt financed property does not qualify for the exclusion. Nor does the exclusion apply to historic structure easements. Finally, there must be a prohibition on more than de minimis commercial recreational activity.

Special-use valuation under Section 2032A is available in addition to the exclusion under Section 2031(c). For capital gains tax purposes, carryover basis will apply to the land excluded from the estate on account of a conservation easement. The exclusion should not reduce generation-skipping transfer (GST) tax. This provision is effective for estates of decedents dying after 1997.

Revaluing Gifts for Estate Tax Purposes
(Act Section 506; Code Section 2001)

Prior to the passage of TRA '76, the law regarding the gift tax statute of limitations was well settled. The statute of limitations for most purposes was three years from the due date of the gift tax return, or three years from the date the gift tax return was filed, whichever was later. If the statute of limitations had run, the value of a gift made in a prior year was the value reported on the return, provided federal gift tax was paid. If no gift tax was paid, the value of the gift could be redetermined.[6] If the taxpayer wanted a binding determination of the tax value of his gift, the gift had to be large enough to cause a gift tax.

With the unification of the estate and gift taxes, and the advent of the unified credit in 1976, a much larger gift was necessary to generate a gift tax. Furthermore, the IRS quickly took the position that Section 2504(c) applied to bar the revaluation of gifts reported on gift tax returns for closed years for gift tax purposes only, and not for purposes of calculating "adjusted taxable gifts." The IRS asserted that the value of adjusted taxable gifts could always be redetermined for purposes of computing the estate tax.

This position was tested in *Boatmen's First Nat'l Bank of Kansas City*.[7] In that case, the IRS attempted to revalue a gift, after the gift tax statute of limitations had run out, for purposes of determining adjusted taxable gifts. The district court ruled in favor of the taxpayer. The IRS did not appeal the decision because it recognized

that it had used the wrong methodology in calculating the gift tax and had not given the taxpayer credit for the gift tax that would have been paid had the increase in value been applied to the gift tax return. Simply put, the IRS attempted to tax the increase in value rather than just use the increase to raise the estate tax bracket.

Two years later, the IRS prevailed in *Estate of Smith*.[8] There, the IRS argued that the value of adjusted taxable gifts could be redetermined in computing the estate tax (even though the gift tax statute of limitations had run out), but that the estate would be entitled to a credit for the gift tax that would have been paid had the corrected value been used on the gift tax return. Since then, the IRS has had a string of victories on this issue.[9]

Although the individual's estate will get credit for the gift tax payable (even though not actually paid) on the increased value of the gift resulting in a tax based solely on the change in brackets, often that change in brackets is from the zero bracket to a very high estate tax bracket. (An example is shown in Figure 36–1.) Consequently, if an individual made gifts of real estate, closely held stock, or other hard-to-value assets, the effect those gifts would have on the individual's estate could never be certain.

This dilemma is resolved in TRA '97. Now, if a gift is reported on a gift tax return or is disclosed on the gift tax return in a manner adequate to apprise the secretary of the treasury of the nature of the gift, the gift may not be revalued for estate tax purposes once the gift tax statute of limitations has run out.

The title of TRA '97 Section 506 specifically applies only to the estate tax provisions of chapter 11 of the code, and not to the gift tax provisions of chapter 12. Nevertheless, in creating new Code Section 7477, TRA '97 does provide for a conforming amendment to Section 2504(c), eliminating the requirement that a gift tax be paid or assessed in order to bar revaluation. This avoids the anomaly of having different figures for prior year's gifts and for adjusted taxable gifts on gift tax returns and an estate tax return filed for the same person.

6. § 2504(c)(pre-1976); Rev. Rul. 84-11, 1984-1 CB 201.
7. 705 F. Supp. 1407, 83 AFTR2d 89-1510, 89-1 USTC ¶13.795 (DC Mo., 1988).

8. 94 TC 872 (1990).
9. Estate of Prince, TCM 1991-208, *aff'd* sub nom. Levin, 986 F.2d 91, 71 AFTR2d 93-2167, 93-1 USTC ¶60.128 (CA-4, 1993); Evanson, 30 F.3d 960, AFTR2d 94-7459, 94-2 USTC ¶60.174 (CA-8, 1994); Stalcup, 792 F. Supp. 714, 68 AFTR2d 91-6057, 91-2 USTD ¶60.086 (DC Okla. 1991).

Figure 36–1

Revaluing Gifts

Example 1A			
Adjusted Taxable Gifts (1990 return)			$ 300,000
Tentative Taxable Estate 1997			700,000
Taxable			$1,000,000
Estate Tax		$345,800	
Less: §2010 Credit	$192,800		
§2011 Credit	18,000		
Tax on ATG	0	210,800	
Net Estate Tax			$ 135,000
Example 1B			
Adjusted Taxable Gifts (1990 return)			$300,000
Audit Adjustment to ATG			250,000
Tentative Taxable Estate 1997			700,000
Taxable			$1,250,000
Estate Tax		$448,300	
Less: §2010 Credit	$192,800		
§2011 Credit	18,000		
Tax on ATG	0	210,800	
Net Estate Tax			$237,500
Estate Tax Before Audit Adjustment			135,000
Tax Caused by Adjustment			$102,500

Unfortunately, the effective date section reference to payment or assessment appears twice in Section 2504(c), and only one such reference is removed by TRA '97. This is addressed in Section 6(e) of the proposed Tax Technical Corrections Bill of 1997 (Technical Corrections Bill).[10] The technical corrections proposal would clarify that in determining the amount of taxable gifts made in preceding calendar periods, the value of prior gifts is the value of such gifts as finally determined, even if no gift tax was assessed or paid on that gift.

TRA '97 modifies the statute of limitations as it relates to substantial omissions. Previously, Section 6501(e)(2) provided for a six-year statute of limitations if there was a substantial omission of gifts. "Substantial omission" is defined as omitting more than 25 percent of the total amount of gifts stated on the return. Under TRA '97, the six-year statute of limitations will not apply if the substantially omitted items are adequately disclosed. On the other hand, the six-year statute of limitations is changed to an unlimited limitations period if the items are not adequately disclosed.

10. H.R. 2645.

The unlimited statute of limitations for gifts not shown on a gift tax return also applies, under Section 6501(c)(9), to valuations determined under Section 2701 or 2702. This expansion of the unlimited limitations period may prove to be extremely troublesome for estate planners who are not fully informed by their clients.

A related feature of TRA '97 is the authority given to the tax court[11] to issue declaratory judgments in controversies involving the valuation of gifts. This change is significant because the tax court previously had no jurisdiction over these matters unless there was an "immediate tax implication." This was a problem because in many cases there was no "immediate tax implication" since the gift was sheltered from tax by the unified credit. An interesting wrinkle under the new law is that the taxpayer—and not the IRS—has the option of whether or not to request a hearing before the tax court.

While TRA '97 brings long overdue relief in the areas of adjusted taxable gifts and the statute of limitations, unfortunately it applies only to gifts made after its effective date. The provision for an

11. § 7477.

unlimited statute of limitations for items not adequately disclosed applies to gifts made in calendar years ending after the date of enactment.

Waiver of Right of Recovery from QTIP
(Act Section 1302; Code Section 2207A)

A decedent's taxable estate for estate tax purposes may include nonprobate property. The question of who is ultimately responsible for the payment of the death taxes on such nonprobate property is generally a matter of state law. However, with respect to QTIP, which is includable in the surviving spouse's estate under Section 2044, and with respect to property in which the decedent retained an interest for life under Section 2036, Sections 2207A and 2207B respectively provide that the estate has a right of reimbursement or contribution, from the person receiving the property, for the estate tax paid with regard to such property. As to QTIP, the estate is entitled to recover the tax paid at the marginal tax rate.[12] As to Section 2036 property, the estate is entitled to recover a proportionate amount of the tax.[13] In both instances, the decedent may direct otherwise and waive the estate's right of recovery, but with different degrees of specificity.

Under pre-TRA '97 law, the right of recovery did not apply in the case of QTIP "if the decedent otherwise directs by will."[14] In the case of Section 2036 property, though, the direction to waive the right of recovery (by either will or revocable trust) had to specifically refer to Section 2207B.[15] This inconsistency could lead to unintended results due to use of imprecise language in wills and trusts.

TRA '97 amends Sections 2207A and 2207B to correct this disparity by establishing a uniform test for both QTIP and Section 2036 property. In both situations, the right of recovery or reimbursement will apply unless the decedent, by will or revocable trust, "specifically indicates an interest" to waive the right of recovery. As indicated in the committee reports, the rationale behind the statute is that a general provision specifying that all taxes be paid by the estate is not sufficient to waive the right to recover. But the statutory language "specifically indicates an intent" can, in itself, be open to interpretation. For this reason,

tax clauses should be drafted to spell out clearly the taxpayer's intent by making specific reference to Sections 2207A and 2207B.

Additional New Provisions

Special-Use Valuation: Defective Elections
(Act Section 1313; Code Section 2032A(d))

For estate tax purposes, Section 2032A permits a reduced valuation of real estate used in farming or in a closely held business. To qualify for this special-use valuation, an election must be made on a timely filed estate tax return and must include an agreement executed by all parties who have an interest in the property, consenting to a recapture of the estate tax savings in the event of the cessation of the special use.[16]

The IRS has traditionally been extremely technical about requiring compliance with the regulations regarding the time and manner of making the election and the form and execution of the recapture agreement. Prior to TRA '97, Section 2032A(d)(3) allowed the personal representative to "perfect" (correct) a special-use valuation decision within ninety days after notice of a defective election by the secretary of the treasury, provided that the personal representative had "substantially complied" with the regulations.

The question of what constituted "substantial compliance" with the regulations has been the subject of much litigation. For example, in *Estate of Doherty*,[17] the personal representatives failed to file an appraisal but were still found to be in substantial compliance. In two other cases, all or some of the signatures were missing from the agreement, yet the court allowed the taxpayers to perfect the elections.[18] In three other cases, no recapture agreement was filed with the return.[19] In two of those cases, *Foss*[20] and *Bartlett*,[21] the court found for the government, holding that the

12. § 2207A.
13. § 2207B.
14. § 2207A(a)(2).
15. § 2207B(a)(2).

16. Reg 20.2032A-8(c).
17. 982 F.2d 450, 71 AFTR2d 93-2155, 93-1 USTC ¶60.125 (CA-10, 1992), *rev'g* 95 TC 446 (1990).
18. Estate of McAlpine, Jr., 96 TC 134 (1991), *aff'd* 968 F.2d 459, 70 AFTR2d 92-6216, 92-2 USTC ¶60.109 (CA-5, 1992); Estate of McDonald, 853 F.2d 1494, 62 AFTR2d 88-5995, 88-2 USTC ¶13.778 (CA-8, 1988).
19. Foss, 865 F.2d 178, 63 AFTR2d 89-1524, 89-1 USTC ¶13.793 (CA-8, 1989); Estate of Merwin, 95 TC 168 (1990); Bartlett, 937 F.2d 316, 68 AFTR2d 91-6015, 91-2 USTC ¶60.078 (CA-7, 1991).
20. 865 F.2d 178, 63 AFTR2d 89-1524, 89-1 USTC ¶13.793 (CA-8, 1989).
21. 937 F.2d 316, 68 AFTR2d 91-6015, 91-2 USTC ¶60.078 (CA-7, 1991).

taxpayers had not substantially complied with the regulations. In the third case, *Estate of Merwin*,[22] the taxpayer prevailed. In yet another case, a multitude of significant information was omitted, including the legal description, an adequate explanation of the FMV of the property, and the identity of all parties with an interest in the property.[23] Nevertheless, the court permitted the taxpayer to perfect the election.

TRA '97 establishes a minimum standard for correcting defective special-use valuation elections without regard to "substantial compliance" with the regulations. Henceforth, if the personal representative makes a timely special-use valuation election, including the timely submission of the recapture agreement, any information missing from the election or any signatures missing from the agreement may be supplied within ninety days of notification by the IRS. The new law (like the pre-TRA '97 version of Section 2032A(d)(3)) refers to correcting the agreement if the signatures of "one or more persons" are missing. What if *all* the signatures are missing? In view of the decision in *Estate of McAlpine, Jr.*,[24] such an agreement should be subject to correction. (In *McAlpine*, the court allowed the election to be corrected even though all the beneficiaries' signatures were missing from the agreement.)

Although this section of TRA '97 is effective for estates of decedents dying after the date of enactment, the conference committee noted that in its view the treasury department had taken an unnecessarily restrictive view of the term "substantial compliance" and that defective special-use valuation elections made prior to the date of TRA '97 should be interpreted in light of its provisions.

Special-Use Valuation: Net Cash Leases
(Act Section 504; Code Section 2032A(c))

TRA '97 Section 504 amends Code Section 2032A(c)(7) to provide that rental of special-use valuation property by a spouse or a lineal descendant of the decedent to a member of the family of the spouse or descendant, on a cash-lease basis, does not cause a termination of the qualified special use for purposes of the recapture tax. (Under pre-TRA '97 law, a similar provision applied to net cash leases to a family member by the surviving spouse.[25]) The new provision is effective for leases entered into after 1976.

Annuities
(Act Section 1311; Code Section 2056(b))

Section 20566(b)(7)(C) allows a marital deduction for spousal survivorship annuities arising out of the decedent's employment that are included in the decedent's gross estate under Section 2039. If, however, a surviving spouse has rights under community property laws in an annuity arising out of the decedent's employment, those rights are taxable under section 2033 and not Section 2039. Congress recognized that there was no practical reason to disallow a marital deduction merely because the annuity was included in the decedent's estate under Section 2033 rather than under Section 2039. TRA '97 amends Section 2056(b)(7)(C) to make it clear that the marital deduction is available for a nonparticipant spouse's interest in an annuity under community property laws where he or she predeceases the participant spouse, regardless of whether the annuity is included in the decedent's estate under Section 2033 or Section 2039.

QDOTs: Withholding Requirement
(Act Section 1303; Code Section 2056A)

The marital deduction is, in effect, a tax postponement. When the surviving spouse is not a U.S. citizen, however, there is a chance that the surviving spouse—and the property left to that spouse—will move offshore, thus avoiding the postponed federal estate tax at the surviving spouse's death. Section 2056A was enacted to protect against that result. If the estate of the first spouse to die elects to have property left to the noncitizen spouse qualify for a marital deduction, a trust known as a qualified domestic trust (QDOT), which contains certain specific provisions, must be created to hold the property and to pay, with limited exceptions, a tax on all distributions from the trust and on the assets remaining in the trust at the death of the surviving spouse.

Prior to the Revenue Reconciliation Act of 1990 (RRA '90), all the trustees of a QDOT were required to be U.S. citizens or domestic corporations. RRA '90 changed the rule to require that

22. 95 TC 168 (1990).
23. Parker, 71A AFTR2d 93-5096, 90-2 USTC ¶60.028 (DC Ark., 1990).
24. 96 TC 134 (1991), aff'd 968 F.2d 459, 70 AFTR2d 92-8216, 92-2 USTC ¶60.109 (CA-5, 1992).

25. § 2032A(b)(5).

only one trustee need be a U.S. citizen or domestic corporation, but added another requirement that the U.S. trustee have the right to withhold taxes from distributions. TRA '97 permits a trust created prior to the enactment of RRA '90 to qualify as a QDOT even though it does not have the withholding requirement, if the trust meets the pre-RRA '90 requirement that all the trustees be U.S. citizens or domestic corporations. Because each trustee is personally liable for the payment of the federal estate tax, the IRS is adequately protected against a loss of revenue.[26] This provision is effective as of the date of RRA '90.

Non-trust QDOTs
(Act Section 1312; Code Section 2056A(c))

Because the laws of some foreign countries do not permit trusts, TRA '97 amends Section 2056A(c) to permit regulations to be issued that could include in the definition of trusts "other arrangements which have substantially the same effect as a trust." This change was necessary because Section 2056A(a), on its face, applies only to trusts. This provision applies to estates of decedents dying after the date of enactment of TRA '97.

QDOTs with No U.S. Trustee
(Act Section 1314; Code Section 2056A(a)(l)(A))

Some countries do not permit U.S. trustees. TRA '97 allows regulations to be issued that would waive the requirement that a QDOT have a U.S. trustee in circumstances to be determined by the secretary of the treasury. This provision is effective for estates of decedents dying after the date of enactment.

Generation-skipping Tax: Predeceased Parents
(Act Section 511; Code Section 2651(e))

If a direct skip is made to a grandchild of the transferor (or of the transferor's spouse or former spouse), and if the parent of the grandchild is deceased at the time of the transfer, the grandchild (and the grandchild's descendants) move up one generation for purposes of the GST tax.[27] Thus, the transferor's grandchild is treated as though he or she were the transferor's child for GST tax purposes. This is known as the " predeceased parent exception."

26. § 2056A(b)(6).
27. § 2612(c)(2).

Prior to TRA '97, the benefit of this provision was limited to the transferor's direct line of descendants and to direct skip transfers. TRA '97 broadens the scope of the predeceased parent exception to include lineal descendants of the transferor's parents (grandnieces and grandnephews), provided that the transferor has no living lineal descendants at the time of the transfer. For transfers in trust, the time of the transfer is the time of the transfer to the trust.

Because this amendment is placed in Section 2651, the application of the new, modified predeceased parent exception is broadened to include taxable terminations and taxable distributions as well as direct skips. The critical date for determining whether the exception applies is the date on which the transfer is first subject to estate or gift tax.

This change is effective for transfers, distributions, and terminations after December 31, 1997. If, however, (1) the parent was deceased at the time of a transfer to a trust; (2) that transfer occurred prior to January 1, 1998; and (3) a distribution or termination occurs after December 31, 1997, this new provision will, in fact, have a retroactive effect.

For example: Uncle dies in 1994 leaving a wife (aunt), but no lineal descendants. Uncle's will provides for a life estate for aunt, followed, at her death, by a life estate to his nephew. At nephew's death, the principal is payable to nephew's daughter (i.e., uncle's grandniece). Nephew predeceases uncle. At aunt's death in 1998, the distribution to nephew's daughter is shielded from GST tax by the new predeceased parent exception. The key features of this example are that (1) Nephew was deceased at the time the transfer to the trust occurred (upon the death of uncle) and (2) Uncle left no lineal descendants.

It is also noteworthy that, because the predeceased parent exception previously applied only to direct skips, it was impossible to apply the exception to charitable lead trusts. Because the exception now applies to taxable terminations and taxable distributions as well as to direct skips, it will apply to charitable lead trusts.

Indexing
(Act Section 501; Code Sections 2631(c), 2503(b), 2032A(a), and 6601(j)(3))

The following amounts are indexed annually by increases to the cost of living based on 1997, effective for gifts made or deaths occurring after 1998:

- The $1 million GST exemption, rounded to the next lowest multiple of $10,000. TRA '97 applies indexing in the case of individuals who die after 1998. The Technical Corrections Bill makes it clear that indexing would apply to all generation-skipping transfers after 1998.
- The $10,000 gift tax annual exclusion, rounded to the next lowest multiple of $1,000.
- The $750,000 maximum reduction for special-use valuation under Section 2032A, rounded to the next lowest multiple of $10,000.
- The $1 million (less exemption equivalent) subject to a reduced interest rate under Section 6166, rounded to the next lowest multiple of $10,000.

The "exemption equivalent" is not indexed after 2006.

Retirement Plans: Excess Distributions and Excess Accumulations
(Act Section 1073; Code Sections 691(c)(l), 2013, 2053(c)(1)(B), and 6018(a); former Code Section 4980A)

Qualified plans are perhaps the most heavily taxed assets in an estate. Not only subject to estate taxes, such plans are also subject to income tax in the hands of the beneficiary. And, if that were not enough, these plans were also subject to a 15 percent excise tax on excess distributions during life and a 15 percent additional estate tax on excess retirement accumulations at death. The 15 percent tax on excess distributions, but not on excess accumulations, was suspended in 1996 for three years beginning after 1996. Now, under TRA '97, both the excess distribution tax and the excess accumulation tax are repealed as of December 31, 1996. Personal representatives who paid the tax in 1997 would be well advised to file for refunds.

Revocable Trusts
(Act Section 1305; Code Section 646)

TRA '97 creates new Code Section 646, which allows a revocable grantor trust (a "qualified revocable trust") to elect to be treated and taxed as part of the decedent-grantor's estate for income tax purposes for (1) a period ending six months after the final determination of the estate tax liability if an estate tax return was required to be filed, or (2) two years from the date of death if

no estate tax return was required. During that period, the trust would also be considered an estate for purposes of the GST tax.

In the past, trusts and estates have been subject to different tax rules. For example, an estate is entitled to a charitable deduction for amounts permanently set aside for charity; a trust is allowed a deduction only for amounts paid to charity. The active participation requirement under the passive loss rules is suspended for the first two years of an estate under Section 469(i)(4). An estate may own S corporation stock, while a trust generally must qualify as a qualified Subchapter S trust (QSST) or an electing small business trust (ESBT). Section 646 will eliminate these distinctions if desired.

Moreover, for purposes of the GST tax, distributions from an estate are treated as direct skips. Transfers from a trust would be treated as taxable distributions and taxable terminations. Because direct skips are taxed on a tax exclusive basis while taxable distributions and taxable terminations are taxed on a tax inclusive basis, the result of treating the trust as an estate is a lower effective GST tax rate.

This provision is effective for estates of decedents dying after the date of enactment.

Separate Share Rule
(Act Section 1307; Code Section 663(c))

Code Section 663 is amended to apply the separate share rule of trusts to substantially separate and independent shares of an estate. This provision is effective for estates of decedents dying after the date of enactment.

Sixty-five-day Rule
(Act Section 1306; Code Section 663(b))

TRA '97 permits the personal representative of an estate to elect to have distributions paid or credited during the first sixty-five days of the tax year treated as if paid or credited on the last day of the prior year. Under TRA '97, this sixty-five-day rule now applies to estates as well as to trusts. This provision is effective for tax years beginning after the date of enactment.

Throwback Rules
(Act Section 507; Code Section 665)

The throwback rules are now repealed for "qualified trusts." "Qualified trusts" generally are domestic trusts created on or after March 1, 1984, and domestic trusts created prior to that date if aggregation with other trusts would not occur under Section 643(f).

Related Parties
(Act Section 1308; Code Sections 1239(b) and 267(b))

Under Section 1239, capital gain treatment is not permitted on sales of depreciable property to related parties. Nor is a deduction allowed for losses on sales to related parties, pursuant to Section 267. Under Sections 1239 and 267, an individual and a trust may be treated as related parties. But prior to TRA '97, neither section applied to an estate and the beneficiaries of the estate. TRA '97 corrects this omission, and treats an estate and its beneficiaries as related parties. This rule does not apply, however, to sales or exchanges from an estate to satisfy pecuniary bequests. Transfers from a trust, in satisfaction of pecuniary amounts, will continue to be subject to the related party rules. The new provision is effective for tax years beginning after the date of enactment.

Gift Tax Returns Not Required for Gifts to Charity
(Act Section 1301; Code Section 6019)

Even though a gift to charity is exempt from tax, the donor was required to file a gift tax return prior to TRA '97. This requirement was more honored in the breach. TRA '97 now exempts donors of charitable gifts from the filing requirement if the gift consists of the donor's entire interest in the property. This provision is effective for gifts made after the date of enactment.

Extension to Pay Estate Tax
(Act Section 503; Code Sections 6166 and 6601(j))

Under the pre-TRA '97 version of Sections 6166 and 6601, a 4 percent interest rate is applied to the deferred estate tax attributable to the first $1 million in value (less the applicable exclusion amount) of the closely held business. Under TRA '97, the 4 percent interest rate on the deferred estate tax attributable to the first $1 million in value (without reduction for the applicable exclusion amount) is reduced to 2 percent. The interest rate on the balance of tax postponed is 45 percent of the interest rate applicable to tax deficiencies. The tradeoff, if Section 6166 treatment

is elected, is that there is no deduction for the interest on tax postponed under this section. The Technical Corrections Bill clarifies that the 2 percent interest rate will not apply, and the 45 percent of the tax deficiency rate will apply, to unmarketable stock or partnership interests indirectly held and to holding company stock.

The provisions of TRA '97 take effect for estates of decedents dying after 1997. Estates that are currently paying the tax in installments under Section 6166 may irrevocably elect, before January 1, 1999, to have the reduced rates apply. That election, however, cannot increase the amount that has already been postponed at the 4 percent rate.

Declaratory Judgments and Section 6166
(Act Section 505; Code Section on 7479)

TRA '97 grants the tax court authority to make declaratory judgments with respect to an IRS decision to disallow a postponement of tax under Section 6166. The new law also provides that the tax court's declaratory judgment is, itself, subject to judicial review. The petition in the tax court may be brought only by the personal representative or any person who has assumed the obligation to make payments under Section 6166, and only after all administrative remedies have been exhausted. This provision applies to estates of decedents dying after the date of enactment. The Technical Corrections Bill makes it clear that the tax court jurisdiction would include the power to decide which businesses in an estate qualify for the deferral.

Consistency Rule
(Act Section 1021; Code Section 6045(f))

Effective for returns of beneficiaries and owners filed after the date of enactment, the income tax return of a beneficiary of a domestic estate or trust must be consistent with the return filed on behalf of the estate or trust unless the beneficiary files with the secretary of the treasury a statement identifying the inconsistency. Failure to comply can result in the discrepancy being treated as a mathematical error which cannot be appealed by petition to the tax court.

Attorney's Fees
(Act Section 1021; Code Section 6045(f))

Under TRA '97, any person engaged in a trade or business, who makes a payment to a lawyer in the course of such trade or business, is required to report the payment to the IRS. This requirement is effective for payments made after 1997.

Qualified State Tuition Programs
(Act Section 211; Code Section 529)

Qualified state tuition programs allow a person to purchase tuition credits on behalf of a beneficiary, which entitle the beneficiary to a waiver of higher education expenses. Under pre-TRA '97 law, such payments were treated as incomplete gifts. As a result, undistributed amounts in an account were includable in the donor's gross estate if the donor died before the entire account was distributed. TRA '97 reverses this treatment. Contributions to such an account will be treated as completed gifts (taxable as present interest gifts), but no amount (except contributions in excess of the gift tax annual exclusion) will be included in the gross estate of the donor.

If the transfer to the account exceeds the annual exclusion, the aggregate contribution may be reported over a five-year period. If the donor dies during the five-year period, any outstanding amounts constitute excess contributions and are includable in the donor's estate. There are no additional transfer taxes if the account is rolled over to a new beneficiary unless the new beneficiary is of a lower generation than the original beneficiary. Amounts distributed by reason of the death of the beneficiary are taxable in the beneficiary's estate.

Conclusion

The estate and gift tax benefits of TRA '97 have been greatly overstated. The increase in the exemption equivalent—loudly trumpeted as a boon to the middle class—will be quickly absorbed by inflation over its nine-year phase-in period. Benefits of other provisions must be weighed against the provisions' complexity. There are benefits in TRA '97, including the prohibition against the revaluation of adjusted taxable gifts and the simplification of the treatment of interest under Section 6166. Nevertheless, practitioners have been handed a hastily and poorly drafted statute with more than the usual loose ends to grapple with. All that can be hoped for is that these loose ends will be tied up via technical corrections. Stay tuned.

37

Congress Offers Taxpayers Relief by Raising the Unified Credit

HERBERT L. ZUCKERMAN AND JAY A. SOLED

The Taxpayer Relief Act of 1997 offers taxpayers estate tax relief by gradually increasing the unified credit over a nine-year period. By the year 2006 taxpayers will be able to transfer up to $1 million of assets tax-free rather than the $600,000 they are presently allowed under current law. As the following chart indicates, however, during the nine-year phase-in period the unified credit is not uniform:

Year	Applicable Exclusion Amount
1997	$ 600,000
1998	625,000
1999	650,000
2000	675,000
2001	675,000
2002	700,000
2003	700,000
2004	850,000
2005	950,000
2006	$1,000,000

While this may be self-evident, we want our readers to understand the implications of this increase in the unified credit. First, the increase will enhance the opportunity taxpayers have to give highly appreciating assets out of their estates. For example, assume Alan has Company X stock worth $1 million and he wishes to give stock to his daughter, Barbara. Under prior law, Alan could only give $600,000 Company X stock

Herbert L. Zuckerman is a partner at the law firm of Sills Cummis Zuckerman Radin Tischman Epstein & Gross, P.A., in Newark, New Jersey. Jay A. Soled is a lawyer and an assistant professor at Rutgers University in Newark, New Jersey.

before being subject to gift tax. Now Alan can give all of his Company X stock to Barbara. If Company X stock doubles in value, the shares of stock held by Barbara (now valued at $2 million) will all escape being subject to transfer tax.

Second, the strategic use by married couples of credit-shelter trusts is even more important. Credit-shelter trusts are those established at the death of the first spouse who holds assets in trust for the surviving spouse. Upon the death of the survivors, the assets held in the trust pass transfer tax-free to the designated beneficiaries. The advantage of a credit-shelter trust is that it enables both spouses to make full use of each spouse's unified credit without jeopardizing the financial well-being of the survivor.

Under prior law, assuming a taxpayer made no prior taxable gifts, a credit-shelter trust was typically funded with assets valued at $600,000. Now, because of the increase in the unified credit, these trusts will eventually be able to be funded with assets valued at $1 million. During the term of the trust (i.e., the balance of the surviving spouse's life, say twenty years), if the value of the assets held in trust triple in value, say to $3 million, all these assets will pass to the trust's designated beneficiaries transfer tax-free.

To institute proper credit-shelter trust funding, it is imperative that each spouse have at least $1 million in his or her individual name. Failure to do so may result in the credit-shelter trust being underfunded. For example, suppose Carol and David are married, each with $500,000 in their individual names and $1 million held in a joint brokerage account. Upon the death of either spouse only the $500,000 held in each individual's name can be used to fund the credit-shelter trust. The assets held in a joint brokerage account will pass automatically to the surviving spouse. In this instance, the value of one-half of the assets in the joint account should be put in each spouse's individual name.

Aside from the funding issue, taxpayers should review their entire estate plan to make sure it is consistent with the increase in the unified credit (e.g., clauses in decedent's will referring to funding the credit-shelter trust should use formulas rather than specific dollar amounts).

In sum, Congress rarely offers relief in the area of estate planning but it did so in the new Taxpayer Relief Act. Failure to avail oneself of these opportunities could be unfortunate.

38
Tax and Estate Planning Issues Facing Seniors Today

CHARLES F. NEWLIN

All of us know that death and taxes are certain. Yet you can ease part of the future sting of both death and taxes for your survivors by having a well-designed tax and estate plan. Seniors today face many issues and questions that make their job of tax and estate planning both more complicated and more immediately necessary than for other groups in our society.

The goal of a well-designed estate plan is to see that your property passes to those whom you wish to receive it, in the manner in which you wish them to receive it, and at a minimum cost. Such costs include administration expenses, court costs, lawyers' fees, and taxes. For seniors, especially, estate planning cannot be separated from planning to reduce income taxes during life. This chapter will discuss three aspects of dealing with death and taxes to reach the goals of the well-designed estate plan. These three aspects are: the *tools* by which you cause property to pass to your beneficiaries; the *taxes* that will affect the use of these tools; and the *techniques* you can use to combine tools and taxes to achieve your planning goals.[1]

Tools: How Your Property Passes to Your Beneficiary

You can use several different methods to pass property at your death to the person you want to receive it (your "beneficiary") (see Figure 38–1). We will next examine the particular uses of each of these tools.

The Will

The will controls disposition of property held in your name alone and property that is payable to

your probate estate after your death. If you have no will, the intestacy laws of the state of which you are a legal resident at the time of your death generally control the disposition of this property. The laws of the state in which real property is located govern disposition of that real property if there is no will.

Joint Tenancy

Property that you and another person hold jointly with right of survivorship will pass entirely to the survivor upon the death of the first to die. Generally the will does not affect the disposition of this property. People often confuse property held in joint tenancy with property held in tenancy in common. Any interest you own as a tenant in common becomes part of your probate estate and passes under the terms of your will or the state intestacy law. Some states also allow married couples to hold property in tenancy by the entirety. This is a particular variation of joint tenancy that can apply only to property held by husband and wife.

Community Property

Under the laws of nine states, husband and wife also may hold property as community property. There are some variations among these states on how community property passes upon the death

Charles F. Newlin is a partner at Sonnenschein Nath & Rosenthal in Chicago and is a fellow of the American College of Trust and Estate Counsel.

1. As you read this chapter, you should keep in mind that the term *estate* has different meanings depending on the context. For example, your *estate* or *probate estate* for state law purposes generally means the property you own in your own name at your death. The probate estate also includes property paid directly to your estate or personal representative after your death. Typically, the probate estate defines the property subject to the spouse's rights and creditors' claims. When referring to this state law concept, this chapter will use the term *probate estate*. For tax and estate-planning purposes, however, your *estate* includes all the property you own or control or in which you have an interest at your death. When referring to this tax concept, this chapter will use the term *tax estate*.

Figure 38–1

How Property Passes to Your Beneficiary

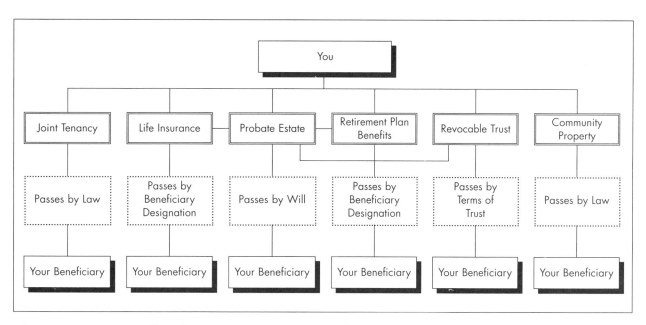

of one spouse. Usually, the surviving spouse receives one-half of the community property. The other half of the community property passes as part of the probate estate of the deceased spouse. If you and your spouse have lived in a community property state, your spouse may have community property rights in assets that you earned or purchased in the community property state. These rights continue to apply, even if you are not living in a community property state at the time of your death. The eight original community property states are Arizona, California, Idaho, Louisiana, Nevada, New Mexico, Texas, and Washington. Wisconsin adopted a community property system by statute in the 1980s.

Revocable (or Living) Trust

You may place property in a trust during your lifetime. The terms of the trust document will then control its disposition during your lifetime and after your death. Usually, the trust is revocable and subject to change by you anytime. You also may create trusts that are irrevocable and unchangeable by you once created. The tax treatment of irrevocable trusts differs dramatically from the tax treatment of revocable trusts. However, irrevocable trusts may be useful for tax planning under certain circumstances.

Life Insurance

The insurance company will pay the proceeds of insurance policies on your life to the beneficiary designated in the policy. You may name a trust as the beneficiary (in which case the trust document will control its disposition). You also may name your probate estate as the beneficiary (in which case the will or intestacy law controls). If you do not designate a beneficiary, or if the designated beneficiary does not survive you, the probate estate will usually receive the proceeds.

Retirement Plan Death Benefits

An employee retirement plan will pay its benefits to the beneficiary designated under the terms of the plan. Again, you could name the probate estate or a trust the beneficiary. Under certain qualified employee benefit plans, you must name your spouse as beneficiary unless your spouse signs a written consent permitting a different designation.

An important point to remember in developing a well-designed tax and estate plan is the distinction among the various tools. Each functions differently; each applies to specific kinds of property. The estate planner must consider the unique strengths and the inherent limitations of each tool and must coordinate the use of the tools appropriate to the specific family situation.

Taxes: The Framework in Which the Estate Plan Operates

We have now experienced several congressional attempts to achieve tax "simplification." Yet the framework of taxes in which your estate plan will operate is no less complex.

Income Taxes

Generally, the property received by your beneficiary upon your death (except retirement plan benefits) will not be subject to income tax. However, you also must consider the effects of your estate plan (1) on your income taxes during your lifetime and (2) on your beneficiary's income taxes after the beneficiary receives your property. Since the general operation of the income tax system is relatively familiar to most of us, we will not attempt an explanation here. We will discuss some income tax planning points later in this chapter.

Federal Gift Taxes

The federal government imposes a tax on the transfer of property by gift. Often the giver owes no tax money to the government because each individual has a unified credit from gift and estate taxes, which we will describe below in more detail. Of all the taxes that the federal government imposes on individuals, the gift tax is probably the least understood by the public. Theoretically, the donor making a gift pays the tax for the privilege of transferring the property to another.

Before the gift tax can apply, the transfer of property must first be a gift. If you receive a payment of equal value in return for the transfer, then the transfer is generally not a gift subject to gift tax. Items of support that the law requires you to furnish to a spouse and minor or dependent children are not gifts and thus are not subject to tax. In addition, payments you make for tuition or medical care directly to the providers of such services for any person are not gifts. Only payments made directly to the service providers are so excluded from the definition of gifts.

The gift tax law provides certain exclusions or deductions for particular gifts. You may give property having a fair market value of $10,000 or less to any number of persons every year without tax. We often call such gifts *annual exclusion gifts*. Your spouse also may agree to split the gifts each of you makes during a calendar year. Thus, together you may give $20,000 to any number of persons during that year. Under the Taxpayer Relief Act of 1997, the IRS will adjust the $10,000 annual limitation for inflation after 1998. The adjusted amount will be rounded down to the nearest $1,000.

You also may make unlimited gifts to your spouse without incurring gift tax if your spouse is a U.S. citizen. However, if your spouse is not a U.S. citizen, the amount that you can give to your spouse without tax is limited to $100,000 each year.

The tax law also allows a gift tax charitable deduction for most transfers to tax-exempt charitable organizations.

Gifts that do not qualify for the annual exclusion or the marital or charitable deduction are subject to gift tax. You have a unified credit to offset the tax. This, in effect, permits you to make additional gifts without paying a gift tax. The cumulative lifetime amount you can give under this provision without tax is $625,000 for 1998. This amount will increase to $1,000,000 by the year 2006. The increase in the exemption will take effect as follows:

Year of Gift or Death	Applicable Exclusion Amount
1998	$ 625,000
1999	650,000
2000	675,000
2001	675,000
2002	700,000
2003	700,000
2004	850,000
2005	950,000
2006	$1,000,000

Current law does not provide for any further adjustment after 2006. For individuals with taxable gifts or a taxable estate more than $1,000,000 but less than $10,000,000, the increase in the applicable exclusion amount will result in gift or estate tax savings of $153,000. For individuals with taxable gifts or taxable estates of more than $10,000,000, the 5 percent additional gift or estate tax imposed under current law will erode or eliminate this potential tax savings.

Although no gift tax may be due, you may have to file a federal gift tax return to report a gift. For example, you must file a return if you make a gift of more than $10,000 and your spouse consents to have half the gift treated as made by your spouse.

After considering the unified credit, gift tax rates now range from 37 percent to 55 percent. The maximum rate applies to aggregate taxable transfers exceeding $3,000,000. There is also a surtax of 5 percent for aggregate taxable transfers exceeding $10,000,000. This surtax phases out the benefits of the unified credit and the lower tax brackets for very large transfers. For aggregate taxable transfers of more than $10,000,000, the actual marginal rate is thus 60 percent. Once the aggregate taxable transfers reach $18,340,000, the benefits have been fully recaptured. The surtax does not apply once the aggregate taxable transfers exceed $21,040,000.

A few states also impose gift taxes on transfers by residents of the state or on transfers of property within that state by nonresidents.

Federal Estate Taxes

The federal government also imposes a tax on all your property at the time of your death. This includes property: (1) that you own; (2) that pays you certain benefits; or (3) that you control in certain ways. Generally, the amount subject to the tax is the fair market value of the property at your date of death. Your tax estate may deduct certain debts, expenses, charitable gifts, and gifts to a surviving spouse (discussed below). The IRS also allows a credit for state death taxes paid.

Most property passing to a surviving spouse qualifies for an estate tax marital deduction. This marital deduction once was limited to 50 percent of the gross estate. But Congress removed all limits on the amount of the marital deduction in 1981. Under current law, you may give your surviving spouse only an income interest in property and still qualify the entire value of the property for the marital deduction. This provides flexibility when you want your spouse to have the use of property for life and assure that it will pass to your children or other specified beneficiaries after your spouse's death.

Generally, the marital deduction is available only if the surviving spouse is a U.S. citizen. If the surviving spouse is not a U.S. citizen, the tax estate may still claim a marital deduction for property passing into a qualified domestic trust for the benefit of the non-citizen spouse.

To the extent you have not used your unified credit for gift taxes, the credit is available to reduce estate taxes. If you have used none of your unified credit during your lifetime, the first $625,000 (increasing to $1,000,000 by the year 2006) worth of property escapes the estate tax. If the estate tax applies, the rates, like those on gifts, now range from 37 percent to 55 percent, with the 5 percent surcharge applying to taxable estates of more than $10,000,000.[2]

The Taxpayer Relief Act of 1997 provided a new, highly technical estate tax provision for some family-owned business interests. A new section of the Internal Revenue Code, Sec. 2033A, will allow the executor of the estate to exclude from the decedent's taxable estate up to $675,000 of such qualified business interests. This provision applies to the estates of decedents dying after 1997. The exclusion is based on the difference between $1,300,000 and the unified credit applicable exclusion amount previously described. As the applicable exclusion amount increases, the family-owned business exclusion decreases. By 2006, the law will thus reduce the family-owned business exclusion to $300,000. To qualify for this exclusion, the value of the family-owned business overall must exceed one-half of the decedent's adjusted gross estate. The business also must have its principal place of business in the United States. In addition, this new provision requires material participation in the family-owned business by the decedent or a member of the decedent's family. This participation must have occurred during an aggregate of five years during the eight-year period ending on the decedent's death. The government will recapture some or all of the benefits of the exclusion if the family members dispose of their interests. A recapture tax also applies if the family members fail to materially participate in the family-owned business during the ten-year period after the decedent's death. This new provision probably will be of limited benefit to many family-owned businesses.

State Inheritance or Estate Tax

Most states impose some kind of death tax. Many states now levy only a so-called "pick-up" tax that

---

2. The changes in the unified credit and the tax rates, discussed above under the gift tax, also apply to the estate tax.

equals a portion of the estate tax otherwise payable to the federal government. In those states, if no federal estate tax is due, then there is no state death tax. Other states use the more traditional inheritance tax system, which taxes the right to receive property from another at death. The state calculates a separate tax on property passing to each beneficiary. The tax rate often depends upon the relationship of the beneficiary to the decedent: the more distant the relationship, the higher the tax rate.

Federal Generation-Skipping Transfer (GST) Tax

Congress intended this tax, first enacted in 1976 and completely rewritten in 1986, to plug certain perceived loopholes in the federal estate tax benefiting the rich. In essence, the law attempts to ensure that when property is placed in trust (or similar devices are employed), the government still collects a tax on the property as it passes to each successive generation. The tax should be roughly the same as if a member of each generation owned the property outright. Transfers directly to grandchildren and more remote descendants, either outright or in trust, also may be subject to GST tax. Generally, each individual has a GST exemption that allows that individual to transfer up to $1,000,000 free of this tax. Under the Taxpayer Relief Act of 1997, the IRS also will adjust the $1 million GST exemption for inflation, in $10,000 increments (rounded down).

Techniques: Using the Available Tools to Accomplish Planning Goals

Income Tax Planning Issues

Retirement Benefits

Probably the most significant income tax planning challenge facing seniors today is planning to reduce income taxes on benefits under a qualified pension or profit-sharing plan. When the benefit is payable in a lump sum, the recipient must report the payment exceeding employee nondeductible contributions as ordinary income. Several detailed rules affect the taxation of this income. The tax treatment of the distribution depends on whether the recipient had attained age 50 before January 1, 1986. If so, the recipient

may subject the payment to a special five-year or ten-year averaging provision. In addition, the recipient may choose to have benefits accrued before 1974 taxed as capital gains rather than ordinary income, at a 20 percent maximum rate. A recipient who did not attain age 50 before January 1, 1986, may use special five-year averaging for a distribution received after the recipient attains age 59½ and before the year 2000. The Taxpayer Relief Act of 1997 repealed five-year averaging for such persons after the year 1999.[3] The first $5,000 of a lump-sum payment from a qualified plan, payable because of the employee's death before August 21, 1996, escapes income tax. Finally, if a surviving spouse receives a lump-sum payment, the spouse can roll it over into an IRA to defer income tax until actual distributions are later made from the surviving spouse's IRA.

When the benefit is payable in installments, the income tax consequences are similar, except that no five-year averaging election is available. There are alternate rules for calculating the taxable portion of each annuity payment, depending on the annuity starting date and the terms of the annuity. If you are recovering part of your annuity tax free under any of these rules, you may wish to recognize other income during the years that this recovery reduces your income. For example, you may wish to sell appreciated assets (such as a home or securities) or to withdraw IRA funds.

Under prior law, distributions from a qualified plan or IRA that exceeded a calculated limit in a single year could be subject to a 15 percent excise tax, besides the income tax otherwise payable. The Taxpayer Relief Act of 1997 repealed the 15 percent excise tax for distributions received after 1996.

The IRS can penalize you still under the current tax rules if you fail to withdraw a minimum amount from your retirement plans. Most qualified retirement arrangements must make certain minimum distributions by April 1 of the year following the participant's attaining age 70½. For tax years beginning in 1989, there is an excise tax imposed on the participant for failure to meet these requirements. This penalty equals 50 percent of the amount by which actual distributions

---

3. The first $5,000 of a lump-sum payment from a qualified plan, payable because of the employee's death before August 21, 1996, escapes income tax. The Taxpayer Relief Act of 1997 repealed this exclusion for beneficiaries of decedents dying after August 20, 1996.

fall short of the required minimum distributions in each calendar year.

The Taxpayer Relief Act of 1997 adopted an exception to the minimum distribution rules for persons who are still working after the year in which they reach age 70½. These persons do not have to begin receiving minimum distributions until April 1 of the year following their actual retirement. The exception does not apply, however, to those who own more than 5 percent of the business for which they are working.

Questions on selecting a payment method for retirement benefits can only be answered as part of the total development of your entire estate plan. They require careful calculation of the tax effects of each option.

IRA Options and Rules

The Taxpayer Relief Act of 1997 made many changes in the law concerning individual retirement accounts (IRAs). Congress revised significantly the rules concerning contributions to and withdrawals from traditional, regular IRAs. This act also created two additional kinds of IRAs: the "Educational IRA" and the "Roth IRA."

Active participants in employer-provided retirement plans may make deductible contributions to a regular IRA, subject to income phaseout rules. The income phaseout range will increase starting in 1998 and continuing through 2007. For a married couple filing jointly, the 1997 phaseout range started at modified adjusted gross income of $40,000, with no deduction allowed if modified adjusted gross income exceeded $50,000. In 1998, this phaseout range begins at $50,000 and is complete at $60,000. By 2007, the law schedules the phaseout range for a married couple filing jointly to be $80,000 to $100,000. Beginning in 1998, the spouse of an active plan participant will no longer be treated as an active participant as well. The IRA deduction limit for such a spouse will be phased out if modified adjusted gross income in 1998 exceeds $150,000, with no deduction allowable above $160,000.

The Taxpayer Relief Act of 1997 also relaxed the penalties for early withdrawal from a regular IRA. The new rules allow a person younger than age 59½ to withdraw up to $10,000 after 1997 without incurring the 10 percent penalty for early withdrawal. The taxpayer, however, must use the funds withdrawn for first-time home-buyer expenses or for higher education costs, including tuition, room and board.

The first-time home buyer can be the IRA owner, or that person's spouse, child, grandchild, or an ancestor of the owner or the owner's spouse. A "first-time home buyer" is a person who has not owned a present ownership interest in a principal residence for two years before the acquisition of the new residence. The $10,000 limit on first-time home-buyer expenses is a lifetime limit, applied to each IRA owner.

The penalty exception for higher-education costs applies if the funds are used by the IRA owner or that person's spouse, child, or grandchild. The allowable costs include tuition, room, board, fees, books, supplies, and equipment for courses starting after 1997.

The "Educational IRA," created by the Taxpayer Relief Act of 1997, can receive up to $500 per year in cash contributions per child beginning in 1998. The law phases out the contribution limit for married couples with modified adjusted gross income between $150,000 and $160,000. No contributions are deductible, but the funds in the Educational IRA accumulate free of tax. Distributions from the Educational IRA will be tax-free as well if the recipient uses them to pay for post-secondary education costs, including tuition, room, board, books, and supplies. Distributions that are not so used are subject to regular income tax, plus a 10 percent penalty tax, whenever distributed.

Finally, the Taxpayer Relief Act of 1997 also created the "Roth IRA." This is another kind of IRA for which no contribution deduction is allowed, but which permits earnings to accumulate tax-free. The contribution to a Roth IRA is limited to $2,000, reduced by contributions to other IRAs for the same year. The Roth IRA also has an income phaseout provision for contributions. A married couple filing jointly is subject to the phaseout if modified adjusted gross income exceeds $150,000, with no contribution allowed if modified adjusted gross income is more than $160,000. A distribution from a Roth IRA is tax-free if it is made more than five years after the year of the creation of the Roth IRA. The taxpayer also must be at least age 59½ or disabled or the distribution must be used for first-time home-buyer expenses of up to $10,000. Distributions that do not qualify for tax-free treatment are subject to ordinary income tax (to the extent they exceed the total contributions to the Roth IRA). They also may be subject to the 10 percent penalty tax if the taxpayer is under age 59½ and none of the exceptions to the penalty tax apply.

Tax on Social Security Benefits

Some Social Security benefits may be includible in gross income if the taxpayer's "provisional" income exceeds $32,000 for married persons filing jointly, $25,000 for unmarried taxpayers, and $0 for married persons filing separately. "Provisional" income includes adjusted gross income (with certain modifications) plus tax-exempt interest plus one-half of the Social Security benefits. Current law may include up to 85 percent of the Social Security benefits in gross income if the taxpayer's provisional income exceeds certain limits.

The only planning steps to reduce the tax on Social Security benefits involve reducing the provisional income. Since provisional income includes tax-exempt interest, shifting to tax-exempt investments does not solve the problem. However, deferring the receipt of income (by investing in savings bonds, for example) delays the tax. You can also plan the timing of income receipts so that you have higher income in alternating years, allowing you to avoid or reduce the tax in the intervening low-income years. For example, you probably can plan for asset sales, IRA withdrawals, and Treasury bill maturities to occur in one year. This may increase the tax on Social Security benefits in that year. It may, however, reduce your provisional income (and the tax on Social Security benefits) in the preceding or following year.

Sale of Principal Residence

Under the Taxpayer Relief Act of 1997, any taxpayer, whatever age, may exclude up to $250,000 ($500,000 for a married couple filing jointly) of gain realized on the sale of a home. To qualify for this exclusion, the taxpayer must have owned and occupied the home as a principal residence for two of the five years before the sale. There is no longer any requirement that the taxpayer acquire replacement property. The exclusion applies every time the taxpayer meets the two-year ownership and principal residence rule. These rules apply to sales on or after May 7, 1997.

Medical and Dental Expenses

Seniors often have significant medical and dental expenses. Maximizing the medical expense deduction can help reduce the burden of these expenses.

You should not overlook the deductibility of various expenses that seniors frequently incur. These include the following:

- Retirement home "founder's fee" or "lifetime care" fee; you can deduct the amount allocable to medical care.
- Wages and meals provided for an attendant who provides nursing services (whether or not a nurse); these amounts are generally deductible.
- Certain costs of sending a mentally or physically disabled person to a special school or home; these costs are often deductible.
- Prescription medication and special medical supplies, eyeglasses, fees for physicians, physical therapists, and other medical care-givers and special transportation to and from health-care appointments; these amounts are generally deductible.
- Special improvements made to a home for medical care; you can deduct the excess of cost over the amount by which the improvement increases the market value of the home. Similarly, the cost of the operation and upkeep of capital expenses or improvements made for medical care are deductible.
- Costs of transportation, meals, and lodging while away from home to obtain medical care; the deductible portion of these expenses depends upon several factors. For example, one case disallowed a deduction for living expenses claimed by a woman who spent part of the year in Florida on advice of her doctor. Since she did not receive particular medical treatment there, her normal living expenses in Florida during that period were not deductible.
- Nursing home; you probably can deduct all costs if the primary purpose of the stay in the nursing home is for medical care and not for personal or family reasons.

You should not only be aware of the kinds of expenses that may be deductible. Also, you should plan to obtain the maximum tax benefit from each dollar of deductible expense. Medical expenses are deductible only in the year paid and then only to the extent they exceed 7.5 percent of adjusted gross income. Accordingly, you can use several techniques to maximize the deductible amount.

If your total medical expenses for a year clearly will not exceed the 7.5 percent floor, consider deferring payment until the next year. You may then have aggregate medical expenses in that following year that exceed the 7.5 percent floor. On the other hand, if you clearly will exceed the 7.5 percent floor in one year, consider scheduling elective procedures for the same year to obtain the deduction for those expenses. You also can decrease the amount of the 7.5 percent floor and increase deductible amounts by decreasing your adjusted gross income. Ways you can reduce adjusted gross income include deferring IRA withdrawals and selecting investments that will not pay income until the next year or that produce tax-exempt income. If you are married, you may also want to consider filing separate returns if the medical expenses of one spouse are much greater.

Other Issues Concerning Itemized Deductions

Similar concerns apply to miscellaneous itemized deductions, which are deductible only to the extent they exceed 2 percent of adjusted gross income. The same considerations also apply to the whole issue of whether to claim the standard deduction or itemized deductions. As with the medical expenses, the key to obtaining maximum tax benefit from such deductions is to attempt to aggregate them in a single year and reduce adjusted gross income for that same year. The law reduces some itemized deductions by 3 percent of the amount by which adjusted gross income exceeds a fixed amount. For 1997, for example, the threshold amount was $121,200 ($60,600 for married persons filing separately). The IRS adjusts the threshold amount each year for inflation. The reduction applies to the amount of itemized deductions otherwise allowable after applying other limitations (like the 2 percent floor for miscellaneous itemized deductions). However, this provision cannot reduce the allowable itemized deductions by more than 80 percent. Deductions for medical expenses, investment interest, nonbusiness casualty and theft losses, and gambling losses are not subject to the reduction. You also must consider these rules in planning to optimize use of the available deductions.

Factors in Selecting Filing Status

The taxpayer's status on the last day of the tax year generally determines filing status for income tax purposes and affects the rate at which income is taxed. The four possibilities are (1) single, (2) married filing jointly or qualifying widow or widower, (3) married filing separately, and (4) head of household. Generally, tax rates are lowest for married filing jointly or qualifying widow or widower and then increase for head of household, single, and married filing separately, in that order.

These differing rates raise several planning considerations and opportunities. When the medical expenses of one spouse substantially exceed those of the other spouse, you should consider filing separate returns to increase the deductible portion of expenses paid by the spouse with greater expenses. If your filing status will change in the next year to a status with lower rates, you should attempt to decrease taxable income for the current year and increase taxable income for the next year. This could occur, for example, if you will change your filing status from single to married filing jointly or head of household next year. On the other hand, if your filing status will change next year to a status with higher rates, you should attempt to increase taxable income for the current year and decrease taxable income for the next year.

Although tax planning obviously should not be a key factor in deciding to marry or divorce, the timing of marriage or divorce can have a tax impact. If a husband and wife have roughly equal amounts of income, they should try not to be married to each other on December 31. When both incomes are roughly equal, the marriage penalty will cause the total tax payable to be higher than the total tax that two single taxpayers would have paid. Such a couple planning to get married should wait until January. Such a couple heading for divorce should complete the divorce before the end of the year. If one person in the couple has much more income than the other, they should try to be married to each other on December 31. Then they can obtain the tax benefit of the lower rates for taxpayers married filing jointly. A couple such as this, planning to get married, should do so before the end of the year. The same couple heading for divorce should wait to complete the divorce until January.

If your spouse died during the tax year, you may continue to file a joint return for the year of death. This return would, of course, include the deceased spouse's income and deductions only to the date of death. A surviving spouse may continue to benefit from joint rates as a qualifying widow or widower for two years after death. The surviving spouse qualifies if he or she has not remarried, could have filed jointly with the deceased spouse for the year of death, and provides more than half the costs of maintaining his or her home that is also the principal residence of a child or stepchild.

Director's and Consulting Fees

Director's fees are earned income for purposes of determining Social Security benefits payable. The IRS treats them as received during the year in which you earn them, whenever you receive them. If you can arrange to receive a consulting fee, rather than a director's fee, you probably can defer payment of the consulting fee. If you receive the fee after you reach age 70, it will not affect the amount of your Social Security benefits.

Estate Tax Planning Issues

Brief Description of Typical Marital Deduction Plan

As noted earlier, each person has a unified credit that shelters a certain amount of property ($625,000 in 1998, increasing to $1,000,000 in 2006) from gift and estate tax. We sometimes call the sheltered amount the *credit-shelter amount*. You may give your credit-shelter amount to any persons you choose, without incurring gift or estate tax. In addition, property passing to a surviving spouse generally escapes tax. The typical marital deduction plan seeks to give the surviving spouse the benefit of the entire tax estate. Simultaneously, it ensures that the government does not tax the credit-shelter amount in the estate of the surviving spouse upon the survivor's later death.

We outline the structure of the typical marital deduction plan in Figure 38–2. Under the will (or trust) we divide your tax estate into two shares. One, the marital share, includes all property subject to federal estate taxation, except the credit-shelter amount. The marital share may pass to your spouse outright or may continue in trust for

your spouse's sole benefit. The trustee will distribute the trust on your spouse's death either as the spouse directs or as you have directed in the will or trust. This share is not subject to tax when you die, but will be taxed as part of your surviving spouse's estate upon his or her later death.

The balance of the estate (the credit-shelter amount plus any property not subject to estate tax) passes to a separate trust, called the family trust.[4] Your surviving spouse can receive all the income produced by this trust and principal for certain purposes. You may give your spouse limited control over where the property will go upon his or her death. This portion escapes tax upon the deaths of both spouses.

The basic marital plan is quite flexible. Besides the variations mentioned above, you may give the credit-shelter amount outright to children or others rather than place it in a family trust. This alternative may be desirable where the spouse has sufficient assets and a gift directly to the children is desirable from a personal point of view. Also, when one spouse's tax estate is much larger than the other's, the family may find tax advantages to having a smaller marital share and correspondingly larger family trust than under the plan outlined above. Doing so would cause the tax estate of the first spouse to die to incur estate tax. Yet the net effect is to subject both spouses' estates to estate tax at lower marginal rates.

The typical marital deduction plan is appropriate when the combined tax estates of husband and wife exceed the credit-shelter amount ($625,000 in 1998, increasing to $1,000,000 in 2006). It may be useful in smaller tax estates as well, depending on individual circumstances.

Brief Description of Basic Generation-Skipping Marital Deduction Plan

As noted earlier, each person has a generation-skipping tax exemption ("GST exemption") of $1,000,000 under current law. (The IRS will adjust the amount of the exemption for inflation after 1997.) This exemption can shelter outright transfers to grandchildren or more remote

---

4. Keep in mind as you consider these various plans that your credit-shelter amount is reduced by your lifetime taxable gifts. Thus, if you make an aggregate of $350,000 in taxable gifts during your lifetime, the family trust under any basic marital deduction plan will be only $275,000 if you die in 1998. That is the amount remaining that your unified credit will shelter from gift and estate tax.

Figure 38–2

Basic Marital Deduction Plan

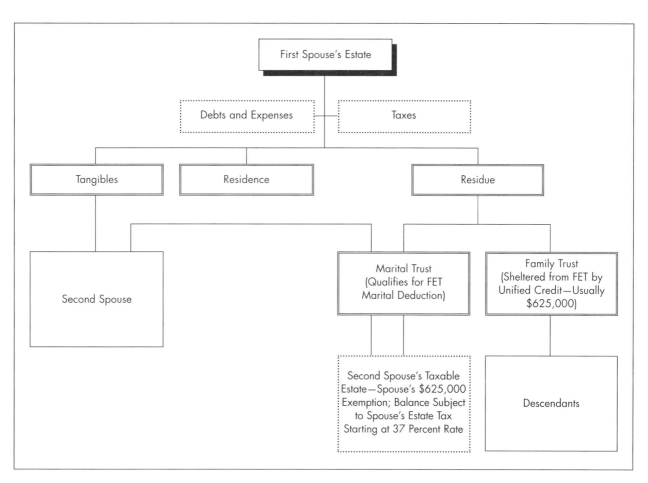

descendants and to shelter trusts that will eventually benefit grandchildren or more remote descendants. The estate plan thus can include trusts that will run for the benefit of children for life. These trusts then pass on to grandchildren or more remote descendants without payment of any gift, estate, or generation-skipping tax at the child's level. The purpose of the generation-skipping marital deduction plan is to secure all the benefits of the marital deduction plan described above. At the same time, it places the maximum amount possible into trusts that will avoid tax at the child's family level.

We outline operation of the basic generation-skipping marital deduction plan in Figure 38–3. The will (or trust) divides your tax estate into three shares. One, the credit-shelter amount ($625,000 in 1998, increasing to $1,000,000 in

2006), passes to a separate trust, called the family trust. It is exempt from generation-skipping tax. The marital share includes all property subject to federal estate taxation, except the credit-shelter amount. We divide the marital share itself into two portions. One portion, the exempt marital trust, receives the rest of the property that your GST exemption can shelter from generation-skipping tax. For 1998, assuming no inflation adjustment in the GST exemption, the exempt marital trust would receive $375,000 (the $1,000,000 GST exemption, minus the credit-shelter amount of $625,000). The other portion of the marital share may pass to your spouse outright or may continue in trust for your spouse's sole benefit. The trustee will distribute this trust on your spouse's death either as the spouse directs or as you have directed in the will or trust.

Upon the death of the surviving spouse, the trustee divides all the property then held in the family trust and the exempt marital trust into separate trusts for each of your children. Each such trust will continue until the child's death. Your spouse's estate plan also would create similar trusts for the children using the spouse's GST exemption ($1,000,000 adjusted for inflation after 1997). Upon a child's death, the remaining trust assets held for the child pass on to grandchildren or others at no additional tax cost, despite the value of the assets then.

This plan can employ the same kinds of alternatives as in the basic marital deduction plan discussed above. This plan allows parents to save taxes when property will pass from their children to their grandchildren. It does, however, increase the complexity and cost of the plan. It may be

Figure 38–3

Basic Generation-Skipping Marital Deduction Plan

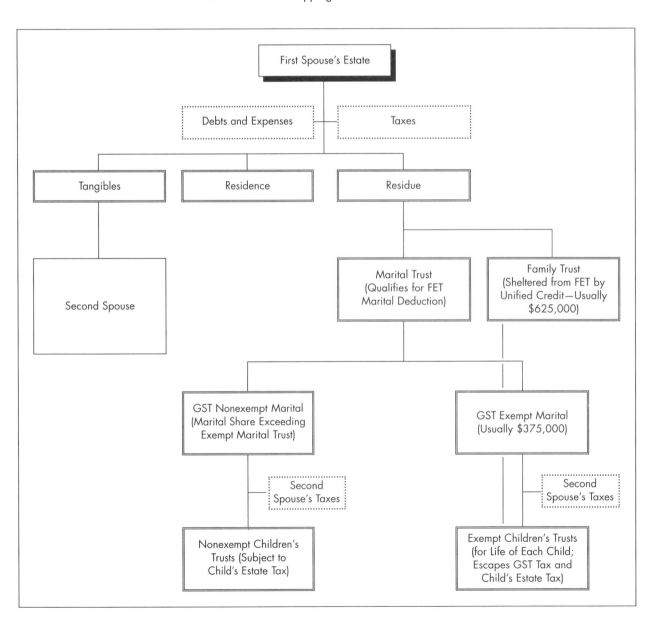

appropriate whenever the combined tax estates of husband and wife exceed the GST exemption amount ($1,000,000 adjusted for inflation after 1997).

Using Gifts to Reduce Estate Taxes

When the combined tax estates of husband and wife exceed twice the credit-shelter amount ($1,250,000 for 1998), the marital deduction plans described above will not alone eliminate the estate tax. You must then combine the marital deduction plan with other techniques to reduce or eliminate the estate tax. Such techniques usually include a program of lifetime gifts, estate "freezing" techniques, and life insurance transfers.

A lifetime gift program is the simplest way to reduce estate taxes when the marital deduction plan alone will not suffice. Before using a gift program, however, you must first be comfortable that your remaining assets will be sufficient for your own needs. Once you have reached that conclusion, you should fully use annual exclusion gifts each year. Husband and wife together can reduce their tax estates each year by $20,000 multiplied by the number of their beneficiaries. If we assume a 45 percent effective estate tax rate, a couple's maximum annual exclusion gifts produce an estate tax savings of $9,000 per beneficiary each year. (Again, note that the IRS will adjust the annual exclusion amount for inflation after 1997.)

You may make major lifetime gifts to use part or all of the unified credit. Of course, use of the unified credit during your lifetime reduces the amount that passes free of estate tax at your death. However, if you give away assets that are likely to increase in value, all those value increases after you make the gift escape gift and estate tax completely.

You probably can maximize the benefits of annual exclusion gifts and the unified credit by making gifts of discounted property. Under the valuation rules used by the IRS, a fractional interest in an asset is worth less than its proportionate share of the total value of the property. (For example, a 10 percent interest in real estate worth $100,000 is worth less than $10,000 because selling a fractional interest would be harder.) You could probably discount the value of gifts somewhat by first placing the property into

a limited partnership or S corporation and then making gifts of the limited partnership interests or the stock.

Congressional Restrictions on Estate "Freezing" Techniques

Since the mid–1970s, various types of estate "freezing" plans have been a popular means of reducing estate taxes. Under the typical plan, the parents would divide their interests in the family business (for example) into an income interest and a growth or equity interest. The parents would then give or sell the growth or equity interest to their children or other family members. The parents thus would retain the right to the income from the family business and all the future growth in the value of the family business would belong directly to the children. Thus, the value of the parents' interests for estate tax purposes would be "frozen" and the subsequent growth in value would escape estate tax. Both corporations and partnerships were used for this purpose.

The Revenue Reconciliation Act of 1990 added a new Code Chapter 14, consisting of Code Sections 2701 through 2704. These code provisions seek to limit abusive estate freeze transactions. The chapter 14 rules apply only to family-owned corporations and partnerships, to trusts, and to term interests in property. Term interests in property are rights in property that last for life or for a specified number of years. Only transactions after October 8, 1990, are subject to the chapter 14 rules. Generally, these new rules apply a gift tax to the full value of the property involved when an estate freeze type of transaction occurs. The new rules also largely eliminate the estate and gift tax benefits of grantor retained income trusts (GRITS), joint life estate/remainder purchases, and family buy-sell agreements. You should review any proposed transaction involving the matters discussed in this paragraph in advance with competent tax counsel.

Estate Freezing with Personal Residence Trusts

Some estate "freeze" opportunities are still available under chapter 14. One of these is the qualified personal residence trust (QPRT). In the typical QPRT arrangement, the creator of the QPRT (whom we call "parent") transfers his or her personal residence to a QPRT specifically designed and drafted for this purpose. The terms of the QPRT allow parent to retain an interest in the personal residence for a specified number of years. During this specified period, parent may use and occupy the personal residence. At the end of the specified period, the personal residence passes to the beneficiaries of the QPRT. Typically these are the parent's children. If parent dies before the end of the specified period, then the personal residence usually reverts to the parent's probate estate.

When the personal residence is first transferred to the QPRT, parent makes a gift to the other QPRT beneficiaries. This gift equals the fair-market value of the personal residence, minus the value of parent's interest. The value of parent's interest equals: (1) the actuarial value of parent's right to use and occupy the residence for the specified period; plus (2) the actuarial value of the possibility that full ownership of the residence might revert to parent's probate estate. We call this possibility a "contingent reversion." The gift tax cost to parent would be much greater if parent used a similar trust that did not meet the technical requirements of the QPRT. In such a case, parent would make a gift equal to the full fair market value of the property placed in the trust. There would be no reduction for the actuarial value of the parent's interest. Consider the results in the following examples:

1. Parent, age 60, creates a QPRT using one personal residence having a fair market value of $1,000,000. Parent retains the right to use and occupy the personal residence for ten years, after which time it will pass to child. If parent dies within ten years, the personal residence will revert to parent's probate estate. The value of parent's interest is determined using the valuation rate announced by the IRS for the month when parent creates the QPRT. Assuming this rate is 10 percent, the parent's interest is worth $685,730. Thus, the gift to the child upon creation of the QPRT is $314,270, computed as follows:

Fair-market value of the residence	$1,000,000
Minus the value of parent's interest	(685,730)
Equals the value of the remainder to child (taxable gift)	$314,270

2. Assume the same facts as Example 1 except the trust parent creates does not qualify as a QPRT. Here, there is no reduction for parent's interest. The gift to the child upon creation of the trust is $1,000,000, computed as follows:

Fair-market value of the residence	$1,000,000
Minus the value of parent's interest	(00)
Equals the value of the remainder to child (taxable gift)	$1,000,000

To obtain an estate tax advantage, parent must survive the specified term. Parent then will have successfully removed the full value of the personal residence from his or her tax estate. If, however, parent dies during the specified term, parent's tax estate will include the full value of the personal residence. However, parent's tax estate will, in effect, receive a credit for any gift tax paid or unified credit used in creating the QPRT. Except for the expense of creating and administering the QPRT and any lost income on any gift tax paid, parent's tax estate basically will be in the same tax position as if parent had never created the QPRT.

The QPRT does have serious disadvantages, which should be carefully considered. The most significant disadvantage is the requirement that parent must be willing to move out of the residence after the specified term. It may be possible for parent to rent the personal residence from the QPRT beneficiaries (parent's children) after the term has expired. However, this arrangement may not be acceptable to everyone. Parent may be able to repurchase the personal residence from the remainder beneficiaries *after* the parent's term interest expires. (Regulations issued by the IRS in 1997 concerning the QPRT require that the trust prohibit a sale of the residence back to parent during the term of the QPRT.) The remainder beneficiaries may generate capital gains on a sale and the additional tax must be considered before using this alternative.

Transferring a mortgaged personal residence to a QPRT presents several problems. These include questions about the gift tax value and the availability of the income tax interest deduction. Generally, you should not create a QPRT using mortgaged property.

Estate Freezing with Grantor Annuity Trusts

The grantor annuity trust (GRAT) is another estate-freeze device still available under chapter 14. It is similar in concept to the QPRT. In the typical GRAT arrangement, the creator of the GRAT (whom we call "parent") transfers income-producing or investment property to a GRAT specifically designed and drafted for this purpose. The terms of the GRAT direct the payment of a fixed annuity to parent for a specified number of years. At the end of the specified period, the remaining trust assets pass to the beneficiaries of the GRAT. Typically these are parent's children. If parent dies before the end of the specified period, part of the GRAT is taxable in parent's estate.

When the property is first transferred to the GRAT, parent is deemed to make a gift to the other GRAT beneficiaries. This gift equals the fair-market value of the property, minus the value of parent's interest. The value of parent's interest equals the actuarial value of parent's right to receive the annuity amount for the specified period. The gift tax cost to parent would be much greater if parent used a similar trust that did not meet the technical requirements of the GRAT. In such a case, parent would make a gift equal to the full fair-market value of the property placed in the trust. There would be no reduction for the actuarial value of parent's interest.

Irrevocable Insurance Trusts

Your tax estate includes life insurance on your life only if the insurance is payable to your probate estate or if you owned the policy at your death. Thus, you can avoid the estate tax on life insurance by having the policy owned by someone else. Usually, the best alternative is for the insurance to be owned by an irrevocable insurance trust, which you establish as part of your estate plan. The trust can use the proceeds of the insurance for the benefit of your family in the same manner as provided under your will or other estate planning documents. If your probate estate needs the insurance proceeds to meet its cash needs, the insurance trust can lend funds to the probate estate or purchase assets from the probate estate.

If you transfer policies you already own to an insurance trust, the IRS will still tax the policies in your estate if you die within three years of the transfer. However, if the insurance trust buys a new policy on your life, there is no such waiting period.

Estate Tax Planning for Retirement Benefits

For decedents dying on or after January 1, 1985, and subject to several transition rules, benefits payable from a decedent's qualified plan are subject to federal estate tax. The tax applies no matter how or to whom the plan pays the benefits. (Previously, we could exclude benefits up to $100,000 from the decedent's tax estate, under certain circumstances.) However, if the benefits are payable to or for the benefit of a surviving spouse, they may qualify for the marital deduction and escape the federal estate tax on that basis. If the decedent's gross estate, including the qualified plan benefits, is less than the credit-shelter amount ($625,000 in 1998, increasing to $1,000,000 in 2006), the entire estate will escape estate tax anyway.

Some Nontax Estate Planning Issues

Revocable Inter Vivos Trusts

Revocable lifetime trusts, also known as *living trusts*, have become a topic of interest, as well as the subject of several books, in the last few years. Such a trust, of course, is not a required component of any estate plan. Many individuals find, however, that a living trust provides significant advantages in the management and disposition of their assets during their lifetimes and at death. The following is a general description of living trusts and some basic factors to be considered when deciding whether to use these trusts in your estate plan.

During your lifetime, you may establish a living trust, to which you then transfer some portion or all of your assets. You may name yourself as trustee of the trust, or you may name one or more other individuals or a corporate entity, such as a bank, as trustee.

The trustee manages the property owned by the living trust under the terms of the trust document. These terms usually require that the trustee pay all the income to you for life. Commonly, the trust terms also allow the trustee to pay you as much of the principal of the living trust as you may direct or as the trustee may decide according to the standards contained in the living trust. The trust terms also may allow the trustee to distribute

265

trust income and principal to other persons, usually members of your family.

Since the living trust is revocable, you may amend or revoke it any time during your lifetime. If the living trust is still in effect upon your death, the trustee continues to hold and administer the trust property as directed under the terms of the trust document. These post- death provisions are the same as those you would normally include in your will. Your will becomes a relatively short and simple document. It often includes a few specific bequests and gives the residue of your probate estate to the trustee of your living trust.

A living trust can provide for the management of your property if you become disabled or incompetent. Suppose that you have placed most of your property in the living trust and later become incompetent. The trustee then has the power to manage the trust property for the benefit of you and your family under the terms of the trust document. This avoids the publicity, costs, and delays involved in guardianship proceedings before the probate court. However, a living trust is not necessary to avoid guardianship proceedings. A durable power of attorney, which is generally less expensive to prepare than a living trust, may also allow your agent to act for you without court intervention.

Generally, you will not incur any gift tax upon the transfer of your assets into your living trust. However, if the trustee then distributes assets from the living trust to another person, you may incur gift taxes depending upon the amount of the transfer and other circumstances. The gift tax consequences generally are the same as if you had made the gifts directly.

A living trust is a grantor trust for income tax purposes. This means that the IRS treats all trust income as if you received it directly and all trust expenses as if you paid them directly.

Assets transferred to the living trust during your lifetime are not subject to probate proceedings at your death. The trustee administers such assets according to the terms of the living trust without any supervision by the probate court. Generally, this simplifies the administration of the assets and may result in some reduction in lawyers' fees and executors' fees. However, in many states, some form of simplified or unsupervised probate proceeding is available to reduce the costs and delays of traditional probate without a living trust. Nonetheless, if you plan to move or retire to a state that has high probate costs, a living trust would normally result in a cost savings for you.

If you own real estate in a state other than the state of your legal residence, separate probate proceedings in that state are often required to transfer title to that property. This occurrence is termed "ancillary probate" and usually requires the executors of your probate estate to retain separate local counsel in each such state. Ancillary probate can significantly increase the costs and delays involved in administering a probate estate. However, if you place the real estate in your living trust during your lifetime, your estate can avoid ancillary probate.

Avoiding probate maintains greater privacy about your assets and the distribution of your estate. Upon your death, your executor will file your will with the court. It becomes a matter of public record, available for inspection by anyone. This makes all the details of your estate plan open to the public. If you use a living trust rather than a will as your primary estate plan document, your assets and the names of the beneficiaries receiving your assets need never become public. However, anyone who holds assets in the name of your living trust may require a copy of the trust. Often this causes the contents of your estate plan (or at least part of it) to become public before your death.

Because you can amend or revoke a living trust during your lifetime, the law will require inclusion of all assets of the living trust in your estate for estate tax purposes. Thus, using a living trust, by itself, produces no tax savings. However, all estate tax planning techniques used in wills (marital deduction gifts, QTIP trusts, and the like) are also available using the living trust.

The living trust offers some benefits that are not available in an estate plan based solely on a will. Its primary disadvantages arise in setting up and maintaining the trust before its real benefits begin to accrue. Your estate plan is more complicated because it involves two documents. You will realize the full benefits of a living trust only if you transfer most of your assets into the trust. Therefore, the living trust plan requires the additional effort and cost involved in actually transferring assets to the trust and preparing and filing income tax returns for the trust (if the grantor is not the trustee). Each situation must be examined carefully to decide whether the benefits of the living trust outweigh the costs involved.

Durable Power of Attorney

All states and the District of Columbia now have statutes that allow an individual to appoint another person (such as a spouse or child) to act as the individual's agent. Such an appointment continues in effect, even if the appointing individual later becomes incompetent and cannot act. The requirements for such a so-called durable power of attorney vary widely from state to state, however, and you must carefully observe local law. For example, Illinois permits its residents to designate any person as an agent. Florida, on the other hand, only recognizes durable powers of attorney given to certain family members. Some states also allow the use of the so-called springing power of attorney. It becomes effective some time after you sign it, rather than immediately upon your signature. The use of a durable power of attorney can often avoid the need to have the individual legally declared incompetent by court proceeding. It also can allow the family to manage the individual's property and pay bills for the individual's benefit. Many states also let an individual designate the person who should act as his or her guardian or conservator if the individual ever needs one. However, the appointment of the guardian or conservator by a court usually revokes the power of attorney. A court-appointed guardian or conservator has sole responsibility for managing the property after that.

Some states also let an individual sign a separate power of attorney for health care, or to include provisions concerning health care in the general durable power of attorney. Such a health-care power of attorney authorizes a specific family member or friend to make decisions regarding any health-care procedure. These decisions include the termination of life-support systems, performance of various kinds of surgery, anatomical gifts, and the disposition of the body. The powers granted may be very broad. This document can be very useful but must be considered carefully before being signed.

Living Will

Most states now have statutes authorizing residents to execute living wills. A living will is a document that instructs a person's physician to withhold or withdraw death-delaying procedures if the physician diagnoses that person as having a terminal condition. It must usually be witnessed or executed with the same formalities required of a regular will for disposing of property. The issues of stopping life-sustaining treatment and physician-assisted suicide have become matters of considerable public interest over the last decade. While a living will may not be the best solution to these concerns, any person with strong feelings or wishes on this subject should take steps to make those wishes known. This may involve using the living will or any other suitable approach that may be available under state law.

Anatomical Gifts and Funeral Instructions

Many individuals wish to donate body organs or provide for special arrangements concerning the funeral and burial. Such instructions may—but need not—be confirmed in a will. The individual should still make other provisions with family or friends to see that these arrangements are carried out. For example, one wishing to donate organs should properly complete and always carry a uniform donor card.

So Many Decisions, So Little Time— Setting Priorities in Tax and Estate Planning Issues for Seniors

As indicated by the scope of the issues discussed in this chapter, seniors today face many difficult decisions in planning for themselves and their families. Often, the solutions for various issues may not be compatible or consistent. The individuals must then choose the goals they will meet. To decide wisely, the issues themselves must be ranked in importance for the individuals involved, or you may sacrifice that which matters most for less-important goals. This section attempts to suggest an order of priorities that may help resolve these issues.

Many seniors would accept the following list of priorities:

1. Personal care for myself and my spouse
2. Financial support for myself and my spouse
3. Management of assets during my lifetime and my spouse's lifetime

4. Maximizing assets available for myself and my spouse (including income tax reduction)
5. Providing for my beneficiaries after my death as I desire
6. Maximizing the benefits available for each beneficiary, including reducing taxes and protecting beneficiaries from creditors and other predators.

Once you have established your own list of priorities, you must apply those priorities in resolving the issues and decisions raised in this chapter. If your priority list were similar to the one given above, you probably would resolve the issues raised in this chapter in the order suggested below.

Assuming your first concern or priority is providing for the personal care of yourself and your spouse, you probably would first need to resolve the following questions: Who will make decisions regarding my personal care and medical treatment if I become disabled? Should I sell my current home? If so, will I rent or purchase a new home?

Most people probably will place as a second priority providing adequate financial support for themselves and their dependents. In doing so, they must consider the following issues: How much do I need for my support? How much do I need for the support of my spouse or other dependents? Do I need to receive my retirement benefits in a lump sum to provide for our support? If so, should I use special averaging for tax treatment? On the other hand, should I receive my retirement benefits in an annuity? If so, should I use an annuity for my lifetime, an annuity for the joint lives of myself and my spouse, or an annuity for our lives with a guaranteed number of payments? If I do not need these retirement funds immediately, should I roll over my retirement benefits into an IRA? When should I start withdrawing funds and how much should I withdraw each year? How will I provide for medical care for myself and my spouse? What private insurance is available? Should I invest in nursing home insurance? Can I afford to start giving away some of my assets now to reduce estate tax or to enjoy providing for my descendants during my lifetime?

Providing for the management of your assets during your lifetime and your spouse's lifetime may be your next priority. If so, you will next need to consider the following issues: How should my property be managed if I become disabled? How much control should my spouse or other family members have over my assets during my lifetime?

Maximizing the value of the assets available for yourself and your spouse may be your next priority. Often this will involve income tax reduction. This goal raises the following issues: How can I reduce taxable income and increase the amount of deductible medical expenses and some other itemized deductions and thus reduce the total amount of income tax? What would be the best tax treatment for receiving my retirement benefits? How does this coincide with the economically best type of benefit for myself and my spouse? How would I treat any gain on the sale of my current residence for tax purposes?

The next priority is typically the focus of estate planning work: providing for your beneficiaries after your death as you desire. This concern focuses on the following questions: How do I want to divide my property at my death? Are there family members or others with special needs for whom I want to make special provision?

After deciding how you want to divide your property after your death, you may want to consider maximizing the benefits available for each beneficiary. This will first involve reducing transfer taxes, so you will want to consider these issues: Should I start giving away some of my assets now? Should the property I leave to my beneficiaries pass to them outright or in trust? Should my spouse and I rearrange the way we hold our assets so that each of us will have the credit-shelter amount ($625,000 in 1998, increasing to $1,000,000 in 2006) to pass tax-free at our respective deaths? Another way to maximize the economic benefit given to beneficiaries is to protect them from creditors and other possible predators. Thus, you may want to consider further: How much control should my spouse have after my death over the property I am leaving to him or her? Should the property I leave to my beneficiaries pass to them outright or in trust?

Summary

Many tools are available to seniors today in completing the complex and important task of estate planning. You can pass property to your beneficiaries using a variety of methods. The selection and coordination of the appropriate methods are crucial aspects of the estate plan. Maximizing the benefits that will eventually pass to your beneficiaries involves thoughtful consideration of the income, gift, estate, and generation-skipping tax consequences of the estate plan. Basic marital deduction planning, generation-skipping planning, and various kinds of trusts can be most useful in reducing the tax burden for beneficiaries. Of course, the tax considerations are not the most important. You should first be comfortable that you and those dependent upon you are adequately cared for. Within that framework, you can then plan to increase the economic value of the benefits you are leaving to your beneficiaries. With this task complete, you can then live with the assurance that you have done all you can to help your family in facing the burdens of death and taxes.

39
Using South Dakota Law for Perpetual Trusts

THOMAS H. FOYE

Perpetual trusts are inter vivos or testamentary trusts that hold significant assets and last for at least the period of the rule against perpetuities of the governing state law or, if there is no such rule, forever. Clients often use perpetual trusts for their $1 million exemption from the federal generation-skipping transfer tax (GSTT). This article first describes the tax and nontax characteristics of perpetual trusts. The article then focuses on perpetual trusts under South Dakota law, which is well-suited to the establishment and maintenance of perpetual trusts because the state has no rule against perpetuities or state income tax.

What Is a Perpetual Trust?

The primary purpose of a perpetual trust is to create a large fund that will be available for future generations of the trustor's family. Although only the drafting lawyer's imagination limits the substantive terms of the trust, a perpetual trust typically gives its trustees complete discretion about whether, when, and how much income or principal, or both, to distribute to the beneficiaries. The beneficiaries often are the descendants of the trustor as a class. The trustor usually does not reserve any interest or power over the trust. Some trustors, however, reserve a limited power to remove trustees, although trustors more often vest removal and replacement powers in an advisory committee or a trust protector. The protector or committee members typically are individuals unrelated to the trustor and may have broader powers, including the addition or deletion of beneficiaries and amendment of the trust.

Wealthy clients often give $1 million during their lifetimes to a perpetual trust to obtain the maximum advantage of their GSTT exemptions. Many lawyers also advise married couples to use perpetual trusts to provide for the continuation of a credit shelter trust after the death of the surviving spouse. The couples' children will be discretionary income and principal beneficiaries during their lifetimes. The trust will typically give the children nongeneral testamentary powers of appointment over their shares of the trust principal. The trust instrument may also give the children a "five and five" power of withdrawal. If the trustee makes a distribution to a child, or the child exercises a right of withdrawal, a waste of the trustors' GSTT exemption allocated to the trust will result. The remaining assets of the trust not appointed or distributed will be held in discretionary trusts for successive generations of the deceased parents' descendants and will provide efficient leverage of the GSTT exemption.

Why Use a Perpetual Trust?

The federal and many state transfer tax systems attempt to impose a transfer tax on assets as they pass from one generation to the next. A person can eliminate transfer taxes at each generation yet still make assets available to family members in a succeeding generation by creating a trust for his or her family over which the younger generations have little control but from which they receive economic benefits. Thus, the longer the trust, the greater the theoretical benefits.

Distributions from a perpetual trust to the trustors' grandchildren and more remote descendants may trigger the GSTT. Code Section 2631, however, allows each person an exemption from the GSTT of $1 million; this amount will be

Thomas H. Foye is a partner with Bangs, McCullen, Butler, Foye & Simmons, LLP, in Rapid City, South Dakota.

indexed for inflation starting in 1999. If a person places his or her GSTT exemption amount in a perpetual trust and allocates GSTT exemption to the trust, he or she will incur gift tax to the extent that the gift exceeds the available unified credit exemption equivalent, which currently is $25,000. If, however, the person limits the gift to the perpetual trust to the amount of his or her available unified credit exemption equivalent and allocates that much GSTT exemption to the trust, the person could avoid a gift tax on the creation of the trust.

The significance of perpetual trusts is highlighted by the fact that if there is a gift tax on the transfer to the trust, that will be the last transfer tax ever paid on the assets of a properly structured trust. If there is no gift tax because the trustor gave only his or her unified credit exemption equivalent, a transfer tax will never be paid on the assets of the trust.

The impact of these facts in dollars is graphically demonstrated when one considers that $1 million invested for eighty-five years at a 5 percent current yield, appreciating at a rate of 7 percent per year and sold and reinvested at a rate of 20 percent per year, will produce a value of $1.9 billion at the end of the eighty-five-year period, assuming no distributions of income and principal and no payment of transfer taxes. The reason for the large principal amount at the end of eighty-five years is that the trust assets have not been subjected to transfer taxes for three generations. It may be possible for the trust to grow even larger if the trustee invests in life insurance or minority positions in family entities at a discounted value or engages in deferred payment purchases of family assets.

Given the attractiveness of the perpetual trust and the fact that trusts are mobile, lawyers and their clients should consider in which state to establish a perpetual trust. Alaska, Delaware, Idaho, Illinois, South Dakota and Wisconsin have no rule against perpetuities. In addition, Alaska and South Dakota have no state fiduciary income tax, making those states even more favorable for a perpetual trust under certain circumstances. Recent changes in the laws of many states and the current proliferation of new state laws (for example, in Alaska and Delaware) have generated increased interest in perpetual trusts. The laws of some states are more favorable to perpetual trusts than others. No one state law is best, however, and laws that are favorable today may not be the best choice tomorrow because of legislative activity in other states. The law of one state may be the best choice to accomplish one purpose of the trust, such as asset protection from creditors, while the law of another state may be best to accomplish a different purpose, such as creation of a private trust company.

Why South Dakota?

Perhaps most important, the South Dakota legislature and state administrative officers have attempted to create a very favorable business climate that encourages the use of perpetual trusts. For example, South Dakota abrogated the common law rule against perpetuities in 1983. SDCL 43-5-8 ("the common law rule against perpetuities is not in force in this state"). Thus, trusts, the validity of which is governed by South Dakota law, literally can last forever; there is never any need to vest interests in or make any distributions to anyone. As a result, transfer taxes need never be incurred on the trust assets following the initial transfer to the trust.

Another attraction is that there is not and never has been any individual or trust state income tax in South Dakota to erode the trust principal. In the earlier example, an eighty-five-year trust could accumulate up to $1.9 billion from a $1 million initial contribution. If a New York resident created an identical trust at the same time under New York law and based on the same assumptions, the New York trust would accumulate only to $488 million. See Pierce H. McDowell III, *The Dynasty Trust: Protective Armor for Generations to Come*, Tr. & Est. 47-54 (Oct. 1993). As discussed below, however, lawyers and their clients should note that, even though South Dakota does not have an income tax, the state of the trustor's domicile may tax the undistributed income and gains of a South Dakota perpetual trust.

Creating Situs in a Favorable State

Lawyers have considerable freedom to choose the law of the state that will govern the validity, construction and administration of the trust. In *Wilmington Trust Co. v. Wilmington Trust Co.*, 24 A.2d 309, 313 (Del. 1942), the Delaware Supreme Court noted that

Contracting parties, within definite limits, have some right of choice in the selection of the jurisdiction under whose law their contract is to be governed. . . . [T]here seems to be no good reason why [a trustor's] intent should not be respected by the courts, if the selected jurisdiction has a material connection with the transaction.

The Restatement (Second) of Conflicts of Laws Section 268-270 (1971) expresses the same philosophy that a court will uphold a trustor's selection of the law governing a trust if, under the law of the state selected, the trust would be valid, even though the law of the trustor's domicile would not recognize the trust as valid.

South Dakota's version of the Uniform Probate Code (SDCL 29A-2-703) provides that the local law of the state selected by the transferor in the governing instrument controls its meaning and legal effect, unless the application of that law is contrary to South Dakota public policy. Therefore, the South Dakota legislature has expressly recognized the freedom of a trustor to choose applicable law in the governing instrument.

But lawyers should be aware of decisions such as *Rudow v. Fogel*, 426 N.E.2d 155 (Mass. Ct. App. 1981), in which the court held that the trust instrument's choice of governing law was only one criterion for determining what law governs the trust. In *Allstate Insurance Co. v. Hague*, 449 U.S. 302 (1981), the Supreme Court indicated that constitutional due process and full-faith and credit principles would prevent enforcement of a provision choosing a foreign state's law if the only contact with that state was simply its designation as the governing law. Accordingly, although it is clear that there must be something more than the expression of the trustor's intention in making a binding choice of law, the necessary number and quality of the trust's contacts with the chosen state is a question of fact. Accordingly, the more contacts the trust's constituent parts—its trustees, beneficiaries, and assets—have with South Dakota, the stronger the case will be that the trust is in fact a South Dakota trust.

At a minimum, in addition to the selection of law and situs provisions in the trust instrument, the client establishing the trust and his or her lawyer should take the following steps to ensure that South Dakota law in fact applies to the trust:

- At least one trustee should be a resident of South Dakota. This requirement could be satisfied by the appointment of a South Dakota "administrative trustee" to act in conjunction with non-South Dakota resident individuals or trust companies. An administrative trustee's duties would typically be limited to holding physical evidence of the trust assets, filing federal income tax returns, preparing accountings, holding legal title to trust assets, and conducting trustee meetings. The other trustees, who would not be residents of South Dakota, would possess powers over discretionary distributions and trust investments.
- Evidence of the trust assets, such as stock certificates, should be physically present in South Dakota.
- As much administrative activity of the trust as possible should take place in South Dakota, including the preparation of trust accountings, trustee meetings, and the preparation and filing of federal income tax returns for the trust.
- The trust instrument should contain a forum selection provision requiring that any disputes arising under the instrument be submitted to a South Dakota court.
- If arbitration is a desirable means of resolving disputes, the trust instrument should specify that the South Dakota arbitration statute applies and that the arbitration take place in South Dakota.

Changing Situs to South Dakota

If a client already has an irrevocable trust in place, it may be possible to change the law governing its validity and its administrative situs to South Dakota. If the governing instrument limits the present term of the trust to the period of the rule against perpetuities of the jurisdiction in which it was created, moving the trust's situs of administration to South Dakota will not overcome that limitation. In that case, the only advantage of moving the trust is the *possibility* of escaping the state income tax of the state under which it was formed, which depends largely on how that state defines a "resident trust" for income tax purposes. If, however, the trust instrument does not expressly limit the term of the trust by the rule against perpetuities, switching the situs to South Dakota may allow for an unlimited term under South Dakota law, provided that an effective change of the law governing the validity of the trust occurs.

One method of changing the situs of a trust from one state to another is by an agreement among the trustor (if living), the present trustees and all beneficiaries to transfer the situs. Alternatively, one or more of the present trustees could resign and the beneficiaries could then appoint a South Dakota resident as successor trustee, if the trust instrument permits. The trustees would then physically transfer the evidence of the trust assets to South Dakota, where they should remain. The trustees or the beneficiaries could also petition a court of the original state to order the change of situs. The method the parties use will depend on the terms of the trust instrument and local law.

Although South Dakota has no fiduciary income tax, changing the situs of administration of a trust to South Dakota will not necessarily result in the elimination of state fiduciary income tax. If, following the move to South Dakota, the trust remains a resident of another state for income tax purposes, the trust will continue to be subject to that state's fiduciary income tax. For instance, under the laws of some states, a trust is a resident trust, and therefore subject to tax on all its undistributed income and gains, if the trustor was domiciled in the state when the trust became irrevocable. See Minn. Stat. Section 290.01, subd. 7b; N.J. Rev. Stat. Section 54A: 1-2(m)(3). Moving such a trust to South Dakota will not eliminate the first state's tax on the trust.

In contrast, some states base trust residency for tax purposes on the administration of the trust in the state or the trustee's residency in the state. See Or. Rev. Stat. Section 128.135; Hawaii Rev. Stat. Section 235-1. If a trust is moved from one of these states to South Dakota, and no trustees reside in the former state, the trust will probably no longer be subject to state fiduciary income tax, except if the beneficiaries reside in a state that bases a trust's residency for income tax purposes on the beneficiaries' residency in that state. See Ariz. Rev. Stat. Section 43-313; Cal. Rev. & Tax. Code Section 17742(a).

Lawyers and their clients should be sensitive to these state fiduciary income tax residency issues when moving a trust to South Dakota. The law in this area is evolving and has significant constitutional overtones. For example, if the trust is being moved from a state that taxes a trust based on the trustor's domicile, but the trust's constituent parts otherwise have no connections to that state, the lack of nexus to the state may make taxation of the trust unconstitutional under the due process clause of the 14th amendment. See *Swift v. Dept. of Revenue*, 727 S.W.2d 880 (Mo. 1987). But see *District of Columbia v. Chase Manhattan Bank*, 689 A.2d 539 (D.C. Ct. App. 1997). For a discussion of these issues, including an analysis of recent case law, see M. Read Moore and Amy Silliman, *State Income Taxation of Trusts: New Case Creates Uncertainty*, Estate Planning, June 1997, at 200–209.

In light of this issue, a lawyer might consider giving notice of a court petition to change situs to the taxing authorities of the original state. The decision about whether to do this would depend on an analysis of the state tax statutes, the trust provisions, the activity in administering the trust and the domicile of the trustor, the beneficiaries and the trustees. If the analysis of those factors convinces the lawyer that a strong case can be made for avoiding the state income tax in the state of origin, an effort should be made to obtain a court order to that effect over the objection (if any) of the state revenue department. If a court order is not necessary to move the situs, the trustee should simply file a final return in the state of origin.

A further issue that lawyers and their clients should consider is whether changing the applicable perpetuities period of a trust by moving it to South Dakota will jeopardize the trust's exemption from the GSTT. If the perpetuities period that applies to a trust grandfathered from the GSTT is changed, thereby extending the trust term, the change is likely to cause a grandfathered trust to lose its GSTT-exempt status. See PLRs 9448024, 9244019 (trusts exempt from GSTT will lose exempt status following a change in quality, value or timing of beneficial interests in the trust). If, however, the trust is exempt from the GSTT by reason of an allocation of GSTT exemption, changing the perpetuities period does not appear to change the exempt status of the trust under current law.

South Dakota Inheritance Tax Considerations

No nonresident of South Dakota would be interested in establishing a trust in South Dakota if doing so might subject the trust assets to South Dakota inheritance tax. Although a detailed analysis of the South Dakota inheritance tax is beyond the scope of this article, nonresidents of South Dakota should be sensitive to the following possible bases for imposition of the South Dakota inheritance tax on a perpetual trust established under South Dakota law:

- Transfer by a nonresident of property physically located in South Dakota. SDCL 10-40-2.
- Transfer of intangible property with a connection to South Dakota intended to take effect in possession or enjoyment at or after the death of the transferor. SDCL 10-40-2.
- Transfer of intangible property with a connection to South Dakota made within one year of death, creating a *rebuttable* presumption that the transfer was made in contemplation of death and is therefore taxable (if it is more than $10,000). SDCL 10-40-1(1).

SDCL 10-40-4 and 10-40-5 erase the concerns of the latter two provisions by providing that transfers of *intangibles* by nonresidents are not subject to the South Dakota inheritance tax if the transferor is a resident of a state or territory of the United States that at the time of the transfer did not impose a transfer tax in respect of intangibles owned by residents of South Dakota. Almost all states have reciprocal exemption statutes or simply exempt a nonresident's intangible property from state death taxes. Accordingly, South Dakota is unlikely to tax transfers by a nonresident of intangible property with a connection to South Dakota, transfers of such property by a nonresident intended to take effect at death and transfers of such property made within one year of death.

Even if the reciprocity statutes do not apply to nonresidents of South Dakota, the only real exposure to the South Dakota inheritance tax is for transfers to a perpetual trust made within one year of the trustor's death. Nevertheless, even the presumptive contemplation of death intent ascribed by that statute is rebuttable on a proper factual showing. If the presumption is rebutted, then the tax should not apply because the transfer to the trust was complete at the time it was made.

A perpetual trust created inter vivos by a South Dakota resident may be subject to the South Dakota inheritance tax even if created more than one year before death. The argument in favor of taxation is that the transfer was intended to take effect in possession at or after death. See *Estate of Crowell*, 128 Cal. Rptr. 613 (Cal. 1976). As shown by the authorities collected at Annotation, *Succession Tax—Postponed Enjoyment*, 6 ALR 2d 223, Sections 11, 12 (1949), this rule seems to be in accordance with the weight of authority. Nevertheless, there is respectable and better reasoned authority to the contrary that all beneficial and legal interests in the trust property pass from the trustor at the time of the creation of the trust, even though the time of distribution is deferred until after the trustor's death. See *Re: Heine's Estate*, 100 N.E.2d 545 (Ohio 1950). Obviously, transfers to a perpetual trust created in a testamentary instrument on the death of the trustor (a South Dakota resident) would be taxed as a transfer at death.

What Is South Dakota Law?

It is easy for lawyers and clients interested in a South Dakota perpetual trust to focus on the state's lack of a rule against perpetuities and an income tax. Several other statutes, however, may affect a South Dakota perpetual trust. The following lists significant South Dakota statutory provisions that affect the administration of a South Dakota perpetual trust.

- SDCL 43-5-1 prohibits suspension of the power of alienation for longer than the lives of persons in being plus thirty years. As long as a trustee has the power to sell assets, a perpetual trust will not violate this rule. SDCL 43-5-4. The existence of the power of sale does not, of course, mean that the trustee must distribute the proceeds of the sale. Rather, the trustee has the freedom to reinvest the proceeds in trust.
- Real estate is not a desirable investment for a South Dakota perpetual trust. If a perpetual trust owns real estate, SDCL 43-6-4 provides that the trustee may not accumulate the income from the real estate for longer than the period of minority of a minor beneficiary. Accumulations in violation of this rule, however, are void only as to the time beyond the minority of the beneficiary.
- South Dakota has adopted the Revised Uniform Principal and Income Act. SDCL 55-13. In a significant departure, South Dakota's version

provides that the increment in value of obligations for the payment of money, such as zero coupon bonds, constitutes income only when distributed by the obligor in cash.

- South Dakota has adopted the Prudent Investor Rule. SDCL 55-5-7 through 55-5-16. Lawyers and their clients should note that SDCL 55-5-16 permits a trustee to prudently delegate responsibilities to others, making it easy for trustees to delegate investment responsibilities to investment experts.

- Under South Dakota's version of the revised Uniform Limited Partnership Act (SDCL 48-7-603), a limited partner has no right to withdraw from a limited partnership except as otherwise specified in the partnership agreement. Although this statute does not apply to partnerships in existence on June 30, 1996, the lack of a statutory right of withdrawal from a limited partnership is relevant to establishing the value of South Dakota limited partnership interests that a perpetual trust might acquire.

- South Dakota has adopted the Uniform Trust Act. SDCL 55-4. The Act prohibits self-dealing between (among others) a trustee and a relative, employer, partner or other business associate in the absence of express authorization in the trust instrument. SDCL 55-4-13 allows a trustor to relieve a trustee from all duties, restrictions, and liabilities otherwise applicable, except these self-dealing provisions. Therefore, lawyers and clients should specifically anticipate transactions between a trustee and related parties, particularly those that are intended to initially fund the trust, and specifically permit them in the trust instrument.

- As part of the Uniform Trust Act, SDCL 55-4-37 provides that a trustee may be a general partner in a limited partnership and the trustee's liability as such is limited to the assets of the trust.

- South Dakota codifies the concept of a trust protector in its "directed trust" statute. SDCL 55-1B. Among other things, the trust instrument may give the trust protector the power to amend a trust agreement to achieve favorable tax status or to address changes in the tax statutes, rulings, or regulations. The trust instrument may also give a trust protector the power to increase or decrease the interests of beneficiaries and to modify the terms of any power of appointment granted by the trust. The statute also allows a trust instrument to give investment duties to trust advisors and permits the trust instrument to absolve such advisors from liability.

- SDCL 51A-6A permits formation of private trust companies in South Dakota. Thus, interested clients may form their own trust company to act as the resident trustee of a perpetual trust in South Dakota. There is a $200,000 capital requirement and a $25,000 application fee, but the administrative officers administering this statute have been quite liberal in the application and fulfillment of the requirements.

Conclusion

Perpetual trusts serve a vital function in the reduction and elimination of transfer taxes for clients with large estates and an interest in making some part of those estates available to their descendants without giving those descendants unfettered control of the client's assets. South Dakota is one of several states that facilitates the use of perpetual trusts and provides the possibility of avoiding state fiduciary income tax. Whether South Dakota is the best state in which to create a perpetual trust depends on a number of factors, which lawyers and clients must carefully consider before making a decision.

40
Heavyweight Competition in New Trust Laws

DOUGLAS J. BLATTMACHR AND RICHARD W. HOMPESCH II

Two states recently enacted laws that permit the creation of asset protection trusts in the United States. The Alaska Trust Act, which Governor Knowles signed into law on April 1, 1997, permits residents of any state to create self-settled spendthrift trusts in Alaska. Delaware quickly followed suit when Governor Carter signed amendments to Delaware's trust law on July 9, 1997. The authors of Delaware's legislation admitted that it was similar to the Alaska legislation and hoped that the law would allow Delaware to compete with Alaska as the most favorable domestic jurisdiction for the establishment of trusts.

This chapter compares Alaska's and Delaware's trust laws as they affect asset protection and examines the merits of each. Alaska's concurrent repeal of its rule against perpetuities is not discussed in this article. Delaware effectively repealed its rule earlier. The repeal of the rules in Alaska and Delaware provide significant transfer-tax savings opportunities, which are discussed in Thomas H. Foye's chapter on South Dakota perpetual trusts in Chapter 39.

The Alaska Trust Act

The most significant change made by the Alaska Trust Act is its repeal of Alaska's version of the rule in the 1571 Statute of Elizabeth, which provided that transfers to a trust for the benefit of the trustor were void as to the trustor's creditors, regardless of whether those claims arose before or after the creation of the trust. Every state had adopted a version of this rule. Although many offshore jurisdictions (most notably the Cook

Douglas J. Blattmachr is president and CEO of Alaska Trust Company in Anchorage, Alaska. Richard W. Hompesch II is the sole principal of Hompesch & Associates P.C. in Fairbanks, Alaska.

Islands) had repealed the rule, arguably Alaska was the first state to do so by statute.

Alaska law now provides that if a person transfers property to a trust for his or her own benefit with a restriction that provides that

> the interest of a beneficiary of the trust may not be either voluntarily or involuntarily transferred before payment or delivery of the interest to the beneficiary by the trustee . . . [the restriction] prevents a creditor existing when the trust is created, a person who subsequently becomes a creditor, or another person from satisfying a claim out of the beneficiary's interest in the trust.

Alaska Stat. (AS) Section 34.40.110(a)-(b).

A court will enforce the spend-thrift provisions in a self-settled Alaska trust if four conditions are met:

1. The transfer to the trust is not fraudulent under AS Section 34.40.010.
2. The trustor cannot revoke or terminate the trust without the consent of an adverse party, which the law defines as a person who has a substantial interest in the trust who would be adversely affected by the exercise of the power. The trustor, however, may retain the power to veto a distribution from the trust, a testamentary nongeneral power of appointment or similar power, and the right to receive distributions of income, principal or both in the discretion of a person, including a trustee, other than the trustor. Nevertheless, the trustor's retention of a power to veto a distribution from the trust or a nongeneral power of appointment over trust assets will prevent any transfer to the trust from being a completed gift and it will also result in the inclusion of the trust assets in the trustor's gross estate for federal estate tax purposes. Code Section 2038.

3. The terms of the trust cannot require that all or a part of the trust's income or principal, or both, must be distributed to the trustor.

4. At the time of the transfer, the trustor cannot be in default by thirty or more days in making a payment due under a child support judgment or order. AS Section 34.40.110(b).

The Alaska Trust Act imposes strict rules on what a trust must include to make it Alaskan. The trust must provide that the laws of Alaska govern the trust. The following four additional tests apply:

1. The trustor must deposit some or all of the trust assets in Alaska.

2. The Alaska assets must be administered by a trust company with its principal place of business in Alaska, a bank with trust powers with its principal place of business in Alaska, or an individual domiciled in Alaska.

3. The Alaska trustee's powers must include "maintaining records for the trust on an exclusive or a nonexclusive basis" and "preparing or arranging for the preparation of, on an exclusive or a nonexclusive basis, an income tax return that must be filed by the trust."

4. Part or all of the administration of the trust must occur in Alaska, including the physical maintenance of the trust records in Alaska. AS Section 13.36.035(c).

The apparent purpose of these four conditions is to bring trust business to Alaska.

The Alaska Trust Act restricts challenges to Alaska trusts under certain circumstances. Except as provided in AS Section 34.40.110, discussed above, a creditor of the trustor cannot challenge or set aside an Alaska trust on the grounds "that the trust or transfer avoids or defeats a right, claim, or interest conferred by law on any person by reason of a personal or business relationship with the settlor or by way of a marital or similar right." AS Section 13.36.310.

Alaska law also limits the time in which a creditor may bring a claim to set aside a transfer to an Alaska trust. A creditor with a claim at the time of trust creation must bring that claim within four years after the trustor transfers property to the trust or one year after the creditor discovered or reasonably could have discovered the transfer. A creditor who becomes a creditor after a trustor makes a transfer must bring its claim within four years after the transfer. AS Section 34.40.110(d).

The Delaware Trust Act

Outside of some definitional differences, most of the essential provisions of Delaware's new trust law are identical, or nearly identical, to those of the Alaska Trust Act. A Delaware trust may provide:

> that the interest of a beneficiary in the trust property or the income therefrom may not be transferred or assigned, whether voluntarily or involuntarily, before the trustor distributes the property or income to the beneficiary.

Del. Code Ann. (DCA) 12 Section 3570(9)(c).

Delaware law requires that "some or all" of the trust property be in Delaware, that the trustee maintain records for the trust in Delaware, that the Delaware trustee prepare or arrange for the preparation of tax returns, and that the trustee "otherwise materially participate in the administration of the trust." DCA 12 Section 3570(8). The trust instrument must also contain a governing law provision incorporating Delaware law. See DCA 12 Section 3570(9)(a).

Delaware law incorporates the same statute of limitations as Alaska: existing creditors must bring their claims to set aside the trust within four years after the transfer to the trust or one year after the creditor discovered or reasonably could have discovered the claim. If the claim arose after the transfer to trust, the creditor must bring the claim within four years. DCA 12 Section 3572(b).

Although a Delaware trust must be irrevocable, the trustor may, as with an Alaska trust, retain the power to veto a distribution, a testamentary nongeneral power of appointment or similar power, or the right to receive a distribution. DCA 12 Section 3572(b). See AS Section 34.40.110(b)(2). As noted above, however, the retention of such a power will result in the inclusion of the trust assets in the trustor's gross estate for federal estate tax purposes under Code Section 2038.

One noteworthy difference is Delaware's less restrictive trustee requirement. For purposes of Delaware law:

> "Trustee" means a person who . . . in the case of a natural person, is a resident of this State or, in all other cases, is authorized by the law of this State to act as a trustee and whose activities are subject to supervision by the Bank Commissioner of the State, the Federal Deposit Insurance Corporation, the

Comptroller of the Currency, or the Office of Thrift Supervision or an successor thereto.

DCA 12 Section 3570(8).

By contrast, an individual trustee of an Alaska trust must be domiciled and not merely reside in Alaska, and a corporate trustee's principal place of business must be in Alaska. Both Alaska and Delaware allow other cotrustees to serve who have no connection with either state.

Delaware improved on Alaska's statutory scheme in two ways. First, Delaware law requires that the trustee be "neither the transferor nor a related or subordinate party of the transferor within the meaning of [Code] Section 672(c)." DCA 12 Section 3570(8). Although Alaska law does not specifically require an independent trustee who is unrelated and not subordinate to the trustor, lawyers drafting an Alaska trust probably should ensure that the trustee is in fact independent and is not related to or subordinate to the trustor. Otherwise a creditor may be able to successfully argue that the trustee was the trustor's alter ego so that the trustor effectively retained sufficient powers over the trust to make it revocable.

Second, Delaware law gives a trustor special rights when a creditor successfully sets aside a transfer to a Delaware trust. Alaska and Delaware both provide that a transfer to a trust will be avoided only to the extent necessary to satisfy the trustor's debt to the creditor who set aside the trust. DCA 12 Section 3574(a); AS Section 34.40.110(c). Delaware, however, goes further than Alaska and provides that:

> If the court is satisfied that the trustee has not acted in bad faith in accepting or administering the property that is subject to the qualified disposition,
> a. the trustee shall have a first and paramount lien against the property that is subject of the qualified disposition in an amount equal to the entire cost, including attorneys' fees, properly incurred by the trustee in the defense of the action or proceedings to avoid the qualified disposition; and
> b. the qualified disposition shall be avoided subject to the proper fees, costs, preexisting rights, claims and interests of the trustee (and of any predecessor trustee that has not acted in bad faith); and
> c. for purposes of this subparagraph (1), it shall be presumed that the trustee did not act in bad faith merely by accepting such property.

DCA 12 Section 3574(b)(1). This provision will be of considerable relief to a trustor who faces a claim by a disgruntled creditor.

Delaware Creditor Rights

Delaware made additional changes to Alaska's statutory scheme. It added DCA 12 Section 3573, which is unlike any provision in the Alaska law. This provision creates a class of "preferred" creditors, including the trustor's spouses and children, anyone making loans to the trustor, and other persons who have claims against the trustor for death, personal injury, or property damage based on acts that occur before the trustor transfers assets to the trust. Delaware law allows these preferred creditors to invade a Delaware trust to satisfy their claims. In addition, it appears that Delaware's four-year statute of limitations does not apply to this preferred class of creditors. See DCA 12 Section 3573. The protection afforded this preferred class of creditors effectively dilutes the creditor protection that otherwise would have been available under Delaware law and limits what could have been effective asset protection and estate planning legislation. The following discussion explores each of the three subparts of Section 3573.

Alimony, Child Support, and Marital Property

Under Delaware law a spouse with a claim for alimony, child support, or the division of marital property is a preferred creditor who may invade a Delaware self-settled spendthrift trust. The spendthrift protection of a Delaware trust

> shall not apply in any respect . . . to any person to whom the transferor is indebted on account of an agreement or order of court for the payment of support or alimony in favor of such transferor's spouse, former spouse, or children, or for a division of distribution of property in favor of such transferor's spouse or former spouse, to the extent of such debt.

DCA 12 Section 3573(a).

At first reading the legislature appears to have directed this provision at preventing a married trustor from defrauding his or her current spouse by transferring assets to a Delaware trust. But the statute does not limit the preference to current spouses; it also protects claims of unknown future spouses. DCA 12 Section 3570(1).

The application of this provision can be illustrated by the following example. W is single and has no children and no debts. She inherits $5 million and transfers $600,000 to a self-settled trust for her benefit, the benefit of her sister, and for the benefit of her unborn descendants. Five years later W meets and marries H. W and H have one child, C. H talks W into investing into a series of unprofitable businesses. W loses all of her wealth that is not in her trust. After ten years of marriage W divorces H. At that time the trust has assets with a fair-market value of $1 million. The court awards H custody of C and orders W to pay alimony of $1,000 per month, child support of $500 per month, and $100,000 for division of marital property.

Delaware law seems to allow a spouse with a claim for alimony, child support, or for division of marital property that arises many years after the creation of the trust to invade a Delaware trust. It is irrelevant under Delaware law whether the trustor's prior transfers to the trust were fraudulent. Under the facts in the example, H can invade W's Delaware trust to satisfy his claim for alimony, child support, and distribution of $100,000 of marital property.

The result would be different in Alaska. When W transferred assets to the trust, she had no debts and owed no child support. Immediately after she transferred assets to her trust, W was solvent; she had remaining assets worth $4.4 million. Assume that: (1) W could not revoke the trust; (2) W was purely a discretionary beneficiary of the trust and was eligible but not entitled to a distribution; (3) the trustee was a qualified person under Alaska law; (4) some of the trust principal was deposited in Alaska; and (5) the trustee had the requisite administrative powers and, in fact, some administration of the trust occurred in Alaska. Given these facts, H could not invade W's self-settled spendthrift trust.

Consider what would happen in this example if W died before the divorce was final. Under Alaska law, W's transfer to an irrevocable trust would not be included in her augmented estate. AS Section 13.12.205(2). In any case, if H did not, as permitted by AS Section 13.12.213, waive his right to claim an elective share of W's estate and his right to statutory allowances, and W died before the divorce while domiciled in Alaska, the trust would be included in W's augmented estate under AS Section 13.12.205(2)(B). See Rev. Rul. 77-378, 1977-2 C.B. 347; Rev. Rul. 76-103, 1976-1 C.B. 117.

Consider a variation of the above example. What would be the result if W inherited her $5

million and transferred $600,000 to her self-settled spendthrift trust while she was married to H? Under Delaware law the result would be the same; H could invade the trust. Under Alaska law, although the facts suggest that H could not invade an Alaska trust, the issue would turn on whether W's transfer to the trust was fraudulent. The argument could be made that if W had no intention of ever divorcing H at the time of the transfer to the trust her transfer was not fraudulent. The $600,000 of assets W transferred were her own property and W was solvent after the transfer. If H was a discretionary beneficiary of the trust, it would be even easier to argue that W's transfer to the trust was not fraudulent.

Creditors Who Make Loans to the Trustor

Under Delaware law, preferred creditors may include financial institutions and other persons who make loans to the trustor after the trustor transfers property to the trust. If the trustor expressly agrees in writing that the assets of a Delaware trust are available to satisfy a particular debt, the trust will be subject to the debt. Delaware law provides that the spendthrift protection of a Delaware trust

> shall not apply in any respect . . . to any creditor who became a creditor of the transferor in reliance upon an express written statement of the transferor that any property that was the subject of the qualified disposition thereafter remained the property of the transferor and was available to satisfy any debt to such creditor incurred by the transferor.

DCA 12 Section 3573(b). This power makes it impossible for a trustor to make a completed gift to a Delaware trust and causes all the assets of the trust to be included in his or her estate for federal estate tax purposes. Under Treas. Reg. Section 25.2511-2(b) and (c), a gift is incomplete if "the donor reserves any power over its disposition . . . [or] in every instance in which a donor reserves the power to revest the beneficial title to the property in himself."

In *Paolozzi v. Commissioner*, 23 T.C. 182 (1954), the court noted that, under Massachusetts law, the taxpayer's creditors had recourse to the full amount of the trust. The court therefore held that the taxpayer's gift to the trust was incomplete and she properly deducted the value of her life estate for gift tax purposes (under pre-Code Section 2702 law). In Rev. Rul. 76-103, 1976-1 C.B. 293, the IRS ruled that a trustor's retained power to, in effect, terminate the trust by allowing his or her creditors to look to the trust assets to satisfy the trustor's debts would cause the trust to be included in the trustor's gross estate under Code Section 2038. Nevertheless, the IRS continued,

> [i]f and when the grantor's dominion and control of the trust assets ceases, such as by the trustor's decision to move the situs of the trust to a State where the grantor's creditors cannot reach the trust assets, then the gift is complete for Federal gift tax purposes under the rules set forth in section 25.2511-2 of the regulations.

Under Alaska law a trustor has no power to allow his or her creditors to reach the assets of an Alaska self-settled spendthrift trust. Absent a secret pre-arrangement with the trustee to pay the trustor a certain amount of the income or principal of the trust, the trustor's transfer of assets to an Alaska trust should be a completed gift for federal gift and estate tax purposes, unless he or she retains a power to veto distributions from the trust or a non-general power of appointment over the trust assets. Accordingly, a trustor of an Alaska trust can decide whether to draft the trust so that his or her gifts to the trust will be complete or to avoid making a taxable gift by making the transfers incomplete. Delaware law does not provide these options.

Personal Injury and Other Claims

The preferred class of creditors under Delaware law also includes any person injured by the trustor's acts or omissions that occurred before transfers to the trust. A Delaware trust will not be protected from the claims of

> any person who suffers death, personal injury or property damage on or before the date of a qualified disposition by a transferor, which death, personal injury or property damage is at any time determined to have been caused in whole or in part by the act or omission of either such transferor or by another person for whom such transferor is or was vicariously liable.

DCA 12 Section 3573(c).

This provision might seem fair to the casual reader. If the trustor injures another person, public policy could justify prohibiting the trustor from hiding assets in an irrevocable trust, retaining the beneficial enjoyment of the assets and, in effect, defrauding the injured person. If, however, the trustor did not know about the claim at the time of the transfer and the transfer to the trust was not fraudulent, the results under Delaware law are surprising.

Consider the following example. S is a careful surgeon who has never been sued by a patient. S has a net worth of $5 million and carries $5 million of malpractice insurance. In 1997, she transfers $600,000 to a self-settled spendthrift trust for her benefit and for the benefit of her spouse, children, and descendants. At the time of the transfer S has no debts. In 2007, S suffers a series of financial losses and loses all of her wealth, other than assets owned by the trust. In 2008, a patient S treated in 1996 discovers that S caused him injuries that could not have been reasonably discovered beforehand. S did not know that she injured the patient until S was served with the summons and complaint. The patient recovers a $7.5 million judgment against S. On the date of the judgment the fair-market value of the trust assets is $1.2 million. S has assets worth $250,000.

Under these facts the patient could invade the trust under Delaware law. It is irrelevant that S did not know of the injury until years after the date of her $600,000 transfer to the trust. It does not matter that, immediately after the transfer to trust, S was solvent. Finally, it does not matter that S had no notice of the patient's claim when she settled the trust and, in fact, the patient did not discover that he was injured until twelve years after being treated by A.

The result would be different under Alaska law. At the time S transferred assets to the trust she owed no child support, and immediately after she transferred assets to her trust, S was solvent. AS Section 34.40.110(b)(4). Under Alaska law, the patient should not be able to invade an Alaska self-settled spendthrift trust.

Future Issues

The Alaska and Delaware laws raise several unanswered questions. Will a bankruptcy court exclude from the debtor's estate under Bankruptcy Code Section 542(c)(2) the debtor's beneficial interest in an Alaska or Delaware trust when the restrictions on its transfer are enforceable? Will the courts of other states recognize the spendthrift provisions of an Alaska or Delaware trust, or will these courts ignore Alaska and Delaware law and drive the domestic asset protection trust business back offshore? Will Delaware be able to correct the flaws in its recent trust legislation? Will another state, such as South Dakota, enact similar laws? And lastly, what other legislative changes will states embrace in an attempt to become leaders of the domestic trust industry in the United States?

Conclusion

Before the passage of the Alaska Trust Act, Delaware and South Dakota had in many ways the best trust laws of any state and were the undisputed leaders of the domestic trust industry. Now Alaska has weighed in with asset protection legislation that is second only to that found in some offshore jurisdictions. Delaware tried to match the Alaska Trust Act but fell short. In any case, Delaware's legislation helps legitimize asset protection planning with domestic trusts by allowing persons to shield assets from the future claims of unknown creditors.

The differences between Alaska and Delaware law are many. Despite the differences and unanswered questions, one thing is certain. As states become aware of the benefits of attracting trust business, much of which now goes offshore, future legislation is likely to make developments in self-settled spendthrift trusts worth watching.

41
Lifetime Tax Planning

ALLAN C. BELL

Tax Overview

Gift Tax

The federal gift tax serves several purposes, one of which is to discourage avoidance of the federal income tax by giving away income-producing property to those in lower income tax brackets than yourself. The "price" for this opportunity is a gift tax at the time the transfer is made. However, the principal purpose of the gift tax is to limit avoidance of the estate tax by lifetime gifts which would remove property otherwise subject to estate tax from your estate upon your death. The gift tax, then, complements the estate tax and, accordingly, the taxes are integrated—the rates for lifetime transfers and transfers upon death are identical. At death, the estate tax is determined by applying the rate schedule to cumulative lifetime gifts and death transfers to arrive at a "tentative tax," and then subtracting the gift taxes payable on the lifetime transfers.

Consistent with the integration of the rates, the law allows a unified credit against the estate and gift taxes. Like an income tax credit, the unified credit is a dollar-for-dollar reduction in the tax. The maximum credit prior to the Taxpayer Relief Act of 1997 was $192,800, which is equivalent to an exemption of $600,000. That is to say, the estate or gift tax upon the transfer of property worth $600,000 would be $192,800 and thus fully absorbed by the unified credit. The estate and gift tax rates for U.S. citizens and residents begin at 37 percent for the first dollar above $600,000 and then rise quickly in a compressed structure to a 55 percent maximum at transfers over $3 million.

Allan C. Bell is a tax lawyer and a partner in the Newark, New Jersey, law firm of Sills Cummis Zuckerman Radin Tischman Epstein & Gross.

The benefit of both the unified credit and the lower estate tax brackets begin to be phased out once the taxable estate exceeds $10 million.

The Taxpayer Relief Act of 1997 gradually increases the unified credit over nine years, resulting in an exemption amount and tax reduction as follows:

Year	Exemption	Reduction
1998	$ 625,000	$ 9,250
1999	$ 650,000	$ 18,500
2000 and 2001	$ 675,000	$ 27,750
2002 and 2003	$ 700,000	$ 37,000
2004	$ 850,000	$ 94,500
2005	$ 950,000	$133,500
2006 and after	$1,000,000	$153,000

Since the new increases are phased in very slowly, considering inflation, the tax savings will be modest even when the exemption is fully in effect. For example, in 2006 the savings on a $1 million taxable estate would be $153,000 with no adjustment for inflation since 1997.

Taxable Gifts

The Internal Revenue Code does not define a gift for gift tax purposes. Any transfer for less than full consideration is a taxable gift as long as the person making the transfer completely parts with control over the subject matter of the gift. Thus, if you transfer property to a revocable trust you have not made a taxable gift because you can revoke the trust and get the property back.

Annual Exclusion

The amount of gift tax you will have to pay depends upon the available deductions and exclusions, and whether you can split the gift with your spouse. The annual exclusion permits an infinite number of annual gifts of present interests of up to $10,000 per donee to be made gift tax-free. The Taxpayer Relief Act of 1997 indexes the $10,000 exclusion annually for inflation after 1998 rounded to the next lowest multiple of $1,000. The annual exclusion is allowed only for a gift of a present interest, not for a gift of a future interest.

Suppose that father irrevocably transfers $50,000 in trust, to accumulate the income until son (age 20) attains the age of 30 or sooner dies, and on son's attaining 30 to pay the principal and accumulated income to son; or, should son die before attaining 30, to pay the principal and accumulated income to son's estate. The gift to son is a gift of a future interest for purposes of the gift tax, and no part of the gift qualifies for the annual exclusion. On the other hand, suppose that father irrevocably transfers $50,000 in trust, to pay the net income to son for life, and at son's death, to pay the principal to son's estate. Father, in this case, has made two gifts to son: (1) a gift of income that is a present interest and thus qualifies for the annual exclusion; and (2) a gift of principal that is a future interest and does not so qualify. You will read more about other ways to obtain the annual exclusion later in this chapter.

Educational and Medical Expenses

There is an unlimited exclusion for educational and medical expense transfers described later in this chapter.

Charitable Deduction

The law allows a gift tax charitable deduction for the value of a gift to charity. There is no limit on the amount of this deduction as there is on the income tax charitable deduction. A partial gift must be in one of several forms in order to qualify for the deduction. As you will see, charitable gifts in trust of income interests and remainder interests not only allow property to be passed on to the next generation at a reduced gift and estate tax cost, but also permit income tax savings.

Marital Deduction

A U.S. citizen or resident has an unlimited marital deduction for qualified gifts made to his or her spouse who is a U.S. citizen. There is a $100,000 annual exclusion for qualified gifts to alien spouses. The marital deduction is also an important estate planning device for the married donor,

the requirements and uses of which are dealt with in Chapter 38.

Gift-Splitting

Gift-splitting—where your spouse consents to being treated as the donor of one-half of any taxable gift made by you to a third person—allows a married couple to use two annual exclusions and unified credits with respect to a single gift. For example, suppose mother gives $20,000 in cash to daughter. Mother gets one $10,000 annual exclusion and so makes a $10,000 taxable gift which requires her to absorb part of her unified credit. However, if father consents to gift-split, father and mother will get two $10,000 annual exclusions or $20,000, and the gift passes completely gift tax-free. Likewise, suppose mother gifts $1,220,000 in cash to daughter prior to 1998. Mother gets one $10,000 annual exclusion and, assuming mother has not previously used any of her unified credit, fully absorbs her unified credit exemption equivalent of $600,000 and so makes a taxable gift of $610,000 to daughter. However, if father consents to gift-split, father and mother will get two annual exclusions and unified credits, and the gift passes completely gift tax-free.

Compliance

Every taxpayer who makes a gift must file a gift tax return (Form 709), unless the gift qualifies for the available exclusions and deductions so that no current gift tax is due. Even where there is no tax owing because a married couple gift-splits for $20,000 or less, a return must still be filed to report the gift-splitting election. A shorter return (Form 709-A) may be used for this purpose if the gift is not more than the $20,000 double annual exclusion. To avoid filing such a return, the donor spouse could transfer $10,000 of the intended $20,000 gift to his spouse who, in turn, would complete the gift to the donee. Gift tax returns must be filed on or before April 15th of the year following the calendar year in which the gifts are made. An automatic extension arises if the taxpayer extends his income tax return filing date for gifts made in the same year. Gift tax must be paid upon the filing date of the return, regardless of any extension of time for filing the return. To avoid late payment penalties, extension of time for payment of the tax should be requested.

Income Taxation of Trusts and Minor Children

Trusts

Under the Revenue Reconciliation Act of 1993, a new rate schedule, effective January 1, 1993, applies to trusts:

Taxable Income	Tax Rate
$0 - $1,650	15 percent
$1,650 - $3,900	28 percent
$3,900 - $5,950	31 percent
$5,950 - $8,100	36 percent
Above $8,100	39.6 percent

A trust that previously paid income tax at a rate lower than the beneficiaries could now be taxed at a higher rate than the beneficiaries. You may want to review your trust arrangements to measure the tax impact of the new law.

Unearned Income of a Minor Under Age 14

Since 1987, all unearned income of a child under age 14, regardless of the source of the assets generating the income, is taxed to the child at his or her parents' top marginal rate. In other words, the tax on all the child's net unearned income will be the amount of additional income tax that would have been owed by the parents if the child's unearned income had been added to the parents' income. In general, the first $650 of unearned income will not be subject to tax and the next $650 of unearned income will be taxed at the child's own rates resulting in a total tax of $97.50 on $1,300 of income. Unearned income in excess of $1,300 will be taxed at the top marginal rate of the child's parents. Any earned income of a child of any age and unearned income of a child who has attained the age of 14 is taxed at the child's marginal rate.

Grandparents and parents desiring to make gifts to minor grandchildren and children where the income will be taxed at the child's marginal tax rates should consider assets that generate taxable income, if at all, only after the child attains age 14. To accomplish this result, you might consider gifting single premium deferred annuities, U.S. Treasury Series EE Bonds, or zero-coupon tax exempt securities to your grandchildren or children under age 14.

Generation-Skipping Transfer Tax

Structure

Assume father establishes a trust for son's benefit under which income is paid to son for son's life and, at son's death, the trust property is distributed to son's children (father's grandchildren). Prior to 1976, father was subject to gift tax upon the establishment of the trust but no estate tax was ever due when son's interest terminated upon son's death. Thus, son's generation was "skipped" for gift and estate tax purposes when the corpus of the trust was distributed to his children. The generation-skipping transfer tax rules of 1976 were imposed to make up for the absence of estate or gift tax in son's generation. This did not deter capable taxpayers. In wealthy enough families, the grandparent would transfer assets, outright or in trust, to his grandchildren. In this way, no generation-skipping transfer taxes would ever be imposed. The Tax Reform Act of 1986 established a new generation-skipping transfer tax and repealed the prior tax. While the new law continues to cover the first scenario where the middle generation has some interest in the generation-skipping transfer trust, the new law now subjects the "direct" skip of the second example to the tax. The new generation-skipping transfer tax is a flat rate equal to the maximum gift and estate tax rate.

Exemptions

There are a number of exemptions to the generation-skipping transfer tax. Each transferor has a $1 million exemption that applies at the time of transfer, thus protecting any future appreciation. For example, father can transfer $1 million to a trust for son's benefit and eventually his grandchild, applying his $1 million exemption to the transfer excepting the trust from generation-skipping transfer tax even if the corpus appreciates to $2 million at the date of termination. The Taxpayer Relief Act of 1997 indexes the $1 million exemption annually for inflation after 1998 rounded to the next lowest multiple of $10,000. Through December 31, 1989, there was a special $2 million per grandchild exclusion for trust or outright direct skips. Also, where the middle generation member (transferor's son/transferee's parent) is dead, no tax is imposed on nontrust direct skips. Lastly, any outright transfer of property that is not treated as a taxable gift because of the annual gift tax exclusion, or because of the exclusion for certain transfers for educational and medical expenses, is not subject to the tax.

Outright Gifts

Uniform Gifts to Minors Act and Uniform Transfers to Minors Act

Every state and the District of Columbia has in effect, in one form or another, laws simplifying the making of gifts to minors which make unnecessary the appointment of a guardian or the establishment of a trust. Under the Uniform Gifts to Minors Act, cash, securities, life insurance policies, and cash equivalents (certificates of deposit, bank accounts, and so forth) may be transferred to a custodian, and invested under a "prudent man" standard provided in the law. The majority of states have now adopted the Uniform Transfers to Minors Act as a successor to the Uniform Gifts to Minors Act. The Uniform Transfers to Minors Act expands the types of property that can be given to minors to include all types of property (money, securities, life insurance, real property, tangible personal property, and partnership interests) and permits the broad use of custodial transfers by trustees and executors.

A gift made under either uniform act is irrevocable. The custodian is under the legal obligation to hold and manage the custodial property, and is authorized to apply as much of the income and principal of the property for the benefit of the minor as he, in his discretion, deems appropriate. All property must be distributed outright to the minor upon his or her attaining the age of majority or to his or her estate in the event of prior death. While the age of majority is set by state law, which varies from state to state, the distribution age under a uniform act may be different.

The chief advantage of a gift under the uniform acts is its simplicity. Additionally, gifts under the uniform acts also qualify for the $10,000 gift tax annual exclusion. Thus, no gift tax return is required and no gift tax is due on transfers of up to $10,000 a year. And if you and your spouse elect to gift-split, no tax is due on transfers of up to $20,000 under the uniform acts. Furthermore, since a custodianship is not a trust for income tax purposes, no trust income tax returns are

required. Rather, the minor donee reports all custodial income, whether or not distributed, directly on his or her own individual income tax return.

You should be aware of the fact that if you, as a parent, are legally obligated under state law to support your child, you will be taxable on any custodianship income to the extent used for support of the minor child. In an increasing number of states, a college education is deemed to be within the parental support obligation. If the custodial funds are used to pay for luxuries not covered by the parents' legal support obligation, this potential income tax problem should be avoided. The uniform laws permit you to serve as custodian of your own gift, but this would not be a wise choice since the value of the property is included in your gross estate for estate tax purposes if you die while serving in that capacity and before your child attains the majority age for distributions. Even with the tax law changes under the Revenue Reconciliation Act of 1993, the uniform acts are still excellent ways to put money aside for your minor grandchildren and children and take advantage of potential tax savings. In fact, it is likely that the new restrictions may have little or no effect on the gifts you may have already planned for your issue.

Grandparents and parents will still be able to set up accounts for grandchildren and children, but the rate at which they will be taxed will now depend on two factors. As you have already read, investments belonging to a grandchild or child younger than 14 are taxed at the minor's rate, unless that investment earns more than $1,300 of income in a year. Should that happen, any amount above the $1,300 limit is taxed at the parents' higher rate. However, for grandchildren and children age 14 and older, all income from their investments are taxed at the minor's rate.

If your grandchild or child is younger than 14, there are two ways to avoid taxation at the minor's parents' higher rate. You can simply concentrate investing in growth-oriented and lower-yielding investments until the minor is age 14. Since this strategy will accrue less income in the short-term, you could avoid exceeding the $1,300 per year income limitation. Or you may consider placing the money in a tax-free municipal investment which will earn income that is 100 percent free from federal taxes.

While a grandparent or parent would usually incur less expense to establish and maintain an account under either one of the uniform acts than to establish a trust for the benefit of a minor grandchild or child, one must consider the ability of the minor to manage the property when distributed. A trustee may control property transferred in trust beyond the required age of distribution under the uniform acts and without the loss of the gift tax annual exclusion. Many grandparents and parents are unwilling to let large sums of money come under the control of an 18- or 21-year-old and will use a trust rather than one of the uniform acts for large gifts. The advantages and disadvantages, then, should be carefully weighed before a decision is made about which transfer is most appropriate for a particular beneficiary.

Educational and Medical Expenses

In addition to the annual exclusion explained above, transfers for educational and medical expenses can be made in unlimited quantities and still not be considered a gift for gift tax purposes. The amounts must be paid directly to the provider of certain medical or educational services to the donee. The unlimited exclusion applies to tuition payments to foreign or domestic educational organizations and to payments for medical care. The purchase of books, materials, and supplies or the payment of laboratory fees, room and board, and other related expenses are not covered by the exclusion.

For example, assume father pays more than $20,000 a year for son's medical school tuition where son is an adult or where father's support obligation under state law does not encompass medical school tuition. The tuition payments constitute gifts from father to son that qualify for the unlimited gift tax exclusion. Also, if son pays $50,000 a year in medical bills to a doctor and a hospital for father, the medical payments are gifts from son to father, but they qualify for the unlimited exclusion. Again, it should be noted that the unlimited exclusion applies only to direct payments to the service provider. The exclusion does not apply to payments that reimburse the donee for his medical care payments nor is the exclusion available to the extent such amounts paid are reimbursed by insurance.

Gifts in Trust

Irrevocable Minor's Trust

If you create a trust for your grandchild or child in which the trustee has the discretion to distribute both income and principal for the grandchild or child's benefit before he or she reaches 21 years of age, at which time any unused income and principal must be completely distributed to him or her, the gift tax annual exclusion will be available for gifts to the trust. Such a trust will shift the income on the corpus away from you, remove the corpus from your estate, and at the same time take maximum advantage of the $10,000 gift tax annual exclusion or, if you gift-split with your spouse, $20,000.

The same nontax factors that are considered when implementing a custodial account are present here in that you must be willing to permit the beneficiary to obtain possession of the trust corpus at age 21. If you will be able to exercise sufficient influence over the beneficiary after he or she reaches the age of 21, you may be able to persuade him or her to voluntarily extend the trust. Furthermore, the issue of discharge of support obligations has to be considered here as well. Lastly, you should neither designate yourself as trustee nor retain the power to remove and appoint a trustee and substitute yourself, as either action would cause the inclusion in your estate of the trust assets in the event you die prior to the termination of the trust.

Current Income Trust

If you desire property held for the benefit of your grandchild or child to remain in trust beyond his or her 21st birthday, you might consider a current income trust. Such a trust does not have to terminate when the minor beneficiary attains 18 or 21 years of age as under the Uniform Gifts to Minors Act or Uniform Transfers to Minors Act, nor does the minor beneficiary have any power to terminate the trust upon his or her attaining the age of 21 as in an irrevocable minor's trust.

As its name applies, a current income trust beneficiary must have an income interest for a fixed number of years or for life; that is, all ordinary income must be distributed to the beneficiary currently during the term of the trust. Gifts to such a trust qualify for the gift tax annual exclusion only to the extent of the actuarial value of the beneficiary's income interest. The remainder interest is a gift of a future interest that requires the filing of a gift tax return and the payment of gift tax or absorption of the unified credit. Thus, a $20,000 gift in trust for the life of a 5-year-old is a present interest (tax-free gift) to the extent of $19,788 and a future interest (taxable gift) to the extent of $212 (based upon Internal Revenue Service actuarial valuation tables assuming a 10 percent interest rate, which rate fluctuates monthly). Because all trust income must be paid currently to the beneficiary, the trust must invest in income-producing assets. Gifts to a trust that allow the trustee to invest in non-income-producing property, even if the trustee never makes such an investment, do not qualify for the annual exclusion. The trustee can have wide discretion concerning principal distributions to the beneficiary. However, no other beneficiary can receive principal.

As with the other trusts we have seen, you can be taxed on any trust income actually used to discharge any legal support obligations you have to the beneficiary. If the trustee pays the income directly to the beneficiary, not to a third-party service provider for his or her benefit, and the beneficiary then makes the payment to the third party, this rule should be avoided. Unlike the irrevocable minor's trust, you may serve as trustee if your discretion to distribute principal can be exercised only for the "health, education, support, and maintenance" of the beneficiary. Such an "ascertainable standard," as the law refers to it, prevents trust income from being taxed to you or the property being included in your estate if you predecease the beneficiary. Lastly, you should remember that income from this type of trust would qualify as unearned income of a minor when distributed to a beneficiary younger than 14 and, to the extent it exceeds $1,300, would be taxed at the top marginal rates of the beneficiary's parents.

Irrevocable *Crummey* Support Trust

If the above trusts inhibit your dispositive intentions by requiring you to give all the property to the beneficiary at age 21 or to distribute all income currently to the beneficiary, you should consider the use of a *Crummey* trust. Named for a landmark case, such a trust is probably the most advantageous method of creating a present interest for purposes of the annual gift tax exclusion and is certainly, for the present, superior to the two other methods.

A *Crummey* trust is one in which the beneficiary is given a withdrawal power over the annual contribution to the trust. The withdrawal power gives the beneficiary a present interest in the trust, thus qualifying transfers to the trust for the annual gift tax exclusion. The Internal Revenue Service requires that proper notice be given to the beneficiary, who must have actual knowledge of his or her legal right to withdraw and must be capable, or have a guardian capable, of exercising the withdrawal power.

To increase the number of available annual exclusions, you may use several *Crummey* power holders. In this way, each trust beneficiary would be given the right to withdraw his or her pro rata share of the transfer. As long as they have some beneficial interest in the trust, there can be several *Crummey* power holders possessing withdrawal rights where a trust has only one beneficiary. (The Internal Revenue Service has taken a contrary position which, however, is outside the scope of the Internal Revenue Code.) This would allow you to exceed the $10,000 or $20,000 per donee exclusion. Of course, in any event, you should be somewhat certain that the power holders will not exercise their rights or your purpose will be defeated. Also, you must avoid using reciprocal powers, where power holders have rights in each of several trusts. Where every power holder has a beneficial interest in the trust and you are concerned with them actually exercising their powers, simply informing them that should they do so, no more gifts to the trust would be made in the future and your goals will probably not be defeated.

Nonetheless, assume you intend to gift-split with your spouse and contribute $20,000 per beneficiary a year to the trust. You would probably want each beneficiary's withdrawal power to lapse after a certain period, typically thirty to sixty days, following each annual contribution. Otherwise, the beneficiary would have a cumulative withdrawal power over ever-increasing amounts that would do little to limit the temptation to exercise that power. However, the withdrawal power is a general power of appointment the lapse of which may cause adverse gift and estate tax consequences to the beneficiary. The law deems a lapse of a general power of appointment in excess of the greater of $5,000 or 5 percent of the trust corpus (commonly referred to as a "5 or 5" limitation) to be a taxable gift made by the beneficiary to the other remaindermen of the trust. Thus, if a beneficiary's noncumulative demand power is limited to the greater of $5,000 or 5 percent of the trust corpus, no such adverse consequences will result.

For example, assume you and your spouse establish a *Crummey* trust for your son and daughter and contribute $40,000 ($20,000 per beneficiary to take advantage of the double annual exclusion). Upon the lapse of each child's right to exercise his or her withdrawal power, each will be deemed to have made a $15,000 ($20,000 – $5,000) gift to the other. For this reason, many *Crummey* trusts limit the beneficiary's withdrawal right to a "5 or 5" power. However, this restriction prohibits you from taking full advantage of the $10,000 annual gift tax exclusion or the $20,000 exclusion if you gift-split with your spouse. Where a beneficiary is given the right to withdraw $10,000, or $20,000 if the donor's spouse consents, no "5 or 5" protection is available and estate and gift tax consequences may result in certain situations to the extent of the excess. Of course, if the power holder is the sole beneficiary of the trust, he or she may be given the right to withdraw property in excess of the "5 or 5" safe harbor without the imposition of estate and gift tax consequences because the beneficiary's lapsed power favors himself or herself, or his or her estate, and one cannot make a gift to oneself. If other trust beneficiaries may benefit from the lapse of the power, a gift may result.

However, there are two methods that may be used to avoid this problem. First, the power holder could be given what is called a "hanging" power, which lapses only to the extent of the "5 or 5" limitation and the excess, if any, is carried over to the next year in which it lapses; again only to the extent of the "S or S" exemption, taking into account any current contribution to the trust during that year. In the alternative, you will recall from the tax overview section of this chapter that for a gift to be complete, the donor must give up sufficient dominion and control over the property. If a *Crummey* power holder is given a testa-

mentary power of appointment over his or her interest in the trust corpus, so that he or she still has control even after the lapse of his or her annual withdrawal power, the gift is then incomplete for gift tax purposes.

Charitable Remainder Annuity Trust

A charitable remainder trust can be used to create an income stream for several years to fund a grandchild or child's education. In such a trust, a specified sum is paid annually to one or more designated noncharitable beneficiaries (grandchildren or children). At the end of the trust term, the principal is paid to charity. To achieve the income, gift, or estate tax deduction, a charitable remainder trust must be in one of two forms: an annuity trust or a unitrust. In a unitrust, a fixed percentage of not less than 5 percent of the net value of trust assets valued annually is payable to the noncharitable beneficiary or beneficiaries for life or for a term of years, which term cannot exceed twenty years. In an annuity trust, a sum certain, not less than 5 percent of the initial fair-market value of the trust corpus, is payable annually for the life or lives of persons in being at the creation of the trust, or for a term of years not in excess of twenty years, unless shortened by a stated contingency. The annuity payment is thus constant in amount. No additional contributions may be made to a charitable remainder annuity trust. Since the actuarial tables, revised monthly to reflect market interest rates, have made the annuity trust generally more favorable than the unitrust, we will consider the annuity trust.

Funding a charitable remainder annuity trust entitles you to a charitable income tax deduction equal to the present (discounted by the actuarial valuation tables) value of the charitable remainder interest in the trust. The value of the noncharitable beneficiary's interest is subject to gift tax but qualifies for the annual gift tax exclusion. Distributions from the trust are taxed to the noncharitable beneficiary. In general, the charitable remainder trust is exempt from federal income tax. However, the exemption is lost if the trust has any unrelated business income, including debt-finance income. In addition, the Internal Revenue Service has published guidelines for drafting charitable remainder trusts (in the form of sample language) which require extreme technical compliance.

For example, assume you transfer $100,000 in appreciated assets to a charitable remainder annuity trust, providing for a $7,000 annual pay-out to the noncharitable beneficiary older than 14 for four years, remainder to charity. You would receive an immediate income tax deduction of approximately $68,300 (based upon IRS actuarial valuation tables assuming a 10 percent interest rate, which rate fluctuates monthly). Assuming you are in the 36 percent income tax bracket, the tax savings would be slightly less than $24,600. The annual payments to the beneficiary are taxed at his bracket, not yours. The beneficiary will receive $7,000 per year or $28,000 over four years. This relieves the beneficiary's parents of a significant financial burden. Should the trust property not be producing a high enough income yield, the trustees may sell the property at no income tax cost since the trust is tax-exempt. If you had sold the property while you owned it, you would, under present law, have capital gains income tax on the sale. After four years the charity receives your original $100,000 contribution, subject to appreciation or depreciation, and you have the satisfaction of making a substantial contribution to charity during your lifetime. Finally, the assets would not be taxed in your estate at your death.

The Taxpayer Relief Act of 1997 imposes two new restrictions on charitable remainder trusts. The act requires that (1) a charitable remainder trust cannot have a maximum payout percentage in excess of 50 percent of the trust's fair-market value and (2) the value of the charitable remainder be at least 10 percent of the net fair-market value of property transferred in trust on the date of contribution to the trust.

Grantor Charitable Annuity Lead Trust

If you have followed an annual charitable giving program, you might consider the establishment of a grantor charitable annuity lead trust. Such a trust involves a gift in trust of enough income-producing property to throw off a certain amount of income for a fixed period of years. Each year the trust is required to pay such income to the designated charities. When the trust terminates, you get the property back. The trust allows you to take a large, up-front charitable deduction in the year you fund the trust for donations that are made in later years.

Suppose in a given year you have an unusually high level of income. In such a year you may wish to accelerate your charitable giving plans for the next few years in a manner which would offset a portion of the income tax that would otherwise be payable currently in respect of your substantial income for the present year. Many taxpayers took advantage of this device in 1986 when the top bracket dropped from 50 percent to 38.5 percent for 1987 in order to take advantage of the 11.5 percent spread.

The creation of the trust entitles you to an income tax charitable deduction in the amount of the actuarial value of the charitable income interest in trust on the date of the transfer. For example, trust payments of income of $10,000 a year to charity for five years will produce an immediate deduction of $37,906 for agreeing to give charity a certain amount annually (based upon IRS actuarial valuation tables assuming a 10 percent interest rate, which rate fluctuates monthly). The deduction is limited to 20 percent of your adjusted gross income.

During the term of the trust, the income earned will be fully taxable to you with no offsetting charitable deduction, notwithstanding the fact that all, or a significant portion, of the income will be paid out to charity. This disadvantage can be avoided by transferring tax-exempt municipal bonds to the trust. Even though you are obligated to report all of the trust's income, none of it is taxable to you since it consists entirely of tax-exempt interest.

The creation of the trust involves a gift of the income interest to the charitable beneficiaries. Inasmuch as the income interest is a qualified annuity interest, it will qualify for the gift tax charitable deduction. Consequently, the establishment of the trust does not result in any taxable gift. Nonetheless, a gift tax return must still be filed.

Since you retained a reversionary interest in the trust, the assets of the trust will be included in your estate if you should die prior to the expiration of the trust term. The value of the income interest remaining at your death, however, will qualify for the estate tax charitable deduction because it is in the form of a qualified annuity.

Grantor Retained Annuity Trust (GRAT)

A GRAT is a way of saving estate tax at a small gift tax cost. You, as grantor, retain the right to receive an annuity from trust property for a fixed term of years. If you survive the annuity term, the trust principal passes to your descendants, and that trust principal, including all appreciation thereon, is excluded from your estate for federal estate tax purposes.

Because you retain a right to an annuity from the trust property, you are treated as making a gift only of the present value of the right to receive the property at the end of the annuity term. You offset your unified credit exemption equivalent in the amount of the gift to avoid paying any current gift tax. In the event you die during the term of the trust, a portion of the value of the trust property is included in your estate, as if you never created the GRAT. However, in the event you are survived by your spouse, the trust property will qualify for the marital deduction, thus not creating any current estate tax liability. If you are not survived by a spouse, special trust provisions would minimize, if not eliminate, the estate tax inclusion.

For example, assume you create a GRAT with income-producing property currently worth $1 million. You reserve an $80,000 annuity for a term of fifteen years with your surviving children as the remaindermen. At the end of fifteen years, the property may be worth $2 million. You have made a gift equal to only $391,512 (based upon IRS actuarial valuation tables assuming a 10 percent interest rate, which rate fluctuates monthly). Since a gift in that amount is covered by your available unified credit exemption, there is no current gift tax. Assuming you survive fifteen years, assets worth $2 million are removed from your estate with a unified credit exemption cost of only $391,512. If you had not created the GRAT and had died when the property value was $2 million, additional federal estate taxes of $780,800 to $1.1 million would have been generated.

You should realize that the $1 million figure is only an amount for illustrative purposes. You may transfer a substantially smaller amount to a GRAT and obtain the same 60 percent discount. To be sure, since after the annuity term all your rights in the GRAT expire, in no event should you transfer any amount that would leave you uncomfortable psychologically or economically. To avoid this financial loss, however, with proper planning you may give your spouse an interest in the GRAT property after termination of your annuity interest, thus retaining the beneficial interests of the GRAT property for your spouse's lifetime.

Personal Residence Trust (PRT)

A PRT is based upon concepts similar to the GRAT, but because the PRT involves personal residences, a much larger gift tax discount can be generated. "Personal" residences, however, are not limited to "primary" residences and may include "vacation" residences.

For example, assume your and your spouse's tenancy by the entirety interest in your residence, with a $500,000 value, is first transferred to you (age 50) who has the longer life expectancy between the two spouses. You, in turn, create a trust that always provides either spouse the opportunity to use the trust property, whether as the initial trust beneficiary (for the greater of fifteen years, if you, as the grantor, survive such term, or the lifetime of your spouse, if your spouse survives you), or as a fair-rent-paying tenant (if your spouse does not survive the term, or if your spouse predeceases you).

At the surviving spouse's death, the real estate may be worth $1 million. The gift and estate tax consequences would be as follows. You have made a gift equal to only $100,839, an 80 percent discount off the $500,000 value of the real estate (based upon IRS actuarial valuation tables assuming a 10 percent interest rate, which rate fluctuates monthly). Since a gift in that amount is covered by the unified credit exemption equivalent, there is no current gift tax. Assuming you survive fifteen years, assets worth $1 million are removed from the surviving spouse's estate with a unified credit exemption equivalent cost of only $100,839 saving additional federal estate taxes of approximately $500,000.

If you die prior to the expiration of the initial fifteen-year term, the then current value of the trust assets will be fully includable in your gross estate for federal estate tax purposes. However, in such an event the amount of the $100,839 unified credit exemption equivalent initially offset on the trust's creation will be restored. If your spouse survives you, the trust property will qualify for the marital deduction, thus creating no current estate tax liability. Thus, there is no gift or estate tax downside as a result of your "premature" death prior to the expiration of your fifteen-year term.

If you outlive your spouse and survive the fifteen-year term, you will have to pay a fair-market rent to continue using the residence. If this represents any risk to your security, a PRT should not be implemented. However, the payment of rent to the trust presents an extraordinary additional planning opportunity. Assuming you can afford to pay the market rent, substantial amounts will be transferred (in the form of rental payments) to your ultimate beneficiaries without gift or estate tax consequences (if it is characterized as rent, and not as a gift or bequest). Of course, the rent will be taxable income to the trust, but it can be partially offset by deductions (depreciation, taxes, and so forth).

Irrevocable Second-to-Die Life Insurance Trust

The majority of estate plans, because of the unlimited marital deduction, will not generate estate taxes until the surviving spouse's death. In addition to the GRAT and PRT, second-to-die life insurance is another method available to reduce the estate tax burden that would otherwise be imposed upon the surviving spouse's estate.

Life insurance proceeds can provide liquidity to permit an estate to pay federal and state death taxes, administrative expenses incurred in probate, and/or debts owed by the decedent. In the estate planning context, life insurance allows the avoidance of the forced sale of estate assets at a depressed price and provides an estate with the ability to meet the immediate and future needs of the surviving family members.

An irrevocable life insurance trust is one of the most important means of providing immediate liquidity for the nonliquid estate, and for providing for the needs of the insured's survivors at no estate, and little or no gift, tax cost. As noted above, a common purpose for obtaining life insurance is to provide liquidity to pay debts, expenses, and taxes of an estate. The irrevocable life insurance trust assures this liquidity by permitting the trustees to purchase assets from the estate at estate tax values, or loan money to the estate, even though the insurance proceeds are excluded from the taxable estate.

A second-to-die life insurance policy insures both your life and your spouse's life but pays only upon the survivor's death. Because the actuarial probability that both of you will die in any particular year is so much lower than the probability that only one of you will die, premiums are significantly lower for a second-to-die policy than for a policy insuring either of you.

For example, you would gift sufficient cash each year to the trustees to enable the trust to purchase and maintain second-to-die insurance on the lives of you and your spouse. At the time of the surviving spouse's death, the trustees would collect the policy proceeds and administer the funds, together with any assets from your estates, for your beneficiaries. *Crummey* withdrawal rights regarding cash contributions to the trust (to cover insurance policy premiums) are included to obtain the gift tax annual exclusions as discussed above. The insurance proceeds should not be taxed in either spouse's estate, but will provide the surviving spouse's estate liquidity by permitting the trustees to purchase assets from the estate and the predeceasing spouse's testamentary trusts or to loan money thereto.

42
Tax-Wise
Charitable Planning!

STEPHAN R. LEIMBERG

This entire chapter is devoted to making the most of current tax law in order to benefit those organizations—and those individuals (including yourself)—whom you love and who are important to you.

> If I am not for myself, who will be for me?
> Being only for myself, what am I?
> And if not now, when?

These three questions, first posed thousands of years ago, sum up the essence of good financial and estate planning and the relationship of these to charitable giving.

Simply put:

- "If I am not for myself" means that we must provide first for ourselves and those we love, for we can rely with certainty on no one else. Before giving, we must first plan and assure financial security for ourselves and our immediate families.
- "Being only for myself" means that if we cared only for ourselves, our lives would amount to very little. So we must reach out and give back to others (especially to those organizations and institutions that enhance the value of life for all of us).
- "And if not now, when?" means that there is an urgency to accomplishing the first two objectives that must not be put off. When we provide nothing and give back nothing, that "nothing" is the legacy we leave.

Read on and you'll learn the smart and creative ways to give.

Tax-wise giving can mean:

- Enhancing your own (and your family's) financial security
- Enriching the lives of others
- Increased retirement income
- A safer investment portfolio
- Reduction in investment management aggravation
- Financial security for incompetent family members
- Increased income tax deductions
- Significant gifts to the charity of your choice
- Substantially reduced death taxes and probate expenses
- A lasting tribute and honor
- Privacy—if desired

Here are three great ways to give (and receive):

1. Set up a charitable remainder annuity trust.
2. Set up a charitable remainder unitrust.
3. Use life insurance.

Set Up a Charitable Remainder Annuity Trust

You can transfer money, securities, or both to a trust. That trust can pay you (or someone else you name) a fixed-dollar amount (an annuity) each year for a specified number of years or for life.

You set the fixed amount you'll receive each year when you set up the trust (no less than 5 percent of the initial value of the assets you place into the trust).

At the end of the specified number of years (or at the death of the income beneficiary), the assets in the annuity trust pass to the specified charity.

Stephan R. Leimberg is CEO of Leimberg and LeClair, Inc., an estate and financial planning software company, and president of Leimberg Associates, Inc., a publishing and software company, in Bryn Mawr, Pennsylvania. He is a best-selling author and a nationally known speaker on estate and financial planning.

You receive an immediate income tax deduction for the gift the charity will receive. That deduction is measured by the present value (the worth today) of the charity's right to receive what remains in the trust (the remainder interest) at the end of the specified term or upon the death of the specified annuity recipient.

A charitable remainder annuity trust (CRAT) can provide pre- or postretirement income for you, a spouse, parent, child, or other relative or friend. A CRAT can also provide income for more than one person; for example, you can keep the right to income for the rest of your life and then have income paid to your spouse for that person's life.

Figure 42–1 illustrates the current deduction allowable against income taxes at various ages assuming you place $100,000 of cash and/or other assets into a CRAT.

Note that the deduction increases with your age. For instance, assuming you were age 45 and took a fixed income for life equal to 5 percent of your initial $100,000 contribution ($5,000 a year), you'd receive a deduction worth about 57

percent of your contribution and worth about 73 percent of your contribution if you were age 75. That's because the shorter period of time the charity must wait for its money, the more the gift to charity is worth—the converse is also true.

The figures shown in Figure 42–1 assume a federal discount rate of 10.6 percent. Your deduction drops if the discount rate drops and increases if the rate goes up.

For example, if the discount rate jumps to 11.6 percent, your deduction at age 45 would increase from $57,029 to $61,393. If the discount rate dropped to 9.6 percent, your deduction would fall to $53,313.

Fortunately, you have the option of selecting the federal discount rate (technically called the "Section 7250 rate") for the month you fund the trust or for the two months prior to that month.

You can pick the most favorable discount rate. In fact, by waiting until the time of month the rate is announced (usually about the 21st or 22nd of each month), you have the choice of four months' rates.

Set Up a Charitable Remainder Unitrust

You can transfer money, securities, or both to a trust. That trust can pay you (or someone else you name) a fixed percentage of the value of trust assets as revalued each year (a variable annuity) for a specified number of years or for life. For instance, if you retain the right to receive a payout of 5 percent, in the first year when the trust was worth $100,000, you'd receive $5,000. In the next year, if the trust assets were worth $200,000 you'd still receive a payment of 5 percent, but it would be $10,000 (5 percent of $200,000).

You set the fixed percentage payout rate when you set up the trust (no less than 5 percent of the initial value of the assets you place into the trust). At the end of the specified number of years (or at the death of the income beneficiary), the assets in the trust pass to the specified charity.

You receive an immediate income tax deduction for the gift the charity will receive. That deduction is measured by the present value (the worth today) of the charity's right to receive what remains in the trust (the remainder interest) at the end of the specified term or upon the death of the specified annuity recipient.

Figure 42–1

Deductions for $100,000 Contribution to a Charitable Remainder Annuity Trust

	Payout Rate			
Age	5 Percent	6 Percent	7 Percent	8 Percent
45	$57,029	$48,435	$39,841	$31,246
50	$58.572	$50,286	$42,000	$33,714
55	$60,501	$52,600	$44,701	$36,801
60	$62,885	$55,462	$48,038	$40,616
65	$65,701	$58,841	$51,981	$45,122
70	$69,014	$62,817	$56,620	$50,422
75	$72,748	$67,298	$61,847	$56,397

A charitable remainder unitrust (CRUT) can provide pre- or postretirement income for you, a spouse, parent, child, or other relative or friend. It can also provide income for more than one person; for example, you can keep the right to income for the rest of your life and then have income paid to your spouse for that person's life.

Figure 42–2 illustrates the current deduction allowable against income taxes at various ages assuming you place $100,000 of cash and/or other assets into a CRUT.

Note that the deduction increases with age. For instance, assuming you took a fixed income for life equal to 5 percent of the value of the CRUT (revalued each year), you'd receive a deduction worth about 24 percent of your contribution if you were age 45 and worth about 62 percent of your contribution if you were age 75. That's because the shorter period of time the charity must wait for its money, the more the gift is worth to the charity—the converse is also true.

The CRAT and the CRUT share important similarities:

Figure 42–2

Deductions for $100,000 Contribution to a Charitable Remainder Unitrust

Payout Rate

Age	5 Percent	6 Percent	7 Percent	8 Percent
45	$23,935	$18,813	$15,028	$12,193
50	$29,005	$23,521	$19,328	$16,084
55	$34,681	$28,941	$24,406	$20,788
60	$40,946	$35,093	$30,321	$26,401
65	$47,621	$41,814	$36,938	$32,817
70	$54,673	$49,101	$44,288	$40,109
75	$61,855	$56,701	$52,131	$48,000

- You receive a sizable income tax charitable deduction in the year you create the trust.
- Generally, you'll pay no income tax even if you transfer appreciated assets to the trust. (You do have to treat any appreciation as a "preference item," which means there may be alternative minimum tax implications.)
- Your deduction for a gift of appreciated securities held for more than one year is based on the full fair-market value rather than on your basis (cost).
- If and when the trustee chooses to sell trust property, any gain is tax exempt to the trust. The trust is tax exempt.
- Your deduction will generally increase if you retain income for only a few years rather than your lifetime.
- Your deduction will be reduced if you retain income not only for your lifetime but for the lifetime of a spouse or other selected beneficiary (but of course your spouse's security and the total income you have retained increases significantly).
- You can save both probate fees and estate taxes since neither the CRAT nor the CRUT are subject to executor's fees or other probate costs in most states. Assets transferred to a qualified charity through a CRAT or CRUT will typically be either fully excludable or totally or partially deductible for estate tax purposes. This may make significant federal estate tax savings possible. For example, if you retain trust income for life, nothing will be in your estate. If you retain trust income for your life and your spouse's life, there will be no tax in either estate. If you have retained an income and a survivor beneficiary other than your spouse receives a continuation of income at your death, only the actuarial value of that portion will be in your estate.
- If you set up either a CRAT or a CRUT in your will, you can provide significant income for the life of one or more beneficiaries and still receive a large charitable estate tax deduction.
- You can use either a CRAT or a CRUT to increase your retirement income by giving low income yielding but highly appreciated stock or other investments to the trust. If you sell the asset, you'd only have the net after-tax proceeds to invest. If you give the asset to the charitable trust (which will be paying you income for a

fixed term of years or for life), the trustee can sell the same asset but pay no income tax and then reinvest (all) the proceeds in higher yielding investments. In fact, this technique also increases investment safety through diversification.

The CRUT differs from the CRAT in a number of important respects:

- A CRUT is more complex (and therefore may be more expensive to administer than a CRAT because the assets in a CRUT must be revalued each year.
- The deduction for a given contribution to a unitrust is significantly lower than the deduction for a gift of the same amount to an annuity trust (see Figure 42–3) because the actuarial value of the charity's interest is much higher with a CRAT.
- The actuarial value of the income interest you retain in a CRUT is significantly higher than the value of the retained income interest in a CRAT (see Figure 42–4). This explains why the deduction for a gift to a CRAT is so much higher than the deduction allowed for a gift of the same amount to a CRUT.
- Because the amount paid to you (and/or your selected beneficiary) reflects any increase in the value of a CRUT's assets, it can serve as a hedge against inflation. Because the CRAT's income is fixed, it is a relatively poor defense against inflation.
- Because the amount paid to you (and/or your selected beneficiary) can fall with a decrease in the value of a CRUT's assets, you may be paid less than anticipated or needed. Because the CRAT's income is fixed, you are more certain of receiving necessary income—even if the trustee must invade the charity's capital to do so.
- The CRUT assures you of income equal to a stated percentage of the trust's value even if the actual income earned by the trust is less than that stated percentage—even if the trustee must invade principal or use capital gains to do so.
- If the actual income earned in a CRUT is more than the percentage you've retained, the excess is added to trust assets and reinvested. That means you'll receive a larger income in later years because you get the same percentage but of a "bigger pie." This is not the case with a CRAT.

Figure 42–3

Two Life Charitable Remainder Trusts
Comparing Annuity with Unitrust
(Deduction for $100,000 Contribution)

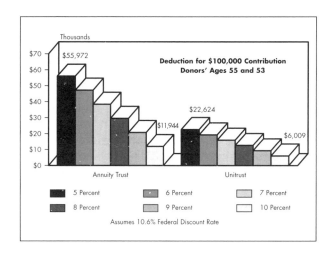

Figure 42–4

Two Life Charitable Remainder Trusts
Comparing Annuity with Unitrust
(Actuarial Value of Income Retained
$100,000 Contribution)

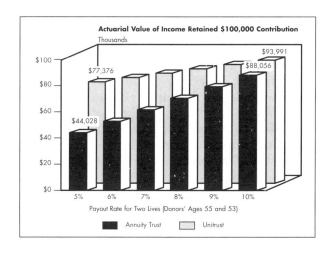

- A CRUT can require the trustee to pay the lower of (a) the actual income of the trust or (b) the stated percentage. If income is less than the stated percentage, any deficiencies in promised distributions could be made up and paid to you in later years when actual trust income is greater than the stated percentage you've

295

retained. This "net income CRUT with makeup provision" enables you to take less income in years you don't need it or when you are in higher tax brackets and receive more in later years when you need it more or are in a lower tax bracket. In contrast the CRAT must pay the specified annuity whether or not there is sufficient trust income. If the principal in the CRAT is real property, such as an apartment house, if rents fall below the specified annuity, the trustee may have to borrow against the property or sell it. With a CRAT, there is much less tax or cash-flow planning flexibility.

- You can choose to make one or more additional contributions to a CRUT after you initially fund it. But you cannot make additional contributions to a CRAT. It is therefore possible to make additional lifetime gifts and also pour over future testamentary bequests from your will into a CRUT. If trust income is less than the required income percentage, you can choose to forgive all or a portion of any year's payment from a CRUT (as if you were making an additional contribution to the trust).

Use Life Insurance

Life insurance is an excellent tool for making charitable gifts for a number of reasons

First, the death benefit is guaranteed as long as premiums are paid. This means that the charity will receive an amount that is fixed (or perhaps increasing) in value and not subject to the potential downside volatile market risks of securities.

Second, life insurance provides an "amplified" gift that enables you to "purchase immortality on the installment plan." Through a relatively small annual cost (the premium), a significant benefit can be provided for the charity of your choice. This sizable gift can be made without impairing or diluting the control of a family business or other investments. Assets earmarked for your family can be kept intact.

Third, life insurance is a self-completing gift. If you live, cash values (which can be used currently by the charity for an emergency or opportunity) grow constantly year after year. If you become disabled, the policy will remain in full force through the "waiver of premium" feature. This guarantees the ultimate death benefit to the charity as well as the same cash values and dividend buildup that

would have been earned had you not become disabled. Even if you were to die after only one deposit, the charity is assured of your full gift.

Fourth, the death proceeds can be received by your designated charity free of federal income and estate taxes, probate and administrative costs, and delays, brokerage fees, or other transfer costs. So your charity receives 100 cent dollars! This prompt (and certain) payment should be compared with the payment of a gift to the same charity under your will.

Fifth, because of the contractual nature of the life insurance contract, large gifts to charity are not subject to attack by disgruntled heirs.

Finally, a substantial gift can be made with no attending publicity. On the other hand, your amplified gift should lead to "amplified honor" and public recognition if desired.

You can use life insurance in a number of ways:

- Name a charity as the annual recipient of any dividends you receive from life insurance. As dividends are paid to the charity, you'll receive a current income tax deduction.
- Use dividends from an existing policy to purchase a new policy and name the charity the owner and beneficiary of the new policy. You'll receive an income tax deduction for the premiums you've paid.
- Name a charity as contingent (backup) beneficiary or final beneficiary under a life insurance policy protecting your dependents.
- Name a charity as the beneficiary of life insurance you currently own or a new life insurance policy. Although this will not yield a current income tax deduction, it will result in a federal estate tax deduction for the full amount of the proceeds payable to charity—regardless of how large the policy.
- Make an absolute assignment (gift) of a life insurance policy you currently own, or donate a new life insurance policy. This will yield a current income tax deduction. Your immediate deduction will be equal to the lower of (a) your cost (premiums paid less any dividends you've received or (b) the value of the policy. You'll also receive a deduction for amounts you pay to the charity in future years to help the charity pay premiums.

Send your check directly to the charity and have it pay the premiums. That way you'll have proof of the date of your contribution and the amount of the gift and assure yourself of the largest possible deduction. (Note that neither deduction will be allowed unless you make the charity owner and beneficiary of the entire policy. The income tax deduction will be lost if you try to keep the cash values and name the charity as beneficiary or if you give away the cash values but name a family member as beneficiary.) In addition to the income tax deduction, the life insurance proceeds will be removed from your estate—thus saving estate taxes.

- Life insurance may make it possible for you to make an immediate gift of land or some other property. This concept is called "wealth replacement." For instance, say you were age 50, a widower, and had three children. Your adjusted gross estate is about $1 million. One of your assets is a $200,000 parcel of undeveloped land you inherited from your late wife (and which will be subject to federal estate taxes at your death). You want to perpetuate the memory of your wife through a memorial scholarship fund but at the same time you don't want to deprive your children of a significant part of your estate.

   You could make your gift of the land immediately (and obtain a very large income tax deduction). You could make tax-free gifts of the income tax savings to your personal beneficiaries (or a trust on their behalf) and they could use those gifts to pay the premiums on life insurance on your life owned by and payable to them. At your death, none of the insurance proceeds will be subject to income, estate, or inheritance tax and your children may actually receive more net after taxes than if you had waited until your death to make the charitable gift.

   Consider coupling a gift in trust (such as the CRAT or CRUT, described above) with this "wealth replacement" concept. The large and immediate income tax deduction generated by the establishment of the charitable trust (with or without the income you'll also receive from the trust) will provide cash to make gifts to your personal beneficiaries. They (or a trust on their behalf) can use those gifts to buy life insurance on your life. In many cases this wealth replacement technique actually enhances wealth; both the charity and your children end up with far more than if you do nothing.

- You can use group term life insurance to meet your charitable objectives. By naming a charity as the (revocable) beneficiary of your group term life insurance for coverage over $50,000, you can not only make a significant gift to charity but also avoid any income tax on the economic benefit. For example. a 63-year-old executive with an average top tax bracket of 28 percent who had $140,000 of coverage would save $353.80 each year. 28 percent of the $1,263.60 annual "Table I cost" (the amount reportable as income). The advantage of this technique was significantly enhanced by the introduction of higher group term rates for individuals older than 65 who receive group term insurance. So you save income taxes every year the charity is named as beneficiary. In a later year if you change your mind, you can change your beneficiary designation and name a new charity or even a personal beneficiary.

Summary

There are many ways you can simultaneously enrich the lives of others while protecting and caring for yourself and your loved ones. Tax-Wise Charitable Planning suggests that you investigate the alternatives with your financial advisors to develop the optimum mix.

43
Handling the Nontax Issues in Business Succession Planning

JON J. GALLO AND DAVID A. HJORTH

Approximately 90 percent of the fourteen million businesses in the U.S. are family owned and managed. Family businesses are responsible for nearly half the gross national product; 50 percent of all the workforce in the private sector is employed in family-owned businesses. Of the Fortune 500 companies, 168 are family owned and managed.

The greatest strength of the family-owned business is the unique blood relationship that exists among family members. This natural kinship can create a competitive edge—a common sense of direction and purpose—that other companies can only dream of matching. Husband-and-wife teams (which account for nearly one-third of the companies on the Fortune 500 list) can generate an unusual, dynamic synergy that adds new depth to the idea of partnership. Then mix in a generation or two of children and siblings. The result can be either a unified common bond or the formula for disaster. Distrust and disagreements among family members can lead to discord, turning clan gatherings into reenactments of scenes from *Cat on a Hot Tin Roof*.

The average family-owned business lasts only twenty-four years. Only 30 percent of family-owned businesses survive the succession from the founder to the next generation. And only 10 percent make it to the third generation.

Jon J. Gallo is a partner with the Los Angeles law firm of Greenberg Glusker Fields Claman & Machtinger LLP. David A. Hjorth is president of DH Financial Consulting Services, Inc., and owner of DH Financial & Insurance Services in Upland, California.

Issues to Be Addressed

If family businesses are so common and many are so successful, why is the likelihood of long-term survival so bleak? The answer lies in recognizing that the term "family business" is a psychological contradiction. Families and businesses have separate and often mutually exclusive psychological profiles. Businesses succeed by being aggressive and confrontational; families avoid confrontations between and among family members. Businesses succeed by changing to meet altered circumstances and new challenges; families succeed by achieving homeostasis and resisting change.

How then can family business succession be prevented from degenerating into chaos? There are few simple answers. But the estate planner can help family members reduce the potential for discord by suggesting a few sound business practices that are based on an understanding of the sometimes contradictory human relations (the "soft" concerns) and financial and estate planning issues (the "hard" issues) that must be confronted.

In dealing with the soft issues, the business owner and his or her advisor must separate (1) employment by the business, (2) control of the business, and (3) ownership of the business. Which family members are employed by the family business? Is the family business a guaranteed source of employment for all family members, whether or not qualified? Who will control the business; how do the family members get along? In dividing the estate, will the family business be owned by all the children or only by those children active in the business?

At the same time, the succession plan must confront such hard issues as whether the business will be able to recruit, reward, and retain key managers. Will the business be able to pay off existing loans and cover lines of credit? Will there be adequate cash flow to provide operating capital? Will (and should) the business be able to pay salaries to family members working in the business as well as provide some form of remuneration to nonparticipating family members? Will the business be able to buy out family members who want to sell their interests? What financial and emotional upheaval among the surviving family members will the death of a family member cause in the business, and what effect will estate taxes have on the successful continuation of the business?

Although some families consider these issues before they become troublesome, most do not. If not analyzed and planned for well in advance, the hard and soft issues can escalate into major problems that will diminish the probability of a favorable business succession. As one of the authors wrote in 1988:[1]

> Too often successful businessmen focus on the current financial visibility of their company and do not look at the human relationships which are so integral in the successful continuation of the business. A few years ago, one of California's largest wineries was in the news, when its president was fired by his mother, the firm's majority stockholder, and replaced by his brother. The father had been the majority stockholder until his death, at which point his will stipulated that his wife receive his stockholdings. His son, however, was his successor as the top manager for the business. The seed for dissension was plain to see: One family member, who was inactive in the business, held the power of ownership, while another managed the enterprise, and yet a third was waiting in the wings.
>
> "You asked mom for an employment contract. The family got together and elected me chairman of the board. And they asked me to look into your performance as president. As a result of that, I've decided that you and Vicki are both to be terminated." (One brother's statement to the other.)
>
> Or as another brother once said regarding sibling rivalry: "I spend a lot of time figuring out how I'm going to get my brother's half of the business."

While separation of management from ownership may be normal—even essential—in publicly held corporations, it can be the cause of a fatal controversy in the smaller, family-owned business. And, without advance planning, disaster is practically an inevitable consequence. As John Ward has observed:

> The process of resolving conflicts must be established long before the children arrive in the business. It must begin in the home: in the lessons children are taught, in the way the family conducts itself. It continues with . . . the children's entry into the business and their preparation for leadership roles . . . families find that considering these challenges ahead of time increases the chances of solving them to everyone's satisfaction.[2]

Guidelines for Success

A family business is most likely to succeed if the advisors recommend the following ten common-sense rules:

Provide leadership. Don't let your client ignore potential problems. Recognize that positive relationships are in everyone's best interest and your clients are the ones who must take the initiative. They must strive for unity and cooperation among family members.

Don't let the client treat the business as a personal playground. Family businesses that treat employment of all family members as a right, rather than a privilege, are unlikely to survive the death of the founder. Employment criteria should be established and adhered to. If the founder determines that positions must be found for family members who are unemployable in the outside world, make certain those individuals are not placed in executive positions where they can harm the business. If the founders lend money to family members (or to themselves) from company funds, be sure that all transactions are treated at arm's length. Have written policies that cover such arrangements without discriminating against minority shareholders. And keep books and records in good order at all times. The bottom line is that it is crucial to create a traceable paper trail.

Help your clients work out their divorce today. Divorce can destroy in a few months a business that took years to build as ownership of the business becomes a pawn in the divorce settlement. This is had enough when husband-wife teams split up. But it can be even worse when a former

1. Hjorth and Connelly, *Estate Planning for the Independent Businessman*, INLAND BUSINESS MAGAZINE (June 1988).

2. John Ward, KEEPING THE FAMILY BUSINESS HEALTHY 54 (San Francisco, Jossey-Bass, 1987).

son-in-law or daughter-in-law becomes a silent partner. Shareholders should be encouraged to enter into buy-sell agreements so that ownership remains in the family in the event of a divorce.

Prepare a succession plan. Have your clients decided what will happen to their business after they die, become incapacitated, or decide it's time to retire?

- Who will be the future owners of the business? What method or combination of methods will be used to transfer legal ownership to successors? What involvement will withdrawing shareholders have in future decisions?
- When will a transition occur and what will it be contingent upon?
- Is active participation in the business required for ownership? Can nonfamily members (key employees) become owners?
- Will (should) there be a distinction in voting rights for different owners? That is, will some owners hold nonvoting stock while others hold voting shares?
- Are there existing shareholder agreements (such as stock redemption or buy-sell agreements) that influence or restrict ownership decisions? Will those agreements need to be amended? What other problems can be anticipated?

While every situation is unique, experience leads to certain commonsense conclusions concerning succession plans. First, children not actively involved in the business usually should not own an interest in the family business. It is common that the key family asset is the business, and only one of the children has chosen it as his or her life's work, while the other children have followed other pursuits. The parent-owner typically wants to leave the business to the child involved in the business yet treat all the children equally. Even if the dollar value of the assets can be mathematically divided into equal shares, the parents are concerned whether any distribution will be truly fair when one child gets a business and the others receive cash or other assets.

Fairness and equality are not easy to define. "Equality" carries with it the notion of a quantitative, measurable sameness in the shares of the estate's assets. "Fairness," on the other hand, is best translated as "equitable." After considering all the issues, we want to do the right thing for each of our children, but the result may not always be mathematically equal.

For lack of a better solution, the business owner may sometimes be tempted to leave the business in fractional shares to all the children, without regard to the fact that only one child may be involved in its operation. The result is usually disastrous to family harmony as well as to the long-term health of the business. Inactive owners of a family business almost invariably wish to withdraw as much cash as possible from the business. In contrast, active owners want to reinvest as much as possible in the business to increase the likelihood of success. In such instances, siblings will view one another as "parasites" or "plunderers." Those not involved in the business will regard those running it as plunderers, "earning all that money and fighting us for every dollar our shares are worth." Meanwhile, the siblings who are running the business view the others as parasites who are taking the profits with them.

Second, if the business will be owned by two or more children, one should be designated as the decision maker. In most family businesses, the founder is the decision maker. The children have usually developed a model based on centralized decision making. Consequently, committees generally do not work.

Don't ignore the rights of minority shareholders. Minority shareholders have rights that can do almost as much harm to the business in as short a time as can a divorce. Most complaints by minority shareholders center around salaries of active managers that are "too high" and dividends that are "too low." If minority shareholders are treated unfairly, the majority shareholder may find himself or herself dealing with court-ordered audits, followed by forced distribution of retained earnings in the form of dividends or liquidation of the business.

Give minority shareholders an easy out. When family members are unhappy with the business, make it possible for them to sell their shares for a fair and equitable price. For everybody's sake, minority shareholders need to be able to convert their ownership interests to cash.

Help provide communication. Nonactive minority shareholders and even active heirs working their way up the ranks can become anxious when they don't know what is going on. The advisor's responsibility is to help all those involved in running the business so that they have realistic expectations with respect to management, succession, earnings, and dividends.

Succession and estate planning is almost hopeless or, at the very least, incredibly frustrating when conflict among family members renders communication impossible. In *Passing the Torch*, Mike Cohn identified three deficiencies that tend to underlie family disputes:

- The inability to communicate, either by lack of listening or trying to see the other person's viewpoint;
- Unwillingness to reach an amicable and well-reasoned solution; and
- Lack of consideration and understanding for others.

Changing such behavior requires a new viewpoint centered on today and the future and directed toward specific goals. Emotional and psychological issues that sustain conflict can, and must, be redirected in healthier, more positive directions. Mediation is an effective tool in improving communication in a contentious family business. Mediation can effectively create this new frame of reference and redirect misguided energy. With the help of an objective third party as mediator, participants can frequently reach agreements cooperatively. Unlike litigation, which is a zero sum game with winners and losers, mediation creates a climate for the parties to solve their own problems.

Help the clients create a mission statement. This process helps provide the family business with a clearer sense of its purpose, identity, and direction, and gives the family members a better understanding of how the business is run. In creating the mission statement, the clients need to consider, among others, the following issues:

- How is the existing business succeeding?
- What changes (if any) are needed in the existing business, and how do we monitor our results?
- What are the basic values that are collectively held by the family in running the business?
- Are all existing and prospective owners able to understand the company's financial statements?
- What planning for the future is necessary (e.g., new product lines, research and development)?

- What risks are acceptable to the family business and what risks are unacceptable?
- What can and should we learn from the past?

Establish a family board. In many family businesses, meetings of the board of directors and shareholders are more myth than reality. But if your clients want family harmony, make a point of scheduling board meetings regularly and inviting shareholders to participate. These procedures help your clients meet their legal responsibilities to minority shareholders while giving smaller shareholders a voice.

Hold shareholders meetings. Such a meeting can be another name for a fun-time family reunion. Each year, many family-owned businesses pay to have the clan meet at a resort. A part of each day may be devoted to family business, with the balance of the time devoted to socializing. This approach strengthens family bonds, resolves problems, and helps initiate new generations into the business.

Once the family succession and transition plan exists, both the advisor and the business owner need to focus on the process of transferring the family business, and must understand that transfer taxes may be minimized most effectively through lifetime transfers. Even though the estate and gift tax system uses the same tax rates for both lifetime gifts and transfers at death, the effective tax rate applicable to transfers at death is more than twice as high as the effective tax rate applicable to lifetime gifts. This difference in effective rates occurs because the estate tax is tax inclusive (that is, the entire estate is taxed, including the funds that are used to pay the estate tax), while the gift tax is tax exclusive (that is, only the gift is taxed).

Conclusion

Advisors must recognize family businesses for what they are: a combination of family and business in which financial, emotional, and estate planning issues are inextricably intertwined. Advisors must help the family balance these issues while maintaining family harmony and achieving an orderly succession of both management and ownership.

44
Estate Planning
for the Remarried Retiree

LEON FIELDMAN AND MARY D. FIELDMAN

Retirees usually are older persons. For them, the prospect of becoming widowed is, unfortunately, not remote. Given the fact that the divorce rate in America is almost 50 percent of the marriage rate, even retirees who have not lost a spouse may get divorced. As a result, many retirees find themselves to be newly single. Many of those newly single persons will remarry.

Estate planning, important as it is in a first marriage, is even more vital—and more complicated—in a second marriage. And estate planning in a second marriage becomes even more crucial for retirees, because of their age and the likelihood that they have more assets to dispose of than a younger person would.

Estate planning presents special problems for spouses in a second marriage. Those marriages seem to vary more widely than first marriages in the circumstances of the spouses. For example, the second marriage may be of the "June-December" variety, where one spouse is 45 while the other spouse is 65. The wife may have more assets or more income than the husband. One spouse may have large tax shelters or be facing a substantial tax delinquency. One spouse may have children, but the other none. Relations may be strained between a prospective stepfather and his stepchildren. One spouse may be healthy and the other sickly. In a second marriage, all of these factors can seriously complicate estate planning.

A good time to do estate planning for a second marriage is before the couple marries. That is

Leon Fieldman - DECEASED - was a senior partner at Jenner & Block in Chicago. Mary D. Fieldman is a vice president of marketing and sales for Concord Investment Company in Chicago. It has not been edited for applicable changes occasioned by passage of TRA '97. The original version of this article appeared in the *Illinois Bar Journal,* vol. 74, no. 2, October 1985. © Illinois State Bar Association.

when binding legal arrangements should be made about future financial obligations of each to the other, during life and at death. Postnuptial agreements exist, of course, but are much more difficult to conclude because the goal of the negotiations—the marriage of the parties—has already taken place.

Statutory Benefits for a Surviving Spouse

If a couple enters a second marriage without making a written contract between them as to how their respective assets are to pass at death, statutory provisions will control the disposition of their assets. Under the laws of most states, a surviving spouse has significant rights:

1. A surviving spouse has priority to be appointed as administrator of the deceased spouse's intestate estate.
2. If a spouse dies testate, the surviving spouse has the right to renounce or elect against the will and to receive a portion of the probate estate.
3. If a spouse dies intestate, the surviving spouse is entitled to receive a share of the decedent's property, with the dead spouse's children getting only the balance.
4. A surviving spouse is entitled to a surviving spouse's award, which is often a fixed sum with a minimum amount.

While both spouses are living, each may have important rights granted by statute. One is the right to be considered for appointment as guardian of a disabled spouse. Another is the homestead right, which for practical purposes gives a spouse the right to grant or withhold signature on a deed of homestead property of the other spouse. And, under federal law, a qualified retirement plan must provide automatic survivor benefits to the surviving spouse of a retiree-participant or of a vested participant who dies before retirement, unless those rights are waived.

The effect of these statutory provisions is that without appropriate estate planning in a second marriage, a husband, for example, may find it impossible to leave his entire estate to his own children, even though his wife may be wealthy in her own right or have substantial income of her own.

Prenuptial Agreements— Essential Elements

The traditional way to avoid the impact of these statutes is for persons about to marry for a second time to enter into a prenuptial agreement, although many intelligent and sophisticated people do enter a second marriage without such an agreement. A prenuptial agreement ideally is a formal written agreement prepared by a lawyer. It must be signed and is often witnessed and notarized. The following elements are also crucial to its validity:

1. Each spouse should have his or her own separate counsel. Lack of separate counsel could lead to the claim, when a spouse dies, that the surviving spouse was not properly represented, due to conflict of interest, by the dead spouse's lawyer. Therefore, the surviving spouse may claim the prenuptial agreement is invalid.
2. Each spouse should reveal in detail his or her own assets and their current values. This is to prevent a later attack on the agreement by the surviving spouse, who might claim that had he or she been fully informed about the spouse's assets, he or she would have negotiated a better deal for himself or herself and that the agreement therefore is not valid.

Bargaining over the Terms

Bargaining between the spouses over a proposed prenuptial agreement can become intense and difficult. Often the impending marriage seems to hang in doubt. A fiancé may complain that if the partner really loved him or her, he or she would not insist on a prenuptial agreement at all. The parties may seem at a complete impasse, and rough give-and-take may be necessary to hammer out the details. Despite the difficulties, with the help of persistent and knowledgeable lawyers, the parties usually can reach a mutually acceptable agreement.

The Agreement's Goals and General Contents

Most agreements have the same goals: (1) to fix the financial obligations of each spouse to the other during the marriage (to the extent state law does not do so) and (2) to allow each spouse to will his or her own assets at death without being required to leave anything to the other spouse. Although some agreements deal with alimony and property settlements in case the couple divorces, this chapter will not examine those provisions. An agreement generally recites the rights each party surrenders and the rights each will gain. It establishes rules governing the financial conduct of the parties with regard to each other during the marriage, as well as the disposition of their assets at death.

A spouse may be asked to surrender some or all of the statutory rights described earlier in this chapter. Each spouse usually retains the right to control his or her own assets during the marriage. The wealthier spouse may promise to support the other spouse during marriage in the style to which he or she was accustomed. The spouse owning the residence in which the couple is to live can agree that the other spouse can continue to occupy that residence for some period of time after the owner dies. Either or both of the spouses can agree to provide at death for the surviving spouse, usually by a provision in a will or living trust. A recital can be incorporated that there are no oral agreements between the parties on the subject matter of the prenuptial agreement.

Specific Provisions— Cash Bequest

A promise to will a specific amount of cash to the surviving spouse has a big drawback. The estate of the promising spouse can grow or shrink between the date of the agreement and death. The cash payment therefore may be a much smaller or a much larger part of the dying spouse's estate than the parties intended.

A better approach is for the promising spouse to agree to will to the other spouse a specific percentage or fraction of his or her estate. To avoid ambiguity, "estate" should be defined as gross or net probate estate or as the gross estate or taxable (as computed without taking a marital deduction for what the other spouse is to receive from the promising spouse) estate for federal estate tax purposes. If the latter approach is to be used, remember that the estate of the promising spouse has to be large enough to be required to file a federal estate tax return. That amount currently is $600,000. If there is no probate estate because, for example, all of the assets are in a living trust, the asset pool from which the bequest is to be made must be carefully defined.

Restriction on Gifts

Obviously, the unrestricted right to give away assets during one's lifetime could result in one dying without any estate at all. A promise to leave part of the estate to the surviving spouse would become meaningless. That is why some agreements put restrictions on gifts by the promising spouse, such as limiting gifts to descendants to no more than the annual gift tax exclusion amount of $10,000 each. Such an agreement could give adequate protection, depending on the size of the donor-spouse's estate. A wealthy donor-spouse may then want to bargain for the right to make annual gifts of $20,000 and to require the other spouse to consent to gift-splitting on the gift tax returns.

Who Pays the Income Taxes?

A provision dealing with who pays the income taxes need not favor either spouse, but can avoid future controversy. In a first marriage, the couple normally files joint returns, and, since the couple likely pools their funds, the question of how the tax liability is divided between them seldom arises. But in a second marriage, one spouse may not want to pay the income tax on the other spouse's separate income. Furthermore, one spouse may have tax shelters or tax-free municipal bonds, while the other spouse's income is all taxable. To deal with these circumstances, the agreement might provide that the couple will file joint federal and state income tax returns, but that each spouse will contribute to the payment of the tax in a specified way, such as:

1. The couple will share the tax payments in the same ratio that their respective taxable incomes bear to their combined taxable income.
2. The wealthier spouse will pay all of the income tax.
3. The less-wealthy spouse will pay no more of the total tax bill than he or she would have paid had he or she remained single, filed his or her own tax returns, and paid his or her own tax.

If avoiding personal liability for the other spouse's income tax is an issue, the agreement can provide that the spouses will file as "married filing a separate return." And if a spouse has reason to believe that his or her intended is careless or worse in reporting income and deductions, he or she should not agree to file joint returns.

In dealing with income tax issues, the couple must keep in mind that Social Security payments are partly income-taxable for taxpayers with higher incomes and, for the spouse who may still be working, that Social Security taxes are large and growing. In today's economic climate, tax statutes very likely will be subject to change, requiring the agreement to be kept current by periodic review and revision.

Amendments and Cancellation

Although many prenuptial agreements do not provide for amendment or cancellation, consider adopting a provision that the agreement will automatically terminate after five years, for example, if the parties are then still married to each other and are living together as husband and wife. This would restore to the second spouse the rights a first spouse would have had. Without such a provision, the parties should regularly review the agreement to determine if it is still appropriate in light of new circumstances.

How to Structure a Bequest at Death

Suppose, for example, a husband wants to provide in the agreement that he will bequeath some assets to his wife on his death. The agreement could specify (1) what sort of assets can be used to satisfy the provision he is to make for her and (2) whether the bequest is to be outright or in trust. Leaving property outright is simple, avoids a long trust entanglement between the husband's children and his wife, and qualifies for the marital deduction for federal estate tax purposes. On the other hand, the wife will be free, on her subsequent death, to leave that inherited property to her own family or to anyone else of her choice, thereby giving her the power to exclude her husband's children and his other family members.

Providing for a trust makes sense if the husband wants to insure against that possibility or if his wife may need trust protection because of illness or age. If a trust is used, it will often be one that qualifies (or can be elected to qualify) for the marital deduction, such as a general power of appointment trust or a qualified terminable interest property (QTIP) trust. Under federal estate tax law, to qualify for the marital deduction, each such trust must give the surviving spouse all of the trust income during her lifetime, even if she subsequently again remarries. In a QTIP trust, principal need not be given to the surviving spouse.

Advantages and Disadvantages of a QTIP Trust

In a QTIP trust, a spouse can designate who is to receive the trust principal upon the surviving spouse's death. This feature accounts for the QTIP's popularity in second marriages, for it permits the surviving spouse to get all of the trust income following his or her spouse's death, yet allows the decedent to leave the trust principal to his or her own children after the second spouse's death. Furthermore, a QTIP trust can be elected to qualify for the marital deduction in the decedent's estate.

The major perceived disadvantage to a QTIP trust is that the decedent's children will have to wait for their stepparent's death before getting the trust principal. Another practical problem is that the trustee will have a duty to the surviving spouse as the income beneficiary, as well as a duty to the decedent's children as the remaindermen. This has a potential for conflict, especially where the survivor's need for income exceeds his or her actual income.

An Alternative to Using a QTIP Trust

To avoid or lessen the disadvantages of using a QTIP trust, one spouse might choose to divide his or her estate in thirds upon his or her death. One-third could go outright to the surviving spouse; another third could go into a QTIP trust, with the survivor as the income beneficiary and the decedent's children as the remaindermen; and the final one-third could go outright to the children at the decedent's death. This arrangement gives everyone a piece of the cake. It may, however, result in a federal estate tax being payable at the first spouse's death (rather than being deferred until the second spouse's death) because the provisions for the survivor may not equal the optimum marital deduction in the decedent's estate. A spouse must decide whether the right of his or her children to receive one-third at his or her death, without having to wait for the surviving spouse's death, is worth the projected estate tax cost.

Irrevocable Insurance Trusts

A spouse owning insurance on his or her own life could remove that insurance from his or her estate by giving the policies outright to his or her children. Or, if that would be unwise, he or she could create an irrevocable insurance trust agreement for the children and transfer ownership of the policies to the trustee, who could be directed to transfer the death proceeds to the children or to retain those proceeds in trust for the children. A gift tax might be payable on the transfer, but federal estate tax savings could be large. The spouse might then be inclined to agree to provide more generously for his or her mate from his or her remaining estate in the prenuptial agreement.

Funding a Payment to a Spouse at Death

In a second marriage, the method of funding a payment for the spouse at death is more sensitive than in a first marriage. In general, a payment to a surviving spouse could be made from (1) insurance or pension or profit-sharing benefits, (2) joint tenancy assets, or (3) the probate estate or living trust assets.

Funding with insurance or pension or profit-sharing benefits has a number of advantages. Payment from the insurance company or from the pension or profit-sharing plan is not subject to being thwarted by an attack on the will, because those payments are almost never made pursuant to the terms of a will. And insurance payments and, to a lesser degree, pension and profit-sharing benefits are usually paid promptly after death and are usually paid directly to the beneficiary. Those payments, therefore, are not subject to funding or time-of-payment decisions by the decedent's executor. This is most important in a second marriage where the executor may not be the surviving spouse but instead the decedent's child or other relative.

If this method or either of the other methods is used to fund the payment, the prenuptial agreement should clearly preclude a renunciation of the will, a will contest, a request for a surviving spouse's award, and any other claim against the probate estate by the surviving spouse. This is to prevent the surviving spouse from receiving more than the intended payment.

A spouse may intend to provide for his or her mate by creating a joint tenancy with him or her in one or more of his or her assets. Joint tenancy does have the advantage of usually not being subject to probate delays or controversy. However, other beneficiaries of the estate could claim that the joint tenancy was created not to pass title at death, but merely as a lifetime convenience between the spouses. The basic problem with a spousal joint tenancy is that the tenancy may be difficult to undo if the marriage fails. For example, a spouse may place some securities into joint tenancy with his or her mate. If later the spouse changes his or her mind and wishes to put the securities back into his or her own name, the other spouse's signature will be required before the transfer agent will reissue the securities. If the marriage is not going well, such a signature may not be forthcoming.

An unexpected result can occur from the use of joint tenancy. Under current federal estate tax law, one-half of all assets held in joint tenancy between spouses is included in the estate of the spouse who dies first, regardless of contribution. Thus, if the prenuptial agreement requires one spouse to leave the other one-third of his or her gross estate for federal estate tax purposes, and one spouse places one-third of his or her estate into joint tenancy with the other spouse, at the first spouse's death, one-half of that one-third will not be a part of his or her estate. Therefore, surviving spouse will take the joint tenancy property and may still be entitled to other property from the decedent's estate to make up the one-third share.

The use of the probate estate as the source for funding a provision for the surviving spouse has some problems. Delay is one. And, where conflict exists between the stepparent and stepchildren, the will could be contested by the children on the ground that their parent was of unsound mind when he or she made the will or that the will is invalid for some other reason. If the decedent's child is executor or coexecutor of the will, bad personal relationships may make the administration of the estate difficult, costly, and prolonged.

Occupancy of Marital Residence after Spouse's Death

Another common provision in a prenuptial agreement gives the surviving spouse the right to reside in the decedent-owned marital residence for some period following the decedent's death. If no such provision is made, when the first spouse dies, the survivor may find himself or herself living in a home that he or she does not own and that is the property of the decedent's children. This can be an uncomfortable if not intolerable situation for the survivor.

A spouse may believe that his or her residence is too valuable an asset to leave outright to his or her spouse. However, a spouse may wish to provide a place for a surviving spouse to live after his or her death, at least for some limited time until the survivor can move into other quarters.

To deal with this situation, some prenuptial agreements provide that a spouse will allow his or her survivor to use the residence rent-free for some period after his or her death. The agreement must be specific as to who pays the real estate taxes, condominium assessments, utility bills, minor repairs, major repairs, and other expenses of the residence. If the survivor is to pay these charges during occupancy after the decedent's death, that places no financial burden on the decedent's children while their stepparent continues to live in the residence they will ultimately receive. However, to preserve the marital deduction, the survivor's obligation to pay expenses should not be greater than the obligation placed on the holder of an income interest by the applicable Income and Principal Act. But if a spouse wants his or her survivor to live cost-free in the residence, those expenses will have to be paid by the takers of the other assets of the decedent after his or her death. This means that the children will have to come up with the money during their stepparent's life, which sets the stage for unhappiness and conflict. A more prudent solution would require creation of a trust, funded with some other assets that can be used (or the income from which can be used) to pay the expenses.

Other points to consider about the use of the residence by the survivor are these:

1. How long is the survivor's use to last? It could be for his or her entire lifetime, but otherwise it is best to specify a fixed period, such as twelve months from the decedent's death, rather than an indefinite period. An indefinite period may, as a practical matter, require agreement between the survivor and the other takers of the decedent's estate, unless an independent nonfamily fiduciary is directed to make that decision.

2. Is the survivor's use limited to the primary residence or can he or she also use a vacation home on the same terms?

3. What if the survivor wishes to move to another residence during the permitted period of rent-free use? This is often permitted, but the terms have to be spelled out in detail.

4. What about the furnishings in the residence? Rent-free use of a residence does not necessarily include use of the contents. It may come as a great shock to the survivor when, shortly after his or her spouse dies, the children remove from the residence all of the furniture and furnishings that belonged to their parent. Therefore, a provision allowing the survivor the rent-free use of the residence should also permit the survivor to use, if not own outright, all of the furniture and furnishings normally located in the residence.

Personal Belongings

Many fierce family battles are waged after the death of a parent about relatively inexpensive personal items, such as clothing, jewelry, and furniture. Disposition of personal belongings is highly sensitive in a second marriage and can worsen when the second marriage has lasted a number of years. Then it is difficult to ascertain which items belong to which spouse and which to both of them. There usually are no title papers to show who owns what. Even records of purchase by one

spouse or the other are not conclusive, because they do not show a possible subsequent gift from the purchasing spouse to the other spouse.

These problems can be avoided if the spouses are willing to have the prenuptial agreement provide that, at death, all tangible personal property will pass outright to the surviving spouse. However, if the wife, for example, has family heirlooms that she wants her children to receive at her death, the agreement might provide that at her death all of her tangible personal property passes outright to her husband except for specifically described items that then pass outright to her children.

If the agreement is silent on chattels, and if each spouse intends to will his or her chattels to his or her children, then the spouses should make and keep detailed records as to which items are owned by which spouse. These records could describe the items that each spouse brought into the second marriage, state the purchase date and the purchaser of important items purchased during the marriage, and note which items originally belonged to one spouse but were subsequently given to the other spouse.

Appointment of Spouse as Fiduciary

Is it wise to appoint a second spouse to a fiduciary position such as executor, trustee, guardian, or as an attorney-in-fact in a power of attorney?

If, for example, the second wife is named as executor of the husband's will, which leaves part of his estate to his children, some of her fiduciary powers loom more important than they would if the marriage were the first marriage. For example, an executor is entitled to a fee. A first spouse often waives the fee; a second spouse may not. The second wife may retain her own lawyers to represent her as executor, rather than the husband's lawyers, contrary to the husband's expectations. Usually, a direction to retain certain lawyers is considered to be precatory, not mandatory.

If the will gives the executor customary powers, under the laws of many states the executor can decide what assets to sell and when to sell them to raise cash, subject to the general rule that the first source for cash requirements is the residue of the estate rather than specific bequests. An executor may have the right to dictate burial arrangements for the deceased spouse. He or she can pass on claims and pay them or contest them. An executor has important elections under the Internal Revenue Code. He or she funds bequests and, within limits, determines the timing of the payment of bequests. The executor can accelerate or delay the closing and distribution of the estate.

A spouse reviewing these broad powers may decide that to keep peace between his or her spouse and his or her children, he or she will name one of the children as coexecutor with the other spouse. This, of course, does not avoid conflict and impasse unless the will states which executor is to prevail in the case of a deadlock. A third executor could be appointed to prevent a deadlock, but in many estates this would be too cumbersome. Perhaps the best solution is the appointment of a non-family executor, such as a bank or a trustworthy and sophisticated individual.

A second spouse might also be appointed as successor trustee or cotrustee of his or her spouse's living trust. Because such a trustee usually has a great deal of discretion in matters of personal care and investments, his or her authority may be perceived by the children as being misused. The same problem exists in the reverse if a child is appointed instead of the second spouse. An independent successor trustee may be the answer.

Retired persons often sign durable powers of attorney for health or property purposes. These highly useful powers delegate responsibility to be effective either at once or when disability occurs. Here, too, the appointment of a second spouse as the sole attorney-in-fact may place him or her in direct conflict with the decedent's children and may lead to strife and litigation.

A living will usually directs that life-sustaining measures shall be withheld or withdrawn when there is a terminal illness or injury with death imminent. When the time comes, someone in the family must notify the patient's doctor of the existence of the living will and see that the patient's wishes are carried out. If the second spouse and the patient's children are not in agreement with the goals of the living will, the patient, while healthy, should be sure to deliver copies of the living will to those who share his or her views on impending death.

Review of the Arrangements

As in all relationships, a second marriage can be successful or it can fail. Failure does not necessarily mean divorce, for the couple may continue to live together unhappily for a long time. In addition to a possible change in the relationship between the spouses, the assets of each may change materially in value. Their incomes may rise or fall. Catastrophic illness may strike one of them. Children from a first marriage may become adults and no longer require support or substantial bequests at death. For all of these reasons, prenuptial agreements and other documents used to carry out the estate plan must be reviewed regularly by spouses in a second marriage. Failure to conduct honest and thoughtful reviews may perpetuate an arrangement that has become outdated and inappropriate. Periodic and careful reviews, on the other hand, with the help of candid and professional lawyers, can keep estate planning for the remarried retiree effective and in mesh with current circumstances.

APPENDIX A
Sample Prenuptial Agreement

This prenuptial agreement is made at Chicago, Illinois, on July 1, 1993, between John Howard ("Howard") of Chicago, Illinois, and Jane Wendell ("Wendell") of Peoria, Illinois.

Howard is a widower and is retired from the practice of law. He has two adult children and three minor grandchildren, who currently are his only descendants. Wendell is a widow and is retired from work as a bookkeeper. She has one adult child and two minor grandchildren, who currently are her only descendants.

Howard and Wendell plan to marry each other on or about August 15, 1993. They intend by this agreement to adjust the rights each will have in the other's assets and estate because of that marriage.

NOW, THEREFORE, in consideration of their planned marriage and of the mutual promises contained in this agreement, Howard and Wendell agree as follows:

1. Howard has consulted John Jones, of Chicago, Illinois, who has advised him about this agreement and his legal rights under it, as well as his legal rights if this agreement were not made. Wendell has consulted Richard Roe, of Peoria, Illinois, who as her lawyer has advised her about this agreement and her legal rights under it, as well as her legal rights if this agreement were not made. Among other things, Howard and Wendell each has been advised that under Illinois law a spouse who has not made an agreement similar to this one may be entitled:

A. To preference to act as administrator of the other spouse's intestate estate;
B. To receive upon the death of the other spouse, if the other spouse dies testate, regardless of the provisions of the deceased spouse's will, at least one-third of all probate property owned by the deceased spouse at time of death;
C. To receive upon the death of the other spouse, if the other spouse dies intestate, at least one-half of all probate property owned by the deceased spouse at the time of death; and
D. To a surviving spouse's award of at least $10,000.

Howard and Wendell each has also been advised that he or she may have or acquire (1) rights under federal law to receive a qualified joint and survivor annuity and a qualified preretirement survivor annuity as the surviving spouse of a retirement plan participant and (2) other rights granted to spouses under the laws of Illinois or other states in which either or both of them

may reside or own property. Except as otherwise specifically provided in this agreement, each party hereby releases all such rights described in this paragraph 1 and all financial rights and claims of every sort arising from their planned marriage, or under any present or future law, in and to the property now owned or hereafter acquired by the other party.

2. Howard and Wendell each acknowledges that he or she is fully conversant with the financial assets and income of the other party and is entering into this agreement voluntarily and with full understanding of its provisions. Howard warrants to Wendell that Exhibit A to this agreement is a true statement of his approximate net worth as of July 1, 1993, and of his 1992 gross income. Wendell warrants to Howard that Exhibit B to this agreement is a true statement of her approximate net worth as of July 1, 1993, and of her 1992 gross income.

3. All property owned or acquired by either party before or during their marriage to each other shall remain the separate property of that party, except as provided in this agreement. There shall be no marital, community, or quasi-community property. Each party shall have the right to control, sell, mortgage, give, or otherwise deal with any and all of his or her respective separate property now or hereafter owned by her or him without the other party joining. A transfer by either party will convey the same title that would be conveyed if the parties were not married. If their marriage is terminated by divorce, or by declaration of invalidity or annulment, the separate property of each party shall remain the property of the party owning it, free of any claim by the other, and shall be assigned to that spouse as her or his separate property, which shall include but not be limited to non-marital property under the Illinois Marriage and Dissolution of Marriage Act.

4. Each party hereby waives, effective when their planned marriage takes place:

A. the right to be or to nominate the personal representative of the other party's estate in the case of intestacy or in case no named executor acts as such, and the right to act as guardian of the person or of the estate, or both, of the other party if the other party is declared legally disabled;
B. the right to renounce the other party's will even if the will makes no provision for the surviving spouse;

C. the right to an intestate share in the other party's probate estate;

D. the right to a surviving spouse's award;

E. her or his dower or curtesy or homestead interest in the other party's real estate; and

F. the right under federal law to receive a qualified joint and survivor annuity and a qualified preretirement survivor annuity under a retirement plan in which either party is a participant. [*Note:* Under developing case law, for the waiver to be valid, it may be necessary for the waiving spouse to reexecute the waiver after the marriage.]

5. Howard shall leave $500,000 outright to Wendell at his death if she survives him for thirty days, if they are married to each other at the time of his death, and if they are living together as husband and wife at the time of his death. Howard shall make no gifts or other transfers during his lifetime or at his death that would endanger his ability to comply with the foregoing provisions of this paragraph 5.

6. Nothing contained in this agreement shall be construed as a waiver or release of the obligation of either party to provide reasonable support for the other party during the marriage to the extent the resources of the other party are insufficient for that purpose. Nothing contained in this agreement shall be construed as a waiver by either party of any gift or bequest that may be made to him or her by the other. Each party may make such disposition of his or her own property for the benefit of the other in excess of the requirements of this agreement as each sees fit.

7. Subject to paragraph 6, each party shall (1) be responsible for the payment of his or her own debts and liabilities, whether incurred before or during their marriage or following termination of the marriage, and (2) not contract any debt or liability with third parties for which the other, or the other's assets, income or estate, shall be liable, and (3) keep the other party free, harmless, and indemnified of and from any debts or liabilities hereafter contracted by the first party with third parties.

8. This instrument contains the entire agreement of the parties on its subject matter and supersedes any oral agreements between them on its subject matter. This agreement may be amended or revoked only by written agreement of the parties, which shall specifically provide that it is intended to amend or revoke this agreement. This agreement shall be construed under Illinois law, despite any later domicile or residence of either party.

9. Each party shall upon request execute any documents necessary to evidence rights waived under this agreement, including but not limited to a binding consent to the other party's election, as a participant in a retirement plan, to waive the qualified joint and survivor annuity form of benefit or the qualified preretirement survivor annuity form of benefit or both.

10. In conveying or otherwise dealing with the separate property of either party, that party shall be and hereby is constituted the other party's attorney-in-fact with power to join in the contemplated transaction and execute documents to effect it on behalf of the other party without the consent or knowledge of the other party, to the same extent as if their marriage had not taken place.

11. The invalidity of any provision of this agreement shall not impair the validity of any other provision. If any provision of this agreement is determined by a court of competent jurisdiction to be unenforceable, that provision shall be deemed to be severable and this agreement shall remain in force with such provision severed.

12. This agreement shall be effective only if the contemplated marriage between the parties occurs. If the marriage does not occur, this agreement shall not be effective.

13. This agreement shall be binding upon, and inure to the benefit of, the parties and their respective heirs, legatees and personal representatives.

IN WITNESS WHEREOF the parties have signed this agreement and Exhibits A and B hereto.

_____	_____
John Howard	Witness
_____	_____
Jane Wendell	Witness

Exhibit A

John Howard's approximate net worth as of July 1, 1993, is comprised of the following:

1. 3,250 common shares of stock in Howard Mfg. Corp., a closely held family corporation with 10,000 common shares outstanding and with no preferred shares outstanding. Current book value is $265 per share: $861,250

2. Self-directed IRA rollover trust invested in marketable commercial paper, bonds, and stocks: $1,375,000

3. Marketable bonds and stocks: $675,000

4. Single-family residence located at 1234 First Street, Chicago, Illinois. The property is mortgage-free: $425,000

5. Bank CDs, checking accounts, and
savings accounts: $65,000
6. Life insurance policies on his life,
all of which are whole life and paid up.
Death benefit is: $260,000
7. Household furniture and furnishings: $10,000

John Howard's 1992 gross income for federal
income tax purposes was $105,000

_____   _____
John Howard   Witness

Exhibit B

Jane Wendell's approximate net worth as of July 1,
1993, is comprised of the following:
1. Marketable stocks and bonds: $230,000
2. Condominium apartment at 2345
Rock Street, Peoria, Illinois. The property
is mortgage-free: $145,000
3. Bank CDs and checking account: $160,000
4. Demand promissory note from son, Elmer,
with interest at 7.75 percent per annum. No
payments of principal have been made: $70,000

5. Jewelry: $30,000
6. Household furniture and furnishings
and 1990 Oldsmobile four-door sedan: $15,000
Jane Wendell's 1992 gross income for federal
income tax purposes was: $48,000

_____   _____
Jane Wendell   Witness

45

How Should I Take My Retirement Benefits? When Can I? When Must I?

THOMAS C. FARNAM AND KATHLEEN DOWLING BROWN

Federal Income Taxation of Distributions

The purpose of this chapter is to review the federal income taxation of retirement distributions and point out some of the options available under current federal tax law. We are not including any specific references to state taxes, but they should also be closely reviewed. Many states exempt some or all of the distributions from a retirement plan from income taxation. The distributions we are looking at in this chapter are those being made from any kind of "qualified retirement plans" described in Code §§401 through 416.[1]

The first question thus becomes "what is a qualified plan." The term is defined by the code in different ways, but generally these are plans which meet the requirements of Code §401(a) and are exempt from federal income taxes under Code §501(a). They operate under a variety of names, including pension and profit sharing plans; 401(k) plans; Keogh (or HR-10) plans; individual retirement accounts (IRAs); individual retirement annuities; simplified employee pensions (SEPs); tax-sheltered (or tax-deferred) annuities (TSAs); employee stock ownership plans (ESOPs); and stock bonus plans.

The principal tax characteristics shared by all of these plans are (1) contributions to them are wholly (or partially) excluded from federal taxes when they go into the plan; (2) the income earned by assets of the plans are exempt from federal tax-ation while they remain in the plan; and (3) the participants in the plan are not taxed on plan contributions or earnings at the time of funding the plans.

General Rule

All distributions are taxable as ordinary income when they are received by the payee.[2] Typically, distributions are taxed as if they were annuities, with a portion of each payment considered a return of the taxpayer's "investment in the contract" and the balance taxed as ordinary income.[3] The "investment in the contract" effectively represents any amounts in the plan that have been previously taxed, either before distribution or while within the plan.

In most cases, the taxpayer has essentially no "investment in the contract" and the benefit payments are entirely taxable as ordinary income. However, many plans permit (or even encourage) participants or beneficiaries to take their benefits in the form of a single payment (often called a lump-sum distribution, even though it may not meet the code definition of that term).

In the case of pension plans and TSAs, the lump-sum settlement is actuarially equivalent to the annuity, which is the "normal form" of payment under the plan, while in profit sharing and stock bonus plans (including 401(k)s, ESOPs, IRAs, and SEPs) it is equal to the participant's account balance. Lump-sum settlements have a variety of tax implications that we will explore in more detail.

Thomas C. Farnam heads The Farnam Law Firm and Kathleen Dowling Brown is a lawyer with The Farnam Law Firm in St. Louis, Missouri.

1. All references herein to the code are to Internal Revenue Code of 1986, as amended.
2. Code §402.
3. Code §72.

1. Distributions of after-tax employee contributions are recovered tax free,[4] as part of the individual's "investment in the contract." While some plans permit the participant (or their beneficiary) virtually unlimited opportunities to withdraw these contributions, distributions of less than the entire account balance may be partially taxable. If all of the employee contributions were made after 1986, or the amount paid exceeds pre-1987 contributions, part of any distribution of the employee contribution account will be taxable.

   These after-tax employee contributions include "deemed contributions" equal to the value of the death protection provided when plan assets are invested in life insurance contracts. These are sometimes known as "PS 58 costs" and are reported to the participant each year on Form 1099.

2. Any other balances in the plan which have been taxed previously are typically considered part of the employee's "investment in the contract." These might occur if the plan loses its tax-exempt status for a period of time. While these are not taxable a second time, they are generally recovered ratably from each distribution (instead of making the first payments nontaxable), based on the ratio of the investment in the contract to the expected return. For annuity starting dates after November 18, 1996, recovery of "investment in the contract" for qualified plans can be calculated by dividing the "investment in the contract" by the anticipated payments to be made.[5] The number of anticipated payments is determined from IRS tables set forth below.

   If benefits are based on a single life, the following table applies:[6]

Age of Annuitant	Anticipated Payments
Not more than 55	360
More than 55, not more than 60	320
More than 60, not more than 65	260
More than 65, not more than 70	210
More than 70	160

Beginning in 1998, if benefits are based on multiple annuitants, the following table applies:[7]

Combined Age of Annuitants	Anticipated Payments
Not more than 110	410
More than 110, not more than 120	360
More than 120, not more than 130	310
More than 130, not more than 140	260
More than 140	210

Caution: Pretax deferrals, such as to §401(k) and §403(b) plans, are not considered "investment in the contract." These are considered employer contributions for tax purposes, even though the employee gave up current income to make the deferrals.

3. Distributions of employer securities are not taxed currently to the extent of the "unrealized appreciation in employer securities" (UA).[8] UA basically consists of any market value of such securities that exceeds the basis of the securities in the hands of the plan. This might occur when a plan purchases stock for allocation under an ESOP and the value of the stock increases.

   UA is taxable upon later sale of the stock, under very specialized rules that we will not review in this chapter.

4. If plan death benefits are paid as a result of the death of a participant, they constitute "income in respect of a decedent" under Code §691. However, a special "spousal rollover IRA" presents a surviving spouse with a unique opportunity to postpone income taxation on such distributions. This is discussed in detail infra.

   Qualified plan death benefits attributable to decedents dying on or before August 20, 1996 are eligible for exclusion from gross income up to $5,000 under the "employees' death benefits" rules.[9] If the death occurred after August 20, 1996, this exclusion is no longer available.

5. If qualified plan benefits are not paid to the participant or beneficiary in accordance with specific rules, they may be subject to special excise taxes, which are discussed in detail infra. Great caution should be exercised in

---

4. Code §72(m).
5. Code §72(d), *as amended by* P.L. 104–188 (Small Business Job Protection Act).
6. Code §72(d), *as amended by* P.L. 104–188 (Small Business Job Protection Act).

7. Code §72(d)(1)(B)(iv), *as added by* P.L. 105–34 (Taxpayer Relief Act of 1997), Sec. 1075(a).
8. Code §§402(e)(4).
9. Code §101(b).

making these payments—the impact of these excise taxes can be enough to eliminate the inherent tax advantages of the qualified plan.

Roth IRAs

Beginning in 1998, a new type of IRA is available, called the Roth IRA.[10] Contributions are made on an after-tax basis and are nondeductible. "Qualified distributions" from a Roth IRA are not included in the individual's gross income. A "qualified distribution" must satisfy a five-year holding period and meet one of the following conditions:

- be made on or after age 59½,
- be made to a beneficiary on or after the individual's death,
- be attributable to the individual's disability, or
- be a distribution to pay for qualified first time home-buyer's expenses.[11]

To satisfy the five-year holding period, the distribution may not be made before the end of the five tax-year period beginning with the first tax year for which distributions were made.[12]

If the distribution is not qualified, the distribution will be taxable to the extent that the amount of the distribution exceeds the individual's contributions to the Roth IRA. Thus, no portion of the distributions from a Roth IRA is included in income until all distributions exceed the total amount of contributions.[13]

Rollovers

A "rollover" occurs when a qualified plan payment is "rolled over" to another qualified plan or an IRA account. *(Note: this discussion applies only to "regular" IRAs, as Roth IRAs have special rules, and rollovers to or from them may be taxable transactions.)* If a rollover is done correctly, income taxation is postponed until payments are made from the successor plan or IRA.[14] For retiring lawyers, rollovers will typically be to an IRA. However, if the lawyer has a Keogh plan based on current or previous self-employment income, it could become the rollover recipient.

Prior to 1993, rollover treatment was only available for a "lump-sum distribution" and certain partial distributions.[15] However, the law was changed significantly in 1992,[16] and now virtually all distributions to participants (or their spouses) are eligible for rollover to an IRA or a successor employer's plan.[17] The significant distributions not eligible for rollovers are (1) minimum required distributions at age 70½[18]; or (2) amounts paid as an annuity or part of a series of substantially equal payments that will last ten years or more.[19] (Payments to nonspouse alternate payees or beneficiaries are generally not eligible for rollover.)

IRA rollovers are a major tool for income tax planning. Even though the participant or beneficiary has virtually complete control of the investment of IRA assets, they are not taxed on the earnings of the account until they are withdrawn from the IRA. (Investments in collectibles, attempts to pledge the account, and certain other technical issues may cause amounts to be treated as distributions).

IRA rollovers are not limited to $2,000 per year or affected by individual 's status as a plan participant. IRA rollovers can be made after the individual reaches age 70½.[20]

1. A rollover may be made of all or any portion of the taxable benefits paid from the plan, but it cannot include any nontaxable portion of the plan payments. For example, any portion of the payment attributable to employee after-tax contributions cannot be rolled over. However, deferrals to a 401(k) or TSA plan can be rolled over, since they have not been previously taxed.

2. Any rollover must be made within sixty days of the day the payment is received.[21] In order for any contribution to an IRA to be treated as a rollover, the individual must *irrevocably* designate this in writing, to the trustee or issuer of the IRA, at the time of the contribution. In order to avoid tax withholding on the distrib-

---

10. Code §408A, *as added by* P.L. 105–34 (Taxpayer Relief Act of 1997).
11. Code §408A(d)(2)(A).
12. Code §408A(d)(2)(B).
13. Code §408A(d)(1)(B).
14. Code §402(c)(1).
15. Code §402(d)(4)(A) defines this as "payment within 1 taxable year of the recipient of the balance to the credit of an employee which becomes payable to the recipient—(i) on account of the employee's death, (ii) after the employee attains age 59½, (iii) on account of the employee's separation from service *(not applicable for the self-employed)*, or (iv) after the employee has become disabled. . . ."
16. Unemployment Compensation Act of 1992.
17. Code §402(c)(1).
18. Code §402(c)(4)(B).
19. Code §402(c)(4)(A).
20. Rev. Rul. 82–153, I.R.B. 1982–35, Private Letter Ruling 7919045.
21. Code §402(c)(3).

ution, many payees will elect direct transfer from the plan to the IRA, instead of taking the distribution and then rolling it over.

3. Rollovers may be of the property received from the plan or the proceeds of the sale of such property. However, the IRS has ruled that a contribution of cash representing the fair-market value of property received from the plan does not qualify as a rollover.[22]

4. A tax explanation to participants is required when any plan pays any benefits that could be eligible for rollover to an IRA.[23] For your information, a sample notice is attached as Appendix A of this chapter.

"Spousal Rollovers"

"Spousal rollovers" provide a unique postmortem income tax planning opportunity for surviving spouses. They are permitted to make an IRA rollover of any qualified plan death benefit distribution. Since these amounts would otherwise be subject to tax as income in respect of a decedent, this avoids current income tax.[24] The spousal rollover technique may be available even in a situation where a trust or estate is named as beneficiary, rather than the spouse directly.[25]

This has no effect on the estate tax treatment of the distribution, which is treated in detail elsewhere in this book. For purposes of this chapter, suffice to say all qualified plan benefits are generally includable in the gross estate.

Partial spousal rollovers are also permitted, which would result in taxation of the portion of the distribution that is not rolled over.

Rollover Rules for Roth IRAs

Rollovers can be made from one Roth IRA to another Roth IRA on a tax-free basis. Rollovers may also be made from an ordinary IRA to a Roth IRA, but only if the taxpayer's adjusted gross income for the tax year does not exceed $100,000 and the taxpayer is not married filing separately.[26] However, such rollover amounts are included in gross income to the extent they would be taxable if they were not part of a qualified rollover. If the distribution occurs prior to January 1, 1999, the taxable amount is included in gross income ratably over a four-year tax period beginning with the year the distribution is made.[27]

Roth IRA rollovers must meet the general rollover rules of Code Section 408(d)(3).[28] However, a rollover from an ordinary IRA to a Roth IRA is disregarded for purposes of the limitation of one IRA rollover per year.

An ordinary IRA can also be "converted" to a Roth IRA either by designation as such or a trustee-to-trustee transfer. The rollover tax rules described above also apply to a conversion of an ordinary IRA to a Roth IRA.

Rollover Rules for SIMPLE IRAs

SIMPLE IRAs are generally taxed under the IRA rules. However, there are some restrictions on rollovers for these arrangements. During the first two years of participation, amounts withdrawn from a **SIMPLE IRA** can only be rolled over to another **SIMPLE IRA**. After the two-year period, distributions can be rolled over to other types of IRAs without tax or penalty.

Federal Income Tax Withholding on Distributions

1. Generally, any distribution paid from a qualified plan (or 403(b) annuity) after 1992 is subject to federal tax withholding equal to 20 percent of the taxable distribution. However, this withholding tax will not apply if the funds are paid, in a "direct transfer," to an IRA or another qualified plan.[29] Like any other federal income tax withholding, this will not affect the ultimate tax liability for the distribution, but is an issue to be considered when a distribution is being made.

2. IRA accounts are *not* subject to the withholding requirements, nor are Simplified Employee Plans (SEPs), which are a collection of IRAs. This results in some payees electing to transfer a plan distribution to an IRA, then take money from the IRA immedi-

22. Rev. Rul. 87–77, I.R.B. 1987–33.
23. Code §402(f).
24. Code §402(c)(9).
25. P.L.R. 9247026 (disclaimer), 9509028 (trust operated like grantor trust in favor of surviving spouse), 9502042 (surviving spouse is sole beneficiary of estate and estate is sole beneficiary of plan benefits). *But see* P.L.R. 9303031 (trust could not make rollover even though sole beneficiary of trust was surviving spouse).
26. Code §408A(c)(3)(B), *as added by* P.L. 105–34 (Taxpayer Relief Act of 1997).

27. Code §408A(d)(3)(A)(iii), *as added by* P.L. 105–34 (Taxpayer Relief Act of 1997).
28. Code §408A(e), *as added by* P.L. 105–34 (Taxpayer Relief Act of 1997).
29. Code §3405(c).

ately.[30] This will avoid the withholding tax but does not affect the ultimate tax liability for the distribution.

3. "Periodic payments" are subject to withholding at a different rate, and the payee must be given an opportunity to elect out of withholding (using IRS Form W-4P). These are payments measured either by (1) the life (or life expectancy) of the employee or the joint lives (or joint life expectancies) of the employee and the employee's designated beneficiary, or (2) a specified period of ten years or more.[31]

4. Minimum required distributions (beginning at age 70½) are not eligible for rollover, nor are they subject to the 20 percent withholding. However, the payee will be subject to tax withholding unless they file IRS Form W-4P requesting no taxes be withheld by the plan.[32]

5. Keogh Plan distributions *are* subject to the 20 percent tax withholding rules. If you, as trustee of your own Keogh Plan, make a distribution to yourself, you must comply with the tax withholding rules or risk penalties for failure to withhold. To avoid the withholding issues, you could make the distribution from the Keogh plan a transfer to an IRA, then take the cash from the IRA without the tax withholding issue.

Special Income Averaging and Capital Gains Treatment

Generally, special five- and ten-year income averaging[33] is available only with respect to "lump-sum distributions." It is not available if the employee whose balance is involved ever made a rollover of a prior distribution from that plan.[34] A lump-sum distribution is the "payment within one taxable year of the recipient of the entire balance to the credit of the employee which becomes payable to the recipient:

1. on account of the employee's death,
2. after the employee attains age 59½,
3. on account of the employee's separation from service *(not applicable for the self-employed)*, or
4. after the employee has become disabled."[35]

Five-year averaging is available (before 1999) to *any* taxpayer (former participant or beneficiary) for the ordinary income portion of a distribution from an *employer plan* (but not an IRA). However, the employee on whose account the distribution is based must have been a participant for five or more taxable years,[36] and:

1. the taxpayer must make a one-time election to use five-year averaging, and
2. the taxpayer must elect to treat all eligible distributions received during the year under five-year averaging, and
3. the election must be made after the employee attains age 59½,[37] and
4. no prior election to use five-year averaging may have been made by any taxpayer with respect to the employee (that is, the participant before his or her death).

Capital gains treatment for lump-sum distributions is still available for participants born prior to 1936 (at a 20 percent tax rate).[38] For those born after 1935, taxation at capital gains rates was phased out over the six-year period between 1987 and 1992. Therefore, this treatment was only available for 1990 with respect to 50 percent of the distribution, 25 percent in 1991, and is no longer available for any distributions paid after 1991.

The portion of a "lump-sum distribution" eligible for capital gains is determined using a fraction:

$$\frac{\text{years of plan participation before 1974}}{\text{years of plan participation after 1978}}$$

which the employer should report on Form 1099-R. In determining this fraction, the IRS bases the calculation on "months of active participation," and for active participation before 1974, any part of a calendar year in which an employee was an active participant counts as twelve months. In determining post–1973 active participation, any part of a calendar month counts as a full month.[39]

If a plan is the successor to prior plans of the employer (or its predecessor), the years of participation may be added together or "tacked" for

30. Temp. Regs. 31.3405(c)-1T, Q&A 1.
31. Code §§402(c)(4)(A) and 3405(a).
32. Code §402(c)(4)(B).
33. Code §402(d)(1).
34. Code §402(c)(10).
35. Code §402(d)(4)(A).

36. Code §402(d)(4)(F).
37. If the employee was born before 1936, they may elect five-year averaging (at current tax rates) or the ten-year averaging (at 1986 rates) before reaching 59½. If this election is made, it eliminates the ability to use five-year averaging or capital gains treatment after age 59½. I. §1122(h)(3)(C) and (h)(5), Tax Reform Act of 1986, P.L. 99–514.
38. Code §402, *as amended by* §1122(h) of the Tax Reform Act of 1986, P.L. 99–514.
39. Prop. Reg. §§1.402(a)-1(a)(9) and 1.402(e)-2(d)(3); T.I.R. 1315, November 12, 1974.

purposes of computing the capital gains fraction. Keogh plan years *may* be combined with corporate plan years if the Keogh plan assets were transferred to the corporate plan or the plans were merged.[40]

Ten-year averaging may only be applied to "lump-sum distributions" made on behalf of participants who were older than 50 on January 1, 1986. For this purpose, the tax rates to be used are 1986 rates. While there is no phaseout of ten-year averaging, the use of 1986 rates means large distributions are at a disadvantage.

The most advantageous averaging method will depend on the amount of the lump-sum distribution. Based solely on 1997 federal tax rates, the results are as follows:

Lump-Sum Amount	Best Method
$0 to $367,700	Ten-year averaging
Over $367,700	Five-year averaging and capital gains (if available—otherwise use five-year averaging)

The tax on a lump-sum distribution is reported on IRS Form 4972. This form can serve as an excellent worksheet for testing the federal tax effect of the alternative tax forms applicable to these payments. This form should be available from your local IRS office or your tax advisor, or will be furnished by the author for $5 to cover postage and handling.

In the final analysis, the decision of what form of benefit payment to take will be dependent principally on the relationships of three factors: (1) the payout period; (2) the marginal tax rate during the payout period; and (3) the rate of return during the payout period.

Excise Taxes on Distributions to Participants

These have been characterized as creating a "benefit payment window" almost like the "launch window" for a NASA rocket. The excise taxes apply if the plan payments are too early, too little, or too late.

Early Distributions

Early distributions from qualified plans, including IRAs, are subject to an excise tax equal to 10 percent of the distribution (however, see special

rule below for distributions from a SIMPLE IRA).[41] This is in addition to all other federal taxes, and is a nondeductible tax. The IRS requires plan sponsors to provide an explanation of this penalty when any payment is made that may be eligible for "rollover".[42] For your information, a sample notice is attached as Appendix A of this chapter.

The early distribution excise tax will not apply to any distribution made as follows:

1. On or after the employee attains age 59½. This can only be elected once for an IRA, but may be used more than once for non-IRA distributions.

2. Made to a beneficiary (or the estate) of a deceased employee.

3. Attributable to the employee's being disabled (defined as unable to engage in any substantial gainful activity).[43]

4. As one of a series of substantially equal periodic payments (no less than annual) for the life or life expectancy of the employee (and beneficiary). (May be subject to tax penalty if the payment method is changed before 59½ or within five years of date payments begin.)

5. After the employee's separation from service at any time after attaining age 55. (Not applicable to self-employed or IRAs.)

6. To an alternate payee pursuant to a qualified domestic relations order. (Not applicable to IRAs.)

7. To the extent they do not exceed the amount that the employee could deduct as medical expenses under IRC Section 213 if they itemized deductions. (Applicable to IRAs after 1996.)

8. From an IRA, to pay health insurance premiums, for an IRA owner who has been receiving unemployment compensation for at least twelve consecutive weeks (or if self-employed, would have been entitled). (Effective after December 31, 1996.)

9. Attributable to dividends on employer securities or meet other special rules covering employee stock ownership plans prior to 1990. (Not applied to IRAs.)

---

40. Private Letter Ruling 8004092.

41. Code §72(t).
42. Code §402(1). Failure to provide this explanation may result in imposition of a $10 penalty for each failure, up to $5,000 per calendar year. Code §6652(i).
43. Code §72(m)(7). Note this may be stricter than many retirement plan definitions of disability.

A special early distribution tax applies to certain withdrawals from **SIMPLE IRAs.** If contributions are withdrawn during the first two years of participation, a 25 percent penalty is assessed.[44] The penalty tax will not be assessed for distributions made after age 59½, distributions after the participant's death, distributions made as part of a series of substantially equal periodic payments, or distributions that otherwise qualify for an exception under Code Section 72(t)(2), outlined above.[45]

"Minimum Required Distributions"

"Minimum required distributions" must be made to avoid a 50 percent excise tax.[46] This tax is imposed on the payee who fails to get the minimum distribution. The actual amount of the minimum payment required to avoid the excise tax depends on when the participant (or IRA holder) reaches age 70½ (or, after 1996, the date of actual retirement, except for 5 percent owners[47]). It is also affected by whether the employee is (or was after age 66½) a "5 percent owner."[48]

Many former participants (or IRA owners), even though they are legally entitled to the entire balance, prefer to take advantage of the tax-deferred accumulation of investment income in the plan or IRA. These payees often seek to postpone the receipt of their distributions as long as possible, and because this also postpones the taxation of these benefits, the IRS became concerned about the loss of tax revenue.

The result was the current minimum distribution rules, which are among the most complex provisions of the code. This chapter cannot begin to deal with all the issues in detail; however, we will at least outline some major issues. The reader is urged to consult with a competent tax lawyer, accountant, or employee benefits consultant before making final decisions on the application of these rules.

These minimum distribution rules apply to par-

ticipants in almost all types of plans, including pension, profit-sharing, 401(k)s, Keoghs, IRAs, SEPs, and ESOPs. (The minimum distribution rules do not apply to Roth IRAs.) Under these rules, the plan must begin payments to a 5 percent owner even if the participant is still actively employed.

Regulations were proposed by the IRS on July 27, 1987 (and amended December 30, 1997) and are not yet final.[49] However, the IRS has stated they may be relied upon until final regulations are published. The proposed regulations provide techniques to determine the minimum distributions in all types of situations.

Calculation Concept:
Required Beginning Date

Payments must commence by the participant's "required beginning date" (RBD). For participants who reached age 70½ after December 31, 1987, the RBD is April 1 of the year following the year they reached age 70½ (not age 70) or in the case of a participant who is not a 5 percent owner, the year of actual retirement, if later. The RBD for a 5 percent owner is April 1 following the attainment of age 70½, regardless of whether he or she continues to work.

Calculation Concept:
Life Expectancy

If the employee (or beneficiary) chooses to minimize the current payment, the use of a life expectancy calculation becomes important. For this purpose, life expectancy is computed using IRS "expected return multiples," which are listed in IRS tables.[50] The choice of table depends on whether the payee is married or single and whether he or she wants to take the absolute minimum payout to satisfy the law.

If the payee is single and payment is *not* made on a basis that guarantees postdeath payments to a designated beneficiary, use Table V: Ordinary Life Annuities, One Life-Expected Return Multiples. If the payee is married, Table V may be used, or if a lower minimum payment is desired, the calculation can be based on Table VI: Ordinary Joint Life and Last Survivor Annuities, Two Lives-Expected Return Multiples.

44. Code §72(t)(6), *as added by* P.L. 104–88 (Small Business Job Protection Act).

45. IRS Notice 98-4, I.R.B. 1998-2, January 12, 1998, Q&A 1-2.

46. Code §4974(a).

47. There are transition rules which apply to those employees who attained age 70½ prior to January 1, 1997. IRS Notice 97-75, I.R.B. 1997-51, December 22, 1997; IRS Notice 96-67, I.R.B. 1996-53, December 30, 1996.

48. Code §416(i). A "5 percent owner" is anyone who owns 5 percent of the corporate stock (or 5 percent of the capital or profits interest) during the plan year ending in the calendar year when the individual attains age 70½, or during any of the four preceding years.

49. Prop. Regs. §1.401(a)(9).

50. Regs. §1.72-9, Tables V and VI. A copy of Table V and portions of Table VI are included at the end of this chapter.

A "designated beneficiary" for this purpose may be either an individual designated by the employee or the terms of the plan or a trust. However, a trust must be written and (1) constitute a valid trust under state law, (2) be irrevocable, (3) have identifiable beneficiaries, and (4) be furnished to the plan.[51] On December 30, 1997, new proposed regulations were issued that permit a designated trust to be revocable while the individual is alive, as long as it becomes irrevocable upon the individual's death.[52]

All of the tables are organized based on age and, in the case of joint life tables, two ages. In either case, the age used for this purpose is the attained age as of the employee's birthday in the calendar year during which he or she reaches age 70½ (and the attained age of the spouse or designated beneficiary in the year the employee reaches age 70½). Life expectancy may be recomputed each year, or may be computed solely at age 70½.[53]

Recalculation of life expectancy will lead to the smallest possible payment during the life of the participant and spouse (or other beneficiary), but has a potential problem. The proposed regulations say that in the year following the death of the employee (or spouse) their life expectancy must be considered zero. Further, they require distribution of the employee's entire remaining interest in the year the last life expectancy is reduced to zero.

Calculating the Minimum:
Living Employee

If the plan participant (or IRA owner) is living at the time distributions commence, the entire interest of the employee must be paid out based on his or her life expectancy. The only options are either (1) complete payout by the RBD, or (2) payments must begin by the RBD and be distributed ". . . over the life of such employee or over the lives of the employee and a designated beneficiary (or over a period not extending beyond the life expectancy of such employee or the life expectancy of such employee and a designated beneficiary)."[54]

If payments are to be made over life expectancy, the minimum to be distributed each year is based on a portion of the account value as of the

last day of the prior calendar year. (The plan may need to adjust the participant's accrued benefit if distribution is postponed beyond age 70½.)[55] For the first year, the payment must be made as of the following April 1, and thereafter the minimum must be paid as of December 31 of each year. Thus, if the first payment is postponed as long as possible, there will be a "double payment" in the year the employee reaches age 71½.

EXAMPLE

An example may help illustrate the operation of these concepts. Assume a single individual born August 1, 1920, has an IRA holding assets valued at $100,000 as of December 31, 1990. Also assume she wants to know what she must take as a payment to meet the minimum distribution requirements. For simplicity, we will assume the additional earnings of the IRA are 8 percent per year during the distribution period. This person will attain age 70½ in 1991, and therefore the IRA must begin payments no later than April 1, 1992.

For 1991, the minimum payment (assuming no designated beneficiary) will be $6,250 (1/16 of $100,000), which must be paid no later than April 1, 1992. The minimum for 1992, which must be paid no later than December 31, 1992, will be $6,750 (1/15 of $101,250), and for 1993 $7,290 (1/14 of $102,060) if life expectancy is not recalculated. Recalculating the life expectancy would change the 1992 minimum to $6,617.65 (1/15.3 of $101,250), and 1993 would be $7,000.20 (1/14.6 of 102,203).

If the individual had a spouse the same age, the first year minimum distribution would be $4,854.37 (1/20.6 of $100,000), the second year would be $5,242.72 (1/19.6 of $102,757.28), and the third year would be $5,662.16 (1/18.6 of $105,315.72), assuming no recalculation. If life expectancies were recalculated, the second year would be $5,189.76 (1/19.8 of $102,757.28), and the third year $5,575.29 (1/18.9 of $105,372.91).

Minimum Death Benefit Payments

If plan distributions have commenced before death, any distributions made after death must be made at least as rapidly as under the distribution method in effect before death. Thus, if the payee were taking benefits based on life

---

51. Prop. Regs. §1.401(a)(9)-1 D-5.
52. Prop. Regs. §1.401(a)(9)-1 D-5, as amended.
53. Prop. Regs. §1.401(a)(9) E-6, 7, and 8.
54. Code §401(a)(9)(A)(ii).
55. Code §401(a)(9)(iii), IRS Notice 97-75, I.R.B. 1997-51, Dec. 22, 1997.

expectancy, the beneficiary must take them at least that quickly.[56]

Caution: In our example above, if the employee died in 1993 and life expectancy was being recalculated, the entire balance would have to be paid out in 1994. On the other hand, if life expectancy is not being recalculated, the beneficiary could continue to take the payments based on the employee's life expectancy. (Assuming this is permitted by the plan.)

If plan distributions commence after the employee's death, there are two methods for computing the minimum distributions to the beneficiary(ies): (1) the entire interest of the employee must be distributed within five years of the employee's death; or (2) any amount payable to a designated beneficiary must be distributed, beginning within one year, over the life (or life expectancy) of the beneficiary.[57] The latter is sometimes referred to as the "exception to the five-year rule."

If the exception to the five-year rule applies and the participant's spouse is the beneficiary, payments to the spouse must begin by the later of (1) December 31 of the year following the year of the employee's death, or (2) April 1 of the year following the calendar year the employee would have attained age 70½.[58]

The plan may designate which of these rules will be applied in any given situation. If the plan is silent, the five-year rule will apply to any beneficiary other than a surviving spouse, and the exception to the five-year rule will apply to the surviving spouse.

"Excess" Distributions

For distributions made prior to 1997, a 15 percent excise tax is imposed upon payments made which exceed $150,000 per calendar year[59] ($750,000 for a lump-sum payment) and for certain "excess accumulations" within a qualified plan.[60] This provision was repealed effective for distributions made after December 31, 1996. For additional information regarding this provision, see *The Lawyer's Guide to Retirement*, second edition, Chapter 14 (Chicago: ABA, 1994) or contact the author.

Conclusion

This chapter has reviewed some of the major elements in the tax analysis of using your retirement benefits. However, the subject has unfortunately become one of the most complex topics in our tax law, and we cannot hope to cover all of the nuances in a few pages. In addition, as our fiscal process becomes more and more sensitive to tax revenues, the "tax expenditures" for retirement benefits loom larger and larger as a legislative target. Therefore, careful consideration of changes in the law is absolutely essential in your analysis.

In the process of planning how to use your retirement savings, we encourage a thorough review of all your options, including the techniques for avoiding the excise tax penalties. While this may require a variety of sophisticated financial calculations, the effect may be to provide all the income you need and avoid payment of unnecessary taxes. In making these calculations, be sure to include all retirement plans, especially Keogh or IRA accounts, which sometimes don't get filed with other retirement plan information.

Last, but certainly not least, contact your tax advisors before you begin taking money out of your retirement plans. Many planning techniques are available, but very few of them can be applied retroactively.

---

56. Code §401(a)(9)(B)(i).
57. Prop. Regs. §1.401(a)(9)-1 C-1 to C-4.
58. Code §401(a)(9)(B)(iv).If the surviving spouse also dies before payments begin, distributions to the surviving spouse's beneficiary must be made in accordance with the exception to the five-year rule, without the special exception for a surviving spouse.

59. Code §4980A.
60. Code §4980A.

Sample, Inc. 401(k) Plan with Annuities
Special Notice Regarding Tax on Plan Payments

This notice contains important information you will need before you decide how to receive your benefits from this plan.

Summary

A payment from the plan that is eligible for "rollover" can be taken in two ways. You may have *all or any portion* of your payment either {1} PAID IN A "DIRECT ROLLOVER" or (2) PAID TO YOU. A rollover is a payment of your plan benefits to your individual retirement arrangement (IRA) or to another employer plan. This choice will affect the income tax you owe.

If you choose a DIRECT ROLLOVER:

- Your payment will not be taxed in the current year and no income tax will be withheld.
- Your payment will be made directly to your IRA or, if you choose, to another employer plan that accepts your rollover.
- Your payment will be taxed later when you take it out of the IRA or the employer plan.

If you choose to have your plan benefits PAID TO YOU:

- You will only receive 80 percent of the gross payment, because the plan administrator is required to withhold 20 percent of the payment and send it to the IRS as income tax withholding to be credited against your taxes.
- Your payment will be taxed in the current year unless you roll it over. You may be able to use special tax rules that could reduce the tax you owe. However, if you receive the payment before age 59½, you also may have to pay an additional 10 percent tax.
- You can roll over the payment by paying it to your IRA or to another employer plan that accepts your rollover within sixty days of receiving the payment. The amount rolled over will not be taxed until you take it out of the IRA or employer plan.
- If you want to roll over 100 percent of the payment to an IRA or an employer plan, *you must find other money to replace the 20 percent that was withheld.* If you roll over only the 80 percent that you received, you will be taxed on the 20 percent that was withheld which is not rolled over.

I. Payments That Can and Cannot Be Rolled Over

Payments from the plan may be "eligible rollover distributions." This means that they can be rolled over to an IRA or to another employer plan that accepts rollovers. Your plan administrator should be able to tell you what portion of your payment is an eligible rollover distribution. The following types of payments cannot be rolled over.

Nontaxable Payments. In general, only the "taxable portion" of your payment is an eligible rollover distribution. If you have made "after-tax" employee contributions to the plan, these contributions will be nontaxable when they are paid to you, and they cannot be rolled over. (After-tax employee contributions generally are contributions you made from your own pay that were already taxed.) Salary deferrals to a 401(k) or 403(b) plan are not after-tax contributions, and are generally eligible for rollover.

Payments Spread Over Long Periods. You cannot roll over a payment if it is part of a series of equal (or almost equal) payments that are made at least once a year and that will last for:

- your lifetime (or your life expectancy), or
- your lifetime and your beneficiary's lifetime (or life expectancies), or
- a period of ten years or more.

Required Minimum Payments. Beginning in the year you reach age 70½, a certain portion of your payment cannot be rolled over because it is a "required minimum payment" that must be paid to you.

II. Direct Rollover

You can choose a direct rollover of all or any portion of your payment that is an "eligible rollover distribution," as described above. In a direct rollover, the eligible rollover distribution is paid directly from the plan to an IRA or another employer plan that accepts rollovers. If you choose a direct rollover, you are not taxed on a payment until you later take it out of the IRA or the employer plan.

Direct Rollover to an IRA. You can open an IRA to receive the direct rollover. (The term "IRA," as used in this notice, includes individual retirement accounts and individual retirement annuities.) If you choose to have your payment made directly to an IRA, contact an IRA sponsor (usually a financial institution) to find out how to have your payment made in a direct rollover to an IRA at that institution. If you are unsure of how to invest your money, you can temporarily establish an IRA to receive the payment. However, in choosing an IRA, you may wish to consider whether the IRA you choose will allow you to move all or a part of your payment to another IRA at a later date, without penalties or other limitations. See IRS Publication 590, *Individual Retirement Arrangements*, for more information (including limits on how often you can roll over between IRAs).

Direct Rollover to a Plan. If you are employed by a new employer that has a plan, and you want to make a direct rollover to that plan, ask the plan administrator of that plan whether it will accept your rollover. If your new employer's plan does not accept a rollover, you can choose a direct rollover to an IRA.

Direct Rollover of a Series of Payments. If you receive eligible rollover distributions that are paid in a series for less than ten years, your choice to make or not make a direct rollover for a payment will apply to all later payments in the series until you change your election. You are free to change your election for any later payment in the series.

III. Payment Paid to You

If payment is made directly to you (instead of being transferred directly to an IRA or new employer's plan), it is subject to 20 percent income tax withholding. The payment is taxed in the year you receive it unless, within sixty days of receipt, you roll it over to an IRA or another plan that accepts rollovers. If you do not roll it over, special tax rules may apply.

Income Tax Withholding

Mandatory Withholding. If any portion of the payment to you is an eligible rollover distribution, the plan is required by law to withhold 20 percent of that amount. This amount is sent to the IRS as income tax withholding. For example, if your eligible rollover distribution is $10,000 only $8,000 will be paid to you because the plan must withhold $2,000 as income tax. However, when you prepare your income tax return for the year, you will report the full $10,000 as a payment from the plan. You will report the $2,000 as tax withheld, and it will be credited against any income tax you owe for the year.

Voluntary Withholding. If any portion of your payment is not an eligible rollover distribution but is taxable, the mandatory withholding rules described above do not apply. In this case, you may elect not to have

withholding apply to that portion. To elect not to have withholding apply to that portion, ask the plan administrator for an election form and related information.

Sixty-Day Rollover Option. If you have an eligible rollover distribution paid to you, you can still decide to roll over all or part of it to an IRA or another employer plan that accepts rollovers. If you decide to roll it over, you must make the rollover within sixty days after you receive the payment. The portion of your payment that is rolled over will not be taxed until you take it out of the IRA or the new employer's plan.

You can roll over up to 100 percent of the eligible rollover distribution, including an amount equal to the 20 percent that was withheld. If you choose to roll over 100 percent, you must find other money within the sixty-day period to contribute to the IRA or the employer plan to replace the 20 percent that was withheld. On the other hand, if you roll over only the 80 percent that you received, you will be taxed on the 20 percent that was withheld.

Example: Your eligible rollover distribution is $10,000, and you choose to have it paid to you. You will receive $8,000, and $2,000 will be sent to the IRS as income tax withholding. Within sixty days after receiving the $8,000, you may roll over the entire $10,000 to an IRA or employer plan. To do this, you roll over the $8,000 you received from the plan, and you will have to find $2,000 from other sources (your savings, a loan, etc.). In this case, the entire $10,000 is not taxed until you take it out of the IRA or employer plan. If you roll over the entire $10,000, when you file your income tax return you may get a refund of the $2,000 withheld.

If, on the other hand, you roll over only $8,000, the $2,000 you did not roll over is taxed in the year it was withheld. When you file your income tax return you may get a refund of part of the $2,000 withheld. (However, any refund is likely to be larger if you roll over the entire $10,000.)

Additional 10 Percent Tax If You Are Under Age 59½. If you receive a payment before you reach age 59½ and you do not roll it over, then, in addition to the regular income tax, you may have to pay an extra tax equal to 10 percent of the taxable portion of the payment. The additional 10 percent tax does not apply to your payment if it is (1) paid to you because you separate from service with your employer during or after the year you reach age 55, (2) paid because you retire due to disability, (3) paid to you as equal (or almost equal) payments over your life or life expectancy (or you and your beneficiary's lives or life expectancies), or (4) used to pay certain medical expenses. See IRS Form 5329 for more information on the additional 10 percent tax.

Special Tax Treatment. If your eligible rollover distribution is not rolled over, it will be taxed in the year you receive it. However, if it qualifies as a "lump-sum distribution," it may be eligible for special tax treatment. A lump-sum distribution is a payment, within one year, of your entire balance under the plan (and certain other similar plans of the employer) that is payable to you because you have reached age 59½ or have separated from service with your employer (or, in the case of a self-employed individual, because you have reached age 59½ or have become disabled). For a payment to qualify as a lump-sum distribution, you must have been a participant in the plan for at least five years. The special tax treatment for lump-sum distributions is described below.

Five-Year Averaging. If you receive a lump-sum distribution after you are age 59½, you may be able to make a one-time election to figure the tax on the payment by using "five-year averaging." Five-year averaging often reduces the tax you owe because it treats the payment much as if it were paid over five years.

Ten-Year Averaging If You Were Born Before January 1, 1936. If you receive a lump-sum distribution and you were born before January 1, 1936, you can make a one-time election to figure the tax on the payment by using "ten-year averaging" (using 1986 tax rates) instead of five-year averaging (using current tax rates). Like the five-year averaging rules, ten-year averaging often reduces the tax you owe.

Capital Gain Treatment If You Were Born Before January 1, 1936. In addition, if you receive a lump-sum distribution and you were born before January 1, 1936, you may elect to have the part of your payment that is attributable to your pre-1974 participation in the plan (if any) taxed as long-term capital gain at a rate of 20 percent.

There are other limits on the special tax treatment for lump-sum distribution. For example, you can generally elect this special tax treatment only once in your lifetime, and the election applies to all lump-sum distributions that you receive in that same year. If you have previously rolled over a payment from the plan (or certain other similar plans of the employer), you cannot use this special tax treatment for later payments from the plan. If you roll over your payment to an IRA, you will not be able to use this special tax treatment for later payments from the IRA. Also, if you roll over only a portion of your payment to an IRA, this special tax treatment is not available for the rest of the payment. Additional restrictions are described in IRS Form 4972, which has more information on lump-sum distributions and how you elect the special tax treatment.

Employer Stock or Securities. There is a special rule for a payment from the plan that includes employer stock (or other employer securities). To use this special rule, (1) the payment must qualify as a lump-sum distribution, as described above (or would qualify except

that you do not yet have five years of participation in the plan), or (2) the employer stock included in the payment must be attributable to "after-tax" employee contributions, if any. Under this special rule, you may have the option of not paying tax on the "net unrealized appreciation" of the stock until you sell the stock. Net unrealized appreciation generally is the increase in the value of the employer stock while it was held by the plan. For example, if employer stock was contributed to your plan account when the stock was worth $1,000 but the stock was worth $1,200 when you received it, you would not have to pay tax on the $200 increase in value until you later sold the stock.

You may instead elect not to have the special rule apply to the net unrealized appreciation. In this case, your net unrealized appreciation will be taxed in the year you receive the stock, unless you roll over the stock. The stock (including any net unrealized appreciation) can be rolled over to an IRA or another employer plan either in a direct rollover or a rollover that you make yourself.

If you receive employer stock in a payment that qualifies as a lump-sum distribution, the special tax treatment for lump-sum distributions described above (such as five-year averaging) may also apply. See IRS Form 4972 for additional information.

IV. Surviving Spouses, Alternate Payees, and Other Beneficiaries

In general, the rules summarized above that apply to payments to employees also apply to payments to surviving spouses of employees and to spouses or former spouses who are "alternate payees." You are an alternate payee if your interest in the plan results from a "qualified domestic relations order," which is an order issued by a court, usually in connection with a divorce or legal separation. Some of the rules summarized above also apply to a deceased employee's beneficiary who is not a spouse. However, there are some exceptions for payments to surviving spouses, alternate payees, and other beneficiaries that should be mentioned.

If you are a surviving spouse, you may choose to have an eligible rollover distribution paid in a direct rollover to an IRA or paid to you. If you have the payment paid to you, you can keep it or roll it over yourself to an IRA but you cannot roll it over to an employer plan. If you are an alternate payee, you have the same choices as the employee. Thus, you can have the payment paid as a direct rollover or paid to you. If you have it paid to you, you can keep it or roll it over yourself to an IRA or to another employer plan that accepts rollovers. If you are a beneficiary other than the surviving spouse, you cannot choose a direct rollover, and you cannot roll over the payment yourself.

If you are a surviving spouse, an alternate payee, or another beneficiary, your payment is not subject to the additional 10 percent tax described in Section III above, even if you are younger than age 59½.

If you are a surviving spouse, an alternate payee, or another beneficiary, you may be able to use the special tax treatment for lump-sum distributions and the special rule for payments that include employer stock, as described in section III above. If you receive a payment because of the employee's death, you may be able to treat the payment as a lump-sum distribution if the employee met the appropriate age requirements, whether or not the employee had five years of participation in the plan.

How to Obtain Additional Information

This notice summarizes only the federal (not state or local) tax rules that might apply to your payment. The rules are complex and contain many conditions and exceptions that are not included in this notice. You may want to consult with a professional tax advisor before you take a payment of your benefits from the plan. Also, you can find more specific information on the tax treatment of payments from qualified retirement plans in IRS Publication 575, *Pension and Annuity Income,* and IRS Publication 590, *Individual Retirement Arrangements.* These publications are available from your local IRS office or by calling 1-800-TAX-FORMS.

46

The Supreme Court Opens an Estate Tax Planning Window

HERBERT L. ZUCKERMAN AND JAY A. SOLED

In a recent case the Supreme Court rendered a decision that gives taxpayers and their estates a tax break. Under *Estate of Hubert* (117 S.Ct. 1124 (1997)), taxpayers now potentially have the opportunity to have administration expenses do double duty by reducing an estate's taxable income and simultaneously preserving the size of the estate's marital and/or charitable deductions. The advantages of the Supreme Court's interpretation of the law will not, however, automatically inure to the benefit of taxpayers. Taxpayers must incorporate specific provisions in their wills to avail themselves of the opportunities offered under *Hubert*.

Over the past few years the IRS has held that if the executors of an estate take a deduction for administration expenses on the estate's income tax return (Form 1041), the executors of the estate are precluded from taking a similar deduction for administration expenses on the federal estate tax return (Form 706), even if the estate, during the course of administration, produces income that could absorb these expenses. Nondeductible administration expenses on a taxpayer's estate tax return are deemed to correspondingly reduce the size of the marital and/or charitable bequests.

To illustrate, suppose taxpayer A dies with an estate worth $8 million. He bequeaths $600,000 to his son and the residue of his estate to his wife. Assume that during the first year of administrating A's estate expenses total $100,000, and assume further that the estate generates an income of $1 million.

The executors of A's estate could elect to use the $100,000 of administration expenses as a deduction on the estate's income tax return. Doing so would reduce the estate's taxable income to $900,000 ($1 million income less $100,000 expenses). However, from the perspective of the IRS, these same administration expenses could not then be deducted on the federal estate tax return and there would be a corresponding reduction in the amount qualifying for the marital deduction. Instead of the estate generating tax on $600,000 ($8 million gross estate less $7.4 million deduction for a bequest qualifying for the marital deduction), the estate would generate estate tax on $700,000 ($8 million gross estate less $7.3 million deduction for the bequest that qualifies for the marital deduction) (that is, the $100,000 of administration expenses reduces the amount qualifying for the marital deduction).

The executors of A's estate could forgo the income tax deduction and take a deduction for the entire $100,000 on the estate tax return. On the one hand, the executors of A's estate would have to pay income tax on the entire $1 million of income earned (with no offsetting deduction). On the other hand, the executors of A's estate would reduce the size of the taxable estate by $100,000 to $600,000.

In *Hubert*, under somewhat similar facts, a plurality of the Supreme Court did not embrace the IRS's either-or position. They instead concluded that, assuming a taxpayer's estate generates sufficient income, the executors of a taxpayer's estate could take a deduction for the estate's administration expenses on the estate's income tax return with no reduction of the amount that would qualify for the marital and/or charitable deduction on the decedent's estate tax return.

Herbert L. Zuckerman is a partner at the law firm of Sills Cummis Zuckerman Radin Tischman Epstein & Gross, P.A., in Newark, New Jersey. Jay A. Soled is a lawyer and an assistant professor at Rutgers University in Newark, New Jersey.

Applying the Supreme Court's holding to the prior example would permit the executors of A's estate to reduce the taxable income of A's estate and simultaneously preserve the size of the marital deduction for purposes of the federal estate tax. The result to the estate is significant overall tax savings.

The tax savings offered under *Hubert* are not automatic, however. Taxpayers must incorporate specific provisions in their wills that permit executors of a taxpayer's estate to charge administration expenses against postmortem income. Failure to incorporate such provisions may pre-clude fiduciaries from doing so, unless state law specifically authorizes to the contrary.

Tax-saving opportunities are not easily found in an environment where Congress is trying to close the budget deficit. When the Supreme Court offers a window of opportunity to taxpayers, they should actively pursue it. Accordingly, those with substantial estates and significant marital or charitable deductions might be well-advised to check with their tax counsel to determine whether any changes should be made in their wills as a result of the *Hubert* decision.

47
Maximizing the Use of Discounts During the Estate Administration Process

HERBERT L. ZUCKERMAN AND JAY A. SOLED

When it comes to minimizing one's transfer taxes, the use of minority and marketability discounts is well known. These discounts permit taxpayers to transfer valuable assets at reduced transfer-tax costs because the Internal Revenue Code mandates the application of a "willing buyer/willing seller" test when valuing assets. Application of this test causes assets that have no readily available market or assets that put the taxpayer at a disadvantage (for example, a minority stock position in a closely held business) to be discounted.

Take, for example, Ann who owns a 49 percent interest in a closely held business worth $1 million. If Ann were to transfer her interest in the company to her daughter, Betty, for transfer-tax purposes, Ann would not have to value her interest in the company at $490,000. Instead, because she is transferring a minority interest in the company, for federal gift tax purposes, she can apply as much as a 50 percent discount to the value of the transferred stock, reducing its value to as low as $245,000 [$490,000 - ($490,000 x 50 percent)]. In the past, courts have recognized minority interest discounts that range anywhere from 5 percent to 60 percent and the fact the donee is a member of the donor's family is ignored.

What is less known is how the use of these discounts can be maximized during the estate administration process for married couples. A

Herbert L. Zuckerman is a partner at the law firm of Sills Cummis Zuckerman Radin Tischman Epstein & Gross, P.A., in Newark, New Jersey. Jay A. Soled is a lawyer and an assistant professor at Rutgers University in Newark, New Jersey.

recent Fifth Circuit opinion (*Estate of Bonner v. Commissioner*) provides instructive advice regarding this planning opportunity and overrules the prior contrary position of the IRS.

Background

A typical estate plan for married couples with larger estates is as follows:

A husband and wife usually establish two trusts: a bypass trust, which is designed to hold the lifetime credit exemption equivalent of $600,000 (less the value of any taxable gifts made by the taxpayer during his or her lifetime) and a marital trust, which holds the balance of the decedent's assets. Because the former trust absorbs the taxpayer's unified credit (the exemption equivalent amount that can pass tax-free under the code) and the latter trust normally qualifies for the marital deduction, no federal estate tax is ordinarily due at the death of the first spouse. On the death of the surviving spouse, no federal estate tax is due on the assets held in the bypass trust. Federal estate taxes, however, are due on the assets held in the marital trust. The latter trust therefore defers, but does not eliminate estate tax.

A number of court cases and IRS rulings clearly indicate that during the estate administration of the first spouse to die, when the bypass and marital trusts are being funded, valuation adjustments must be made to account for the fact that certain interests require a minority discount or a control premium (for example, the converse of a minority discount in which certain interests have enhanced value because they provide the owner with governance abilities).

In recognition that minority and marketability discounts and control premiums are recognized in funding these testamentary trusts, estate administrators usually consider the following strategy: To the extent possible, assets that command a control premium are used to fund the marital trust and, conversely, assets that command a minority or marketability discount are used to fund the bypass trust. The underlying reason for such an allocation is the opportunity it provides the trustee, during the administration of the marital trust, to exercise his or her powers to rid the trust of the control premium through sales or other dispositions.

Consider, for example, Cal who is married and dies owning only one asset, stock in Widget, Inc., a company worth $2 million. Assuming Cal's estate plan follows the norm, on his death, his executor should consider putting 49.99 percent of the Widget stock in the bypass trust and the balance in the marital trust. If the executor of Cal's estate can justify a 40 percent discount, the executor can fund the bypass trust with almost half the stock of Widget, Inc. If the other 50.01 percent of the stock of Widget, Inc. qualifies for a control premium of 40 percent, the marital trust will hold this stock and no federal estate taxes will be due.

During the term of the marital trust some Widget stock may be sold to a third party. If this occurs, when the surviving spouse dies, the Widget stock held in the marital trust may be discounted to reflect its minority ownership in the company.

Estate of Bonner

While the IRS and the taxpayer may have differing views about the size of the discount and/or control premium, neither will differ regarding the tax effects analysis described above. A recent controversy, however, has arisen regarding how the stock of Widget, Inc. should be valued on the death of the surviving spouse if the surviving spouse also owns such stock in his or her individual name.

In the past, the IRS has taken the position that on the death of the surviving spouse, for valuation purposes, any interest held in trust for the surviving spouse's benefit that is includable in her gross estate (that is, the marital trust) should be considered as if owned by the surviving spouse outright. If, in the prior example, Cal's spouse owned Widget stock independently of the marital trust, the problem of a control premium continues. By requiring fictional ownership, the IRS has attempted to curtail the taxpayer's use of discounting.

The Fifth Circuit, however, reached a conclusion different from that of the IRS. It held that assets owned by the marital trust should not be deemed owned by the surviving spouse. The court based its conclusion on the fact that the marital trust, though established for the surviving spouse's benefit and includable in her gross estate for federal estate tax purposes, was not controlled by the surviving spouse and, therefore, assets owned by it should not be taken into account during the valuation process.

Reconsider Cal's situation, but suppose that upon Cal's death he bequeathed 49.99 percent of the company outright to his wife, Dale, and 50.01 percent of the company to a marital trust to hold the stock for her benefit. Because both bequests qualify for the marital deduction, no estate tax would be due upon Cal's death. During the trust administration process, suppose the trustee of the marital trust sells a .2 percent interest in the company to Cal's son, Ed. Upon the death of Cal's wife, Dale, though she and the marital trust each owned 49.99 percent of Widget, Inc., both interests may be discounted for federal estate tax valuation purposes.

The Fifth Circuit opinion thus paves the way for taxpayers and trust administrators to use discounting to their advantage when funding testamentary trusts and to exercise foresight during the trust administration process. More specifically, an astute trust administrator of the marital trust should consider ridding herself of a portion of any assets held by the trust (even a fraction of a percent) to drop below a control position. In this way, upon the death of the surviving spouse, the assets held in the marital trust may enjoy discounted treatment, after an initial funding at premium levels.

48
Save a Ton on Taxes by Two Methods of Discounting

HERBERT L. ZUCKERMAN AND JAY A. SOLED

Over the years, Congress has made it progressively more expensive to transfer wealth. Gift and estate tax rates now range as high as 55 percent, and a recent addition—the generation-skipping transfer tax—can make the effective transfer rate as high as 80 percent. In addition, the tried-and-true wealth transfer techniques of the past, such as Clifford trusts and grantor-retained income trusts, have been eliminated or curtailed by a government anxious to enhance revenue.

With many tax-saving wealth transfer techniques now obsolete, estate planners are giving greater emphasis to the issue of valuation. Obviously, this has always been the starting point when a person uses any transfer-tax-saving techniques. In valuation, the form of ownership and method of transfer are structured to take advantage of qualities that depress the value of assets.

Two of the most important value depressors are minority and marketability discounts. By lowering the value of a person's taxable gifts and estate, these discounts result in a corresponding reduction of transfer taxes. As we'll see, sometimes the savings can be huge.

What exactly are minority and marketability discounts? At death, a minority discount is triggered when a transferor holds less than a 50 percent interest in the equity or control of a business. In life, it is triggered when the transferor gifts less than a 50 percent interest in the equity or control of a business or property. Because a minority interest has no control, it is considered less valuable than an equal or controlling majority interest.

Herbert L. Zuckerman is a partner at the law firm of Sills Cummis Zuckerman Radin Tischman Epstein & Gross, P.A., in Newark, New Jersey. Jay A. Soled is a lawyer and an assistant professor at Rutgers University in Newark, New Jersey.

The second type of discount, the marketability discount, can apply when the property in question does not have a readily ascertainable fair-market value because it is not widely traded. Consider a closely held family business. Unlike the records of a publicly listed company such as IBM, GM, or GE, the records of a small business are not generally audited, and no broad range of investors is analyzing its net worth. Its shares therefore are much more difficult to value, and potential purchasers tend to discount its value below what a balance sheet and individual asset appraisals would show. A marketability discount can also apply to a thinly traded public issue. This discount (frequently called blockage) is meaningful if it can be shown that the market could not absorb a large block of stock without depressing the listed price.

The range of minority and marketability discount rates varies. In the closely held or family business context, these two discounts are almost always amalgamated into one. Courts typically have allowed combined discounts from between 30 and 60 percent. Because of the somewhat inherently amorphous nature of discounting, courts rarely ascribe individual percentages to either form of discount. Factors that courts consider salient when discounting include the rights of the minority shareholder, the dividend history of the enterprise, and the nature and value of the underlying business assets.

To illustrate, suppose someone owns a 49 percent interest in a family partnership that holds real estate worth $1 million. When that person dies, instead of valuing the decedent's family partnership interest at $490,000 (49 percent x $1,000,000), the executor may discount the value of the partnership interest by 50 percent because the decedent has a minority interest that is not readily marketable. This valuation technique results in a dramatic estate tax savings of approximately $122,500 (50 percent x $490,000 x 50 percent), assuming a 50 percent estate tax rate.

In the valuation process, the law does not consider to whom the property is bequeathed or gifted—even if the recipients are family members. If, in the example above, the decedent bequeathed his or her minority interest to a child who is the 51 percent majority shareholder, the child's controlling interest is irrelevant and does not affect the value of the decedent's shares.

But in valuation, timing matters. It is critical whether the transfer occurs at death in the form of an estate, or during life in the form of a gift. The focus of the valuation inquiry at death is what the decedent owned. All of the decedent's interests are aggregated, and the estate tax applies to whatever property the decedent transfers.

If, on the other hand, the transfer takes the form of a gift during the life of the transferor, then the aggregate method is not followed. Instead, in figuring the gift tax, the value of each gift is analyzed separately. An example will best demonstrate the difference between these two methods.

Suppose transferor owns all 100 shares of Company X, which is worth $1 million. If transferor were to die owning all the stock of Company X, its entire $1 million value would be included in the gross estate. But if, while still alive, the transferor were to gift an equal number of company shares to each of four children, then each gift would not be valued at $250,000, but at

$125,000, because the 50 percent discount would apply. Though the magnitude of this tax break seems somewhat illogical, last year the Internal Revenue Service sanctioned this outcome.

With minority and marketability discounts offering such potentially great tax savings, some strategizing is clearly called for. The client should evaluate his or her portfolio to see if there are existing opportunities to take advantage of—or if there are opportunities that can be created. For example, the client could establish a family business in which he or she would be a minority shareholder or have a minority vote.

A common concern among clients, though, is a loss of control. They do not wish to be ruled by the whims of the children who may be, or may become, the majority owners of the business. And yet to obtain a discount, the transferor may have to sacrifice some control. A full retreat, however, often is not necessary. Corporate and partnership agreements can be structured so that minority shareholders have some say over important decisions and their voices are heard. Unanimous consent requirements are one example of such advantageous structuring. Discounting does not come free, but relinquishing unilateral control over the family business may be a small price to pay for the opportunity to realize significant transfer-tax savings.

In sum, in this atmosphere of federal belt tightening, estate planners have to look where they never looked before for opportunities. In certain situations, valuation discounts may just what the estate planner ordered.

49
Saving on Funeral Costs

RICHARD JAMES STEVENS

All humans are mortal. I am a human. Therefore, I am mortal. While this syllogism is logically correct, I really do not believe it. I, like most other individuals, refuse to face up to the fact that, sooner or later, I will die. That is one reason few individuals make any plans in connection with their funerals. We do not need to go as far as the ancient Egyptians, who spent a good part of their lives building pyramids and otherwise preparing for death, but prudence suggests that some prior thought should be given to planning one's funeral.

Usually a funeral is the third most expensive purchase a family makes. A house and a car may cost more than a funeral, but few other things are more expensive than a funeral, particularly an unplanned funeral. At time of death, the surviving family wants to be sure that proper respect is shown the deceased. No one is in a mood to do any shopping or bargaining about funeral prices, and the sympathetic funeral director knows how to encourage the family to spend generously as the last thing that can be done for the deceased. Of course, it is too late now to do anything meaningful for the deceased, but that obvious fact somehow is overlooked.

Some individuals and some cultures strongly encourage the lavish expenditure of funds on funerals. If this is what is desired, that is a choice that may be made, and many funeral directors can be found who will gladly help in spending your money. If that is your wish, stop reading now and turn on the TV. However, if you are interested in saving money on your funeral, keep on reading.

Richard James Stevens, retired, practiced law in Chicago since 1938. He was a founding member of the Chicago Memorial Association and served as its president for thirty years.

Basically there are two ways to save money on funerals. First, careful preplanning; second, joining a memorial society.

Preplanning involves two things: considering the alternative options available and shopping for those alternatives. The typical funeral involves two different functions. First, the disposition of the body. Second, a ceremony celebrating the life of the deceased and expressing grief at his or her death.

Basically there are three ways to dispose of a body. The body may be buried; the body may be cremated; or the body may be donated to a medical school to be used as a cadaver for medical students. The donation of a body to a medical school tends to be the least expensive method, but it may be necessary to hire a funeral director to obtain the necessary permit and to transport the body to the medical school. This seemingly brief task by the funeral director may result in a surprising bill, so it is wise to check on the funeral director's charges for this service in advance. Also, it usually is necessary to execute a document that gives your body to a medical school in advance of death. In some states there are organizations that help medical schools obtain bodies and help individuals who desire to make such donations. In Illinois, the organization is The Anatomical Gift Association of Illinois located at 2240 West Fillmore, Chicago, Illinois 60612; phone (312) 733-5283. In other states, a call to a local medical school usually will give one a lead to possible methods of body donation.

Cremation is a relatively inexpensive way of disposal of the body. An increasing number of individuals are choosing cremation, with a memorial service held after the body is cremated. The cremation can be purchased through a funeral director, but as there is a wide variation in the charges made by funeral directors for cremations, shopping definitely is in order. This shopping can be done over the telephone. Under the Federal Trade Commission Funeral Rule, a funeral director is required to give a caller the price range for direct cremations. In making the inquiry, you should ask what charges are made for the cremation, what charges are made for a container, what charges are made for the funeral director's services in addition to the cremation, and what charges are made for the delivery or scattering of the ashes.

In some areas, there are cremation societies. These are not consumer societies as their owners want the public to believe. They are businesses, usually funeral directors, that provide cremations to the public. The "societies" usually charge membership fees, but there is no organization to which the members belong. Nevertheless, these cremation societies usually provide low-cost cremations. Generally, the cremations provided by the cremation societies are cheaper than those provided by funeral directors. Again, care should be exercised in determining what charges are made for containers and for delivery of the ashes.

If cremation is chosen, some thought should be given to the disposition of the ashes. The ashes may be buried in a cemetery. The cost of such a cemetery lot and the charge for opening the grave are much less than the charges for a normal grave. The ashes may be scattered in some appropriate place. The ashes may be placed in an urn. Some churches and most cemeteries have niches that may be purchased for the disposition of ashes. The crematory may dispose of the ashes, usually by burial.

If burial is chosen, one relatively inexpensive option is to have immediate burial with a graveside service. This eliminates the use of the funeral home for a service and may eliminate the need for embalming. In such a service, usually an inexpensive casket is appropriate as there is no viewing. Frequently, a graveside service with a memorial service in a church, home, lodge, or other appropriate place at a later date is feasible.

Burial preceded by a full-scale service in a funeral home is the most expensive procedure. Even here there are options that may save. One of the variable items is the cost of the casket. Heavy metal caskets tend to be the most expensive. There are several cloth-covered wooden caskets lined in satin that are quite inexpensive, yet quite presentable. If the service is not held in the funeral home, but is held in a church or other appropriate place, the cost of the funeral may be reduced, depending on the negotiations with the funeral director. The rental of flower cars and limousines can add significantly to the cost of the funeral. One possible place to save on the cemetery cost is in the cost of the grave-liner. Many cemeteries require that there be some sort of a solid encasement for the casket so the ground at the grave site will not sink. Metal grave-liners are quite expensive, while a cement grave-liner does just as good a job and is much cheaper.

The Federal Trade Commission has a rule that has two basic requirements for funeral directors. First, the funeral director must provide the purchaser with a casket price list. This enables the purchaser to be aware of the alternatives that are available. Second, the funeral director is required to give the purchaser at the conclusion of the discussion of arrangements a written statement listing the funeral goods and services selected and the prices for each of them. It may be helpful to review those goods and services to see if they all are wanted.

Probably the easiest and best way to save on funeral costs is to join a memorial society. In 1959, Leroy Bowman wrote a book, *The American Funeral*, that was highly critical of the funeral industry. About four years later, two very popular books, Ruth Harmer's *The High Cost of Dying* and Jessica Mitford's *The American Way of Death*, generated widespread criticism of the funeral industry. Spurred on by this publicity, a number of funeral-reform societies were formed. They used the name "memorial society" because one option urged by the societies was to have a prompt disposition of the body followed by a memorial service celebrating the life of the deceased. Today there are about 120 memorial societies in the United States. Generally, they are of two types. Some, the least effective, are sources of information as to prices charged by funeral homes. The second type of memorial society has a contract or arrangement with a funeral home to render services to members at predetermined prices. These are very cost-effective because the funeral industry is grossly overbuilt. There are about twenty-three thousand funeral homes in the nation, and about 2.1 million individuals die each year. That means that each funeral home gets fewer than two funerals a week if it gets its share of funerals. Most of the time, the typical funeral home has no business, and the overhead and salaries continue to mount up. Consequently, when a family comes in the door, the funeral director must load all the overhead charges on that one funeral. Memorial societies that are successful have thousands of members. By making a deal with a funeral director sympathetic to the society's aims that all the society's funerals will be directed to that funeral director, the funeral director can spread his or her overhead over a large number of funerals, can reduce the price of each individual funeral, and can still make a profit. For example, Chicago Memorial Association has about fifteen thousand members in the Chicago area. Through arrangements with one funeral director, the cost of a cremation is $445; the cost of a graveside service is $495 plus cemetery costs; and the price of a standard funeral with a cloth-covered casket, embalming, use of the funeral home for one visitation and the funeral service, obtaining the necessary permits, and transportation to the cemetery is $1,150 plus cemetery costs. These prices compare to the $5,000 costs that are frequently incurred.

There is a national organization of memorial societies: Funeral and Memorial Societies of America, Inc. Its address is P.O. Box 10, Hinesburg, Vermont 05461; phone (802) 482-5246; E-mail famsa@funerals.org; Web site http://www.funerals.org/famsa. The name and address of a memorial society in your area can be obtained from Funeral and Memorial Societies of America.

The cost of membership in any memorial society is nominal. For example, the membership fee for Chicago Memorial Association is $20 for an individual, $25 for a family, $15 for a senior citizen (65 or older), or $20 for a senior couple. There are no annual dues. The Chicago Memorial Association may be reached at P.O. Box 2923, Chicago, Illinois 60690; phone (312) 939-0678.

There are about 120 memorial societies in the United States. The most successful ones are on the West Coast. Peoples Memorial Association is at 2366 Eastlake Avenue, Seattle, Washington 98102; phone (206) 325-0489. Oregon Memorial Association's address is P.O. Box 649, Madras, Oregon 977414; phone (541) 475-5520. Bay Area Funeral Society can be reached at P.O. Box 264, Berkeley, California 94701; phone (510) 841-6653.

Part VI
Tax and Estate Planning Vehicles

50
Trust Me:
A Nutshell Primer on Trusts

STEPHAN R. LEIMBERG

This chapter is devoted to how to do two things: (1) how you can use trusts to solve personal problems and (2) how to use trusts to save thousands of dollars in taxes and probate costs. What you are about to read explains the secrets of how to keep wealth in the family through trusts.

What Is a Trust?

Trust Defined

Picture in your mind a box. Let's call that fictional box a "trust." Into that box you can put cash, stocks, bonds, mutual funds, the deed to your home, or even life insurance. You can put almost any asset into a trust. When you put property into the box, you are "funding" the trust. Additional assets can be put into the trust at some later date. For example, you can even name the trust as the beneficiary of your group life or personal life insurance, your pension plan, IRA, or HR-10. So at your death, the trust would be funded.

A trust is therefore a legal relationship that enables one party, the *trustee*, to hold money or other property (trust *principal*) transferred to the trust by a second party (called the *grantor* or *settlor* or *trustor*) for the benefit of one or more third parties (the *beneficiaries*) according to the terms and conditions of a written document called a *trust agreement*. That document spells out (a) how the assets of the trust are to be managed and invested, (b) who will receive income and assets from the trust, (c) how that money is to be paid

out, and (d) when principal or income is to be paid (for example, at what ages or upon what circumstances each of the beneficiaries will receive his or her share).

The key is that the trustee—for investment, management, and administration purposes—holds legal title to the property in the trust. But the trustee may only use the property—and the income it produces—for the benefit of the beneficiaries you have selected (which may include yourself).

Trustee Defined

We need someone to safeguard and invest the assets in the "box" and then pay out—to the people you specify—the income and/or capital from those assets. This obligation may last only a few years or it may run for generations. The party you select to shoulder those responsibilities is called a *trustee*. You can have more than one. In fact you can name two or three trustees and backup trustees in case one you've named can't serve or for some reason or refuses to serve. You can name one or more individuals and/or a corporate trustee such as a bank as trustee. When several parties are named, they are *cotrustees* and make decisions jointly (and are jointly liable for mistakes).

Beneficiaries Defined

The people for whom you've set up the trust (which may include yourself) are called the trust's *beneficiaries*. They receive income from trust assets—and/or principal—at the ages and under the terms and conditions you specified when you had your lawyer draft the trust. The first people to receive distributions from the trust are called the *primary beneficiaries*. For instance, if you said in the trust instrument that you were to be paid all the income for as long as you live, you would be

Stephan R. Leimberg is CEO of Leimberg and LeClair, Inc., an estate and financial planning software company, and president of Leimberg Associates, Inc., a publishing and software company, in Bryn Mawr, Pennsylvania. He is a best-selling author and a nationally known speaker on estate and financial planning.

the primary beneficiary. If you stated that your child was to receive what remained in the trust at your death, he or she would be the *remainderman*.

Living Trust Defined

If you set up that trust during your lifetime, it would be a *living (inter vivos) trust.* That trust could hold assets you put in during your lifetime or could receive assets you own when you die. Your will could "pour over" assets into the previously established trust.

Testamentary Trust Defined

If the trust is created under your will when you die, the trust is called a *testamentary trust.* Assets you own in your own name would pass from your will into the trust. Lawyers use a testamentary trust to reduce the number of documents: With a testamentary trust your will and trust are both in one document. A living trust and will would require two separate documents (and if you fund the living trust during your lifetime there will be ongoing expenses). The drawback of the testamentary trust is that, if your will is not probated or is successfully attacked, the testamentary trust may never come into existence. Testamentary trusts save neither income nor estate taxes since you own the assets and the income those assets produce until you die.

Revocable Trust Defined

Now picture a string on the fictional box we call a trust. That string enables you to pull back the box, reach in, and take out what you've put in the box. You can revoke your trust, take back what you've transferred to it, alter it, amend it, or even revoke and terminate it. A box with a string on it is a *revocable trust.*

Irrevocable Trust Defined

Cut that string and you've created an *irrevocable trust.* You can't get the property back once you've put it into the box. You can't change the terms or alter, amend, or revoke an irrevocable trust.

Why Set Up a Trust?

People set up trusts for many reasons. You may want to create a trust because:

1. You feel your beneficiary is unwilling or unable to invest, manage, or handle the responsibility of an immediate outright gift. Families with minor, handicapped, or merely financially or emotionally immature children should consider trusts.
2. You would like to postpone full ownership until your beneficiary is in a position to handle the property or income properly or until you (or someone you name) are ready or able to part with it. For example, you may want to keep the income from a trust for a given number of years—or for your life—and then have the principal remaining go to charity (a *charitable remainder trust*).
3. You want to spread the financial security of property among a number of individuals but the asset you have in mind (for instance an apartment house or life insurance policy) does not lend itself to fragmentation.
4. You have particular dispositive plans in mind and control is essential. For example, you may want to prevent your beneficiary from disposing of the family business or family home to persons outside the family.
5. You'd like to protect assets from the claims of your own creditors.
6. You want to treat your children or grandchildren equally—yet you own some property that may appreciate and some property that may fall in value. By placing both properties in trust and giving all your children equal shares of that trust, you equalize both benefits and risks among the children.
7. You want to avoid the mysterious and uncertain (and sometimes costly) process of probate.
8. You want to reduce the probability of a will contest or an "election" by a spouse to take a state-mandated portion of your estate (roughly one-third) regardless of what your will provides.
9. You would like all the details of your finances kept as private as legally possible.
10. You would like to relieve yourself of the burden of investing and managing property and would like to protect yourself in the event of a physical, emotional, or mental incapacity. (You may want a *step-up trust,* a trust that steps up and takes over when you don't want to or can't manage property.)

In summary there are many management, conservation, and dispositive objectives available through one or more types of trust that are not possible with a direct gift.

Trusts That Don't Save Taxes But Do Lots of Other Great Things!

Revocable living trusts (RLTs), the kind you hear about all the time on the radio and TV are not designed to produce income or estate tax savings. Because you can regain the assets you put into a revocable trust, you are taxed on the income the trust produces. The principal in an RLT will also be included in your estate.

So if there are no tax savings, why are RLTs so popular?

- All your assets (such as life insurance, pension plan, IRA, and personal property) can be "poured into" a revocable living trust. The trust serves as a unifying receptacle for the collection of assets from a variety of sources. This unification is particularly important if you own property in more than one state (and may save your heirs a great deal of aggravation aside from avoiding multiple probates)
- There is no publicity and so the amount you leave, the people you leave it to, and the terms of your gifts to them will be completely private.
- Setting up a trust during your lifetime gives you the opportunity to see how well the trustee manages property—and to see how well the beneficiaries handle the income or other rights you give them. If you don't like what you see, you can make changes.
- A revocable living trust allows you to pick a state where the laws will be most favorable to accomplishing your objectives. You don't have to use the laws of your own state.
- You reduce the likelihood of an attack on your will—if you've put assets into the trust and had it going for some time before your death.

Here are some things to think about:

- Don't set up an RLT as a cure-all: it isn't!
- Don't set up an RLT solely to save income or estate taxes. In spite of what you may have heard, it wouldn't!
- Don't set up an RLT to save big on probate costs. In most states the bogeyman of probate isn't nearly as scary as it's been portrayed by

people trying to sell you their books or their "revocable trust kits." The highly publicized advantage of a living trust avoiding probate comes with the disadvantage of avoiding court supervision of how the trustee you've named manages, invests, and distributes your wealth to those you love. In other words, no one is officially looking over the trustee's shoulder.

- Don't set up an RLT to "beat the lawyers." The laws involved are too numerous and a trust .s much too complex a document to draft yourself—or to rip out of a formbook—unless you are the type of person who buys one-size-fits-all clothes or who would take out your own appendix or who would attempt do-it-yourself brain surgery. Even with an RLT, you'll still need an up-to-date will.

Let me repeat: A revocable living trust is a highly useful estate and financial planning tool—but only when used as part of an overall plan, and only when established and maintained by knowledgeable planners.

Trusts to Save Taxes

You're probably wondering why tax savings weren't listed among "top ten" reasons to set up a trust. The truth is that more trusts are set up to achieve nontax objectives than those set up to merely save taxes.

But the right type of trust can result in big tax savings. In fact, a properly arranged trust may be the only way to keep wealth—in the family and out of the hands of the IRS.

There are many types of trusts that yield significant tax savings under current law: Two of the most important of these are (1) the marital deduction trust and (2) the irrevocable life insurance trust.

The Marital Deduction Trust

When lawyers draft a marital deduction trust, designed to qualify the property that goes into it for the "marital deduction" (which eliminates federal estate tax in virtually unlimited amounts), they also draft a second "nonmarital" or "family trust," also called the *credit equivalent bypass trust* (CEBT).

Why two trusts? Mainly because it's no great legal trick to save estate taxes when the first spouse of a married couple dies. The federal estate tax law allows you to pass an unlimited amount of property to your spouse (assuming he or she is a U.S. citizen) and pay no federal estate tax—if you leave the asset outright or in a manner tantamount to outright. The marital trust is set up so that whatever goes into that trust qualifies for this very special deduction. Transferring property to this trust—either during your lifetime or at your death—wipes out the federal estate tax no matter how much you place in the trust!

The big trick is to minimize taxes when the surviving spouse dies. That's when the estate gets hit with "the second death whammy." Since there's no marital deduction when the survivor dies, the estate gets clobbered! Federal estate tax rates start at 37 percent and actually go as high as 55 cents on every dollar you own!

The CEBT is where the real taxes are saved; instead of giving the surviving spouse everything you own and having it all taxed in that person's estate at higher and higher rates, you hold back an amount roughly equal to a credit allowed to all taxpayers called the *unified credit.* Currently that amount is $600,000. Some of your assets, up to $600,000, go into the CEBT for the express purpose of bypassing taxation in the surviving spouse's estate.

Obviously, if you can bypass the estate tax on $600,000, you've saved a considerable amount of taxes. But the savings on the $600,000 ($235,000 if your estate is $1,200,000 after debts and settlement expenses) is only the beginning. If your spouse survives you by, say, ten years and the $600,000 is invested at, say, 7.2 percent, the $600,000 will have grown to $1,202,539. In twenty years that $600,000 grows to $2,410,166! By using a marital trust/credit equivalent bypass trust, not one nickel of that money will be taxed in either spouse's estates. Think of the tax savings at your surviving spouse's bracket!

The price for this incredible tax savings is that the surviving spouse cannot be given carte blanche over the assets in the CEBT. That doesn't mean your surviving spouse gets no benefit. To the contrary, the CEBT typically pays all income to the surviving spouse for life. Furthermore, the spouse can be given a power to use trust assets to provide for health, support, and maintenance—even education—without making the trust estate taxable. Best of all, the surviving spouse can be given the tax-free power to use trust assets to make gifts to

his or her children or grandchildren under what is called a *limited power of appointment.*

So the classic marital/CEBT trust combination looks like this:

Marital Deduction Trust	Credit Equivalent Bypass Trust
Income to spouse for life	Income to spouse for life
Spouse has power to consume use, give, or leave property to anyone	Spouse has no power to use or dispose of principal
Remainder goes to party specified by spouse	Remainder goes to party specified by first to die
Additional flexibility for spouse can be built in	Additional flexibility for spouse can be built in
Assets in this trust will be subject to estate tax when spouse dies	Assets in this trust will not be subject to estate tax when surviving spouse dies

There are two types of marital trusts that are important. The first is called a *qualified terminable interest property trust* (QTIP). Its characteristics are very similar to the CEBT except that (1) much more than $600,000 can be placed into the QTIP and (2) the assets of the QTIP will be included in the surviving spouse's estate.

Why then is the QTIP so popular? Because it qualifies your assets for the marital deduction but does not give the surviving spouse the right to choose who will gee those assets. You make that decision. QTIPs are understandably appropriate in second-marriage situations where you want your property to go to the children of your first marriage but you want to provide income to your new spouse without jeopardizing the marital deduction.

The second type of special marital deduction trust is called the *qualified domestic trust* (QDT). If your spouse is not a U.S. citizen. transfers to her during your lifetime or at your death will not qualify for the estate tax marital deduction—unless you transfer assets to a QDT.

A QDT requires that the trustee be a U.S. citizen or U.S. corporate trustee, that all income be paid at least annually to the surviving spouse, and that certain other tests be met. But the moment the surviving spouse dies or the QDT fails any requirement, or if the QDT distributes anything other than trust income to the surviving spouse, a federal estate tax is imposed on the value of trust assets.

Irrevocable Life Insurance Trust

For the highly successful individual, aside from marital deduction/CEBT planning, no means exists under current law to transfer large amounts of wealth and provide financial security that are as certain or as dramatic as the *irrevocable life insurance trust* (some call it the "super trust").

The *Wall Street Journal* quoted me as saying, "The irrevocable life insurance trust is the best game in town right now." Here's why:

- Federal estate taxes on millions of dollars can be avoided—not only when you die but also when your spouse dies. That's right. This trust can bypass death taxes in both of your estates. The total tax savings can be staggering!
- With relatively little or no gift tax, high amounts of life insurance can be simultaneously created and sheltered from both federal and state death tax—thus leveraging the tax-free estate you can effectively pass to your heirs.
- There will be no probate expenses or delays or uncertainties with respect to the assets in the irrevocable life insurance trust.
- You specify the disposition of the assets in the trust in the trust document.
- By making loans to your estate or purchasing assets from your estate, the trustee can use trust assets at your death to help provide estate liquidity and prevent a "forced sale" (pennies on the dollar of your business, real estate, or securities portfolio).

As is the case with every tool or technique of estate and financial planning, "there is no free lunch." The price you must pay for all these advantages is that you must be willing to give up:

1. the income produced by trust assets,
2. the use and enjoyment of trust property,
3. the right to name or change trust beneficiaries,
4. the right to regain the assets in the trust, and
5. the ability to alter, amend, revoke, or terminate.

Transfers you make to an irrevocable life insurance trust are technically gifts you are making to the trust's beneficiaries. Fortunately, under current law, with proper drafting and planning, huge amounts can be placed into your trust—leveraged many times over through life insurance—and yet no gift tax will be payable.

Imagine—at your estate tax bracket—how much can be saved through the multiplying effect of an irrevocable trust! No wonder some of these trusts are called *dynasty trusts*.

Where Do I Go from Here?

Remember, trusts are among dozens of estate and financial planning tools and techniques. None of these is a panacea; they all have costs and none should be used in a vacuum—any more than you'd expect a doctor to prescribe pills over the phone to a patient she's never met. Insist that your advisors create a plan that (1) measures your needs and objectives, (2) establishes an order of needs and objectives, and most of all (3) gives priority to those needs and objectives you feel are most important.

You probably have lots of questions at this point—such as "Do I need a trust?" "Which type of trust would work best for me?" "What will a trust cost?" "Who should I name as trustee?" "Where do I go for competent advice?"

A good place to start is with a financial services professional. But don't stop there: Educate yourself—and those you love—about the basics of financial and estate planning.

51
Simple Revocable Living Trust and Pour-Over Will

DAVID A. BRIDEWELL

One of the principal objectives in estate planning is, of course, to avoid federal estate taxes as far as possible because the rates now are from 37 percent to 55 percent of the value of the estate in excess of the "Unified Credit," which will be increased to $625,000 in 1998 by the Taxpayer Relief Act of 1997 and will be further increased over the next seven years at the rate of approximately $25,000 each year.

In moderate estates, the tax bite can be reduced if, for example, a husband transfers ownership of assets in an amount equal to the Unified Credit to his wife thus assuring that the Unified Credit exemption to which she too is entitled is not waived and those assets taxed. Of course, he could leave his entire estate to her and he would then have no federal estate tax to pay, but this usually is not the best practice because the tax on the assets of both their estates would have to be paid when she dies.

The Revenue Reconciliation Act of 1993, under which we are now in part operating, does provide, under the provisions of the generation-skipping transfer tax, a $1,000,000 exemption for each estate owner and a $1,000,000 exemption for his or her spouse with respect to children and grandchildren that does permit tax planning in larger estates. To take advantage of this exemption, it is necessary to make use of trusts that will pass the estate, or part of it, down to them. For that reason, if it is desired to provide for children and grandchildren and their heirs, it is possible to extend the benefits down for up to one hundred years without incurring the 55 percent to 60 percent generation-skipping transfer tax rate that could be collectible from them upon their death in addition to the regular federal estate tax that would be collectible from the original taxpayers. Trusts to provide for said exemptions must be carefully drawn by expert professional planners.

Following are drafts of a very simple self-declaration revocable trust (Exhibit 51–1) and a pour-over will (Exhibit 51–2). They can be used in small estates where the total asset value is below the Unified Credit. If the assets exceed the Unified Credit amount, more complex provisions are required and the advice of a tax and estate consultant should be obtained.

For a far more exhaustive treatment of this subject, see the chapter 52, "Living (Revocable) Trusts for the Retiring Attorney," by Thomas A. Polachek. Also, see chapter 37, "Congress Offers Tax Payers Relief by Raising the Unified Credit," by Herbert L. Zuckerman and Jay A. Soled

---

David A. Bridewell serves as counsel to the Chicago law firm of DeWolfe, Poynton & Stevens.

Exhibit 51–1
Self-Declaration
Revocable Living Trust

I, _____ , of _____ , individually, as the grantor-settlor, hereby transfer to myself, as trustee, the property described in Schedule A and all other property belonging to me to be held in trust as follows:

ARTICLE I

During my life, I, as trustee, shall pay to myself, or upon my order, all of the net income of the trust, or so much of the principal thereof as I from time to time request in writing. During any period in which I am, in the judgment of the successor trustee, unable properly to administer any payments otherwise due me, the preceding sentence shall not apply, and the successor trustee hereinafter named shall distribute for my benefit so much or all of the net income and principal of the trust as the successor trustee named believes to be desirable for my support, comfort, companionship, enjoyment, and medical care, taking into consideration my resources known to the trustee, and shall add to principal any income not applied for such purposes.

ARTICLE II

Upon my death, my _____ , _____ , as successor trustee, or any successor trustee hereinafter named, shall take title as trustee to all my real and personal property, wherever situated, in which I may have any interest at the time of my death not otherwise effectively disposed of, but not including any property over which I have a power of appointment. The trust property (including proceeds of insurance and any other property to which the trustee is entitled) shall be held and disposed of as follows:

A. After my death, my said successor trustee shall pay from the trust estate, directly or through my personal representative, without apportionment or reimbursement, all of my debts, all expenses of administration of property wherever situated passing under my Will (if probate is instituted) or this instrument or otherwise, and all estate, inheritance, transfer, and succession taxes which become due by reason of my death (including interest and penalties thereon, if any) other than any tax on a generation-skipping transfer which is not a liability of my estate, and shall distribute the balance of principal and interest remaining as provided for in Article II. None of the foregoing payments shall be made out of any asset not otherwise includible in my estate for federal estate tax purposes.

B. My said successor trustee shall then give all my personal and household effects not otherwise effectively disposed of, such as jewelry, clothing, automobiles, furniture, furnishings, silver, books, and pictures, including policies of insurance thereon, to my wife/husband, _____ , if she/he survives me, but in the event she/he predeceases me, then to my children in equal shares, to be divided between them as they may determine. If they shall fail to agree upon said division within sixty (60) days, I leave the final decision as to said division to my _____ , _____ ; and, in the event he/she is unable or unwilling to act, to my _____ .

C. My successor trustee after first making the payments or transfers provided above, shall then transfer the remaining principal and any accrued or undistributed income in the trust to my wife/husband, _____ , if she/he survives me, but, in the event she/he predeceases me, then in equal shares to my children, namely:
   (a)
   (b)
   (c)

ARTICLE III

1. If any beneficiary to whom the trustee is directed in a preceding provision to distribute any share of trust principal is under the age of twenty-one (21) years when the distribution is to be made, and if no other trust is then to be held under this instrument for his/her primary benefit, his/her share shall vest in interest in him/her indefeasibly, but the trustee may in his/her discretion continue to hold it as a separate trust for such period of time as the trustee deems advisable, but not after the time the beneficiary reaches that age. In the meantime, the trustee may use for the beneficiary's benefit so much of the income and principal as the trustee determines to be required for his/her support, welfare, and education, adding any excess income to the principal.

2. (a) If at any time any beneficiary to whom the trustee is directed in this instrument to pay any income is under legal disability or is in the opinion of the trustee incapable of properly managing his/her affairs, the trustee may use such income for his/her benefit.

   (b) Upon the death of any such beneficiary any accrued or undistributed income shall be held and accounted for, or distributed, in the same manner as if it had been received and accrued before the beneficiary's death.

343

3. The trustee either may expend directly any income or principal which he/she is authorized in this instrument to use for the benefit of any person, or may pay it over to him/her or for his/her use to his/her parent, guardian, or custodian under any Uniform Gifts to Minors Act or to any person with whom he/she is residing, without responsibility for its expenditure.

4. In determining whether and to what extent to make discretionary payments of income or principal to, or for the benefit of, any beneficiary, the trustee may, but shall not be required to, take into account any other property or sources of income or support of the beneficiary known to the trustee. Discretionary payments of income or principal shall not be considered as advancements.

5. No interest under this instrument shall be transferable or assignable by any beneficiary or be subject during his/her life to the claims of his/her creditors or to any claims for alimony or for support of his/her spouse.

ARTICLE IV

1. (a) No trustee shall be required to give any bond as trustee; to qualify before, be appointed by, or in the absence of breach of trust to account to any court; or to obtain the order or approval of any court in the exercise of any power or discretion.

   (b) No person paying money or delivering any property to any trustee need see to its application.

   (c) Any trustee shall be entitled to reasonable compensation for services in administering and distributing the trust property, and to reimbursement for expenses.

   (d) The trustee may rely upon any notice, certificate, affidavit, letter, telegram, or other paper or document believed by him/her to be genuine, or upon any evidence deemed by him/her to be sufficient, in making any payment or distribution. The trustee shall incur no liability for any payment or distribution made in good faith and without actual notice or knowledge of a changed condition or status affecting any person's interest in the trust.

   (e) Whenever the context requires or permits, the gender and number of words shall be interchangeable.

2. The trustee shall have the following powers, and any others that may be granted by law, with respect to each trust, to be exercised as trustee if in his/her discretion he/she determines it to be in the best interests of the beneficiaries.

   (a) To retain any property or undivided interests in property received from any source, including residential property, regardless of any lack of diversification, risk, or nonproductivity;

   (b) To invest and reinvest the trust estate in bonds, notes, stocks of corporations regardless of class, real estate or any interest in real estate, interests in trusts or in any other property or undivided interests in property, wherever located, without being limited by any statute or rule of law concerning investments by trustees;

   (c) To sell any trust property, for cash or on credit, at public or private sales; to exchange any trust property for other property; to grant options to purchase or acquire any trust property; and to determine the prices and terms of sales, exchanges, and options;

   (d) To operate, maintain, repair, rehabilitate, alter, improve, or remove any improvements on real estate, to make leases and subleases for terms of any length, even though the terms may extend beyond the termination of the trust; to subdivide real estate; to grant easements, give consents, and make contracts relating to real estate or its use; and to release or dedicate any interest in real estate;

   (e) To borrow money for any purpose, either from any bank or lending institution, and to mortgage or pledge any trust property; and, also, to lend money, at his/her discretion, to prospective beneficiaries of this Trust for their education, medical needs, and general welfare, but only to that prospective extent of the amount they would ultimately receive under this Trust themselves or from their parents *per stirpes;*

   (f) To employ attorneys, auditors, depositaries, and agents, with or without discretionary powers; to exercise in person or by proxy all voting and other rights with respect to stocks or other securities; and to keep any property in bearer form or in the name of the trustee or a nominee, with or without disclosure of any fiduciary relationship;

   (g) To determine in accordance with the Principal and Income Act of Illinois in effect at the time of the determination, or in an equitable manner in those cases not then clearly covered by that law, the allocation or apportionment of all receipts and disbursements between income and principal;

   (h) To take any action with respect to conserving or realizing upon the value of any trust property and with respect to foreclosures, reorganizations, or other changes affecting the trust property; to collect, pay, contest, compromise, or abandon demands of or against the trust estate wherever situated; and to execute contracts, notes, conveyances, and other instruments, including instruments containing covenants, representations, and warranties binding upon and creating a charge against the trust estate and containing provisions excluding personal liability;

(i) To receive additional property from any source and add it to the trust estate;

(j) To enter into any transaction authorized by this Article with trustees, executors, or administrators of other trusts or estates in which any beneficiary has an interest, even though any such trustee or representative is also trustee under this instrument; and in any such transaction to purchase property, or make loans on notes secured by property, even though similar or identical property constitutes all or a large proportion of the balance of the trust estate, and to retain any such property or note with the same freedom as if it had been an original part of the trust estate;

(k) To make any distribution or division of the trust property in cash or in kind or both, and to continue to exercise any powers and discretion for a reasonable period after the termination of the trust, but only for so long as no rule of law relating to perpetuities would be violated;

(l) To allocate different kinds or disproportionate shares of property or undivided interests in property among the beneficiaries or trusts, and to determine the value of any such property; and to make joint investments of funds in the trusts, and to hold the several trusts as a common fund dividing the net income among the beneficiaries of the several trusts proportionately;

(m) To transfer the assets of any trust to another situs and to appoint as a special trustee any person or corporation authorized under the laws of the United States or of any state to administer trusts and to remove any special trustee and reappoint itself.

ARTICLE V

1. (a) Any trustee may resign by giving written notice, specifying the effective date of his/her resignation, to the beneficiaries to whom the trustee is to or may distribute the income at the time of giving notice.

(b) If any individual trustee dies, resigns, or refuses or is at any time unable to act, the successor trustee shall have all the powers and discretion of the trustee named herein without the appointment by a court of a successor trustee.

(c) Any trustee or successor named herein shall be the custodian of the trust property and of the books and records of the trustees, and may perform all acts necessary for the acquisition and transfer of personal property and money, including the signing and endorsement of checks, receipts, stock certificates, and other instruments, and no person need inquire into the propriety of any such act.

(d) If at any time any trust property is situated in a jurisdiction in which the trustee is unable or unwilling to act, any trustee able and willing to act, or, if none, such person as may be appointed in an instrument signed by _____ , my then acting successor trustee shall act as trustee with respect to that property, and such trustee shall have all the title, powers, and discretion with respect to that property that are given to him/her. The net income from that property and any net proceeds of its sale shall be paid over to the principal trustee in this state.

2. (a) The approval of the accounts of the trustee, in an instrument signed by a majority in number of the beneficiaries to whom the trustee is to or may distribute the income at the time of approval, shall be a complete release and discharge of such trustee with respect to the administration of the trust property for the period covered by such accounts, binding upon all persons.

(b) No successor trustee shall be personally liable for any act or omission of any predecessor trustee. Any successor trustee shall accept without examination or review the accounts rendered and the property delivered by or for a predecessor trustee without incurring any liability or responsibility. Any successor trustee shall have all the title, powers, and discretion of the trustee succeeded, without the necessity of any conveyance or transfer.

3. The guardian or conservator of the estate of a beneficiary under legal disability, or the parents or surviving parent or guardian of the person of a minor beneficiary for whose estate no guardian has been appointed may, in carrying out the provisions of this Article, act and receive notice for the beneficiary and sign any instrument for him/her.

ARTICLE VI

A. I, as trustee, may resign at any time by giving thirty days' written notice to the persons described in this Article.

B. If I, as trustee, cease to act, I appoint _____ as my successor trustee. If said _____ ceases or is unwilling to act, I appoint a second successor trustee, and, if he/she is unable or unwilling to act, I appoint the _____ Bank of _____ , as their successor trustee. Each successor trustee shall have the powers and discretions herein granted to his/her predecessor.

C. As often as the trustee deems such action to be advantageous to any trust or beneficiary, he/she may, by written instrument, resign and appoint as substitute trustee any bank or trust company, wherever situated. Said substitute trustee shall have all of the powers and discretions of the trustee, but shall exercise the same under the supervision of the trustee. The trustee may at any time remove the substitute trustee and appoint himself/herself again as sole trustee.

ARTICLE VII

I reserve the right from time to time during my life, by written instrument delivered to the trustee, to amend or revoke this agreement, but no amendment may change the trustee's duties, powers, and discretions without the trustee's consent.

ARTICLE VIII

This agreement shall be governed by and interpreted in accordance with the law of Illinois.

We have executed this agreement on _____ , 19 _____ .

_____
Grantor-Settlor and Initial Trustee

_____
First Successor Trustee

NB Schedule A is to be attached with list of initial assets deposited in trust under this Trust Agreement.

SUBSCRIBED and SWORN to before me this _____ day of _____ , 19 _____ .

_____
Notary Public

Exhibit 51–2
Last Will and Testament
of

_____

I, _____ , of _____ , make this my Will and revoke all prior wills and codicils.

FIRST

My Executor shall pay all expenses of my last illness and funeral, costs of administration including ancillary, costs of safeguarding and delivering legacies, other proper charges against my estate. My Executor shall pay from the residue of my estate all estate and inheritance taxes assessed by reason of my death, except that the amount, if any, by which the estate and inheritance taxes shall be increased as a result of the inclusion of property in which I may have a qualifying income interest for life or over which I may have a power of appointment shall be paid by the person holding or receiving that property. Interest and penalties concerning any tax shall be paid and charged in the same manner as the tax. I waive for my estate all rights of reimbursement for any payments made pursuant to this Article.

My Executor's selection of assets to be sold to make the foregoing payments or to satisfy any pecuniary legacies, and the tax effects thereof, shall not be subject to question by any beneficiary.

My Executor shall make such elections under the tax laws as my Executor deems advisable, without regard to the relative interests of the beneficiaries. No adjustment shall be made between principal and income or in the relative interests of the beneficiaries to compensate for the effect of elections under the tax laws made by my Executor.

SECOND

My wife's name is _____ and she is herein referred to as "my wife." I have ___ children now living, namely: _____ , _____ , and _____ .

THIRD

I give all my personal and household effects not otherwise effectively disposed of, such as jewelry, clothing, automobile, furniture, furnishings, silver, books, and pictures, including policies of insurance thereon, to my wife, or in the event she should pre decease me, to our children in equal shares, and if said division is not accomplished within sixty (60) days, I leave the final decision as to said division to my executor, _____ in the event he/she is unable or unwilling to act, to my _____ , _____ .

FOURTH

All the residue of my estate, wherever situated, I give to the Successor Trustee named in my Self Declaration Revocable Living Trust dated ___ , a copy of which is attached hereto, to be disposed of as therein stated.

FIFTH

I appoint my _____ , _____ as Executor of this Will. If for any reason he/she is unwilling or unable to act as Executor, I appoint my _____ , _____ as Successor Executor, and in the event he/she is unable or unwilling to act, I appoint the _____ Bank of _____ , _____ as Second Successor Executor, and grant to each of them in succession all the powers and discretions herein granted to my Executor. I direct that no security on the Executor's bond be required of any Executor named herein. I give my Executor power to invest in bonds, stocks, notes, bank deposits, shares of registered in vestment companies, or other property, lease, borrow with or without security from any lender, sell or exchange all or any part of my estate, real or personal, for such prices and upon such terms as my Executor deems proper; to compromise, contest, prosecute, or abandon claims in favor of or against my estate; to distribute income and principal in cash or in kind, or partly in each, and to allocate or distribute undivided interests or different assets or disproportionate interests in assets (and no adjustment shall be made to compensate for a disproportionate allocation of unrealized gain for federal income tax purposes), and to value my estate in order to make allocation or distribution, and no action taken by my Executor pursuant to this power shall be subject to question by any beneficiary; to deal with the fiduciary of any trust or estate in which any beneficiary under this Will has an interest, though an Executor hereunder is such fiduciary; to deal with a corporate executor hereunder individually or a parent or affiliate company; and to execute and deliver necessary instruments and give full receipts and discharges. The foregoing powers shall be exercised by my Executor without authorization by any court and, as to property subject to administration outside the state of my domicile, only with the approval of my domiciliary Executor. If permitted by law and if not in consistent with the best interests of the beneficiaries as determined by my Executor, the administration of my estate shall be independent of the supervision of any court.

IN WITNESS WHEREOF, I have signed this will, consisting of five (5) pages, and for the purpose of identification have placed my initials at the foot of each preceding page, this _____ day of _____ , 19 _____ .

_____ (SEAL)

We certify that the above instrument was on the date thereof signed and declared by him or her, as his or her Will in our presence and that we, at his or her request and in his or her presence and in the presence of each other, have signed our names as witnesses thereto, believing _____ to be of sound mind and memory at the time of signing.

Address _____

_____

Address _____

_____

STATE OF ILLINOIS   )
) SS.
COUNTY OF COOK   )

We, the undersigned, whose names are signed to the foregoing instrument, and being first duly sworn, do hereby declare to the undersigned authority that the testator, in the presence of the foregoing witnesses, signed the instrument as his or her Last Will and that he or she signed willingly; and that each of the witnesses, in the presence of the testator and in the presence of each other, signed the Will as a witness and that to the best of his or her knowledge the testator was at the time of legal age, of sound mind, and under no constraint or undue influence.

_____

_____

SUBSCRIBED and SWORN to before me this _____ day of _____ , 19 _____ .

_____
Notary Public

52
Living (Revocable) Trusts for the Retiring Attorney

THOMAS A. POLACHEK

AUTHOR'S NOTE: When this chapter was initially written in 1993, there were a number of differences, primarily for income tax purposes, between a living trust, postmortem, and the administration of a will in probate. In addition, the Internal Revenue Service (the "IRS") had continually taken the position, with success, that transfers from a living trust, even where the grantor was acting as the sole trustee, to a third party constituted taxable gains which could be included in the grantor's federal estate tax return. The Taxpayer Relief Act of 1997 ("so-called"), referred to herein as the "1997 Act," has eliminated a number, but not all, of these differences. Other changes that affect estate planning also result from the 1997 Act, particularly the increase in the unified credit equivalent, which will reach $1 million in the year 2006. These changes are not included within the scope of this chapter.

As one begins to consider retirement, it is quite appropriate to also give consideration to one's estate plan. This is equally as true for the practicing lawyer as it is for others. One integral tool used in an estate plan is the living ("revocable") trust. The purpose of a living trust is to provide a vehicle for the administration of assets during one's lifetime and to include in the trust document the disposition of those assets at death. A living trust should be an alter ego for a will. Living trusts do not, however, dispose of joint tenancy assets or the proceeds of third-party beneficiary contracts (for example, life insurance policies, IRAs, and profit and pension plans).

It cannot be emphasized too strongly that a living trust should be the document that constitutes the individual's estate plan; that is, serves as the instructions for the disposition of an individual's assets at death. The living trust, however, may add additional elements to an estate plan by pro-viding a device for probate avoidance and allowing a successor trustee to step in should an individual become mentally disabled. Although these additional elements are laudable objectives, a living trust is by no means a simple answer to the complex issues raised in planning for the disposition of an individual's estate. Other alternatives are also available and must be considered.

A trust, in its simplest terms, is a legal document designating one or more individuals or a corporation to act as trustee(s) ("fiduciaries") to receive and hold legal title to property and to administer such property in accordance with the terms of the document. For a trust to be legally effective, there must be one or more individuals or entities with a beneficial interest in the property held in the name of the trustee. A living trust is a trust created during an individual's (whether called a "grantor," "donor," or "settlor") lifetime and is revocable (that is it can be changed, amended, or terminated, in whole or part, by the grantor).[1] An irrevocable trust, one that cannot be changed, amended, or terminated, is beyond the scope of this chapter.

There are two fundamental concepts that must be understood about living trusts. First, a living trust should constitute the individual's "estate plan"[2] except for the limited circumstances dis-

---

Thomas A. Polachek is a partner with Wilson & McIlvaine in Chicago. The author wishes to thank his partner Sarah M. Linsley for her assistance in preparing this chapter.

1. A form of living trust and pour-over will prepared by David A. Bridewell can be found in chapter 51.

2. An estate plan is much more than simply a will or living trust. The estate planning process should address inter vivos transfers, whether by gift to individuals or to trusts; the use of revocable (living) trusts; the disposition of joint tenancy assets, third-party beneficiary contracts, and interests in closely-held businesses; and the use of durable property and health care powers of attorney, to mention just a few additional considerations. In preparing your estate plan, you should think beyond the mere disposition of assets and give consideration to the postmortem administrative process. Anticipating the postmortem administrative process while crafting the estate plan will provide for the orderly and efficient (less costly) fulfillment of your objectives.

cussed in the following paragraph. There can be serious detriment if an individual executes a living trust simply for the purpose of probate avoidance and does not take into consideration tax laws and other legal issues regarding the orderly disposition of property following the individual's death. Second, living trusts are not tax avoidance devices. With a few exceptions,[3] the assets held in a living trust at the date of the grantor's death will be subject to transfer ("death") taxes in exactly the same manner as if the assets had been held individually and were subject to probate administration. Similarly, so long as the grantor is competent and acting as his or her own trustee during life, there will be no income tax implications to having assets titled in the grantors living trust. No additional income tax returns are required to be filed, nor is a new taxpayer identification number required. Further, the grantor will not be required to file accounts or disclose any information with regard to the trust or its administration to any other party. In effect, in these circumstances, the grantor can deal with the trust assets just as if the living trust were not in existence.

One exception to the first point made above is the avoidance of ancillary probate administration. If an individual owns real estate, including working interests in oil or gas wells, out of the state of his or her domicile, the execution of a simple form of living trust to avoid ancillary administration is frequently appropriate. Depending on the individual's situation, however, holding such property in joint tenancy with a spouse or children can accomplish the same purposes.

It is assumed that those reading this chapter have an understanding of the basic trust and tax laws relating to estate planning, including inter vivos transfers, trust and estate administration issues, and postmortem tax planning. Accordingly, with a few exceptions, citations of authority and technical explanations have been omitted.

A Comparison of a Living Trust and a Will as the Primary Estate Planning Document

The assets held in a living trust on the date of the grantor's death will not be subject to probate

administration. To effectively avoid probate, the individual who has executed a living trust must transfer all of his or her assets to the trust. In addition, subsequently acquired assets must also be titled in the trust's name rather than the individual's name, otherwise a probate administration may be required. Bear in mind that there are other alternatives for the avoidance of probate such as joint tenancy, third-party payee (beneficiary designation) contracts, contracts (other), "payable" or "transfer" on death accounts, Totten Trusts, and administrative procedures to transfer certain types of assets such as traveler's checks, automobiles, and tax refunds.

It has long been argued that probate avoidance is more convenient and may save some costs. With the advent of "informal" (independent or unsupervised) probate administration in many states,[4] the additional costs of probate administration are relatively modest in terms of the time spent and fees charged by professional executors ("personal representatives") and lawyers, except in those jurisdictions that allow personal representatives and lawyers' fees as a percentage of the value of the probate estate.[5] Informal probate administration usually requires the preparation of fairly standard pleadings and an initial court appearance. Then, shortly prior to closing the estate, the preparation of a fairly simple inventory and account and one additional court appearance. (If informal probate administration has been elected, the inventory and account will not be a part of the public record.) The postmortem administration of a living trust will, as with a probate administration, also requires the preparation of an inventory and accounts, although no court appearances are required. The greatest amount of time spent in a postmortem administration relates to (1) the identification of assets (an inventory); (2) the collection of third-party beneficiary payments; (3) the valuation of assets; (4) the allocation of assets to fund bequests, trusts, and so forth; (5) investment review and possible sales; (6) the preparation and filing of the decedent's final income tax returns; (7) postmortem income tax planning matters and the

---

3. For example, some jurisdictions exempt life insurance proceeds held in a living trust from transfer taxes.

4. See, for example, Haw. Rev. Stat. §§ 560: 3-301 et seq. (1992); Idaho Code §§ 15-3-301 *et seq.* (1992); 755 ILCS (Ill.) §§ 5/28-1 *et seq.* (1992); Minn. Stat. §§ 524-3-301 *et seq.* (1992); and N.M. Stat. Ann. §§ 45-3 301 *et seq.* (1992).

5. See, for example, Cal. Prob. Code § 10800 (1993); MA Gen. Laws. c. 206, § 16 (by custom); Mo. Rev. Stat. § 473-153 (1991); N.Y. S.C.P.A. § 2307.

preparation of fiduciary income tax returns; (8) the preparation and filing of federal and state estate or inheritance tax returns, if required; and (9) the reregistration of assets in the name of the personal representative or successor trustee and, again, to the beneficiaries, when distributed. Substantially all of these activities and services are also required even though a properly drafted, fully funded and operating living trust is in effect.

It is frequently suggested that probate administration will delay the distribution of assets. In the vast majority of cases, I do not agree that this will be true, particularly when a surviving spouse (or other family member) is acting as the estate's personal representative. Frequently, assets are retained in a probate administration for two years or more, first because of the potential for a federal estate tax audit and second to sustain a separate income tax entity. While professional fiduciaries (banks) are reluctant to distribute the entire estate until the federal estate tax return has either been audited and approved or a closing letter is received, an individual acting as a trustee of a postmortem living trust, whether a family member or not, would also be prudent to adopt the same course of conduct. If no federal estate tax return is required to be filed, it would also be prudent in a probate administration to retain some assets pending the expiration of the claims period but, again, distributions can be made at any time.

While it has been my experience that the cost of preparing a living trust and a pour-over will as an estate plan is substantially equivalent to the cost of incorporating the same estate plan in a will, there may be some additional costs associated with creating a living trust. These generally relate to the time needed to identify and transfer assets. See L. William Schmidt, Jr., "How to Fund A Revocable Living Trust Correctly," *Estate Planning*, March/April, 1993. Obviously the amount of time (and fees) associated therewith will depend upon the type of assets and the manner in which they are titled. Consider the following examples:

- Many married couples own their residence as joint tenants. There may need to be a severance conveyance between the joint tenants and a transfer of title to the trust.
- The mortgage should be reviewed to determine whether there is an acceleration on transfer

clause. If there is, I suggest, despite the provisions of the Garn-St. Germain Depository Institutions Act of 1982, 12 U.S.C.A. Section 1701j-3, a "comfort" letter be obtained from the mortgage lender. (For an example, see Exhibit 52–1 at the end of this chapter.)

- Bills of sale for personal property need to be prepared. (For an example, see Exhibit 52–2 at the end of this chapter.)
- If stocks and bonds are held in certificate form, proper stock powers must be prepared and the certificates delivered separately to the transfer agents by insured mail.
- The name of street (brokerage), bank, mutual fund, and money market accounts will be changed to the name of the trustee.
- Ownership of insurance policies should be transferred to the trust and beneficiary designations (insurance, IRAs, pension and profit sharing plans, and so forth) reviewed and, perhaps, changed. Under current law and the provisions of many qualified employee benefit or retirement plans, either the spouse must be named as the beneficiary or his or her consent to a change in the beneficiary designation must be obtained.
- Transfer of closely held business interests to a living trust may pose special problems that require careful analysis, particularly if the interests are subject to some form of restriction, stock redemption, or stock purchase agreement.
- Partnership agreements need to be reviewed and appropriate assignments made.
- Be alert for and transfer working (realty) and royalty (personality) interests in oil and gas wells.
- Safe deposit box rental agreements should also be changed to the trustee's name to avoid having cash, bearer bonds, or other unregistered property considered to be probate assets.

The transfer requirements should not be a reason to avoid a living trust, but are examples of the care that must be exercised to insure that one of the purposes of the living trust—probate avoidance—is accomplished.

To fully fund a living trust effectively, joint tenancy property needs to be divided and conveyed to the owners' trusts. A living trust will not dispose of joint tenancy property at the death of the second joint tenant, unless following the first joint tenant's death the property is transferred to the surviving joint tenant's living trust, a point frequently overlooked. Although a pour-over will may cause the property to pass to the survivor's living trust, probate will not be avoided.

When funding a living trust, you should carefully consider whether certain types of property should be transferred:

1. The S corporation stock election is not jeopardized by a transfer to a living trust assuming the requirements of IRC Section 1361 (c)(2) are met. S corporation stock, however, may be held in an estate for a "reasonable" period of administration, see IRC Section 1361(b)(1)(B), but only for two years after the grantor's death in a living trust, post-mortem, provided such stock had been owned by the living trust as of the date of the grantor's death. See IRC Section 1361(c)(2)(A). This two-year rule may force an earlier distribution than is appropriate for tax and administrative purposes. See Treasury Regulation Section 1.641(b)-3(a) regarding estate termination for income tax purposes. See also Revenue Ruling 76-23, 1976-1 C.B. 264 for the definition of a "reasonable" period of administration.

2. Generally, property generating passive activity losses (frequently rental or real property) should not be used to fund a living trust. See IRC Section 469(i).

3. Where real property with potential environmental clean-up liability is involved, the use of a living trust to avoid probate may cause the fiduciary or beneficiaries to lose the so-called "Inheritance Defense" against such liability. The statute expressly states that the defense applies if "[t]he defendant acquired the facility by inheritance or bequest." 42 USC Section 9601 (35)(A)(iii). An argument may be made that the word "bequest," rather than the correct term "devise," intended a nontechnical meaning of "property received as a result of the death of the previous owner." The need to make such an argument can easily be avoided by the use of a probate estate.

A will is a public document that anyone can read following an individual's death, while a living trust is not required to be filed of public record and, therefore, is not subject to public scrutiny. Creating this zone of privacy is important to many individuals. Even with a living trust, a simple "pour-over" will should be executed to ensure that any assets not owned by the trust at the grantor's death are transferred to the trust to be distributed as part of the grantor's estate plan. It is essential for an individual to have a pour-over will if the individual has minor children, so that guardians of the person (and the estate, if necessary) of the minor children may be appointed. In this circumstance, it will be necessary to admit the will to probate to confirm the appointment of the designated guardian. While the pour-over will must be filed of public record, the act of filing the will does not require a probate administration for an estate if there are no assets held in the decedent's individual name or if the value of such assets is below a specified amount, allowing the use of a Small Estate Affidavit.

If, during the course of an individual's lifetime, he or she experiences physical or mental deterioration, a funded living trust provides an effective vehicle to enable a successor trustee to administer assets for the individual's benefit without the necessity of seeking a court adjudication of disability, although removing a disabled grantor/trustee may be difficult, in the absence of well-drafted remover provisions in the living trust. If the purpose of creating a living trust is to anticipate the disability of the grantor, an alternative approach may be to execute the living trust naming a third-party trustee, not fund the trust (to allow the grantor to retain control), and provide a durable property power to an agent. Then, in the event of the disability of the grantor, the agent acting pursuant to the authority of the property power can transfer assets to the executed living trust, whose trustee is someone other than the now disabled grantor.

You need to discuss the disability issue with representatives of banks, brokerage firms, insurance companies, and others. My experience suggests that financial institutions and transfer agents are willing to rely on trust language where the grantor/trustee has become disabled and the successor trustee is attempting to assume responsibility for the administration of the trust. Further, numerous jurisdictions have adopted statutory relief to address this situation. For example, the

Illinois Trust and Trustees Act, 760 ILCS Section 5/8 (1992) states: "Relation with third persons. Anyone dealing with the trustee is not obliged to inquire as to the trustee's powers or to see to the application of any money or property delivered to the trustee and may assume that the trust is in full force and effect, that the trustee is authorized to act, and that his act is in accordance with the provisions of the trust instrument." Conversely, representatives of financial institutions are concerned that multiple property powers of attorney may exist and may be unwilling to rely on a power that is more than five years old.

In some jurisdictions, assets held in a living trust will not be subject to a surviving spouse's statutory right to "renounce" and receive a share of the deceased spouse's property. In other jurisdictions, legislation or judicial decisions grant a surviving spouse the right to receive an elective share of his or her deceased spouse's "Augmented Estate," including all assets held in the deceased spouse's living trust.[6] As a lawyer who may be representing his or her own spouse, you must be very careful in advising your spouse with regard to the use of a living trust in the context of avoiding spousal rights. Clearly, there would be a conflict of interest in these circumstances absent a complete explanation to your spouse of the consequences and a knowledgeable waiver of those consequences, if such is possible in these circumstances.

It would appear that a living trust may make it more difficult to contest the disposition of the decedent's (grantor's) assets. The reported cases tend to address the questions of undue influence or competency with no real distinction between the execution of a will and a living trust. It is suggested, however, that the grantor/trustee's continuing management tends to dispute claims of incompetency, assuming that the management is done in a competent manner. More importantly, in probate, a disgruntled heir only needs to intervene in the probate proceeding; while with a living trust, the heir may first have to institute a court proceeding even to learn the terms of the trust. Also, the need to comply with the Statute of Wills upon execution of a will provides additional opportunities for challenge, not available against a living trust. The fact that there are very few reported cases on challenges to living trusts,

6. See Uniform Probate Code § 2-202 (1975).

as opposed to wills, suggests that they may be less subject to postmortem attacks. Accordingly, where there is a second marriage, children by different spouses, or no children and a risk of collateral heirs making claims, a living trust may be more appropriate than a will.

The Internal Revenue Service had regularly and successfully challenged transfers made from a living trust to third parties within three years of the grantor's death as being includible in the grantor's estate for federal estate tax purposes, even though the grantor was competent and acting as the trustee. See TAM 8609005; TAM 8940003,TAM 9010004; TAM 9018004; TAM 9318004; PLR 9010005; PLR 9017002; PLR 9016002; *Perkins v. United States*, 90-2 USTC 86, 142 (N.D. Ohio 1990). This problem could be avoided if the trust included language that any distribution made to someone other than the grantor would be deemed a transfer directly from the grantor individually, and a gift to the third party or by the cumbersome fiction of first transferring the asset to the grantor in his or her individual name and then making a second transfer to the donee. See, *Estate of Jalkut v. Comm'r.*, 96 T.C. 675 (1991); TAM 9309003. The 1997 Act eliminates this distinction by stating that a transfer from a revocable trust is treated as a transfer made directly by the grantor/decedent. Please note this will not apply to a transfer of life insurance on the grantor's life if the grantor held incidents of ownership at the date of the transfer.

The assets of a living trust are subject to claims of creditors under the current law of most jurisdictions, just as in a probate administration. While the benefit of a statutory bar to probate creditors has been diminished, but not eliminated, by *Tulsa Professional Collection Services. Inc. v. Pope*, 485 U.S. 478 (1978), nevertheless, a disadvantage to living trusts is that there generally is no short statutory bar to the time an unknown creditor's claim may be filed.

It is also suggested that without a living trust, access to the decedent's safe deposit box will be delayed. In most jurisdictions, upon the death of an individual with access to a safe deposit box, the box is sealed, except for access by a joint tenant owner, and is opened pursuant to specified procedures. This may be as simple as having a bank officer clear the box or as complex as requiring a representative of the state taxing authority to be present and inventory the contents of the box. The use of a living trust does not change these procedures.

If the grantor of a living trust is neither the sole nor a cotrustee of the trust, the third-party trustee of the trust must obtain a taxpayer identification number (Treasury Form SS-4—Application for Employer Identification Number) for the trust and file a fiduciary income tax return (Form 1041), although all items of income, deductions, and credits will be reported on the grantor's personal returns. In addition, Treasury Form 56 (Notice Concerning Fiduciary Relationship) and W-9 (Request for Taxpayer Identification Number and Certification) must also be prepared.

The IRS has suggested that certain income tax benefits (in this instance, the one-time post-age 55 exclusion from capital gains on a sale of a residence under IRC Section 121, eliminated by the 1997 Act) may not be available to the grantor taxpayer if the grantor is adjudicated a disabled person during his or her lifetime. See PLR 8549046. The 1997 Act now provides for a $250,000 exclusion of gain ($500,000 for married persons filing a joint return) on the sale of the principal residence, once every two years, if the taxpayer (1) owned the residence and (2) used it is a principle residence for periods aggravating at least two years during the five years prior to the sale date. While it seems silly, conceivably, the IRS could argue that a residence titled in a living trust would not meet the ownership requirement.

It is at least arguable under the literal language of Treasury Regulations Section 25.2511-2(b) that in the event a grantor was adjudicated a disabled person, the assets of the trust would constitute a completed taxable gift of a future interest in trust property; although no judicial or other authority in support of this position has been identified. The IRS, however, held, in Technical Advice Memorandum 8901006, that the mental disability of a holder of a general power of appointment did not preclude its inclusion in the power-holder's estate since the power could have been exercised by the power-holder's guardian. This is important with regard to the avoidance of inadvertent gains by a grantor either to remaindermen and/or through the power to revoke or direct inter vivos gifts. One way to address this issue is to give the grantor a continuing testamentary power to appoint the trust funds. See Treasury Regulations Sections 25.2511-2(b) and (c), and 25.2511-3.

In most jurisdictions, there are statutes that specifically address questions relating to anti-lapse issues, revocation of a will by dissolution of marriage, providing for an after-born child, and the acceleration of interest in the event of a disclaimer. It is not clear, however, whether these statutory provisions apply to a living trust. The law of your jurisdiction must be reviewed and these issues addressed in the trust document.

While beyond the scope of this chapter, I would suggest that joint trusts have all the estate planning and tax issues applicable to planning for the use of separate living trusts and for wills. See Williams, "The Benefits and Pitfalls of Joint Revocable Trusts," *Trusts and Estates*, November 1992, at 41; and Adams & Abendroth, "The Joint Trust: Are You Saving Anything Other Than Paper?" *Trusts and Estates*, August 1992, at 39.[7]

Some Postmortem Tax Issues and Other Considerations

As noted above, living trusts do not save federal estate taxes and, in most jurisdictions, state death taxes; nor during the grantors lifetime do they have any income tax implications to the grantor. If not properly drafted as an estate plan, and particularly when a single "joint" living trust is used for a husband and wife, a living trust can increase transfer taxes by not taking advantage of available tax avoidance opportunities, such as the appropriate use of the unified credit equivalent and GST exemption.

If probate avoidance is an objective, then the use of a living trust eliminates one postmortem tax entity, including its $600,000 exemption and one opportunity for postmortem income tax planning and can increase the overall income tax burden to the beneficiaries. If income tax margin rates (and surtaxes) increase, this will become an increasingly important consideration.

The 1997 Act has eliminated some, but not all, of the income tax differences between a postmortem trust administration and a probate administration. It would appear that the most significant change created by the 1997 Act is to

7. For a critical look at the use of joint and mutual wills see Hess, *The Federal Tax Consequences of Joint and Mutual Wills*, 24 REAL PROP. PROB. TL. J. 469 (1990).

allow an executor and trustee to file an election to treat a revocable trust, postmortem, as part of the decedent's probate estate for income tax purposes. While the 1997 Act states that "both" the executor and trustee must agree to the election, it modifies "executor" by the phase ("if any"). It would appear that the trustee, if no personal representative is appointed for the estate, which is expected in situations where living trusts are utilized, may make the election alone. In other words, it is suggested that if no probate administration is required, an appointment of a personal representative is not needed for the simple purpose of making the election. There are specific time requirements for making this election.

At first blush, it would seem that the election described above eliminates any differences in postmortem tax treatments. I suggest, however, that this may not be the case as an election may not be made. This is an all-or-nothing election and, in effect, a consolidated income tax return would be filed if there were in fact both probate and living trust, postmortem, administrations in process. Finally, I also suggest that if the election is made, then the fiduciaries cannot elect to utilize any benefit that might be available to a living trust, postmortem, but not available to a probate estate.

Some other changes resulting from the 1997 Act and some continuing differences are:

1. Estates do not have to make estimated income tax payments for taxable years ending within two years of a decedent's death. IRC Section 6654(1). A living trust postmortem will also qualify for the application of this rule, if specific requirements are met. IRC Section 6654(1)(2)(B).

2. An estate may elect a fiscal year other than one ending on December 31. A trust may not.

3. IRC Section 213(c) allows a deduction on the decedent's final 1040 return for medical expenses paid "out of his estate" within one year of death. There is no authority that payments from a decedent's living trust also qualify, although I suspect practitioners claim them.

4. The 1997 Act has extended to estates of decedents dying on or after May 7, 1997, the separate share rule under IRC Section 663(c) for determination of DNI, previously only available to postmortem trust administrations.

5. The throwback rules, IRC Sections 644 and 665, which are not applicable to estates, are repealed by the 1997 Act for most domestic trusts created on or after March 1, 1984.

6. An advantage of a living trust, postmortem, had been the sixty-five-day distribution rule, IRC Section 663(b), not applicable to estates. The 1997 Act extends the rule to estates for taxable years beginning after May 7, 1997.

7. IRC Section 194 provides for a deduction of up to $10,000, amortized over a seven-year period, for costs incurred in a taxable year for reforestation or forestation of timber property. The deduction is allowed to estates, but is expressly denied to trusts. IRC Section 194(b)(3).

8. In the absence of a probate administration, the trustee is deemed to be a statutory executor and liable for the payment of the federal estate tax with respect to property in the trust. See, IRC Section 2203. While a personal representative may obtain a discharge from personal liability for the payment of federal estate taxes, this is not available to the postmortem trustee. Revenue Ruling 57-424, 1957-2 C.B. 623.

9. A personal representative (not a statutory executor) or, if no personal representative has been appointed, the surviving spouse may elect or refuse to file a joint income tax return. IRC Section 6013(a)(3). This election is not available to the postmortem trustee. Treasury Regulation Section 1.6013-4(c).

10. If an estate plan includes a trust where the income may be used for a surviving spouse's benefit, the amount of such income, whether or not so used, will reduce the allowable Medicaid benefits to the surviving spouse unless the trust is "established by will." 42 USC Section 1396a(k).

One frequently overlooked tax trap for living trusts is the postmortem funding of a pecuniary unified credit equivalent trust (or other pecuniary gifts) created after the grantor's death. Assets used to fund a pecuniary gift must be valued as of the date of funding and, if there had been appreciation in value, a recognition of capital gain. If, on the other hand, there has been a decline in the value of assets since the date of death, a loss will be recognized but will be disallowed under IRC

Section 267 as a transaction between related parties. Similarly, the transfer of depreciable property from a revocable trust, postmortem, to a beneficiary, whether an individual or a trust, would not be entitled to capital-gain treatment under IRC Section 1239 as a transaction between related parties. The code did not recognize a transfer from an estate to its beneficiaries as being between related parties. The 1997 Act changes this and now will treat an estate and its beneficiaries as related parties. This rule will not apply to an estate in satisfying pecuniary gifts. Thus, there remains an advantage to having an estate administration, although the election to treat the living trust as being part of the descendant's estate will likely eliminate this problem. One other answer to the problem in the trust situation is to sell assets before funding, but fiduciaries should not be placed in a situation where they are forced to sell assets to avoid tax problems.

While the use of living trusts is an integral and important part of the estate planning process and serve a number of valid purposes, a living trust is not a panacea. Simply executing a living trust, particularly a standard form, will not have any material effect in terms of the disposition of one's assets, will not save death taxes, and will not, in any significant way, reduce postmortem administration costs. In fact, using a standard form living trust can create many problems and, certainly for clients whose net worth is in excess of the unified credit equivalent, can result in the incurrence of otherwise avoidable death taxes. The retiring lawyer should first consider her or his objectives for the transfer of wealth, both during life and at death, and the tax implications of implementing those objectives. The last decision in the estate planning process should be whether to use a living trust, rather than a will, as the primary dispositive document.

Exhibit 52–1
Form of Request for Mortgage Comfort Letter

Date

Name
Address of Mortgage Lender

Attention: _____ , Loan Representative

Re: Name of Borrowers:
    Loan Number:

Gentlepersons:

Please be advised that we represent Mr. and Mrs. Thomas A. Client, and are writing with regard to the above-captioned loan. Mr. and Mrs. Client hold title to the real estate, which is the subject of the loan as joint tenants with right of survivorship. For estate planning purposes, it would be advantageous if title were transferred to separate living (revocable) trusts executed by Mr. and Mrs. Client on [date] to be held as tenants in common. Certified abstract copies of these trust agreements are enclosed.

We have in our possession a copy of the above-identified Mortgage Agreement dated _____ which includes a payment on transfer clause (Section ___).

We are requesting, on behalf of Mr. and Mrs. Client, a letter stating that the lender, or its authorized representative, consents to the proposed transfer to the trusts and a written representation that such transfer will not give rise to an acceleration of the principal of the mortgage loan. We are enclosing for your information the form of Quit Claim Deeds to be used to make the transfer. We understand that your consent to such a transfer does not constitute a release of either Mr. and Mrs. Client's liability with regard to the mortgage.

The following is suggested language for the type of letter we have in mind, which should be addressed to the attention of the undersigned:

As requested in your letter of _____ , 19 ___ , relative to the above-identified loan, we are consenting to the transfer of the above-identified property from Susan W. and Thomas A. Client, as joint tenants, to Susan W. Client as Trustee U/A/D/ _____ and Thomas A. Client as Trustee U/A/D _____ , as tenants in common, and represent that such transfer does not constitute a default under the loan documents and will not result in an acceleration of the payment of the principal.

If you should require any additional information or documentation, or if you should have any questions, please contact the undersigned.

Very truly yours,
WILSON & McILVAINE

By:
Thomas A. Polachek

Exhibit 52–2
Bill of Sale

Seller, _____ , in consideration of Ten and no/100 ($10.00) dollars, receipt whereof is hereby acknowledged, does hereby sell, assign, transfer and set over to Buyer, _____ , as Trustee of the _____ Revocable Trust U/A/D _____ all the tangible personal property owned by Seller, including, but not limited to such property located in or about the premises _____ .

Seller hereby represents and warrants to Buyer that Seller is the absolute owner of said property, that said property is free and clear of all liens, charges and encumbrances, and that Seller has full right, power and authority to sell said personal property and to make this Bill of Sale. All warranties of quality, fitness and merchantability are hereby excluded.

IN WITNESS WHEREOF, Seller has signed and sealed this Bill of Sale at _____ , this day _____ of _____ , 19 ___ .

_____
[SELLER NAME]

STATE OF _____   )
) SS.
COUNTY OF _____   )

I _____ , a notary public in and for said County, in the State aforesaid, DO HEREBY CERTIFY that _____ is personally known to me to be the same person whose name is subscribed to the foregoing instrument, appeared before me this day in person and acknowledged that he/she signed, sealed and delivered the said instrument as his/her free and voluntary act, for the uses and purposes therein set forth.

Given under my hand and official seal this day of _____ , 19 ___ .

_____
Notary Public
My Commission Expires: _____

Exhibit 52–3

_____

Trust

I, _____ of _____ , _____ , declare myself to be the Trustee of, and deliver to myself as Trustee, the property described in Exhibit A, which, together with any other property subsequently delivered to the Trustee (by Will or otherwise, by me or any other person), shall be held, administered and distributed as provided in this Agreement, as a separate trust designated as the "_____ TRUST." My (wife/husband) is _____ and my children now living are _____ , born _____ , _____ , born _____ , _____ , born _____ , and _____ , born _____ . I intend by this Agreement to provide for all of my children, including any hereafter born or adopted.

ARTICLE 1
Power to Alter, Amend, Revoke or Terminate

1.1 I reserve the right to alter, amend, revoke or terminate this Agreement in whole or in part in any respect by a writing signed by me and delivered to the Trustee during my life. This Agreement shall become irrevocable upon my death.

ARTICLE 2
Distributions During My Life

2.1 During my life, the Trustee shall distribute the income and principal as I direct in writing, provided that while I am acting as Trustee, I may act without written direction. My disability shall revoke such written direction. In the absence of my written direction, the Trustees may distribute the income and principal in such amounts and at such times as the Independent Trustee deems advisable among a class of beneficiaries comprised of me, my (wife/husband), my descendants and any person dependent upon me for support, including such amounts as appropriate to continue a program of annual gifts to members of my family, whether I made such gifts by my own actions or that of any agent of mine pursuant to an effective power of attorney. Each distribution to someone other than me shall be deemed to be a revocation of the trust by me (to the extent of the distribution) and a gift from me to the distributee.

ARTICLE 3
Payments Upon My Death

3.1 Upon my death, the Trustees, in the Independent Trustee's sole discretion, may pay from the principal any taxes payable by reason of my death, including interest and penalties, and proper charges (whether or not filed) against the trust or my estate, including real estate taxes on my residences but excluding all other obligations secured by encumbrances on real estate.

3.2 I waive all rights of apportionment or reimbursement for payments under this Article, except with respect to debts arising from joint and several obligations and taxes payable (A) by reason of the inclusion in my taxable estate of property over which I had a power of appointment or with respect to which I am considered to have retained a taxable power or interest for federal estate tax purposes or (B) from any trust which contains an express right of reimbursement for taxes payable by reason of my death.

[*NOTE:* Consider apportionment of tax on retirement plan interests.]

ARTICLE 4
Distributions Upon My Death

4.1 Upon my death, the Trustees shall distribute all tangible personal property (including collections) owned by the trust to my (wife/husband), if (she/he) survives me, otherwise, *per stirpes* to my descendants who survive me to be divided as they shall agree, or, if they fail to agree within six months after my death, then the Independent Trustee shall divide and distribute the property, or the proceeds thereof, with respect to which no agreement was reached. I may leave a memorandum concerning distribution of items of tangible personal property to certain individuals, and I request that my wishes be honored.

ARTICLE 5
Creation of Separate Trusts

5.1 Upon my death, if my (wife/husband) survives me, the Trustees shall set aside from the principal to hold, administer and distribute as hereinafter provided (A) as the "Family Trust" a pecuniary gift equal to the amount, if any, which when added to all other gifts included in the determination of the federal estate tax is required to make full use of the unified credit allowable upon my death, (B) as the "Marital Trust" a pecuniary gift equal to the amount, if any, of my unused "GST exemption" for federal generation-skipping transfer tax purposes, less the amount of the gift to the Family Trust and (C) as the "Residuary Trust" the balance of the trust (excluding property over which I have a power of appointment).

5.2 Upon my death, if my (wife/husband) does not survive me, the Trustees shall distribute from the principal (A) a pecuniary gift equal to the amount, if any, of

my unused GST exemption to the Family Trust established under the ___ Trust of even date hereto as in effect as of the date of my (wife/husband)'s death ("my (wife/husband)'s _____ Trust") if the provisions are substantially similar and for the same beneficiaries as my Family Trust to be held, administered and distributed as a part of such trust and (B) the balance of the trust (excluding property over which I have a power of appointment) to the Children's Trusts established under my (wife/husband)'s _____ Trust, if the provisions are substantially similar and for the same beneficiaries as my Children's Trust, to be held, administered and distributed as a part of such trust, provided, however, if either such trust is not in existence at the date of my death, the Trustees shall hold such amount as the "Family Trust" or "Children's Trusts" as established herein.

ARTICLE 6
Residuary Trust

6.1 From the date of my death, the Trustees shall distribute the income from the Residuary Trust at least quarterly to my (wife/husband) during (wife/husband)'s life.

6.2 The Trustees may distribute the principal of the Residuary Trust to my (wife/husband) in such amounts and at such times as the Independent Trustee deems advisable.

6.3 Upon my (wife/husband)'s death, the Residuary Trust shall be held in trust for the benefit of, or distributed to, any one or more of my descendants, their surviving spouses and charity in such manner and proportions, upon such terms, trusts and conditions and with such powers (including additional powers of appointment) as my (wife/husband) shall appoint by Will specifically referring to this power of appointment.

6.4 To the extent not effectively appointed, the Residuary Trust shall terminate upon my (wife/husband)'s death. Upon termination, subject to the payment of taxes, if any, as hereinafter provided, (A) Residuary Trust property to which my (wife/husband)'s unused GST exemption is allocated shall be added to the Family Trust to be held, administered and distributed as a part thereof and (B) the balance, if any, of the Residuary Trust shall be set aside to be held, administered and distributed as the Children's Trusts as hereinafter provided.

[*CAUTION:* The power to allocate GST exemption and thereby add property to the GST–exempt Family Trust should not be held by a beneficiary of the Family Trust.]

ARTICLE 7
Marital Trust

7.1 From the date of my death, the Trustees shall distribute the income from the Marital Trust at least quarterly to my (wife/husband) during (wife/husband)'s life.

7.2 The Trustees may distribute the principal of the Marital Trust to my (wife/husband) in such amounts and at such times as the Independent Trustee deems advisable.

7.3 Upon my (wife/husband)'s death, the Marital Trust shall be held in trust for the benefit of, or distributed to, any one or more of my descendants, their surviving spouses and charity in such manner and proportions, upon such terms, trusts and conditions and with such powers (including additional powers of appointment) as my (wife/husband) shall appoint by Will specifically referring to this power of appointment.

7.4 To the extent not effectively appointed, upon my (wife/husband)'s death, the Marital Trust, subject to the payment of taxes, if any, as hereinafter provided, shall be added to the Family Trust to be held, administered and distributed as a part thereof.

ARTICLE 8
Family Trust

8.1 The Trustees may distribute the income from the Family Trust in such amounts and at such times as the Independent Trustee deems advisable among a class of beneficiaries comprised of my (wife/husband), my descendants and the surviving spouses of my descendants.

8.2 The Trustees may distribute the principal of the Family Trust in such amounts and at such times as the Independent Trustee deems advisable among a class of beneficiaries comprised of my (wife/husband) and my descendants.

8.3 Upon my (wife/husband)'s death, the Family Trust shall be held in trust for the benefit of, or distributed to, any one or more of my descendants, their surviving spouses and charity in such manner and proportions, upon such terms, trusts and conditions and with such powers (including additional powers of appointment) as my (wife/husband) shall appoint by Will specifically referring to this power of appointment.

8.4 To the extent not effectively appointed, the Family Trust shall terminate upon the earlier to occur of (A) 21 years after the death of the survivor of my (wife/husband) and such of my descendants and their surviving spouses as are living on the date this Agreement becomes irrevocable or (B) the death of my (wife/husband), all of my descendants and all surviving spouses of my descendants. Upon termination, the Family Trust shall vest in and be distributed per stirpes to my then living descendants, if any, otherwise, _____ .

[*NOTE:* Consider distribution on *non per stirpes* basis and equalization provisions.]

ARTICLE 9
Children's Trusts

9.1 The Children's Trusts shall be divided into as many separate shares, equal in value, as there are the following: (A) children of mine living on the date of my death and children of mine who predeceased me leaving one or more then living descendants (for property distributable to the Children's Trusts by reason of my death) or (B) children of mine living on the date of my (wife/husband)'s death and children of mine who predeceased my (wife/husband) leaving one or more then one living descendants (for property distributable to the Children's Trusts by reason of my (wife/husband)'s death). Each share for a predeceased child shall be distributed *per stirpes* to the predeceased child's then living descendants. Each share for a then living child shall be held as or added to a separate trust ("the trust") designated by such child's name ("the child") and administered and distributed as hereinafter provided.

9.2 The Trustees may distribute the income and principal of the trust in such amounts and at such times as the Independent Trustee deems advisable among a class of beneficiaries comprised of the child and the child's descendants, including amounts to help the child purchase a home or start, continue or advance in a business, trade or profession.

9.3 The child, by written direction delivered to the Trustees, may from time to time withdraw the trust in the following fractional shares (in the aggregate) after attaining the following ages: (A) One-____ at ___ years of age; (B) one-____ of the balance remaining (after set aside or distribution of the one-____ fractional share) at ___ years of age; and (C) the balance at ___ years of age.

9.4 Upon the child's death, the trust shall be held in trust for the benefit of, or distributed to, any one or more of my descendants and their surviving spouses, charity and the creditors of the child's estate in such manner and proportions, upon such terms, trusts and conditions and with such powers (including additional powers of appointment) as the child shall appoint by Will specifically referring to this power of appointment.

9.5 To the extent not effectively appointed, the trust shall terminate upon the child's death. Upon termination, subject to the payment of taxes, if any, as hereinafter provided, the balance, if any, of the trust shall vest in and be distributed *per stirpes* to the child's then living descendants, if any, otherwise, *per stirpes* to my then living descendants, if any, otherwise _____ , provided, however, assets distributable to a child for whom a separate trust is then held under this Article shall be added to such trust to be held, administered and distributed as a part thereof.

ARTICLE 10
General Provisions

10.1 For all purposes under this Agreement:

10.1.A in determining the persons who from time to time are "descendants," only those persons shall qualify who at the time the determination is made had been born in lawful wedlock, legitimatized by a subsequent marriage or other action, or adopted prior to attaining 18 years of age (but a person adopted by me shall qualify at any age), regardless of whether such event occurred prior to or after the date of this Agreement, provided, however, if a descendant of mine has an illegitimate child who is raised by such descendant as his or her child, that child shall be treated as a child born in lawful wedlock to a descendant of mine;

10.1.B a child of mine shall be deemed to have predeceased me, unless such child is living on the 90th day following my death;

10.1.C an individual's "surviving spouse" shall mean the person who was married to and living as husband and wife with the individual at the date of the individual's death;

10.1.D "Trustees" shall mean the Trustee or Trustees from time to time acting;

10.1.E whenever an action or determination may be taken or made in a Trustee's "sole discretion," such action or determination shall be free from liability and binding upon all beneficiaries and co-Trustees;

10.1.F where income or principal may be distributed (i) "in such amounts and at such times," distribution may be withheld or made in whole or in part at any time or times, (ii) as a Trustee "deems advisable," the distribution decision shall be made in the Trustee's sole discretion and the Trustee may take into consideration such factors as the Trustee deems appropriate, such as other income and assets known to the Trustee to be available to a beneficiary, the desirability of supplementing income or assets for any purpose, the exempt or non-exempt status of the trust for transfer tax purposes and the effect of present or future tax laws, (iii) among a "class of beneficiaries," equal or unequal distributions may be made among any one or more then living members of the class and any one or more members may be excluded from any distribution, (iv) among "descendants," distributions may be made to descendants of any degree, whenever born and whether or not an ancestor is then living and (v) no distribution shall be treated as a charge against any distribution upon termination;

10.1.G "disability" shall mean a legal, mental or physical condition which renders a person incapable of properly managing financial affairs and the determination of a disability with respect to (i) a beneficiary shall be made by the Independent Trustee, in the Independent Trustee's sole discretion and (ii) a Trustee shall be made by a co-Trustee (and if there is no co-Trustee, successor Trustee as provided herein) based upon the affidavit of an attending physician or a family member of the Trustee alleged to be under a disability;

10.1.H "power" shall include every right, duty, option, election, privilege, discretion, judgment and immunity; and

10.1.I "charity" shall mean any organization to which contributions are deductible for federal estate tax purposes.

10.2 In the Independent Trustee's sole discretion, income or principal which otherwise would be distributed to a beneficiary may be expended directly by the Trustees for the beneficiary. If a beneficiary is under 21 years of age or under a disability, income or principal which otherwise would be distributed to the beneficiary shall vest in the beneficiary but instead may be distributed, in the sole discretion of the Independent Trustee: (A) outright to the beneficiary, even though a minor or under a disability, (B) to the guardian of the estate of the beneficiary or (C) to any person or entity (including a Trustee hereunder) either as custodian under any gifts or transfers to minors act or as Trustee of a separate trust. A Trustee under these General Provisions shall have all powers of the Trustees under this Agreement, including the power to distribute income and principal to the beneficiary in such amounts and at such times as the Trustee deems advisable. Each trust under these General Provisions shall be distributed to the beneficiary upon the later to occur of removal of the disability or attainment of 21 years of age, or to the beneficiary's estate if death occurs first. Notwithstanding the foregoing, no Trustee shall have any power under this Section which would reduce the federal estate tax marital deduction otherwise allowable.

[*NOTE:* Consider increasing ages in both places.]

10.3 If income or principal distributable to a trust would be immediately distributed to a beneficiary of the trust, the distributing Trustees instead may distribute such income or principal directly to such beneficiary.

10.4 The following persons, in the order named, who are of legal age, under no disability and stand in the relationship indicated to a beneficiary who is under 18 years of age or under a disability, are authorized to act for such beneficiary in connection with the administration of a trust under this Agreement, including selecting tangible personal property, appointing a successor Trustee and giving and receiving any accounting, notice, receipt, approval, waiver or release, all without appointment of a guardian *ad litem:* then acting guardian of the estate, then acting guardian of the person, attorney-in-fact, spouse, parents (or surviving parent), children (or surviving child), nearest blood relative, or person standing in *loco parentis.*

10.5 Notwithstanding any provision to the contrary, (A) no beneficiary shall have any right to compel a distribution which is in a Trustee's sole discretion and (B) if a beneficiary of a trust is eligible to receive government assistance, a Trustee's discretionary authority to distribute income or principal to the beneficiary shall be restricted to providing benefits beyond those which the government otherwise provides.

10.6 Present or future interests in income or principal shall not be subject to claims for alimony or support, claims of any creditor or others, or to legal process, and may not be voluntarily or involuntarily alienated or encumbered. This Section shall not limit any disclaimer or release or the exercise of any power of appointment.

10.7 Distributions which the Trustees elect for tax purposes to treat as having been made on the last day of the preceding tax year shall be similarly treated for trust accounting purposes. Subject to such election, undistributed income of a trust which is not required to distribute all of its income currently may be allocated to principal from time to time and, if it is not so allocated during the year, shall be added to principal as of the end of each year.

10.8 Accrued and undistributed income at the termination of an interest in a trust (other than by reason of my death) shall retain its character as income and be held and distributed as if it had accrued or been received after such termination. Upon my death, all accrued and undistributed income shall be added to principal.

10.9 Claims under insurance policies which provide indemnity for the loss of or damage to property shall pass, respectively, to those persons who shall or would have become the owners of such property had such property not been lost or damaged.

10.10 Any power, including those given to a Trustee, may be irrevocably released, in whole or in part, in the manner provided by the Illinois Termination of Powers Act. In the sole discretion of each then acting Trustee, one or more Trustee powers may be released, and, if the written release expressly so provides, such release shall forever extinguish the power, otherwise, the release shall extinguish the power only as to the Trustee giving the release.

10.11 If my (wife/husband) survives me, in determining the amount to be set aside as the Family Trust (A) the credit for state death taxes shall be taken into account only to the extent such state taxes are not thereby incurred or increased, (B) all tax elections

actually made shall be taken into account, except no reduction or increase in such amount shall be made by reason of a qualified terminable interest property election of less than 100% or a disclaimer and (C) the amount so determined shall be reduced by all unreimbursed Article 3 payments which were not allowed as federal estate tax deductions. In funding the Family Trust, the Trustees first shall use assets which would not qualify for the marital deduction if given to my (wife/husband), and, if the value of such non-qualified assets exceeds the amount to be set aside as such trust, the excess shall be added to the Family Trust notwithstanding any other provision of this Agreement.

10.12 If no personal representative for my estate is appointed, the Independent Trustee may (A) elect, in whole or in part, a marital deduction for qualified terminable interest property, (B) allocate my unused GST exemption to property set aside as the Family and Marital Trusts or distributed to the Family Trust under my (wife/husband)'s _____ Trust, and (C) elect for federal generation-skipping transfer tax purposes to treat the property in the Marital Trust as though no qualified terminable interest property election has been made (even though such election may in fact be made for federal estate tax purposes). This Agreement shall be given that construction which gives full effect to such elections and allocation and any provision of this Agreement which would defeat the effectiveness of such elections and allocation shall not apply.

10.13 The Marital and Residuary Trusts shall terminate as of my death with respect to each interest my (wife/husband) disclaims and property which thereupon becomes distributable (A) from the Marital Trust shall be added to the Family Trust and (B) from the Residuary Trust shall be added to the Children's Trusts, to be held, administered and distributed as a part of the trust to which such property is added. My (wife/husband) shall have the same interests in and powers over property added to the Family and Children's Trusts as my (wife/husband) has with respect to other property in such trusts, except my (wife/husband) shall have no power or interest which my (wife/husband) has specifically disclaimed or released or the possession of which would prevent the disclaimer from being a "qualified disclaimer" for federal estate and gift tax purposes.

10.14 With respect to apportionment of taxes on the assets in the Marital and Residuary Trusts and each child's trust:

10.14.A Unless my (wife/husband) otherwise directs in (wife/husband)'s Will, if any portion of the taxes incurred by reason of my (wife/husband)'s death is attributable to the existence of the Marital or Residuary Trust, then an amount equal to the difference between the taxes actually incurred and the taxes which would have been incurred if neither trust existed shall be paid from the principal of the Residuary Trust (and to the extent the principal of the Residuary Trust is insufficient, taxes attributable to the existence of the Marital Trust shall be paid from the principal of the Marital Trust); and

10.14.B unless a child of mine otherwise directs in the child's Will or revocable trust, if any portion of the taxes incurred by reason of the child's death is attributable to the existence of a child's trust, an amount equal to the difference between the taxes actually incurred and the taxes which would have been incurred if the trust had not existed shall be paid from the principal of the child's trust.

[*NOTE:* Broaden tax clause if an Irrevocable Trust or other source also is to contribute.]

10.15 Unproductive assets in the Marital and Residuary Trusts shall be converted to productive assets upon my (wife/husband)'s written direction.

10.16 My (wife/husband) may personally occupy rent-free any residential real estate held in a trust from which (she/he) may receive income on the condition that (she/he) shall be responsible for all real estate taxes and interest payments on any mortgage with respect to such real estate.

10.17 My (wife/husband) shall be deemed to have (survived/predeceased) me if we die under such circumstances that there is no sufficient evidence that our deaths were other than simultaneous.

ARTICLE 11
Administrative Provisions

11.1 Any Trustee may resign from any one or more trusts at any time. A vacancy in the office of a Trustee shall occur upon the Trustee's death, disability, resignation or refusal or inability to act.

[NOTE: Consider Independent Trustee removal provisions.]

11.2 If I cease to act as Trustee, I appoint my (wife/husband) and _____, as successor Trustees. I designate _____ as the initial Independent Trustee.

11.3 Subject to the preceding Section, each then acting Trustee may from time to time (A) designate a successor or series of successors to fill a vacancy in the office of such Trustee and (B) revoke, in whole or in part, a designation previously made by such Trustee. The oldest unrevoked designation, whether made by a current or prior Trustee, shall have priority. If no designated successor Trustee (other than a Trustee under the General Provisions) accepts appointment to fill a vacancy, I substitute, in the order named, (A) _____ , then _____ as successor Independent Trustee, and (B) _____ , then _____ to fill any other Trustee vacancy.

11.4 Each vacancy in the office of a Trustee not filled pursuant to the preceding Sections may (and, in the case of the office of Independent Trustee, shall) be filled by the appointment of a successor Trustee by me, if I am not then under a disability, otherwise, a majority of my (wife/husband) and children who are then living, if any, otherwise, a majority of the persons to whom income then would be distributed from the trust or trusts affected if income were distributed *per stirpes* to my then living descendants.

11.5 Any bank or trust company authorized by law to administer trusts or any individual may become a successor Trustee, provided, however, no individual may become a successor Independent Trustee if such individual, or any person such individual is legally obligated to support, then could receive income or principal distributions from the trust or trusts affected. Each successor Trustee shall have the same estates, trusts and powers as the prior Trustee without the necessity of a conveyance. No successor Trustee shall be required to examine the accounts or records or be responsible for the acts or omissions of any prior Trustee. Each successor Trustee may accept a final accounting of the prior Trustee as conclusive of the amount, nature and allocation of trust assets.

11.6 The Trustees, other than my (wife/husband) or a descendant of mine, may receive reasonable compensation for services. The Trustees' regular compensation shall be charged half against income and half against principal, except that the Independent Trustee may charge a larger portion or all of the Trustees' fees against income.

11.7 No Trustee shall be required to give any bond or security or be liable for any error in judgment or good faith reliance on advice of counsel. No Trustee shall be required to qualify before or, in the absence of an alleged breach of trust, account to any court.

11.8 The Trustees shall send an accounting within a reasonable period after the end of each tax year to each person to whom income could have been distributed during such year from the trusts affected, provided, however, if distribution could have been made to "descendants" or "surviving spouses" the accounting shall be sent only to (A) those descendants and surviving spouses who received a distribution during the accounting period and (B) those descendants who would have received a distribution had the distribution been made *per stirpes* to descendants. Approval of the accounting (including a final accounting) and ratification of the acts of a Trustee by a majority of the persons to whom such accounting is required to be sent under this Section shall be final and binding on all beneficiaries.

11.9 Persons dealing in good faith with a Trustee under this Agreement shall not be required to see to the application of any money or property delivered to such Trustee and may rely without inquiry upon such Trustee's certificate that the trust involved is in full force and effect, the Trustee is authorized to act and the Trustee's act is in accordance with the provisions of this Agreement.

11.10 From time to time a Trustee may (A) delegate to a co-Trustee any or all powers under this Agreement (including the power to convey real property) and (B) revoke, in whole or part, a delegation previously made by the Trustee or the Trustee's predecessor. Powers given only to the Independent Trustee may not be delegated.

11.11 Each resignation, designation, appointment, acceptance, delegation and revocation shall be in writing signed by the maker and placed with the trust records.

[*NB:* Consider adding the following: . . . and copies shall be delivered to each then acting co-Trustee, if any, and to me, if I am then living.]

ARTICLE 12
Trustee Powers

12.1 The Trustees shall have, without authorization from any court, the following enumerated powers, and, in addition, all powers otherwise granted to fiduciaries by law:

12.1.A to sell, exchange or grant options to purchase any property at public or private sale, for cash or on credit; to enter into leases for any period of time, even though extending beyond the termination of the trust;

12.1.B to invest in or hold undivided interests in property, to make joint investments for any two or more trusts, crediting each trust with an undivided interest in such investment in proportion to its contribution, and to consolidate or merge any separate trust hereunder with any other trust or trusts established by me or any other person with substantially similar provisions for the same beneficiaries if, in the Independent Trustee's sole discretion, such merger or consolidation is in the best interests of the beneficiaries of the trust under this Agreement (and if prior to consolidation or merger the trusts had different rule against perpetuities ending dates, the shorter date shall apply to the consolidated or merged trusts);

12.1.C to acquire, invest, reinvest, exchange, retain, sell and manage principal and, pending distribution or accumulation, income in every kind of property, real or personal, and every kind of investment, without being limited by any statute restricting investments by fiduciaries, without being required to maintain any particular ratio between fixed income securities and equity investments and regardless of lack of diversification;

12.1.D to inspect and monitor businesses and real property (whether held directly or through a partnership, corporation, trust or other entity) for environmental conditions or possible violations of environmental laws; to remediate environmentally damaged property or to take steps to prevent environmental damage in the future, even if no action by public or private parties is currently pending or threatened; to abandon or refuse to accept property which may have environmental damage; to expend trust funds to accomplish the foregoing; to exercise the foregoing powers in the Trustees' sole discretion, and no action or failure to act by the Trustees pursuant to such power shall be subject to question by any beneficiary;

12.1.E to borrow money or extend existing loans, including from a Trustee, and to mortgage, pledge or otherwise encumber any property, to guarantee obligations of a beneficiary or with respect to an asset of a trust hereunder;

12.1.F to grant easements, to subdivide real estate, to operate, maintain, repair, rehabilitate, alter, erect, demolish or remove any improvements on real estate, to give consents and enter into contracts relating to real estate or its use, and to dedicate or release any interest in real estate;

12.1.G to transfer from time to time the situs of any trust or property to another jurisdiction, to designate or appoint a Trustee to act in such other jurisdiction as sole Trustee or Co-trustee of any trust or property, to pay the appointed Trustee reasonable compensation, to confer upon the appointed Trustee any or all powers of the Trustees under this Agreement, to remove the appointed Trustee, to appoint another Trustee, including one or more of the appointing Trustees, at will (the Trustees may act as advisers to the appointed Trustee and receive reasonable compensation for so acting);

12.1.H to exercise all powers of an individual owner with respect to securities, partnership interests and other investments, including exercising stock options, voting, giving or receiving proxies, entering into voting trusts or shareholder or partnership buy-sell or other restriction agreements, participating in mergers, acquisitions, foreclosures, reorganizations or liquidations, and exercising or selling subscription or conversion rights, provided, however, at such times as the Trustees may be unable to exercise any voting or other rights with respect to securities and other interests held by any trust, and at such other times as the Trustees deem appropriate, the adult persons who are under no disability and to whom income then may be distributed from the trust holding such securities or interests shall be entitled to exercise such rights in such manner as the majority of such persons shall determine;

12.1.I to pay taxes, including interest and penalties, and reasonable expenses incurred in administering and distributing the trust;

12.1.J to employ, with or without discretionary powers and with reasonable compensation, attorneys, accountants, investment counsel, managers and other agents, even though a Trustee may be a partner or shareholder thereof or affiliated therewith;

12.1.K to contest, prosecute, compromise, release or abandon claims, including taxes and interest and penalties thereon, or other charges in favor of or against the trust;

12.1.L to execute contracts, notes, conveyances and other instruments, including indemnities in connection with securities offerings and the like, whether or not containing covenants and warranties binding upon and creating a charge against trust property or excluding personal liability;

12.1.M to receive additional property from any source and, in the absence of any direction, to hold, administer and distribute such property as part of the trust (provided, however, if any additional property would be added to a trust that for federal generation-skipping transfer tax purposes has an inclusion ratio of zero before such addition and such addition would cause the trust to have an inclusion ratio of more than zero, including an addition resulting from a qualified disclaimer, the Trustees instead shall hold, administer and distribute such additional property in a separate trust under the same terms and conditions as the trust under this Agreement to which such property otherwise would have been added), to divide a trust into two or more separate trusts, in the Independent Trustee's sole discretion including (i) one or more with a GST tax inclusion ratio of zero and one or more with an inclusion ratio of more than zero and (ii) into separate trusts of equal value, one for each line of descent ("per stirpes") of any beneficiary;

12.1.N to establish, increase, decrease, discontinue or re-establish in the Independent Trustee's sole discretion reasonable reserves for obsolescence, depreciation, depletion or the like for property which is subject to the creation of such reserves under generally accepted accounting principles;

12.1.O to satisfy pecuniary gifts and distribute assets or divide trusts in kind using date of distribution values or in cash or both, and to distribute different kinds or disproportionate shares of assets to the various trusts and beneficiaries, irrespective of the income tax basis of such assets and without adjustment for variations in such basis, and for that purpose to value assets divided or distributed in kind (assets which are eligible for federal estate tax credit for foreign death taxes shall be used to fund the Marital and Residuary Trusts only to the extent other available assets which qualify for the marital deduction are insufficient);

12.1.P to deal with the fiduciary or counsel of any other trust or estate notwithstanding the fact that such person is a fiduciary of, or counsel to, a trust under this Agreement;

12.1.Q to exercise every power, including the right to allocate my GST exemption as provided herein, to make qualified terminable interest property elections in whole or in part, to file with my surviving spouse joint income tax returns and consents to split gift treatment for gift tax purposes, to defer or make installment payments of any taxes, to value assets on a date or dates other than that of my death or according to a special use, and to deduct expenses from either income or principal in computing taxes (no adjustments between income and principal or between different beneficiaries shall be made to compensate for the effect of any election);

12.1.R to cause securities and other investments, real or personal, to be registered and held in the name of a nominee without mention of the trust in any instrument or record constituting or evidencing title thereto and individual Trustees shall not be liable for the acts of nominees selected in good faith;

12.1.S to presume that the holder of a power died without exercising such power unless within three months after such holder's death the Trustees have actual notice of the exercise of the power; to rely upon a court order, certificate, affidavit, letter or other evidence reasonably believed to be genuine, and on the basis of any such evidence to exercise any power or make any payment, distribution, or reimbursement (these provisions shall protect the Trustees from liability for actions taken in good faith, but shall not affect any rights an appointee, taker in default, or other beneficiary may have against persons to whom distributions are erroneously made);

12.1.T to utilize capital gains in determining the amounts of principal to be distributed in any tax year and from time to time to distribute any portion or all of the capital gains so utilized by so designating on the books of account and tax returns if, in the sole discretion of the Independent Trustee, significant over-all income tax savings may be gained by making such distribution;

12.1.U to disclaim, in whole or in part, any gift to which I may have been entitled;

12.1.V to continue or enter into any business and participate in its management, directly or indirectly, with appropriate compensation from the business, even though a Trustee also may have an interest in the business, to enter into new partnerships, corporations or other entities, to participate in securities offerings, to increase or decrease the investment in the business, to make secured or unsecured loans to the business or to pledge property for debts of the business, to waive the filing by the surviving partners of any partnership inventory, appraisal, account, bond or security, to make all decisions and exercise all powers with respect to the business that the Trustees could do if the Trustees were the individual owners;

12.1.W to continue operation of any farm or ranch property, to lease on shares, to purchase, lease and sell farm or ranch equipment, livestock and produce of all kinds, to participate in government programs, and to engage agents, managers and employees and delegate powers to them;

12.1.X to drill, mine and otherwise explore and operate for the development of oil, gas and other minerals, to enter into contracts relating to the installation and operation of absorption and repressuring plants, to enter into unitization or pooling agreements for any purpose including recovery, to place and maintain pipe and utility lines, and to execute oil, gas and mineral leases, division and transfer orders, grants and other instruments; and

12.1.Y to do all other acts relating to investment, management, disposition and control of property which shall be advisable for the proper and advantageous management of the trust.

Each of the foregoing powers shall be exercised by the Trustees during the administration of a trust under this Agreement and for a reasonable period after termination of such trust, but only for so long as no rule concerning perpetuities would be violated.

12.2 The Trustees may invest trust assets primarily or entirely in common stocks, including stock of foreign corporations, whether or not listed on an exchange or paying a dividend, including new or emerging companies, real estate or similar types of investments, having in mind appreciation in value of the principal as well as the attainment of a reasonable income. I have not made the foregoing types of investments mandatory since I realize that economic conditions will change and there may be periods when the Trustees may deem it appropriate to invest trust assets primarily or entirely in bonds, notes, mortgages or similar types of investments. In making investments, the Trustees may (A) consider the trust estate as a whole and determine the appropriateness of any particular investment as part of the overall investment portfolio rather than in isolation and (B) give consideration to the other income, investments and assets of individual beneficiaries including assets and investments in which the beneficiaries may have an indirect interest. No Trustee shall be liable for any loss resulting from an investment decision made in good faith in accordance with the foregoing provisions.

ARTICLE 13
Governing Law

This Agreement and the trusts created hereunder shall in all respects and for all purposes be construed, administered, regulated and governed solely by the internal laws of Illinois.

IN WITNESS WHEREOF, I have executed this Agreement as Settlor and Trustee this _____ day of _____ 19 ___ , at _____ , Illinois.

_____

_____ , Settlor and Trustee

STATE OF ILLINOIS)
) SS.
COUNTY OF _____)

The foregoing instrument was acknowledged before me this _____ day of _____ , 19 ____ , by _____ , as Settlor and Trustee.

(SEAL) _____
Notary Public

Exhibit 52–4
Will
of

_____

I, _____ of _____ , _____ declare this to be my Will and revoke all prior Wills and Codicils

My (wife/husband) is _____ and my children now living are _____ _____ , and _____ . I intend by this Will to provide for all my children, including any hereafter born or adopted.

ARTICLE 1
Payments Upon My Death

1.1 The Executor shall pay from my probate estate, wherever situated, all taxes payable by reason of my death, including interest and penalties, and proper charges against my estate (whether or not filed); provided, however, the then acting Trustee of the

_____ Trust under Agreement of even date (but executed before this Will) created by me as Settlor and Trustee, as in effect at my death ("my Trust Agreement"), has authority to make any of the foregoing payments, and I request that the Executor and the Trustee consult with each other regarding such payments.

1.2 I waive all rights of apportionment or reimbursement for payments under this Article, except with respect to debts arising from joint and several obligations and taxes payable (A) by reason of the inclusion in my taxable estate of property over which I had a power of appointment or with respect to which I am considered to have retained a taxable power or interest for federal estate tax purposes, or (B) from any trust which contains an express right of reimbursement for taxes payable by reason of my death.

ARTICLE 2
Specific Gifts

2.1 I give all my tangible personal property (including collections) to my (wife/husband), if (she/he) survives me, otherwise, *per stirpes* to my descendants who survive me to be divided as they shall agree, or, if they fail to agree within six months after my death, then the Executor, in the Executor's sole discretion, shall divide and distribute the property, or proceeds thereof, with respect to which no agreement was reached. I may leave a memorandum concerning distribution of items of my tangible personal property to certain individuals, and I request that my wishes be honored.

ARTICLE 3
Residuary Estate

3.1 I give the rest, residue and remainder of my estate (excluding property over which I have a power of appointment) to the then acting Trustee of my Trust Agreement to hold, administer and distribute as provided therein.

ARTICLE 4
General Provisions

4.1 For all purposes under this Will:

4.1.A "disability" shall mean a legal, mental or physical condition which, as determined in the Executor's sole discretion, renders a person incapable of properly managing financial affairs;

4.1.B "power" shall include every right, duty, option, election, privilege, discretion, judgment and immunity;

4.1.C whenever the Executor may take an action or make a determination in the Executor's "sole discretion," such action shall be free from liability and binding upon all beneficiaries;

4.1.D "Executor" shall mean the Executor or Executors from time to time acting; and

4.1.E in determining the persons who from time to time are "children" or "descendants," only those persons shall qualify who at the time the determination is made had been born in lawful wedlock, legitimatized by a subsequent marriage or other action, or adopted prior to attaining 18 years of age (but a person adopted by me shall qualify at any age), regardless of whether such event occurred prior to or after the date of my death, provided, however, if a descendant of mine has an illegitimate child who is raised by such descendant as his or her child, that child shall be treated as a child born in lawful wedlock to a descendant of mine.

4.2 The Executor may distribute directly to a beneficiary under my Trust Agreement any property which, if distributed to the Trustee, would then be immediately distributed to such beneficiary.

4.3 In the Executor's sole discretion, income or principal that is distributable to a beneficiary who is under 21 years of age or under a disability may be distributed in any manner available to fiduciaries by law or to the Trustee under the General Provisions of my Trust Agreement.

4.4 The following persons, in the order named, who are of legal age, under no disability and stand in the relationship indicated to a beneficiary who is under 18 years of age or under a disability, are authorized to act for such beneficiary in connection with the administration of my estate, including selecting my tangible personal property and giving and receiving any accounting, notice, receipt, approval, waiver or release, all without appointment of a guardian ad litem: then acting guardian of the estate, then acting guardian of the person, attorney-in-fact, spouse, parents (or surviving parent), children (or surviving child), nearest blood relative, or person standing in *loco parentis*.

4.5 Claims under insurance policies which provide indemnity for the loss of or damage to property shall pass, respectively, to those persons who shall or would have become the owners of such property, under the provisions of this Will or otherwise, had such property not been lost or damaged.

4.6 The Executor, in the Executor's sole discretion, may elect, in whole or in part, to claim a marital deduction for qualified terminable interest property, including property set aside under my Trust Agreement as the Marital and Residuary Trusts. The Executor shall (A) allocate my unused GST exemption to the property set aside as the Family and Marital Trusts under my Trust Agreement or distributed to the Family Trust established pursuant to the _____ Trust of even date herewith created by my (wife/husband), as Settlor and Trustee, and (B) elect for federal generation-skipping transfer tax purposes to treat the gift to the Marital Trust as though no qualified terminable interest property election had been made (even though the Executor may in fact make such election for federal estate tax purposes). My Will shall be given that construction which gives full effect to such elections and allocation and any provision of my Will which would defeat the effectiveness of such elections and allocation shall not apply.

4.7 My (wife/husband) shall be deemed to have (survived/predeceased) me if we die under such circumstances that there is no sufficient evidence that our deaths were other than simultaneous.

ARTICLE 5
Administrative Provisions

5.1 I nominate _____ , of _____ , _____ as the Executor. In the event of the death, resignation or refusal or inability to act of the Executor, I nominate as successor Executor, in the order named, _____ , of _____ , _____, then _____ , of _____ , _____ .

5.2 The Executor may receive reasonable compensation for services.

5.3 No Executor shall be required to give any bond or security or be liable for any error in judgment or good faith reliance on advice of counsel.

ARTICLE 6
Executor Powers

6.1 The Executor shall have, without authorization from any court, the following enumerated powers, and, in addition, all powers granted to the Trustee under my Trust Agreement:

6.1.A to sell, exchange or grant options to purchase any property at public or private sale, for cash or on credit;

6.1.B to employ, with or without discretionary powers and with reasonable compensation, attorneys, accountants, investment counsel, managers and other agents, even though the Executor may be a partner or shareholder thereof or affiliated therewith, and to deal with the fiduciary or counsel of any other estate or trust notwithstanding the fact that such person is a fiduciary of, or counsel to, my estate;

6.1.C to contest, prosecute, compromise, release or abandon claims, including taxes and interest and penalties thereon, or other charges in favor of or against my estate;

6.1.D to acquire, invest, reinvest, exchange, retain, sell and manage principal and, pending distribution or accumulation, income in every kind of property, real or personal, and every kind of investment, without being limited by any statute restricting investments by fiduciaries, without being required to maintain any particular ratio between fixed income securities and equity investments and regardless of lack of diversification;

6.1.E to establish, increase, decrease, discontinue or re-establish reasonable reserves for obsolescence, depreciation, depletion or the like for property which is subject to the creation of such reserves under generally accepted accounting principles, as determined by the Executor, in the Executor's sole discretion;

6.1.F to exercise every power, including the right to allocate my GST exemption as provided herein, to make a qualified terminable interest property election in whole or in part, to file with my surviving spouse joint income tax returns and consents to split gift treatment for gift tax purposes, to defer or make installment payments of any taxes, to value assets on a date or dates other than that of my death or according to a special use, and to deduct expenses from either income or principal in computing taxes (no adjustments between income and principal or between different beneficiaries shall be made to compensate for the effect of any election);

6.1.G to continue or enter into any business and participate in its management, directly or indirectly, with appropriate compensation from the business, even though the Executor may also have an interest in the business, to enter into new partnerships, corporations or other entities, to participate in securities offerings, to increase or decrease the investment in the business, to make secured or unsecured loans to the business or to pledge property for debts of the business, to waive the filing by the surviving partners of any partnership inventory, appraisal, account, bond or security, and to make all decisions and exercise all powers with respect to the business which the Executor could make if the Executor were the individual owner;

6.1.H to disclaim, in whole or in part, any gift to which I may be entitled; and

6.1.I to make distribution of my estate in undivided interests or wholly or partly in kind.

6.2 If the appointment of an executor is necessary or desirable in any jurisdiction in which the Executor is unable or unwilling to act, I nominate in that jurisdiction such executor as the Executor may designate in writing, with reasonable compensation and without bond or other security and to have all powers with respect to my estate in that jurisdiction, exercisable without court order, that the Executor is given under this Will (including the power to sell real or personal property at public or private sale, for any purpose). If an executor is appointed in any jurisdiction which is not my domicile at the date of my death, it is my desire that such executor shall make distributions directly to the persons entitled thereto under this Will.

ARTICLE 7
Guardian for Minor Children

7.1 If my (wife/husband) does not survive me (or if (she/he) survives me and does not nominate a guardian for our minor children), I nominate _____ and _____ , of _____ , _____ , or the survivor of them, as guardian of the person (and, if necessary, the estate) of each minor child of mine.

7.2 No bond or other security shall be required of any guardian.

ARTICLE 8
Provisions for (Wife/Husband)

8.1 Although I have made certain provisions for my (wife/husband) under this Will and there may be certain provisions for me under my (wife/husband)'s Will, our Wills have not been made pursuant to any contract and each Will is independently revocable at any time in any manner authorized by law. The provisions I have made for my (wife/husband) are in lieu of a surviving spouse's award and any other rights (she/he) may have.

IN WITNESS WHEREOF, I have executed this Will this _____ day of _____ , 19 ___ , at _____ , _____ .

_____
[Name]

The foregoing instrument was, on the date thereof, signed, sealed and declared by the Testator, _____ , to be the Testator's Will, in the presence of us, who, at the request and in the presence of the Testator and in the presence of each other, subscribe our names as attesting witnesses and certify that we saw the Testator sign and believe the Testator to be of sound mind and memory and under no constraint or undue influence.

_____ residing at _____

_____ residing at _____

_____ residing at _____

STATE OF ILLINOIS)
) SS.
COUNTY OF _____)

The undersigned Testator and witnesses whose names are signed to the foregoing instrument, being first duly sworn, state that in the presence of the witnesses the foregoing instrument was signed, sealed and declared by the Testator to be the Testator's Will and to be the Testator's free and voluntary act for the purposes therein expressed; that the witnesses saw the Testator sign the foregoing instrument; and that each of the witnesses, at the request of the Testator, in the Testator's presence and in the presence of each other, signed the Will as a witness, believing the Testator to be 18 or more years of age, of sound mind and memory and under no constraint or undue influence at the time of signing.

_____
TESTATOR

_____
WITNESS

_____
WITNESS

_____
WITNESS

Signed, sworn to and acknowledged before me by the foregoing Testator and witnesses this ____ day of _____ , 19 __ .

_____
Notary Public

(SEAL)

53

The Case of the
Unauthenticated Revocable Trust

LEONARD L. SCOTT

Sounds like a Perry Mason headline, does it not? It really is a little misleading, because the authenticity of revocable trusts is not the sole subject matter of this article. However, out of the numerous articles on revocable trusts, none seem to deal with the basic problems of authenticating such an instrument or the difficulties that may arise when such a document is not and cannot be readily authenticated.

When I was young (many years ago) and going to high school, there was a cheer that went something like, "Two, four, six, eight; who do we appreciate?" We then shouted the name of "Jones, Jones, Jones" or some other current hero. I suppose there is some remnant of that cheer even today. However, I would change it a little bit to say, "Two, four, six, eight; how do we authenticate?"

In a recent, well-written article on revocable trusts (regrettably, not mine), the author points out that the trustee must satisfy himself or herself that the trust has not been revoked or amended and that the trustee (very often a successor to the settlor) must have an accurate copy of the trust and amendments thereto.

I heartily agree. But how *do* we authenticate a revocable trust? A "pour-over" will making reference thereto surely helps. However, that is not a satisfactory remedy by any means, because usually the will refers to a trust "as same may be amended." Even if it does not, the applicable statute validates the later amendments to the trust, even if made after the will.[1]

A revocable trust, as the name implies, is revocable, and, in the context we are addressing, by its terms is revocable or amendable by the settlor at any time and from time to time, usually, but not necessarily, by written notice or delivery of some sort to a cotrustee or the settlor as trustee alone. True, a revocation attempted by some method not specifically reserved or at least implicitly authorized by the original trust is ineffective. But we are here addressing an amendment or revocation in the manner reserved in the original document itself.

Let us assume a revocable trust with the settlor and T as cotrustee, with the power to amend or revoke permitted the settlor in a written instrument delivered to either trustee. (I believe that, technically, the creator of a trust is the "settlor," but the Internal Revenue Code always refers to a "grantor," so I assume either term is acceptable.)

The settlor, or grantor, revokes or amends the trust in writing and *accepts the amendment as trustee,* but puts the amendment in an already-cluttered desk drawer or in the inner pocket of an old, tattered jacket or overcoat, intending to deliver it to the cotrustee. Thirty days later, or perhaps ten months later, the settlor dies without making the delivery. The document is not located for four or six or eight years thereafter.

Or suppose the amendment or revocation, albeit irrefutably delivered to the cotrustee, was clearly procured by undue influence or fraud—unbeknownst to the cotrustee. Upon the death of

Leonard L. Scott of Eichenbaum, Liles, Heister & Bauman, P.A., in Little Rock, currently specializes in estate, trust and probate law. He was chair of the Senior Lawyers Division Committee on Wills, Probate and Trusts (1990–1992) and vice chair in 1993.

1. The statutes I will be referring to are the Arkansas statutes and this particular statute is Ark. Code Ann. § 28-27-101 (Michie 1987). Although obviously there will be different statutes and procedures in most states, all of them will generally have something in common with the broad nature of the statutes I am referring to, so to make my points, I am simply going by the statutes in Arkansas. The particular statute I refer to, incidentally, is an enactment of the Uniform Testamentary Additions to Trust Act.

the grantor, the duly designated cotrustee and/or successor trustee proceeds under the instrument he or she believes governs. What limitations, rights, and obligations are involved?

If the documents involved were a will and/or a codicil thereto, in Arkansas, the document could be established against claims of incompetency, fraud, or undue influence by notice to possible contestants within a relatively short period (three months), but if not given notice except by publication, within a longer period.

However, if the ground of objection is that there is a later will (or codicil), such objection must be filed (again, in Arkansas) before final distribution of the estate is ordered. That can vary from a very short time in a small estate (three to six months) to two to three years where taxes or disputes are involved.

The point is that, at least as far as the executor is concerned, a will can be finally and firmly established in some manner within some reasonably fixed period. I would doubt if such procedures exist for revocable trusts except in some states that have provisions for revocable trusts that are not dissimilar to the provisions with reference to wills.

Assuming, however, there is no particular governing statute, what does the supposed trustee do? I suppose he or she could file some sort of declaratory judgment proceeding in court, with notice to all possible legatees or distributees. However, secrecy is one of the major arguments that advocates of the revocable trust advance. So, I assume that the usual trustee would simply let sleeping dogs lie in that connection. Further, by hypothesis, the trustee thinks what he or she has is "it," anyway.

As noted later in this article, revocable trusts are usually accompanied by a "pour-over" will. We will assume the trustee probates such a will and gives statutorily prescribed notice to heirs, legatees, and creditors. We will also assume such a trustee protects himself or herself reasonably well by making sure that the various tax liabilities (estate, income, and gift) that could be asserted against the settlor are satisfied before he or she makes distributions. However, under our assumption, the trustee is still naked so far as the true beneficiaries are concerned.

In Arkansas, there is a special statute that gives rights of recovery against parties receiving property improperly distributed for a period of three years from death or two years from distribution, whichever is longer. However, this statute is limited to distributions from an estate. I do not know what statute, if any, would govern such an improper distribution by a trustee, nor do I know what statute, if any, would govern the rights of the true recipients against the distributees thus unduly enriched by the improper distribution. I assume that even in the absence of statute, the general rules permitting quasi-contractual recovery of money or property so received would govern, even in the complete absence of improper action by the transferee and despite negligence by the transferor.

How long a period must elapse before a claim of undue influence, fraud, or incompetency would be barred? How long can a later trust or amendment thereto be successfully presented? I think we have to assume that there is some general limitations statute applicable to the situation (although determining which one it is might give us pause); but if we inject the further element of fraud, more troubling questions arise—for example, is any otherwise applicable statute extended because of concealment of the fraud?

Is recovery limited to the (incorrect but innocent) distributees, or is the trustee liable for improper distribution? Some say not, but surely the trustee would be held to a high fiduciary standard of care. Not only time but a change of circumstances would seem to limit recovery rights against the distributees. In any event, the above situation could spawn some interesting litigation and, further, the guidelines are not as fixed and established as those governing wills.

A related problem: How can you prove a trust that you absolutely "know" was the last and controlling document, duly executed and free from fraud or undue influence? You cannot find the "original." However, the successor, or cotrustee, has an executed copy. Is this sufficient? One would suppose so, although a related and well-established doctrine in the field of wills states that an original will known to have been in the possession of the testator or testatrix but not located is presumed to have been destroyed with the intention of revoking same—even if the will was executed in duplicate and the duplicate still exists! Does the same presumption exist with reference to revocable trusts?

Again, if this is the situation, the problem of authentication raised earlier makes such authentication even more difficult and frustrating in a situation such as this. You might "know" that the document you have is "the" trust, but you cannot find the original. You think the copy is enough, but you would like to have it authenticated in some way. I can conceive some problems in that connection.

I do not have the answers to the above questions. Indeed, I really do not have all the questions that may arise due to lack of ability to authenticate or delayed ability to authenticate. I simply remind us all that there is a definite sea of uncertainty in this area, and we had best proceed with caution.

In a recent circular I received, one of the advantages mildly urged for revocable trusts was that they did not require the formalities of execution prescribed for wills. I find it slightly ironic that for 200 years our several states (except for a holographic instrument) have uniformly required two or more witnesses for a will—requirements that, when complied with, surely tend to portend authenticity, competency, lack of fraud, and undue influence more reliably than their absence—and that this should be seen as a disadvantage!

I suppose what I am saying is that there is no satisfactory way of dealing with questions such as these unless statutes not dissimilar to probate procedures are enacted with reference to revocable trusts. In such eventuality, we have really chased ourselves in a circle, from probate to trust to probate.

There is another practical troublesome spot in this field. A person during his or her lifetime will certainly average three (and conceivably as many as ten) testaments and/or codicils. This is obviously true because there are changes in fortunes and misfortunes, in emotions and relationships; there are deaths; there are marriages; there are births; there are changes in the tax laws and changes in the nontax laws. In short, there are myriad things that recommend, and almost command, that we do change our testamentary dispositions. Thus, three or four such instruments of alteration would be a minimum, and ten, twelve, or even fifteen not improbable.

Let us take an average of five, merely for discussion. No matter how long or involved the first

(or third or fourth) wills or codicils are, they can be revoked and reestablished with a simple one-page document or, no matter how simple the first or later documents are, they still can, no matter how complex or lengthy the change, be revoked and recreated by a single document. In either event, ordinarily there is no necessity of retaining more than the last document, or possibly one codicil if the will is extremely lengthy and only a small change was desired.

What about revocable trusts?

Let us assume the original revocable trust was carefully thought out and, because of various trust provisions, whether marital trusts, generation-skipping trusts, or otherwise, required some length to portray the settlor's desires. However, some minor thing comes along and amendment 1 is made. Then, a major event or idea comes along, and a rather substantial alteration is made in amendment 2. Amendment 3 is minor, but amendment 4, because of a change in tax laws or family fortunes, or simply the desires of the settlor, is again rather lengthy. Even though it really covers the waterfront, can we just keep the last document as the dispositive one? I think not.

We must remember that the original trust document is an instrument of title. It conveys title to the settlor's assets (by hypothesis, virtually all) to the trustee or trustees. The settlor no longer owns them, qua settlor. The subsequent amendments do not change that title. They merely change the governing provisions. Even if new or different trustees are named, the tracing of title and the determination of the currently applicable provisions necessarily have to go back to the original document. Thus, on the ultimate death of the settlor, to determine what "the" trust is at death, one has to go through, retain, and administer all of the trust documents. This is not only bulky and time-consuming, but it tends to make errors in drafting more likely.

One, and perhaps the only, alternative is to revoke the trust entirely, have title conveyed back to the settlor, and recreate the trust the next day or the next minute and retransfer the title to the trustee with the latest trust provisions. Such a process is time-consuming, no doubt expensive, and certainly annoying. It, no doubt, was hard enough to get a lay settlor to gather his or her assets and titles together for the initial trust and transfer them to himself or herself and the corporate trustee, or even to himself or herself as sole trustee. To have the trust revoked and to have instruments executed reconveying title no doubt will strain his or her patience, to say the least. And if you, the retiring lawyer, are doing your own carpentry, it will strain your patience also.

I further suspect that even if the trust, as amended five or six times, was completely revoked and a newly created and titled trust governs, the knowledge of the new (or latest) trustee (particularly if an understandably cautious corporate fiduciary), or the beneficiary thereof, that the trust was recreated may still suggest a review of the old documents to make certain that the new trust itself is what it purports to be. This is a very real practical problem.

The practical problems mentioned above are noted neither to praise nor decry the use of a revocable trust, but to point out that these matters and circumstances should be considered when one goes about the creation of such a document, particularly when compared to or contrasted with the same or similar problems that might exist if the settlor simply used the available testamentary procedures.

Then, let us—and perhaps briefly—refer to the other items that seem to to be elements for consideration in the utilization of a revocable trust.

One item that has been brought to my attention is the suggestion that the assets can be identified and marshalled more readily and easily by the settlor while alive than by his or her executor or trustee after his or her death. This statement certainly has merit; however, if a client (or you yourself) could bring himself or herself to do it, he or she could do it just as well without a trust as with a trust. If he or she has enough motivation to do it for a trust, he or she could have the same motivation to do it without a trust. The excellent article by Philomene Gates in *Experience* (Winter 1993 edition) suggests the importance of this. It is one thing to have very prim and precise requirements that a client list each and every asset, where it came from, and so on, on the one hand, and then have the client, on the other hand, just give you a rough generalization by category of all the property he or she has, how much joint property, and how much stocks, how much real property (and where), and how much life insurance. For the most part, the client just does not want to go into that—and we are talking about

clients not only with one or two thousand dollars, but with several million. And, peculiarly enough, for the most part, those generalizations will suffice, if you insist on the client sitting still long enough to answer your questions.

One good thing may come out of this discussion. Whether you use a trust or will, try to make some reasonable inventory and/or written instructions for those who follow you. In the first edition of *The Lawyer's Guide to Retirement*, at least three separate articles suggested something along this line (as did Philomene Gates' aforementioned article), not as a recommendation for use of a revocable trust as opposed to a will, or vice versa, but because it is the practical course to follow, regardless. If your assets lie mostly in stocks and bonds, you can put them in some brokerage account, which will make it not only easier for you to manage during life, but to transfer at death, and to have a record of it. If your assets are cash or CDs, certainly they are easy to list. If you go through the Federal Reserve Bank to get your Treasuries, they will give you an accurate list of whatever you have bought there, at reasonable intervals. If you have any life insurance of substance, your agent, particularly the one who has most of your policies, will be glad to list them for you. And you get 1099s on your CDs every year from every bank or institution.

Your real estate holdings, however vast, probably are not very numerous and certainly could be easily identified. If any are located in another state, a revocable trust with respect thereto is urged in order to avoid ancillary probate.

Actually, your income tax returns for the last four or five years are the initial and possibly the most valuable guide to your assets and income. One other suggestion: A good secretary is indispensable.

The problems that cause the most trouble are the left-handed antique chair that you want to go to Aunt Jennie or the pearl-handled letter opener that you want to go to Cousin Susie. To handle these, of course, you need to include them in your pour-over will, or a written attachment thereto permitted by many states. The pour-over will, of course, is a necessity (not only to prevent technical questions arising because of pretermitted children or spouse) but because, no matter how accurately you may think you marshal, some assets are overlooked or forgotten or, once in a great while, you become an heir without realizing just exactly what you have received, or even that you are an heir, before you die.

Even more troublesome as a practical matter are the old files, drawers, and cabinets full of old checks, bank statements, documents and papers, mementos and objets d'art (or lack thereof) that you can never bring yourself to sift through and the importance of which, or lack thereof, is probably lost even to you. How much more difficult and time-consuming will it be for your loved ones?

What are other considerations to help you decide: will or revocable trust? Don't worry about the estate or generation-skipping taxes; they are just as much or just as little whether you use a trust or a will. And your executor/trustee has the same problems of being subject to liability with respect thereto whichever way you go. Actually, under IRC Section 6903 and regulations thereunder, a fiduciary (executor or trustee) must give notice (Form 56) of his fiduciary relationship and tax notices desired. Otherwise, a notice of deficiency with respect to the tax involved sent to the last known address of the taxpayer is sufficient.[2]

Surely, there is less light shown on your assets and your mode of disposition if you use the revocable trust, and you need to consider how important that is to you. To me, people are not as curious about others' assets as one would think; they are too busy looking after their own fortunes. The more fortunate parties seem to have the amounts of their assets known pretty well anyway, through various SEC, banking, and state and federal public official laws and regulations, as well as credit reports. As one person of substance recently said to me: There are very few people today whose fortunes are not pretty generally known. Secrecy does not seem to be very secret, but it is certainly something you should consider.

There is not going to be too much secrecy if your trust does not "fairly" treat one heir as contrasted with another. This is particularly true if you have no spouse or descendants and you tend to go to one side of the family and leave the other out. The next of kin simply want to know about what you have done and they will be apt to attack a disposition contrary to their innermost feelings.

Whether they attack or not, they surely want (and are entitled) to find out about it, and their lips are hardly sealed. A fortiori, spouses and descendants must be informed.

If, through a living trust, you only leave $1,000 to a friend, relative, or charity, and the bulk of your estate elsewhere, the whole document presumably has to be exposed to that beneficiary, although possibly the value of the entire estate need not be exposed. And, of course, substantial beneficiaries are entitled to full information with no requirement that they remain silent.

Remember, further, that to be really effective, you have to have two instruments. You have to have the pour-over will (pouring over all your assets that you have not transferred to the revocable trust into that trust on your death). So, you have got two instruments that you have to keep up with one way or another; and the one has to be probated.

Remember also that whether you use a trust or will, the assets are not going to automatically transfer themselves to the intended recipients on your death. Someone has to transfer them, whether it be the executor under your will or the trustee under your revocable trust, and someone has to see that it is done correctly. And there is going to be time, trouble, and expense involved in such transfers, whichever way you go. Expenses of probate are not as great as they have been said to be. Those expenses, as I pointed out in another article, primarily relate to tax problems, to creditor problems, and to beneficiary problems, although the size of the estate is considered. It is really not improper to consider the size of the estate, inter alia, because, whether it be a trust or a will, the potential liability of the executor/trustee and lawyer handling (or mishandling) the estate is increased accordingly.

Nor, as a practical matter, are the transfers to beneficiaries after death going to be made any more quickly because they emanate from revocable trusts rather than wills. A responsible trustee realizes that he or she must make sure that not only are all creditors paid but that all estate, gift, and income taxes are provided for. Actually, an executor who wants to risk liability can probably transfer many assets immediately. All the bank or transfer agent involved generally requires is a certified copy of letters testamentary, particularly where no estate taxes are involved. If they are

2. Further, under § 646 of the Taxpayer Relief Act of 1997, on the election of an executor and the trustee of a qualified revocable trust, the trust may be treated and taxed as part of the estate for tax years ending after the taxpayer's death.

involved, similar transfer requirements will be imposed, be it trust or will.

Although nonresidents can, of course, qualify as your executor in most states, if they cannot, or the particularly trusted nonresident relative desires to handle matters personally from his or her own domicile, or pursuant to its laws, the revocable trust should be considered.

If you own real estate in other states, revocable trusts as to those properties can reduce the aggravation of ancillary probate in that respect. Such trusts of all or most of your property can also serve if you are in present or have apprehension of future ill health or disability, although, generally, durable powers of attorney will suffice.

Of course, you do not want to forget the other simple procedures that "avoid" probate. If you have life insurance, it goes outside both the trust and the will (if you so provide). If you have joint bank accounts or jointly owned properties, they also go outside of both.

Actually, the gift and estate taxation of joint properties is so relatively complex that I always hesitate to recommend such holdings except for a home or a bank account sufficient to provide for needs of the survivor until distributions from the estate or trust can reasonably be expected. But there are additional and greater nontax reasons, especially when the other tenant is not the spouse: Is the joint tenant the owner on death or is he or she simply holding for convenience? The amount of litigation arising in this area is incredible.

Life insurance and joint ownership are primarily beyond the scope of this article, but I mention them because they also avoid probate. However, I do want to mention one potential use of revocable trusts, not as a will or probate substitute, but as an additional protection against malpractice exposure—a particularly sensitive area of exposure for the retiring lawyer. I refer to the "revocable-irrevocable" trust, noted in the 1992 report of the chair of the ABA Senior Lawyers Division Committee on Wills, Probate and Trusts, which in turn relies on an article in 42 *Arkansas Law Review* 713 (1989).

The central theme is simple. A transfer by a financially independent senior citizen—lawyer, doctor, or otherwise—to a trust for his or her spouse for life, remainder to children, of a substantial part of his or her estate (one-fourth, one-third, and so on, revocable only with the consent of a third party, the more independent the better) is or should be free from attacks by future creditors, including malpractice creditors. The Internal Revenue Service seems to regard this technique as valid (*if* the party whose consent is required has no adverse pecuniary interest); and only if one gets too greedy will such conveyances be subject to attack (any more than if made outright) as one in fraud of creditors.

As indicated in the article, it is *not* an estate tax avoidance program inasmuch as the property remains in the grantor's estate, but so do all revocable trusts. Whether will or revocable trusts are used, they ordinarily are structured (except for the exemption equivalent) to qualify for the marital deduction. Why not make an additional lifetime trust for the benefit of the spouse thus revocably "irrevocable"? It is going there anyway, so the testamentary plan is not altered; but substantial additional protection against malpractice or, indeed, any tort liability may well be afforded.

Finally, we suggest that a "revocable-irrevocable" trust with grantor as beneficiary and a third-party trustee and "consentor" can be most effective for preserving assets for senior citizens, to guard against their own imprudence. For the same reason, such a trust might be considered as superior by some to the purer form, as a protection against disability.

Now, after the above diversion, back to the primary underlying topic—the revocable trust as a will substitute. If you have estate tax problems, and it is not within your area of expertise, by all means, consult someone with knowledge in that field, whether you use revocable trust or will. This is true even though it should be repeated over and over again—there is no different estate tax treatment of either.

Finally—and I am speaking to the retiring lawyer—for a practical resolution to assist you in determining whether to use a will or revocable trust, look about you. What is good for others may not be good for you, and vice versa. You are in a better position than John Q. Public to make informal inquiry. What are your partners, associates, and friends at the bar doing? For the most part, I believe you will find they simply do not want to take the trouble with the latter. They know there is no tax saving, and they are not really afraid of probate. They will all probably urge you to leave behind some sort of instructions and a rough inventory, and you should follow their recommendation (even though they might not be doing so themselves).

If because of a second marriage or other situations there is the slightest hint or suggestion of family disharmony (or you are fearful of same whether for any reason), by all means go the route of the will. That is where disputes are best resolved.

In summary, we think a discussion with your friends at the bar, including a conference with a lawyer with a reasonable degree of expertise in these fields, can help you decide which way you want to go. A revocable trust is certainly an appropriate instrument if you decide to go that route. Just do not do so for the wrong reasons or, as one friend has suggested, because it is the "stylish" thing to do.

54

Disclaimer Will: Is It Right for You?

HERBERT L. ZUCKERMAN AND JAY A. SOLED

The Internal Revenue Code allows every taxpayer to transfer up to $600,000 exempt from gift and estate tax through what is known as the unified credit. A taxpayer can use part or all of the unified credit during a lifetime in the form of taxable gifts (those over the $10,000 per donee annual exclusion) and use the balance, if any, at death. A fundamental premise in estate planning is that, whenever possible, each taxpayer's unified credit should be used totally, with none of it wasted.

Often, however, waste is the case. Take, for example, a married man, worth $600,000, who dies with an "I love you" will in place. The widow receives the bequest outright and, because of the unlimited marital deduction, no estate tax will be due when the husband dies.

Assume further that the widow is also worth $600,000 in her own right and, until her death, continues to live off the interest generated from her assets and her late husband's bequest. The last estate, valued at $1.2 million, would be subject to an estate tax of $235,000.

Taking a "Bypass"

But let's imagine a different approach. Let us assume that this same couple, in order to mitigate the estate tax when the surviving spouse dies, chooses to execute a will that automatically creates a so-called "bypass" trust when the first spouse dies. This trust would be funded with an amount equal to the exemption equivalent ($600,000) less any taxable gifts (in excess of the $10,000 per donee annual exclusion) made by the first spouse during life.

Herbert L. Zuckerman is a partner at the law firm of Sills Cummis Zuckerman Radin Tischman Epstein & Gross, P.A., in Newark, New Jersey. Jay A. Soled is a lawyer and an assistant professor at Rutgers University in Newark, New Jersey.

The terms of this trust may vest the surviving spouse with an income interest and other benefits, but the terms must not create any "incidents of ownership" to cause the underlying corpus of the trust to be included in the surviving spouse's gross estate. Under this scenario, when the surviving spouse dies, only the $600,000 owned outright would be includable in his or her gross estate, but the tax due on it would be offset by the unified credit (assuming no taxable gifts during lifetime). Result: No taxes would be due the federal government.

The danger of an automatic bypass trust plan, however, cannot be overstated: Should the couple's assets diminish in value between the time the will is executed and the first spouse dies, the surviving spouse faces the risk of possible impoverishment. In the example cited above, suppose the surviving spouse's assets become worthless. Although the assets of the decedent spouse may pass automatically into a bypass trust for the benefit of the surviving spouse, depending on the trust terms and trustee(s), the surviving spouse might have a difficult time maintaining an existing lifestyle.

Disclaimer to the Rescue

Is there anything this couple could have done to lessen the impact of the estate tax while simultaneously safeguarding against the surviving spouse's possible impoverishment? If this couple had used what is known as a disclaimer will, they could have had the best of both worlds: The entire federal estate tax of $235,000, or a portion of it, could have been avoided, and the surviving spouse could have ensured his or her own well-being.

An example illustrates the dynamics of a disclaimer will. Again, suppose that the husband's will had left everything to his wife, but that the will further provided that if she disclaimed any or all of this bequest, the disclaimed assets would be placed in trust for her benefit until her death, when the assets of the trust would pass to the couple's children. Suppose further that the wife disclaims her entire bequest of $600,000 passing to her under her husband's will. The assets disclaimed would be held in a disclaimer trust (essentially, a bypass trust) for the benefit of the wife during her lifetime.

When the wife dies, the trust's assets would not be includable in her gross estate because she would not have had incidents of control over that property. Her own $600,000 of assets would be subject to estate tax, but when her unified credit is applied, no estate tax would be due.

Underlying the success of this estate planning technique is the fact that the husband's estate does not use the marital deduction, which defers, but does not eliminate, estate tax. Instead, the husband's estate makes maximum use of his unified credit, which actually eliminates estate tax. Net result in dollar savings to this couple and family: $235,000.

The salient feature of this planning technique is that the surviving spouse, at the time of her spouse's death, is in the best position to evaluate her financial condition to determine whether or not she should exercise the disclaimer option.

Getting It Right

What does a widow or widower need to do to ensure that the disclaimer is handled correctly when a spouse dies?

- The disclaimer must be an irrevocable and unqualified refusal to accept an interest in property;
- The refusal must be in writing;
- Such writing must be received by the transferor of the interest, the legal representative of the first dying spouse, or by the holder of the legal title to the property to which the interest relates. This receipt must occur sooner than nine months after the later of (1) the date on which the transfer creating the interest in such person is made, or (2) the day on which such person attains age 21;
- Such person has not accepted the interest or any of its benefits; and
- As result of such refusal, the interest in the property passes without any direction on the part of the person making the disclaimer and passes either (1) to the spouse of the decedent, or (2) to a person other than the person making the disclaimer.

One important point to make is that the treasury department regulations sanction this sort of planning by permitting a surviving spouse to disclaim part or all of a bequest and still receive indirect benefits (for example, an income interest) from the assets held in the disclaimer trust. Finally, we need to note that for a couple to take maximum advantage of this technique, each spouse should have about one-half of the family's combined assets. A tax-free interspousal transfer can achieve this goal.

55
Techniques for Estates Under $625,000

HERBERT L. ZUCKERMAN AND JAY A. SOLED

Estate planners understandably devote the bulk of their time to techniques for the big estate, where the big money is, to the virtual exclusion of the medium and small estate. We admit we have been similarly preoccupied, but we are ready to make amends.

A taxpayer need not indulge in sophisticated estate planning—at least from a tax perspective—unless the estate exceeds $625,000 (minus any lifetime taxable gifts). The reason is simple: The Internal Revenue Code provides a credit to shield the first $625,000[1] of a taxpayer's assets from the gift and estate transfer tax. Therefore, for example, if a person dies owning a bank CD worth $195,000, a house worth $400,000, and no other major assets, then no federal transfer tax would be due on the estate of $595,000, nor would a federal estate tax return have to be filed.

In the discussion that follows, we suggest certain proposals for the small to medium-sized estate. These proposals also hold true for married couples whose combined assets do not exceed $625,000 in value.

The Worth of a Will

The person for whom the will is written, the testator, needs a simple instrument that specifies, among other things, how the assets of the estate will be disposed; what people are to serve as fiduciaries (guardians, executors, and trustees); and who will be successors to these fiduciaries in case they cannot serve. Finally, the will should specify

Herbert L. Zuckerman is a partner at the law firm of Sills Cummis Zuckerman Radin Tischman Epstein & Gross, P.A., in Newark, New Jersey. Jay A. Soled is a lawyer and an assistant professor at Rutgers University in Newark, New Jersey. This article originally appeared in the Summer 1993 issue of Experience, which is published by the ABA.

the source for paying any tax. For instance, the source could be the residuary of the estate. The testator needs to keep in mind that although the estate may not owe any federal transfer tax, it may owe state inheritance or similar tax.

Just as a will should specify certain things, it should also avoid others. First of all, where practicable, the will should not contain precatory language, which is language expressing a wish. One illustration is the following sentence: "I would like my grandson to have my car, if possible." Such wishful wording confronts the executor with uncomfortable choices and may lead to litigation down the road. The will also should not attempt to give burial instructions since wills, in most states, are probated after a person has been buried. A much better idea is to give one's next of kin written nontestamentary burial instructions; in this way, the decedent's wishes can be carried out in a timely way.

To draft an effective will, the lawyer should examine how title to the testator's assets is held. To the extent that any or all of the property is held in joint names with right of survivorship, the disposition of the property will be controlled by the laws where the property is located. Generally, this means the will has no effect on how the property

1. Note that the Taxpayer Relief Act of 1997 gradually increases the unified credit over a nine-year period, which will eventually insulate estates in excess of $625,000 from the federal estate tax. The following table indicates how this phase-in will be instituted:

Year	Unified Credit Exemption Equivalent
1998	$ 625,000
1999	$ 650,000
2000	$ 675,000
2001	$ 675,000
2002	$ 700,000
2003	$ 700,000
2004	$ 850,000
2005	$ 950,000
2006	$1,000,000

is ultimately handled. In many cases, it is preferable to avoid joint ownership. If the estate is small, it may be especially convenient to have the marital residence kept in joint names (or in a tenancy by the entirety, the married person's equivalent of a joint tenancy).

Other Instruments

Durable Power of Attorney

Because there is a distinct possibility that many of us will become either mentally or physically disabled at some point in our lives, it is routine in the estate planning world to suggest a durable power of attorney. This instrument authorizes another person to act as one's agent or lawyer, allowing that person to engage in a whole range of transactions, including banking, gift giving, engaging in sales and leases, and so on. The durable power allows the authorized agent or lawyer to continue to act despite the principal's mental or physical disability, whereas a regular power of attorney is void upon just such an occurrence, obviously limiting its usefulness. A durable power of attorney can become effective when it is executed or, as is commonly recommended, it can spring into effectiveness when a disability occurs. This is commonly referred to as a "springing power."

Living Will/Health-Care Power of Appointment

Given the inevitability of death, a client may wish to execute a living will. This is an instrument that instructs the health-care provider not to resuscitate the client if a life-threatening disability or coma-inducing event occurs, and if there is no reasonable chance for recovery. The quality of life and its deterioration are equal concerns of the wealthiest and the poorest.

Functioning much like the power of attorney is an instrument known as a health-care power of appointment. But there is a crucial difference: The health-care power of appointment grants a particular person—known as a health-care surrogate—authorization to make health-care decisions (for example, the execution of an informed consent) if the principal becomes incapacitated. However, some clients are reluctant or squeamish to delegate such power to anyone.

In setting up a durable power of attorney, living will, or health-care power of appointment, a lawyer needs to consult state statutes for the legal requirements needed for drafting effective and enforceable instruments. This is necessary because the statutes vary among the states.

Revocable, or "Living," Trust

Though most knowledgeable estate planners have many reservations about such trusts, they are helpful in certain estates, large or small. For example, if a client owns real estate in a number of states, we might recommend establishing a revocable trust and funding it with these various properties. In this way, the executor can avoid the expense and delay of obtaining ancillary administration in other jurisdictions. Another reason to create a revocable trust is if the client wants or needs special management of assets, either because the client is mentally or physically unable or lacks the expertise. But hiring a property manager, rather than setting up a revocable trust, may be a simpler and less costly way to accomplish this.

Odds and Ends

In fashioning a sensible plan for a small or medium-sized estate, it is important to consider compiling a master list of assets. Such a list helps the executor administer the estate. What could happen, for example, if municipal bearer bonds are lodged in a home safe and no one but the deceased homeowner knew they were there? It is easy to see that someone buying the house could get more than was bargained for.

Another item to consider is whether the client should engage in an annual gift-giving program, particularly if the client is close to the taxable estate threshold of $625,000. If he or she happens to earn more money, or if other assets grow in value without the earnings or growth being spent, the result will soon be a taxable estate. To prevent this, interest gifts can be made annually to whomever the client wishes. As long as the value of these gifts does not exceed $10,000 per donee, the client will not incur any gift tax, exhaust any part of the unified credit, or be required to file a gift-tax return. Assuming the client has three children, a gift to each of $10,000 could be made annually, thereby depleting the estate of $30,000 without incurring tax.

In this day and age, however, even a client with, say, a $700,000 estate needs to be careful about such a substantial gifting program. Further, the client needs to consider the maturity and ability of the children to handle these gifts.

Finally, a client should also consider disposing of tangible personal property by a handwritten letter rather than by a will, if state law permits. The use of such a letter permits the client to change his or her mind as often as desired prior to death without going through the time and expense of having a codicil or new will drawn up.

Not Just for Well-to-Do

This article has merely outlined some of the major considerations that a person planning a small or medium-sized estate needs to keep in mind. There is much that a person of modest means needs to know about property conservation and disposition. These concerns do not solely belong to the wealthy.

56
How to Structure an Of Counsel Agreement for Tax Advantage

HAROLD G. WREN

If you think it is time to move into an of counsel relationship with your firm, how you structure the agreement can directly affect what you owe Uncle Sam. Most of counsel agreements are negotiated on the retirement of a senior lawyer who desires to take a less active role in the practice. The parties to the agreement are usually the law firm and the retired or retiring partner. In this setting, most lawyers and law firms find that the independent contractor, rather than the employer-employee, relationship is more tax advantageous to both sides.

Using of counsel for a retiring partner is only one of several situations where such an agreement is useful. Large firms also use of counsel for probationary partners-to-be or for intermediate employees, known variously as "counsel," "senior attorney," and the like. In these other situations, from the firm's perspective at least, the employer-employee relationship may be preferable, and realistically the lawyer may have little, if anything, to say about what the contractual arrangement should be.

But when a partner is retiring, the independent contractor relationship will usually be the better choice. The former partner will want to retain the independence that the relationship connotes and gain some substantial tax advantages as well.

The principal advantage for the retiree will be to take the business deductions "above the line" (meaning before the adjusted gross income is determined), on Schedule C of Form 1040. He or she then will have the option of itemizing or taking the standard deduction. The person will not be limited by the 2 percent floor on miscellaneous business deductions applicable to employees, since these amounts will be shown as part of the cost of doing business on Schedule C. For 1998, the independent contractor will pay Social Security taxes of 15.3 percent on the first $68,400 of income, and receive a business expense deduction of 50 percent of the amount of Social Security taxes paid, so that his or her final tax position is precisely the same as that of the wage earner.

The law firm also gains substantial tax advantages from the independent contractor relationship in that it is not required to withhold income taxes for amounts that it pays the lawyer according to the of counsel agreement. Instead, it files an information return, using Form 1099. The firm need not be concerned about withholding Social Security taxes, since the lawyer will compute these taxes on Form SE.

The Internal Revenue Service has recently moved vigorously to enforce the tax rules regarding the employer-employee, as distinct from the independent contractor, relationship. The agency has required that lawyers practicing as of counsel who characterize themselves as independent contractors must answer elaborate questionnaires. These are designed to elicit factual data about the extent to which one party has "control" over the other. If the common-law element of control is present, the relationship is that of employer-employee; if not, then the parties are independent contractors.

Harold G. Wren is of counsel to the law firm of Voyles & Johnson, P.S.C., in Louisville, Kentucky. This article originally appeared in the Spring 1993 issue of *Experience*, which is published by the ABA.

To the extent that the questions proffered earlier in Chapter 7, pages 44–45, are answered in the affirmative, the relationship of the firm with the lawyer will be that of *employer-employee*, rather than independent contractor:

No single affirmative answer—or even several affirmative answers—necessarily determines whether the firm is in fact in "control" of the lawyer.

The questions, though, provide a guide for one drafting an of counsel agreement to ensure that a particular contract between a lawyer and a law firm will be construed as establishing an independent contractor, rather than an employer-employee, relationship.

The drafter of the agreement should make certain that more than half the above questions will be answered in the negative. This should not be too difficult, since only a few of the questions (for example, the sixth question, dealing with the continuing relationship of the parties), *must* be answered in the affirmative to maintain the of counsel relationship.

57

Basic Estate Planning and Irrevocable Life Insurance Trusts

STEPHEN A. FROST

Each taxpayer may transfer a certain amount of property during his or her lifetime or at death free of gift and estate taxes. Historically, the amount was $600,000. After 1997, the amount of property that can be transferred free of gift and estate taxes is called the "applicable exclusion amount." The "applicable exclusion amount" is $625,000 in 1998, but increases in subsequent years. By the year 2006, the applicable exclusion amount is $1.0 million. The applicable exclusion amount for each tax year after 1997 is as follows:

Year	Applicable Exclusion Amount
1998	$ 625,000
1999	$ 650,000
2000	$ 675,000
2001	$ 675,000
2002	$ 700,000
2003	$ 700,000
2004	$ 850,000
2005	$ 950,000
2006	$1,000,000

Full use of each taxpayer's "applicable exclusion amount" is critical to basic estate tax planning. The following four rules capture the essentials of estate tax planning:

Rule 1: Calculate the size of the estate in round numbers. You can do this part in your head or on the back of an envelope. An individual's taxable estate generally equals the fair-market value of his or her property less any debts—that is, fair-market value of the house less the related mortgage. See Internal Revenue Code Section 2000 et seq. Each spouse considers his or her half of any joint property. Life insurance is considered at its face

value. If the client is married, add the spouse's estate to arrive at the combined family estate.

Rule 2: If the combined family estate (husband and wife) is less than the applicable exclusion amount, no sweat. Combined family estates of less than the applicable exclusion amount escape estate taxes altogether. The applicable exclusion amount applies to each taxpayer, so it doesn't even matter which spouse owns the property. Most of your clients fall into this category.

Rule 3: If the combined family estate (husband and wife) is between one and two times the applicable exclusion amount, married taxpayers can pass everything to the next generation tax-free with proper planning and the correct documents. Single taxpayers with estates greater than the applicable exclusion amount should skip to rule 4 because his or her estate is taxable.

Because each taxpayer is granted an applicable exclusion amount, most married couples can transfer up to two times the applicable exclusion amount to the next generation without triggering estate taxes. First, the family's assets must be titled so that each spouse has at least the applicable exclusion amount in his or her estate, minus marital deduction property. If each spouse's individual estate is less than the applicable exclusion amount, retitle the family assets. Having less than applicable exclusion amount in each estate may cause your client to needlessly waste some of the applicable exclusion amount available to each spouse. Second, each spouse's will or operative trust document must provide for an A/B trust arrangement, which is explained as follows:

An A/B trust arrangement consists of two trusts created upon the taxpayer's death. The A trust is eligible for the marital deduction and is deducted from the first spouse's taxable estate under IRC Section 2056. However, this trust is included in the taxable estate

Stephen A. Frost is a lawyer and a certified public accountant associated with Laser, Pokorny, Schwartz, Friedman & Economos in Chicago, where he concentrates in estate planning, tax, and probate matters.

of the second spouse to die under IRC Section 2044. The A trust is funded with the property that cannot be protected from tax by the first spouse's applicable exclusion amount. If the first spouse's applicable exclusion amount can shield all of the taxpayer's assets from tax, no property will be transferred to the A trust.

The B trust is funded with property that can be shielded by the first spouse's applicable exclusion amount. The B trust usually provides income to the surviving spouse, but will not be included in the surviving spouse's taxable estate upon his or her death.

If your married client does not have an A/B trust arrangement, both spouses should get one immediately. If either spouse lacks an A/B trust, estate taxes may be needlessly triggered. If your client is single, rule 3 does not apply, and any estate over the applicable exclusion amount poses a rule 4 problem.

Rule 4: If the combined family estate (husband and wife) is more than two times the applicable exclusion amount, estate taxes will be due when the second spouse dies. Consider reducing the taxable estate by creating an irrevocable life insurance trust.

Farm and business owners may be in this category, of course, but rule 4 may also apply in less obvious cases. For example, a middle manager with a house, a 401(k) plan, some profit-sharing benefits, and a $1 million life insurance policy may be in a position to owe estate taxes without even recognizing it. Maybe you are, too. Without additional planning, estate taxes will be due when the second spouse dies.

When the combined family assets exceed two times the applicable exclusion amount and both spouses have A/B trust arrangements in their wills, the only way to reduce or avoid estate taxes is to reduce the size of the taxable estate. The techniques to do this are varied and often exceedingly complicated, and you may want to retain an experienced estate planning lawyer as cocounsel.

Reducing Combined Taxable Estates

The primary way to avoid estate taxes for combined family estates over two times the applicable exclusion amount (or the applicable exclusion amount for singles) is to reduce the taxable estate before death. How? By giving away assets or giving up sufficient control over them that they are no longer considered your client's property. Your client will probably chafe at this idea. He or she has worked hard to accumulate wealth and knows that old age is on the horizon. However, a client who sees how much the government is willing to take in estate taxes is usually open to suggestion.

Calculating potential estate tax savings requires two steps. First, calculate the combined family estate taxes (husband and wife) assuming the status quo. Next, calculate the estate taxes assuming that the assets in excess of two times the applicable exclusion amount are excluded from the combined family estate. (Each spouse's estate taxes are computed separately, then added together to arrive at a combined total.) Compare the difference. This is what your client stands to gain by using more sophisticated estate tax planning techniques. It usually is an impressive number. Assuming $500,000 can be removed from a combined family estate of $1.7 million in 1998, your client could save $174,500 in estate taxes. That's an additional $174,500 of accumulated wealth that can be passed on to the next generation.

Determine how much to remove from the taxable estate in dollars, then identify specific assets. Remember, the goal is to reduce total family assets to around two times the applicable exclusion amount or, for a single person, to around the applicable exclusion amount. The difference between the family's accumulated wealth and the target amount equals the needed reduction in the taxable estate.

Once you determine how much needs to be removed, you must decide which assets should be removed from your client's taxable estate. The assets must total about the right value either individually or in aggregate. Look for assets that will not be particularly missed by the taxpayer, or whose transfer will not substantially interfere with his or her control of the business. Also, strongly prefer assets that have a high value at death compared to their current value. Life insurance polices are an obvious choice because they meet these criteria.

Outright giving is seldom preferable to gifts in trust. After deciding what and how much to get out of your client's taxable estate, you must consider who to give it to and in what form. Children and surviving spouses are the most common choices, but any provisions for a surviving spouse should be limited to keep assets out of his or her estate. Grandchildren are possibilities, but generation-skipping tax implications should be considered first. See IRC Section 2601 et seq. Parents are seldom a good choice, because they're likely to die sooner—and be taxed earlier—than your client. Life estates for spouses and parents should be considered. Perhaps a particular charity is important to your client.

Deciding how to make a gift is far more difficult than identifying the recipient. The problems with giving directly to children are obvious: (1) they may be minors and require some type of legal supervision; (2) they may not be mature enough to manage large sums of money; (3) they may be spendthrifts; or (4) they may have creditors that your client does not wish to pay.

Also, income from direct gifts cannot be routed to the surviving spouse, because it will accrue to the property's new owner. Finally, outright gifts mean no strings attached. Since your client is shedding assets primarily to save estate taxes, the idea of passing property to an immature donee with no strings attached is usually objectionable. Using a trust is a simple solution to this problem.

Giving to a trust avoids the problems of outright gifts. Trusts can hold property for the beneficiaries' benefit without giving them control of the property. Your client gets to pick a trustee to manage the property. Restrictions on disbursements can be built into the trust to protect against spendthrifts and creditors. Trust agreements can provide that the trust will be liquidated and disbursed to beneficiaries after they attain specified ages. The surviving spouse can retain rights to income and principal. It is the perfect vehicle.

Putting It All Together: Irrevocable Life Insurance Trusts

Your client probably has insurance policies that could be transferred out of your client's estate without affecting him or her much. Beneficiaries are clearly identified and your client has ideas about who could manage the property effectively until they reach the appropriate age. It's up to you to package this information and draft a trust agreement to accomplish your client's goals. A good technique is the irrevocable life insurance trust. Here's how it works.

Basic trust elements must be met. A trust needs a res, a trustee, and a beneficiary. The insurance policies will be the res. The trustee can be any competent adult or an institution (for example, a bank or trust company), but it should not be your client. Beneficiaries can be identified specifically ("Sue" or "Tom") or as a class ("my children").

You will need to draft a trust agreement that clearly outlines your client's wishes. Be sure that it reflects a distribution pattern consistent with your client's overall estate plan. Then fund the trust with the life policies desired by transferring title into the trustee's name.

The trust must be irrevocable. The biggest drawback to an irrevocable trust is that it is irrevocable. Your client will not be able to revoke, amend, or alter the agreement once it is exercised and the trust is funded. Given that financial circumstances can change dramatically overnight, marriages do not always endure, and tax laws are never constant, transferring property irrevocably should not be done lightly.

Yet the trust must be irrevocable for the trust assets to be effectively removed from your client's taxable estate. Nor can your client retain any "incident of ownership" in the life insurance policies transferred to the irrevocable trust. But all is not lost. Some protections can be built into the trust agreement, and your client can retain a critical role in the very life of the trust.

Premium funding is the ultimate solution to your client's need for control. Because insurance policies require premiums, your client's policies will stay in force only if the premiums are paid. Unless your client has contributed income-producing assets to the trust, the trust cannot internally generate income to pay the premiums. Your client can essentially choke the life out of an irrevocable life insurance trust by not contributing additional cash. Without cash, the trustee cannot fund the premiums.

Your client should not retain control over the trust or the trustee. Your client should not retain any control over the trust or the trustee that may cause the IRS to challenge the arrangement and include trust assets in your client's taxable estate. (Litigating a great planning idea dissipates the trust estate even when your client wins.) Nor does your client want to retain any "incidents of ownership" over the life insurance policies.

The most conservative approach is to select an independent trustee who is prudent, trustworthy, and unrelated to your client. Your client should never act as trustee or cotrustee. Nor should your client's spouse be named trustee or cotrustee if the spouse can exercise any powers or incidents of ownership for the spouse's own benefit. For taxpayers who cannot afford a costly battle with the IRS, select a nonspousal trustee that cannot exercise any powers or incidents of ownership for his or her personal benefit.

Your client may retain the right to remove a trustee for cause under some very limited circumstances, but your client should *never* retain a discretionary right to replace the trustee.

Gift taxes need to be considered before the trust is initially funded. Transferring life insurance policies to a trust is considered a gift. Gift tax issues related to life insurance trusts are particularly messy, so be prepared for long discussions with your client. The bottom line is that you should never make gifts to the trust of more than $5,000 per beneficiary per year unless you know exactly what you are doing. Also, never forget that a renegade beneficiary can disrupt your client's well-laid plans by actually withdrawing a contribution to the trust.

Gift taxes: general. Gifts of future interests—including life insurance policies in trust—are not eligible for the annual $10,000 gift tax exclusion. However, life insurance trusts can be converted to gifts of present interests by giving beneficiaries the current right to withdraw contributions made to the trust. These withdrawal rights are often called "Crummey powers" after the landmark case establishing them. Withdrawal rights are the best way to be sure your client's contributions to the trust (policies or premiums) are eligible for the annual gift tax exclusion.

Gift taxes: withdrawal rights. Unfortunately, withdrawal rights are considered general powers of appointment. The lapse of a general power of appointment in excess of certain limits triggers gift taxes. If the annual lapse amount is too large, gift taxes will be triggered.

Gift taxes: lapses. Lapses of general powers of appointment are excludable from gift tax up to the greater of $5,000 or 5 percent of the value of assets from which the exercise of the lapsed power could be satisfied. Each trust beneficiary is entitled to the $5,000 or 5 percent exclusion. To avoid gift taxes, therefore, contributions and the related withdrawal rights should be limited to $5,000 per donee each year.

Because the specter of gift taxes haunts all contributions, selecting and valuing which life policies are to be transferred to the trust is very important. Remember that the $5,000 lapse exclusion applies to each donee each year. Each beneficiary of the trust is considered a donee. If the value of a particular policy is over the annual lapse exclusion limit, your client can use some of his or her applicable exclusion amount to shield taxable gifts. But the better approach is to save the applicable exclusion amount and transfer only those policies that do not trigger gift taxes.

Since the $5,000 lapse exclusion is an annual one, several life policies can be contributed to the trust over several years without triggering estate taxes. However, do not unknowingly contribute so many polices that future premiums and the related cash contributions will exceed the $5,000 per donee exclusion in the outlying years.

Valuing life policies. Life insurance for estate tax purposes is taxed at its face value. For gift tax purposes, however, the value of a life insurance policy essentially equals its replacement cost. In other words, the value of the policy is the amount the insurer would charge for a similar policy on that particular date. This creates a terrific planning opportunity because your client can give something with a low current value and a high estate tax value.

Determining replacement cost depends on the type of the policy. A term policy is generally valued at zero, unless there is any unamortized premium remaining. The value of a whole life policy is generally its cash surrender value plus any unamortized premium. It is usually wise to get a value quotation from the insurer by requesting an IRS Form 712.

If a whole life policy's surrender value exceeds the applicable annual exclusion limit, consider advising your client to borrow against the policy to reduce its cash value before making the gift. However, be aware that the transfer for value rule may apply and income tax can be triggered under some circumstances when the loan amount is too much.

Future contributions of cash for premiums must also be subject to withdrawal rights and meet annual lapse restrictions. Future premiums must be planned for carefully. Your client should plan on contributing cash to the trust as premiums come due in the future. The trustee will pay future premiums with the cash.

385

As noted above, the ongoing need for cash is your client's greatest protection related to the irrevocable life insurance trust, but it is also the greatest weakness. Because each beneficiary is given the right to withdraw assets from the trust—including cash—your client's estate plan may be temporarily placed at the mercy of the beneficiaries. A renegade beneficiary could withdraw the needed cash and disrupt your client's estate plan.

Second, gift taxes must always be considered before making any contributions to the trust. Because your client will be contributing cash to the trust annually, you must consider the gift tax exclusion every year. Because withdrawal rights are always an issue, the annual $5,000 lapse exclusion must also be considered. In years when premiums (plus any policies contributed in the same year) exceed the $5,000 annual lapse exclusion per donee, your client will generally trigger gift taxes. Fortunately, the annual lapse exclusion limit is not usually a problem if the trust has multiple beneficiaries. Obviously, premiums for elderly clients can become large and may require using some of your client's applicable exclusion amount.

Crummey *notices should be delivered at least annually.* The IRS has held that it will not recognize withdrawal rights unless they are communicated to the beneficiaries. The trustee should give notices to each trust beneficiary each time a gift to the trust is received. At a minimum, the trustee should give a written notice to each beneficiary at least annually and get a written acknowledgment from each. The IRS also says that the withdrawal period must be reasonable.

The trustee operates as a separate legal entity. An irrevocable life insurance trust operates as a separate legal entity for tax purposes. It will have its own tax identification number and file its own tax returns, if necessary.

The trustee should be given the authority, but not the obligation, to loan life insurance proceeds to your estate. Your trustee may also be given the authority, but not the obligation, to purchase assets from your client's estate. This will allow the irrevocable trust to provide your client's estate with additional liquidity should your client's taxable estate be composed of illiquid assets.

Three-year throwback period. Gifts of life insurance policies are returned to your client's taxable estate whenever your client dies within three years of the gift. Be absolutely sure that your client is made aware of this risk. The only way to avoid the risk is to have the trustee buy a brand new policy. Cash can be contributed and used to buy a new policy, thereby avoiding the three-year throwback rule under some circumstances.

58
Title Insurance for Estate Planning Transfers

JONATHAN RIVIN AND THOMAS J. STIKKER

Under many estate plans, an individual will make a pre-death transfer of real property to a revocable or irrevocable trust, limited or general partnership, limited liability company or corporation. Often, estate planning or corporate lawyers prepare and record the deeds that transfer title to the trust or other title holding entity, and they do not consider the title insurance implications of the transfer. Without some planning, any title insurance coverage benefiting the individual may be lost.

The typical title insurance policy is not assignable, does not continue coverage for the transferor after these transfers (except for deed warranties) and does not include a transferee in its definition of "insured." See generally Joyce Dickey Palomar, *Limited Liability Companies, Corporations, General Partnerships, Limited Partnerships, Joint Ventures, Trusts—Who Does the Title Insurance Cover?*, 31 Real Prop., Prob. & Tr. J. 605 (1997) (discussing who qualifies as an insured). In some circumstances, title insurance coverage may be preserved at a nominal cost or by paying a new title insurance premium. Other circumstances may justify proceeding without title insurance coverage for the new owner. This article considers this problem and proposes some solutions.

Estate Planning Transfers

An estate plan frequently involves the owner's conveyance of real estate during his or her lifetime. The most common transfer occurs when the owner establishes a revocable living trust. These popular estate planning devices can avoid probate proceedings following the transferor's death, provide a management vehicle for assets if the transferor is incapacitated before death, and assure family privacy and ease of administration. A transferor typically establishes the trust and transfers all of his or her assets to the trustee (often the transferor) before death.

Lifetime gifts of real estate interests also are common for estate planning purposes. These gifts may be made outright to children or other beneficiaries to take advantage of the $10,000 per person annual gift tax exclusion or the unified credit for estate and gift tax purposes ($625,000 in 1998 and rising to $1 million by 2006). A donor may even make taxable lifetime gifts instead of taxable transfers at death because the donor pays the federal gift tax, the donee receives the entire gift and the donor is not paying gift tax on the amount of the gift tax. In contrast, in a taxable transfer at death, the entire estate is subject to estate taxes, so that funds used to pay the estate tax on the transfer are themselves subject to the estate tax (requiring considerably more value in the estate to yield the same net benefit to the donee).

Often lifetime gifts of real estate interests are made to irrevocable trusts for the benefit of children or other beneficiaries. These trusts allow a designated trustee to control and manage the property until the beneficiaries have reached an appropriate age to receive the property outright or even to hold the property in trust for the lifetime of the beneficiaries to take advantage of generation-skipping tax planning opportunities.

Individuals frequently transfer real estate to family corporations, partnerships, and limited liability companies. These conveyances can permit the transferor to retain some control over the

Jonathan Rivin and Thomas J. Stikker are partners with Springs Rivin Detwiler Dudnick & Stikker L.L.P. in San Francisco, California. Mr. Rivin is chair of the Real Property Division's Decisions Committee.

entity while making gifts of interests to family members and other beneficiaries. Substantial valuation discounts for transfer-tax purposes are often available through this type of planning because the transfer is of an interest—typically a minority interest at that—in an entity, rather than a transfer of the property itself.

A transferor will usually make estate planning conveyances of real estate interests by limited warranty deed or quitclaim deed. The transferor and his or her advisors will frequently not analyze title insurance considerations in the context of these conveyances.

Who Is an "Insured"?

The most commonly used forms of owner's title insurance policy do not expressly cover the transferees in pre-death estate planning transfers. The American Land Title Association (ALTA) 1992, 1990, 1987, and 1970 forms of owner's policy all define "insured" as the party named as the insured in the policy and "those who succeed to the interest of the named insured by operation of law as distinguished from purchase including, but not limited to, heirs, distributees, devisees, survivors, personal representatives, next of kin, or corporate or fiduciary successors." The ALTA 1979 and 1987 forms of residential policy both provide continuation of coverage for "anyone who receives your title because of your death."

Clearly, transferees by operation of law and on death are intended to be covered by the standard owner's policy, but purchasers are not. The estate planning transfers addressed in this article are typically gifts, not sales, and are not considered transfers by operation of law. If a claim is made, the title insurer may assert that the transferee is not an insured and deny coverage.

This defense might be considered extreme when the transfer is from the named insured to a revocable trust of which the named insured is trustee. Under the express language of the policy, however, the trust or trustee is not an insured. If the loss is large, a title company may well deny coverage. In a more complex transfer, such as to a family limited partnership, limited liability company, or subchapter S corporation, through which family members acquire interests in the property or the transferee, a title company is likely to deny coverage on the same basis.

Newer forms of title insurance policies may be available in some states for an additional premium to address pre-death transfers to trusts. For example, in California, First American Title Insurance Company's "Eagle Protection" owner's policy expands the continuation of coverage provisions of the typical residential policy. That policy form includes protection for the "trustee or successor trustee of a trust in which you are the trustor/settlor to whom you transfer your title after the Policy Date." If that form of policy was issued and the named insured transfers the property to the trustee of a trust of which the insured is the trustor, then coverage continues and the discussion that follows is moot. In general, however, title to property transferred pursuant to pre-death estate planning transfers is probably not insured by the transferor's title policy.

Techniques to Continue Coverage

If this gap in title insurance coverage is recognized at the time of the transfer or shortly thereafter, there are several possible solutions that may be achieved with the title insurer.

Additional Insured Endorsement

The most common technique to close the gap is for the title company to issue an "Additional Insured" endorsement to the existing title insurance policy. An Additional Insured endorsement will specifically amend the policy to add the trust or other new titleholder as a named insured.

The cost of an Additional Insured endorsement may be minimal—$100 or less. Many title companies will issue the endorsement on request for donees (including trustees of inter vivos trusts) who are acquiring title from the insured owner. Especially for transfers to entities other than trusts, the title company will require full disclosure of all particulars of the transaction, including the status and relationship of all parties. For its underwriting, the title company will want to determine whether the transfer is truly donative in nature and whether the transaction will otherwise expand the insurer's risk.

The coverage of an Additional Insured endorsement is no greater than that afforded by the original policy. Thus, the additional insured has no coverage for title defects arising after the original issuance date of the policy and the liability limit of the policy will not reflect any increase in property value from the original issuance date of the policy. Additionally, the endorsement provides no protection for the additional insured if the deed to the donee is itself defective for some reason. This last concern may result in malpractice exposure to the estate planner for errors in the deed. For example, in some states the property should be deeded to the trustee rather than to the trust itself. Many title companies consider transfers to a trust rather than the trustee as voidable, undermining title insurance coverage.

New Policy

The issue of continuing coverage and the problems attendant to an Additional Insured endorsement can be resolved by obtaining a new title insurance policy effective on recording the estate planning transfer, naming the transferee as insured, and increasing the coverage to the current value of the property. The obvious downside to this approach is cost. A full premium will be due that, depending on the jurisdiction, can be considerable. In some jurisdictions, a lower reissue rate may apply.

Warranty Deed

The ALTA owner's policy forms generally provide that coverage continues "so long as the insured shall have liability by reason of covenants of warranty made by the insured in any transfer or conveyance of the estate or interest." The named insured involved in an estate planning transaction may be able to preserve the coverage of the original title policy by warranting title to the transferee (subject to the matters excepted in the original title policy), thus activating the continuation of coverage provision. If a title defect is discovered, the transferee could make a claim back against the transferor, who would be able to tender the claim to the title insurer. An obvious advantage of this solution is that there is no title insurance premium payable on the transfer.

In some states this technique would not be effective in an estate planning context because recovery under a warranty deed is limited to the consideration paid. Because the transferee has paid no consideration, the warranty would be ineffective. Thus, the named insured would have no liability for the warranty, and the continuation of coverage provision would not apply.

Even in states where the warranty is enforceable, the effectiveness of this technique is limited by the scope of the initial policy. As with the Additional Insured endorsement, the coverage would be limited to the initial date of policy issuance, would not afford coverage for defects in the transfer in question, and would be subject to the dollar limits of the initial policy.

The derivative nature of the transferee's claim under the title policy creates several additional concerns. Perhaps most basic is that the transferee must make a claim back against the transferor for breach of warranty to trigger any title insurance coverage. Although intended ultimately to be a claim against the title company, this claim may appear to the transferor as a personal attack and may result in family squabbles. The transferor is faced with a suit by a seemingly ungrateful family member arising from an attempted gift. Also, the warranty ordinarily runs with the land and could be enforced against the original transferor by a successor property owner. These problems could be mitigated, perhaps, with a limitation on the transferor's warranty liability to the amount of recovery, if any, under the title insurance policy and a limitation of the warranty so that it only runs to the initial transferee.

Another defect in this approach is that the transferor's warranty covenant is personal to the transferor. Thus, if the transferor dies, claims must be made against his or her estate within the applicable statute of limitations. Nevertheless, title defects may not be discovered until after the limitations period has expired. In that case, there is no transferor liability on the warranty and, thus, no title insurance liability under the continuation of coverage provision.

Fairway Endorsement

If the estate planning transfer involves the substitution of the estate planning entity as a general partner into an existing partnership or a change of form from general to limited partnership, limited liability company, or corporation, then title insurance coverage that would otherwise be lost may be preserved by negotiating a so-called *Fairway* endorsement to the existing title policy. The *Fairway* endorsement assures that the new partner or newly constituted partnership (depending on the jurisdiction's legal theory of partnerships) is considered an insured. This endorsement was first requested by insureds and issued by title companies in response to *Fairway Development Co. v. Title Insurance Co. of Minnesota*, 621 F. Supp. 120 (N.D. Ohio 1985). In *Fairway*, the court held that the transfer of the interests of two partners in an insured partnership to the remaining partner and a new partner terminated the original partnership and its title insurance coverage.

Many title insurers have become accustomed to underwriting and issuing *Fairway* endorsements. Even if an estate planning transfer does not involve a partnership or does not fit the parameters of a *Fairway* endorsement, an insured may be successful in obtaining a similar endorsement by analogizing it to a *Fairway* endorsement.

Mountain or Molehill?

The risk of losing title insurance coverage when an individual transfers title to himself or herself as trustee is quite real. When that risk can be eliminated for the nominal cost of an Additional Insured endorsement, the money is well spent.

If the title company will not issue the endorsement for a nominal cost, the lawyer and client are faced with a more difficult question of whether the significant premium cost is justified to avoid the risk of losing title insurance coverage. A similar question is posed for increases in property value that may have occurred after issuance of the initial title insurance policy, even if an Additional Insured endorsement is issued (or, indeed, whether or not any transfer has occurred). Should the transferee purchase a new title insurance policy or increased coverage endorsement to increase the amount of the title insurance?

Most real estate owners do not purchase new title insurance coverage as their properties increase in value. As time passes, title insurance is forgotten. Title risks that seemed so real on initial acquisition (missed mortgages, forgeries, and the like) fade from memory. An owner may reason that if many years have passed and no title problems have surfaced, the likelihood that they will ever arise is remote. If the use of the property and neighboring properties is static, the risk of this approach may be minimal. But, in a dynamic environment, where construction is anticipated or occurring, uses are intensifying and values are escalating, long-dormant title issues may surface, including boundary problems, defective legal descriptions, disputes over access and other easements and encroachments. Lawyers should advise their clients that these risks can be addressed by buying new title insurance coverage. Otherwise, the lawyer may be exposed to future malpractice claims.

Miscellaneous Issues

Other title insurance concerns may arise in the context of estate planning transfers, including coverage for outright gifts of partial interests and the effect of not recording estate planning real estate transfers. Of course, new title insurance resolves any questions about partial interest transfers. An Additional Insured endorsement can cover the definition of who is an insured, but it will not address problems arising since the issuance of the original policy.

To avoid transfer taxes and increased property tax assessments and to protect confidentiality of the transaction, some lawyers may be tempted to execute and deliver deeds for estate planning transfers but then not record them immediately. Failure to record may enable the parties to try to unwind a transaction privately. In the event of a title insurance claim, the title company may never become aware of the transfer or its reversal and so may never assert a coverage defense to the claim. This approach is not recommended. It may subject the parties to defenses and exposure for concealing material facts relating to the claim, not to mention possible tax fraud.

Conclusion

For their clients' and their own protection, when completing inter vivos transfers for estate planning purposes, lawyers should carefully consider the necessity for obtaining title insurance coverage, at least in the form of endorsements to existing title insurance policies. The safest course is to obtain a new title insurance policy, but the premium cost may be difficult to justify if the client would not be increasing its title insurance coverage in the absence of the estate planning transfer. Nevertheless, at a minimum, lawyers should discuss the consequences of not obtaining such coverage with their clients when making estate planning real estate transfers.

59
Family Limited Partnerships: The Secret to Tax-Free Wealth Transfer

BRIAN T. WHITLOCK

I. Impediments to Utilizing the Annual Exclusion and Unified Credit

A. The Future is Uncertain

1. How much is enough—to keep?

   "I want to retain a secure stream of income for life."

   "I don't want to ask for anything from my kids."

2. How much is too much—to give?

   "I don't want to ruin the kids."

   "I don't want to take away their incentive to be productive."

B. Liquid Gifts: Kid's temptation to spend

C. "The Secret": Creating methods that allow the parent to transfer value yet keep control.

II. Partnerships as Part of the Solution

Partnerships are one of the oldest forms of doing business known to man. They have existed both formally and informally since the time of creation. Today, as a result of two significant changes, the partnership represents the foundation of the hottest wealth transfer vehicle available—the Family Limited Partnership.

A. Background

There generally are two types of partnerships available under state law: general partnerships and limited partnerships.

General partnerships may be informal (that is, a mutual understanding to cooperate or a handshake agreement) or formal (that is, a written partnership agreement).

Limited partnerships require certain formalities under state law. These requirements generally include a written agreement, registration with state and county governmental authorities, and a partner residing within the state to accept notice. It is the adoption of this act that effectively expanded the use of limited partnerships. The members of the limited partnership can be individuals, corporations, foreign or domestic trusts, other partnerships, or combinations of any of the above.

B. Limited Partnerships: An Ugly History

For many people the simple mention of the words "limited partnership" can recall horrible memories. In the 1970s and early 1980s many "tax shelter promoters" used limited partnerships that they controlled to bilk millions of unsuspecting investors out of their hard-earned dollars. Investors purchased limited partnership interests that offered tax refunds in excess of their investment, and if the partnership made money, then they stood to reap huge returns. Too good to be true? It was.

Greed took over. Unsavory promoters set up questionable schemes, loaded them down with up-front fees and massive debt, and then dumped them in the laps of the limited partners. To add insult to injury the IRS disallowed the income tax refund

Brian T. Whitlock is a partner and the director of business succession planning for Blackman Kallick Bartelstein, L.L.P.

claims of the investors and hit them with interest and penalties. Limited partnerships and tax shelter schemes were abandoned wholesale after the 1986 income tax act.

C. Family Limited Partnerships: Why Now? What's Different?

A family limited partnership is simply a limited partnership that is controlled by members of your family. It bears no resemblance to the tax shelter partnerships of the past. There are no outsiders or promoters skimming the cream off of your investment.

Three recent developments have brought family limited partnerships into the limelight as a family investment tool. First, since 1985, thirty-three states have adopted the Revised Uniform Limited Partnership Act (RUPLA), as their state law governing the formation and operation of limited partnerships. Only Louisiana is different. RUPLA put in place numerous provisions that protect the partnership from the claims of a limited partner's creditors.

Second, Section 2701 was added to the Internal Revenue Code in 1989. This provision specifically clarifies the gift and estate tax valuation rules governing the transfer of voting and nonvoting partnership interests.

Third, in March 1993, the Internal Revenue Service issued Revenue Ruling 93-12, in which the IRS changed its long opposition to valuation discounts on gifts of stock and partnership interests to members of the same family.

These three changes, taken together, have encouraged numerous families to embrace the family limited partnership as a family investment management vehicle and as a tool that can help minimize gift and estate taxes.

D. Nontransfer Tax Advantages of Limited Partnerships: Business Reasons

Key Point: The IRS cannot disregard the existence of a partnership if it is determined that either (1) the partnership was formed for a nontax reason or (2) the partnership, in fact, did engage in a business or investment activity. *Moline Properties, Inc. v. Commissioner,* 319 US 426 (1946).

1. The general partner controls the management and investment of the portfolio.
2. The general partner controls all distributions of cash and/or property to the partners and can reinvest significant portions of the cash flow.
3. Partnerships allow families to foster the modern portfolio theory of investing. Pooling investment assets gives the family greater ability to diversify the families investments.
4. Pooling of securities investments reduces account charges and investment fees and allows the family access to sophisticated money manager expertise where minimums exist.
5. Real estate held by the partnership as a consolidated investment can be developed and/or managed in an orderly manner.
6. Senior family members can preserve their spendable assets by giving nonspendable limited partnership units rather than cash and securities to younger family members.
7. The limited partnership protects assets from the claims of future creditors of any of the limited partners. Creditors may not force cash distributions, vote, or own the interest of a limited partner without the consent of the other partners.
8. The limited partnership protects assets from the claims of spouses of failed marriages.
9. Buy-sell agreements can prevent valuable assets from getting outside the family.
10. Partnerships have a proven track record in the management of family assets, unlike LLCs and LLPs. Partnerships are flexible: they can be amended or changed, unlike irrevocable trusts.
11. A limited partnership provides as opportunity to avoid probate of the assets held by the partnership. Out-of-state real estate and assets held in partnership in foreign countries are intangible personal

property. Probate only applies to the partnership interests. Probate of the partnership interests also can be avoided by using joint tenancy or living trusts.

12. Partnership agreements may require arbitration of family disputes.

E. Income, Gift, and Estate Tax Advantages

1. Partnerships are not subject to federal income tax. Pursuant to IRC Section 702, each item of income and/or loss flows through to the individual partner, regardless of the distribution of cash or property.

2. Taxable income may be split among junior members owning limited partnership interests in lower income tax brackets.

3. Transfers of limited partnership interests to junior family members will be eligible for the annual gift tax exclusion ($10,000/$20,000 per person per calendar year).

4. Transfers of limited partnership interests to junior family members will reduce the taxable estate of senior family members.

5. Transfers of limited partnership interests to junior family members are eligible for valuation discounts for lack of marketability and lack of control.

6. Leveraged transfers of partnership interests can be structured by adding preferences to some but not all of the partnership interests.

7. Future appreciation of assets inures to the benefit of the donee, thus escaping transfer taxes.

8. The partnership may qualify under Internal Revenue Code Section 6166 for partial deferral of estate tax payments if the partnership represents a closely held business. Retained partnership interests would thus be eligible to pay the decedent's estate tax in installments over a fifteen-year period following the decedent's death.

9. Partnerships are easier to liquidate tax-free than a corporation, and nontaxable distributions may be easily made from partnerships.

III. General Strategies for Funding the Partnership

A. Good Selections

1. High basis assets (gifts)
2. Vacant real estate (Section 1031)
3. Cash and marketable securities
4. C Corporation stock (double discounts)

B. Acceptable, but . . .

1. Low basis assets (capital gains)
2. Business real estate (built-in gains and *Cirelli*)
3. Equipment leasing could raise sales tax issues (loss of exemption, loss of state investment tax credits, loss rental taxes, and *Cirelli*).
4. Farm and timber land transfer could cause loss of subsidy
5. Vacation (rental) property
6. Life insurance (PLR 9309021); business buy-sell the only purpose, *Estate of Knipp,* 25 TC 153 (155); no incident of ownership (PLR 9131006); no Section 2036 or 2038 risk with insurance.
7. Active businesses with exposure to product or personal liability (unless safeguards are met, for example, corporate general partner).

C. Unacceptable

1. S Corporation stock; partnership not a permitted shareholder
2. Professional practices, IRC Section 704(e)
3. Personal residence. Watch for loss of homestead real estate tax exemption or rollover of capital gain under IRS Section 1034. Strictly personal assets without more lack business purpose.

D. Income Tax Issues in Funding

1. Avoiding classification as an investment company—IRC Section 721(b)—gain on contribution

   a. Avoid multiple contributors of marketable securities. Note: Not an issue where initial partners are only spouses. No deemed sale under IRC Section 1041.

   b. Include property other than cash, municipal bonds, bonds, and securities as more than 20 percent of capital contributions to avoid IRC Section 721(b).

   c. Example in regulations would permit de minimis amount (1 percent) of cash without diversification. Treasury Regulation Section 351.

  2. Liabilities in excess of basis. Assumption of liabilities by partnership may be deemed an exchange, subject to gain. IRC Sections 752, 731(a)(1), 741.

E. Ancillary Funding Issues

  1. Some states may not allow farms to be owned by limited partnerships.

  2. Transfers may cause loss of government subsidy.

  3. Transfer may result in loss of real estate tax, farm or open space valuation.

  4. Consider nominee ownership to preserve subsidy.

  5. Transfer may cause loss of farm water rights.

IV. Midwest Manufacturing Case Study

A. Selection of Assets

  1. Current Business Operations

    a. Midwest is a mature corporation, producing a healthy stream of income. Operating as a flow-through entity allows Frank to access the earnings of the corporation for his future income needs without being subject to multiple levels of income taxation.

    b. The stock of Midwest could not be placed into the partnership without losing the corporation's S status. Therefore, the operations should either continue as a C Corporation or be rolled out into a partnership. Here's how the rollout might work:

     i. The business assets of Midwest would be contributed to a limited partnership together with cash and other assets from Frank, Sam, and Diane.

     ii. Midwest (an S Corporation) would receive the general partnership interest. Frank, Sam, and Diane would receive various limited partnership interests.

     iii. Over time, Frank, Sam, and Diane could transfer their limited partnership units to their children and grandchildren (or trusts for their benefit) by utilizing their unified credit shelter equivalent amounts and annual exclusion gifts (see Figure 59–1).

  2. Future Business Operations

    a. Midwest, acting as the general partner, could enter into new lines of business with the children and grandchildren (or trusts for their benefit) as the limited partners. Frank could similarly receive limited partnership interests for his financial contributions to the new partnership.

    b. Instead of receiving an interest in the partnership, Frank could take back a note. This would freeze Frank out of future growth in the new business and keep his income to a fixed level (the stated interest rate).

  3. Marketable Securities and Real Estate

    a. Frank and his spouse could contribute the company plant and marketable securities (less that 80 percent) to a new limited partnership. Sam and Diane (and their children, if desirable) would also contribute some cash and marketable securities.

    b. Frank and his spouse would receive the general partnership interest and some of the limited partnership interests. The others would receive limited partnership interests.

    c. Frank and his spouse could hold the general partnership interest in joint tenancy or in a living trust. If it was held by a new S Corporation, it would be necessary to fund the new corporation with sufficient assets to avoid classification as a taxable association rather than as a partnership.

    d. Over time, Frank, Sam, and Diane could transfer their limited partnership units to their children and grandchildren (or trusts for their benefit) by utilizing their unified credit shelter equivalent amounts and annual exclusion gifts (see Figure 59–2).

B. Additional Features for Consideration

1. Create drawing accounts for the accumulation or distribution of income/cash without altering the capital interests of the partners.

2. Consider purchasing life insurance on Frank and spouse with excess partnership cash flow. This will aid the family at death to meet liquidity needs. Insurance is also useful at the time of liquidation. It allows one family to keep the plant and another to receive only cash.

3. Consider creating guaranteed payments or preferred limited partnership interests to direct cash flow in favor of Frank to meet his objective. The preferred partnership interest can also use cash flow to leverage transfer.

   a. Common limited partnership interests can be additionally discounted for gift purposes.

   b. Preferred limited partnership interests can be transferred to a grantor retained annuity trust or similar "leveraged transfer vehicle." (See Figure 59–3.)

Figure 59–1

Family Limited Partnership

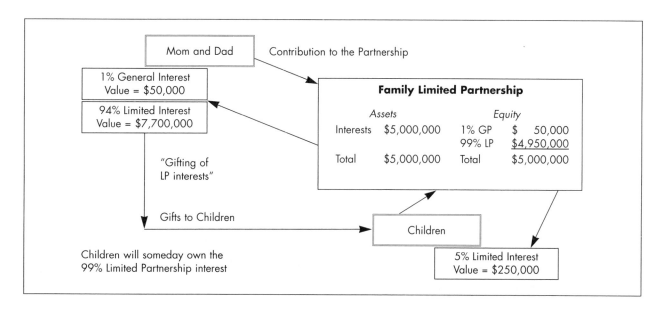

Figure 59–2

Family Limited Partnership with Preferred Partnership Interest

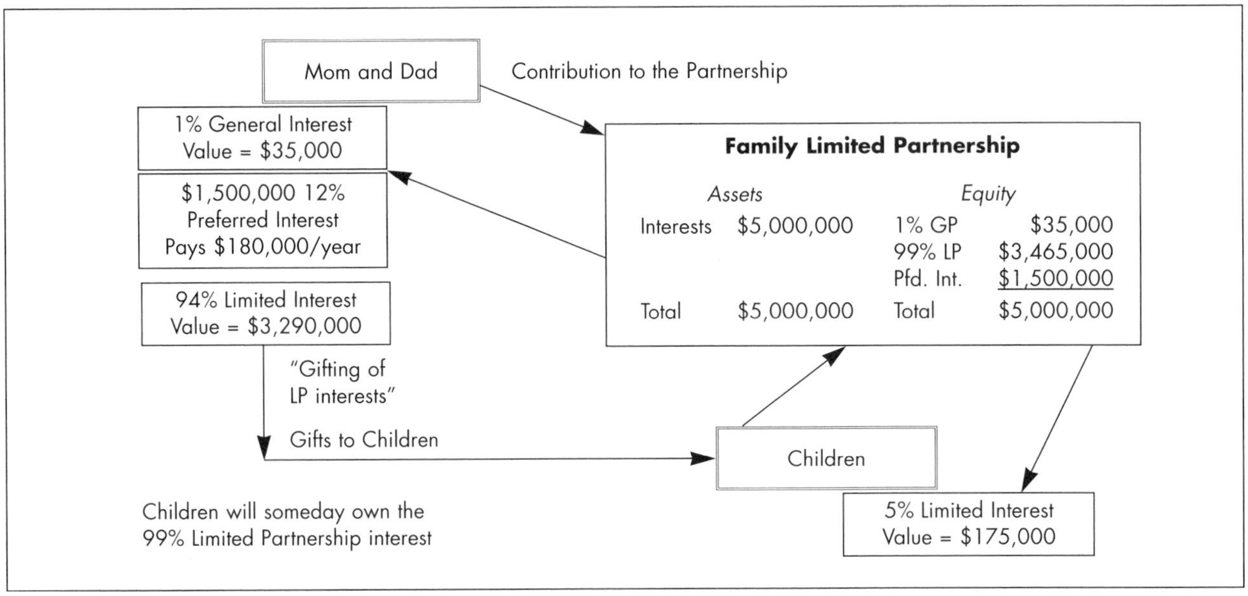

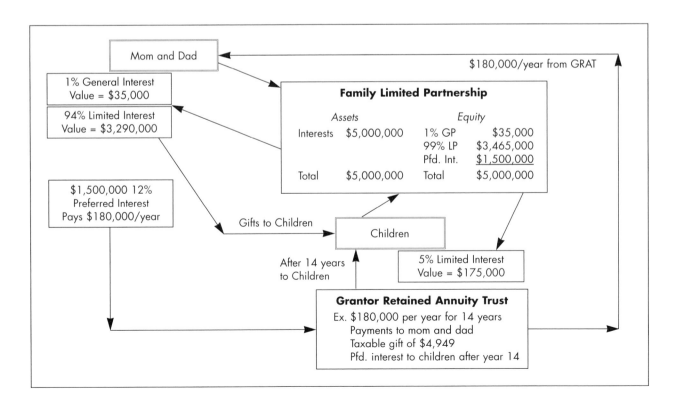

Figure 59–3

Family Limited Partnership with Preferred Partnership Interest Placed Into GRAT

60
Personal Residence Trusts

HERBERT L. ZUCKERMAN AND JAY A. SOLED

Many of you may be concerned about the recent rash of insurance company failures and the government's tightening of the "rules" in the Revenue Reconciliation Act of 1990, wondering what's left in the area of estate planning that involves minimal risk but has a high reward. One opportunity Congress still has not foreclosed is placement of your personal residence into what is known as a grantor retained income trust.

The advantages of using this trust for personal residences, known by the acronym "PRIT," are that it allows a deep discount of the value of the gift being made to the trust's remaindermen (for example, your children), permits subsequent appreciation to pass tax-free, and involves modest sacrifice by you and/or your spouse.

Discount. The reason for the deep discount is twofold: First, because you (as grantor) retain an income interest in the trust for a term of years, say ten, that interest has value that will not immediately inure to the remaindermen. Second, if you should die during the trust term, the entire value of the trust, including any appreciation thereon, reverts to your gross estate for estate tax purposes. The values of both the retained interest and the reversion right are subtracted from the value of the residence funding the PRIT in determining the present value of the gift.

For example, suppose you were to place your residence, currently worth $500,000, into a PRIT for a term of ten years. Suppose further that according to tables provided by the treasury department the values of your retained interest and reversion right are $375,000 and $25,000, respectively. The value of the gift you have made,

therefore, is only $100,000 ($500,000 – $375,000 – $25,000). Should your house appreciate in value to $1 million over the next ten years, you will have effectively made a $1 million gift with a $100,000 gift tax reporting requirement.

Sacrifices. A properly drafted PRIT should not involve substantial disruption of your lifestyle and/or that of your spouse. Indeed, during the trust term, you can be the sole trustee of the PRIT and, needless to say, you and your spouse can continue to occupy the residence and make all necessary repairs and improvements. Real estate taxes paid remain deductible to you and likewise, should the residence be sold during the term, you could defer the gain if you reinvest the funds in another principal residence of equal or greater value or if you use the $250,000 (or $500,000 for couples) exemption applicable to principal residences to offset any gain.

Problems arise, say some practitioners, at the end of the trust term; that is, when you can no longer be your own trustee and must now worry about being "kicked-out" of your own home. Yet, as long as you carefully select your trustee, as the following discussion points out, you should not need to worry about such an event.

At the end of the trust term, it is preferable that the PRIT provides that the corpus of the trust will be held in further trust for the benefit of the grantor's spouse or children (of course, there are other alternatives, such as giving the corpus outright to the children, but few will be willing to lose "control" of their homes). Whichever is the case, you hope the trustee will maintain the trust's investment in the personal residence. This means that, if the trustee is holding the trust's assets for the benefit of your spouse, she (and you) can continue to reside there rent-free. If instead the trustee is holding the assets of the trust for the benefit of your children, both you and your spouse must pay market rental if you wish to continue to reside in the house.

Herbert L. Zuckerman is a partner at the law firm of Sills Cummis Zuckerman Radin Tischman Epstein & Gross, P.A., in Newark, New Jersey. Jay A. Soled is a lawyer and an assistant professor at Rutgers University in Newark, New Jersey.

A couple of points should be made clear here. First, the trustee and his successors should be chosen on the basis of their past and future willingness to act in a responsible manner and not counter to you or your spouse's interests. Obvious candidates include your close friends, your lawyer, or your accountant.

Second, the payment of rent is in itself an excellent estate-planning device. Remember, any rent you and/or your spouse pay—all the benefit of which inures to your children—further reduces your estate at no gift tax cost to you. However, because of certain income tax consequences regarding grantor trust rules, this option requires careful consideration and planning.

Finally, at the end of the initial trust term, should you have any concern about losing your home, you could buy it back from the trust. This means that at the end of year ten, if the house is then worth $1 million, you write a check to yourself, in your capacity as trustee, for its then fairmarket value No income taxes are due on the gain because of the special nature of the trust (that is, grantor) and yet, this strategy allows you all the estate planning advantages of using the PRIT because you are still able to get $1 million out of your estate at one-tenth the price and have your house back in your name.

Odds and Ends. There are some other odds and ends those seeking to create a PRIT must consider

In particular, for the PRIT to be of estate tax advantage, you must survive the trust term, lest the entire value of the trust assets is included in your gross estate.

Congress also sought to curtail the use of PRITs by limiting their use to one principal residence and a vacation home. What this means is that married couples can create a maximum of three PRITs, using their principal residence and one vacation home each.

In line with this limitation approach, proposed regulations issued by the treasury department provide that if the residence is sold during the trust term the proceeds must be either invested in another personal residence within two years or converted into a special type of trust known as a grantor retained annuity trust. Failure to take either of these steps will cause a termination of the PRIT, with all the trust assets reverting to the grantor, thereby defeating the purpose behind the creation of the PRIT.

Despite these limitations, in a world where the solvency of life insurance companies is no longer a certainty and Congress keeps looking for new sources of revenue to meet the needs of FISC, PRITs do offer an opportunity, not one free from risk, but one where the risks are containable and well worth taking.

61
Tax-Deferred Exchanges

SUZANNE GOLDSTEIN BAKER

A typical estate and retirement planning conversation covers many tax and investment strategies, but tax deferred exchanges are not usually among those discussed. They ought to be.

The Situation

Let's assume that you own a couple of apartment buildings with a present fair-market value of $1 million. You acquired these apartment buildings many years ago and have a current tax basis of a mere $100,000. At this point in your life, you have several significant concerns:

- You are concerned about proper management of this investment at some future point when you are no longer capable of or interested in active management responsibilities.
- You recognize that your three adult children do not share your enthusiasm for owning and managing these multifamily residential properties.
- You also have had a serious "reality check" conversation with yourself and strongly suspect that your children, two of whom reside in other states, may not successfully work together, and thus there exists the potential for your hard-earned and long-nurtured investment to be dissipated through acrimonious or simply inattentive mismanagement in the event your children inherit the apartment buildings.
- If you sell the buildings and convert this investment to cash, you will recognize a gain of $900,000 and suffer an immediate reduction in value due to capital gains taxes of nearly $200,000.

The Solution

A tax-deferred exchange can provide the best solution to this smorgasbord of dilemmas. You

Suzanne Goldstein Baker is vice president of American National Exchange Corporation in Chicago.

can sell your apartment buildings and replace them with a real estate investment more acceptable to your future personal and estate planning needs. By structuring this sale and replacement purchase as a like-kind exchange under Section 1031 of the Internal Revenue Code,[1] you can defer recognition of gain on the transfer of these apartment buildings and, thus, defer indefinitely all of the federal capital gains taxes which ordinarily would be due.

There are two options under the like-kind exchange structure which will resolve these needs. First, you can acquire as replacement property an undivided percentage interest in a long-term triple net lease, such as a Walgreen's or Wal-Mart property. This option immediately reduces your active management duties to cashing a check. It also provides an asset easily transferable after death to your children. Finally, it preserves the value of your million dollar investment through nonrecognition of gain and tax deferral.

Conversely, you can ask each of your three adult children to go out and select the exact parcel of real estate, located anywhere in the United States, having a value of approximately $333,500 (one-third of $1,000,000) that they would actually like to take responsibility for at some time and ultimately inherit. You can acquire these three parcels as replacement property and then provide in your will or other estate planning documents for each property to pass, upon your death, to the child who selected it. This allows you to continue active management duties for as long you wish, but provides the comfort of knowing that each child will inherit exactly the parcel of real estate he or she wants, and further eliminates any need for cooperative management among these geographically remote

1. All references to the code are to the Internal Revenue Code of 1986, 26 USCA, as amended. All references to Treasury Regulations are to 26 C.F.R.

siblings. Once again, no gain has been recognized, so a million dollars is still a million dollars.

Section 1031

Now that we have established why a tax-deferred exchange is a valuable tool, let's back up and discuss what it is and how an exchange is accomplished. Any such discussion must begin with the synonym list. To the confusion of many, this tax advantaged vehicle is known variously as: a "Starker Trust," Like-Kind Exchange, Tax Deferred Exchange, Section 1031 Exchange, or Property Swap. There is absolutely no distinction between these terms.

Section 1031[2] provides that no gain or loss will be recognized on the transfer of an asset that

- has been held for investment or
- used productively in a trade or business, if that asset
- is exchanged for like-kind property
- that also will be held for investment or
- used productively in a trade or business.

The same rules govern real estate exchanges as well as personal property swaps. The exchange does not have to be simultaneous. In fact, most exchanges are nonsimultaneous, for the simple reason that a purchaser of an investment or business use asset is not likely to have acceptable property to exchange back to the selling taxpayer. In a nonsimultaneous exchange, the buyer's purchase money is used to acquire replacement property from a third-party seller.

Like-Kind Real Estate

Once the investment or business use criteria has been satisfied, the question to be answered is whether the property sold ("Relinquished Property") and the property acquired ("Replacement Property") in the exchange are like-kind to one another. Real estate enjoys an incredibly broad definition of like-kind. All real estate located within the United States is like-kind to all other domestic real estate.[3] A taxpayer may exchange a strip mall for farmland, an apartment building, an office building, a nursing home, a quarry pit, mineral rights, or a long-term leasehold. The simple answer is, "If it has dirt on it, and it's in the United States, it is like-kind."

2. Code § 1031(a)(1)
3. Code § 1031(h)(1); Treas. Reg. § 1.1031(a)-1(b)

Like-Kind Personal Property

Personal property is defined much more narrowly. Tangible depreciable personal property must be either like-kind or like-class to qualify for exchange treatment.[4] Like-kind refers to two objects that are the same, such as a noncommercial airplane for another noncommercial airplane or a backhoe for a backhoe. To be like-class, the relinquished and replacement properties must both be included in the same general asset class, or if there is no general asset class covering those particular assets, then they must fall within the same product class.[5] There are thirteen general asset classes.[6] Product classes are set forth in the Standard Industrial Classification Manual and are identified with the same four-digit SIC code.[7] Under the like-class definition, a noncommercial airplane could be exchanged for a helicopter because they both fall within the same general asset class. Similarly, the backhoe may be exchanged for a bulldozer, dredging machinery, a road grader, or a log splitter, because these assets all are included within the construction machinery and equipment product class.[8]

Nondepreciable personal property, such as collectibles or artwork, unfortunately must fit the narrower definition of like-kind. These assets are not afforded the latitude given by the general asset classes or product classes, which are specifically limited to depreciable property.[9] However, unlike other classifications of assets for which the capital gains tax was reduced in 1997, gains on collectibles are penalized with a maximum individual capital gains rate of 28 percent.

The Problem You Never Imagined

Perhaps you have seriously invested in artwork over the years and are considering a testamentary donation of your art collection to a museum. Due to burgeoning collections and increasingly limited wall space, some museums have had to become much more selective about what pieces of artwork they will accept. Museums frequently find themselves in the position of turning away potential donations because the composition of

4. Treas. Reg. § 1.1031(a)-2(b)(1).
5. *See id.*
6. Treas. Reg. § 1.1031(a)-2(b) (2)
7. Treas. Reg. § 1.1031(a)-2(b) (3)
8 SIC Code 3531
9. Treas. Reg. § 1.1031(a)-2(c)(1)

the collection is not consistent with the permanent collection needs of the museum. The last thing you want is for your trustee or executor to be told "No thanks!" to the generous donation of your beloved collection. Section 1031 affords you the opportunity to work with the museum to upgrade or modify your collection so that future patrons of the arts will enjoy your artwork collection proudly displayed on the museum walls. By using a like-kind exchange, you can sell the necessary artworks, acquire as replacement property those pieces suggested by a museum curator as appropriate for future incorporation into their permanent collection, and defer all of the capital gains taxes that would be due on a pure sale.

Transacting an Exchange

Step 1: The Qualified Intermediary

So how do you actually accomplish an exchange? A tax-deferred exchange can be safely, easily, and painlessly accomplished through the use of a qualified intermediary. The Treasury Regulations which set forth the safe harbors for a successful nonsimultaneous like-kind exchange prohibit the taxpayer from having any rights to receive, pledge, borrow, or otherwise obtain the benefits of the exchange funds while the exchange is pending.[10] The qualified intermediary is the independent third party who will receive the sale proceeds directly from the buyer, hold them in a restricted account, and subsequently disburse directly to the seller of the replacement property.

Be careful who you select as a qualified intermediary. Most of the population is defined as disqualified: a related party, an agent of the taxpayer, including the taxpayer's lawyer, accountant, employee, investment banker, or broker, unless the professional has provided no services other than those related to a Section 1031 exchange within the past two years.[11] The few notable exceptions to the definition of disqualified agent are financial institutions, title insurance companies, and escrow companies, which provide routine financial, title insurance, escrow, or trust services for the taxpayer.[12] However, even these entities can potentially be disqualified. Your safest bet is to look for a reputable institutional qualified intermediary that is a separate corporation from the bank or title company. A subsidiary or affiliate of a bank, title, or escrow company is fine. Although an individual may be qualified intermediary, an institutional qualified intermediary will protect your exchange from disaster caused by a very untimely bankruptcy, death, disability, or other legal difficulty to which individuals are prone.

Financial strength and stability is also an often overlooked issue. Do you really want your very large deal to be 50 percent of the capitalization of the entire qualified intermediary? No. You really want to know that your money will be there, safe, sound, and available, when you need it, no matter what other difficulties the qualified intermediary may have. Not all qualified intermediaries are created equal. Look for one who employs a knowledgeable, professional staff who can work with you and your tax advisors to assist you through the morass of fine print known as the Internal Revenue Code and Treasury Regulations. Make sure that you will receive a decent rate of interest, such as an institutional money market rate, on your exchange funds for the entire period during which they are on deposit. Finally, look for a qualified intermediary who is truly responsive. A first-rate qualified intermediary should understand and accommodate the "fire drills" inherent in this type of transactional business, be able to liquidate funds, and disburse on short notice.

Step 2: The Initial Closing

Now that you have selected a qualified intermediary you will enter into a written Like-Kind Exchange Agreement between only the taxpayer and the qualified intermediary.[13] The best qualified intermediaries provide a complete set of forms necessary to document the like-kind exchange. Next, you must assign the sale contract for the relinquished property to the qualified intermediary and notify the buyer of the assignment.[14] It is not necessary that the qualified intermediary enter into the chain of title. Assignment of contract rights is sufficient. Now you can close the deal. At closing, the buyer will tender all net proceeds directly to the qualified intermediary. Prorations and loan payoffs are typically paid to third parties as they would be in any closing.

---

10. Treas. Reg. § 1.1031(k)-1(g)(4)(i) and (ii)
11. Treas. Reg. § 1.1031(k)-1(k)
12. Treas. Reg. § 1.1031(k)-1(k)(2)(ii)
13. Treas. Reg. § 1.1031(k)-1(g)(4)(iii)(B)
14. Treas. Reg. § 1.1031(k)-1(g)(4)(iv)(B) and (v)

Step 3: Identification of Replacement Property

You have forty-five calendar days from the date of the sale of the relinquished property to identify replacement property.[15] The identification must be in writing, signed by the taxpayer, must specifically and unambiguously identify the replacement property, and is usually given to the qualified intermediary, although there are a few other acceptable recipients of this notice.[16] If no identification is made, the exchange will terminate and you will be entitled to receive funds on deposit on the forty-sixth day. Real estate may be identified by street address; by other specifically identifiable common name, such as the Empire State Building; or by legal description.

You do not need to be under contract within this time. You may even identify alternate replacement properties to protect your exchange in the event your favorite property is not attainable. The basic rule is the "3 Property/200 Percent Rule" which allows you to identify (1) up to three properties without regard to value or (2) four or more properties so long as the aggregate value of all identified properties does not exceed 200 percent of the fair-market value of the relinquished property.[17] If you sold for $1 million, you could identify the Sears Tower, the Empire State Building, and the Trump Tower, because value is irrelevant to an identification of three or fewer. However, if you identified four properties, the total aggregate value of all identified properties must not be more than $2 million. There is an exception to this rule, the "95 Percent Rule." You may successfully violate the "3 Property/200 Percent Rule" if you actually acquire at least 95 percent of what you identified.[18] For example, you could reinvest your $1 million apartment sale proceeds, along with other cash or debt, in thirty rental resort condominiums valued at $3 million.

15. Code § 1031(a)(3); Treas. Reg. § 1031(k)-1(b)(2)(i)
16. Treas. Reg. § 1031(k)-1(c)(2) and (3)
17. Treas. Reg. § 1031(k)-1(c)(4)(i)
18. Treas. Reg. § 1031(k)-1(c)(4)(ii)

Step 4: Acquisition of Replacement Property

Once you have successfully negotiated a purchase contract for the replacement property, you must assign your rights under that contract to the qualified intermediary and notify the seller of the assignment.[19] You must actually close on the acquisition of the replacement property within the earlier of 180 calendar days following the sale of the relinquished property or the due date for filing your tax return for the year in which the relinquished property was sold.[20] Diary the forty-five-day and 180-day deadline dates well; there are no extensions. When you need earnest money, or a final disbursement for closing, so advise the qualified intermediary who will then disburse directly to the seller who will, in turn, deliver title to you. After your exchange is concluded, you are entitled to receive the earnings on your exchange funds.[21]

Conclusion

In summary, a Section 1031 like-kind exchange is a tax-deferral vehicle useful for investors of all ages. It can be a creative tool to satisfy changing needs required by aging, retirement, and estate planning. The basic criteria for benefit is a taxpayer who wishes to sell an investment or business-use asset, in which he has a gain, and replace that asset with like-kind investment or business-use property within 180 days. Structuring the sale and replacement purchase in conformance with the requirements of a like-kind exchange can avoid recognition of gain and defer all federal capital gains taxes that otherwise would be due upon transfer. The appointment of a professional qualified intermediary can make this process a simple and very cost-efficient tool.

19. Treas. Reg. § 1031(k)-1(g)(4)(iv)(C) and (v)
20. Code § 1031(a)(3); Treas. Reg. § 1031(k)-1(b)(2)(ii)
21. Treas. Reg. § 1031(k)-1(g)(5)

62

On the Flip Side: A New Spin on Charitable Remainder Trusts

CHRISTOPHER P. CLINE

Few estate planning devices have proven as useful as the charitable remainder trust (CRT). Lawyers have touted CRTs as the estate planning jack-of-all-trades: charitable giving vehicle, installment sale substitute, nonqualified retirement plan, and life insurance funding source. Over the past few years, the IRS, concerned that lawyers and others have sold CRTs as devices to defer or avoid taxes, has closely scrutinized the uses of CRTs. In some cases the IRS has even denied the tax-exempt status of CRTs when it disagreed with the use of the CRTs. Critics argued that these pronouncements had no basis in law and were unenforceable. On April 17, 1997, the IRS took a new tack by issuing proposed regulations concerning CRTs under Code Sections 664 and 2702 (CRT regulations). The CRT regulations, if issued in final form, will officially promulgate many of the IRS' previously informally stated positions on CRTs and will allow donors and their lawyers more flexibility in the creation and operation of CRTs.

This chapter discusses various uses for CRTs invented by lawyers and other professionals, the IRS response to those uses and the effect that the CRT regulations will have on both existing and future CRTs. After briefly describing the way CRTs work, the article looks at a variety of creative CRT planning techniques and some of the IRS attacks and restrictions on those techniques. Finally, the article describes the operation of the CRT regulations, along with some planning ideas to consider in light of the regulations.

Christopher P. Cline is a partner with the law firm of Lane Powell Spears Lubersky, LLP, in Portland, Oregon.

CRTs

A CRT pays a specified amount to one or more individuals (noncharitable beneficiaries) either for their lives or for a fixed term not exceeding 20 years. A charitable remainder annuity trust (CRAT) pays a fixed amount equal to at least 5 percent of the trust assets on the creation of the trust to the noncharitable beneficiary each year. For instance, a 6 percent CRAT funded with $1 million will pay $60,000 to the noncharitable beneficiary per year, regardless of the increase or decrease in the value of the trust assets over time.

A charitable remainder unitrust (CRUT) pays to the noncharitable beneficiary a fixed percentage (unitrust amount) of the trust assets revalued each year. For example, a 6 percent CRUT funded with $1 million will pay $60,000 to the noncharitable beneficiary in the first year of the trust. If, however, the trust assets appreciate in value to $1,100,000 in the second year, the noncharitable beneficiary will receive 6 percent of that amount, or $66,000.

The net income with makeup CRT (NIMCRUT) is a variant of the CRUT. The noncharitable beneficiary of a NIMCRUT receives the lesser of the specified unitrust amount or the trust's net accounting income. Any deficiency between the amount of net income paid and the unitrust amount in any year is paid in a future year when the trust income exceeds the unitrust amount. For example, assume a donor creates a 6 percent NIMCRUT with assets worth $1 million. If the trust has $50,000 of income in the first year, the noncharitable beneficiary will receive $50,000, which is the lesser of income or the unitrust amount ($60,000).

Assume in its second year that the trust again has $1 million of assets but now has $80,000 of income. The noncharitable beneficiary will receive $60,000 (the lesser of the unitrust amount or trust income) *plus* $10,000 from the excess income to make up for the deficiency between the unitrust amount and actual income paid to the noncharitable beneficiary in year one. The remaining $10,000 of excess income is added to principal.

A significant benefit of a CRT is that the donor receives a current income tax charitable deduction equal to the actuarially determined present value of the remainder interest passing to charity on the date the donor makes the gift to the CRT. Calculation of the deduction depends on the type of CRT, the percentage payment, the term of the CRT (either the term of years or the life expectancies of the noncharitable beneficiaries if the CRT runs for their lifetimes) and the Code Section 7520 interest rate published for either the month in which the CRT is created or one of the two months before the creation. Choosing the highest of those rates maximizes the amount of the deduction. For example, if a 60-year-old donor funds a 6 percent CRUT with $1 million and retains an interest in the trust for his or her lifetime and the Code Section 7520 rate is 8.2 percent, then the donor will receive a $362,000 charitable income deduction.

Another benefit of a CRT is that it is not subject to federal and state income tax unless it has unrelated business taxable income under Code Section 512. The noncharitable beneficiary, however, is subject to income tax on payments he or she receives under a four-tier system. Payments are treated first as ordinary income to the extent the trust has ordinary income in the current year or undistributed ordinary income from prior years, second as capital gains in the same manner, third as other income in the same manner and, finally, as trust principal.

CRTs are also subject, through Code Section 4947, to certain penalty taxes and restrictions applicable to private foundations. Most significantly, Code Section 4941 imposes a penalty tax on a disqualified person (defined in Code Section 4946 but typically the donor) for any act of "self-dealing" between the trust and the disqualified person. The penalty tax initially equals 5 percent of the amount involved and 200 percent if the act is not corrected within the taxable period.

Using CRTs in Estate Planning

In its simplest form, a CRT can provide a cash stream to the donor or another beneficiary and serve as a deferred charitable giving vehicle. The CRT can also provide other benefits. Because the trustee of a CRT can sell assets without incurring income tax, a donor can use a CRT to defer the tax liability on appreciated assets (often real property or a closely held business), thereby allowing the CRT to act as an installment sales substitute. If a donor transfers appreciated assets to a CRT, the donor can obtain a return of a fixed percentage of the full value of the assets over time, rather than immediately losing a significant portion of that value to capital gains tax. The donor pays income tax at his or her marginal rate on CRT distributions to the extent the CRT has income and at capital gains rates to the extent of the balance of the payment.

The donor who intends to sell a business or other asset through a CRT will, however, face an unpleasant choice. Either the donor can use a CRUT and take the chance that the trust will not sell the asset immediately, which will require the trust to satisfy its distribution requirement through a piece of the asset, or the donor can use a NIMCRUT and take the chance that the trust's income will never equal the unitrust amount, thereby reducing the amount the donor receives from the trust. To solve this dilemma, lawyers have suggested using a CRT that begins life as a NIMCRUT but that converts to a straight CRUT after the trust sells certain assets—a flip unitrust. A flip unitrust has the advantage over a straight CRUT of not requiring the trustee to distribute trust assets until the CRT sells the business or other asset. After the sale, the CRT would convert to a straight CRUT and the CRUT would pay the noncharitable beneficiary the original unitrust amount.

A CRT also can provide a noncharitable beneficiary with an income stream, the source of which probably is protected from the beneficiary's creditors. The degree of protection afforded depends on the state law under which the CRT is governed and is not uniform, but an irrevocable trust that has a charity as a remainder beneficiary probably is an unattractive asset to creditors. If the donor has appreciated assets, the donor also can take advantage of the installment sale characteristics of a CRT in this situation.

Many lawyers and insurance professionals have also marketed CRTs as an alternative to a qualified retirement plan. In this situation, the donor creates a NIMCRUT that invests only in high-growth, low-income assets during its early years. Because the trust has little or no accounting income, the actual distributions from the trust are low, thereby increasing the amount of future makeup payments. When the noncharitable beneficiary retires, the NIMCRUT trustee shifts the trust's investments to income-producing assets and, by using a combination of the unitrust amount and the makeup payments, replaces the income lost on retirement. The problem with using a CRT in this manner is finding investments that generate income sufficient not only to meet the unitrust amount but also to exceed it so that the makeup payments can be made.

Lawyers came up with two solutions to this problem. The first was to include a provision in the trust instrument deeming capital gains to be accounting income. This provision allowed the trustee time for the sale of trust assets to generate income at the time when the noncharitable beneficiary needed it. The second was to advise the trustee to invest in partnerships, life insurance, or deferred annuities and have the trust administered under the law of a state (such as Indiana or Delaware) that deems distributions to the trustee from those investments to be accounting income. This allowed the trustee to time distributions from the investments, which would be deemed trust accounting income when distributed to the trustees and thus distributable to the noncharitable beneficiary.

Finally, lawyers and clients came up with a way to use CRTs to make gifts to a client's children at a small gift tax cost, known as a "near-zero CRUT." Under this plan, a donor would establish a NIM-CRUT, usually with a capital-gains-as-income provision that named the donor as a noncharitable beneficiary for a term of years, after which the donor's children succeeded the donor as the noncharitable beneficiaries. During the term of years in which the donor was the noncharitable beneficiary, the trustee would invest trust assets in high-growth, low-income assets. The donor would accordingly receive few, if any, trust distributions, causing a significant buildup in the makeup account. After the term ended and the children became noncharitable beneficiaries, the trustee

would switch investment strategies and sell appreciated assets to produce greater income. The trustee would then distribute both the unitrust amount and the makeup account to the children. The gift of the interest to the children, however, would be valued at the time the donor created the trust under the IRS tables, with the assumption that the donor would actually receive the unitrust amount each year. This valuation technique greatly reduced the amount of gift tax due on the gift of the unitrust interest to the children.

IRS Reactions to CRTs— Some Recent History

Although the IRS has continued to support the use of CRTs that it deems "legitimate," it has made several pronouncements condemning certain uses for CRTs that it deemed abusive or inconsistent with the purposes of CRTs. For instance, in 1994 the IRS issued Notice 94-78, 1994-2 C.B. 555, in which it stated that it would closely scrutinize "accelerated" CRTs. The example provided in the Notice is of a two year, 80 percent CRUT funded with a highly appreciated asset. By deferring the sale of the asset and the first year distribution from the CRUT into the early part of the second year, which was allowable under the regulations in effect at the time, no income tax liability would attach to the first year payment to the noncharitable beneficiary because the trust would have no income, the sale having taken place in the second year. This resulted in the noncharitable beneficiary paying $44,800 in income taxes during the two-year CRT term on an asset with $1 million of built-in gain. The IRS stated that it would not respect the form of this transaction, that gain from the sale might be attributable to the donor under the assignment of income doctrine, that the CRT might not qualify as a CRT under Code Section 664 and that the entire transaction might constitute self-dealing under Code Section 4941. In short, the IRS said that it did not know exactly what the accelerated CRT was but that it would fight it.

Also in 1994 the IRS issued PLR 9442017, in which it privately ruled that a provision in a CRT that allowed the trustee to deem a reasonable amount of capital gains from the sale of unproductive assets to be accounting income did not disqualify the CRT. Although this provision prob-

405

ably gave the trustee slightly greater authority than that provided under state law, the provision was not out of line with most states' principal and income acts.

In 1995 the IRS again ruled that a capital-gains-as-income provision in a CRT would not disqualify the CRT. PLR 9511007. The IRS, however, noted that the provision worked only because the CRT also required that the trustee treat any shortfall between the unitrust amount and the amount actually distributed in any year as a liability in determining the unitrust amount for future years. The provisions in the CRT described in PLR 9442017 and those in the CRT de-scribed in 9511007 differed in that the former dealt only with gains from unproductive assets, whereas the latter dealt with all gains.

Also in 1995 the IRS determined that flip unitrusts were contrary to the legislative intent behind Code Section 664 and therefore ruled that a court reformation to convert a NIMCRUT to a straight CRUT would disqualify the trust as a CRT. PLR 9506015. The IRS later ruled that such a reformation would be self-dealing. PLR 9522021. Neither ruling, however, considered a CRT that included a conversion provision in the trust agreement.

In 1996 the IRS made three significant pronouncements regarding CRTs. In PLR 9609009, the IRS approved a CRT with a capital-gains-as-income provision, following the rationale of PLR 9511007. The trust agreement involved in PLR 9609009, however, provided that only *post-contribution* capital gains were deemed to be income. Second, in PLR 9643014, the IRS again approved a NIMCRUT that deemed *post-contribution* capital gains to be income and included the "liability" provisions, although the IRS "express[ed] no opinion on whether the trustee's control over the timing and amount of realized income from the sale of trust assets would constitute an act of 'self-dealing.'" Third, and most important, the IRS told its agents in its training manual that use of NIMCRUTs to defer payouts to noncharitable beneficiaries in years when a beneficiary is in a lower tax bracket, which the IRS referred to as "income deferral NIMCRUTs," constituted self-dealing under Code Section 4941. This mandate is Topic K of the *1996 (for FY 1997) Exempt Organizations CPE Technical Instruction Program Textbook* and is quoted in full in the October 1996

issue of *Taxwise Giving*. This approach is consistent with PLR 9643014 and explains why the IRS refused to express an opinion on the self-dealing issue.

In 1997, in addition to issuing the CRT regulations, the IRS issued Rev. Proc. 97-23, 1997 I.R.B. 17, in which it provided that it would not privately rule on whether a trust qualifies as a CRT if it is a NIMCRUT and a grantor, trustee, beneficiary, or a person related or subordinate to any of those parties could control the timing of the trust's receipt of income from a partnership or deferred-annuity contract. This is an area currently under study by the IRS. This Revenue Procedure appears to be a further step toward eliminating the use of retirement plan CRTs.

The CRT Regulations

The CRT regulations attempt to make fast some of these recent informal IRS positions. The CRT regulations, if made final, will do the following:

- allow donors to create flip unitrusts under certain circumstances;
- eliminate the ability of a trustee of a CRUT or CRAT, but not of a NIMCRUT, to make the payment to a noncharitable beneficiary for a given year within a reasonable time after the end of that year;
- impose appraisal requirements on CRT donors or related or subordinate parties serving as trustees of CRTs holding hard-to-value assets;
- eliminate the use of near-zero CRTs; and
- require the allocation of the proceeds of sale of any trust asset to trust principal to the extent those proceeds represent the fair-market value of the asset at the time the donor contributed the asset to the trust.

Flip Unitrusts

The CRT regulations state that a CRUT agreement may provide that the trust will pay the lesser of income or the unitrust amount during the "initial period" of the CRUT and will pay the unitrust amount for the remaining period of the CRUT if four conditions are met.

First, 90 percent of CRUT assets, either immediately after the initial contribution of assets to the trust or after a subsequent contribution, must consist of "unmarketable assets" (90 percent test).

Second, the CRUT instrument must trigger the change of payment method on the earlier of (1) the sale or exchange of a specified asset or group of assets that the donor contributed to the trust on its creation; or (2) the sale or exchange of "unmarketable assets" if, immediately afterward, the fair-market value of the unmarketable assets in the trust equals 50 percent or less of the total fair-market value of all trust assets.

Third, the payment method must change at the beginning of the first calendar year following the sale or exchange that triggered the change.

Fourth, after the payment method has changed, the trustee must pay at least annually only the unitrust amount and not any makeup amount that accrued while the trust was a NIM-CRUT. This fourth provision eliminates any benefit from the "makeup" feature, but most donors who create flip unitrusts will likely want to convert the trust to a straight CRUT soon after they fund the trust. For purposes of these provisions, "unmarketable assets" are any assets other than cash, cash equivalents or "marketable securities" as defined under Code Section 731(c) and the applicable regulations. Prop. Treas. Reg. Section 1.664-3(c).

Lawyers should pay particular attention to the effective dates for flip unitrust provisions in the CRT regulations. The provisions allowing a CRT to change payment methods apply to CRTs created on or after the date the IRS publishes the final regulations in the Federal Register. If a CRT created *before* that date has a defective "flip" provision in it, it may be reformed or amended to comply with the provisions of the CRT regulations. A CRT created after that date with a defective "flip" provision, however, must be reformed or amended to require that its initial period payment method be used throughout the term of the trust or it will cease to qualify as a CRT. Finally, a CRT, whether created before or after the CRT regulations become final, that is reformed or amended to add a "flip" provision, will cease to qualify as a CRT. Prop. Treas. Reg. Section 1.664-3(f)(vi).

The rules governing flip unitrusts have several important ramifications. First, a flip unitrust created by a donor that converts to a straight unitrust following an asset sale before the date that the CRT regulations become final presumably will be subject to the same scrutiny applied under PLRs 9505015 and 9522021, with the result that

the CRT will not qualify as a CRT and may result in an excise tax under the self-dealing rules. Second, lawyers can probably begin drafting flip unitrusts for donors, so long as the "flip" provision does not become effective until after the CRT regulations become final. Third, an improperly drafted flip unitrust created after the CRT regulations become final cannot be amended to save the "flip" feature, but only to keep the CRT from becoming disqualified. Finally, a donor cannot use an existing CRT to jump on the "flip" bandwagon by simply amending or reforming the CRT to add a "flip" provision.

Lawyers also should be wary of the effects of the 90 percent test. Because 90 percent of the trust assets must consist of unmarketable assets, which will be hard to value, it may be difficult to determine whether a CRT qualifies as "flippable." If the donor wishes to contribute both unmarketable assets and cash or publicly traded securities, the donor should consider creating two CRTs, one that will hold only the unmarketable assets and contain appropriate "flip" provisions, and the other that will hold the cash or publicly traded securities assets. Alternatively, the donor could contribute the cash or publicly traded securities to the CRT only after the trustee sells the unmarketable assets and the CRT has "flipped."

Timing of CRT Payments

Effective for taxable years ending after April 18, 1997, the governing instrument of a CRT that pays a unitrust or annuity amount only must require that the trustee pay that amount to the noncharitable beneficiary for each taxable year "no later than the close of the taxable year for which the payment is due." Prop. Treas. Reg. Section 1.664-2(a)(1)(i) (for CRATs); Prop. Treas. Reg. Section 1.664-3(e) (for CRUTs). The CRT regulations, however, allow NIMCRUT agreements to continue to give the trustee a reasonable time after the close of the year for payments to the noncharitable beneficiary. Inasmuch as the "reasonable time" provision for payment drove the accelerated CRT, this timing provision eliminates a donor's ability to create an accelerated CRT.

Although the IRS intended the timing-of-payment provision to correct a perceived abuse, it also is a trap for the unwary because it affects both the administration of existing CRTs and the preparation of new ones. Lawyers should consider making all of their clients who are acting as trustees of fixed percentage CRTs aware of this change and advise them to make distributions accordingly. Lawyers who draft fixed percentage CRTs to require distributions to noncharitable beneficiaries quarter-annually should consider providing the trustee with greater flexibility for the timing of payments, at least allowing the quarter-annual payments to be made before the end of the quarter.

Appraisal Requirements for Hard-to-Value Assets

If a CRT that holds assets other than cash, cash equivalents, or marketable securities has as a trustee the grantor, a noncharitable beneficiary, or a party that is related or subordinate to the grantor or noncharitable beneficiary, the trustee must use a current qualified appraisal (defined under Treas. Reg. Section 1.170A-13(c)(3)), from a "qualified appraiser" (defined in Treas. Reg. Section 1.170A-13(c)(5)), to value those assets. Prop. Treas. Reg. Section 1.664-1(a)(7). This provision addresses the portion of the legislative history of Code Section 664, in which Congress expressed concern that a trustee who is the grantor or a beneficiary of a CRT, or a party related or subordinate to either, should not have the power to independently value such assets for purposes of determining the unitrust amount. Before the issuance of the CRT regulations, many lawyers appointed a special trustee, who was not the grantor, a beneficiary, or a related or subordinate party to either, specifically to value such assets of a CRT, much to the chagrin of the donor. This new provision allows the donor to act as trustee in that situation—provided he or she obtains a qualified appraisal.

Elimination of Near-Zero CRTs

Under the CRT regulations, for transfers made on or after May 19, 1997, a transfer to a CRT (other than a CRT that pays a fixed percentage only) or a pooled income fund is subject to the valuation rules under Code Section 2702. Prop. Treas. Reg. Section 25.2702-1(c)(3). This eliminates a donor's ability to derive benefit from a near-zero CRT because under Code Section 2702 the value of the

interest retained by the donor or any applicable family member will be zero when someone other than the donor, his or her spouse, or both the donor and spouse are noncharitable beneficiaries of the trust.

Allocation to Principal of Pre-Contribution Gains

The CRT regulations state that, when determining "income" for purposes of NIMCRUT distributions, proceeds from the sale or exchange of any asset the donor contributes to the trust must be "allocated to principal and not to trust income, at least to the extent of the fair-market value of those assets on the date of contribution." Prop. Treas. Reg. Section 1.664-3(a)(1)(i)(b)(3). In other words, a NIMCRUT agreement can deem only post-contribution gains as accounting income. This provision, together with Rev. Proc. 97-23, under which the IRS announced its refusal to rule on whether NIMCRUTs holding certain partnership interests or deferred annuity products qualify as CRTs, appears to be part of the IRS attack on retirement plan CRTs.

The CRT regulations formalize the requirement articulated by the IRS in PLRs 9609009 and 9643014 that pre-contribution capital gains cannot be allocated to principal, but the CRT regulations are silent about the liability account requirement. Because lawyers roundly criticized the liability account as unnecessary and unjustified, lawyers could read the CRT regulations as an IRS retreat on the liability account requirement. The careful lawyer may, however, want to continue including liability account provisions until the IRS affirmatively states that they are no longer required.

Example for Computing Income

Finally, the CRT regulations contain an example of how a trustee should compute income distributable to a noncharitable beneficiary of a NIMCRUT. The example merely confirms that the trustee should make the computation in the same manner as in all other CRTs; that is, a distribution is deemed first as ordinary income to the extent the CRT has such income, then as capital gains, then as other income, and finally as a return of principal. This example answers the lawyers who wondered whether those computations should be different from those made for other CRTs. Prop. Treas. Reg. Section 1.664-1(d)(1)(iii). This example breaks no new ground.

Taxpayer Relief Act of 1997

After this chapter was written, President Clinton signed into law the Taxpayer Relief Act of 1997 (TRA '97), which enacts several changes to the law regarding CRTs (none of which affect the CRT regulations). TRA '97 is discussed in Chapter 35 by Grace Allison and David Hirschey. Two aspects of TRA '97 should be noted, however. First, the percentage payment to the noncharitable beneficiary (of either a CRAT or a CRUT) cannot exceed 50 percent of the trust assets. Second, the value of the remainder interest passing to the charity must be at least 10 percent of the fair-market value of the trust assets on the date of contribution to the CRT (TRA '97 also contains relief provisions if this requirement is violated).

Conclusion

The CRT regulations, for the most part, are a welcome arrival. The flip unitrust should prove an effective tool for lawyers and donors interested in planned giving, and the ability of a donor to act as trustee of his or her own CRT, even if it holds hard-to-value assets, makes the lawyer's life much easier. There will be many, particularly those who have championed retirement plan CRTs and accelerated CRTs, who will find the CRT regulations less helpful. Finally, as with all attempts by the IRS to correct behavior it perceives as abusive, the CRT regulations present traps for inattentive lawyers. Those who recommend CRTs as a routine estate planning device for their clients should take a spin around the CRT regulations to avoid skipping the grooves that the IRS has laid out in these pronouncements.

63
Near-Zero CRUT Expands the Estate Planning Possibilities of Charitable Trusts

SIMON LEVIN AND JAY A. SOLED

The charitable remainder unitrust (CRUT) can provide significant estate and income tax savings to a donor while guaranteeing substantial benefits to worthy charities. CRUTs can be used to increase the donor's cash flow from assets; augment support of needy relatives; create wealth replacement by funding premiums needed to maintain life insurance; provide for college educations of children and grandchildren; and, through what is known as the next income makeup CRUT (NIM-CRUT), serve as a private retirement plan. A new form of CRUT—the near-zero CRUT—permits a donor to make large gifts that have low value for gift tax purposes under IRS actuarial tables.

Forms of CRUTs

An understanding of traditional CRUTs is the starting point for an analysis of the near-zero CRUT.

Standard CRUTs

There are three permissible ways for a taxpayer to use a trust to make a deferred gift to charity with favorable gift and estate tax consequences. One is a CRUT; the other two ways are a charitable remainder annuity trust and a pooled income fund.

Under the Internal Revenue Code (code), a governing instrument of a CRUT must provide that a

Simon Levin is a member of the firm and chairman of the tax law group at Sills Cummis Zuckerman Radin Tischman Epstein & Gross, with offices in Newark and Atlantic City, New Jersey, New York City, and Washington, D.C. Jay A. Soled is a lawyer and an assistant professor at Rutgers University in Newark, New Jersey.

unitrust recipient (that is, the donor or other noncharitable beneficiaries) receive a fixed percentage (not less than 5 percent) of the net FMV of the trust assets, valued annually. During the trust term, the noncharitable income beneficiary receives this variable-annuity-type benefit that fluctuates with the value of the trust assets. On the death of the noncharitable income beneficiary or the termination of a fixed number of years (not to exceed twenty), the remainder must pass to a qualified charity.

The tax consequences of a CRUT are as follows:

1. The donor gets an immediate income tax deduction. This deduction is the value of the CRUT remainder interest payable to charity.
2. The trust itself is a tax-exempt entity. Thus, any internal income or loss it generates (for example, interest and gains or losses from sales and exchanges) is not taxed to the trust. Distributions to the noncharitable beneficiary during the term of the trust, however, retain their character and may be taxable.
3. The creation of a CRUT results in a gift of the remainder interest to the charity.
4. If the donor transfers the noncharitable interest to someone else, gift tax may apply. If the income beneficiary is the donor's spouse (and a U.S. citizen), the gift qualifies for the unlimited gift tax marital deduction. If the income beneficiary is not the donor's spouse, the gift is taxable to the extent that it exceeds the annual exclusion.
5. If the donor is the sole income beneficiary for a term of years and survives the term, none of the trust property is includable in the donor's

gross estate. Likewise, if the donor transfers the noncharitable income interest to someone else, either for a term of years or for life, the value of the trust assets are not includable in the donor's estate. On the other hand, if the donor dies during the term of the trust or the trust lasts for the donor's lifetime, the code includes the property in the donor's gross estate, but with an offsetting estate tax charitable deduction. Inclusion in the donor's gross estate, with only a partial offsetting charitable deduction, occurs if the donor dies while receiving unitrust payments and there is an intervening noncharitable interest (that is, a second noncharitable income interest arises before the charity obtains its remainder).

NIMCRUT

A variation on the standard CRUT is the NIMCRUT, and the same transfer-tax rules apply to both. The sole difference between the two arrangements is that a NIMCRUT distributes the *lesser* of trust income or the unitrust amount. When trust income is less than the unitrust amount, a distribution buildup accrues. If the income of the trust *exceeds* the unitrust amount in subsequent years, the excess can be paid out to the extent of the aggregate distribution buildup.

Ordinarily, a NIMCRUT is packaged as a retirement planning technique particularly suited to clients who already have made maximum use of other tax-deferral vehicles. During the donor's working years, the NIMCRUT's investment orientation is generally slanted toward growth assets generating little current income. When the donor reaches retirement age, the trustee may change the investment orientation to income-generating assets, triggering the makeup provision. As an added benefit, if the donor is in a lower tax bracket than in preretirement years there will be overall tax savings.

Near-Zero CRUT

Although the near-zero CRUT and the NIMCRUT are conceptually quite similar, there are two significant differences:

1. Unlike the term of an ordinary NIMCRUT, which typically is for the donor's life, the term of a near-zero CRUT is bifurcated into a term of years to the donor, followed by a noncharitable beneficiary's interest for either a term of years or for that beneficiary's life.

2. Although both ultimately provide substantial benefits to charity, the underlying goals of the two instruments differ. A NIMCRUT is formulated to provide for the donor's retirement, while the near-zero CRUT is designed to pass wealth to a noncharitable beneficiary with as little transfer tax as possible.

The code sanctions both of these variations from the ordinary NIMCRUT. The length of payments from a charitable trust can be (1) "for life," (2) "for a term of years," or (3) a combination of the two. The second and third categories are the key to the near-zero CRUT. A term interest for the donor, perhaps five years, may be followed by another term interest for the donee, say ten years. As long as the two terms do not total more than twenty years, the trust qualifies as a CRUT. Furthermore, a life interest for the second noncharitable beneficiary may follow a term interest for the donor as long as that beneficiary is living when the near-zero CRUT is created.

As noted, the trustee of a NIMCRUT generally would manage the trust's investments with an objective of growth during the donor's working years and income in the donor's retirement years. The trustee of a near-zero CRUT would follow a parallel growth investment strategy during the donor's retained term, but switch investment strategies on the termination of the donor's interest. If the growth strategy is successful, the noncharitable beneficiary could come into a wealth of cash because of the makeup provision. Nevertheless, no additional gift tax would be due because the value of the taxable gift was fixed when the donor's initial contribution to the trust was made, as explained below.

The near-zero CRUT also normally contains a higher percentage payout than the usual unitrust. The higher percentage payout increases the value of the donor's retained interest, causing a corresponding reduction in the value of any gift to the noncharitable beneficiary. When that beneficiary's term commences, that same high unitrust percentage payout provides an opportunity for large gift-tax-free distributions. (Of course, the donor also has a much smaller charitable deduction, but that appears to be a small price to pay for the rather substantial transfer tax savings.)

Uses of Near-Zero CRUTs

A few detailed examples illustrate the actual mechanics of a near-zero CRUT. In each example, a 60-year-old father holds appreciated stock worth $1 million with a cost basis of $100,000. The stock pays an annual dividend of $2,000. Father establishes a near-zero CRUT that he funds with this stock, which will pay out annually the lesser of trust income or 25 percent of the FMV of the trust assets. Unless stated otherwise below, father retains the income for ten years, followed by a ten-year income interest vested in his son. On the termination of the trust after twenty years, the assets pass to a section 501(c)(3) charity.

If what is known as the applicable federal rate is 9.6 percent and the trust makes one annual payment at the end of the year, the transfer-tax results are as follows:

- On contribution of the stock on January 1 to the near-zero CRUT, the father has made simultaneous gifts to his son and the charity of $69,456 and $5,640, respectively.
- There would be an offsetting gift tax charitable deduction for the gift made to the charity, and the transfer of property to the son may be exempt from gift tax if the father had sufficient unused unified credit.

During the father's term, the trust continues to hold the stock. The trustee, therefore, pays the father $2,000 a year which is taxable to him. Meanwhile, each year a potential distribution buildup of $248,000 [(25 percent x $1,000,000) – $2,000] accrues-for a total of $2.48 million by the end of year ten.

Example 1: By the beginning of year eleven, the stock triples in value to $3 million and is sold. The proceeds are reinvested in a highly profitable real estate venture yielding 30 percent. For each of the next ten years the trustee of the near-zero CRUT must make a $900,000 payout to the son, consisting of a combination of the unitrust amount (25 percent of $3 million, or $750,000) and a part of the unused potential distribution buildup [$900,000 (that is, 30 percent of $3 million) less the $750,000 unitrust amount, or $10,000]. Over the son's ten-year term, $9 million is distributed to him. At the end of year twenty,

the trust terminates and $3 million of property passes to charity.

Example 2: The stock's value remains at $1 million by the beginning of year eleven. It is sold and the proceeds invested to yield 10 percent. The $100,000 annual income is distributed to the son, and the potential distribution buildup increases by $150,000 [that is, 25 percent of $1 million ($250,000) less the $100,000 payout]. Although this buildup is never used, the near zero CRUT still remains quite attractive—while a potential taxable gift of less than $70,000 was reported, the present value of the annual $100,000 payments of $249,968.

Example 3: The facts are the same as in Example 2, except the father's interest is followed by a life estate (rather than a ten-year term) in his 40-year-old son. The son reaches his life expectancy of age 82.5, thus collecting annual payments of $100,000 for thirty-two years (that is, from year eleven to year forty-two). On contributing the stock to the near-zero CRUT, the father has made simultaneous gifts to his son and the charity of $70,166 and $4,930, respectively. Again, there is an offsetting gift tax charitable deduction for the gift made to the charity, and the father can use his unified credit to shelter the gift to his son from tax. Thus, the son receives distributions totaling $3.2 million, with a present value of $394,342.

Potential Risks

Figure 63–1 compares the transfer-tax savings, assuming a 50 percent tax rate, resulting from each of the three above examples. These savings should outweigh the potential risks of using a near-zero CRUT.

The IRS could challenge the bona fides of the near-zero CRUT by claiming that it fails to meet the definition of charitable remainder trusts. With a near-zero CRUT that pays out the lesser of trust income or a fixed percentage of the trust assets, however, the charity receives at least the initial FMV of the trust corpus (unless the FMV of those assets declines). That the charity itself is a true benefactor of the near-zero CRUT under most, if not all, circumstances calls into question any purported "abuse" resulting from this planning.

What is the worst-case scenario if the IRS successfully challenges the bona fides of the plan?

Figure 63–1

Comparison of Tax Savings

	Present Values		
Example	Reportable Gift	Actual Gift	Tax Savings (assuming 50% tax rate)
1	$69,456	$2,249,914	$1,090,229
2	69,456	249,968	90,256
3	70,166	394,342	162,088

Aside from the costs of battling the IRS, the investment strategies of the near-zero CRUT might persuade a court to rule that the IRS tables are inappropriate for valuing the gifts to both the noncharitable and charitable donees. Thus, the donor would be deemed to have made larger gifts to both donees. The larger charitable gift would be sheltered by the charitable gift deduction, and the larger noncharitable gift would not generate any gift tax if the donor had a sufficient amount of unused unified credit.

Although such a challenge should not exceed, two measures can reduce exposure:

1. The donor should not serve as a trustee of the near-zero CRUT to diminish the risk that a court might find that the trust failed to qualify as a CRUT because the donor retained the power to affect or alter beneficial enjoyment of the distributions.
2. The annuity payout percentage should be in line with ordinary growth rates (for example, 10 percent to 15 percent, rather than 25 percent).

If the near-zero CRUT is properly structured, the IRS should not seriously threaten the tax benefits.

A more serious threat, however, may be the premature death of either the donor or the non-charitable beneficiary. If the donor dies while entitled to receive the unitrust payments, the FMV of the assets in the unitrust are includable in the donor's gross estate. Also, although the donor's estate should receive a restoration of the donor's unified credit, if any, expended when the contribution was made and a credit for any prior gift taxes paid, a large estate tax can still be generated. Despite this hazard, the donor would be in no worse position than if the gift had not been made and the property was instead distributed by a testamentary trust to the noncharitable donee.

Another and perhaps more serious problem arises if the noncharitable beneficiary dies prior to or shortly after the commencement of his life interest. In that event, the donor's transfer intentions are thwarted because the assets of the near-zero CRUT will flow directly to the charity rather than remaining inside the family unit. This risk may be avoided by giving the noncharitable beneficiary a term-of-years interest that follows the donor's term of years. That way, the advantages of the near-zero CRUT can still flow to the noncharitable beneficiary's estate during the second term.

Conclusion

As a planning device, the near-zero CRUT permits transfers to the next generation at minimal transfer tax cost, compared with other CRUTs that channel wealth only to the donor and charity. Potential IRS challenges appear limited by the code provisions that sanction the building blocks of this technique. For charitably minded donors in appropriate circumstances (that is, low-income appreciated assets with additional growth potential that can generate a distribution buildup inside the trust, and no need for additional current income themselves), this technique may accomplish several goals.

64
GRATS:
Sophisticated Estate Planning Alternative for Shifting Future Appreciation to Younger Generations

STEVE R. AKERS

The Grantor Retained Annuity Trust (GRAT) should be considered by the client who is looking for ways to transfer assets to a younger generation without having to pay federal gift taxes. For example, assume the client is already making the full amount of annual exclusion gifts available (that is, $10,000 per donee annually). Any additional gifts will use some of the client's lifetime "applicable exclusion amount" of $625,000 for 1998 (the exemption amount will be increasing to $1 million by the year 2006). Any gifts beyond that exempted amount will generate current federal gift taxes. Assume that the client has a $1 million stock portfolio that the client wants to transfer to children in 1998 so the future income and appreciation on the stock portfolio will not be subject to estate tax. If the client has not previously used any of his or her $625,000 "exemption equivalent amount," a gift of the $1 million stock portfolio will require paying a current gift tax of $143,750.

Alternatively, the client might transfer the $1 million stock portfolio to a GRAT. The trust agreement would provide that an annuity be paid annually to the client for a specified number of years. The planner could structure the amount and term of the annuity payments so that the actuarial value of the retained right to receive the payments, using the appropriate treasury valua-

tion tables, would be almost $1 million. The value of the retained annuity payments can be subtracted to determine the amount of the gift, as long as all the technical requirements of Section 2702 of the Internal Revenue Code are followed. Therefore, the amount of the gift would be nominal and any appreciation and income from the portfolio in excess of the annuity payments would be removed from the client's gross estate without the client making a substantial gift for federal gift tax purposes.

Example of Benefits

Assume a $1 million stock portfolio is transferred to a three-year GRAT by a 60-year-old individual in a month when the "Section 7520 rate" (the rate that is used by the IRS for determining the present value of annuities) is 6.8 percent. The GRAT could be structured to make three annuity payments to the donor as follows:

End of Year One	$ 315,410
End of Year Two	378,492
End of Year Three	454,190
Total Payments to Grantor	$1,148,092

The present value of the annuity, using a discount rate of 6.8 percent, is $999,998. If the stock pays annual dividends of $20,000, and if the stock market continues to have substantial gains and the stock grows at 25 percent per year, there would be about $594,000 remaining in the GRAT at the end of the three year term. The $594,000 amount could pass to the client's children or to

Steve R. Akers is a director of Ernst & Young Center for Family Wealth Planning.

trusts for the client's children. No gift or estate taxes would be payable on that $594,000 amount. The client would make a small gift when the trust is created of either (1) $1 million minus $999,998, or $2.00, or (2) under an approach urged by the IRS about $22,540 (because of the "example 5 problem" discussed below in the discussion about determining the amount of the taxable gift.) The net bottom line result would be that the client would have made a gift of, at most, $22,540 (which would not result in the payment of any current gift taxes, and would leave almost all of the client's "applicable exclusion amount" intact to shield estate taxes, and the client would have transferred almost $600,000 to his or her children after three years without paying any gift taxes or estate taxes.

General Description

A GRAT is an irrevocable trust designed to minimize the amount of gift that is made when the trust is initially created. The grantor would transfer stock (or other appreciation assets) to the irrevocable trust and retain an annuity interest for a specified term of years (such as, for example, three years) at the end of the specified term, any assets remaining in the trust could pass to the grantor's children (or to trusts for the children). No gift taxes or estate taxes would be due when the trust terminates.

How It Works

Typically, the GRAT is designed so that the present value of the annuity payments to the grantor equals the value of assets initially contributed to the GRAT. The present value is determined using the 7520 rate, which is the rate used by the IRS for valuing annuity interest. This rate changes each month. For example, if the rate is 6.8 percent, the annuity payments would be set at a level so that if the trust assets had combined appreciation and income of 6.8 percent per year, the trust would exactly run out of money when the last annuity payment was made back to the grantor. This means that if the assets appreciate at more than 6.8 percent per year (assuming that is the appropriate Section 7520 rate when the trust is created), the excess growth would remain in the trust to pass to the children without any gift or estate tax.

Caveats: Survival Requirement and GST Exemption

If the grantor dies before the end of the specified term of the GRAT, the IRS will take the position that all of the assets of the GRAT will be includable in the grantor's estate for federal estate tax purposes. Therefore, the grantor needs to survive the specified terms of years in order for the GRAT to "work" by removing the appreciated assets in the GRAT from the grantor's estate for federal estate tax purposes.

It is not possible for the grantor to allocate any of his or her GST exemption to this trust until the end of the stated term of the GRAT. Accordingly, if the assets remaining in the GRAT at the end of the specified term were to pass directly to the grantor's grandchildren, that transfer would be a generation-skipping transfer. If it cannot be fully covered by the grantor's $1 million GST exemption amount (which will be indexed for inflation in future years), GST taxes may be due when the GRAT terminates and passes to the grandchildren. Contrast this situation with a direct gift to a "standard irrevocable trust" that does not have donor-retained annuity payments. GST exemption can be allocated to that trust at the outset. Therefore, if all gifts to the "standard irrevocable trust" can be covered by the donor's available GST exemption, all future income and appreciation can pass to grandchildren or more remote descendants without the imposition of any generation-skipping transfer tax.

Determining Amount of Taxable Gift

The amount of gift is determined by subtracting the present value of the donor's retained annuity rights from the full value of property transferred to the GRAT.

In determining the present value of the retained annuity payments, the IRS takes the position that only the present value of payments that would be received during the grantor's lifetime, taking into account the actuarial likelihood that the grantor would survive to receive each payment, may be subtracted in determining the amount of the gift. The IRS' position is based on Treasury Regulation Section 25.2702-3(e), example 5. Under this approach, the amount of the taxable gift will increase as the age of the donor and the length of the GRAT term increases. The example discussed at the beginning of this article assumes that a three-year GRAT is created with $1 million of assets by a 60-year-old individual. The amount of the taxable gift, taking into account the actuarial likelihood that the donor will not receive each of the three annuity payments, is $22,540. If a six-year GRAT were used, the amount of the gift would increase to $51,484. If a ten-year GRAT were used, the amount of the gift would increase to $101,216. (This is the reason that short-term GRATs of approximately three years are typically used rather than longer term GRATs of ten to fifteen years.) Similarly, if the donor's age increases above age 60, the amount of the gift will also increase. If the donor is age 60, the amount of the gift is $22,540. If the donor is age 65, gift amount is $33,506. If the donor is age 75, the gift amount is $72,390.

One approach to reduce the GRAT taxable gift that was previously recognized by the IRS is to use a "revocable spousal contingent annuity." The trust document would provide that if the grantor dies during the specified term of the trust, the grantor's spouse would receive an annuity for a fixed term if the spouse is surviving at the grantor's death. The IRS previously ruled in a variety of letter rulings (for example, PLR 9449012, 9449013, 9451056, and 9353017) that the spouse's contingent interest was considered a qualified annuity interest, in accordance with Treasury Regulation Section 25.2702(a)(5) and (d)(2), example 7. Adding a "revocable spousal contingent annuity" significantly decreased the amount of the gift, because the retained annuity interest was valued for the term of the trust or the sooner death of *both* the grantor and the grantor's spouse. Taking into account two lives can dramatically reduce the amount of taxable gift that is generated when a GRAT is created, because the actuarial likelihood that two people will both die before the end of the specified term of the GRAT is very low. In the example discussed above, of a 60-year-old individual creating a three-year GRAT with $1 million, the amount of the gift is $22,540. If the donor's spouse is also age 60 and the revocable spousal contingent annuity is used and is recognized by the IRS to further reduce the value of the gift, the gift would be reduced to $709.

Unfortunately, the IRS has publicly changed its position on revocable spousal annuities, and now takes the position that they cannot reduce the size of the gift. Under the IRS current guidelines, the revocable spousal annuity will be ignored in determining the value of the retained annuity interest. The IRS has taken this approach in several rulings, including Technical Advice Memorandum 9707001.

Creative planners might attempt to reduce the amount of the gift produced when the GRAT is created by choosing an annuity payment amount that is greater than the level at which the trust property would exhaust itself at the end of the trust term, assuming a growth rate precisely equal to the IRS discount rate used to value the annuity. However, under Revenue Ruling 77-454 and Treasury Regulation Section 25.7520-3(b)(2)(i), if the trust would actuarially be exhausted before the end of the fixed term if the assets grow at the assumed discount rate, the annuity will be valued as though it were to be paid for the number of years and months prior to the point of exhaustion. Because of this position, planners do not typically set the annuity amount greater than the amount that would result in the present value of the annuity determined at the Section 7520 rate for the full specified term of the GRAT being equal to the amount contributed to the GRAT.

Income Tax Effects

The GRAT should be structured so that it is treated as a "grantor trust" for federal income tax purposes, at least during the term of the trust in which the donor has retained the right to receive annuity payments. If the trust is a "grantor trust," the grantor would be taxable on all of the income of the trust.

Under current law, the grantor's payment of tax on the GRAT income should not be considered income to the GRAT beneficiaries regardless of whether the grantor actually receives all the income the grantor is taxed on. However, in order to obtain a ruling on a GRAT from the IRS, the IRS insists that the trust contain a provision that reimburses the grantor for income taxes borne by the grantor with respect to income in excess of the annuity amount. The IRS suggested in Letter Ruling 9444033 that the failure to reimburse the grantor for taxes would be considered a gift by the grantor to the remaindermen. However, the

IRS subsequently reissued that ruling without that sentence.

Because the trust is a grantor trust, neither the donor nor the trust will recognize any gain or loss for income tax purposes as a result of any of the following:

- The donor's initial transfer of appreciated property to fund the trust;
- Transfer of appreciated property from the trust to the donor in satisfaction of any annuity payments; or
- Donor's purchase of appreciated property from the trust for cash or other property.

Furthermore, the payment of the annuity amount by the GRAT will not create additional taxable income for the grantor. (Instead, as discussed above, the grantor simply reports all income of the trust on the grantor's income tax return.)

There are several different techniques that are used to cause the GRAT to be a "grantor trust" for income tax purposes but still not treat the GRAT as being owned by the grantor for federal gift and estate tax purposes. For example, the grantor could be given a non-fiduciary power to reacquire trust corpus by substituting other property of an equivalent value, as described in Section 675(4)(c) of the Internal Revenue Code. (However, the IRS has taken the position in various recent rulings that whether the grantor holds the power in a *non-fiduciary capacity* for purposes of Section 675 is a question of fact, not to be determined by a letter ruling.) Several private letter rulings, including Letter Ruling 9642039, have ruled that a substitution power held in a non-fiduciary capacity would not cause the grantor to be treated as the owner of the trust for estate tax purposes. Another power that is sometimes used to cause the GRAT to be treated as a grantor trust is to give a nonadverse party (other than the grantor) a power to add beneficiaries (other than "after-born or after-adopted children"), as described in Section 674(a). For example, the power of a trustee to add charitable organizations as beneficiaries can cause the trust to be treated as a grantor trust for income tax purposes. Another method that can be used to assure that the trust is a grantor trust as to the income of the trust is to require that all of the GRAT income be distributed to the grantor even if the

income exceeds the amount of the annuity payments. As a practical matter, the annuity payments will almost always exceed the amount of the trust income, so inclusion of this clause typically would not require any additional amounts to be returned to the grantor. (However, the last method would not, by itself, also make the trust a grantor trust as to the corpus or principal of the trust.)

Planning Considerations

Formula Annuity Amount

The annuity amount may be defined by reference to a percentage of the originally contributed property. This substantially reduces the risks of any significant gift tax adjustment in a gift tax audit. A determination by the IRS that the property was undervalued will operate to increase the amount of the annuity payments and will not significantly increase the amount of the taxable gift.

Use Increasing Annuity Amount

The annuity amount may increase by 20 percent each year. Using an increasing annuity amount (as in the example at the beginning of this article) is generally desirable, because the highly appreciating assets are left in the GRAT as long as possible before having to be distributed to the grantor in satisfaction of the annuity payments.

Short-Term or Long-Term GRAT?

Using a short-term GRAT reduces the amount of the gift that results from taking into account the actuarial likelihood that the grantor will die before all of the annuity payments are received. Also, a shorter term reduces the chance that outstanding growth in the trust assets in the GRAT's early years will be diluted by sub-par performance later on. Finally, using a short term reduces the risk that the donor will die before the end of the specified term, thus causing all of the trust assets to be includable in the donor's estate for federal estate tax purposes. The IRS generally will not grant a favorable ruling on a GRAT for less than six years. However, there is nothing in the treasury regulations requiring that a GRAT be this long. The regulations may suggest that a GRAT must be in existence for at least two taxable years. GRATs are often structured to last from two to five years.

Separate GRAT for Each Asset

If a particular asset transferred to a GRAT does not produce sufficient income and growth to make all of the specified annuity payments, when there is no further value left in the GRAT, it would simply terminate for lack of any trust corpus. If other assets had been gifted to the same GRAT, the other assets would have to be used to make up the deficiencies. In order to avoid this result, it is best to use a separate GRAT for each individual asset so that poor performance results of one asset will not adversely affect the trust with respect to other assets.

Use with S Stock or Partnership Interests

If the GRAT is a grantor trust as to the entire trust for federal income tax purposes, the GRAT may be funded with stock of an S corporation. Furthermore, partnership interests may be contributed to a GRAT. A particular advantage of funding a GRAT with S corporation stock or a partnership interest is that the grantor would be taxable on a pro rata share of all income of the S corporation or partnership, thus reducing, to some extent, the net amount brought back into the grantor's estate by the annuity payments. In addition, cash can be distributed from the S corporation or partnership to each shareholder (including the GRAT) without dividend treatment.

Planning Considerations for Payment of Annuity Amounts

The GRAT will typically use any available cash first to make the required annuity payments. If the trust assets do not produce enough income or cash flow to pay the annuity amount, some of the trust assets could be distributed in kind in payment of the annuity amount each year. (As long as the trust is a grantor trust, such distributions will not result in taxable income for the trust or the beneficiary.) Some planners have questioned whether the GRAT can issue a note bearing interest at the applicable federal rate in satisfaction of the annuity payment. There appears to be no technical reason prohibiting the use of a note to

pay the annuity amount. However, the IRS is taking the position in Technical Advice Memorandums 9604005 and 9717008 that issuance of notes by GRAT in satisfaction of annuity payments is not recognized, and prevents the ability to reduce the amount of the taxable gift when the GRAT is created by the present value of the annuity payments. If property is distributed in kind in satisfaction of the annuity payments, it is important that valuation discounts be taken into consideration in determining the value of any minority or fractional interests distributed by the GRAT.

Selection of Trustee During GRAT Term

There are no restrictions preventing the grantor from serving as the trustee during the annuity payment period. The IRS takes the position that the entire trust corpus will be included in the grantor's estate in any event if death occurs during the trust term, so there is no added estate tax risk by having the grantor serve as trustee. If the GRAT relies solely on the non-fiduciary substitution power under Section 675(4) of the Internal Revenue Code, it may be a little clearer that the grantor holds that substitution power in a "non-fiduciary capacity" if the grantor is not serving as the trustee. If the property remains in trust for the benefit of children after the end of the annuity payment period, the grantor generally should not be the trustee during that continuing period of the trust. Furthermore, the grantor should not retain the power to vote any stock in the trust that is stock in a "controlled corporation" as described in Section 2036(b) of the Internal Revenue Code.

Summary

The GRAT is a sophisticated estate planning technique that involves a significant degree of tax planning and structuring. However, it is a very powerful planning technique for the client who wants to transfer much of the future appreciation from a highly appreciating asset without making a large current gift for federal gift tax purposes.

65
Roth IRAs:
Estate and Income Tax
Planning Tool for the 21st Century

STEPHEN P. MAGOWAN

The Roth IRA is perhaps the best piece of "relief" in the Taxpayer Relief Act of 1997 (TRA '97). A Roth IRA differs from a traditional IRA in many respects, most importantly in that contributions to a Roth IRA are not tax deductible and that qualified distributions from a Roth IRA are not taxable to the recipient. In creating the Roth IRA, Congress gave taxpayers within a certain income range the opportunity to convert traditional IRAs to Roth IRAs but, in such a conversion, taxpayers must pay income tax on the full value of the traditional IRA, generally for the year of conversion. Accordingly, clients considering a conversion must determine whether the Roth IRA benefits of tax-free qualified distributions and lack of required minimum distributions outweigh the tax triggered by the conversion. The conversion question is more compelling in 1998 because, as described below, Congress created an income tax incentive for 1998 conversions.

A consensus appears to have emerged among financial advisers and the popular press that taxpayers who are younger than age 50 are the most likely to benefit from converting a traditional IRA to a Roth IRA. In at least three situations, however, a client older than 50 should consider converting his or her traditional IRA to a Roth IRA as a way to save estate taxes and create increased estate planning flexibility. These situations most generally will occur when:

- a client has passed his or her required begin-

ning date (RBD) but has failed to designate a beneficiary for his or her traditional IRA;
- a client's designated beneficiary, usually a spouse, has died after the client has passed his or her RBD; or
- a spouse has inherited a traditional IRA and will have a taxable estate.

This chapter examines when a client should consider converting a traditional IRA to a Roth IRA, even though the holder would not generally benefit from such a conversion, and demonstrates that a conversion to a Roth IRA offers an excellent planning opportunity for elderly clients with large IRA assets to move their IRA assets to their descendants in a tax-efficient manner.

Differences Between Roth IRAs and Traditional IRAs

The key differences between a Roth IRA and a traditional IRA are:

- Contributions to a Roth IRA are not tax deductible, regardless of the account owner's income.
- Distributions from a Roth IRA are not taxed if the owner keeps the funds in the IRA for the period required under the statute and if the owner takes only "qualified distributions" from the IRA.

Code Section 408A(d). The maximum contribution to all Roth IRAs and traditional IRAs a person with compensation income can make for any taxable year is $2,000. Code Section 408A(c)(2). A person can mix and match contributions, however, such as $1,000 to a traditional IRA and $1,000

Stephen P. Magowan is a lawyer with the law firm of Gravel and Shea in Burlington, Vermont, where he concentrates on estate, pension, and compensation planning.

to a Roth IRA. Congress phased out the $2,000 amount for married couples filing joint returns with incomes from $150,000 to $160,000 and for single filers with incomes from $95,000 to $110,000. No additional restrictions apply to persons who participate in tax-qualified retirement plans. Thus, if a Roth IRA owner and his or her spouse jointly earn $130,000 a year and are both active participants in a qualified plan, they could each contribute $2,000 to a Roth IRA.

These Roth IRA rules differ significantly from traditional IRA rules. A person can deduct a contribution to a traditional IRA if he or she does not participate in a tax-qualified plan or if he or she participates in a tax-qualified plan and his or her income does not exceed certain levels. The precise nature of these rules is not critical to this article and will not be examined further.

Roth IRA Distribution Rules

Two key general rules govern distributions from a Roth IRA. First, the Code Section 401(a)(9) minimum distribution rules do not apply to the owner of the Roth IRA. Accordingly, the owner need not take distributions from the IRA beginning on April 1 of the calendar year following the year he or she reaches age 70½. The minimum distribution rules *only* apply to a Roth IRA after the owner dies, and even then they can be postponed by a spouse (but no other beneficiary) who inherits the Roth IRA and elects to treat it as his or her own.

Second, the Roth IRA owner or his or her successors pay no federal income tax on a "qualified distribution." A "qualified distribution" is any payment or distribution:

- made on or after the date on which the owner reaches age 59½;
- made to a beneficiary (or to the estate of the owner) on or after the death of the owner;
- attributable to the owner being disabled; or
- that is a qualified "special purpose distribution."

Code Section 408A(d)(2). Under these rules, a beneficiary, such as a spouse, child or grandchild, will pay no federal income tax on distributions from the Roth IRA after the owner's death.

A payment or distribution is not a qualified distribution if made within the five-taxable-years period beginning with the first taxable year for which the individual made a contribution to a Roth IRA. Note, however, that the code treats the owner as having withdrawn his or her contributions—which were already taxed—first on a "first-in, first-out" approach. Code Section 408A(d)(1)(B). Thus, the owner of a Roth IRA who has contributed $10,000 to the IRA can always withdraw up to that amount tax free.

Problems with Estate Planning for Traditional IRAs

A traditional IRA often complicates estate planning, primarily because a traditional IRA is an item of income in respect of a decedent (IRD). As a result, the assets of the IRA are subject to both estate tax and income tax on the owner's death. How does this happen?

Assume, for example, that a client leaves 100 shares of Bigco stock to her daughter. The client bought these shares for a total of $1 per share, and the client's total basis in the shares equals $100. Assume also that at the client's death the shares are trading at $100 per share, and that the daughter sold all of the shares for $10,000 six months after the client died. Under income tax rules, the daughter's basis for calculating gain on the sale would be the value of the shares at client's death, that is, $100 times 100 or $10,000. Code Section 1014. Thus, the daughter would have paid no income tax when she sold the shares in the above example. If the daughter sold the shares for $110 per share, she would pay capital gains tax on the difference between $110 and $100, or $10, multiplied by the number of shares sold.

Assets in a traditional IRA, however, do not enjoy the benefit of a new basis on the owner's death. Assume that instead of leaving Bigco shares to her daughter, the client left a $10,000 traditional IRA to her daughter and that six months after the client's death, the daughter withdrew all the funds from the traditional IRA to pay for funeral and related expenses. In this instance, the daughter would have to pay income tax on the full $10,000 at ordinary income tax rates.

The daughter may have the benefit of an income tax deduction equal to the amount by which the inclusion of the IRA assets in her mother's estate increased the federal estate tax on the estate. Code Section 691(c). Because this is an income tax deduction and not a tax credit, it will not reduce the income tax dollar-for-dollar for each estate tax dollar paid. Thus, the assets passing from a traditional IRA to the owner's beneficiary are subject to both estate and income tax. As a result, the ultimate amount passing to the owner's beneficiary will be greatly reduced because the estate tax is as high as 55 percent and the federal income tax is as high as 39.6 percent. State death taxes and income taxes may further increase the tax burden.

Benefits of the Roth IRA in Estate Planning

A Roth IRA is very different from a traditional IRA because no federal income tax applies to "qualifying distributions" from a Roth IRA. Thus, after the owner's death, the assets of his or her Roth IRA will be subject only to estate tax, not income tax. This places Roth IRA assets on the same playing field as capital assets. In fact, the Roth IRA is superior to a capital asset because the post-death appreciation in the Roth IRA is never subject to income tax, while post-death appreciation in a capital asset is subject to federal income tax on the sale of the asset.

Consider the previous example. If the Bigco stock doubles to $20,000, the daughter will have to pay tax on a $10,000 capital gain if she sells the stock. If, however, the traditional IRA were a Roth IRA, and if the Roth IRA assets doubled to $20,000, the daughter would pay no income taxes if she sold the assets and liquidated the account.

This income tax exemption is very valuable. For example, assume that a client leaves a $100,000 Roth IRA to a 27-year-old beneficiary. Assume also that the IRA earns a total return of 8 percent free of income tax, that all distributions from the IRA earn an after-tax total return of 5.76 percent and that the 27-year-old lives until age 83. When the beneficiary reaches age 83, the Roth IRA assets, plus the after-tax investment account, would equal $4,744,471. Using the same assumptions, a traditional IRA, plus the after-tax investment account, would be worth about $2 million less because the distributions to the beneficiary would be taxable when he or she received them, and these taxes would increase as his or her minimum required distributions increased.

These differences become even more remarkable when the analysis uses younger beneficiaries and larger account numbers. A Roth IRA of $150,000 left to a 7-year-old beneficiary, under the same earnings and investment assumptions, would be worth more than $25 million when the beneficiary reached age 83. A $150,000 traditional IRA for the same 7-year-old would be worth "only" about $14 million when the beneficiary reached age 83 because, as the beneficiary's minimum required distributions increased, the income taxes on those distributions would go up.

Although these examples may be extreme, they show that at any given point, amounts sitting in a Roth IRA are available for college expenses, housing costs, and other qualified expenses on a tax-free basis. Thus $20,000 in a Roth IRA buys $20,000 worth of educational expense, not some other after-tax amount.

Conversion of Traditional IRAs

One way out of the conundrum posed by the IRD rules for a client with a large traditional IRA is to convert it to a Roth IRA. When the client makes the conversion, income tax will result. For instance, if a client converts a $100,000 traditional IRA to a Roth IRA, he or she would have to pay income tax on $100,000.

Not all clients can convert traditional IRAs to Roth IRAs. Only clients whose adjusted gross income for the taxable year of a conversion is $100,000 or less can make the conversion. The income from the conversion does not count in determining the limit. Further, a married client who files a separate return may not make a rollover contribution.

Rollover contributions are not subject to the 10 percent excise tax of Code Section 72(t) or the $2,000 annual limitation on contributions to a Roth IRA. Moreover, TRA '97 has another benefit for eligible taxpayers making the conversion in 1998. For rollovers in calendar year 1998, any amount required to be included in gross income is included ratably over the four taxable year period (that is, one-quarter is included each year) beginning with the tax-able year in which the payment or distribution is made. As a result, clients can defer paying the tax on the traditional IRA without paying any interest on the deferred tax.

The Planning Opportunity

Estate planning lawyers should review the possibility of converting a traditional IRA to a Roth IRA with many of their elderly clients. In particular, lawyers should pay attention to single clients who have their own IRAs with significant assets. In many instances these clients will have named a spouse as primary beneficiary and elected to recalculate life expectancies to determine their required minimum distributions. For these clients, the potential for a high amount of estate and income tax after death is significant.

To understand the planning possibilities, consider the following example. A 77-year-old client owns a $600,000 traditional IRA and $600,000 in other estate taxable assets. The client's spouse died two years before, when the client was 75, after the client's RBD. The client had named the spouse as beneficiary of the traditional IRA. The client and the spouse were recalculating their life expectancies for minimum required distribution purposes. The client's income is expected to be about $60,000 for 1998. After the spouse's death, the client cannot name a new younger beneficiary to restart the required minimum distribution clock. In fact, because the client and his or her spouse were recalculating life expectancies, the client's IRA must be distributed by the end of the calendar year following the year of the client's death.

Should this client consider converting his traditional IRA to a Roth IRA? Yes. If the client did nothing and died in 2002 owning the same assets, assuming no growth, the client would have a taxable estate of $500,000 ($1.2 million less the $700,000 exemption available in 2002). The client's estate would be subject to an estate tax of approximately $155,800. Also, under Code Section 401(a)(9), the client's traditional IRA would have to be distributed about one year after the client's death and would be subject to an additional $200,000 in income taxes, taking the Code Section 691(c) credit for estate tax on the IRA into account. The total tax cost to the client's estate would be $355,800.

What if the client had converted his or her traditional IRA to a Roth IRA in 1998? The client would have to pay approximately $300,000 in income taxes over four years, subject to adjustment for state income taxes. If the client died in 2002, he or she would have a taxable estate of $200,000 ($900,000 less $700,000 exemption equivalent) subject to an estate tax of approximately $54,800. Thus, the client's total taxes over the period would be $354,800, or about the same as if he or she had kept the traditional IRA.

If the client had converted, however, further distributions from the client's new Roth IRA would not be subject to income tax after the client's death. In addition, once the client converted the traditional IRA, he or she could stop taking minimum distributions during his or her lifetime. Finally, the client could also name new beneficiaries of the Roth IRA after the conversion, perhaps setting aside the account for his or her grandchildren's use in trust for education.

This could be an extraordinarily valuable opportunity for a client. Return to the example of a $150,000 Roth IRA left to a 7-year-old, with the same earnings assumptions described above. In that case, the beneficiary could take out $45,000 a year for his or her eight college and graduate school years and take $200,000 out when he or she turned 34 for a housing deposit, in each case from both the Roth IRA and the "after-tax" investment account. When the beneficiary reached age 75, the grandchild's Roth IRA and after-tax account would total more than $1 million.

All in all, a client's loved ones could benefit from careful and professional consideration of the idea of converting a traditional IRA to a Roth IRA and paying some income taxes up front over four years or, after 1998, one year, rather than waiting until later. Moreover, a client's beneficiaries would have a powerful nontaxable savings account from which to draw for college expenses, home buying, and other expected expenses.

Which clients should consider converting? Any client with a large taxable estate and a large traditional IRA should seriously review the option. Paying the income taxes early will remove the assets used to pay the tax from the client's estate and the conversion will create planning flexibility. Clients who earlier may have considered drawing out a traditional IRA to avoid the IRD rules, and then using the money to purchase life insurance, should also review the Roth IRA option. A client who has passed his or her RBD but failed to name a designated beneficiary for a traditional IRA should also consider converting it to a Roth IRA. Finally, if a client's designated beneficiary dies after the client passes his or her RBD, converting a traditional IRA to a Roth IRA will allow the client to choose new beneficiaries who will be able to use their own life expectancies for the required distributions after the client's death.

Dealing with the Income Limit

Lawyers considering whether their clients should convert traditional IRAs to Roth IRAs will need to review with their clients how to keep their income below the $100,000 limit for the year of the conversion. Of course, this may not be possible. Nevertheless, the client may have the ability to defer income into later years if, for example, he or she owns shares of a dividend-paying close corporation or if he or she has discretion about whether to take income out of a trust set up by his or her spouse. A surviving spouse might also consider converting any stepped-up assets to municipal bonds for a year and then restructuring the investments after year-end to have a more balanced portfolio. By doing this, the client might bring adjusted gross income below $100,000 for the year in question.

Conclusion

Estate planning lawyers should view the Roth IRA as a new weapon in the arsenal for reducing taxes and increasing planning flexibility. Although this is a complicated area of law with many intricate rules, in many situations a conversion of a traditional IRA to a Roth IRA can make considerable sense.

66

Use of the Private Annuity and Self-Cancelling Installment Note in Estate Planning

HERBERT L. ZUCKERMAN AND JAY A. SOLED

In the development of a lawyer's estate, if he or she has prospered and invested wisely, there may come a time when he or she may wish to reduce transfer taxes by assigning estate assets to a younger generation at minimal transfer-tax expense, but retain an income stream for a term of years or for life. Suppose the lawyer is already engaged in an annual gift-giving program, has created irrevocable insurance trusts, and has a will that makes maximum use of the unified credit, the generation-skipping transfer-tax exemption, and the marital deduction. Are there any less traditional techniques for furthering estate planning objectives by reducing death and transfer taxes?

This chapter explores the opportunity to use two devices, the self-cancelling installment note (SCIN) and the private annuity. The goal of both is to transfer appreciating assets out of a taxable estate at little or no transfer tax and, at the same time, to provide an income stream for retirement.

The Basics

SCIN

In an ordinary installment sale that is not self-cancelling, the buyer purchases property using a note calling for periodic payments that are not dependent upon the seller surviving the note's term. The buyer (or maker of the note) satisfies

Herbert L. Zuckerman is a partner at the law firm of Sills Cummis Zuckerman Radin Tischman Epstein & Gross, P.A., in Newark, New Jersey. Jay A. Soled is a lawyer and an assistant professor at Rutgers University in Newark, New Jersey.

his or her obligation under the note when it is paid in full. Should the seller die before the note is fully paid, the seller's estate (or successors, heirs, and assigns) is, of course, entitled to the note and to the payments made thereon. On the seller's estate tax return, the present value of the remaining installment payments would be fully included in the seller's gross estate and would be exposed to estate tax rates currently as high as 55 percent.

If there is a cancellation feature in the installment note by which the maker of the note is relieved of further liability upon the seller's death, the United States Tax Court has ruled that there is no fair-market value to the note for transfer-tax purposes. It ceases to have any value at the moment of the seller's death since there are no monies due to the seller, his or her estate, or his or her heirs. It is this cancellation feature that unlocks estate planning opportunities.

A SCIN obligates a buyer to make payments for the shorter of the payment term or the seller's life. As long as the fixed payment term is less than the life expectancy of the seller at the time of the sale, the transaction will be characterized as an installment sale with a contingent sales price. However, if the fixed payment term is longer than the seller's life expectancy at the time of the sale, the structure cannot be a SCIN; instead, it will be characterized as a private annuity.

The cancellation feature is of obvious value to the buyer. The negotiating of this feature into the note represents an enhancement to the deal, representing a potentially taxable transfer by the seller to the buyer were a premium not charged. Because the seller wants to avoid making a taxable gift to the buyer, he or she must charge the buyer a premium for the note's cancellation feature. This premium is necessary to reflect the seller's additional risk in possibly failing to recoup the full fair-market value of the item sold in the event that he or she dies before receiving all payments. In the absence of a premium (either in a higher sales price, higher interest rate, or both), the Internal Revenue Service could and probably would contend that the seller has engaged in a part sale/part gift with the buyer at the time of the exchange.

Determining the exact amount of the premium the seller should charge can be a complicated task. It depends on the age of the seller and the actuarial likelihood that he or she will survive the note's maturity. As noted, the premium itself can be reflected in an upward adjustment of the purchase price, the interest rate charged, or a combination of both. The services of an actuary or specially designed computer software can be invaluable in determining the premium.

Private Annuity

In a commercial setting, one can purchase an annuity from an insurance company that will pay proceeds to the annuitant during his or her lifetime. Assuming it is a straight annuity and not a term-certain or a refund annuity, at the annuitant's death, the annuity is extinguished and is not includable in the annuitant's gross estate.

The tax treatment of a private annuity corresponds with that of a commercial annuity. The twist with a private annuity is that the annuity is not issued by an organization that normally issues annuities. Instead, in a typical case, a member of one's family purchases property from an elder member, issuing in return a note or other undertaking in the form of an annuity obligation.

As with the case of a SCIN, the seller of property to a family member in return for an annuity has to be alert to the possibility of the transaction being treated as a direct or indirect gift. Unlike the SCIN situation, in which a premium for the self-cancelling feature must be exacted in order to avoid a taxable gift, in the private annuity context, the present value of the future annuity payments must equal the fair-market value of the property transferred on the date of sale. If the present value of the annuity is less than the fair-market value of the property, then the seller has

made a taxable gift at the time of transfer equal to this difference. To illustrate, suppose a 65-year-old mother, with a life expectancy of twenty years under the IRS's mortality tables, transfers a painting with a fair-market value of $100,000 to her son for a $10,000 annual annuity. If the present value of the annuity is $97,500, then the mother has made a taxable gift to her son of the difference between $100,000 and $97,500, or $2,500.

Advantages and Disadvantages

Assuming the seller has sold property to a member of the younger generation of the family in return for a SCIN or a private annuity, the advantages to the seller and his or her estate are obvious. First and most important is the fact that the seller has removed the transferred property (and its subsequent appreciation) from his or her taxable estate; under no circumstances will the property sold be subject to estate tax. Second, the seller will receive a fixed sum of money for a term of years (in the case of SCIN) or for the remainder of his or her lifetime (in the case of a private annuity), obviously facilitating or enriching the seller's retirement. Finally, since the buyer is presumably a family member, the property transferred remains under family control, opening the opportunity for the younger generation to manage the property while the seller is still available to render sage advice.

However, the disadvantages of SCINs and private annuities cannot be ignored. First, in the case of a SCIN, should the seller survive the entire term of the note, there may be minimal estate tax savings in light of the seller's recoupment of the entire purchase price of the property sold and the SCIN premium. Likewise, in the case of the private annuity, should the superannuated transferor-seller outlive his or her life expectancy, the buyer may pay more than originally bargained for. Second, in both the SCIN or private annuity context, to the extent that the seller cannot consume the installment or annuity payments, his or her taxable estate will correspondingly grow. Third, the buyer may have a difficult time making installment or annuity payments, especially if the property itself is an asset, such as undeveloped land, that does not produce income, and, in the case of a private annuity, in the event that the buyer defaults, the seller's only recourse is to sue for recovery as an unsecured creditor. This is due to the tax law requirement that a private annuity be unsecured. Finally, if the seller dies prematurely, in the case of a SCIN, the unrealized gain, if any, on the property sold must be included on the seller's estate income tax return; in the case of the private annuity, though there is no inclusion on the seller's estate income tax return of the unrealized gain, the buyer's tax basis is reduced from fair-market value on the date of sale to the amount of the annuity payments to date.

Income Tax Consequences

Aside from the gift and estate tax consequences of a SCIN or a private annuity, both the buyer and seller should also consider the income tax implications of both of these estate-planning techniques.

SCIN

*Income Tax Consequences
for the Seller*

Because a SCIN meets the requirements of being an installment note, the seller may use the installment method to report income. Under the installment method, each payment the seller receives (in addition to interest payments on the outstanding balance of the principal due, which is subject to tax as ordinary income) must be separated into two components: return of basis and gain (capital gain if the property sold is a capital asset).

This bifurcation process is accomplished by first determining the gross profit ratio, which is equal to the seller's gain (the difference between the sales price less adjusted basis) over the sales price. This ratio is then multiplied by each payment to determine the taxable gain. The difference between the payment and the taxable gain represents the seller's nontaxable return of basis.

On the seller's death, any deferred gain on the sale of the property must be included on the seller's estate income tax return.

*Income Tax Consequences
for the Buyer*

The buyer includes the face amount of the note as his or her basis in the purchased property, which is not adjusted even if the seller dies before the note's maturity. In addition, the interest portion of the SCIN payment is deductible, subject to normal deductibility limitations under the Internal Revenue Code (for example, if the purchased property is investment in nature, the buyer must have sufficient investment income to use the interest expense).

Private Annuity

*Income Tax Consequences
for the Seller*

In general, transferring property in exchange for a private annuity of equal value does not trigger immediate income tax consequences. This deferral of tax, however, does not mean its elimination: each annuity payment must be broken into three components: (1) a return of basis of the property transferred; (2) capital gain; and (3) annuity income.

To calculate the return-of-basis portion of an annual annuity payment, the seller must determine the exclusion ratio. This ratio is equal to the seller's investment in the contract—his or her adjusted basis in the property transferred—divided by the expected return (annual annuity payments multiplied by the seller's life expectancy). Once determined, each annuity payment is multiplied by this ratio, and the resulting product is the seller's nontaxable return of basis.

To calculate the capital gain portion of an annual annuity payment, the seller divides the gain attributable to the transfer—the difference between the present value of the private annuity contract and the seller's adjusted basis in the property—by his or her life expectancy in years at the time of transfer. This portion of each payment will be subject to capital gain rather than ordinary income tax rates, assuming the property sold is a capital asset or is treated as a capital asset (for example, Section 1231 property). Finally, in order to calculate the ordinary annuity income portion, the seller simply subtracts the sum of the return-of-basis component and the capital gain component from the annuity payment.

When and if the seller recovers all of his or her basis and capital gain by attaining his or her life expectancy (determined at the time of the initial property transfer), then both of these components of the annuity payment are merged and become ordinary annuity income. On the other hand, if the seller dies prematurely, the decedent is entitled to a loss on his or her final income tax return for the unrecovered basis in the private annuity contract.

*Income Tax Consequences
for the Buyer*

The buyer receives a basis in the purchased property equal to its fair-market value (assuming the present value of the annuity does not reflect any donative element). Once total payments exceed fair-market value, the buyer's basis will increase thereafter corresponding to each additional annuity payment. Conversely, should the seller die before this break-even point (that is, where payments equal the fair-market value of the property), his or her basis will be reduced to the accumulation of annuity payments to date, less any depreciation deductions taken with respect to the property.

In contrast to a SCIN arrangement, the buyer may not deduct any portion of his or her annuity payment as an interest expense.

Comparison

An example illustrates the mechanics of a SCIN and a private annuity. Suppose a father, age 75, with a life expectancy of twelve-and-a-half years (as determined under IRS actuary tables), purchased investment real estate in 1985 for $200,000, and it is currently worth $500,000. He has already exhausted his unified credit in the form of large taxable gifts, and he now wishes to transfer his investment real estate to his daughter, because he anticipates that the property will greatly appreciate over the course of the next few years, and he does not want the property to be includable in his gross estate. He can opt to use either a SCIN or a private annuity to accomplish all of his goals. Even for those who are not too number-oriented, the calculations presented are straightforward.

SCIN

With the aid of a computer software program or an actuary, the father is able to determine the SCIN premium amount (reflecting the cancellation feature in the note) to be $40,000. He transfers title to the property to his daughter, who, in return, gives her father a SCIN with a ten-year term and a face value of $540,000 containing an annual payment schedule of $54,000. Assume further that the SCIN bears interest of 7 percent (the amount, using the IRS monthly tables, that will not be considered below-market and, consequently, not be considered a gift).

The gross profit ratio is equal to 62.96 percent, or the amount of gain ($540,000 less $200,000) over the purchase price ($540,000). Therefore, $34,000 of each payment (62.96 percent of the $54,000 annual payment) is subject to capital gains tax on the father's income tax return, and the remaining $20,000 ($54,000 less $34,000) constitutes a nontaxable return of the father's basis. The 7 percent interest payment the father receives is subject to tax as ordinary income on the father's income tax return (for example, in the first year, the outstanding balance of the note, $540,000, generates $37,800 of taxable income—$540,000 times 7 percent).

Meanwhile, during the SCIN term, the daughter can deduct her interest payments as investment interest expense (subject to Internal Revenue Code limitations), and her basis in the real estate would equal $540,000.

Private Annuity

With the aid of tables provided by the IRS, given the father's age and the current applicable federal interest rate (which we assume to be 7 percent), one can determine the annual annuity to be $75,987.84. This annuity in conjunction with the father's life expectancy produces an overall expected return of $949,848. The exclusion ratio is equal to the father's investment ($200,000) over the expected return ($949,848), or 21.056 percent. What this means is that $16,000 (21.056 percent of $75,987.84) of every annuity payment represents the father's nontaxable return of basis. The capital gain portion of each annuity payment is equal to the gain or the sale of the property ($300,000) over the father's expected life span (twelve-and-a-half years), which is equal to $24,000. The remaining $35,987.84 ($75,987.84 less $16,000 less $24,000) represents annuity income and is subject to tax as ordinary income. Should the father live beyond age 87½, any additional payment would be subject to tax as ordinary income; on the other hand, should the father not attain age 87½, on his final income tax return, his executors could take a loss for his unrecovered basis in the annuity contract.

During the father's life, while the daughter makes her annuity payments, she is precluded from deducting any portion of the annuity payment as an interest expense. Her initial basis in the property is equal to $500,000, but it would be subject to adjustment depending on when her father passes away.

Figure 66–1 facilitates comprehension of SCIN and private annuity dynamics.

Figure 66–1

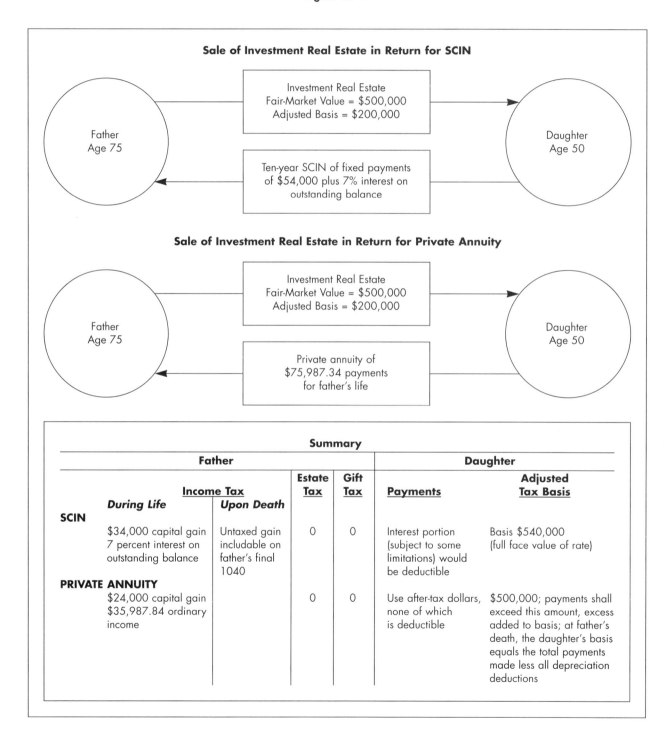

Sale of Investment Real Estate in Return for SCIN

Father
Age 75

Investment Real Estate
Fair-Market Value = $500,000
Adjusted Basis = $200,000

Daughter
Age 50

Ten-year SCIN of fixed payments
of $54,000 plus 7% interest on
outstanding balance

Sale of Investment Real Estate in Return for Private Annuity

Father
Age 75

Investment Real Estate
Fair-Market Value = $500,000
Adjusted Basis = $200,000

Daughter
Age 50

Private annuity of
$75,987.34 payments
for father's life

	Father				Daughter	
	Income Tax		**Estate Tax**	**Gift Tax**	**Payments**	**Adjusted Tax Basis**
	During Life	*Upon Death*				
SCIN	$34,000 capital gain 7 percent interest on outstanding balance	Untaxed gain includable on father's final 1040	0	0	Interest portion (subject to some limitations) would be deductible	Basis $540,000 (full face value of rate)
PRIVATE ANNUITY	$24,000 capital gain $35,987.84 ordinary income		0	0	Use after-tax dollars, none of which is deductible	$500,000; payments shall exceed this amount, excess added to basis; at father's death, the daughter's basis equals the total payments made less all depreciation deductions

Summary

The tax savings realized through a SCIN or a private annuity can be substantial. In the examples just cited, suppose (1) that the father were to die one year after the date of sale, and (2) that the investment real estate appreciated in that same year by 20 percent, to a fair-market value of $600,000. In the case of a SCIN, the father is able to rid his estate of a $600,000 asset and receives in return a payment of $94,800 ($54,000 installment payment plus 7 percent interest on the unpaid balance of $540,000), netting him an estate tax savings of $252,600 (the difference between $600,000 and $94,800 times an assumed effective estate tax rate of 50 percent). In the case of a private annuity, the savings are even more dramatic: the father is able to rid his estate of the same $600,000 asset and receives in return a payment of $75,987.84, netting him an estate tax savings of $262,006 (the difference between $600,000 and $75,987.84 times an assumed effective estate tax rate of 50 percent).

On the father's final income tax return, his executors would report $37,800 in interest with respect to the SCIN and $24,000 of capital gain plus $35,987.84 in ordinary income with respect to the private annuity. In addition, with respect to the SCIN, the father's executors would also report $340,000 of capital gain on the estate's income tax return.

As should be self-evident, the estate tax savings may be further enhanced to the extent that the father consumes the installment or annuity payments made to him by his daughter and/or the investment real estate appreciates further in value.

Conclusion

Unlike grantor-retained income trusts, grantor-retained annuity trusts, and grantor-retained unitrusts (discussed elsewhere in the book), which depend on the longevity of the client, both the SCIN and the private annuity work most advantageously for the individual who is in ill health or who, given his or her present age, is not expected to survive a certain number of years or reach his or her normal life span. The IRS has ruled, however, that the valuation and actuarial tables necessary to implement SCINs and private annuities may *not* be used where death is "clearly imminent." Where death though is not "clearly imminent," the advantage of a SCIN or a private annuity is that death annuls all obligations for future payments; the installment or annuity obligation is deemed valueless and therefore not includable on the seller's estate tax return.

Consternation on the part of the buyer is certainly a likely by-product if the seller surprisingly regains health or just "hangs on." The seller's longer-than-expected life means the buyer remains obligated to make payments well beyond the anticipated installment or annuity time period. At the same time, the seller's taxable estate grows correspondingly, waiting for the day of reckoning when it will ultimately be subject to estate tax.

67
Adding Names to Bank Accounts

RICHARD V. WELLMAN

Aided by funding provided by the American Association of Retired Persons (AARP), the Wills, Probate and Trust Committee, Senior Lawyers Division, ABA, developed a pamphlet describing the advantages and disadvantages of joint and other forms of money accounts naming two or more persons with interests in the deposit. The project followed a survey showing that banks rarely advertise or explain available multiple-name account options. This finding helped observers realize that some effort should be made, possibly by lawyers working through state and local bar associations, to generate more consumer-friendly information for depositors interested in adding names to their deposit accounts.

The information in this chapter, made up of portions of the AARP-SLD pamphlet and subsequent drafting efforts, should be helpful in all parts of the country to reduce consumer confusion about joint accounts and litigation attributable to this confusion.

The Joint Account

Joint accounts are the oldest, most familiar, and most troublesome type of multiple-name account. A joint account names two or more individuals as account owners (referred to here as "parties"). Each is entitled to the entire account balance. Each party has full control of the account, without regard to whose money was deposited in the account or whether the deposi-

tor is alive or deceased, competent or incompetent, or agrees with the purpose of a withdrawal. Ownership between the parties is a matter with which the bank has *no* concern (other than as a possible witness). Indeed, ownership is important only when one party withdraws money from a joint account in excess of sums he or she deposited *and the other party objects*.

Thus, the bank will not be directly involved in ownership disputes between joint account parties and their successors, including the probate estate of a deceased party. Persons involved in these disputes frequently are forced to compromise because of difficulty in determining the exact amounts to which each is entitled as between the parties. These amounts depend on who made deposits into the account, the intentions of those making the deposits, interest earned, and the purpose and application of withdrawals.

If a joint account includes survivorship, the ownership interest of a party who dies ends and passes by survivorship to the other party. This transfer at death occurs outside the probate process, even though the question of survivorship may require a court determination. See the text below under the heading "Questionable Survivorship." For now, simply note that each party to a joint account agreement has the power to *withdraw* from the account *before or after* the death of any other party, *even if survivorship is not part of the deposit contract*. A party who withdraws more than his or her ownership interest owes the excess to the other party or that party's estate, but litigation may be required to enforce the obligation. A bank may decline a withdrawal request if it is notified by a party or a party's estate that another party's withdrawal would be wrongful, but the bank is not required to do so.

Richard V. Wellman is professor of law, emeritus, at the University of Georgia School of Law, Athens, Georgia, and chair of the ABA's Senior Lawyers Division Wills, Probate and Trusts Committee.

Advantages of Joint Accounts

The joint account is an all-purpose financial management tool that serves several objectives.

Probate Avoidance

If survivorship is part of the joint account (it normally is, but *not always*), a party's interest in the account balance at death passes outside probate to the surviving owners. Survivorship cannot be prevented by the deceased party's will because a will controls probate assets only and a deceased party's interest in a joint and survivor account is not part of the decedent's probate estate when survivorship applies. Avoiding probate does *not* mean avoidance of federal and state taxes on transfers of property at death, however, so this benefit only avoids any cost or delay of probate, which can be minimal.

Access on Party's Incompetence or Disability

The funds in a joint account are not frozen when a party loses the ability to handle banking matters. No durable power of attorney or guardianship is necessary to access the funds in a joint account if another party is willing and able to transact with the bank.

Financial Partnership

Happily married couples and others in comparable personal relationships often want to commingle funds because it is convenient and reflects the trust they have in each other. A joint account suits these persons because each is willing to risk any loss caused by the other's activities and wants the account to belong to the other in the event of death.

The Dangers of Joint Accounts

Joint accounts also involve risks that lead well-informed advisors to discourage this account form and recommend other alternatives that offer the same benefits with reduced risks. These alternatives are described following more elaboration about the perils of joint accounts.

Risk of Loss

Each joint account party may take the money and run. Even if a depositor's trust is not misplaced,

joint deposit contracts routinely enable the bank to seize the entire account balance to recover money owed it by *either* party. For example, a depositing party's money in a joint account can be taken from the joint account by the bank to repay an earlier or a subsequent bank loan to the other party even though the depositing party knew nothing about the loan and was unaware of the deposit contract provision putting his or her money at risk. The debtor would be obligated to repay the depositing party the amount taken for the debt, but the debtor may not be good for the money. This risk may be acceptable to couples who expect to share financial rewards and risks, but may be terrifying to others.

Questionable Survivorship

Some joint account forms do not mention the survivorship feature that avoids probate when a party dies. Examples include an account payable to "A or B," an account payable to "A and B as joint tenants," and an account payable to "A and B." In a few states, if no express mention of survivorship appears in the deposit contract, a joint account deposit creates an arrangement without survivorship commonly referred to as a "tenants in common" account. In most other states, the opposite rule applies and survivorship is a part of a joint account unless the deposit contract specifies that the parties are "tenants in common" or otherwise expressly *rejects* survivorship.

If survivorship is not a part of the joint account, a party's death is likely to precipitate a squabble between the surviving party and the probate estate of the decedent over the size of each party's share. These disputes are difficult to resolve unless careful records of deposits, interest, and withdrawals are available.

There also is the significant risk of survivorship rights that were unintended and attributable to depositor confusion. For example, consider the following case:

> Mary died recently, leaving a will giving her entire estate in equal shares to her closest relatives, her five nieces and nephews. One niece (Amanda) lived in Mary's community. The other four lived in other states.
>
> A few weeks before her unexpected death, Mary sold her house and deposited the proceeds in her savings account. The account was in Mary's sole name when she signed her will, but a year or so

before her death Mary signed a new account agreement setting up a joint account with Amanda. The account remained in this joint form after the real estate sale and until her death.

Amanda claims the entire balance of the account. Indeed, shortly after Mary's death, Amanda closed the joint account and moved the money into an account in her own name. If her claim is valid, Amanda will keep the money from Mary's account *and* receive one-fifth of Mary's other assets passing through probate.

Mary's case raises many questions. Why did Mary establish the joint account? Would she have deposited the proceeds from the property sale in the account if she had known that Amanda could claim the account balance despite the provisions in Mary's will? Is it possible that Mary only wanted a dual *signature* arrangement on her account to enable Amanda to help Mary with financial matters if she became disabled? Was Mary aware that ownership was involved or did she merely request that Amanda's name be added to her account? Did Mary just accept the form offered by the bank without knowing about the legalities involved? Indeed, was Mary aware that the bank offered other arrangements that would have authorized Amanda to draw on the account without having owner rights? How can these important questions be answered now that Mary is gone?

Cases like this can invite bitter feelings, litigation, and results that are unsatisfactory to all concerned. Thousands of cases have litigated post-death disputes involving survivorship rights in joint accounts. The typical theory urged in these cases is that the deceased party was unaware of the survivorship feature and opened the joint account solely to authorize an assistant to access the account in case of emergency or disability.

Limited Purpose Multiple-Name Accounts

Given the uncertainties and risks implicit in joint accounts, persons should be interested in alternative account forms that offer joint account advantages but avoid joint account risks. Joint accounts may be desirable to (1) assure access to funds in spite of a depositor's loss of capacity; (2) transfer the account balance at death via the survivorship right avoiding probate; and (3) permit full commingling of funds by persons in close

relationships who trust each other. Years ago, persons who wanted only some of these features had to choose between all or none because the joint account was the only multiple-name account offered.

The good news is that most banking institutions now offer two basic alternatives to the joint account that meet the needs of most persons interested in less than all features of a conventional joint account. One is an account describing the depositor's selection of a beneficiary who is entitled *only* to balances in the account at the depositor's death. The other is a dual access account naming a person who will be recognized by the bank as the depositor's agent with authority to access the account for the depositor but who is not intended to have a beneficial interest in account balances immediately or at the depositor's death.

Death Beneficiary Only Account

Two account forms enable a depositor to retain sole ownership and control of an account that designates beneficiaries who receive the account by a nonprobate transfer at the depositor's death. One is known as a pay on death (p.o.d.) account. The other, called a trust account or "Totten" trust, takes the form of an account in the name of the depositor who is described as "trustee" for, or as holding "in trust for," the person named as beneficiary. For example, a p.o.d. account title would appear as "John Q. Owens, p.o.d. Nancy Owens." A trust account title would appear as "John Q. Owens, trustee for Nancy Owens."

Both forms signal that the depositor (John Q. Owens) has sole ownership and control of the account. The person designated to take at the depositor's death (Nancy Owens) is merely a death beneficiary who need not sign the deposit form when the account is established and acquires no rights until the depositor's death. If not previously terminated, either form passes funds in the account at the depositor's death to the beneficiary, in each case free of any delay and expense of probate. The depositor may change or terminate the arrangement at any time and the beneficiary need not even know of the account. Although depositors with death-beneficiary-only accounts should inform the beneficiary to apply to the bank for payment after the depositor's death (because banks normally do not assume responsibility for notifying account beneficiaries of their rights), the depositor can leave these instructions in a will or other document to be read after death.

In effect, these death-beneficiary-only accounts function like wills: they provide a revocable death benefit for the beneficiary of whatever is in the account at the depositor's death, but they differ from wills because they need not be probated or handled by an estate administrator (and may not be subject to other rules that apply to wills and probate estate property). Note, too, that the death beneficiary designation in these accounts usually cannot be changed by the depositor's will. If the depositor decides to eliminate or change the death benefit provision, he or she needs to contact the bank or credit union and sign a new account contract. If the beneficiary dies before the depositor, the account will remain the property of the depositor and, unless changed or closed, will be included in the depositor's probate estate to be controlled by a will if there is one.

A p.o.d. or trust account beneficiary designation probably can be added to a joint and survivor account title for added flexibility. For example, a married couple might want a joint and survivor account that, unless changed by either or the survivor, will take effect at the death of the survivor of them to pass the account on to a designated beneficiary. This combination would describe the couple as joint and survivor owners followed by p.o.d. (or in trust for) beneficiaries.

The Agency Account

A single owner account that can be accessed by a second person acting as an assistant of the sole owner is available everywhere though described by names that differ from state to state. This type of account offers the convenience of the dual access feature of a joint account but avoids the risk of loss to creditors of the assistant and the risk of an undesired survivorship benefit for the assistant.

One form serving this purpose is a single owner account that designates another person as an "additional authorized signatory" with authority under the deposit agreement to act for the owner. Another is an account in which the owner shares authority to access account balances with another person described in the account as the owner's "agent," or as authorized to act by the owner-depositor's "power of attorney." In some states, the term "convenience account" is used to refer to this arrangement.

Some banking companies may insist on an accompanying "power of attorney" document incident to opening an agency account, and some may also insist that the power of attorney document be provided by the depositor and be satisfactory to bank personnel. More commonly, power of attorney language will be included in the forms to be completed when an agency account is opened.

Authority to access an owner's account as the owner's "assistant," "agent," or "additional authorized signatory," ends when the owner gives written notice to the bank or credit union of revocation of the agency, or removes the additional authorized signatory's name from the account. This authority also ends when a bank or credit union receives notice of the owner's death. Sums remaining on deposit at that time belong to the deceased owner's probate

Most banks will recognize that the same person may be designated as the depositor's agent *and*, by an additional signal, as a death beneficiary. For example, an account might be entitled: "Owner: Randolph Jones. Additional authorized signatory: Randolph Jones, II: p.o.d. Randolph Jones, II, and Betty Jane Jones." This form offers the advantage of dual access during the depositor's lifetime, freedom from risk of loss to the son's creditors during the father's life, and a nonprobate transfer at father's death with no need to favor the one beneficiary who was his father's agent to handle account business.

Some Concluding Advice

1. Do not select a joint account unless you are comfortable with the risks of loss through the co-depositor's acts or carelessness,(and intend that the other become sole owner on your death.

2. If your primary interest is merely in transferring the account balance at your death, choose the p.o.d. beneficiary designation and have the account list you as sole owner, with or without another also listed as a banking assistant.

433

3. Unless otherwise bound by private contract with the account owner, a person you name as account death beneficiary may do as he or she pleases with money withdrawn from the account at your death. If you are counting on that person using the money for a special purpose (such as for funeral expenses, or to divide with others), consult a lawyer about a trust agreement that the p.o.d. beneficiary should be asked to sign.

4. Do not select the joint account simply to get the convenience of giving another person authority to access your account. Ask for an authorized additional signatory form, an agency account, a power of attorney arrangement or whatever your bank or credit union offers that does *not* involve survivorship, *and* offers you the standby assistant, non-coowner arrangement that you desire.

A Statutory Form Aiding Account Selection

A model state statute designed for enactment by all states encourages banking institutions to offer depositors a menu of available multiple-name accounts. This menu is reprinted here to illustrate what you may encounter when opening an account (see Figure 67–1). This information will help you ask the right questions when you consider a multiple-name account, or wish to discuss the topic with your advisors.

Figure 67–1

Uniform Single- or Multiple-Party Account Form

PARTIES [Name one or more parties]

_____   _____

OWNERSHIP [Select one and initial]:

____ SINGLE-PARTY ACCOUNT

____ MULTIPLE-PARTY ACCOUNT

Parties own account in proportion to net contributions unless there is clear and convincing evidence of a different intent.

RIGHTS AT DEATH [select one and initial]

____ SINGLE-PARTY ACCOUNT

At death of party, ownership passes as part of party's estate.

____ SINGLE-PARTY ACCOUNT WITH P.O.D. DESIGNATION

[Name one or more beneficiaries]:

_____   _____

At death of party, ownership passes to P.O.D. beneficiaries and is not part of party's estate.

____ MULTIPLE-PARTY ACCOUNT WITH RIGHT OF SURVIVORSHIP

At death of party, ownership passes to surviving parties.

____ MULTIPLE-PARTY ACCOUNT WITH RIGHT OF SURVIVORSHIP AND P.O.D. DESIGNATION

[Name one or more beneficiaries]:

_____   _____

At death of last surviving party, ownership passes to P.O.D. beneficiaries and is not part of last surviving party's estate.

____ MULTIPLE-PARTY ACCOUNT WITHOUT RIGHT OF SURVIVORSHIP

At death of party, deceased party's ownership passes as part of deceased party's estate.

AGENCY (POWER OF ATTORNEY) DESIGNATION [optional]

Agents may make account transactions for parties but have no ownership or rights at death unless named as P.O.D. beneficiaries.

[To add agency designation to account, name one or more agents]:

_____   _____

[Select One And Initial]:

____ AGENCY DESIGNATION SURVIVES DISABILITY OR INCAPACITY OF PARTIES

____ AGENCY DESIGNATION TERMINATES ON DISABILITY OR INCAPACITY OF PARTIES

68
Billion Dollar Babies: Annual Exclusion Gifts to Minors

BRADLEY E.S. FOGEL

One ubiquitous issue in estate planning is how to provide for young children—frequently, the client's children or grandchildren. If the client is willing to make lifetime gifts for the benefit of the child, then the client can make use of the federal gift tax annual exclusion to transfer substantial sums to the child free of gift or estate tax. The federal gift tax annual exclusion allows a donor to give up to $10,000 to any individual in any calendar year free of gift tax. Code Section 2503(b). If the donor is married and the spouse consents to splitting the gift, then $20,000 may be transferred free of gift tax each year. Code Section 2513. Congress indexed these amounts for inflation beginning in 1999. Code Section 2503(b)(2).

This is a powerful technique. For example, if a donor and her spouse were to transfer $20,000 to a child on the day he was born and on every subsequent birthday until the child reached age 18, then at age 18 the child would have received about $750,000, assuming a 7 percent net annual return. At age 21, the child would have almost $1 million.

A problem arises because the federal gift tax annual exclusion is not available if the gift is of a "future interest" in property. Treas. Reg. Section 25.2503-3(a). Thus, to make use of the annual exclusion, the donor must give to the donee a present interest in property, such as outright ownership. Treas. Reg. Section 25.2503-3(b). This requirement is particularly problematic when the gift is made to a minor. For obvious reasons most donors do not wish to give minors substantial outright gifts. Certain devices, however, allow a donor to make gifts that qualify for the annual

exclusion to a child while still allowing the gifts to be managed for the minor by a custodian or trustee.

This chapter describes three of these devices and the tax rules associated with them. The chapter first addresses gifts to a custodian for a minor under a uniform gifts or transfers to minors act; then considers the "2503(c) Trust," which is, not surprisingly, permitted by Code Section 2503(c); and concludes with a discussion of trusts with *Crummey* withdrawal powers.

Minors Acts

All states and the District of Columbia have some form of the Uniform Gifts to Minors Act or Uniform Transfers to Minors Act, which this chapter collectively refers to as "Minors Acts." Gifts to a custodian under a Minors Act qualify for the federal gift tax annual exclusion. Rev. Rul. 59-357, 1959-2 C.B. 212; Rev. Rul. 56-86, 1956-1 C.B. 449.

The forerunner of the Minors Acts was the "Act Concerning Gifts of Securities to Minors," sponsored by the New York Stock Exchange and the Association of Stock Exchange firms in the 1950s. In 1965 the National Conference of Commissioners on Uniform State Laws (NCCUSL) adopted the Uniform Gifts to Minors Act (UGMA). The UGMA broadened the earlier act by allowing custodial accounts to cover gifts of money as well as securities. In 1983 NCCUSL updated the UGMA and renamed it the Uniform Transfers to Minors Act (UTMA). One of the most significant changes that NCCUSL made in the UTMA was to expand the scope of property that a custodian could hold in a custodial account to include any property, real or personal, tangible or intangible. UTMA Section 1. In contrast, the UGMA allowed custodial accounts for only secu-

Bradley E.S. Fogel is a visiting assistant professor at Widener University School of Law in Harrisburg, Pennsylvania.

rities, life insurance policies, annuity contracts, and cash. UGMA Section 1(e).

It is well settled that gifts to a Minors Act custodian qualify for the federal gift tax annual exclusion. Rev. Rul. 59-357; Rev. Rul. 56-86. Thus, gifts of $10,000 (or $20,000 if the donor is married and his or her spouse elects to split gifts) to the minor in a custodial account will qualify for the federal gift tax annual exclusion.

Minors Act custodial accounts are, in many ways, statutory trusts. The custodian of the account, who may be any person, including the donor or trust company, holds property for the benefit of the minor. The custodian has the power to pay any property in the account ("custodial property") to or for the benefit of the minor. UGMA Section 4(d); UTMA Section 14(a). Neither the UGMA nor the UTMA distinguishes between the income from and the corpus of the custodial property. Both the UGMA and UTMA provide that a court may compel a custodian to distribute to custodial property.

Generally, the custodianship will terminate when the minor attains age 18 or 21, depending on the state. UGMA Section 4(d); UTMA Section 20; D.C. Stat. Section 21-230 (age 18); La. R.S. 9:770 (age 18); Pa. Stat. Section 5320 (age 21); N.Y. EPTL Sections 7-6.20, 7-6.21 (generally age 21; age 18 under some circumstances). California's version of the UTMA is unique in that it allows the donor to specify that the custodian will hold the property until the beneficiary reaches age 25. Cal. Prob. Code Section 3920.5. When the beneficiary reaches the designated age, the custodian must distribute the custodial assets outright to the beneficiary. If the beneficiary dies before reaching the designated age, the custodian must pay the property to the beneficiary's estate.

The class of eligible custodians is relatively broad. The donor, the minor's parents, another adult, or a trust company may act as custodian. If the donor acts as custodian, however, the custodial property will be included in the donor's gross estate for federal estate tax purposes if he or she dies before termination of the custodianship. Code Section 2038; Rev. Rul. 70-348, 1970-2 C.B 193. If the custodian has a legal obligation to support the minor, such as a parent, then if the custodian dies before the termination of the custodianship, the IRS may argue that the parent's gross estate will include the custodial assets.

Gen. Counsel Memo. 37840. Nevertheless, to avoid the issue (and possible litigation with the IRS) the donor should select a person other than the parent as custodian. As discussed below, in light of the fact that donors frequently create custodianships without benefit of advice of counsel, the donor may be unaware of the estate tax ramifications of his or her choice as custodian.

An important benefit of a custodial gift is its simplicity. To create a custodial account, the donor simply transfers the property to a custodian under the applicable act. UGMA Section 2; UTMA Section 9. Because of this simplicity, donors frequently create a custodianship without the assistance of a lawyer. The simplicity of a custodianship, however, has side effects. No substantial body of precedent exists concerning the legal rights and duties of a custodianship under a Minors Act, which may lead to uncertainty. See, for example, *In the Matter of Levy*, 412 N.Y.S.2d 285, 287 (Sur. Ct. Nassau Cty. 1978) (noting that the "paucity of cases" is indicative of the success of UGMA in creating a simple method for making gifts to minors). Moreover, some courts in custodianship cases have refused to draw analogies from the more developed body of precedent regarding trusts and trustees, which exacerbates this problem. *Id.* This uncertainty may make custodianships inappropriate for substantial gifts or gifts of property that may be more difficult to administer, such as partnership interests.

A custodial gift indefeasibly vests the custodial property in the minor. In contrast, trust beneficiaries have only a beneficial interest in trust property. One significant result of this indefeasible ownership is that the IRS does not recognize a custodial account as a separate taxpayer and taxes the income from the custodial assets to the minor. Rev. Rul. 56-484, 1956-2 C.B. 23. If the minor is under age 14, the "kiddie tax" rules may tax income at the parents' marginal tax rates. See Code Section 1(g).

The taxation of the income directly to the minor has both positive and negative aspects. The custodian does not need to file a separate tax return for custodial property. By contrast, if a trustee held the property, the trustee would be required to file a federal income tax return, subject to relatively minor exceptions. Moreover, considering the complexities of trust income taxation, it is unlikely that an individual would be able to properly complete the necessary tax returns for the trust.

On balance, the lack of a requirement for a separate income tax return is, at most, a relatively minor benefit of a custodianship. If, however, the value of the custodial property is small, the lack of a separate tax return may tip the balance in favor of the custodianship. An added advantage is that federal individual income tax rates are, as a general rule, more progressive than the federal fiduciary income tax rates. See Code Section 1. For this reason, the fact that the code taxes the income directly to the minor, as opposed to taxing it to a fiduciary with higher marginal rates, may provide an income tax savings. Of course, whether or not a custodianship results in income tax savings depends on the income earned, the minor's income tax brackets, the minor's parents' income tax brackets, and the hypothetical trust.

Applicable state statutes set the terms of a custodianship, and donors generally cannot vary those terms. For example, Minors Acts dictate:

- the number of custodians that may serve (one);
- the mechanism of the appointment of successor custodians (the current custodian may appoint a successor);
- whether the custodian is required to give a bond (generally not);
- the permissible investments for the custodial property (generally very broad); and
- compensation to the custodian (UTMA provides for reasonable compensation).

For the most part, NCCUSL and state legislatures have drafted Minors Acts with terms that will be acceptable to most donors. The donor is unlikely to be interested in deviating from the terms of the Minors Act merely for the purpose of, for example, requiring the custodian to give a bond. Some Minors Act provisions, however, are likely to be quite distasteful to a donor.

The last significant drawback to a custodianship is that the custodian must distribute the custodial property to the minor at age 18 or 21, depending on the state. This requirement may be acceptable to a donor if the value of the custodial property at that time is expected to be relatively small. If, however, the donor plans to make frequent annual exclusion gifts to a minor via a custodian, the value of custodial property distributed to the beneficiary when he or she reaches the age of majority may be significant. If so, the donor will likely be interested in a gift-giving device that will allow the donor to ensure that the minor will use the substantial sums the donor gives to the minor to pay for the minor's college tuition, rather than a Caribbean extravaganza. A partial answer to this concern may be the use of a minor's exclusion trust or *Crummey* trust.

2503(c) Trusts

A "2503(c)" trust is a trust that meets the requirements of Code Section 2503(c). Gifts to a minor's exclusion trust allow a donor to make gifts to a minor in trust and receive the benefit of the federal gift tax annual exclusion. Code Section 2503(c) imposes three requirements for a 2503(c) trust. The first is that the trust instrument permit the trustee to expend the trust assets for the benefit of the minor. Code Section 2503(c)(1). A trust will meet these requirements if the trust instrument allows the trustee to make wholly discretionary distributions to or for the benefit of the minor.

If, however, the trust instrument places substantial restrictions on the exercise of the trustee's discretion to make distributions, the trust will not qualify as a 2503(c) trust. Treas. Reg. Section 25.2503-4(b)(1). For example, in Revenue Ruling 69-345, 1969-1 C.B. 226, the IRS ruled that a trust that required the trustee to consider other assets available to the minor in determining whether to make distributions did not qualify as a 2503(c) trust. The IRS reasoned that the minor's parents as well as the minor had substantial other assets available, making distributions from the trust unlikely in light of the requirement to consider other assets.

Some restrictions on the trustee's discretion will pass muster with the IRS. In Revenue Ruling 67-270, 1969-2 C.B. 349, the IRS ruled that a trust instrument may limit a trustee's discretion by a standard that has no objective limitation, such as "welfare," "happiness," or "convenience" without running afoul of Code Section 2503(c). More limited standards, such as health or education, may, however, be too restrictive. For example, in *Mueller v. United States*, 1969 WL 20748 (IRS 1969), the IRS argued that a trust that directed the trustee to make distributions as necessary for "support, health, and education" of the beneficiary did not qualify as a 2503(c) trust because of the restriction. The tax court held for the taxpayer only after concluding that the standard was comparable to the standard used for a guardian under Missouri law. *Id.*

Therefore, although a trust that places more restrictive standards on the trustee's ability to make distributions to the minor may qualify as a 2503(c) trust, the safer course seems to be to provide the trustee with unfettered discretion or, at the very least, to include words such as "comfort" or "welfare" in the standard in reliance on Revenue Ruling 67-270.

The second requirement is that if a minor dies before age 21 (when the trust terminates), then the trustee must pay the trust assets to the minor's estate or as the minor appoints pursuant to a general power of appointment. Code Section 2503(c)(2)(B). The purpose of this requirement is to include the trust assets in the minor's gross estate if he or she dies before termination of the trust. Code Sections 2033, 2041. The power of appointment may be exercisable either by will or inter vivos. Treas. Reg. Section 25.2503-4(b). The trust instrument must place no "restrictions of substance" on the donee's exercise of the power. The fact that a legal disability (such as minority) may prevent the donee from exercising the power does not, however, prevent the trust from qualifying as a 2503(c) trust. Treas. Reg. Section 25.2503-4(b).

The third, and most problematic, requirement for a minor's exclusion trust is that the principal and income of the trust must pass to the donee on attaining age 21. Code Section 2503(c)(2)(A). Clients may hesitate to transfer substantial assets to a trust, the assets of which will be distributed to a minor beneficiary outright when he or she reaches age 21. This is similar to the problem discussed above for custodianships. When a minor reaches age 21, the assets of a 2503(c) trust may have considerable value. Consequently, the donor will likely be anxious to find a way to prevent the young donee from squandering his or her windfall.

The most common way to address this problem is to provide in the trust instrument that the beneficiary may elect to continue the trust or provide in the trust instrument that the trust will continue unless the beneficiary elects to terminate it. The regulations expressly provide that the trust will not fail to qualify as a 2503(c) trust merely because "[t]he donee, upon reaching age twenty-one, has the right to extend the term of the trust." Treas. Reg. Section 25.2503-4(b)(2). Thus, the trust instrument may allow the beneficiary to elect to continue the trust. The regulations, however, do not address a trust that continues unless the beneficiary elects to terminate it. For the most part, donors will probably not be satisfied with this option. Rather, donors generally prefer that the trust terminate only if the beneficiary affirmatively elects to terminate it.

In Revenue Ruling 60-218, 1960-1 C.B. 378, the IRS considered a trust that provided that, unless the beneficiary elected to terminate the trust after his 21st birthday, the trust would continue until he reached age 33. The IRS ruled that "[a] power conferred, as in the instant case, upon a donee to require immediate distribution of the property to him upon attaining the age of twenty-one years does not meet the statutory requirement [of Code Section 2503(c)] that the property must pass to [the beneficiary] upon attaining the age of twenty-one years." In Revenue Ruling 74-43, 1974-1 C.B. 285, however, the IRS revoked Revenue Ruling 60-218 and held that a trust may qualify as a minor's exclusion trust if the beneficiary, on reaching age 21, has the right for a limited period of time to terminate the trust. The IRS has privately approved a trust provision allowing a beneficiary to elect to terminate the trust within sixty days of his or her 21st birthday. PLR 8817037. See also PLR 8334071 (ninety days). Drawing an analogy from the context of *Crummey* powers, discussed below, a termination power that lasts only thirty days may also pass muster. See PLR 9232013, PLR 9030005, PLR 8922062.

No published authority requires a trustee to notify the beneficiary of his or her power to terminate the trust. If, however, the trustee does not so notify the beneficiary, the IRS may argue that the beneficiary's power of termination was illusory by analogy to situations involving trustees' failure to notify *Crummey* power holders of their powers. See Rev. Rul. 81-7, 1981-1 C.B. 474; TAM 9532001. Thus, the trust would not qualify as a minor's exclusion trust and the IRS could deny the annual exclusion for gifts to the trust. Considering this potential cost, the trust instrument should require the trustee to provide the beneficiary with notice of his or her right to terminate the trust when he or she reaches age 21.

Regardless of whether the trustee gives the beneficiary notice of the right to terminate the trust at age 21, a 2503(c) trust that gives the beneficiary only a temporary right to terminate the trust is likely to be much more attractive to the donor than a trust that requires outright distribution at age 21. As discussed above, a common concern of clients considering 2503(c) trusts or other devices for making gifts to minors is the risk that the minor beneficiary may squander the assets if he or she receives the assets outright at an early age. A 2503(c) trust that continues unless the beneficiary elects to terminate it significantly alleviates that risk. Even if the trust principal is substantial, it is likely that the donor and other members of the donee's family will be able to exert subtle familial pressure on the beneficiary to prevent him or her from exercising his withdrawal power. Moreover, human nature and the laws of inertia being what they are, and considering the fact that the beneficiary must take the initiative and affirmatively act to terminate the trust, it seems likely that the beneficiary would allow the trust to continue beyond age 21.

The donor, however, should be aware that for a period after the beneficiary reaches age 21, probably at least thirty to sixty days, the beneficiary must have an unfettered opportunity to terminate the trust. The donor may decide to run that risk, sensing that the beneficiary will be unlikely to exercise this power, thus allowing annual exclusion gifts to remain in trust until the donee reaches a more suitable age. Nevertheless, the donor must realize that, if the trust assets are substantial, it may be difficult to persuade the beneficiary not to exercise the termination power. This is particularly true if some family disharmony has transpired since the creation of the trust. Further, the donor must decide to give the beneficiary a termination power when the donor establishes the trust, when the donee is quite young. For these reasons, many donors are uncomfortable with the fact that the beneficiary will have the right, on reaching age 21, to terminate the trust and receive a potentially very substantial amount of assets outright.

Transfer-tax reasons tend to restrict the choice of a trustee of a 2503(c) trust in a manner similar to the restrictions on the choice of a custodian. If the donor serves as trustee of a 2503(c) trust and dies before termination of the trust, the donor's gross estate will include the trust assets because of the donor's ability to make discretionary distributions of the trust assets. Code Section 2038; Rev. Rul. 59-357, 1959-2 C.B. 212. In addition, as discussed above, the IRS believes that a similar result will occur if the trustee is a parent or other individual who has a legal obligation to support the beneficiary. Code Section 2041. Thus, neither the parent of the beneficiary nor the donor should serve as trustee of a 2503(c) trust. The minor's parent, however, could serve as cotrustee without adverse transfer-tax consequences, provided that the trust instrument gives the nonparent trustee the power to make distributions that might satisfy the parent's legal obligation. This option is not available in the context of custodianships because only one custodian may act.

Crummey Trusts

Gifts to a trust other than a 2503(c) trust generally do not qualify for the federal gift tax annual exclusion. Treas. Reg. Section 25.2503-3(a). If, however, the trust instrument provides that a beneficiary has a presently exercisable right to withdraw property transferred to the trust, the IRS will consider the gift to the trust to be a gift of a present interest and will allow an annual exclusion for the gift. These powers are known as "*Crummey* powers," based on the seminal Ninth Circuit case that approved the use of a withdrawal power held by a minor to create a present interest that qualified for the annual exclusion. *Crummey v. Commissioner*, 397 F.2d 82 (9th Cir. 1968).

A *Crummey* power works relatively simply. After a donor makes a gift to the trust, the beneficiary has a period of time, generally at least thirty days, to withdraw the assets of the trust with a value equal to the gift. See PLR 9232013, PLR 9030005, PLR 8922062. If the beneficiary does not withdraw the gift within the allotted time, the *Crummey* power lapses and the gift stays in trust. This thirty-day window, however, makes the gift to the trust a present interest for gift tax purposes, thereby allowing the donor to take advantage of the federal gift tax annual exclusion.

An important advantage of *Crummey* trusts over minor's exclusion trusts or custodianships is their versatility. After the *Crummey* power lapses, the trust may continue as long as the donor wishes, subject only to any applicable rule against perpetuities. The donor also has great flexibility regarding the other terms of the trust. For example, the trust could provide that before age 35 the trustee may make distributions of income and principal only for the beneficiary's school tuition. This flexibility, however, comes at a cost of the added administrative complexity of *Crummey* trusts as compared to 2503(c) trusts or custodianships.

If the donor is married, he or she may transfer up to $20,000 per beneficiary to the *Crummey* trust each year free of gift tax, provided the donor's spouse elects to split gifts with the donor on a timely filed federal gift tax return. In most cases, the beneficiaries will not exercise *Crummey* powers and will allow them to lapse. If a power to withdraw more than $5,000 (or 5 percent of the trust principal, if greater) lapses, then the excess is deemed a taxable gift made by the beneficiary to the other beneficiaries of the trust. Code Section 2514(e). For example, if a beneficiary allows a $20,000 *Crummey* withdrawal power to lapse, he or she may be deemed to have made a $15,000 taxable gift.

Some lawyers simply ignore the potential taxable gift resulting from the lapse of a *Crummey* power. These lawyers reason that, although the taxable gift will use some of the beneficiary's unified credit, gift and estate taxes are unlikely to become a serious issue for the beneficiary for many years. Thus, the argument goes, it is unwise to plan for the estate tax owed by the beneficiary's estate when it is possible or even likely that there may be no (or a very different) estate tax payable at that time. Further, if the minor beneficiary died at a relatively young age, it is unlikely that his or her estate would owe death taxes due to the unified credit.

A second approach is to prepare the trust instrument so that no person other than the beneficiary has an interest in the trust. In this situation, the fact that the beneficiary allows a *Crummey* power to lapse will not result in a taxable gift because the only possible gift made is by the beneficiary to himself or herself. To accomplish this result, the trust instrument should provide that the trustee may make distributions from the trust only to the beneficiary. If the beneficiary dies before termination of the trust, the trust instrument should direct the trustee to pay the trust principal to the beneficiary's estate or as the

beneficiary appoints under a general or nongeneral power of appointment. If the donor is worried that the beneficiary may exercise the power of appointment in an inadvisable manner, the trust instrument can, for example, limit the class of potential appointees or make the power exercisable only with the consent of a nonadverse third party.

It is important to note that a *Crummey* trust drafted so that no individual other than the minor beneficiary has an interest in the trust still gives the donor substantially more leeway to choose the terms of the trust than either a custodianship or a 2503(c) trust. Particularly, the requirement that the assets held in a 2503(c) trust be paid to the beneficiary's estate (if he or she dies before termination of a trust) or be expended for the minor's benefit during his or her lifetime, would alone eliminate any other party's interest in a *Crummey* trust. Thus, lapse of a *Crummey* power over such a trust bears no adverse gift consequences to the beneficiary. Further, such a *Crummey* trust has the added advantage of flexibility because it need not meet the other requirements of Code Section 2503(c).

If the potential taxable lapse of a *Crummey* power does not concern the donor (for example, if no gifts over $5,000 per beneficiary are planned), then a *Crummey* trust with a group of beneficiaries may be attractive. In this case, a donor may be able to create one *Crummey* trust for all of the donor's nieces and nephews, children or grandchildren (subject to the generation-skipping transfer tax issues discussed below). In contrast, if the donor used a 2503(c) trust, he or she would have to establish a separate trust for each beneficiary.

The most significant drawback of a *Crummey* trust, compared to a 2503(c) trust or a custodianship, is its administrative complexity. The IRS requires that every time a donor makes a gift to a *Crummey* trust, the trustee must notify the holder of a *Crummey* power of the gift and of the power holder's right to withdraw his or her proportionate share of the gift from the trust. See Rev. Rul. 81-7, 1981-1 C.B. 474; TAM 9532001. Courts have been much more lax than the IRS in requiring a trustee to send *Crummey* notices. For example, in *Crummey*, the court noted that it was "likely" that some, if not all, of the beneficiaries had no knowledge of their withdrawal rights or even when contributions were made to the trust. 397 F.2d at 88. The court nevertheless allowed the annual exclusions claimed by the taxpayer. Subsequent rulings by the IRS, however, leave little doubt that the IRS believes that the law requires a trustee to notify *Crummey* power holders of their powers for the donor to receive an annual exclusion for the gift. Rev. Rul. 81-7, 1981-1 C.B. 474; TAM 9532001.

A trustee typically sends *Crummey* notices to a beneficiary when-ever a donor makes a gift to the trust. If the beneficiary is a minor, the trustee must send the notice to the minor's legally appointed guardian or the minor's parents. See PLR 8143045. If the minor's guardian is also the trustee, the IRS has privately ruled that the trustee need not notify himself or herself of the minor's withdrawal right. TAM 9030005.

If a *Crummey* notice is required, the beneficiary (or the guardian) may be asked to acknowledge receipt of the notice in writing. These acknowledgments should be retained by the trustee or the lawyer. The acknowledgments are important because the IRS, when auditing the donor's estate tax return, may seek proof that the notices were sent and, thus, the annual exclusions were properly allowed, which may occur years after the gifts. The beneficiary's acknowledgments are powerful proof that notices were sent, which should preclude the IRS from denying annual exclusions.

The acknowledgments should be carefully drafted to prevent the beneficiary from releasing the withdrawal power by expressly declining to exercise it. Instead, the beneficiary should allow the power to lapse. If the beneficiary releases the power, then the $5,000 or 5 percent exclusion discussed above is not available and the entire unwithdrawn amount may be deemed a taxable gift by the beneficiary. Code Section 2514(e).

The requirement that the trustee send *Crummey* notices to the beneficiaries is a complication of *Crummey* trusts not found in either custodianships or minor's exclusion trusts. The comparative flexibility of the *Crummey* trust, however, makes up for the added complexity. Suppose, for example, that a donor wishes to create a trust for the benefit of her grandchild and the donor is anxious for the child's parent to be sole trustee. As discussed above, the IRS would likely argue that the use of a minor's exclusion trust or a cus-

todianship would lead to inclusion of the principal in the parent's estate if the parent were to die before termination of the trust or custodianship because the parent could use the trust assets to discharge her legal obligation to support the beneficiary. Gen. Counsel Memo. 37840. In contrast, a lawyer can prepare a *Crummey* trust to prevent a parent serving as trustee from using the trust principal to discharge his or her obligation of support. Such an arrangement has the added advantage that the IRS apparently will not require the trustee-parent to send *Crummey* notices to himself or herself. TAM 9030005.

On the downside, if the trustee-parent dies during the "window" in which the beneficiary could have exercised a *Crummey* power, the IRS is likely to argue that the amount the beneficiary could have withdrawn should be included in the trustee-parent's estate because the trustee-parent had the power to withdraw the gift and use it to satisfy his or her legal obligation of support. Code Section 2041. One should not overemphasize this factor, considering that the maximum amount included should be $20,000 (if the donor is married and his or her spouse elects to split gifts). Furthermore, for this to be an issue, the trustee-parent must die within the period of time for the exercise of the *Crummey* power, frequently thirty days following the gift.

An additional drawback of *Crummey* trusts is that for some period of time, frequently thirty days, after a donor makes a gift to the trust, the beneficiary has a power to withdraw trust assets. If the beneficiary is a minor, then as a general rule the beneficiary's court-appointed guardian or parent may exercise the power on the child's behalf. PLR 8143045. In some situations the donor may be uncomfortable giving the beneficiary or the beneficiary's guardian the right to withdraw contributions made to the trust. In this case, the client should not use a *Crummey* trust. Nevertheless, in the *Crummey* trust context, the power of withdrawal only covers the gift made to the trust at that time. In contrast, the withdrawal power in a 2503(c) trust allows the beneficiary to withdraw all of the assets held in the trust when he or she reaches age 21.

Beneficiaries or their guardians frequently realize that the donor would prefer that the beneficiary not exercise the *Crummey* power and, in practice, trust beneficiaries do not often exercise their *Crummey* powers. Indeed, this infrequency of exercise forms the basis for the Clinton administration's proposal to prohibit the use of *Crummey* powers to obtain an annual exclusion. The donor should not express his or her wish that the donees not exercise the *Crummey* power to the beneficiaries, especially in writing. The IRS could use such a request to argue that the *Crummey* power was illusory and deny the annual exclusion for the gifts subject to the power.

GST Tax Issues

If the beneficiary is the donor's grandchild, then in addition to assuring that the gifts to the trust or custodianship are exempt from federal gift and estate tax, the lawyer must also be mindful of the potential generation-skipping transfer (GST) tax issues. For the most part, a gift that qualifies for the federal gift tax annual exclusion under Code Section 2503 has a zero inclusion ratio and is, therefore, exempt from the GST tax. Code Section 2642(c)(1). If, however, the gift is to a trust, the gift will be GST tax exempt only if (1) no trust income or principal may be paid to anyone other than one particular beneficiary; and (2) if the beneficiary dies during the trust term, the trust principal will be included in the beneficiary's gross estate. Code Section 2642(c)(2).

Analogizing a custodianship to a trust, the custodianship would meet the requirements of Code Section 2642(c)(2) because no distributions may be made to anyone other than the minor and if the minor dies before reaching age 21, the custodian must distribute property to the beneficiary's estate. Similarly, a 2503(c) trust will meet the requirements of Code Section 2642(c)(2) and will, therefore, be GST tax-exempt. See PLR 8334071.

The issue is more difficult in the context of *Crummey* trusts. As discussed above, a lawyer can draft a *Crummey* trust to prevent the beneficiary's failure to exercise a $20,000 withdrawal power from being a taxable gift. Fortunately, similar provisions would make gifts to the trust GST tax-exempt. Code Section 2642(c)(2). In such a *Crummey* trust, only one beneficiary receives distributions from the trust and the trust assets will be included in the beneficiary's estate if he or she dies before termination of the trust. Accordingly, the trust terms will satisfy Code Section

2642(c)(2). If, however, the trust has more than one beneficiary, or if the assets will not be included in the beneficiary's estate for tax purposes, then gifts to the trust will not be automatically exempt from GST tax.

If gifts to a *Crummey* trust are not automatically GST tax-exempt, then a portion of the donor's GST tax exemption may need to be allocated to the trust if grandchildren or other "skip persons" are beneficiaries. This may not be a significant drawback if the client has no plans to otherwise make use of his or her GST exemption and is willing to take the risk that no such plans will develop in the future. If substantial gifts that are potentially subject to GST tax are likely, the client must consider whether this is an efficient use of the GST exemption. In such a case, it is probably wise to avoid the use of *Crummey* trusts gifts that are not GST tax-exempt under Code Section 2642(c)(2).

Conclusion

The three methods discussed above all allow the donor to make federal gift tax-free transfers to a minor beneficiary. In addition, gifts to a custodianship or a 2503(c) trust will always be GST tax-exempt. A lawyer can also draft a *Crummey* trust so that gifts to it will be exempt from the GST tax without the use of the donor's exemption.

To some extent, these three methods fall on a spectrum. Custodianships are, administratively, the simplest of the three, but the donor has the least control over the terms governing the disposition of the property after he or she makes the gift. *Crummey* trusts, at the other end of the spectrum, allow far greater flexibility for the trust terms. With flexibility comes greater administrative burdens, including the requirement of sending *Crummey* notices. Between custodianships and *Crummey* trusts, 2503(c) trusts allow for greater flexibility than custodianships, although not as much as *Crummey* trusts, and are administratively simpler than *Crummey* trusts, although not as straightforward as custodianships.

If the donor plans to make significant gifts to minors, the donor's main concern will likely be the possibility that the minor will receive the assets outright at what the donor feels is an inappropriate age. In this case, a custodianship, which requires distribution of the custodial property to the minor at age 18 or 21, will likely be inappropriate. A 2503(c) trust that continues unless the beneficiary affirmatively elects to terminate the trust at age 21 may satisfy the donor. The donor, however, must be made aware of the potential for the beneficiary to terminate the trust. *Crummey* trusts allow the donor to delay outright distribution until the beneficiary reaches a more suitable age, but the trust instrument must give the beneficiary (or his or her guardian) the temporary power to withdraw any contribution made to the trust, and the trustee must take on the added administrative difficulties in administering these powers.

Before employing any of these methods, the lawyer should discuss the pros and cons of each with the client. This discussion should involve the amount of property that the client plans to give because this will directly affect the selection. Regardless of the method that the client chooses, the lawyer should not overlook the use of the federal gift tax annual exclusion to make transfer tax-free gifts for the benefit of a minor beneficiary. Use of any of these methods allows the client to make very substantial gifts free of federal gift tax and remove the amount of these gifts (and any future appreciation on them) from the client's estate—an enormous transfer-tax savings.

Part VII
Elder Law

69

The Emergence of Elder Law

WALTER T. BURKE

While the question, "What is elder law?," has not echoed through the ages, it is a question that has been asked more frequently over the past ten years. As the American population grows older, a number of issues have become more relevant to seniors and their lawyers, leading them to focus on legal problems confronting this group and bringing into being the specialty known as elder law.

Elder law is often confused with Medicaid planning. It is much broader in that it encompasses a number of subspecialties ranging from long-term care planning to traditional trusts and estates. Unlike contracts or criminal law, elder law is not devoted to one substantive area of practice. Now, issues requiring the attention of specialists emerge almost daily as, for example, when elder citizens are victimized by domestic abuse or when legislation shifts the cost of long-term care to the consumer.

From guardianship issues to health-care decision-making and from housing options to managed health care, the elder law practitioner must have a firm grasp on a number of areas under the general heading of this emerging specialty. In addition, perhaps most importantly, the lawyer must have compassion and patience.

No Age Limit

When should a client seek advice from an elder law lawyer? At age 40? At age 50? At age 65? Or when it becomes necessary to enter a retirement community or be admitted to a nursing home? The answer is that the services of an elder law lawyer may become necessary at any age depend-

Walter T. Burke is a partner in the law firm of Burke and Casserly, P.C., in Albany, New York, and chair of the Elder Law Section of the New York State Bar Association.

ing upon the services sought. Often clients are in their 30s or 40s seeking counsel on how best to help aging parents.

An elder law lawyer must be able to assist younger clients in dealing with future costs associated with retirement and health care, since financial planning for one's retirement should begin as soon as one is employed. The government's attempts to shift the cost of long-term health care to the consumer makes this planning even more important.

It has been projected that by the year 2000 there will be 47.2 million people receiving Social Security benefits, an increase from 35.6 million in 1980 and from 3.5 million in 1950. As the pool of retirees grows, private investment becomes an integral part of financial planning. Also, as one advances in age, the investment strategies change. A younger individual currently investing in growth funds may need to switch to more conservative funds as retirement approaches, or sometimes senior clients should be advised not to become too conservative, given that their savings may have to meet expenses for a generation or more.

Estate planning is also an integral part of elder law. The lawyer practicing in this field must have knowledge of federal and state tax law in assisting clients during will preparation, account titling, designating beneficiaries, and estate administration. Elder law lawyers must know when credit-shelter trusts and other estate planning vehicles may be appropriate. In addition to traditional trust and estate concerns, elder law lawyers will routinely discuss with clients issues such as advanced directives and durable powers of attorney. While those issues and documents are important to an individual at any age, their relevance and priority are obviously more significant to an elder person than one in his or her 30s.

Changing Roles:
New York's Article 81

An example of the changing role of the elder law lawyer and society's expectations for seniors can be seen in New York's approach to guardianship. That state's conservatorship and committee laws regarding incapacitated individuals were changed in 1992 to provide for their person and their property. Prior to 1992 the approach in New York toward incapacitated individuals was one of governmental intervention, that is, the notion that seniors and those incapacitated (and the mind-set was that those terms were interchangeable) required the care and attention of third parties not only for their personal needs, but also for the protection of their property.

New York State's new Article 81 of the Mental Hygiene Law brought about a significant change in this philosophy. The court may now appoint a guardian over the person if it determines that such appointment is necessary to provide for his or her personal needs or if the person agrees to the appointment, but emphasis is placed on the least restrictive level of guardianship. This may be viewed as an approach which, from the government's point of view, is the least intrusive and least expensive. The elder law lawyer might represent those in need of assistance or their families to strike a balance between independence and the use of assets versus the risk of falling prey to financial or physical disaster. Elder law lawyers provide essential services to seniors and their families from the commencement of a guardianship proceeding through the guardian's final report.

Housing alternatives for seniors pose their own set of challenges, including congregate housing (adult homes), adult foster homes, and adult day care. At one end of the spectrum, assisted living may be appropriate for a senior desiring a residential setting but not needing a medical or skilled nursing facility. At the other end, nursing homes provide intermediate care and skilled nursing for those who need nursing care but not acute care associated with a hospital.

And then there is the issue of financing the decision. Medicare and Medicaid may pay for certain medical services offered by skilled nursing facilities but will not reimburse for most care received in an intermediate care or assisted-living facility. Only Medicaid, and not Medicare, will pay for long- term custodial services.

Elder law encompasses more than calculating the mechanics of Medicaid eligibility and often involves administrative proceedings to assure proper benefits. Frequently, the elderly and frail need advice and assistance in this area. The elder law lawyer must speak for those unable to speak for themselves.

New Legislation, New Challenges

Recent federal legislation effective August 5, 1997, presented a new challenge to many clients and elder law lawyers. In essence, the statute imposes criminal penalties on anyone who, for a fee, counsels or assists any senior to transfer or otherwise dispose of assets to become eligible for Medicaid benefits.

The American Bar Association, the New York State Bar Association, the Ohio State Bar Association, and the National Academy of Elder Law Attorneys, among others, have opposed this statute and have called for its repeal.

The constitutionality of this legislation may be questioned because it forbids one from advising someone about activities that are constitutionally permitted. As of this writing, the statute remains in effect and has imposed much fear and confusion in the minds of many seniors. However, on December 4, 1997, the New York State Bar Association initiated a lawsuit in the Northern District of New York challenging the law because of its infringement upon a lawyer's right to free speech and the chilling effect it has on the right of a senior to obtain counsel.

Enhancing the Quality of Life

Long-term care insurance has been developed to meet some of the costs associated with home care and nursing home care not covered by government programs. Elder law lawyers help clients understand the restrictions and options in their insurance contracts. This is another area of growth and concern for many seniors. Some states, such as New York and Connecticut, for example, also have approved contracts with provisions impacting their residents only, so that if a senior moves to another state, what may have been a good choice in one may become inappropriate in the other.

Elder law lawyers also assist the state and federal government in addressing budgetary issues regarding long-term care costs. They may make suggestions on how health-care dollars may be more appropriately spent, or they may be advocates for maintaining or increasing expenditures of health-care dollars. The elder law lawyer will also assist clients in becoming financially able either independently or through government assistance to help pay for institutional care.

Elder law lawyers may provide counsel to seniors in discrimination actions in employment, health care, and housing. In an era of corporate "downsizing" seniors face potential discrimination and loss of job security. The decisions regarding age discrimination have led to increased protection of the employment of older Americans.

With the integration of managed care into the health-care market, the elder law lawyer must have a grasp on the alphabet soup of managed care and how seniors are affected by the decisions of such organizations. While physicians and health maintenance organizations (HMOs) are competing for consumers, the development of new health-care delivery systems from IPAs (Independent Physician Associations) to MSOs (Medical Service Organizations) affect the cost and type of medical care. Because seniors consume a major percentage of health-care dollars, elder law lawyers are necessarily concerned with the health-care consumer protection movement.

Since the inception of "capitation," whereby the health-care provider receives a fixed, predetermined payment per covered life by a health plan for provision of specific services to covered individuals for a specified period, the issue of patients being denied health-care coverage and treatment options has become a critical issue in the managed-care controversy. Elder law lawyers are, therefore, reviewing the decisions of physicians and managed-care providers to ensure that seniors are afforded appropriate health-care coverage and medical treatment.

The Supreme Court's recent decision in *Washington v. Glucksberg* (1997) regarding physician-assisted suicide presents elder law lawyers with many unanswered questions. The Court declared that there is no constitutionally protected right to hasten one's death, thus leaving it to the states to permit or prohibit physician-assisted suicide. Presently, only Oregon has a statutory plan for its legalization. The full impact of the Supreme Court decision cannot be ascertained, therefore, until we see how the other state legislatures react.

Currently, people older than 50 control 70 percent of the total net worth of households in the United States. Further, by the year 2030, people older than 65 will represent 22 percent of the U.S. population. According to the 1995 Census Bureau, 81 percent of individuals between ages 65 and 69 own their own homes, as do 80.9 percent of people between ages 70 and 74, and 74.6 percent of those older than 75. This amount of wealth and property will be transferred to the next generation in the coming decades. The legal, financial, and tax implications of this enormous transfer of wealth to the next generation will severely impact the nation's economy.

Elder law lawyers must be capable of more than drafting trust agreements and testamentary documents. They also must be able to assist clients faced with depression, shock, and loneliness, providing them not only with legal support but also empathy and moral support. Because many older clients do not seek legal advice on an ongoing basis, it is often a catastrophic illness or the loss of a spouse that causes a client to meet with an elder law lawyer. It is imperative that the elder law lawyer not only have the requisite legal knowledge but also the patience, compassion, and understanding to help the client through such difficult times.

In 1991, the average life expectancy for men and women was 72 and 79, respectively-an increase from 70 and 77 in 1980. As medical technology becomes more sophisticated, the duration and quality of Americans lives will continue to increase. Elder law has, thus, become an acknowledged specialty. Younger lawyers are attracted to it partly because it is new and dynamic with a large client base that is projected to increase dramatically. In addition, it permits the lawyer to work closely with individuals who often have seen the full measure of life and with whom they may establish a rewarding relationship.

70

Senior Home Equity Conversion: Reverse Mortgages and Other Options

DAVID A. BRIDEWELL, CELESTE M. HAMMOND, AND CHARLES NAUTS

The reverse mortgage—one home equity conversion device—is a desirable senior housing planning tool from both an individual and public perspective. It allows senior homeowners to use their homes, often their most substantial asset, to increase individual choice and financial independence.

By allowing the elderly to convert this asset into an income flow, the reverse mortgage reduces the dependency of the elderly upon public funds. For example a recent Cornell University study estimates that more than 620,000 elderly homeowners in poverty could be raised above the poverty line if they obtained a HUD-insured Home Equity Conversion Mortgage (HECM) tenure reverse mortgage. These households constitute 29 percent of all poor elderly homeowners in the United States.[1]

This chapter is divided into three main parts. The first part describes reverse mortgages. The second part compares alternative home equity conversion options. The final part reviews reverse mortgage borrower counseling, the elder law lawyer's role in providing the counseling, and how the home equity conversion tool fits into a comprehensive elder plan.

David A. Bridewell serves as counsel to the Chicago law firm of DeWolfe, Poynton & Stevens. Celeste M. Hammond is professor and director of the Real Estate Law Center and the LL.M. program in real estate law at John Marshall Law School, Cleveland, Ohio. Charles Nauts is of counsel to Harris & Harris in Lincoln, Illinois.

Reverse Mortgages

What Is a Reverse Mortgage?

A "reverse mortgage" is a mortgage loan against home equity. The total loan amount is based on current appraised value plus anticipated appreciation, and on the life expectancy of the borrower. This loan does not require any monthly payment. Instead, it provides monthly cash advances or a line of credit to a borrower, and requires no repayment until some future or determinable time—usually when the last borrower dies, sells, or leaves his or her home. A reverse mortgage is the "reverse" of a forward mortgage, where the borrower, at loan closing, starts with less equity, makes monthly payments, reduces the loan balance, and increases equity. At the outset of a reverse mortgage the borrower owes relatively little (other than the costs and lender's charge for making the loan, which can be substantial) on the reverse mortgage and has substantial remaining equity. The lender makes monthly payments to the borrower, the loan balance rises, and equity declines (see Figure 70–1). The reverse mortgage is structurally similar to all three of an open-ended mortgage, a negative-amortization mortgage, and a balloon mortgage. Like an open-ended mortgage, such as a line of credit loan, the proceeds are paid to the borrower over time. Also, the reverse mortgage has negative amortization; that is, the interest due from time to time is not paid, but added to principal, which results

1. Nandinee K. Kutty, *The Scope for Poverty Alleviation among Elderly Homeowners in the United States through Reverse Mortgages*, 35 URBAN STUDIES, no. 1, 113–129, at 113 (University of Glasgow, Scotland, 1998), [hereinafter Kutty].

Figure 70–1

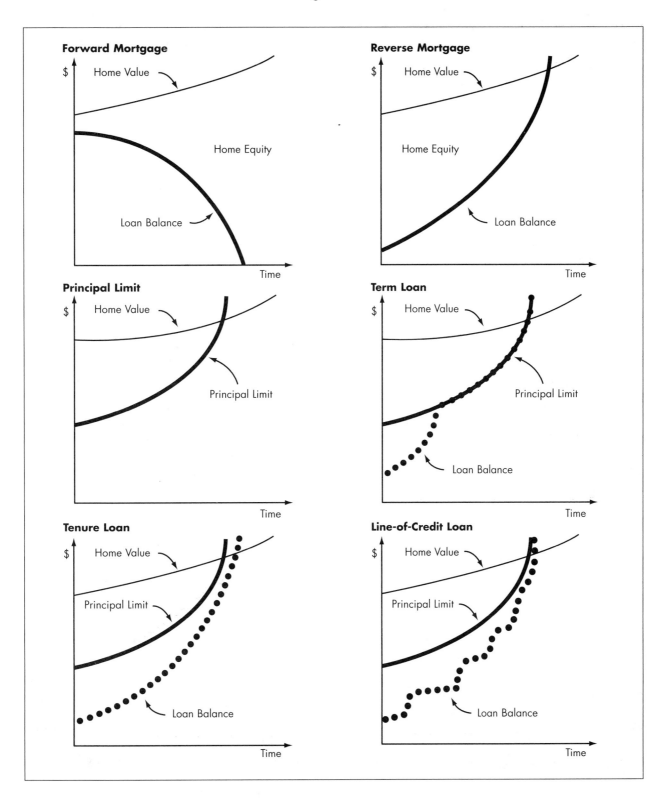

in interest on interest. Also, the reverse mortgage is a classic balloon mortgage, because the whole amount of the indebtedness becomes due in a single payment at the end of the loan term.

Advantages of a Reverse Mortgage

Today, three different types of reverse mortgages are available to elderly homeowners: (1) the uninsured loan, (2) the lender-insured loan, and (3) the FHA-insured loan (HECM).

The Uninsured Reverse Mortgage[2]

This type of reverse mortgage is written for a maximum fixed term from five to ten years, with a loan-to-value ratio of perhaps 80 percent of appraised value. It has no insurance feature to protect the borrower against lender defaults, or to protect the lender against the risk that, over time, the loan balance may exceed a home's market value. The loan becomes due before the end of the term if the borrower dies, sells the property, or moves. The lender does not take the risk of the life term, or "tenure" reverse mortgage, that the borrower might outlive the lender's expectations. The loan-to-value ratio limits any lender's risk that the loan might exceed home value before the loan becomes due. This type of loan generally is not suitable for the elderly homeowner who wants a guaranteed right to live in the home until death. It may be useful, however, for those who need additional income for a short period, for example, to pay for home care if terminally ill, to bridge a gap until an anticipated pension is received, or to obtain cash before a planned move to alternative housing.

The FHA-insured Reverse Mortgage[3]

The HECM reverse mortgage has the most attractive features for seniors who qualify as borrowers. It is the program most seniors who have a reverse mortgage have used and, to the extent HECM remains available, seniors will continue to use. Under HECM, all co-borrowers must be at least 62 years of age and own the home free and clear or have an outstanding mortgage balance low enough to be refinanced with the HECM proceeds. Advantages of the HECM reverse mortgage are:

- HECM reverse mortgages are nonrecourse. The principal amount available is based in part on the assumption that the borrower's home will appreciate by an assumed 4 percent a year, compounded annually. If, instead, the home goes down in value, the HECM lender must continue to make advances until the HECM loan is due. The difference is made up by FHA insurance.

- The due date for a HECM reverse mortgage is most favorable for seniors. The due date is when: (1) the last borrower dies; (2) a borrower conveys his or her title to the property and no other borrower retains title or a long-term leasehold interest; (3) the property is no longer any borrower's principal residence; (4) a borrower fails to occupy the property for more than twelve consecutive months because of physical or mental illness and the property is not the principal residence of at least one other borrower; or (5) a loan obligation of the borrower is not performed. The principal amount available is based in part on the HECM program mortality tables. If any co-borrower outlives these assumptions, again, the HECM lender must continue to make advances until the HECM loan is due.

- HUD will fund HECM loan advances to the borrower if a lender defaults. The defaulting lender may incur significant penalties. Other than some delay in receiving payments from HUD, however, little risk from lender default exists for a HECM borrower.

- Obtaining the HECM reverse mortgage depends on age and home ownership, not the borrower's income, credit, or assets.

The Lender-Insured Reverse Mortgage[4]

The lender-insured loan has advantages for the borrower similar to the HECM reverse mortgage, except that the borrower has to rely on the lender's continuing financial strength, since there is no FHA insurance backing up the lender's commitment to make future advances. In some lender-insured reverse mortgages, the lender makes an initial advance to fund an annuity, so that the borrower also can rely on the financial strength of the annuity provider. Since the lender has made the advance to buy the annuity, the borrower no longer has to worry about the lender's financial strength.

---

2. *See generally* DAVID A. BRIDEWELL & CHARLES NAUTS, eds., REVERSE MORTGAGES: A LAWYER'S GUIDE TO HOUSING AND INCOME ALTERNATIVE, at 172, 173 (American Bar Association, 1997) [hereinafter REVERSE MORTGAGES].

3. *See generally* REVERSE MORTGAGES, *supra* note 2, at 21–30, 173, 174.

4. *See generally* REVERSE MORTGAGES, *supra* note 2, at 20, 26, 28, 29, 83, 118, 172, 173.

The primary advantage of the lender-insured loan, as compared to a HECM loan, is that the amount that may be borrowed is not capped. The HECM loan is capped by the maximum FHA mortgage limit for the area, which varies, as of January 1998, from $86,317 to $170,362, depending on local housing costs. Larger advances are possible under a lender-insured mortgage where property values are higher than the HECM area limit. For example, for a borrower age 75 with a home value of $350,000 and an expected annual interest rate of 9 percent, the monthly advance under a tenure HECM reverse mortgage (the borrower receives monthly payments for as long as the borrower occupies the home as a principal residence) would be $576. The monthly advance under a lender-insured reverse mortgage, with a 9.5 percent fixed annual interest rate, would be $1,298.[5]

One lender-insured reverse mortgage product, House Money, offered by TransAmerica Home-First, has an annuity feature, which results in an additional option that may be particularly beneficial to the borrower when home values appreciate at an unanticipated high rate. If this happens, the borrower can refinance with a new reverse mortgage, or sell and move while, in either case, continuing to receive the annuity.[6]

Another lender-insured reverse mortgage alternative is Fannie Mae's Home Keeper Mortgage™, which Fannie Mae offers through participating lenders. Like HECM, the home value on which the amount loaned is based is capped by a mortgage limit. The HomeKeeper Mortgage™ limit, $203,150 as of January 1998, is higher than HECM. There also is an "equity share" alternative, which results in even higher advances.

Figure 70-2, "Reverse Mortgage Resources," compiled in April 1998 by Stephanie Edelstein of the ABA Commission on Legal Problems of the Elderly, tells how to obtain more detailed information about the HomeKeeper Mortgage™ and about other reverse mortgages.

Disadvantages of Reverse Mortgages

The benefits of a reverse mortgage are dependent on the particular situation of the borrower. A

5. The other factors can be found in REVERSE MORTGAGES, *supra* note 2, at 47–51. For further comparisons, see *id.* at 83–118, 173.
6. REVERSE MORTGAGES, *supra* note 2, at 95–114, reprints TransAmerica HomeFirst's House Money.

Figure 70-2

Reverse Mortgage Resources

Stephanie Edelstein
ABA Commission on Legal Problems of the Elderly
740 15th Street
Washington, DC 20005
Phone (202) 662-8694; Fax (202) 662-8698

Maintaining a home can be a tremendous financial burden for older adults and, when coupled with health and living expenses, can quickly deplete savings. A reverse mortgage may help older homeowners tap home equity to generate extra income. The following resources, compiled for a 1998 Law Day program, provide valuable information for consumers and service providers alike.

AARP Home Equity Information Center
AARP Foundation
601 E Street, NW
Washington, DC 20029
(202) 434-6042 (Publications Order Line);
Internet at http://www.aarp.org

- Home Equity Conversion Fact Sheet
- Basic Facts About Reverse Mortgages
- How to Select Reverse Mortgage Counselors and Lenders
- Home Made Money (consumer booklet)

Fannie Mae
3900 Wisconsin Avenue, NW
Washington, DC 20016
(800) 732-6643;
Internet at http://www.fanniemae.org

- Money from Home (information and workbook)
- HomeKeeper™: It Pays to Keep You in Your Home (pamphlet)
- Home Equity Conversion Mortgage (HECM) Information (flyer)

National Center for Home Equity Conversion
Ken Scholen, Director
7373 147th Street West, #115
Apple Valley, MN 55124

- List of "preferred" counselors and lenders. Send $1 (for postage and handling) and a self-addressed stamped envelope.
- Reverse Mortgages for Beginners (consumer guide, $14.95)
- Reverse mortgage estimates on-line at http://www.reverse.org (Note: fun and informative)

HUD Housing Counseling Clearinghouse
(888) 466-3487

- To locate a counseling agency for free (and required) HECM counseling reverse mortgage can be invaluable to elderly persons who can no longer afford to live in their residences. Nevertheless, by utilizing the reverse mortgage, a borrower must realize that his or her home, which is often the most significant estate asset, is becoming encumbered, and will not be left to the heirs debt-free. The owner remains liable to make all repairs and to maintain the property, and must pay real estate taxes, assessments, and other costs.

The major disadvantage of reverse mortgages is their high total annual loan costs (TALCs) if the borrowers die or sell after a short time.[7] Conversely, if the borrowers outlive the mortality assumptions, or the house fails to appreciate at 4 percent, compounded annually, as assumed by HECM when it determines the principal limit of a HECM loan, the TALC may be very low.

As a general rule, the longer a borrower keeps a reverse mortgage, the lower the total annual loan cost will be, because costs such as mortgage insurance, closing costs, interest, and servicing costs will be spread over an extended period.

It is important to remember that, as the elderly population of this country increases, so do continuing problems of fraud and elder abuse. There have been examples of so-called "estate planners" or mortgage finders who have charged outrageous fees to the elderly for matching up borrowers and reverse mortgage lenders. For example, one 69-year-old borrower was charged $5,571 (10 percent of her loan amount) by an estate planner; another elderly couple, one of whom was disabled, were charged $4,000 (8.5 percent of their loan amount); and a 75-year-old borrower paid $4,200 to a HECM mortgage finder. This latter victim later said, "I never thought I would have to pay that much money (to someone) for simply coming to my house a few times and giving me the name of a lender."[8] HUD has estimated that hundreds of elderly homeowners have been victimized by mortgage finders who charged thousands of dollars for information on reverse mortgages. HUD's position is that for people of limited means who are trying to find a way to stay

in their homes for the remainder of their lives, the charging of these excessive fees is unconscionable.[9] Several bills are pending in the 105th Congress to prevent funding of unnecessary or excessive costs for obtaining a reverse mortgage.[10]

Also, several class action suits are pending against lender-insured reverse mortgages, claiming excessive fees or insufficient disclosures.[11] However, the present required TALC disclosures seem sufficient to adequately explain the total annual loan cost to prospective borrowers.[12]

The Application Process

In order to qualify for a reverse mortgage, borrowers will generally have to meet certain requirements. If the mortgage is federally insured, then borrowers will be eligible if they meet the HECM requirements as to age and home ownership discussed earlier in this chapter. In addition, the borrower will be able to choose from five payment options (tenure, term, line of credit, modified tenure, and modified term), and may accrue interest at a fixed rate, adjustable rate, or with shared appreciation to the lender. As a condition to obtaining a reverse mortgage, prospective borrowers will be required to receive independent counseling on the financial ramifications of the loan and on other equity-conversion alternatives. The number of qualified counselors has been limited, and has sometimes acted as an obstacle to more widespread availability of federally insured reverse mortgages.

For transactions that are not governed by state or federal statutes or regulations, the relationship of the parties to a reverse mortgage will be governed in large part by the promissory note, the mortgage, the loan agreement or, if a sale-leaseback alternative is used, the terms of the lease. Protections that the borrower should look for

---

7. For an example of the required TALC disclosure, *see* REVERSE MORTGAGES, *supra* note 2, at 57, Appendix B, Exhibit 4. In respect to the HomeKeeper Mortgage™, see additionally a special fact sheet on its TALC offered by the National Center for Home Equity Conversions (see Figure 70–2 on how to obtain this).

8. *Patriot, Inc. v. Dept. of Housing and Urban Dev.*, No. 97-0586, D.C.; amicus brief of AARP at 10, 11 (Apt. 2, 1997).

9. HUD News Release No. 97-31, Mar. 17, 1997. HUD has issued a proposed rule designed to curb these practices. 63 Fed. Reg. 12930-12933 (Mar. 16, 1998). The rule would prohibit disbursements from HECM loan proceeds to estate planners, and would require mandatory per-loan counseling as to whether an estate planner is involved. The proposed definition of estate planning service firm would exclude payment of fees for bona fide tax or legal or financial advice.

10. S.562, the Senior Citizens Home Equity Protection Act; H.R. 1297, the Senior Homeowner Reverse Mortgage Protection Act; and H.R. 1474, the HUD Reverse Mortgage Program Protection Act.

11. *See* REVERSE MORTGAGES, *supra* note 2 at 24, 25, 27, 28, 57, Appendix B, Exhibit 4.

12. Jean Reilly, *Reverse Mortgages: Backing Into The Future*, 5 ELDER L.J. 17, 20–26 (1997) summarizes the issues raised in these cases.

during the application process include the following provisions:

1. No prepayment penalty or penalty if the borrower decreases or discontinues the number or amount of payments disbursed;

2. Protection from acceleration of repayment in the event that the borrower is absent from the home for specified periods due to illness;

3. Protection from acceleration if liens are put on the home without the first lienholder's approval, or if the property is transferred between spouses;

4. If the lender defaults, at least cessation of interest accrual and waiver of the lender's right to seek repayment until the borrower's death or the sale of the home;

5. If the interest rate is adjustable, a reasonable cap on rate increases or a lower uncapped rate; and

6. A prohibition against a deficiency judgment (nonrecourse provision) if the loan balance is not satisfied by the sale of the home (either through foreclosure or a voluntary sale).

Alternatives to a Reverse Mortgage

Sale-Leaseback[13]

Sale-leasebacks, common in commercial real estate, are another possible home equity conversion device as an alternative to the reverse mortgage. A residential sale-leaseback involves a homeowner (seller) who transfers title of the home to a buyer (for example, an individual or commercial investor). In exchange, the homeowner either receives a cash down payment and an installment note to be satisfied by monthly payments or is paid off by financing obtained by the buyer. The buyer, in turn, allows the seller to remain in the home pursuant to a lease (usually for a term determined by the sellers life expectancy, unless the lease specifies otherwise) in exchange for rent. Typically, the buyer is responsible for the payment of real estate taxes, major maintenance, the buyer's mortgage payment, and insurance.

A frequent barrier to a sale-leaseback transaction is finding an investor. Before 1986, owners of rental property received substantial tax deduction for depreciation and expenses, and favorable capital gains treatment. These benefits were sig-

nificantly reduced with passage of the Tax Reform Act of 1986.[14] Today, potential investors are limited to three general categories: outside investors who expect the property to appreciate considerably; those who anticipate using the home for their own future retirement and are, therefore, willing to negotiate a long-term lease; and family members or friends of the homeowner who want to help the older person remain in the home, and who are also willing to assume the business relationship necessary for tax purposes.[15] The conclusion of tax advisors who have—from a family-planning perspective—addressed the sale-leaseback alternative to a reverse mortgage is that the family unit will realize more from this alternative than from a reverse mortgage.[16]

Home Equity Sharing

Home equity sharing was developed in the 1980s to enable renters to become homeowners without the down payment necessary to obtain a mortgage loan.[17] Section 280A of the Internal Revenue Code, enacted in 1981 to extend certain joint ownership tax benefits to homeowners, enables the co-owners to agree that the tenant ("occupier") under a fair rental lease will pay and deduct mortgage interest and property taxes while the landlord ("investor") can deduct depreciation, and can agree to pay other expenses deductible by the investor but not by the occupier, such as insurance, maintenance, and any association dues.[18]

14. Tax Reform Act of 1986, Pub. L. No. 95-514, 100 Stat. 2085 (1986) (codified as amended in scattered sections of 26 U.S.C.).

15. Ken Scholen, *Your New Retirement Nest Egg*, at 222 (1996).

16. *See generally*, D. Murphy *Converting Home Equity Into Cash: A Comparative Analysis of Reverse Mortgages and Sale-Leasebacks*, 70 Taxes 622–29 (1992); R. Taylor, *Sale-leaseback May Offer More Benefits Than Reverse Mortgages*, 23 Tax Advisor 360–62 (1992).

17. *See generally*, Marilyn D. Sullivan, *The New Home Buying Strategy* (1997) (hereinafter Sullivan); David Andrew Sirkin, *The Home Equity Sharing Manual* (1974) (hereinafter Sirkin).

18. Sullivan, *supra* note 1, at 152–159; Sirkin, *supra* note 1, at 41–63. Provisions of the Taxpayer Relief Act of 1997 allow a taxpayer to exclude from income up to $250,000 or, for married taxpayers filing jointly, up to $500,000 of gain realized on the sale or exchange of a residence (Act Sec. 312(a) amending Code Sec. 121; Act Sec. 312(b), repealing Code Sec. 1034; Act Sec. 312(c), adding new Code Sec. 6045(e)(5); and Act Sec. 312(d), amending Code Secs. 25(e), 32(c), 56(e), 143(i) and (m), 163(n), 216(e), 280A(i), 464(f), 512(a), 1016(a), 1033(h) and (k), 1038(e), 1223(7), 1250(d) and (e), 1274(c), 6012(c), 6334(a), 6504, and 7872(f); and Act Sec. 312(d) [e]. This exclusion replaces the former rollover of gain provisions of Code Sec. 1034 and the one-time $125,000 exclusion for taxpayers age 55 or older. These changes affect but do not invalidate the Sullivan and Sirkin analyses cited in this note.

13. *See generally*, Reverse Mortgages, *supra* note 2, at 119–125.

A main reason for home equity sharing has been to enable a parent to supply the down payment necessary for an adult child to finance the purchase of a first home. The parent co-owner would become the investor and the adult child co-owner would become the occupier, as tenant under a lease that met the fair rental standards of Internal Revenue Code Section 280A.[19] To meet the standard, the rent is based on the investor's share of ownership. The two co-owners would enter into a cotenancy agreement that met the requirements of a "shared equity financing agreement" under Section 280A.[20] The ownership would be as tenants in common, with the shares determined by the parent investor's contribution, the expected return, and the term of the agreement. For example, where the parent investor was to contribute 20 percent, the expected term, prior to sale, was to be five years and the expected investor return, assuming 4 percent appreciation, was to be 12 percent, the parent investor would own 55 percent and the occupier child would own 45 percent, as tenants in common.[21] The remaining 80 percent would be financed by a first mortgage from both cotenants. The cotenancy agreement, at a minimum, would provide for buyouts, the term (during which the right to partition is suspended), a lease to the occupier co-owner, as tenant, mortgage payment responsibilities, allocation of tax benefits, adjustments to equity for mortgage principal payments, and default provisions.[22] The typical cotenancy agreement, prior to the Taxpayer Relief Act of 1997, contemplated that, on the sale of the home at the end of the shared equity financing agreement, the investor-tenant-in-common might either buy out the occupier or enter into an Internal Revenue Code Section 1031 tax-free exchange while the occupier-tenant-in-common might either buy out the investor or purchase a new residence under the former Code Section 1034 rollover provisions or, if over 55, exclude gain under the former Section 121 $125,000 gain exemption.[23]

The Taxpayer Relief Act of 1997 repealed former Code Sections 1034 and 121 for sales after May 7, 1997, but amended Code Section 121 to exclude from income up to $250,000 of gain realized on the sale or exchange of a residence.[24] The individual seller must have owned and occupied the residence as a principal residence at least two of the five years during the five-year period ending on the date of sale. The amount of excludable gain is increased to $500,000 for married individuals filing jointly.[25]

This change may increase the possibility of using home equity sharing by seniors as an alternative to a reverse mortgage or sale-leaseback. Like a sale-leaseback, because of the investor's credit and ownership participation, home equity sharing should result in the co-owners' ability to obtain a forward mortgage at a lesser interest rate than the reverse mortgage effective rate, which includes interest on interest compounding.[26] Further, home equity sharing may be preferable to the sale-leaseback where it is desirable to preserve some ownership tax deductions for the occupier-senior.[27] Last, the seniors who sell an existing home to downsize while realizing excludable gain may find themselves in a situation analogous to a first-time home buyer. If a relative is willing to make the 20 percent down payment and join in an 80 percent conventional forward mortgage on the new downsized home, the senior co-owner-occupiers, under the equity sharing arrangement, will be able to free up whatever part of their gain is not necessary for rent and their share of mortgage payments on their new house.

Other Alternatives

Other chapters in this book discuss estate planning techniques for the home when the senior has sufficient income to make a reverse mortgage, sale-leaseback, or equity sharing unnecessary.[28]

Retaining a life estate,[29] or selling and moving to a retirement community,[30] are additional alternatives to a reverse mortgage, which may be

19. I.R.C. § 280A (d)(3)(B)(ii) (1998).
20. I.R.C. § 280A (d)(3)(B)(i)-(C)-(D) (1998).
21. Sullivan, *supra* note 1, at 107.
22. Sullivan, *supra* note 1, at 324–349; Sirkin, *supra* note 1, at 129–174.
23. Sullivan, *supra* note 1, at 219–221, 227–248, 345; Sirkin, *supra* note 1, at 56–63.

24. I.R.C. § 121 (1998).
25. *See generally*, The Taxpayer Relief Act of 1997, par. 129 (CCH 1997).
26. *See generally*, D. Murphy *Converting Home Equity Into Cash: A Comparative Analysis of Reverse Mortgages and Sale-Leasebacks*, 70 Taxes 622–29 (1992); R. Taylor, *Sale-leaseback May Offer More Benefits Than Reverse Mortgages*, 23 Tax Advisor 360–62 (1992).
27. *See* discussion at note 18 above; Reverse Mortgages, *supra* note 2, at 33–35, 59, 60, 184, 185.
28. *See* Herbert L. Zuckerman and Jay A. Soled, "Personal Residence Trusts," chapter 60 of this book; Steve R. Akers, "GRATs," chapter 64 of this book.
29. Reverse Mortgages, *supra* note 2, at 171, 172.
30. *See generally*, Reverse Mortgages, *supra* note 2, at 195–272.

appropriate for senior clients. This discussion has centered on alternatives that, at least to some extent, are like the reverse mortgage, which allows the elderly homeowner to use up the equity in the home while living there and receiving a monthly payment.[31]

Reverse Mortgage Borrower Counseling

A recent analysis on evaluating public policies related to age note that, according to a 1991 survey, elderly people often are happier than nonelderly people.[32] Further, they value privacy and, when they can afford to stay in their homes, they resist moving from their homes.[33] This analysis discusses a multiple-self concept.

> Aging brings about such large changes in the individual that there may well come a point at which it is more illuminating to think of two or more persons "time-sharing" the same identity than of one person having different preferences, let alone one person having the same preferences, over the entire life cycle.[34]

This multiple-self concept appears to be consistent with consumer attitudes toward home mortgages.

Typical consumer attitudes of younger homeowners who have paid off their mortgage and are saving toward retirement are:

- Do not borrow in general.
- Do not borrow against your home in particular.
- Do not spend your savings.

The retirement version of these typical attitudes changes to:

- When should I use savings?
- How much should I use?
- What should I use it for?

Home equity is a major part of savings for these seniors. Seniors need professional counseling to help them determine what are their housing alternatives, and to evaluate the costs of available alternatives, particularly the TALC costs of reverse mortgages.[35]

Today, there is a need for informed legal counseling to prospective reverse mortgage borrowers.

HECM now makes HUD insurance available for its 50,000 authorized HECM reverse mortgage loans through September 30, 2000. As of March 1997, HUD estimates about 20,000 HECM reverse mortgages have been insured by the FHA. Because of certain difficulties in understanding the reverse mortgage procedures, HECM requires free counseling by a HUD-approved counseling agency (none of which, at present, is made up of lawyers) and a certificate of borrower counseling, signed by the agency and the borrower, before the loan closes to prove that the counseling has occurred.[36] The counseling agency certifies, in part, that the counselor has made a disclosure to the borrower

> . . . that a Home Equity Conversion Mortgage may have tax consequences, affect eligibility for assistance under Federal and State programs, and have an impact on the estate and heirs of the borrower(s). . . .[37]

As to estate impact, HUD's suggestion, in its 1989 comments on its regulations, was

> . . . to reduce the potential for adverse legal action by heirs, borrowers will be urged to invite heirs to counseling sessions. . . .[38]

In practice, the counseling, which, due to demand, now can be done by phone, if necessary ". . . when face-to-face counseling is not possible, (i.e., if it is too far for the homeowner to travel, or if the counselor is unable to travel to a distant area . . .),"[39] is unlikely to include the heirs.

During the comment period in 1989, private reverse mortgage lenders suggested to HUD that

> . . . the counsel of any adult advisor who is not connected to the lender and whose counsel is trusted by the prospective borrowers should be acceptable to the Department. . . .[40]

HUD did not adopt the lending community's further suggestion that the borrowers' lawyer should be an acceptable advisor to satisfy HUD's counseling requirement. The HUD Counselor Training Manual states:

---

31. REVERSE MORTGAGES, *supra* note 2, at 184, 185, discussing the implications of the reverse mortgage for estate planning.
32. Richard A. Posner, *Aging and Old Age*, 87, 110 (1995).
33. *Id.* at 145–148.
34. *Id.* at 86.
35. *See generally*, REVERSE MORTGAGES, *supra* note 2, at 119–125.

36. 12 U.S.C. § 17152-2D (1998); 24 C.F.R. § 206.41 (1997).
37. The required Certificate of Borrower Counseling appears in REVERSE MORTGAGES, *supra* note 2, at 71.
38. 54 Fed. Reg. 24829, 24830, at 16D (June 9, 1989).
39. Bronwyn Belling and Ken Scholen, *Home Equity Conversion Mortgage*, INSURANCE DEMONSTRATION COUNSELOR TRAINING AND REFERENCE MANUAL at 70 (U.S. Dept. of Housing and Urban Dev., rev. Feb. 29, 1996), [hereinafter HUD COUNSELOR TRAINING MANUAL].
40. 54 Fed. Reg. 24829, 24830, at 16D (June 9, 1989).

A. Counselors should always determine if there are local family members who might participate in the counseling process. On the other hand, it is ethically inappropriate to insist that this occur. Yet all homeowners have the right to make financial decisions independently. It would be erroneous to generalize that all homeowners want or need family guidance in their decision-making. However, it should be encouraged.

B. On the professional side, there are only a few people in ANY fields (sic) (attorneys, bankers, ministers, accountants, etc.) who are qualified to advise older homeowners about reverse mortgages. . . .[41]

The HUD Counselor Training Manual itself calls to the counseling agencies' attention the Commission on Legal Problems of the Elderly's commitment to develop a network of qualified attorneys who can advise homeowners about the legal implications of HECM transactions. The HUD Counselor Training Manual then gives this advice to its approved counseling agencies:

> As counselors and the media increase public attention to this topic, a cadre of qualified professionals will emerge to serve this need. To further this goal, share information with local colleagues, and maintain lists of those with whom you have worked.
>
> Always remember to give a choice of selections to any homeowner. Do not recommend any one program, agency, service, or professional advisor.[42]

At present and for the past several years a significant part of the "free" reverse mortgage counseling by the HUD-approved counseling agencies appears to be funded by the government, through HUD. HUD's pleading in the *Patriot* case describes this process:

> There are currently 705 HUD-approved local housing counseling agencies who are eligible to provide counseling regarding HECM loans. . . . In FY 1995, a total of $6,000,000 to fund all HUD counseling services, including HECM counseling, was awarded to 240 of these agencies. . . . In addition, $650,000 was provided by HUD specifically to train housing counselors in HECM counseling. . . . In FY 1994, HUD provided $11,375,000 for comprehensive housing counseling services, and an additional $250,000 to train counselors in HECM. . . . In that year, 431 counseling entities were funded. . . . (citations omitted).[43]

HUD's borrower counseling is intended to be supplemented, at the borrower's option and expense, with further legal and financial counseling as needed.

HUD requires its agency counseling to cover alternatives to a HECM reverse mortgage, such as sale-leaseback or sale and moving into a congregate-facility residence.

Due to training and experience, a lawyer can often anticipate and analyze problems that HUD's approved counseling agency may not. For example, under applicable state law, who are the heirs; what property powers of attorney, trusts, wills or other dispositions for transferring wealth exist or should exist; what other alternatives, such as property tax deferrals, sale-leaseback, or sale and moving into a congregate-facility residence are there?

The American Bar Association Position

The American Bar Association, in August 1995, adopted a resolution recognizing home equity conversion as a viable option for older homeowners to access the equity in their homes. By the resolution, the American Bar Association ". . . supports the development and promulgation of local, state and federal policies ensuring that loan proceeds are disregarded in determining borrowers eligibility for governmental benefits. . . ."[44]

Adequate borrower counseling must consider the impact of reverse mortgages on some government benefits, particularly SSI and Medicaid benefits. Generally, equity in an applicant/recipient's principal place of residence is not counted as a resource, and proceeds from a reverse mortgage should not be defined as income under present Social Security law. However, loan proceeds retained by the borrower beyond the month in which they are received become a resource and may adversely affect SSI (and Medicaid) eligibility if the resource limit is exceeded. Careful attention must be paid to federal and state resource limits when structuring the payments to the borrower.[45]

---

41. HUD COUNSELOR TRAINING MANUAL, *supra* note 32, at 70.

42. *Id.* at 70.

43. *Patriot, Inc. v. Department of Housing and Urban Development*, No. 97-586 (HHC), D.C., HUD memorandum of law in opposition to plaintiff's motion for summary judgment, at 9 (April 1997).

44. The resolution appears in REVERSE MORTGAGES, *supra* note 2, at 4.

45. *See generally* REVERSE MORTGAGES, *supra* note 2, at 35–37; Jon M. Zieger, *The State Giveth and the State Taketh Away: In Pursuit of a Practical Approach to Medicaid Estate Recovery,* 5 ELDER LAW J. 359–393 (1997); Louis D. Torch, *Spousal Impoverishment or Enrichment? An Assessment of Asset or Income Transfer By Medicaid Applicants,* 4 ELDER LAW J. 359–392 (1996).

In its resolution supporting the development of reverse mortgages, the American Bar Association also supports the need for consumer education and safeguards about home equity conversion, including counseling about other housing options, which is now being provided by the Senior Lawyers Division. Since this counseling requires becoming familiar with both federal benefits law and with the state benefits laws, which vary from state to state, as well as understanding the multiple-self concept in dealing with seniors, it seems particularly appropriate for elder lawyers to counsel seniors about reverse mortgages and other home equity conversion options.[46]

46. An excellent starting point, in addition to this book, is Susan J. Hemp and Cheryl Rae Nyberg, *Elder Law: A Guide to Key Resources*, 3 ELDER LAW J. 1–71, which, in Appendix A, 64–84, identifies state-specific resources.

71
Senior Housing: Zoning for the Future

VICTORIA M. de LISLE

In 1996 there were 33.8 million people in America older than 65. Each day, this population increases by an average of 1,600 people, and it will double by the year 2030. (See Gabrielle DeGroot, *Elderly Housing Market Has Exploded to Meet Demands of Older Population,* Warfield's Bus. Record, April 15, 1996, at 11.) These demographics have fueled tremendous growth in the senior housing industry. A spectrum of housing options is now available to seniors who are willing to move out of their homes. Most housing options are service driven and accommodate needs ranging from the "young old"—active seniors aged 65 to 75—to the "frail elderly" whose activities are severely limited and who often require institutional care.

There are three primary senior housing alternatives: congregate-living facilities (CLFs), assisted-living facilities (ALFs) and continuing-care retirement communities (CCRCs). CLFs provide housing, meals, and an array of recreational and social activities to residents who are generally in good health and functionally independent. Health and medical services are typically not provided, but some CLFs affiliate with nearby medical institutions. ALFs offer studio or one-bedroom furnished or unfurnished units with kitchenettes and common living and dining areas. ALFs are designed for elderly residents who need some assistance with daily living activities, such as bathing, eating, dressing, and grooming. ALFs provide minimum health care or nursing assistance as needed. CCRCs offer a continuum of care from independent living to assisted living to nursing care. Some CCRCs have skilled nursing facilities on site, while others contract with nearby nursing homes. The residential contract generally specifies the amount of long-term care services that the monthly fee includes. In a "life care" community, the resident's entrance fee carries with it the right to full lifetime health care.

Zoning Obstacles

Both charitable and for-profit senior housing facilities face regulatory obstacles of various kinds, including state licensing criteria, statutory inconsistencies about the appropriate regulatory agency, fire and building code requirements, and land use issues. This chapter examines zoning obstacles to the development of senior housing.

Traditionally, local governments have treated homes for the aged and nursing homes as disfavored uses and sometimes have attempted to exclude them from certain districts. More recently, municipalities have come to view senior housing facilities as a fiscally advantageous use. They generate more taxes than charges on local services. This benefit is due to several factors, including the absence of school-age residents, the recent increase in the median income of those older than 65, and the fact that seniors have fewer cars and generate fewer traffic and parking problems. (See J. Gregory Richards, *Zoning for Direct Social Control,* 1982 DUKE L.J. 761, 799-818 (1982).) Developers and state and local governments are now grappling with where they should permit senior housing facilities and how best to integrate them into surrounding neighborhoods.

Zoning Code Inadequacies

Unfortunately, most municipal zoning regulations provide only a limited array of housing cat-

Victoria M. de Lisle is a lawyer with Stone, Pigman, Walther, Wittmann & Hutchinson, L.L.P. in New Orleans and is chair of the Real Property, Probate and Trust Section Elderly Housing Committee.

egories that can accommodate modern senior housing options. For the most part, the market has outpaced the incorporation of appropriate definitions into zoning codes. The long-term goal is to "modernize" zoning codes to facilitate and integrate senior housing options. For the moment, though, it is necessary to work within existing definitions.

The issues vary from state to state and municipality to municipality. New York City is an interesting case study in contradictions. New York City passed the first zoning resolution in the United States in 1916 and has continued to develop new ways for controlling land use to shape the city. (see Norman Marcus, *Air Rights in New York City: TDR, Zoning Lot Merger and the Well-Considered Plan*, 50 BROOK. L. REV. 867, 868 (1984).) New York has three basic zoning districts: residential, commercial, and manufacturing. The key issue is whether to classify senior housing as a "residential use" or a "community facility use." (See Rachel D. Tanur, *Housing the Elderly in New York*, N.Y. LAW J., Mar. 24, 1997, at S1.) The only existing category in which to place elderly housing as a residential use is a "nonprofit residence for the elderly" (NPR). This category covers facilities that are owned by or constructed with financial assistance from a governmental agency and maintained by a nonprofit corporation. NPR residents must be 62 or older and have fixed incomes. NPRs are permitted in all residential zoning districts (except those limited to single-family homes) and receive certain zoning perks, such as higher density thresholds.

Increased participation by for-profit developers in the senior housing market has meant that the NPR category is no longer sufficient by itself. A for-profit senior housing developer in a residential zoning district must file either as an "apartment," an "apartment hotel," or "rooming units." None of these categories is particularly suited for senior housing. Apartment hotels and apartments are permitted as a matter of right (that is, there is no need to obtain prior approval from the planning commission), but no medical care may be provided on site. Rooming units by definition do not contain full kitchens or baths and are not permitted in lower-density residential districts that otherwise permit multifamily buildings.

It may be more desirable to qualify as a community facility use. The existing community facil-

ity categories include "domiciliary care facilities," "nursing homes," and "philanthropic or nonprofit institutions with sleeping accommodations." Community facilities can sometimes have a higher floor area ratio than residential uses in the same district. Nevertheless, a facility with sleeping accommodations is entitled to a higher floor area ratio only in a commercial district. As a matter of public policy, in residential districts, New York treats community facilities with sleeping accommodations the same as other residential uses. To further complicate matters, the zoning does not permit some existing community facility categories that could accommodate senior housing facilities without first obtaining discretionary review and approval by the city planning commission.

New York City's planning commission is currently trying to revise the zoning resolution to cover the continuum of senior housing options, to eliminate references to obsolete programs and financing criteria, and to grant modest zoning benefits to these facilities. The commission is also considering whether to eliminate the different treatment of for-profit and nonprofit operators. These efforts may be instructive for other local governments facing similar senior housing obstacles.

A municipality's efforts to modernize its zoning regulations may be met with resistance from local neighborhood associations, planning boards, and even other developers. For example, in *B&G Associates v. Zoning Board of Stamford*, 1997 Conn. Super. LEXIS 779 (Conn. Super. Ct. Mar. 20, 1997), Marriott Senior Living Services, a for-profit developer, filed an application for a text change to Stamford's zoning regulations. The application proposed to include within the definition of "Senior Housing and Nursing Home Facility Complex" the term "Assisted Living Residence" and to permit this use as a special exception in certain residential zones, subject to zoning board review and approval. *Id.* at *2. The planning board unanimously recommended approval of the application. A facility that fell within the old definition challenged the board's decision on the grounds that the text change ran counter to the town's comprehensive zoning plan and that there was no adequate definition of "assisted living" in the zoning regulations. *Id.* at *4. The suit was an effort to exclude a potential

461

competitor from the market. Although the court upheld the board's decision and dismissed the suit, the case illustrates that resistance to zoning changes can come from the very group that the changes are designed to benefit.

FHAA Litigation

Zoning ordinance inadequacies are exacerbated when local planning and zoning commissions routinely deny petitions for zoning changes and variances in connection with senior housing developments. Aggrieved parties are more aggressively challenging denials under various constitutional theories and federal statutes, most notably the Fair Housing Amendments Act of 1988, 42 U.S.C. Sections 3601 et seq. (FHAA). The FHAA prohibits discrimination in housing on the basis of handicap and familial status. Most of the controversy has centered around the handicap discrimination provisions because the FHAA specifically exempts "housing for older persons" from the prohibition against discrimination based on familial status. 42 U.S.C. Section 3607(b)(2)(C).

The results of FHAA handicapped discrimination challenges have been mixed. Sometimes the developers prevail. In *Hovsons, Inc. v. Township of Brick*, 89 F.3d 1096 (3d Cir. 1996), the developer applied for a variance from the zoning board to build a nursing home in a "rural-residential-adult community zone." That zone was designed for residential use with a focus on less traffic and a quiet, secluded environment. Under the township's zoning ordinance, nursing homes were permitted only in "hospital support zones," which were commercial in nature. The zoning board denied the developer's application for the variance. The developer filed suit, alleging intentional discrimination and that the zoning ordinance had a disparate impact on handicapped persons. Specifically, the developer alleged that the variance denial violated the FHAA's requirement that "reasonable accommodations" be made for handicapped persons.

Although the district court dismissed the developer's claims, the Third Circuit reversed on appeal. As an initial matter, the court found that a nursing home qualifies as a "dwelling" for FHAA purposes. *Id.* at 1102. The court also found that authority to build a nursing home in a hospital support zone was insufficient to satisfy the township's legal obligation under the FHAA.

Granting a variance to the developer would neither have created an "undue financial and administrative burden" nor fundamentally undermined the township's zoning scheme. Thus, the township was required to make the necessary reasonable accommodations. *Id.* at 1105. Notwithstanding the township's substantial interest in enforcing its zoning law, the court granted injunctive relief to prevent the enforcement of the zoning ordinance provisions that barred the nursing home at the proposed location. *Id.* at 1106. Nevertheless, the court did not invalidate the zoning ordinance itself.

Not all litigation has been resolved in favor of senior housing developers. In *People's Council for Baltimore County v. Mangione*, 584 A.2d 1318 (Md. Ct. App. 1991), Baltimore's planning commission had denied a special exception for a nursing home in a residential district. The court upheld the denial, finding that there was sufficient evidence of an adverse impact, including incompatibility with the surrounding landscape, exacerbation of drainage problems, and increased traffic.

In *East Coast Investments, Inc. v. Zoning Commission of Bridgeport*, No. 95-1231, Conn. Super. 1992 LEXIS 2925 (Conn. Super. Ct. Oct. 5, 1992), a senior housing developer appealed a denial of its petition for a zone change and for a special permit to construct a senior housing facility. The zoning commission denied the petition on several grounds, including excessive density and traffic, inadequate parking and, ironically, the absence of zoning regulations or guidelines applicable to elderly housing in the city regulations. The court summarily upheld the commission's decision, stating that zoning commissions have broad discretion and, when the reasons for a decision are stated, courts should not probe beyond them. *Id.* at *3.

Bryant Woods Inn, Inc. v. Howard County, Maryland, 911 F. Supp. 918 (D. Md. 1996), involved a plaintiff that operated group homes for disabled seniors. The plaintiff petitioned for planning board approval to increase the size of one of its group homes. The board denied the request. The plaintiff filed suit, alleging intentional discrimination and disparate impact under the FHAA. The court found that the plaintiff failed to produce any colorable evidence of intentional discrimination against the elderly or disabled, notwithstanding evidence of political pressure from local residents opposed to expansion of the home and transcripts from the board hearing indicating the use of stereotypes to evaluate the petition. *Id.* at 928–37. The court also found that the board's decision did not have a "disparate impact" on the elderly because only one group or class of persons was affected by the decision. *Id.* at 937–39. Finally, the court found that the denial of the petition was not a failure to make a reasonable accommodation; otherwise, group housing for the elderly would be "beyond the reach of zoning regulations in Howard County." *Id.* at 943.

In *Apfelbaum v. Town of Clarkstown,* 428 N.Y.S.2d 387 (N.Y. Sup. Ct. 1980), the court upheld a zoning ordinance that placed certain size and distance limitations on senior housing complexes. The ordinance was challenged on the grounds that it discriminated against senior citizens because those restrictions were not imposed on other dwellings located in multiple-residence zones. The court held that the restrictions were a reasonable exercise of the town's legitimate objective of zoning for the public health and welfare and for the special housing needs of the elderly. *Id.* at 388–89. Finally, in *Gamble v. City of Escondido,* 104 F.3d 300 (9th Cir. 1997), the court rejected the fair housing claims of a landowner who applied for a variance to construct a facility for handicapped seniors in a single-family zone. The court held that the city was not required to make a reasonable accommodation because the facility provided day health care, which does not fall within the protection of the FHAA. See also *Smith & Lee Assoc., Inc. v. City of Taylor, Michigan,* 102 F.3d 781 (6th Cir. 1996).

Constitutional Challenges

In an attempt to meet elderly housing needs, some municipalities have amended their zoning ordinances to create special districts with minimum-age requirements or to create special overlay zones with age-specific requirements. See, for example, Mesa, Ariz. Ord. 1905 tit. XI, ch. 3 Sections 11-3-9.5. Zoning has always been a sensitive subject because historically it has been used to exclude certain segments of the population. Not surprisingly, age-restrictive zoning has been challenged on various constitutional grounds, including denial of equal protection and substantive due process, and as illegal "spot zoning." (See Robert M. Anderson, American Law of Zoning Section 5.08 (2d ed. 1976).)

Although senior housing zoning has not yet been specifically challenged as exclusionary zoning that singly or collectively excludes undesirable persons from an area, a few courts have struck down ordinances that restrictively define a "family" for purposes of regulating dwelling unit occupancy. In *Baer v. Town of Brookhaven,* 537 N.E.2d 619 (N.Y. 1989), five elderly women lived in a house located in an area zoned for single-family dwellings. Under the local zoning ordinance, any number of persons related by blood, adoption, or marriage could live in a dwelling unit, but no more than four unrelated persons could constitute a family. Id. at 619. The court held the ordinance unconstitutional because there was no defensible public purpose for restricting "the size of a functionally equivalent family but not the size of a traditional family." *Id.* See also *McMinn v. Town of Oyster Bay,* 488 N.E.2d 1240 (N.Y. 1986) (declaring this form of exclusionary zoning unconstitutional).

Some local ordinances prohibit age discrimination in housing with-out including an exception for senior housing facilities. In *Metropolitan Dade County Fair Housing and Employment Appeals Board v. Sunrise Village Mobile Home Park,* 511 So. 2d 962 (Fla. 1987), the defendants operated a mobile home park retirement community. When the 29-year-old plaintiff was denied entrance, he brought charges before Dade County's Fair Housing and Employment Appeals Board, which ruled in favor of his admittance. The trial court reversed the board's decision and overturned the antidiscrimination ordinance, finding that it did not contain reasonable age restrictions. On appeal, the Florida Supreme Court reversed and upheld the ordinance despite evidence that it would, in effect, make retirement communities almost impossible to maintain in Dade County. The court held that the ordinance was a legitimate exercise of police power and well within the county's broad authority to legislate for public health, safety, and morals. *Id.* at 965. See also *Gibson v. County of Riverside,* No. 96-56369, 1997 U.S. App. LEXIS 36408 (9th Cir. Dec. 31, 1997).

Exclusion of the young from unlicensed senior apartment complexes or retirement communities should be upheld if other suitable multigenerational housing is available in the community. In that case, the zoning does not exclude a sizable segment of the population. Retirement communities are most likely to survive if they are only part of a zoning district that is multigenerational overall or if only the elderly want to live there, thus avoiding any challenges. (See Peter J. Stauss, Robert Wolf, and Dana Shilling, AGING AND THE LAW 719 (1992).) The best safeguard to these types of challenges are state laws that specifically authorize age-restrictive housing for senior citizens. See, for example, 65 Ill. Comp. Stat. Ann. 5/11-29.3-1; Mass. Gen. Laws ch. 151B, Section 6.

Other Zoning Obstacles

The most commonly cited reasons for denying zoning changes or variances are inadequate parking and density problems. One of the more creative challenges involves the adverse environmental impact of senior housing. In *Getz v. Pebble Beach Community Services Dist.*, 268 Cal. Rptr. 76 (Cal. Ct. App. 1990), a couple sought to add a "senior housing unit" to their home and applied for a use permit. After a hearing, the zoning administrator granted the use permit subject to the condition that sewer service be provided to the housing unit. The relevant service district refused to issue a sewer connection permit, citing excessive sewerage discharge. California has an express legislative policy of encouraging the creation of residential units for persons older than 60. (Cal. Gov't Code Section 65852.1.) Nevertheless, the court held that the policy supporting senior housing must yield to the competing state policy mandating protection of coastal waters and to the local land use plan implementing that policy. (*Getz*, 268 Cal. Rptr. at 79.) Notably, the zoning administrator initially found that adequate sewerage disposal and water supply facilities were readily available to the site.

A similar issue arose in *Sutton v. Board of Trustees of Endicott*, 505 N.Y.S.2d 263 (N.Y. 1986). There, the village board granted the zoning change necessary to build the first phase of a two-phase elderly housing complex and skilled nursing facility. At the hearing, the board found that the first phase of the project would not create any significant environmental impact. Several local homeowners challenged the zoning

change. The court remanded the case to the board on the grounds that it failed to evaluate properly the environmental effects of the second phase of the facility, which was not to be constructed for another ten years. *Id.* at 265.

In some cases, courts fail to specify the grounds for denying a zoning variance and instead cite generalized concerns about nonconformance with the existing neighborhood or the municipality's plan of development. In *Mackowski v. Stratford Zoning Comm'n*, No. 309582, 1995 Conn. Super. LEXIS 3522 (Conn. Super. Ct. Dec. 12, 1995), a developer proposed to construct a senior citizen apartment complex in a district that permitted residence apartments only with zoning commission approval. The project complied with the general requirements for apartments in the zoning regulations, and there was evidence in the record that the complex would create minimal interference with the neighborhood. *Id.* at *19. The court, however, found that certain public welfare concerns were implicated. Construction of the housing project would necessitate razing a historic, but abandoned, boarding house on the proposed site. Notwithstanding the photographic and testimonial evidence about the deplorable condition of the boarding house, the court held that the commission was justified in denying the plaintiff's application. *Id.* See also *Constantine v. Wadsworth City Planning Comm'n*, No. 2519-M, 1996 Ohio App. LEXIS 2328 (Ohio Ct. App. June 5, 1996) (upholding the issuance of a conditional zoning permit for an ALF over objections that the ALF would not be harmonious and appropriate in appearance with the existing and intended zoning area).

Conclusion

The senior housing industry will continue to grow well into the 21st century. As the population ages, the need for elderly housing grows. States and municipalities eventually will adopt more modern statutes and codes that address the special circumstances of senior housing. The goal for developers, local citizen groups, state and local governments, and their lawyers should be to cooperate in that effort to ensure that senior citizens have sufficient workable housing alternatives from which to choose.

72
Competency and Undue Influence: Issues for Elder Estate Planning

HOLTEN D. SUMMERS

Introduction

The elderly constitute the fastest growing segment of our society. Along with the growth in numbers comes a growing emphasis on elder law, due largely to the unique legal problems of the elderly. The children of the elderly are grown, and thus guardianships for minor children and college educations are no longer an issue in the estate plan. The elderly client focuses on financing retirement, facing the prospect of declining health, and transferring wealth to heirs. The elderly client will ask how to avoid probate and reduce or avoid estate taxes, and how to pay for long-term care.

While some elderly clients enjoy good health, others are not as fortunate. Some ailments have been around for some time but, like Alzheimer's disease, were never identified. Diseases that do not impair cognition, such as Parkinson's disease, are now sometimes treated with medication that interferes with the ability to think clearly and rationally.

In addition to these sources of confusion, the elderly may be generally more susceptible to the suggestions and influence of family members, close friends, and associates, all of which present problems for the estate planner. While clients' abilities at motives in estate planning should not be suspect simply because they are older than 65, lawyers must be sensitive and recognize that elderly clients may be vulnerable.

What Does the Problem Look Like?

Scenario One

A client calls to say that her spouse has been diagnosed with Alzheimer's disease. "We want to

Holten D. Summers is a shareholder with Webber & Thies, P.C., Urbana, Illinois.

change our estate plan so that my husband is taken care of in case something happens to me. We thought that we should change our wills and maybe create a trust or two." Just about now, you should be feeling uneasy. The problem may not be whether the transfers are appropriate, but whether the husband is competent to execute the necessary documents.

Scenario Two

You receive a phone call from a client who would like to come to see you with her parent about some estate planning. Yes, her mother has a will, but it was prepared many years ago and is out of date. "Mom gets confused easily and we thought it would be a good idea to get her in to see an attorney to make sure everything is properly prepared—you know, for when something happens to her." An appointment is made and mom and daughter show up. Mom is elderly and obviously frail.

Seated across from you, the daughter says "Mom wants a new will and everything is to go to me, because I'm the only child. She also needs a power of attorney so that I can do everything for her. We just came from the bank and she added me to her checking and savings accounts so that I can sign on them, It's my understanding that mom can make gifts to me in the amount of $10,000 each year without any tax consequences. We want to do that, too. Oh by the way, she is also going to give my son $10,000 a year for a while, too. She might have to go into a nursing home someday and we don't want to spend everything on that, right mom?"

Again, that uneasy feeling. When you ask mom if this is right, she simply echoes that she wants everything to go to her daughter and needs the power of attorney because she gets confused and sometimes and forgets things. Of course, you can ask the daughter to leave the room and ask the mother these questions, but you're likely to get the same answer.

Obviously, mom may indeed want everything to go to her only child. Also, powers of attorney are a valid and effective tool, and there is nothing wrong with conferring such power on a grown child, who sees to the everyday needs of the parent. Gift giving is an effective method of transferring wealth from one person to another, especially when the annual exclusion is considered.

There are lots of variations on these scenes, but the basic issue here is whether the elderly client is competent to make these kinds of decisions, and whether he or she is being subjected to undue influence to make the kinds of transfers contemplated. What have the courts said about competency and undue influence—what is the responsibility of the lawyer—and does it matter that the person is incompetent, or being subjected to undue influence?

Competency

The issue of competency has been addressed by the courts for decades. The Illinois Supreme Court in 1910 defined competency as follows:

> [A]lthough the mind may be impaired by disease incident to old age, still, if the grantor in a deed be capable of transacting ordinary business,—if he understand the nature of the business in which he is engaged and the effect of what he is doing and can exercise his will with reference thereto,—his acts will be valid.[1]

It is obvious that no action taken by an elderly person should be invalidated, or even subject to suspicion, simply because of his or her age. In fact, in Illinois, as in most jurisdictions, the presumption is that every person is sane until the contrary is *proved*.[2]

When there is a challenge to an individual's capacity to execute a will, transfer property through a deed, and make gifts, it must address the capacity at the time the act was undertaken.

Lack of capacity for medical reasons has been classified by the courts as, for example, old age,

illness, or insane delusions.[3] But whatever the label, the affliction must have interfered with the individual's capacity at the time that the act is undertaken. The fact that the person was confused or suffered delusions before and after the event does not establish that he or she lacked capacity at the time.

The effect of this position by the courts is that the individual who suffers from Alzheimer's disease can be capable of executing documents to alter his or her estate plan. Alzheimer's patients are often confused, and may not always be able to grasp the significance of their acts. However, if they do at the time the documents are executed, the execution would be effective and would withstand challenge. This is the importance of doing estate planning early in the diagnosis of Alzheimer's, when the individual has periods of unquestionable lucidity.

There are subtle differences in the criteria for competency applicable to wills, deeds, and gifts. For a will, the courts have held that

> [t]estamentary capacity requires that the testator have sufficient mental ability to know and remember the natural objects of her bounty, to comprehend the kind and character of property held, and to make disposition thereof according to some plan formed in the testator's mind.[4]

For a deed, the grantor must have the ability to transact ordinary business and the "mental ability to cope with an antagonist and to understand and protect his own interests."[5] For a gift, the question is whether the donor at the time of the gift had the ability to comprehend the nature and effect of his or her act.[6]

The important point is that all standards of competency test the individual's *ability* or capacity, not his or her actual knowledge at the time of execution.[7] The fact that your client is mistaken about some element of the transaction does not invalidate the transfer due to competency. The client is only required to have the *ability* to comprehend.

---

1. Kelly v. Nusbaum, 244 Ill 158, 91 NE72, 74, (1910).
2. Wiszowaty v. Baumgard, 257 Ill App 3d 812, 629 NE2d 624 (1st D 1994), citing *In re* Estate of Ciesiolkiewicz, 243 Ill App 3d 506, 611 NE2d 1278 (1st D 1993).

3. *In re* Estate of Kline, 245 Ill App 3d 413, 613 NE2d 1329 (3d D 1993).
4. Matter of Estate of Osborn, 234 Ill App 3d 651, 599 NE2d 1329, 1333 (3d D 1992).
5. Moneta v. Hoinacki, 394 Ill 47, 67 NE2d 204, 210 (1946); see also *In re* Estate of Cunningham, 207 Ill App 3d 72, 565 NE2d 301 (4th D 1990).
6. In the Matter of the Estate of Clements, 152 Ill App 3d 890, 505 NE2d 7, 9 (5th D 1987).
7. George v. Moorhead, 399 Ill 497, 78 NE2d 216 (1948).

Undue Influence

A more common problem in estate planning for the elderly is undue influence. Certainly one spouse has influence over the other. Certainly a grown child has influence over an elderly surviving parent. However, the issue of undue influence arises when the elderly person in question engages in transactions contrary to his or her original intent or plan. An individual who seeks to set aside a will, deed, or gift can raise a presumption of undue influence (which is rebuttable) simply by establishing four elements. An excellent discussion of the presumption and how it operates appears in a third district opinion:

> A rebuttable presumption of undue influence arises when a petitioner is able to establish four elements:
> "'(1) a fiduciary relationship between testator and a person who receives a substantial benefit under the will . . .;
> (2) a testator in a dependent situation in which the substantial beneficiaries are in dominant rolls;
> (3) a testator who reposed trust and confidence in such beneficiaries; and
> (4) a will prepared or procured and executed in circumstances wherein such beneficiaries were instrumental or participated.'"[8]

Translating these criteria into a scenario, consider the following: A parent gives a child property and health care powers of attorney. The parent is frail and depends on the child for transportation and day-to-day care. The parent changes his or her will, giving the bulk of their estate to the child, and the will is prepared by the child's lawyer. Given these facts, it would appear to be sufficient to raise the presumption of undue influence. It does not mean that there actually was undue influence—only that the presumption is raised.

"A presumption is not evidence and cannot be treated as evidence," the supreme court has written. "As soon as evidence is produced which is contrary to the presumption which arose before the contrary proof was offered the presumption vanishes entirely."[9] Therefore, the respondent (presumed to be the grown child in our scenario) would have to present evidence showing that one of the criteria is not met. Rebutting the presump-

tion does not remove the question of undue influence, but simply removes the presumption. "The prevailing theory regarding presumptions that Illinois follows . . . is Thayer's bursting bubble hypothesis: once evidence is introduced contrary to the presumption, the bubble bursts and the presumption vanishes."[10]

However, the issue of undue influence remains and the trier of fact must decide the issue based of the evidence presented.[11]

In spite of the many cases on undue influence, there are no fixed words to describe it. The court has stated that undue influence is defined by the circumstances of each case.[12] In other words, we don't know how to describe it, but we know it when we see it.

Role of the Lawyer

The lawyer's role in estate planing is to assist the client in developing an estate plan, drafting the necessary documents in support of the plan, and overseeing the execution of the documents. However, as the scenarios in this chapter illustrate, lawyers must be mindful of who their client is—whose plan they are implementing—as well as what their responsibility is regarding the competency of the client, and whether or not the client is being subjected to undue influences.

If the client is a long-standing one, then it is easier for the lawyer to determine (1) that the plan is consistent with the client's intent and desires; (2) that the client has the capacity or ability to execute the necessary documents; and (3) that the client is not being subjected to influences that may be contrary to his or her intent and plan.

For clients who have been diagnosed with an ailment (such as Alzheimer's disease) that will interfere with the ability to make decisions, you should review the estate plan to assure their care when they become totally incompetent. Recommending the creation of trusts and durable powers of attorney is simply good advice. To mitigate the likelihood of a challenge to documents that have been executed by the client, take the following steps:

---

8. *In re* Estate of Kline, 245 Ill App 3d 413, 613 NE2d 1329, 1337 (3d D 1993).
9. Franciscan Sisters Health Care Corporation v. Dean, 95 Ill 2d 452, 448 NE2d 872, 876 (1983).
10. *Id*, 448 NE2d at 877.
11. Manning v. Mock, 119 Ill App 3d 788, 457 NE2d 447 (4th D 1983).
12. *In re* the Estate of Hoover, 155 Ill 2d 402, 615 NE2d 736 (1993).

1. The elderly person with cognitive problems, like the Alzheimer's patient, is generally more lucid in the morning. Fatigue and confusion go hand in hand. Check with family members to confirm this fact and schedule the document signing for the morning.

2. See if the client is taking any medication that may affect his or her ability to understand instructions or recognize people. If medication might interfere, check with the doctor about delaying it on the day of signing documents.

3. At the signing, review each document with the client, and have the witnesses present. Ask the client if he or she understands the intent and effect of the documents. Converse with the client so that the witnesses can see that he or she can understand what is being done and why. Remember, the questions asked at the signing of a will are not for the benefit of the client, but for the witnesses, to establish testamentary capacity.

4. Consider video- or audiotaping the signing to provide an independent record of the client's lucidity, or having witnesses prepare memos to refresh their memories in the event they are called to testify on the individual's competency.

Prepare a memo to the file after the meeting. Document all meetings, even those in which the client was not in condition to execute documents. The fact that you postponed the meeting to a time when the client was lucid will support your assertion that he or she was competent at the signing.[13] This procedure should be effective for any client, not just for Alzheimer's patients.

To reveal undue influence, compare the documents to those you have prepared in the past to see if the client's previous testamentary intent is being altered. For example, if the new trust is consistent with the present will, it is unlikely that the client is being subjected to undue influences. However, if the will states that the estate is to pass to nephew "A" and the new trust will pass everything to niece "B," you should investigate further to ascertain, if you can, that the change in testamentary intent is the client's choice.

Serving clients with whom you have no previous relationship is more difficult. Competency should be addressed as indicated above. Ask questions designed to convince you and the witnesses that the testator/grantor/donor can understand what is taking place. Whether or not the new client is being subjected to undue influence is, without question, a more difficult call.

13. *Kline*, 613 NE. 2d 1329.

73

A Brief Look at the Uniform Custodial Trust Act

RICHARD V. WELLMAN AND EUGENE F. SCOLES

Introduction

The Uniform Custodial Trust Act (UCTA), a 1987 product of the Uniform Law Commissioners, presently on the statute books in twelve states, was studied in 1993 by two committees of the ABA Senior Lawyers Division: the Wills, Probate and Trusts Committee and the Durable Power of Attorney and Living Wills Committee. This chapter examines the sources and content of UCTA and the points that should be considered by bar and legislative committees interested in the legislation.

Gifts to Minors Legislation and UCTA

Gifts to minors legislation teaches that enormous benefits can flow from statutes designed solely to simplify otherwise complex legal transactions. Before the advent of gifts to minors legislation in the early 1950s, gifts to minors in outright form or in trust were familiar but complicated. Of course, a minor could simply be designated as owner in a transfer document, but expensive court guardianship proceedings to manage the property prior to the donee's majority were likely to follow. Present-interest trusts for minors avoided guardianships but entailed expensive preparation and management assistance. Savings incentives and tax advantages, as well as parental concern for the educational needs of children and grandchildren, nevertheless impelled financially comfortable persons to make such gifts in spite of high transaction costs.

Gifts to minors legislation responded to the problem and, since 1950, has become a highly popular feature of the law in all states. A simple reference to the gifts to minors statute in a title document incorporates a well-conceived, tax-sensitive, and practical form for a gift to a minor. No special drafting is required because the statute replaces the need by providing the details of this statutory fiduciary arrangement. The legislation has benefited millions of donors and their beneficiaries. Lawyers have readily accepted this new method for accomplishing a client's estate-planning goals. Even though the development meant less drafting and guardianship business for lawyers, it enabled lawyers to meet the client's need at a minimum cost.

A similar need for commonly desired property arrangements to be simplified by legislation is present in the problems attending ownership by elderly persons. The 1950s minors are now highly mobile, aging adults with longer life expectancies and increased risk of outliving their ability to manage their affairs. They must anticipate the perils of guardianships that may well follow if they fail to establish a plan for management of their assets in case they become unable to do it themselves. The risks and advantages of alternative management arrangements such as shared ownership with dual controls, living trusts, and durable powers of attorney must be considered, as well as potential probate costs on assets left to pass through probate at death. Prodded by federal tax burdens and tax savings opportunities available to personal holdings exceeding $600,000, the wealthier elderly frequently resort to individually prepared living trusts to serve their estate-planning and management objectives. Others who

Richard V. Wellman is Alston Professor of Law Emeritus at the University of Georgia Law School in Athens, Georgia, and Eugene F. Scoles is the Max L. Rowe Professor of Law Emeritus of the University of Illinois, Distinguished Professor of Law Emeritus of the University of Oregon, and former Dean of the University of Oregon Law School.

have fewer assets and for whom tax savings are not so significant are worried about the cost of trusts and are unsure of what they should do.

The concept of aiding elderly owners with a statutory trust modeled after gifts to minors legislation surfaced in Massachusetts about twenty years ago when three sections were added to that state's trust law to describe "statutory custodianship trusts." The legislation was directed at difficulties encountered under durable powers of attorney in getting insurance companies, banks, and other third parties to honor requests for sales or transfers on behalf of incapacitated owners. Third-party concerns often related to lack of specificity in the power or to the risks of unknown revocation or expiration implicit in agency arrangements. The Massachusetts statute offered the new trust form as a valuable alternative to durable powers because of the greater protection to third persons who deal in good faith with a title-holding trustee. The Massachusetts law makes transfer of property to another who is designated as "statutory custodianship trustee" sufficient to create a revocable trust that directs the trustee to "apply income and principal by payment to the transferor or by direct expenditure as may be necessary for the comfortable and suitable maintenance and support of the transferor and his family" and to transfer any unused trust assets to the transferor's estate at death.

The Joint Editorial Board for the Uniform Probate Code (JEB-UPC) and the Uniform Law Commissioners (ULC) were also concerned in the late 1970s about numerous reports of difficulties with durable powers. In response, the Uniform Durable Power of Attorney Act (1979) and corresponding revisions to the Uniform Probate Code included new provisions designed to improve acceptance of durable powers of attorney. At the same time, the JEB-UPC undertook to pursue the Massachusetts custodial trust concept as an alternative standby method of management for assets of an owner who might later become unable to manage them. As a result, the UCTA was promulgated by the ULC in 1987 and endorsed by the ABA at Philadelphia in 1988.

The Uniform Custodial Trust Act

The UCTA is considerably more extensive than the earlier Massachusetts model. A brief prefatory note in ULC's UCTA pamphlet serves as a comprehensive description. The pamphlet, with full text and section-by-section commentary, is recommended for careful reading by all lawyers. It is available on request to ULC, 676 St. Clair Street, Suite 1700, Chicago, Illinois 60611.

The most important features of the UCTA are as follows:

1. The statutory trust is created when an asset is transferred to a person designated "as custodial trustee under the [enacting state] Uniform Custodial Trust Act" and another person (who may be the transferor) is designated as beneficiary. Only assets then or later transferred to the same trustee for the same beneficiary are subject to the particular trust.

2. An owner may, by written declaration of trust, cause a described asset to become the subject of a custodial trust of which the declarant is trustee and another is designated as beneficiary. Such a trust, though terminable on demand by the beneficiary, cannot be revoked by the declarant former owner. An owner may not, by declaration, create a custodial trust of which he or she is both sole trustee and beneficiary. Drafters of the uniform act sought assurance that someone other than the beneficiary would have legal title for use if and when the beneficiary becomes incompetent. Note that acceptance of the UCTA does not preclude conventionally drawn, self-declared trusts which normally include provisions serving to shift title to a successor trustee in the event of the trustee-beneficiary's incompetence. Though valid, such a conventional trust would not be a custodial trust under the UCTA.

3. A person who is able to control a future transfer can cause the transfer to be directed to a custodial trust for a designated beneficiary. Hence, a future benefit under a contractual arrangement (for example, a life insurance policy or retirement plan benefit) or a trust can be made the subject of a custodial trust.

4. The beneficiary is full owner of the beneficial interest in all assets of a custodial trust and while not incapacitated may direct the trustee to pay income or any or all assets in the trust to the beneficiary at any time. When the trustee determines that the beneficiary has become

incapable of managing the assets, the trust automatically, without any court proceeding, becomes a discretionary support trust, with the trustee obligated to expend so much of the trust property as the trustee deems advisable for the use and benefit of the beneficiary and individuals dependent on the beneficiary. The beneficiary or any person interested in the trust property or the welfare of the beneficiary may challenge a trustee's determination of beneficiary incapacity in court.

5. Upon the death of the beneficiary, the trustee of a custodial trust has a duty to pay or deliver remaining trust property to the person last designated in a writing signed by the beneficiary that was delivered to the trustee in the beneficiary's lifetime. In the absence of such a direction, the remaining property in the deceased beneficiary's trust goes to the beneficiary's estate, except when the trust is for the benefit of two persons and survivorship rights control. Another exception avoids payment to a beneficiary's estate if the trust was created by a third person who designated a death beneficiary to take in the event the primary beneficiary did not terminate the trust and made no death benefit designation.

6. The UCTA specifies that appointment of a guardian or conservator for a custodial trust beneficiary does not terminate a custodial trust. However, prior to a beneficiary's death, a duly appointed conservator may exercise a beneficiary's power to terminate, meaning that the trustee will always be answerable to another even if the beneficiary and sole owner becomes totally incapable.

7. Although designed to serve typical needs for senility insurance and nonprobate transfers of persons whose assets do not generate significant tax concerns, the custodial trust is also useful for other purposes—for example, as an alternative to a power of attorney for management of real estate during an owner's absences from the jurisdiction, as a device for avoiding ancillary administration of out-of-state real estate, or to make a gift to a surviving spouse that will qualify for marital deduction purposes and, in the event of the spouse's death and failure to end the trust or designate a death beneficiary, pass to a death beneficiary designated by the donor.

8. The statute suggests the following simple form for establishing a custodial trust by transfer:

Transfer Under the [Enactment State] Uniform Custodial Trust Act

I _____ name of transferor or name and representative capacity if a fiduciary), transfer to _____ (name of trustee other than transferor), as custodial trustee for _____ (name of beneficiary) as beneficiary and _____ as distributee on termination of the trust in absence of direction by the beneficiary under the [enacting state] Uniform Custodial Trust Act, the following: (insert a description of the custodial trust property legally sufficient to identify and transfer each item of property).
Dated: _____
(Signature)

It also provides ten illustrations of "customary methods of transferring or evidencing ownership of property [that] may be used to create a custodial trust." Included are:

Registration of ownership of a life or endowment insurance policy or annuity contract with the issuer in the name of a trust company, an adult other than the transferor, or the transferor if the beneficiary is other than the transferor, designated in substance: "as custodial trustee for _____ (name of beneficiary) under the [enacting state] Uniform Custodial Trust Act.

Execution, delivery, and recordation of a conveyance of an interest in real property in the name of a trust company, an adult other than the transferor, or the transferor if the beneficiary is other than the transferor, designated in substance: "as custodial trustee for _____ (name of beneficiary) under the [enacting state] Uniform Custodial Trust Act.

9. Administrative powers of custodial trustees and suitable statutory protections for third persons dealing in good faith with custodial trustees are detailed in UCTA, as are rights and remedies of beneficiaries and needed protections for custodial trustees.

UCTA Enactment Prospects

To date, the UCTA's enactment record has been somewhat disappointing to proponents. Rhode Island became the first UCTA state in 1988. Hawaii and Idaho enactments occurred in 1989, Minnesota and Virginia in 1990, Arkansas and Wisconsin in 1991, and New Mexico in 1992. Missouri enacted a custodial trust law a year before the UCTA was promulgated by ULC, and 1989 amendments largely conformed Missouri's law to the UCTA making Missouri the ninth state with the UCTA. Arizona, Massachusetts, New Mexico, and North Carolina enactments after 1992 brought the number of enacting states to twelve.

Except for Missouri and Virginia, the enactments do not appear to have resulted from bar association studies. Indeed, in some infrequent instances where a state's uniform law commissioners have succeeded in persuading the state bar to study the proposal, resulting reports have tended to nit-pick details in generally unenthusiastic conclusions. For example, an Oregon report fretted over the possibility that a trustee's income tax return would be involved, though surely none would be if a husband and wife are made cotrustees for the benefit of either the husband or the wife. A New York committee suggested that a dollar value ceiling, say $50,000 or $75,000, should have been imposed on custodial trusts and speculated that donors using the statutory trust form to make gifts of beneficial interest to another as beneficiary would be surprised and possibly upset to learn that a UCTA trust is revocable only by the beneficiary. Such surprise seems doubtful inasmuch as the statutory trust aligns with existing conventional trust law. Virginia slightly modified the fiduciary standards under that state's enactment by changing the standard from a prudent person's handling of the *property of another* to the handling of the trustee's *own property*. The Virginia statute also deviates from the UCTA in that a conservator must obtain a court order before terminating a custodial trust arrangement established by or for one for whom a conservator is later appointed.

No bar study of which we are aware expressly criticizes the UCTA as being a threat to lawyers' fees for preparation of trust instruments or as being dangerous in the hands of ill-advised persons. However, statutory forms for wills have proved unpopular with many lawyers because of imagined concerns about loss of fees or ill-advised use, and it would not be surprising if reservations about the UCTA, disguised as technical objections, were not similarly rooted. Such concerns might give pause if one could find a connection between any propensity of consumers to act foolishly and a new, simplified trust form. Joint asset registrations and commercial and homemade forms for deeds, trusts, wills, and powers of attorney are freely available for use by all, including the foolish, making it difficult to

argue that suppression of the custodial trust is vital for anyone's *protection*.

What can be said about future prospects for UCTA enactments? The prospects are good. In early 1993, the American Association of Retired Persons' (AARP) national office dedicated to state legislative concerns of elderly persons issued a ringing AARP endorsement to interested legislators. Following a description of UCTA, the AARP statement observes:

> Most persons will need professional assistance in setting up a custodial trust and in understanding the rights and duties of trustee and beneficiary. Lawyers called upon to assist may decide that a particular client needs a custom-made arrangement serving estate planning needs beyond those served by the "senility insurance" and nonprobate transfer at death functions of the statutory trust. However, for clients with estates below federal transfer tax exemption levels, the custodial trust frequently will be all that is needed, especially in cases where a close friend or family member is willing to serve as trustee. In consequence and with the statute in place, law office trust service at a price well below that usually charged for drafting trust instruments should become available.
>
> Enactment of the custodial trust statute should be followed by education of consumers about the new law by AARP, columnists and other sources, along with education of lawyers regarding appropriate uses and fees for counseling about custodial trusts. Ideally, "custodial trust" might replace the over-promoted "living trust" label and come to be recognized as a familiar, low-cost, law office service that is useful to avoid the threat of guardianship and conservators for persons approaching old age.
>
> Proper implementation of a new custodial trust statute will depend heavily on whether [a state's] lawyers will use the custodial trust in serving limited estate planning needs of persons without federal transfer tax problems for fees below those now charged for preparation of complex wills and trusts. AARP recognizes that such implementation may or may not occur. Nonetheless, AARP urges enactment of the Uniform Custodial Trust Act. With the act in place, educational efforts aimed at consumers and lawyers can hasten the day when clear and affordable protection against loss of an owner's ability to manage for self and associated guardianship risks will become available.

One of the authors of this article recently forwarded a copy of the AARP statement to the chair of a major state's probate and trust law committee. In the letter, note was made of recent action by that committee declining to undertake a serious study of UCTA. That action was contrasted with the same group's responses to a lengthy report of a subcommittee investigating estate planning by nonlawyer financial planners. The letter continued:

> So, at successive meetings, the committee rejected recommendations to support [state name] enactment of a custodial trust proposal, and signaled continuing sharp interest in promotions by nonlawyers of "living trusts."

Is there reason for concern about the committee's actions as reflected by these agenda items? There is no surprise here. Bar leaders plainly must be concerned, if anyone is to be, about any threatened displacement of lawyers in estate planning by hit and run hucksters holding themselves out as "financial planners." Just as plainly, it is unsurprising that a committee of busy practitioners might see little reason to devote the hours and energy necessary to analyze a new and complex proposal for a "custodial trust" statute, especially when cursory inspection of the proposal reveals that it is designed merely to facilitate production of one kind of limited purpose trust and adds nothing by way of new or changed substantive law.

The lawyers in your state, like their counterparts in many other areas of the country, have a public image problem in the probate area. They need to develop and promote greater efficiency in law office services to estate planning clients if they hope to stay ahead of or with financial counselors and others anxious to tap a market fueled by increased affluence and consumer hesitation to seek advice from lawyers. The custodial trust is complex enough to discourage amateur advisors and do-it-yourselfers, meaning that it is likely to be, like the will, primarily a law office product. The proposed custodial trust statute is designed to enable lawyers to give needed service with a minimum investment of time and equipment. It could aid the profession to develop a low cost item that might lend itself to improving the public's image of what lawyers do and for how much. More importantly, if properly nurtured as a friendly connecting link between 30 million plus AARP members and the legal profession, lawyers might discover an answer to the "financial planner" risk and an affirmative response to some very troublesome image problems that plague the profession.

Subsequently, the committee decided to revisit the UCTA proposal but ended up reaffirming its original position. Bar committees can be difficult!

Recommendation

The Wills, Probate and Trusts and the Durable Power of Attorney and Living Wills committees have recommended that lawyers in states that have yet to enact the UCTA give serious consider-

ation to the proposal and, as they do so, to keep in mind the AARP position that its members should use law offices for trust preparation. Many members of the ABA Senior Lawyers Division and their counterparts in state bar associations across the country practiced law a generation or so ago when firms were much smaller and much less specialized than at present. Their experience should help younger colleagues understand that law offices need the contacts and client goodwill that can grow from low-cost client service. Trust preparation by lawyers presently carries a reputation of being complicated and expensive. However, with the UCTA on the statute books, a living trust fitting the foreseeable needs of many clients can be prepared and put into effect with the addition of a few words in a transfer or registration document. Surely a modest fee, rather than the higher living-trust rates currently reported, would mean more clients and more opportunities for advice about tax and other benefits.

Probate avoidance and living-trust promotions have generated a confusing array of property arrangements and a host of aggressive new financial experts and planners striving to become dominant in assisting families with money management and estate planning. Lawyers need to reestablish their credentials in these areas. The custodial trust proposal offers a rare opportunity for generating a new public awareness of the usefulness of lawyers that bar committees should not be allowed to let slip away.

Conclusion

Senior lawyers can play a special role in stimulating local bar studies that can lead to UCTA enactments and the wide availability in law offices of low-cost trusts that can go far toward calming the turmoil generated by probate law's notorious reputation. This article is a call endorsed by two committees of the ABA Senior Lawyers Division for interest in the UCTA and assistance in getting it enacted so that it can be implemented by lawyers interested in giving good service to clients. Public interest will be well-served if persons owning modest estates can be made comfortable about consulting law offices for advice about trusts and other estate-planning opportunities.

Part VIII
When a Lawyer Dies

74
What Happens When a Lawyer Dies: Survey Responses of the Organized Bar

STEPHEN N. MASKALERIS AND VIVIENNE K. COOPERMAN

The information contained in this article was culled from a nationwide survey conducted by the authors of 118 ABA-affiliated bar associations and is presently in the process of publication. All fifty states responded to the survey.

Preface

Lawyers die as all humans do. But when a solo or small practitioner dies suddenly without plans in place for the continuance, transfer, or closure of his or her practice (files, financial and fiduciary accounts, practice business records, and so on) chaos frequently results. It is very real and personal to every lawyer, his or her family and friends and, significantly, to the clients of the law practice.

A recent completed survey of all ABA-affiliated entities conducted for the ABA by the authors addresses this most serious problem, and the responses received suggest actions that might be taken by the organized bar to improve the situation.

The survey is expected to be published in its entirety in the near future with all of the state responses appended. This chapter is but a brief summary of some of the survey responses.

Stephen N. Maskaleris is the principal of Maskaleris & Associates, a litigation law firm in Morristown, New Jersey. He is in the House of Delegates and presently chair of the Planning for Retirement Committee of the Senior Lawyers Division. Vivienne K. Cooperman is an associate lawyer in the firm.

The Problem

In large law firms and the corporate world, lawyers are fungible. One leaves; another takes his place. On the other hand, a solo practitioner has complete ownership of his or her case load and responsibility for clients. It is in this "solo" world "where the rubber meets the road" that the problem arises. A lawyer's practice, clients, estate, and family are integrally bound together when death occurs and the necessity for appropriate action is urgent and real.

Close to 300,000 lawyers are in solo practice today and some 12 percent are 65 or older, suggesting that in any given year 36,000 lawyers could die and leave millions of clients adrift and rudderless.

The Survey and Responses

The survey question of "What Happens When a Lawyer Dies" was presented to the bar associations of fifty states, five U.S. territories, and sixty-one county and city bars—116 bar groups in total—in three successive mailings between August 1996 and January 1997. Responses were received from all fifty state bar associations, and from half of the local bars' groups, a clear indication of the topic's importance.

Twenty-nine of the *responding* state and territorial bars answered that they have plans to deal with the death of a member through court rules, disciplinary rules, state bar programs and, occasionally, by informal conservatorships or through "buddy" relationships. Twenty-two states, however, have *no plan* at all!

Of the sixty-one local bar groups surveyed, nine responding county bars and eight city bar groups said they employed existing state procedures; but even those states and localities with formal plans in place observed that requests for action are infrequent. Whether this was from lack of awareness or lack of need is not known.

Although twenty-nine states and territories answering said they had some sort of procedure in place, in fact, most were informal. Their comments suggested difficulties resulting from state administration: little or no staffing, too long a time-lag to respond, cost to the bar association, cost to lawyers, taking responsibility, and so on.

Wisconsin, a state with a well-defined plan, combined theory with *effective procedures,* which seemed to be lacking in many other jurisdictions. Established in 1994, Wisconsin's plan utilizes the state's Lawyer Assistance Corporation to guarantee malpractice protection to trustee-attorneys handling the closure of deceased lawyers' practices, making them employees of the nonprofit corporation set up by the state bar to procure and maintain professional liability insurance coverage in these matters.

Under the Wisconsin plan the process begins when an interested person files a petition certifying that a lawyer has died and there is no satisfactory arrangement to wind up his or her affairs. The petition is served upon the administrator or executor of the estate, an adult heir, or someone appointed by the court. Special administrators may be appointed if necessary. A court hearing is then held to determine whether satisfactory representation exists. The county circuit court will then *promptly* appoint a trustee counsel to protect clients' rights, files, and property. The personal representative or estate heirs have a right to nominate a trustee counsel. The deceased lawyer's estate is liable for fees and expenses under this system established by supreme court rule.

The appointed trustee may also assist the estate's personal representative in the termination or sale of the deceased lawyer's law practice under another state court rule modeled after ABA Model Rule 1:17, which deals with the sale of a law practice. Trustee-attorneys or their firms, however, may not serve in any other capacity in

the administration of the deceased lawyer's firm, nor be permitted to act as successor lawyer unless the trustee is eligible to become a purchaser of the practice under the court rules. The trustee-attorney is compensated from assets of the estate for services rendered and for reasonable and necessary expenses.

By contrast, among states reporting on their *informal* procedures, Michigan, which encompasses both urban and rural practices, allows the sale of a law practice, and the state bar has pending its own proposed rule on law practice receiverships because the ABA Model Rules are thought to be inadequate. Guidelines are being developed. Maryland, on the other hand, has not adopted ABA Model Rule 1:17 because the rule is considered to be a violation of attorney-client confidentiality. Maryland considers management of the practice of the deceased lawyer to be an essential part of the estate planning process and relies on its Client Security Trust Fund rule and an eight-year-old ethics opinion in these cases.

In New Jersey, when nothing else avails, any interested party may apply to the assignment judge in the county where the deceased lawyer practiced for appointment of a trustee-attorney under rule 1:20-19 of the court rules to protect clients' interests and then the interests of the lawyer. The trustee-attorney is extended immunity from liability for conduct in the performance of official duties and may accept offered employment from any client with the client's consent. Legal fees and costs for services may also be applied for from the law practice of the deceased lawyer. Significantly, by New Jersey Rule of Professional Conduct (RPC 1.1.7), a deceased lawyer's law practice may be sold by his or her estate, thus facilitating the entire closure procedure.

Among states and territories which responded that they had no plans in place, the less populous ones pointed out the difficulties in assuming another lawyer's files in locales where client confidentiality could be too easily breached by this action. And on the other hand, a state's assumption of responsibility ultimately could result in moving client files too far away from the locality where the deceased lawyer practiced to be effective.

Wyoming and Montana, although claiming no policy, indicated some solo lawyers had "mutual assistance pacts" to deal with death when it occurs. Interestingly, Kings County, New York, one of New York City's five boroughs, handles the situation in much the same way; although geographically part of the largest city in the United States, most of its lawyers are to be found in solo or small firm practice. In Brooklyn, as in Montana and Wyoming, an informal "buddy" system functions efficiently and effectively to conclude the practices of deceased lawyers.

Clearly, these responses indicate regional differences in responding to the death of a lawyer and suggest that statewide mandatory rules are often difficult to administer and of little use.

County and City Bar Association Responses

Eighteen county bars and thirteen city gars responding to the survey indicated they had no formal programs in place, usually relying on state procedures to deal with the unexpected or unplanned-for death of a practicing lawyer. Some of them sponsor informal committees that, while having little or no formal authority, effectively manage the closure of decedents' practices and protect the clients left adrift.

It must also be recognized that *every* lawyer has a professional responsibility under the American Bar Association Code of Professional Responsibility to provide for a transition when a lawyer retires, dies, disappears, becomes disabled, or is disbarred. Without advance planning, however, this obligation is more honored in the breach than in practice. The articulated need when practice management plans were discussed in the survey responses was "planning." The survey made clear that this occurred too infrequently.

The Existing ABA Position

A review of the current scene reveals the many difficulties involved in structuring a comprehensive program that would work in every locale for every eventuality. The survey responses clearly indicate that a single and uniform national program would be ineffective. One size will not fit all.

Although the *American Bar Association Model Code of Professional Conduct* makes reference to ethical obligations touching upon the death of a lawyer, our national bar association itself offers

and has no comprehensive program of action. The American Bar Association Model Rules No specific ABA policy addresses the death of a lawyer. ABA Model Rule 1:17, dealing with the sale of law practices, is the rule most frequently cited by the survey respondents. This rule, added new in 1990, deals *only* with the sale of a law practice and as of this time has been adopted by only fifteen states. The other thirty-five states have no such rule or procedure although some are working on it. The official comment to Rule 1:17 states that the rule applies both pre- and postmortem and permits the sale of a practice by representatives of a deceased lawyer. The seller may also be represented by a nonlawyer representative who is not subject to Bar rules. Such transactions obviously work best if planning and preparations precede the lawyer's death.

Disciplinary rules are mandatory in character; they define action that must be taken. Disciplinary Rule 28 directs the actions to be taken when a lawyer dies. The rule provides for appointment of counsel to protect clients' interests when a lawyer dies, becomes disabled, disappears, is suspended or disbarred. It also sets procedures for inventory of lawyers' files, and for the confidentiality of records inventoried. When no partner, executor, other responsible and capable party exists to conclude the affairs of the deceased or disabled lawyer, this rule directs a presiding judge in the relevant judicial district, upon a proper showing, to appoint a trustee-attorney to inventory the files and take such action as is necessary to protect the interests of the lawyer concerned and his or her clients.

According to the commentary to the rule, when a lawyer is "not available" to protect clients, the rule mandates an obligation to protect them. Inventory costs are paid from fees owed the lawyer whose files are inventoried, or from funds made available for this purpose by state and local bar associations. A trustee so appointed may *not* represent the clients, however.

ABA Formal Opinion 92-369 of the Standing Committee on Ethics and Professional Responsibility addresses the disposition of deceased solo practitioners' client files and property under the Model Rules. The opinion places an ethical obligation on all lawyers to prepare a future plan for the maintenance and protection of client interests upon his or her death and the guiding ethical principles of the <u>Model Rules of Professional Conduct 1.1</u> (Competence) and <u>1.3</u> (Diligence), underscore this obligation and emphasize its fiduciary nature.

This critical opinion further stresses the duty of confidentiality for lawyers who assume responsibility for client files. The trustee-attorney should only examine those materials that are essential to disposition and proper maintenance of the client files. <u>Model Rule of Professional Conduct 1.15</u>, providing for the safeguarding of property separate from the lawyer's own property must be punctiliously observed by the trustee-attorney. The importance ABA Rule 28 is also stressed as the only rule that focuses on the "how to" of practice closure.

State and Local Programs

The survey shows that state bars for the most part rely upon ABA Rule 28 as the foundation of their system, but how the rule is implemented is what makes the difference. In states with large urban populations and concentrations of lawyers, state bar procedures, backed by reasonable resources, can be effective. In states of more rural character, special problems militate against a statewide approach. In rural areas, the state administrative agency is too far away to reasonably ship files for inventorying and to inventory them in an acceptable timeframe. On the other hand, rural respondents also point to the very limited ability of a local lawyer to inventory the files of a deceased colleague for reasons of confidentiality. In the small community, colleagues are often opponents, or have family or other connections with clients of the deceased lawyer, so there is no way to maintain the overarching requirement of confidentiality in this particular setting. One thing is clear: *one size does not fit all*. It is essential that state bar programs be adaptable to the character of the various locales within the state.

Implementation Needs

Resources

While a local judiciary has resources to appoint trustee-attorneys to inventory files and respond to the dictates of <u>ABA Rule 28</u>, the question of resources for the trustee-attorney is primary. While the ethical disposition of the practice of a deceased lawyer is typically less arduous than the management and disposition of the practice of a disbarred or disabled lawyer, the time involvement and consequent expenses to the inventorying lawyer are far from trivial.

Some state rules allow fees only for extraordinary costs to the inventorying lawyer: some very few indicate that the lawyer should be paid for his time, but this is unusual. The issue is similar to the pro bono requirement that, ideally, all lawyers intend to fulfill, but practically cannot find the resources or time to give their best. Accordingly, making funds available to assist a lawyer in closing down practices, or making paralegal and secretarial services available for that purpose, must be considered. While some funds for this may be available from an ABA or state bar grant, in today's world this is not likely. Assessing lawyers yearly as part of their ethical obligations for a fund to provide for such services or even taxing deceased lawyers' estates that were left unprotected, are alternatives.

Referrals

<u>Rule 28</u> mandates that the trustee-attorney must take such action as seems indicated to protect the interests of the deceased lawyer and his or her clients, but referrals are frowned upon in many states and, practically, not possible in small communities. Questions abound: should a local or state bar group maintain an agency for this purpose, or should the local judiciary maintain a registry to deal with it? Should the inventorying lawyer be allowed to accept such clients of the deceased lawyer as do not conflict with his interests or client confidentiality? This can be done in New Jersey. Is a single statewide decision adequate, or must each locale develop a policy to suit?

In this same vein, some states allow the purchase of the law practice of the deceased lawyer, and some do not. Some allow a trustee-attorney to take on the cases of the deceased lawyer when agreeable to the client and himself. Others do not. These and other issues need resolution, as now there is no uniformity.

The Need for Planning

The ethical principle that every lawyer plan for his or her own succession cannot be overemphasized. Procedures for practice management should be made known and broadly distributed to all lawyers when they are inducted into the legal profession, with special emphasis, perhaps, on the responsibilities of solo practitioners, with an eye to practice turnover whenever that eventuality should occur. This is as important to the lawyer, new or old, as is the maintenance of his attorney and trust accounts; but, unfortunately, less is done in training new lawyers in ethical practice-management issues than in teaching them to manage their trust accounts.

Problems and Solutions

Among the problems noted in the survey were confidentiality, liability, immunity, conflicts of interests, malpractice considerations, and limitations of actions. Recognition of and accounting for the handling of each one of these issues is essential to an effective program if the survey respondents, many of whom requested assistance, are to be served.

Among the positive values suggested by the survey responses, the following should be highlighted:

- Volunteers are trained and are given a procedural outline in California.
- In Illinois, protocols for closure, procedural outlines, and accompanying forms are provided to trustee-attorneys by the Administrator of Lawyer Registration and Disciplinary Commission.
- In New York, a requirement provides for the designation of successor signatory for a lawyer's accounts.
- In Oregon, a professional liability fund is maintained that affords funds for inventorying procedures. The state bar also maintains a practice-management group to deal with the closing of practices.
- "Time is of the essence" in Texas so that requests to the court to appoint trustees get top priority.
- In West Virginia, as in a number of other states, the bar can act on its own to petition the court to appoint a trustee/inventorying-attorney.

The Next Steps

Despite the number of good ideas and effective programs revealed by the survey, it is clear from the majority of responses that much must still be done. Existing rules and procedures, while conceptually correct, fail badly in providing effective implementation. Some state and local bars are now attempting to design and disseminate procedures independently; others have told us that they await the ABA response to this survey.

We conclude the problem is difficult and complex. There is no universal prepared protocol for a practice management following the death of a lawyer. The Senior Lawyers Division has presented a recommendation to the ABA House Of Delegates urging state, local, and territorial jurisdictions to develop and implement, through court rule or other appropriate means, effective procedures for the protection of clients' interests and property and the ethical closure or disposition of the practices of deceased lawyers and offers some suggested procedures to that end. Admittedly, the problem affects solos more than any other group of lawyers but solos are concerned they will be singled out for special attention, rather than mandating programs for all lawyers regardless of practice setting.

Conclusion

The response of the organized bar to the question of "What Happens When a Lawyer Dies" is not about sending flowers. It has to do with the development and implementation of plans to protect clients' interests, the practice of the decedent lawyer, and the welfare of his family and staff.

Solving the problem is not for the fainthearted. Every state is different under the all-embracing umbrella of the ABA.

Despite a number of good ideas and effective programs suggested by the survey responses, it is clear that much must be done because existing rules and procedures, while conceptually correct, fail badly in their implementations. The independent action through state and local bars is laudable, yet the direction and imprimatur of the ABA is missing. As the job is so big, the authors recommend a global solution through the appointment of an ABA task force or commission to prepare a protocol for practice management following the death of a lawyer comprised of representatives from various segments of lawyer demographics. Throughout this process, the needs and problems highlighted in the survey can be considered and acted upon in an organized way.

Exhibit 74–1
Action Checklist

1. Adhere to <u>ABA Disciplinary Rule 28</u> for the appointment of counsel to protect clients' interests upon the disappearance, disability, death, or disbarment of a lawyer outlining procedures for inventorying lawyers' files and protecting client confidentiality.
2. Implement and comply with <u>ABA Model Rule 1:17</u>, Sale of Law Practices, both pre- and postmortem.
3. Safeguard clients' files and property according to *Formal Opinion 92-369.*
4. Recognize the need for flexibility among jurisdictions in designing plans to account for various types of practices and practice settings.
5. Require the designation of survivor-signatory trustees as a condition of practice.
6. Provide for the appointment of fiduciaries to close or dispose of practices under jurisdictional supervision and protect the interests of the lawyer's clients, estate, and family.
7. Provide expense reimbursements for trustees and fiduciaries closing practices and give consideration to compensation for such services.
8. Implement bar rules to train lawyers how to keep and maintain client files, financial records, and trust accounts.

75
Basic Financial Decisions for Survivors

WALTER T. BURKE

One of the most difficult things a married couple can do while they are together is to plan for the time when they will only be one. This is particularly important when one spouse is a lawyer and has some familiarity in understanding legal documents, title, taxes, and finances and the other spouse does not.

Over the years we have discovered that the best approach is to be proactive and positive in the planning; in that way, the surviving spouse is also prepared for the worst because he or she becomes familiar with major decisions that will need to be made, often alone.

At its most basic level the survivor will need a working knowledge of money and finances. There should be an ability to intelligently project savings and earnings in a realistic manner. One of the first steps in doing that is identifying the value of your estate.

For many people irrevocable decisions about retirement payouts form the backbone of their cash flow during their later years. It is imperative that the surviving spouse has an idea of what implications, if any, the death of one spouse will have on payments and options. Will pension payments continue, be reduced, or stop totally?

While in most instances, one spouse is charged with the responsibility of investing funds, it is important that both spouses have a working knowledge of where their fumds are, the risks and returns of the investments, and what the surviving spouse may choose as an investment plan in the event that there is only one spouse.

The changing years and circumstances often

call for new thinking about a traditional asset, your personal residence. There comes a time when you must view this old asset in a new light. This should be done not only as a married couple, but also in the event that there is only a surviving spouse in the family residence.

The following materials—often presented as questions—address these issues and include a final summary of things to do and a checklist. If read carefully and followed closely, they also contain the secret for providing for your loved ones in a very troubling time.

Basic Financial Decisions for the Survivors

How Much Money Is Enough?

A. For growth of various amounts of initial capital at 8 percent annual total return, see Figure 75–1.

B. A review of your current basic budgeting information is imperative in order to quantify your financial security (see Figure 75–2).
1. Although it is often a cumbersome and annoying task, it is important to identify the following type of expenses and determine their impact on your total spending:
   a. monthly fixed expenses
   b. monthly discretionary expenses
   c. annual fixed expenses
   d. annual discretionary expenses
   e. those expenses subject to inflation
   f. those expenses with a maturity (mortgages and car loans, for example)
2. You should be able to identify expenses and savings approximately totaling your current income.

Walter T. Burke is a partner in the law firm of Burke and Casserly, P.C. in Albany, New York, and chair of the Elder Law Section of the New York State Bar Association.

Figure 75–1

Total Principal Growth of Various Amounts
of Initial Capital
(At 8% Annual Total Return)

Assuming $100,000 at 8% total return

	Amount	Interest	Total
Year 1	$100,000	$ 8,000	$108,000
Year 5	$136,049	$10,884	$146,933
Year 10	$199,900	$15,992	$215,892
Year 15	$293,719	$23,498	$317,217

Assuming $250,000 at 8% total return

	Amount	Interest	Total
Year 1	$250,000	$20,000	$270,000
Year 5	$340,122	$27,210	$367,332
Year 10	$499,751	$39,980	$539,731
Year 15	$734,298	$58,744	$793,042

Assuming $500,000 at 8% total return

	Amount	Interest	Total
Year 1	$ 500,000	$ 40,000	$ 540 000
Year 5	$ 680,244	$ 54,420	$ 734,664
Year 10	$ 999,502	$ 79,960	$1,079,462
Year 15	$1,468,597	$117,488	$1,586,085

C. The Eleventh Commandment: "Thou shalt not invade principal." Must it always be obeyed?
   1. It depends on your circumstances—it may make sense for some, but definitely not all. Factors that must be considered include the following:
      a. Time requirement: How long do you anticipate relying on your savings?
      b. Quantity: How much do you need from your savings in comparison to how much you have?
      c. Other sources of income: Are there any other sources of income and/or savings that should be considered as well?
   2. Figure 75–3 illustrates the effect on $100,000 of principal if an individual spent 2 percent more than what he or she earned annually and Figure 75–4 shows the effect of spending 4 percent more than what is earned annually.

D. Important documents to locate and be familiar with (see Figure 75–5):
   1. Estate planning documents
   2. Bank accounts (registration, account numbers, value)

3. Investment accounts (registration, account numbers, value)
4. Real estate holdings (deeds, municipal property tax bills, insurance policies)
5. Automobiles (title, registration, insurance policies)
6. Life insurance policies (name of owner, insured, death benefit, cash value, premiums payable)
7. Business interests (including law practice)
8. Vested retirement benefits (identify and quantify all sources)
9. Money owed to you (identify and quantify all sources)

Lump Sum vs. Annuity

A. Is the irrevocable decision irrevocable?
   1. Many pension and retirement benefits can be paid in a lump sum at retirement, or the participant can choose to receive an annuity benefit that will generate income for a period of time.
   2. Considerations of selecting an annuitized payment:
      a. Generally involves some degree of interest rate sensitivity; and
      b. Typically cannot be undone.
   3. Considerations for selecting a lump-sum payment:
      a. Provides you with investment control to customize your investment objectives;
      b. Enables you to control the taxation of the benefits when they are distributed;
      c. Allows you greater access to your funds in the event of unforeseen circumstances;
      d. Can still opt to purchase an annuity product with the funds if you later change your mind.

B. The four typical annuity distribution options are as follows:
   1. Single life option: This option provides a monthly allowance for the life of the retiree; on the retiree's death, all payments end.
   2. Joint and survivor: This option provides a retiree a continuing monthly retirement allowance that, upon death, continues for the rest of the life of the retiree's beneficiary. The monthly payment is less than the single life option.

Figure 75–2

Burke Casserly & Associates, Ltd.
Investment Management Services/Financial Planning
Estimated Household Expenses

	Monthly Now	Monthly Retired	Total		Annually Now	Annually Retired	Total
HOUSING				**EDUCATION**			
Rent/Mortgage	___	___		School Loans	___	___	
Utilities	___	___		Investment Fund	___	___	
Telephone	___	___		Other	___	___	___
Maintenance	___	___		**VACATIONS**	___	___	___
Insurance	___	___		**GIFTS**			
Garbage	___	___		Birthdays	___	___	
Lawn & Garden	___	___		Holidays	___	___	
Security System	___	___		Weddings	___	___	
Pool Care	___	___		Other	___	___	___
House Cleaning Services	___	___		**READING MATERIALS**			
Furniture	___	___		Books	___	___	
Driveway & Sidewalk	___	___		Magazines	___	___	
Other	___	___	___	Newspapers	___	___	
FOOD				Other	___	___	___
Groceries	___	___		**CHARITY**	___	___	
Restaurant Costs	___	___		**PERSONAL INSURANCE**			
Other	___	___	___	Disability	___	___	
TRANSPORTATION				Life	___	___	
Car Payments	___	___		Liability	___	___	
Car Insurance	___	___		Other	___	___	___
Maintenance/Gas	___	___		**OTHER ANNUAL**	___	___	___
Car Phone	___	___		**TAXES**			
Parking	___	___		Federal Withholding	___	___	
Other	___	___	___	State Withholding	___	___	
MEDICAL				Estimated Taxes	___	___	
Prescriptions	___	___		Other Deductions:			
Doctor/Dental Visits	___	___		Social Security	___	___	
Eye Care	___	___		Medicare	___	___	
Other	___	___	___	Other	___	___	
PERSONAL CARE				Property Taxes—Municipal	___	___	
Cosmetics/Hair	___	___		Property Taxes—School	___	___	
Health Club/Gym	___	___					
Other	___	___	___		**ANNUAL TOTAL:**		___

CLOTHING
Wardrobe/Shoes ___ ___
Laundry/Dry Cleaning ___ ___
Other ___ ___ ___
ENTERTAINMENT
Cable TV ___ ___
Children's Activities ___ ___
Country Club ___ ___
Movies, Theater ___ ___
Other ___ ___ ___
OTHER ___ ___ ___

TOTAL MONTHLY: ___

Additional Information

Current balance remaining on mortgage: ___
Year you will make your last mortgage payment: ___
Other notes:

Sources of Household Income

Please indicate the source and gross amount (before any deductions) of all income, and frequency of payment.

Source	Gross Amount	Frequency
_____	_____	_____
_____	_____	_____
_____	_____	_____
_____	_____	_____
_____	_____	_____
_____	_____	_____

Figure 75–3

Invasion of Principal
(Spending 2% Above Earnings)

Year	Principal	6% Earnings	8% Spending	Balance
1	$100,000	$6,000	$8,000	$98,000
5	$ 91,251	$5,475	$8,000	$88,726
10	$ 77,017	$4,621	$8,000	$73,638
15	$ 57,970	$3,478	$8,000	$53,448
20	$ 32,480	$1,949	$8,000	$26,429
24	$ 6,008	$ 361	$8,000	($1,631)

Figure 75–4

Invasion of Principal
(Spending 4% Above Earnings)

Year	Principal	6% Earnings	8% Spending	Balance
1	$100,000	$6,000	$10,000	$96,000
5	$ 82,502	$4,950	$10,000	$77,452
10	$ 54,035	$3,242	$10,000	$47,277
15	$ 15,940	$ 956	$10,000	$ 6,896
16	$ 6,896	$ 414	$10,000	($2,690)

Figure 75–5

Burke Casserly & Associates, Ltd.
Investment Management Services/Financial Planning
Document Location Data

Name(s): _____

Social Security Number(s): _____

Date: _____

This record should be kept in a secure location known to husband or wife, if married; or to a friend or relative, if not married. Complete the information now and bring it up to date each year.

Note the following *important* information:

1. I have written a personal letter/burial instructions to: _____ . Such letter is located _____
2. I have made a living will: Yes ____ No ____
   The following people have copies of this will: _____
   _____
3. I have made all arrangements to donate _____
   for transplant. Please call _____
   immediately in case of death.
4. I have made a Last Will and Testament: Yes ___ No ___
   The original is located at _____ .
   Conformed copies of this Will are located at _____
   _____ .

AUTOMOBILE PAPERS
1. Registration _____
   Bill of Sale _____
   Finance Agreement/Lease _____
2. Registration _____
   Bill of Sale _____
   Finance Agreement/Lease _____

BANK ACCOUNT BOOKS & PAPERS
Checking Acct. # _____
Bank & Address _____
Other Signature _____

Checking Acct. # _____
Bank & Address _____
Other Signature _____

Savings Acct. # _____
Bank & Address _____
Other Signature _____

Savings Acct. # _____
Bank & Address _____
Other Signature _____

Certificate of Deposit _____
Bank & Address _____
Other Signature _____

Certificate of Deposit _____
Bank & Address _____
Other Signature _____

BAPTISMAL CERTIFICATE
_____

BIRTH CERTIFICATE
_____

DEEDS
Primary Residence _____
Secondary Residence _____
Mortgage—Primary _____
Mortgage—Secondary _____
Leases _____
Cemetery Plot _____

DIVORCE PAPERS
_____

Figure 75–5 (Continued)

EMPLOYEE BENEFIT DATA
Group Insurance Plans _____
Pension Plan _____
Savings/Profit Sharing Plan _____
Other Employee Benefits _____

INCOME TAX RETURNS
Federal _____
State _____
Other _____

INSURANCE POLICIES
Life _____
(attach schedule if necessary)
Accident/Health _____
Disability _____
Property/Casualty _____
Major Medical _____
Other _____

MARRIAGE CERTIFICATE
_____

MEDICAL & DENTAL INFO (location of records, doctors, etc.)
_____
_____
_____
_____

POWER OF ATTORNEY
_____
_____
_____

SAFE-DEPOSIT BOX
Location _____
Box Number _____
Other Persons with Access to Box _____
_____
Location of Keys _____
Contents _____
_____

SECURITIES CERTIFICATES
(attach schedule if necessary)
Stocks _____
_____
Bonds _____
_____
Money Market Funds _____

SOCIAL SECURITY CARDS
_____
_____

TRUST AGREEMENTS
Original _____
Conformed Copies _____

OTHER IMPORTANT DOCUMENTS
_____
_____
_____
_____
_____

The following are to be contacted in the event of my death

ATTORNEY
Name _____
Firm _____
Address _____
Phone _____

TAX ADVISOR
Name _____
Firm _____
Address _____
Phone _____

EXECUTOR
Name _____
Firm _____
Address _____
Phone _____

TRUSTEE
Name _____
Firm _____
Address _____
Phone _____

EMPLOYEE BENEFITS MANAGER
Name _____
Firm _____
Address _____
Phone _____

I belong to the following organizations, which I would want notified in the event of death:
_____
_____
_____
_____
_____
_____
_____

3. Joint with partial benefit to survivor: This option provides a retiree with a monthly benefit that, on death, continues to the retiree's beneficiary at a reduced level—typically 25 to 50 percent less.

4. Term certain guaranties: Typically available in five- and ten-year increments, this option will guarantee that payments continue at a minimum for the period of guaranteed payments, even if the retiree or beneficiary should die before the guaranty period ends. This option does not limit or reduce your benefit in the event the retiree or beneficiary lives beyond the period of guarantee.

The Danger in Choosing Safety

A. Inflation. See Figures 75–6, 75–7, and 75–8.

Figure 75–6

Effects of 4% Inflation

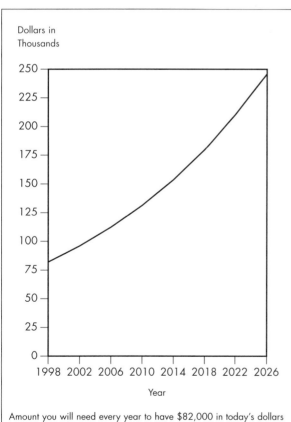

Dollars in Thousands

1998 2002 2006 2010 2014 2018 2022 2026

Year

Amount you will need every year to have $82,000 in today's dollars
Inflation is a culprit!
Your contributions and investments need to grow faster than inflation!

Figure 75–7

Impact of Inflation and Taxes on CD Investments, 1973–1992

Year	6-Month CD Avg. Return	Federal Tax Rate (at $100K)	Inflation (CPI)	6-Month CD after Taxes and Inflation
1973	8.31	69.00	8.80	– 6.22
1974	9.97	69.00	12.20	– 9.11
1975	6.89	69.00	7.01	– 4.87
1976	5.62	69.00	4.81	– 3.07
1977	5.92	69.00	6.77	– 4.93
1978	8.61	69.00	9.03	– 6.36
1979	11.44	68.00	13.31	– 9.65
1980	12.94	68.00	12.40	– 8.26
1981	15.79	68.00	8.94	– 3.89
1982	12.57	50.00	3.87	2.42
1983	9.28	50.00	3.80	0.84
1984	10.71	50.00	3.95	1.41
1985	8.24	50.00	3.77	0.35
1986	6.50	50.00	1.13	2.12
1987	7.01	38.50	4.41	– 0.10
1988	7.91	33.00	4.42	0.88
1989	9.08	33.00	4.65	1.43
1990	8.17	33.00	6.11	– 0.64
1991	5.91	31.00	3.06	1.02
1992	3.76	31.00	3.23	– 0.64

B. Long-term care costs.
1. Successfully meeting long-term care costs requires a certain amount of flexibility and advance planning. A primary consideration is to have someone authorized to act over your savings in the event you are no longer able to manage your investments yourself. This can be done in numerous ways but should be carefully planned and reviewed periodically. Some tools include the following:
   a Durable power of attorney
   b. Trust agreements
   c. Joint accounts
   d. Outright gifts
2. The goal of long-term care planning is to protect some amount of your savings from the costs of long-term care so that they may be passed on to future generations. This type of planning involves reviewing the title, or registration, of your investments and, if necessary, performing some sort of transfer of these assets in order to protect them.

Figure 75–8

Growth of $1,000 Adjusted for Inflation
(December 31, 1925 through December 31, 1992)

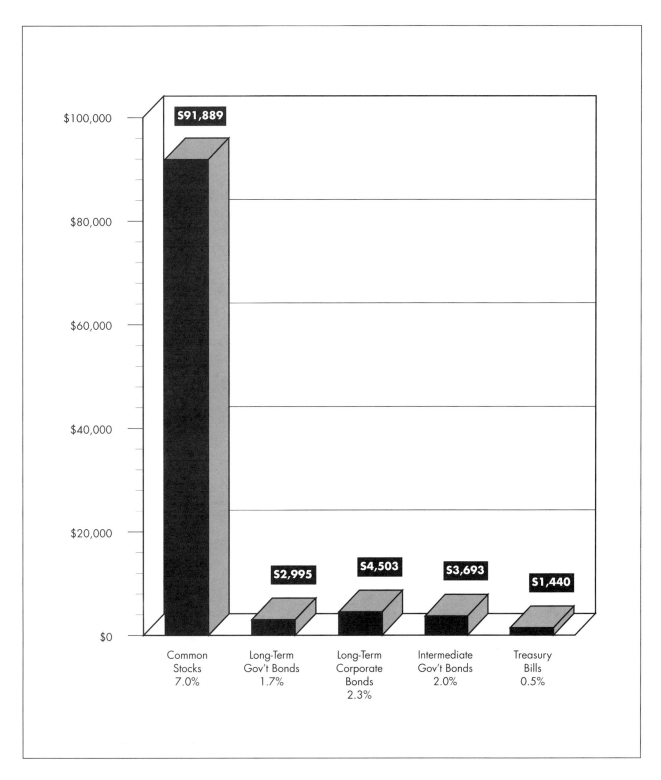

3. The danger of safety may lie in limiting your ability to manage investments and to perform any necessary planning.

C. Estate planning. Similar to planning for long-term care, the danger with excessive safety regarding your investments and estate planning lies in being unable to perform tax-saving planning techniques because you are limited by the structure of your investments. Estate planning techniques generally involve the transfer or retitling of certain assets, or the income they produce, to limit or avoid estate taxation. This is particularly significant in estates of more than $600,000, where the federal estate tax rates range from 37 to 55 percent.

Where Should You Invest Your Money: A Basic Primer

A. Determining risk tolerance. Although the quantity of your retirement savings and the extent of your income needs play a large role in choosing your individual investments, there is another factor that should never be overlooked: your own comfort level with fluctuations in the valuation of your investments.
   1. There are many types of investments, each with its own risks and rewards. Select investments that meet the following objectives:
      a. your personal tolerance of risk is not exceeded;
      b. more risk is not assumed than necessary to achieve your goals;
      c. all elements of risk are identified; and
      d. your portfolio is designed so that the risks associated with individual investments act in opposition to each other. This can protect a portion of your portfolio value, contrary to all individual investments simultaneously declining in value in response to a particular event.
   2. Model portfolios: some samples. The following are general concepts to consider in light of your own personal situation.
      a. For those approaching retirement, there is a mutual objective of continued growth and stability of your portfolio value. In addition, however, it is commonly accepted that there should be a component of the portfolio invested in equity based investments (stocks, growth mutual funds) to enable your entire portfolio to outpace the effects of inflation and accommodate unforeseen expenses. The amount to be held in cash should reflect possible unforeseen emergencies and must meet your specific needs. See Figure 75–9.
      b. For those already in retirement, there is a definite need to protect the stability in value and income of your investment portfolio. In addition, however, it is commonly accepted that there should be a component of the portfolio invested in equity based investments (stocks, growth mutual funds) to enable your entire portfolio to outpace the effects of inflation and accommodate unforeseen expenses. See Figure 75–10.

Thinking of Your Home in a New Light

A. Your home as a source of income.
   1. The use and marketing of "reverse mortgages" has recently received much publicity. A reverse mortgage enables older homeowners to convert the equity in their homes into cash. Unlike a conventional mortgage, the bank makes monthly payments to you. The principal, interest, and possibly loan fees are not paid back until you sell the house or die (in which case the estate would pay off the loan).
   2. Some considerations involving the use of a reverse mortgage:
      a. A lien will be placed against the property to secure the loan, thus ensuring the loan will be repaid upon sale of the property or death of the owner.
      b. The amount owed on the loan will compound over time.
      c. Monthly payments are usually fixed and, therefore, lose purchasing power over time.
   3. Three sources for more information:
      a. The ABA Commission on Legal Problems of the Elderly offers "Attorney's Guide to Home Equity Conversion." Contact them at 740 15th Street NW, Washington, DC 20005.
      b. The AARP offers a booklet, "Consumers' Guide to Home Equity Conversion:

Figure 75–9

Model Portfolios
Approaching Retirement

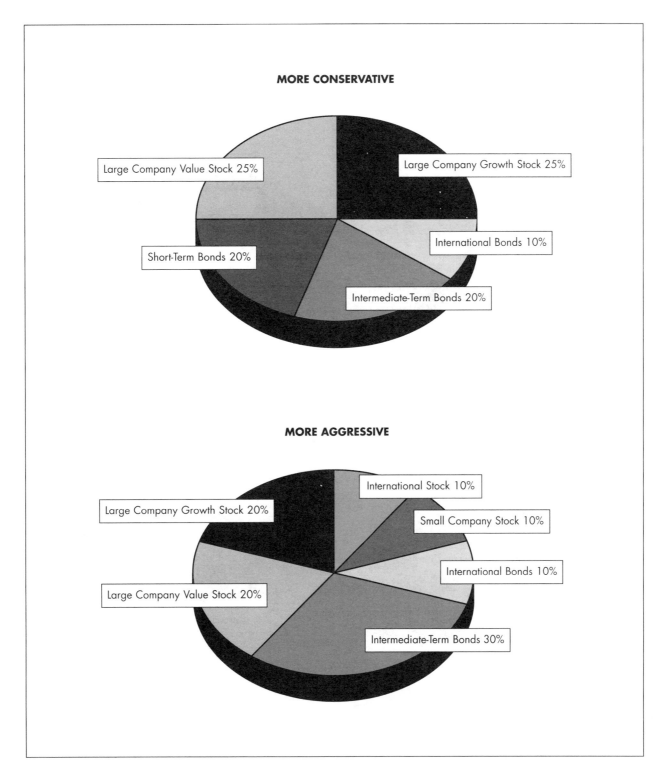

MORE CONSERVATIVE

Large Company Value Stock 25%

Large Company Growth Stock 25%

International Bonds 10%

Short-Term Bonds 20%

Intermediate-Term Bonds 20%

MORE AGGRESSIVE

International Stock 10%

Large Company Growth Stock 20%

Small Company Stock 10%

International Bonds 10%

Large Company Value Stock 20%

Intermediate-Term Bonds 30%

Figure 75–10

Model Portfolios
During Retirement

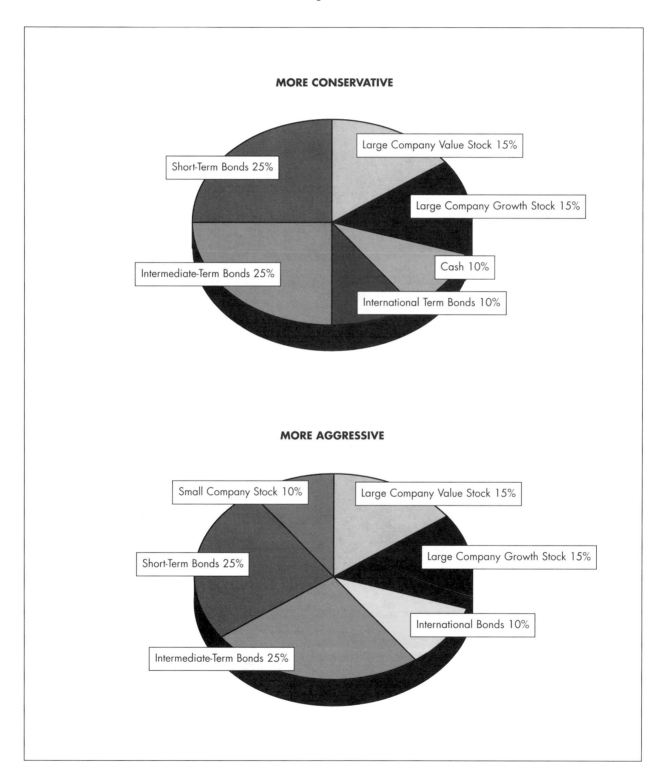

Homemade Money." Contact them at 601 E Street NW, Washington, DC 20049.

c. "Options for Elderly Homeowners: A Guide to Reverse Mortgages and Their Alternatives" is published by the U.S. Department of Housing and Urban Development. Contact them at HUS USER, P.O. Box 6091, Rockville, MD 20850. Use reference number ACCN:5395.

B. Your home as a source of capital. A home-equity loan is more like a conventional mortgage in the sense that the bank provides an up-front sum of money to the homeowner, which then must be repaid along with interest in regular monthly payments.

C. Is your home now a liability?
1. For some people, the financial, physical, and emotional implications of retaining their family home are not appropriate. From time to time, couples should assess whether it really is in their best interests to retain ownership of their current home.
2. Among the factors to be considered are:
   a. Maintenance costs and physical effort required;
   b. Municipal taxes;
   c. Whether homeowner responsibilities are preventing you from traveling for recreation or to see family;

d. The emotional impact of staying or leaving;
e. Whether there are children or grandchildren possibly interested in living in the home in the future.
3. These issues are best discussed and analyzed prior to the death of a loved one.

Conclusion: Planning Is Key to a Financially Successful Future

A. Use time to your advantage!
1. Inventory income and resources for funding your retirement.
2. Identify cash-flow needs during the foreseeable future.
3. Determine if income tax, estate tax, or long-term care planning is needed.
4. Periodically review your objectives and financial performance throughout your lifetime; revise as necessary.
5. Do it now.

B. Going forward from here
1. Talk to each other.
2. Don't avoid the unknown.
3. Don't create the unknown for your loved ones.
4. Control what you can, when you can—while you are both here.

Exhibit 75-1
Basic Financial Decisions for the Survivor Checklist

- Understand and quantify all income sources.
- Maintain a current, accurate budget of your fixed and discretionary expenses.
- Know exactly where all your important documents and financial information is kept.
- Know the value of all your investments and savings.
- If your family is receiving a retirement payment, know what financial impact there will be when the pensioner dies.
- Review the need, cost, and availability of long-term care in your area.
- Be familiar with the estate plan for your family and make sure all beneficiary designations and titled assets comply with your plan.
- Understand the risks associated with any investments, even the most conservative, and determine what you are willing to accept together and alone.
- Review the appropriateness of your current investments and anticipate how they may be changed in the future.
- View your home as an investment and determine what capital and income may be available to you from this investment.
- Discuss frankly whether or not your current home would be where you would want to spend the balance of your life if you were alone. If not, then discuss alternatives when you are not dealing with a crisis.
- Schedule a meeting, *now*, to review these issues with your spouse, family, and advisors.
- Actually hold the meeting.

76

When a Lawyer Dies: A Spouse's Point of View

CORINNE P. MASKALERIS

What happens when a lawyer/spouse dies? Aside from the shock, grief, planning a funeral and the tears that follow . . . PAPERWORK! How much, depends on the various sources of income the deceased had and the preparations made by the deceased beforehand as to what to do to carry you through the transition from joint lives to being alone.

Among the things that must be done promptly is to obtain several death certificates from the funeral director with whom you must deal carefully when making funeral arrangements and spend only as much on the funeral that *you* as a surviving spouse want to spend; find and read the will of the decedent; start probate proceedings; notify all insurance companies, the Social Security Administration, and all sources of pensions and income.

Planning before death can lessen the paperwork and stress.

Several Examples

Procrastination and Mental Disability

Robert's attention to detail was legendary, but a few years before his death, he developed an illness that slowly weakened his memory, much like Alzheimer's. His wife had forms she wanted him to fill out so that his will, insurance policies, bank accounts, and other important papers could be located, but when Robert died, his wife found only the blank forms in his desk drawer. Because of his illness, he had not been able to fill them out.

Corinne Maskaleris, trained as an educator, is a writer and lecturer on topics of interest to lawyers. This chapter is based on a paper she prepared for an August 1997 seminar sponsored by the ABA's Senior Lawyers Division.

Mental disability can be devastating when preparing for one's future. Keep important documents together in a safe place. Legal incompetence may cost you a fortune.

Procrastination, Cupidity, and Stupidity

Bill was an accountant who became a lawyer in his late 40s. He practiced in a limited manner with a local law firm and became the court administrator of his county. He was widowed and married Lil, a widow, who brought a summer home in her name to the marriage. Bill's home, which became the marital home, was in his name. Lil called the marriage a "50–50 marriage" because the household expenses and cost of a new kitchen and redecorating of his house were shared. Lil had two grown children; Bill had four. After fifteen years of marriage, Bill decided to draw wills. He wanted the ownership of both homes to become joint, with the surviving spouse having the use of both homes, and then, when both were dead, the survivor's estate would be divided equally among the children. Bill then drew up the papers for joint ownership of Lil's house, which she signed and he recorded, but he didn't get around to giving her joint ownership of his house because he now directed all his attention to how his law firm would compensate his estate at his death. He drew and redrew these papers; however, nothing had been signed when he died suddenly.

Lil received Bill's IRA, but she had to buy back *her* shore house from *his* daughters. His law firm gave all his fees to his estate under his old will, which named his daughters as beneficiaries. The daughters also received his house because their deceased mother's name was on the title.

All this could have been avoided if Bill and Lil had a prenuptial agreement and will before marriage. Later, an estate lawyer could have updated the wills and worked out the logistics of transferring their properties, arranged for disbursement of legal fees due him from his firm, and dealt with the tax ramifications involved.

So the lesson to be learned here is, if your spouse does not *specialize* in estate planning *insist* on seeing a lawyer who does.

Stay in Control

Another instance of lawyer incompetence, or a lawyer who is borderline incompetent, is this:

When Amy's mother-in-law died twenty-five years ago, she left a capable lawyer in charge of the estate and he did a good job. Now this lawyer is becoming confused and forgetful and will have to be replaced. You may find yourself "giving the ax" to a lot of experts.

Experts You Will Need

When your lawyer/spouse dies, you will need a lawyer, a financial advisor, and an accountant, at a minimum. While they may be costly, remember estates are complicated things. Chances are, you will have a financial advisor or broker and an accountant already. If you find you cannot work with either or both of these people, discuss this with your spouse and change them during life. After all, if you outlive your spouse, *you* will have to be working with them and you both might as well find someone whom you agree upon now, before death. If your spouse balks at this suggestion, look around, ask your friends for suggestions, and have two or three people in mind as backups who are *younger* than you are.

When many lawyers reading this entered the profession, there were only five professions: (1) clergy, (2) architects, (3) teachers, (4) doctors, and (5) lawyers. At that time, that which distinguished a profession from a vocation was a code of ethics. Today, there are professional bartenders, professional plumbers, professional meter readers, and so on. Not all of them are ethical.

Banks, brokers, and financial planners all render the same services: they watch over the estate and make the assets grow. Whichever you choose, choose with care. We have attended estate planning seminars run by "financial planners." This is an unregulated field, and the client pays on a flat-fee basis or on a percentage of the money being managed. When a speaker at one of these seminars starts off by telling a "lawyer joke" and later makes disparaging remarks about how limited a lawyer's knowledge is in these affairs, it's time to leave.

Today, many banks are being swallowed up by mergers. The executor you wanted and worked with yesterday may have transferred, left the business, or retired; so keep current on this.

Jill, a coexecutor for a family trust with a bank, finds discrepancies in her statements almost monthly. The new representative assigned to her account "buys" when she says "sell" and vice versa, but always laughs humorously when she catches him. Give this fellow the hook—fast! And if the bank doesn't cooperate, change banks. There are good and bad financial planners, banks, and accountants. *You* have to find the right one.

The death of a spouse is debilitating. The survivor feels grief stricken and paralyzed, but this is the time a widow must keep a clear head. My spouse, Stephen, counsels my widowed friends to take their time making disbursements. The bills do not have to be paid in three months, and funeral costs should be paid with a charge card, where you have recourse and get frequent flyer miles as well! After all, you never know when you'll be traveling around the world—whether to assuage your grief or for a trip with a new spouse.

You and your spouse should plan ways to turn over you assets to your heirs in a manner that will save as much as possible from taxes. Estate taxes can consume more than half the money in one's estate. There are three basic ways to give away assets and reduce taxes, bearing in mind that *you should only give away assets that you don't need.*

1. Unified Credit, or the $600,000 exemption. This benefit will grow to a million dollars within the next few years. You can transfer $600,000 tax free *before* or *after* death, but *before* is *better.* If you leave $3 million in cash to your children and have used your unified credit, your children will pay 50 percent estate tax on the $3 million, leaving them with $1.5 million. If you give your children $2 million now, you will pay a gift tax of $1 million. Your heirs will be ahead by half a million dollars.
2. Annual Exclusion. You may also transfer $10,000 a year to anyone. You and your

spouse may each transfer $10,000 to the same person or a total of $20,000 a year to the same person. You may do this to as many people as you wish per year.

3. <u>Insurance Trust</u>. The sooner this is done, the lower the premiums. In a "second to die" insurance trust, the death benefit is tax free. This will keep this part of the estate intact. If the heirs of this trust are sued or attached by creditors or former spouses, the amount of this trust cannot be disclosed. It cannot be reached by litigants, creditors, or former spouses. This is also a solution for protecting wealth from a child who might mismanage the money, while at the same time providing for that child. It also can be used to pay estate taxes.

Inheritance taxes are state taxes. Estate taxes are federal taxes and are paid by the inheritor on the value of the estate. The U.S. government gives the executor of the estate nine months to pay what is owed. A second-to-die insurance policy purchased before both husband and wife die can pay these taxes and preserve the value of the estate.

When a spouse dies, a lawyer is needed to change beneficiaries on insurance policies, change the limited power of attorney, draw a new will and a living will if none exists.

An accountant is needed to file tax returns. Should your spouse die on January 1, 2000, you will still have income tax for the deceased in the year 2000.

A financial planner, bank, broker, and sometimes a lawyer can help you plan for the disbursement of your estate after death and suggest ways to provide income for you. Any one of these people can show you how to give away as much money as is legal to your heirs and charities before your death to preserve as much of the estate as possible.

Keep a separate calendar of bills that must be paid for estimated income taxes—both state and federal—property taxes, long-term care policies, and so on. Also, mark the calendar with the dates you expect income from social security, banks, dividends, investments, and the like.

Husbands and wives should alternate paying the household bills every month so that both know how to do it if they don't now.

Grief

Grief can last a long time. This is the time you need the support of friends and family. If you're a man, you'll be invited to all sorts of social events and women will probably show up at your door with casseroles. If you're a woman, expect to be dropped from party lists and most events where you can enjoy the conversation of an intelligent man.

Anger at the deceased is normal. Sadness provoked by thoughts, a song, or memories will drag you to the depths of grief. There is also the tendency to place the deceased on a pedestal. "Harry was the most caring man that ever lived," or "Susie was loved by everyone" is the way the memory will evolve. And the mood can change from day to day: "I was so fed up having to pick up his socks all the time," or "She was always late, the late Mary Ann!"

Widows have told me they "killed their husbands" with their French cooking, and a man may wish he had spent more time with his spouse. Guilt, anger at the spouse and God, and painting a rosy picture of the deceased are to be expected, as well as other emotions. Group and individual counseling may be helpful, and pursuing interests can divert the mind.

Women who want to travel will have to find a single friend if they don't want to go alone. Women will have to create a whole new circle of friends because their married friends do not want to leave their husbands. Widows need friends who are spontaneous, who will go out to dinner or the theater without much planning because it sounds like a good idea. These are positive and important steps to overcoming grief.

Finally, something must be said about "little girl wives." They are the ones whose husbands sheltered them by not allowing them to participate in any financial aspects of the marriage, the ones who were accompanied to the doctor's office, the ones who never assumed responsibility for planning a trip, making a major purchase, and so on. These "little girl wives" will have a hard time standing on their own two feet and functioning. They will be like Janet, who is now widowed and does not realize what a burden she is to her married daughters whose time and attention she demands.

In time there will be an end to each widow's grief, a time when she will become a separate and independent entity and go forward with hope and inner peace as she walks down the long road, but she will have to have done a lot of work to have reached that point.

Life After Death?

Is there life after death? Two true stories follow:

1. Betty helped her husband by keeping the books for his small factory. She had no plans to become further involved, but the day after her spouse's funeral she went to the office and found that she had to take it over or lose it. Today, the business is more profitable and she has a better relationship with the employees than her husband ever did.

2. Mary's husband was a diabetic. He lost his job when he was in his 40s and never tried to get another. Mary had spent years as a Girl Scout volunteer taking different kinds of training and learning about fund-raising. She started her own fund-raising business, and when her husband eventually died, she was able to support herself well. She has her special accounts but also travels the country giving seminars.

There is also the option to remarry, but *never* without a prenuptial agreement and a new will. Studies find that married men live longer than single men, and single women live longer than married women.

This should be the time of your life when you do whatever you want: always fly first-class, spend a year in Europe or Hawaii, learn to tap dance, join the Peace Corps, never cook another meal, go ballooning. You can be sure that your children and grandchildren will enjoy your money and "treat" themselves often with your generosity, so you might as well have fun with it yourself.

Finally, remember: When in doubt, do nothing. This applies to selling your home, giving your daughter-in-law the sterling, or making other no-turning-back decisions.

Death is not an option, and all of us should plan for it.

In the words of the great philosopher, Cher: "Life is not a dress rehearsal," to which we add, "Death is not an option," and we should all plan for it.

Exhibit 76–1
Checklist
A Spouse's Point of View

- Plan before death
- Is your spouse mentally disabled?
- Is your lawyer legally competent?
- Use Experts
    Estate lawyers
    Financial planners
    Accountants
    Banks
- Candidates for the ax
    Estate lawyers

    Financial planners
    Accountants
    Banks
- Using a financial calendar
- Life after death
    A fulfilling career
    Remarriage
    Having fun
- Do not feel pressured to act on anything!

77
A Solo Practitioner's Letters of Instructions

WILLIAM D. HAUGHT

Introduction

Written instructions to your family, personal representative, and office staff containing information and guidance will minimize uncertainty, confusion, and possible oversights following your death. The information you furnish should ease the settlement of your estate and provide for an orderly winding up of your law practice. It is important to tell your survivors and successors what you have, where it is, how to get it, and what to do with it once gotten. You need to share what you know with those who (often suddenly and without warning) must step into your shoes and carry on your affairs. Otherwise, there is a substantial risk of financial loss and potential malpractice claims.

You should review and update your letters of instructions periodically to be certain they are complete and current. Likewise, any records and files to which the reader is referred should be well organized and regularly updated. In most cases, you should personally discuss the contents of the letters with the persons to whom they are addressed, especially so with your spouse and secretary, to amplify or clarify the instructions given and answer any questions. In all events, it is advisable to give the letters of instructions once written to the addressees so they will be aware that the letters call for certain actions promptly after your death.

The letters of instructions that you prepare for your family, personal representative, and office staff should really be road maps pointing the way to, or keys to gain access to, specific detailed

information stored elsewhere. Consequently, the letters do not need to contain all the information the reader might require but rather should refer the reader to those documents, records, or files that contain the necessary information. For example, the letters of instructions can direct the reader to binders or files containing personal and family financial information, insurance papers, contents of safe-deposit boxes, client and matter directories and files, and so on. In a sense, you are creating a system for the settlement of your own estate and the orderly winding up of your law practice. The letters of instructions can tell the reader what information is important, where it can be found, and what action should be taken (or considered) with respect to that information. Like a probate lawyer, you are anticipating and preparing for the steps your family, personal representative, secretary, and other office staff will need to begin taking on the day of your death.

It is likely that your spouse knows many things that your personal representative (if someone other than your spouse) and your secretary do not know. It is equally probable that your secretary knows many things relating to your law practice and business activities that your spouse may not know or fully understand. There is an obvious need for your family, personal representative, and office staff to share information and coordinate their activities in the event of your death. As a solo practitioner, your family, your estate, and your law practice are all necessarily interrelated, and what happens with one affects the others.

The general types of information to cover are:

1. Personal and family information. Include the names, addresses, phone numbers, Social Security numbers, and other data concerning family members, beneficiaries, and heirs.

William D. Haught is a member of the Haught and Wade law firm in Little Rock, Arkansas, and specializes in estate planning and administration.

2. Personal financial information. Identify the assets and liabilities of your estate, tell where they (or their documentation) are located, and indicate what you think they are worth. Very often, you are the best judge of the value of the assets you own, particularly those having no ready market, and you should share your opinion of value with your survivors and successors. Personal financial information should also show how your assets are titled or to whom they are payable, if a beneficiary designation has been made. The same descriptive information should be furnished as to your liabilities. In addition to assets and liabilities, include information about your income and expenses, and indicate where copies of your prior tax returns (income and gift tax) are kept.

3. Estate planning documents. Identify the documents governing your estate plan, such as wills, inter vivos trusts, and business buy-sell agreements, and note where they are located.

4. Professional advisers. Identify the professional advisers you use or recommend, whose services may be needed in settling your estate and closing out your practice, including certified public accountants, appraisers, brokers, trust officers, insurance agents, investment advisers, and property managers.

5. Personal insurance records. Identify coverages you have under any life, property, medical, hospital, accident, and credit life policies, and note where the policies are located.

6. Funeral, burial, anatomical gifts, and other arrangements for disposition of remains. Include instructions as to your funeral and burial (or cremation) and any intended anatomical gifts, or other arrangements concerning disposition of your remains.

7. Law office records. Identify and locate client files and documents, accounting and billing records for your firm and clients, and internal systems, as well as office leases, insurance coverages, equipment ownership, maintenance agreements and records, and other contractual matters pertaining to your law office and practice, and outline steps to take in closing out your practice.

8. Persons to be notified in the event of your death. Identify family, friends, business associates, and colleagues in bar association and civic activities to be notified upon your death, and note any special instructions or messages to them.

What Should Your Letters of Instructions Cover?

Letter to Your Family

Typically, this letter would be written to your spouse, but you may also want to address the letter to your children, if they are primary beneficiaries of your estate or they will be called upon to assist your spouse directly in the settlement of your estate and business affairs. Some possible points to cover in the family letter are these:

1. Funeral and burial arrangements: Where, by whom, what kind, and at what cost?

2. Anatomical gifts: Identify the nature and location of any anatomical gift declarations you have made.

3. Memorials and contributions: Identify what organizations or institutions might be appropriate recipients of memorials or charitable donations made in your memory.

4. Preparation of obituary: Should your obituary be prepared in advance and be updated periodically? To which newspapers should it be sent?

5. Notification of friends, relatives, business associates, and colleagues in bar or civic groups: Identify those persons to be contacted upon your death, noting any particular requests or messages to be given and listing their current addresses and phone numbers.

6. Location of your safe-deposit box and its key.

7. Location of your will and other estate-planning documents: Including any trusts, buy-sell agreements, or extraneous writings incorporated in your will.

8. Medical and hospital coverages and location of the policies.

9. Social Security and Veterans Administration benefits: Identify current or potential benefits.

10. Life insurance: Indicate where policies are located and what steps should be taken to collect policy proceeds.

11. Location and explanation of title documents and other records relating to your assets: Include deeds, stocks, bonds, bank accounts and deposits, retirement plans, and vehicle titles.

12. Identify obligations involving periodic payments, such as your home mortgage, car loans, and other debts, including amounts and to whom payable.
13. Identify professional advisers (including your accountant, broker, trust officer, and insurance agent) you currently use or recommend.

Letter to Your Personal Representative

If your spouse or other family member will be the personal representative of your estate, the following matters can be combined with the letter to your family. Many of the points covered in the letter to your family should also be included in the letter to your personal representative. Among the special items to mention in the letter to your personal representative (in addition to the more general matters relating to family and personal financial information) might be these:

1. Engaging a lawyer to wind up your law practice.
2. Notifying clients of your death.
3. Transferring active files to the client or to the successor lawyer designated by the client.
4. Disposition of closed or inactive files.
5. Making arrangements to complete work on active files.
6. Securing agreements with the successor lawyers as to the handling of open files.
7. Billing and collecting fees and expenses on all open files.
8. Closing your office and disposing of your office furniture, equipment, library, and other tangible assets.
9. Determining who shall be authorized to draw checks on the office account (including any trust accounts for client funds).
10. Continuing of employment of your secretary or other staff while your office is being closed out.
11. Explaining the basis of your office space occupancy (whether you own or lease your space and equipment), locating the title or lease papers, financing documents, and property insurance policies, and offering suggestions as to possible sublease or sale.
12. Paying current liabilities (such as utilities, rentals, debt service, salaries and wages, payroll taxes and benefits, service agreements, subscriptions).
13. Making appropriate arrangements to discontinue phone directory and other listings and professional memberships.
14. Collecting accounts receivable and writing off uncollectible accounts.
15. Providing guidance to your personal representative as to the probable value of your law practice for federal estate tax purposes.

Letter to Office Staff

If you have an experienced and well-trained secretarial and bookkeeping staff, as well as systems in place for monitoring and handling your law practice, extensive instructions to your office staff may not be necessary. In effect, you have already given them through your standing procedures and systems. It is useful, however, to cover with your secretary, office administrator, bookkeeper, or other staff members certain specific items that may require their attention in the event of your death, such as:

1. Immediately checking your calendar to determine what appointments, court dates, and deadlines are scheduled or pending and making necessary arrangements in each instance to cancel (or reschedule) such appointments and meet such deadlines.
2. Checking to determine when any applicable statutes of limitation relating to your clients and their cases will run, noting the date the limitation expires, and making necessary arrangements to take appropriate action before the limitation runs.
3. Notifying the carrier of your professional liability insurance, as well as other coverages related to your office and practice, of your death, and determining if new or converted coverages are required or advisable during and beyond the winding-up period.
4. Notifying all courts, boards, or administrative agencies where you practice, as well as opposing or associated counsel, of your death, determining what cases are on their dockets for which you are the responsible lawyer, and advising them of the lawyer who will succeed you on such cases.
5. Transferring all of your open client files either to the client or to the lawyer the client has designated to succeed you.

6. Disposing of closed or inactive files (through delivery of such files to the clients, placing files in storage, or arranging for their destruction).

7. Sending and collecting statements for unbilled fees and expenses on all files.

8. Closing your office, including the termination, sublease, or assignment of any office leases; sale or other disposition of furniture, supplies, and equipment; and sale or other disposition of your law library.

9. Collecting accounts receivable.

10. Reviewing the contents of any firm safe or other depository for client documents and records held for safekeeping, and turning over such documents and records to the client or the successor lawyer.

11. Reviewing trust account records and making appropriate disposition of any client funds being held on account.

12. Making appropriate disposition of any client retainers carried on the books that have not been fully earned.

13. Coordinating with the accountant for your law practice as to preparation of income tax returns for the year of death, with respect to your business income and expenses.

Conclusion

While the preceding lists contain possible topics to be covered in your letters to your family, personal representative, and office staff, the lists are by no means exhaustive. A number of these items may not be applicable in your situation, and probably there are many others that are applicable. The important thing is to spend some time now considering what you should tell those most closely associated with you to facilitate their handling of your affairs upon your death, and then write those matters down as soon as possible.

Each of us has his or her own style of letter writing. Especially when we are writing our loved ones and close associates, a special and personal form of communication is needed. In preparing the following sample letter from a solo practitioner to his wife, we are mindful that each such letter should be unique and that there is no "best way" to compose the letter. Hopefully, however, this sample will give you some useful ideas of what to cover.

Illustrative Letter of Instructions to Spouse

Dear Mary,

When I die, there will be a good many things you need to know and do to settle my estate, to wind up my law practice, and to plan and prepare for your own future. Although we have talked about most of these things, I know that when my death occurs it will help you and our family to have down in writing at least some of the important steps to take and matters to consider—and that is the reason for this letter.

Although I would rather not think about my own death (even though I know that it and taxes are the two inevitable facts of life), my practice has taught me the importance of planning for the personal and financial consequences of death and the need to fully share those plans with you. I have handled the estates of many husbands who shared very little of their financial and business affairs with their wives who—as widows—were completely in the dark about the nature and value of their husband's estate or their own financial circumstances as surviving head of the family. I don't want to be guilty of this sin of omission. I have made a solemn resolution to keep the information you will need upon my death as current as possible, so that your path at that time will be easier and surer.

Listed below are some of the things you need to know or do, arranged pretty much in the order they will arise after my death:

(1) *My funeral and burial.* We have talked a little bit about our respective wishes on the subject of our funerals and burials. Both of us agree, I believe, that whichever of us survives should decide the kind of funeral service to be arranged and at what cost. We also agree that as little should be spent for this purpose as possible, consistent with the type of service chosen. I would like for my funeral service to be held at our church and for our minister to conduct the services. As you know, we both have burial lots in Oakcrest Cemetery, the deed to which is in our safe-deposit box at First National Bank.

(2) *Donation of organs.* I would like for you to consider, in consultation with our doctor, the possibility of donating my eyes or any other organs that could be used for transplant or other medical

purposes. Your decision will need to be made immediately following my death, so it would be advisable for you to discuss the matter with our doctor before my body is transported to the funeral home.

(3) *Memorials.* I feel you should decide to whom any memorials or contributions might be made in my name. Since virtually all of our civic and charitable activities have been done together, any organization in which we have jointly participated would have my wholehearted approval. One I certainly favor is the Edgemont Youth Foundation.

(4) *Obituary.* While there might be some perverse pleasure in doing so, I would not presume to write my own obituary. You should decide its content, but my preference is for a short and simple one. I would like an obituary to appear not only in our local newspaper, but in the *Star City Beacon* and *Dumas Register* as well, since many of my relatives live in that area.

(5) *Persons to notify.* While there is no need for me to list the persons to be notified of my death among our family, relatives, friends—you know as well as I do—I should mention that my secretary, Sally Donohue, has a listing of my clients, business associates, and bar association colleagues who should receive notice of my death, as well as any special messages or instructions they should be given. Sally will take care of those contacts and also be available to help you with any other calls or letters.

(6) *Safe-deposit box.* As you know, our safe-deposit box is located at First National Bank (box #34265). You and I both have access to the box, and we each have a key. Even after my death, you will have unrestricted access to the box. The box rental is paid in advance for twelve months each January.

(7) *Our wills.* The originals of our wills are in the safe-deposit box at First National Bank. As soon as it is convenient, you should retrieve the original of my will from the safe-deposit box. As indicated below, I suggest you ask my good friend, Bob Johnson, who specializes in estate administration, to help you with the settlement of my estate. I have named you as executor of my will. At your first meeting with Bob you should deliver the original of my will to him, so he can arrange to have it admitted to probate and have you appointed and qualified as executor. There is

no fixed time limit for doing this, but the sooner the better. From the time my will is probated and notice published in the newspaper of your appointment as executor, a three-month period must elapse before my estate can be distributed and closed. This is a period provided for the presentation of any claims against my estate. Consequently, the sooner you start the administration, the sooner it can be completed.

(8) *Medical insurance.* We have a family hospital and medical expense insurance policy written by Blue Cross/Blue Shield (policy #5543768), which will cover most of the costs of my final illness. The policy (and a booklet explaining the benefits and procedure for making claims) is in a file folder in my personal file cabinet at the office. Sally can assist in handling the preparation and submission of any necessary claims.

(9) *Social Security benefits.* You will be entitled to receive certain Social Security benefits upon my death. Initially, you may apply for and receive a $255 lump-sum payment. Subsequently, you will be eligible to draw survivor's benefits (based on my earnings and contributions), but these benefits will not commence until you are 65 (or 60, if you elect to take reduced benefits). Under the current law, your monthly benefit would be approximately $1,500. You should visit the district office of the Social Security Administration to complete the paperwork necessary to collect the lump-sum benefit and establish your eligibility for survivor's benefits.

(10) *Life insurance.* In my personal file cabinet at the office is a folder containing my life insurance policies, as well as blank claims forms for each policy. All of my insurance is payable to you as primary beneficiary (in a lump sum), with our children being designated as contingent beneficiaries if you do not survive me. As quickly as my death certificate is available from the state health department (and it is not uncommon to wait seven to ten days for the certificate), the claims should be completed and executed and sent (with the death certificate and policy) to each company. Normally, the claims should be processed and the policy proceeds paid to you within three or four weeks. In the file folder is a sheet summarizing my policies and showing which will pay additional benefits if my death is the result of an accident. At present, the policy proceeds payable to you if I were to die from natural causes total

$450,000. An additional $100,000 is payable if I die in an accident. There is a $4,000 loan against one of the policies, which will simply be deducted and paid off from the proceeds. All of my insurance has been purchased through Tom Roberts, whose office is next to mine; should you encounter any problems or delays in collecting the policies, Tom will be able to help.

(11) *Property insurance.* We have an "all-in-one" property insurance policy that covers our home, household goods and other personal property, and our cars. The premium is paid yearly (in March), and you will want to be sure this coverage is kept up. Tom Roberts is also our agent for this policy. He will send you a renewal notice when the policy is due to expire.

(12) *Assets and liabilities.* In my personal file cabinet at the office is a loose-leaf notebook with the label "Personal Finances," which lists all of our assets, liabilities, income, and expenses. The listing is fairly detailed and (hopefully) current. Each time we make any change in our financial situation, I update the listing. It includes a description of the asset or liability, how it is registered or titled (whether in my name, your name, or our joint names), and the present value or amount. I have also included information about the original cost of the assets we own and the date they were acquired. Finally, the listing reflects the amount of income presently being generated by each investment asset or (in the case of our debts and liabilities) the amount of monthly expense they represent. All of the original documents relating to our assets and liabilities—such as stock and bond certificates, bank deposit certificates, deeds, notes, mortgages—are kept in our safe-deposit box, although you will find a copy of all such documents in the loose-leaf binder.

(13) *Retirement plan and IRAs.* I have a retirement plan established through my office (termed an "HR-10" plan), to which I have made tax-deductible contributions over the years of a portion of my income. In addition, both you and I have IRAs at First National Bank. You are designated to receive my HR-10 plan benefits and IRA in the event of my death. Taken together, there is a fairly substantial amount of money in these plans—approximately $375,000—and they are growing rapidly, since the earnings are also tax free. When I die and the proceeds become payable to you, the money at last becomes taxable. You have some choices or elections as to how you will receive these funds and the opportunity to at least postpone the inherent tax liability. The law on this subject changes regularly, and my best advice is that you consult with Bob Johnson and Mike Smith, our accountant, to decide which option is best from your standpoint at the time.

(14) *Home mortgage.* Other than our usual living expenses, monthly utility bills, insurance premiums, and various taxes (property, state and federal income, and so on), the only money we owe is on our home mortgage. The rate of interest and monthly payments are sufficiently low that I suggest you not prepay the mortgage, even though you will have enough money to do so. The mortgage is assumable by whomever might buy our home, should you decide to sell and move to another place, and thus is an attractive feature.

(15) *Advisors.* You will undoubtedly receive a great deal of advice following my death from many sources—some good, some not so good. It is important for you to have several people to whom you may turn, in confidence, for advice and guidance. I have already recommended that you retain Bob Johnson as your lawyer to handle the administration of my estate. In that connection, Bob and I have discussed this possibility and he knows my intentions. Bob will probably want to undertake this work on a reduced-fee basis, out of our long-standing friendship, but you should insist on paying him his regular fee. Although you may feel uncomfortable in doing so, you should discuss fees and expenses with Bob on the front end, frankly and openly. I have also suggested that you contact Tom Roberts on any insurance matters, and consult with Mike Smith (as well as Bob) on tax matters. Mike has handled the preparation of our income tax returns for many years, and he also supervises our accounting systems at the office (although Sally keeps our books and handles the office accounts on a daily basis). You will probably be bombarded with investment proposals once it is learned you are a widow with some inheritance. Steadfastly resist all unsolicited sales pitches for investments. You should, however, sit down with Bob, Mike, and also Ed Mitchell—who is the broker and investment advisor we have used for several years—reasonably soon, to evaluate your income and expense situation and the appro-

priateness of different investments to meet your needs, and to determine how best to invest the insurance and retirement plan benefits that will be coming to you in cash. In my estimation, you should have a very comfortable income from the investments available to you, even with a fairly conservative investment approach, and it is advisable to budget your expenses so that your income will be sufficient without invading or depleting your principal. It is also very important to maintain good comprehensive medical and hospital coverage, since prolonged serious illness is one of the greatest threats to your invested capital.

(16) *Closing my law office.* I have prepared and given to Sally rather comprehensive instructions on winding up my law practice and closing the office. Since you are my executor, you and Sally will need to work together in accomplishing these steps. Sally can do most of the legwork and paperwork required, but she will be responsible to you (since my practice is an asset of my estate under your authority) and she should (and I know will) keep you informed as the winding up proceeds. Insofar as my estate is concerned, there are several specific matters to be accomplished, as follows:

- Engaging a lawyer to supervise the winding up of my practice. (Bob and I have similar practices and we have an informal understanding that he would serve in this role if called upon, and I would do likewise for him.
- Notifying by letter all my clients of my death and requesting their instructions on the disposition or further handling of their files.
- Transferring all active files to the client or to the successor lawyer designated by the client, and making appropriate disposition of closed or inactive files. (Bob will carefully review the active files to determine if impending deadlines or due dates must be met, courts or agencies and other counsel notified if trials or hearings need to be rescheduled, and so on.)
- Billing and collecting fees and expenses. (Bob, Mike Smith, and Sally will collaborate on this but they should keep you advised, since the net collections belong to my estate and ultimately to you, and you should be consulted if they propose to write off any unbilled time and expense or accounts receivable as uncollectible.)
- Selling or otherwise disposing of my library, office equipment, furniture, and other tangible assets. (I have indicated to Sally that any furnishings or other items you would like to keep should be delivered to you, but otherwise all such property should be offered for sale. As Bob knows, there is a market—although slow and depressed—for used law books within the state bar association.)
- Canceling the office lease. (Our office lease will expire on September 30, 2005, but with an option to renew for another five years. In the lease we have with the Main Street Office Tower, the lease can be canceled in the event I die. You, Bob, and Sally will need to determine whether the lease should be immediately terminated or continued for some additional period. Sally will need an office from which to work and a place to keep our files during the winding-up process, so you may want to retain the office. Sally will also need to be kept on the payroll for as long as she is needed to help close out my practice and office.)

A final word—I love you very much.

John

78
Handling Files of a Dead Lawyer

PETER GERAGHTY

A lawyer who has a large solo practice dies suddenly. The lawyer has hundreds of client files. Some of these files concern probate matters, others involve civil litigation and real estate transactions. Most of the files are inactive, others involve ongoing matters. While the lawyer kept the active files at his office, most of the inactive files he removed from the office and kept in storage at his home.

- What steps should lawyers take to ensure that their client's matters will not be neglected in the event of their death?
- What obligations do lawyers for the estates of deceased lawyers have with regard to the deceased lawyer's client files?

Discussion

In 1992, The ABA Standing Committee on Ethics and Professional Responsibility issued Formal Opinion 92-369, "Disposition of Deceased Sole Practitioners' Client Files and Property." This opinion addressed (1) the need for a lawyer to have a plan in place that would provide for the protection of the client's interests in the event of his or her death, and (2) guidance for the lawyer who assumes responsibility for the deceased lawyer's files.

The first part of the opinion discusses a lawyer's duty to have a plan in place to protect the client's interests in the event of his or her death. The opinion states:

> The death of a sole practitioner could have serious effects on the sole practitioner's clients. . . . Important client matters, such as court dates, statutes of

limitations, or document filings, could be neglected until the clients discover that their lawyer has died. As a precaution to safeguard client interest, the sole practitioner should have a plan in place that will ensure insofar as in reasonably practicable that client matters will not be neglected in the event of the sole practitioner's death.

The opinion drew support for its conclusions from rules 1.1 (Competence) and 1.3 (Diligence)[1] of the ABA Model Rules of Professional Conduct, and from the lawyer's fiduciary duties to their clients:

> According to Rule 1.1, competence includes "preparation necessary for the representation," which when read in conjunction with Rule 1.3 would indicate that a lawyer should diligently prepare for the client's representation. Although representation should terminate when the attorney is no longer able to adequately represent the client, the lawyer's fiduciary obligations of loyalty and confidentiality continue beyond the termination of the agency relationship.

The opinion notes that lawyers have been disciplined for the neglect of client matters due to ill health or personal problems and further suggests

1. The comment to Rule 1.3 states:

    A client's interests can often be adversely affected by the passage of time or change of conditions; in extreme instances, as when a lawyer overlooks a statute of limitations, the client's legal position may be destroyed. Even when the client's interests are not affected in substance, however, unreasonable delay can cause a client needless anxiety. . . .

    Ethical Consideration 4-6 of the ABA Model Code of Professional Responsibility provides as follows:

    . . . A lawyer should also provide for the protection of the confidences and secrets of his client following the termination of the practice of the lawyer, whether termination is due to death, disability or retirement. For example, a lawyer might provide for the personal papers of the client to be returned to him and for the papers of the lawyer to be delivered to another lawyer or to be destroyed. In determining the method of disposition, the instructions and wishes of the client should be a dominant consideration.

Peter Geraghty is the director of ETHICSearch, the ABA Ethics Research Services at the ABA Center for Professional Responsibility in Chicago.

that lawyers who have failed to make preparations to protect their client's interests in the event of their death should be sanctioned both in the hope of encouraging other lawyers to make such preparations, and to restore confidence in the bar, even though the sanctions would obviously have no deterrent effect on deceased lawyers.

There are state bar associations that have issued opinions on this general topic. See, for example, Maine Board of Overseers of the Bar Opinion 143 (1994), and Oregon State Bar Opinion 1991-129 (1991).[2]

The Maine Board of Overseers of the Bar made the following suggestions as to what should be included in a plan for the protection of clients in the event of the solo practitioner's death:

1. A plan should include as one of its elements the engagement of a lawyer to supervise the winding down of the practice.

2. The plan ought to provide that clients be promptly notified of any termination. They should be advised of the name of the supervising lawyer and key staff who might be employed to assist in the transition. They should be invited to retrieve the files and seek replacement of legal counsel if further legal services are required to complete a task.

3. For those files that are not seasonably retrieved by clients, a determination should be made by a lawyer, presumably the supervising lawyer described in the first suggestion, as to what to do next. Can the file be delivered even if the client makes no effort to retrieve it? Is destruction possible and permissible?

4. What is to be done with those remaining files where destruction appears unreasonable at the time of transition and no client takes custody of the material? In those cases, a suit-

able custodian ought to be engaged by the lawyer, or the lawyer's estate, who is willing to assume custody of the files.

5. Finally, the commission suggests that the supervising lawyer notify the Board of Overseers of the Bar of the location of the unclaimed files. This gives former clients who were unable to be contacted during the transition period a chance to locate the file at some later date.

Florida Opinion 81-8M(1981) involved a situation where a lawyer was anticipating termination of his practice because of a terminal illness. A digest of the opinion reads as follows:

> After a diligent attempt is made to contact all clients whose files he holds, a lawyer anticipating termination of his practice by death should dispose of all files according to his client's instructions. The files of those clients who do not respond should be individually reviewed by the lawyer and destroyed only if no important papers belonging to the clients are in the files. Important documents should be indexed and placed in storage or turned over to any lawyer who assumes control of his active files. (See Florida Opinion 81-M at page 801:2502 of the *ABA/BNA Lawyers' Manual on Professional Conduct*.)

In 1986, the ABA General Practice Section, Sole Practitioners and Small Firms Committee sponsored a program entitled, "Preparing for and Dealing with the Consequences of the Death of a Sole Practitioner." One of the papers presented at this program, "A sole practitioner's letters of instruction regarding things to be done upon his or her death," listed the following as items the solo practitioner should mention in a letter to the personal representative of his estate:

- The need to engage a lawyer to wind up the law practice
- Notifying clients of the sole practitioner's death
- Transferring active files to the client or to the successor lawyer designated by the client
- Disposition of closed or inactive files
- Making arrangements to complete work on active files
- Securing agreements with the successor lawyers as to the handling of open files

The second part of ABA Formal Opinion 92-369 discusses the obligations of a lawyer who assumes responsibility for a deceased solo practitioner's client files:

---

2. Oregon Opinion 1991-129 states:

> For an attorney who has no partners, associates or employees . . . there could well be a significant lapse of time after the attorney's death or disability during which the attorney's telephone would go unanswered, mail would be unopened, deadlines would not be met and the like. The duty of competent representation includes, at a minimum, making sure that someone will step in to avoid client prejudice in such circumstances. This person may, but need not be an attorney. Depending on circumstances, it may be sufficient to instruct this person that in the event of the attorney's death or disability, the person should contact the presiding judge of the county circuit court so that the procedure called for by ORS 9.705–9.750 can be commenced.

A lawyer who assumes . . . responsibility (for the deceased sole practitioner's client files) must review the files carefully to determine which files need immediate attention; failure to do so would leave the clients in the same position as if their attorney died without any plan to protect their interests. The lawyer should also contact all clients of the deceased lawyer to notify them of the death of their lawyer and to request instructions in accordance with Rule 1.15. . . . Because the reviewing lawyer does not represent the clients, he or she should review only as much of the file as is needed to identify the client and to make a determination as to which files need immediate attention.

Earlier ABA opinions touch peripherally on the issues presented in the second question. Informal Opinion C-475 discussed the appropriate form an announcement could take when sent by a lawyer who was temporarily acting as an associate counsel of an incapacitated lawyer to clients of the incapacitated lawyer. Informal Opinion 648 (1963) discusses the propriety of an agreement between a lawyer and his associate whereby the associate would agree to take over the lawyer's practice upon the lawyer's death.

Several state and local bar association ethics opinions discuss the obligations of a lawyer who assumes responsibility for a deceased solo practitioner's client files. Most of them address the duties of lawyers who are either the executors of the deceased lawyers' estates, or who are partners of or shared office space with the deceased lawyers. These opinions stress the importance of the executor/partner/office-mate's careful review of the files to determine if any action need be taken to protect client's interests. See, for example, New York County Lawyers' Association Opinion 709(1996), (Partner of deceased lawyer must give notice of the death to clients for whom the deceased lawyer was handling ongoing matters); Connecticut Bar Association Opinion 95-13 (1995), Nassau County Opinions 89-43 (1989), 92-27 (1992) (lawyer who received all active and closed files of deceased lawyer has the same ethical obligations for the files as if they were his or her own files or if designated a "guardian" of the files by agreement with the deceased lawyer or estate); Mississippi Opinion 114 (1986), Wisconsin Opinion E-87-9 (1987)[3] and 89-23 (1989), Maryland Opinion 89-58 (1989):

3. State Bar of Wisconsin Opinion E-87-9 lists the following as guidelines for a lawyer who is winding up a deceased lawyer's practice:

A lawyer who shared office space with another lawyer and handled that lawyer's cases when he died (1) must review every file in his possession and notify clients or third parties if the lawyer has property belonging to them, (2) the lawyer may dispose of files in cases he handled for the deceased lawyer's estate as he would dispose of his own clients files, (3) the lawyer must turn over all other client files to the representative of the deceased's estate and explain the legal significance of retaining those files, (4) the lawyer must keep information contained in the files confidential regardless of whether or not he handled the cases. See Maryland Opinion 89-58 at page 901:4327 of the ABA/BNA Lawyers' Manual on Professional Conduct.

These opinions also discuss the obligations lawyers have with regard to the retention and disposition of the deceased lawyer's client files. Many of the opinions cite to ABA Informal Opinion 1384 (1984) *(Disposition of a Lawyer's Closed or Dormant Files Relating to Representation of or Services to Clients)* for authority on this point.[4]

1. Notifying past and present clients about the termination of the practice and telling them how they can obtain their files;
2. examining files and financial records to render an accounting of monies owing to the lawyer whose practice is being terminated, or to the lawyer's estates;
3. retaining copies of files involving potential grievance, malpractice or fee dispute exposure;
4. cooperating in representation relating to proceedings under (3) above;
5. providing emergency legal services to avoid prejudice to immediate client rights;
6. cooperating in substitution of counsel; and
7. storing or destroying files no longer needed and not requested by clients, all in strict accordance with court authorization and clients' rights.

4. Informal 1384 states as follows:
A lawyer does not have a general duty to preserve all of his files permanently. Mounting and substantial storage costs can affect the cost of legal services, and the public interest is not served by unnecessary and avoidable additions to the cost of legal services. . . . But clients (and former clients) reasonably expect from their lawyers that valuable and useful information in the lawyers' files, and not otherwise readily available to the clients, will not be prematurely and carelessly destroyed to the clients' detriment.

The opinion also lists eight guidelines that lawyers should consider when deciding whether to retain or discard closed or dormant client files. Guidelines 2, 3, and 4 state:
2. A lawyer should use care not to destroy or discard information that the lawyer knows or should know may still be necessary or useful in the assertion or defense of the client's position in a matter for which the applicable statutory limitations period has not expired.
3. A lawyer should use care not to destroy or discard information that the client may not need, has not previously been given to the client, and which the client may reasonably expect will be preserved by the lawyer.
4. In determining the length of time for retention of disposition of a file, a lawyer should exercise discretion. The nature and contents of some files may indicate a need for longer retention than do the nature and contents of other files, based upon their obvious relevance and materiality to matters that can be expected to arise.

These opinions also stress that any lawyer reviewing client files musts take steps to preserve client confidentiality and may not disclose client confidences without the client's consent. See, for example, North Carolina Opinion 16 (1986), Mississippi Opinion 114 (1986), and Alabama Opinion 83-155 (1983). (Digests of all state and local bar opinions cited in this chapter are available in the *ABA/BNA Lawyers' Manual on Professional Conduct*.)

Some states have statutory guidelines for the appointment of a receiver to manage a deceased lawyer's practice in the event that no partner, associate, executor, or other responsible party capable of conducting the lawyer's affairs is known to exist. See, for example, Illinois Supreme Court Rule 776, Appointment of Receiver in Certain Cases, Ill.Ann.Stat. ch. 1100A, Par. 776 (Smith-Hurd 1991). See also Rule 28 of the *ABA Model Rules for Lawyer Disciplinary Enforcement* (1989). This rule also outlines procedures for the appointment of a receiver after the lawyer's death.[5]

Lawyers should have a plan in place that will protect their client's interests in the event of their death. This is especially true for solo practitioners who do not have partners and/or associates that can manage the practice in their absence. Lawyers who assume responsibility for a deceased lawyer's client files should review them carefully to determine which files need immediate attention. The lawyer should also contact the deceased lawyer's clients, notify them that their lawyer has died, and request instructions. In the event that the lawyer is unable to locate clients whose files are now in his possession, the lawyer must make reasonable efforts to contact them. Depending on the nature and contents of the client files, the lawyer may have an obligation to preserve them if there are items in them that clearly belong to the client if they contain information that "the lawyer knows or should know may still be useful in the assertion or defense of the client's position in a matter for which the applicable statutory limitations period has not expired." (ABA Informal Opinion 1384 (1977).)

---

5. Rule 28. APPOINTMENT OF COUNSEL TO PROTECT CLIENTS' INTERESTS WHEN RESPONDENT IS TRANSFERRED TO DISABILITY INACTIVE STATUS, SUSPENDED, DISBARRED, DISAPPEARS, OR DIES.
A. Inventory of Lawyer Files. If a respondent has been transferred to disability inactive status, or has disappeared or died, or has been suspended or disbarred and there is evidence that he or she has not complied with Rule 27, and no partner, executor or other responsible party capable of conducting the respondent's affairs is known to exist, the presiding judge in the judicial district in which the respondent maintained a practice, upon proper proof of fact, shall appoint a lawyer or lawyers to inventory the files of the respondent, and to take such action as seems indicated to protect the interests of the respondent and his or her clients.
B. Protection for Records Subject to Inventory. Any lawyer so appointed shall not be permitted to disclose any information contained in any files inventories without the consent of the client to whom the file relates, except as necessary to carry out the order of the court which appointed the lawyer to make the inventory.

APPENDIX
Power of Attorney
for Health Care

Caution: **The attached Power of Attorney for Health Care is provided for your convenience. It may or may not fit the requirements of your particular state. A growing number of states have special forms or special procedures for creating health care powers of attorney. If possible, seek legal advice before signing any power of attorney. If not clearly recognized by law in your state, the document may still provide the best evidence of your wishes if you should become unable to speak for yourself.**

Instructions

Section 1—DESIGNATION OF HEALTH CARE AGENT: Print your full name here as the principal or creator of the power of attorney.

Print the full name, address, and telephone number of the person (over age 18) you appoint as your health care attorney-in-fact or agent. Appoint *only* a person whom you trust to understand and carry out your values and wishes. Do not name any of your health care providers as your agent, since some states prohibit them acting as your agent.

Section 2—EFFECTIVE DATE AND DURABILITY: The sample document is effective if and when you become unable to make health care decisions. That point in time is determined by your agent and your doctor. You can, if you wish, specify other effective dates or other criteria for incapacity (such as requiring two physicians to evaluate your capacity). You can also specify that the power will end at some later date or event before death. In any case, you have the right to revoke the agent's authority at any time by notifying your agent or health care provider orally or in writing. If you revoke, it is best to notify both your agent and physician in writing and to destroy the power of attorney document itself.

Section 3—AGENT'S POWERS: This grant of power is intended to be as broad as possible so that your agent will have authority to make any decision you could make to obtain or terminate any type of health care. Even under this broad grant of authority, your agent still must follow your desires and directions, communicated by you in any manner now or in the future. You can specifically limit or direct your agent's power, if you wish, in Section 4.

POWER OF ATTORNEY FOR HEALTH CARE

1. DESIGNATION OF HEALTH CARE AGENT.

I, _____ hereby appoint:
(Principal)

_____
(Attorney-in-fact's name)

_____
(Address)

_____

Home: _____

Work: _____

as my attorney-in-fact (or "Agent") to make health and personal care decisions for me as authorized in this document.

2. EFFECTIVE DATE AND DURABILITY.

By this document I intend to create a durable power of attorney effective upon, and only during, any period of incapacity in which, in the opinion of my agent and attending physician, I am unable to make or communicate a choice regarding a particular health care decision.

3. AGENT'S POWERS.

I grant to my Agent full authority to make decisions for me regarding my health care. In exercising this authority, my Agent shall follow my desires as stated in this document or otherwise known to my Agent. In making any decision, my Agent shall attempt to discuss the proposed decision with me to determine my desires if I am able to communicate in any way. If my Agent cannot determine the choice I would want made, then my Agent shall make a choice for me based upon what my Agent believes to be in my best interests. My Agent's authority to interpret my desires is intended to be as broad as possible, except for any limitations I may state below. Accordingly, unless specifically limited by Section 4, below, my Agent is authorized as follows:

A. To consent, refuse, or withdraw consent to any and all types of medical care, treatment, surgical procedures, diagnostic procedures, medication, and the use of mechanical or other procedures that affect any bodily function, including (but not limited to) artificial respiration, nutritional support and hydration, and cardiopulmonary resuscitation;

B. To have access to medical records and information to the same extent that I am entitled to, including the right to disclose the contents to others;

C. To authorize my admission to or discharge (even against medical advice) from any hospital, nursing home, residential care, assisted living or similar facility or service;

D. To contract on my behalf for any health care related service or facility on my behalf, without my Agent incurring personal financial liability for such contracts;

E. To hire and fire medical, social service, and other support personnel responsible for my care;

F. To authorize, or refuse to authorize, any medication or procedure intended to relieve pain, even though such use may lead to physical damage, addiction, or hasten the moment of (but not intentionally cause) my death;

G. To make anatomical gifts of part or all of my body for medical purposes, authorize an autopsy, and direct the disposition of my remains, to the extent permitted by law;

H. To take any other action necessary to do what I authorize here, including (but not limited to) granting any waiver or release from liability required by any hospital, physician, or other health care provider; signing any documents relating to refusals of treatment or the leaving of a facility against medical advice, and pursuing any legal action in my name, and at the expense of my estate to force compliance with my wishes as determined by my Agent, or to seek actual or punitive damages for the failure to comply.

Section 4—STATEMENT OF DESIRES, SPECIAL PROVISIONS, AND LIMITATIONS:

Paragraph A. Here you may include any limitations you think are appropriate, such as instructions to refuse any specific types of treatment that are against your religious beliefs or unacceptable to you for any other reasons, such as blood transfusions, electroconvulsive therapy, sterilization, abortion, amputation, psychosurgery, admission to a mental institution, etc. State law may not allow your agent to consent to some of these procedures, regardless of your health care power of attorney. Be very careful about stating limitations, because the specific circumstances surrounding a future health care decision are impossible to predict. If you do not want any limitations, simply write in "No limitations"

4. STATEMENT OF DESIRES, SPECIAL PROVISIONS, AND LIMITATIONS.

A. The powers granted above do not include the following powers or are subject to the following rules or limitations:

_____

_____

_____

_____

_____

Paragraph B: Because the subject of life-sustaining treatment is particularly important to many people, this paragraph provides a place for you to give general or specific directions on the subject, if you want to do so. The different paragraphs are options—choose only one, or write your desires or instructions in your own words (in the last option). If you already have a Living Will, you can simply refer to it by choosing the first option. Or, the instructions you provide here can do what a Living Will would do.

B. With respect to any Life-Sustaining Treatment, I direct the following: (INITIAL ONLY ONE OF THE FOLLOWING PARAGRAPHS)

REFERENCE TO LIVING WILL. I specifically direct my Agent to follow any health care declaration or "living will" executed by me.

GRANT OF DISCRETION TO AGENT. I do not want my life to be prolonged nor do I want life-sustaining treatment to be provided or continued if my Agent believes the burdens of the treatment outweigh the expected benefits. I want my Agent to consider the relief of suffering, the expense involved, and the quality as well as the possible extension of my life in making decisions concerning life-sustaining treatment.

DIRECTIVE TO WITHHOLD OR WITHDRAW TREATMENT. I do not want my life to be prolonged and I do not want life-sustaining treatment:
a. if I have a condition that is incurable or irreversible and, without the administration of life-sustaining treatment, expected to result in death within a relatively short time; or
b. if I am in a coma or persistent vegetative state that is reasonably concluded to be irreversible.

DIRECTIVE FOR MAXIMUM TREATMENT. I want my life to be prolonged to the greatest extent possible without regard to my condition, the chances I have for recovery, or the cost of the procedures.

DIRECTIVE IN MY OWN WORDS: _____

_____

_____

_____

Paragraph C: Because people differ widely on whether nutrition and hydration is something that ought to be refused or stopped under certain circumstances, it is important to make your wishes clear on this topic. Nutrition and hydration means food and fluids provided by a nasogastric tube or tube into the stomach, intestines, or veins. This paragraph allows you to include or not include these procedures among those that may be withheld or withdrawn under the circumstances described in the preceding paragraph. Either choice still permits nonintrusive efforts such as spoon-feeding or moistening of lips and mouth.

C. With respect to Nutrition and Hydration provided by means of a nasogastric tube or tube into the stomach, intestines, or veins, I wish to make clear that . . . (INITIAL ONLY ONE)

I *intend* to include these procedures among the "life-sustaining procedures" that may be withheld or withdrawn under the conditions given above.

I *do not intend* to include these procedures among the "life-sustaining procedures" that may be withheld or withdrawn.

Section 5—SUCCESSORS: If you wish to name alternate agents in case your first agent becomes unavailable, print the appropriate information in this paragraph. You can name as many successors in the order you wish.

Section 6—PROTECTION OF THIRD PARTIES WHO RELY ON MY AGENT: In most states, health care providers cannot be compelled to follow the directions of your agent, although in some states, they may be obligated to transfer your care to another provider who is willing to comply. This paragraph is intended to encourage compliance with the power of attorney by waiving potential civil liability for good faith reliance on the agent's statements and decisions.

Section 7—NOMINATION OF GUARDIAN: The use of a health care power of attorney is intended to prevent the need for a court-appointed guardian for health care decision-making. However, if for any reason, court involvement becomes necessary, this paragraph expressly names your Agent to serve as guardian. A court does not have to follow your nomination, but it will normally comply with your wishes unless there is good reason not to.

Section 8—ADMINISTRATIVE PROVISIONS: These items address miscellaneous matters that could affect the implementation of your power of attorney.

5. SUCCESSORS.

If any Agent named by me shall die, become legally disabled, resign, refuse to act, be unavailable, or (if any Agent is my spouse) be legally separated or divorced from me, I name the following (each to act alone and successively, in the order named) as successors to my Agent:

A. First Alternate Agent _____

    Address: _____

    Telephone: _____

B. Second Alternate Agent _____

    Address: _____

    Telephone: _____

6. PROTECTION OF THIRD PARTIES WHO RELY ON MY AGENT.

No person who relies in good faith upon any representations by my Agent or Successor Agent shall be liable to me, my estate, my heirs or assigns for recognizing the Agent's authority.

7. NOMINATION OF GUARDIAN.

If a guardian of my person should for any reason be appointed, I nominate my Agent (or his or her successor), named above.

8. ADMINISTRATIVE PROVISIONS.

A. I revoke any prior power of attorney for health care.

B. This power of attorney is intended to be valid in any jurisdiction in which it is presented.

C. My Agent shall not be entitled to compensation for services performed under this power of attorney, but he or she shall be entitled to reimbursement for all reasonable expenses incurred as a result of carrying out any provision of this power of attorney.

D. The powers delegated under this power of attorney are separable, so that the invalidity of one or more powers shall not affect any others.

SIGNING THE DOCUMENT: Required procedures for signing this kind of document vary from signature only to very detailed witnessing requirements or, in some states, simply notarization. The suggested procedure here is intended to meet most of the various state requirements for signing by noninstitutionalized persons. The procedure here is likely to be more detailed than is required under your own state's law, but it will help ensure that your Health Care Power is recognized in other states, too. First, sign and date the document in front of two witnesses. Your witnesses should know your identity personally and be able to declare that you appear to be of sound mind and under no duress or undue influence. Further, your witnesses should not be:

- your treating physician, health care provider, or health facility operator, nor an employee of any of these;
- anyone related to you by blood, marriage, or adoption
- anyone entitled to any part of your estate under an existing will or by operation of law. Even a creditor of yours should not be used under these guidelines.

If you are in a nursing home or other institution, be sure to consult state law, because a few states require that an ombudsman or patient advocate be one of your witnesses.

Second, have your signature notarized. Some states permit notarization as an alternative to witnessing. Others may simply apply the rules for signing ordinary durable powers of attorney. Ordinary durable powers of attorney are usually notarized. This form includes a relatively typical notary statement, but here again, it is wise to check state law in case a special form of notary acknowledgment is required.

BY SIGNING HERE I INDICATE THAT I UNDERSTAND THE CONTENTS OF THIS DOCUMENT AND THE EFFECT OF THIS GRANT OF POWERS TO MY AGENT.

I sign my name to this Health Care Power of Attorney on this _____ day of _____ , 19 __ .

My current home address is: _____

_____

Signature: _____

Name: _____

WITNESS STATEMENT

I declare that the person who signed or acknowledged this document is personally known to me, that he/she signed or acknowledged this durable power of attorney in my presence, and that he/she appears to be of sound mind and under no duress, fraud, or undue influence. I am not the person appointed as agent by this document, nor am I the patient's health care provider, or an employee of the patient's health care provider. I further declare that I am not related to the principal by blood, marriage, or adoption, and, to the best of my knowledge, I am not a creditor of the principal nor entitled to any part of his/her estate under a will now existing or by operation of law.

Witness #1:

Signature: _____ Date: _____

Print Name: _____ Telephone: _____

Residence Address: _____

_____

Witness #2:

Signature: _____ Date: _____

Print Name: _____ Telephone: _____

Residence Address: _____

_____

NOTARIZATION

STATE OF _____)
) SS.
COUNTY OF _____)

On this _____ day of _____ , 19 ___ , the said _____ , known to me (or satisfactorily proven) to be the person named in the foregoing instrument, personally appeared before me, a Notary Public, within and for the State and County aforesaid, and acknowledged that he or she freely and voluntarily executed the same for the purposes stated therein.

My Commission Expires: _____

_____   NOTARY PUBLIC

Index